Party Systems and Voter Alignments

International Yearbook of Political Behavior Research

GENERAL EDITOR: Heinz Eulau, *Stanford University*

CONTRIBUTORS

Robert R. Alford, *University of Wisconsin*

Erik Allardt, *University of Helsinki*

Mattei Dogan, *Center of Sociological Studies, National Center of Scientific Research, Paris*

Juan J. Linz, *Columbia University*

Seymour M. Lipset, *Harvard University*

Robert T. McKenzie, *London School of Economics and Political Science*

Pertti Pesonen, *University of Tampere*

Alan D. Robinson, *Victoria University of Wellington*

Stein Rokkan, *University of Bergen and The Christian Michelsen Institute*

Allan Silver, *Columbia University*

Glaucio Ary Dillon Soares, *Latin American Faculty of Social Sciences, Santiago*

Immanuel Wallerstein, *Columbia University*

Joji Watanuki, *University of Tokyo*

Volume 7, International Yearbook of Political Behavior Research

Party Systems and Voter Alignments:

Cross-National Perspectives

Edited by

Seymour M. Lipset
Harvard University

and

Stein Rokkan
University of Bergen and The Christian Michelsen Institute

THE FREE PRESS, *New York*

COLLIER-MACMILLAN LIMITED, *London*

To the memories of our fathers:
defenders of the periphery

S.M.L.

S.R.

Preface

This is the last volume of the *International Yearbook of Political Behavior Research*. The reason for terminating the series is a very simple one: since it was conceived in the middle fifties, and since the first volume was published in 1961, the need for the enterprise has steadily decreased. In the fifties, the professional journals of political science were still largely edited by men suspicious of or hostile to the behavioral approaches in the study of politics, and most commercial publishers had not as yet come to appreciate the merchandizing potential of the new wares. All this has drastically changed in the last few years. The editorial policies of the journals not only welcome but encourage the kind of research that is fertilized by behavioral theories and methods, and the publishers vie with each other in contracting scientific research monographs. The end of this series, then, symbolizes the success of the new beginning in the study of politics. Hopefully, it contributed to the change in intellectual atmosphere. But the new atmosphere makes its continuance unnecessary. For to publish for the sake of publishing was certainly not one of our objectives.

This is not to say that the publication problem has been solved. But it has taken on a quite different character. Not paucity but abundance has become the problem. As the market is flooded by journals hospitable to behavioral research, by monographs reporting larger research projects, by symposia of conference papers, and by books on behavioral theories and methods, keeping up with the scholarly output in highly specialized sub-fields has become a heavy burden. The immediate need, therefore, is for media of communication that critically summarize and evaluate the flow of publications. For there is a very real danger that as we are forced to read only in our specialties, we are losing our common discipline. Fortunately, works performing this service are in the offing. The first volume of *Political Science Annual: An International Review,* has just been published.[1] The new *International Encyclopedia of the Social Sciences* will be available in early 1968.[2] And there is an interest in publishing a *Handbook of Political Science.* These developments should contribute to maintaining the unity of the discipline.

This being a swan song of sorts, I want to take the opportunity to say thanks to all those who made this series possible. The idea of a yearbook devoted to empirical research, as at least one means of bridging the publication gap that in the mid-fifties was so severely felt by behavioral researchers in the field of politics, came out of a small group assembled at the Michigan Survey Research Center in the summer of 1954 under the auspices of the Political Behavior Committee of the Social Science Research Council. Robert E. Lane, in particular, was the spark plug that ignited our concern. The series itself would never have come off the ground without the enthusiastic intellectual support of Jeremiah Kaplan, the imaginative editor of The Free Press, now president of The Macmillan Company. Thanks are due to the distinguished International Advisory Board who legitimized the undertaking and gave me a free hand in planning and expediting the series. I cannot appreciate enough the patience of our contributors who sometimes had to wait longer for a volume to appear than they could reasonably be expected to. But the final credit must go to my friends and colleagues who served as special editors of the seven volumes—Morris Janowitz, Dwaine Marvick, Samuel J. Huntington, Glendon Schubert, David Apter, J. David Singer, Seymour M. Lipset, and Stein Rokkan. The individual volumes were their creations and theirs alone. It was fun working with them.

Stanford University

Heinz Eulau

1. Edited by James A. Robinson and published by The Bobbs-Merrill Company.
2. Edited by David L. Sills and to be published by The Free Press and The Macmillan Company.

Prologue

This volume has been in the making for many years. It originated in a suggestion by the general editor of this series, Heinz Eulau, that we undertake a volume bringing together the findings of electoral research in various countries. Following conventional procedure, we invited several scholars who had been involved in research to write articles. Since we were interested in facilitating comparative generalizations, we asked the authors to present data concerning the bases of support over time of the major political tendencies. The resulting articles are naturally disparate in character, reflecting the different intellectual orientations of the authors, the character of the political systems of the various nations, and the availability of research findings. Writing about party developments in West Africa obviously requires a framework very different from that of any analysis for the United States.

Where possible, we sought articles that dealt comparatively with a group of similar nations. Thus Robert Alford has brought together the results of his researches on the bases of party support in the four major Anglo-American democracies. To this has been added an article reporting on the smallest of them, New Zealand, a nation that until recently has been outside the range of comparative social science. We were also able to enlist a contribution by two students of British electoral politics, the pioneering analyst of party histories Robert McKenzie and his American colleague Allan Silver. They have explored the "rightward deviants" within the British working class in greater depth than in any analysis so far published. The political systems of Latin Catholic Europe have a great deal in common, and a comparative treatment of electoral alignments in the two major countries, Italy and France, seemed to be in order. We were fortunate that the leading scholar of this subject, Mattei Dogan, undertook this task. The third important Latin country, Spain, obviously could not be handled within the same body of analysis, but Juan Linz, who knows more about Spain than any other living social scientist, agreed at our invitation to analyze the cleavages within his country and to risk some predictions about the future party system. As is evident from his article on Spain, Spanish politics have much in common with those of Italy and France. Perhaps the most obvious unit for comparative treatment is the northern countries of Europe: for these, however, we have not been able to present any systematic comparisons, but the chapters by Erik Allardt, Pertti Pesonen, and Stein Rokkan are very similar in structure and suggest important themes for future cross-national research. In dealing with central Europe, we were fortunate in being able again to call upon Juan Linz to report on some of the findings of his comprehensive analysis of German voting behavior in the early fifties. We originally hoped to obtain a second article reporting on more recent elections in various countries in this area, particularly in Germany. Unfortunately, for reasons beyond our control, this article could not be completed, and we decided, in view of the many delays, to put out this volume without commissioning this article anew.

The most glaring gap, both from a territorial and an intellectual point of view, is the lack of coverage of the various nations of Asia, Africa, and Latin America. To some extent this omission reflects the political and intellectual situation in these areas. Relatively few third world countries have an institutionalized system of competitive politics. There have been few empirical studies of elections and political behavior. The three articles dealing with non-Western nations, those by Watanuki for Japan, Wallerstein for West Africa, and Soares for Brazil, do, however, point to the kind of research that should be undertaken in these countries. The chapters clearly show that *Kulturkampf* politics is still characteristic of these regions: most of the countries within them are still faced with struggles between traditional and modern institutions and values. Even Japan, the most developed country among them, still reflects this tension in its party politics. The better educated, although disproportionately in privileged positions, tend to support leftist parties, because leftism and socialism are identified with modernism.

The long introductory essay by the editors was undertaken *after* most of the articles were completed. It was the last chapter finished. As should be obvious to readers, many of the issues with which it deals stem from problems raised in the succeeding chapters. While we hope that the Introduction will furnish the reader with a fruitful perspective for evaluating the findings presented in the substantive section of the book, it is important to note that these ideas of the editors were not available to the authors of the regional and national chapters. The Introduction represents an effort to synthesize the knowledge about party systems presented by the chapter authors. It is our hope, of course, that both the Introduction and the substantive chapters will serve to stimulate research elaborating on the ideas presented here.

Although this book does not represent a coordinated effort at comparative analysis in which each section deals with comparable ideas and categories, we do believe that the different sections do contain common elements. The volume in a real sense is a product of the Committee on Political Sociology of the International Sociological Association. The two editors are Chairman and Secretary of this Committee, respectively. The Committee, which has been in existence since 1959, has met regularly over the years in different parts of Europe. Almost all of the authors are either members of the Committee or are former students or co-workers of one of the editors. This background in sustained personal contact underlies the communal character of the volume, and we hope is reflected in its contents.

We would like to acknowledge various indebtednesses, both intellectual and institutional, which have helped bring this volume to fruition. Our most important continuing debt is to our fellow members of the Committee on Political Sociology. Those who have not contributed to the book have given generously of their time and intellectual capital. These include the late Polish sociologist Julian Hochfeld, Mark Abrams, Raymond Aron, Shmuel Eisenstadt, Gino Germani, Morris Janowitz, Radomir Lukic, Giovanni Sartori, Otto Stammer, and Jerzy Wiatr. There are others who have met regularly with us, and who would have been formal members of the Committee, had we not been limited in size by the regulations of the I.S.A. These include, in particular, Angus Campbell, Harry Eckstein, Hans Daalder, Klaus Liepelt, Peter Nettl, Erwin Scheuch, and Henry Valen. With respect to this volume, we must express also our great intellectual obligations to Talcott Parsons and Juan Linz. Both gave unstintingly of their knowledge in helping us conceptualize the problems dealt with herein.

On the institutional level, production of this book was greatly facilitated by the research institutes with which we have been connected. These are the Center for Advanced Study in the Behavioral Sciences at Stanford, where this book was first planned and finally completed, the Christian Michelsen Institute of Bergen, Norway, the Institute of International Studies of the University of California, and the Center for International Studies of Harvard University. Each institution contributed heavily both in terms of funds and in providing a stimulating working atmosphere. Funds from a Carnegie Corporation grant to Professor Lipset also are gratefully acknowledged. And last but not least, we would like to express our gratitude to Heinz Eulau, the editor of this series, for his editorial aid and patience.

Seymour Martin Lipset
Stein Rokkan

Contents

Party Systems and Voter Alignments

Cleavage Structures, Party Systems, and Voter Alignments: An Introduction

Seymour Martin Lipset and Stein Rokkan

INITIAL FORMULATIONS

Questions for Comparative Analysis

The analyses brought together in this collection bear on a series of central questions in the comparative sociology of politics.

The first set of questions concerns *the genesis of the system of contrasts and cleavages* within the national community: Which conflicts came first and which later? Which ones proved temporary and secondary? Which proved obdurate and pervasive? Which cut across each other and produced overlaps between allies and enemies, and which reinforced each other and tended to polarize the national citizenry?

A second group of questions focuses on *the conditions for the development of a stable system of cleavage and oppositions* in national political life: Why did some early conflicts establish party oppositions and others not? Which of the many conflicting interests and outlooks in the national community produced direct opposition between competing parties, and which of them could be aggregated *within* the broad party fronts? Which conditions favored extensive aggregations of oppositional groups, and which offered greater incentive to fragmented articulation of single interests or narrowly defined causes? To what extent were these developments affected by changes in the legal and the administrative conditions of political activity, through the extension of the rights of participation, through the introduction of secret voting and the development of strict controls of electoral corruption, and through the retention of plurality

1

decisions or the introduction of some variety of Proportional Representation?

A third and final set of questions bears on *the behavior of the mass of rank-and-file citizens* within the resultant party systems: How quickly were the parties able to recruit support among the new masses of enfranchized citizens, and what were the core characteristics of the groups of voters mobilized by each party? Which conditions helped and which conditions hindered the mobilization efforts of each party within the different groups of the mass citizenry? How quickly did the changes in economic, social, and cultural conditions brought about through economic growth or stagnation translate themselves into changes in the strengths and the strategies of the parties? How did political success affect the rates of mobilization and the inflow of new support to each party? Did the parties tend to recruit new clienteles and change their followings as they established their viability as useful channels of influence in the decision-making processes?

These are some of the questions we hope to throw light on in this volume. We have assembled analyses of data on the economic, the social, and the cultural conditions of party oppositions and voter reactions in twelve currently competitive and one erstwhile competitive political systems and have added, for purposes of contrast and perspective, a chapter on cleavage structures in a group of new states. Ten of the twelve competitive systems are Western: five English-speaking, three continental European, and two Nordic polities. The "erstwhile competitive" but currently authoritarian system covered is Spain. The two cases outside the West are Brazil and Japan. The final chapter, by Immanuel Wallerstein, covers developments in West Africa in the wake of the movements of liberation and independence.

All these analyses have an important *historical* dimension. Most of them focus on data for elections in the fifties, but they all in one way or another confront us with tasks of *developmental comparison:* to understand the current alignments of voters behind each of the parties, we have to map variations in the *sequences of alternatives* set for the active and the passive citizens within each system since the emergence of competitive politics. Parties do not simply present themselves *de novo* to the citizen at each election; they each have a history and so have the constellations of alternatives they present to the electorate. In single-nation studies we need not always take this history into account in analyzing current alignments: we assume that the parties are equally visible "givens" to all the citizens within the nation. But as soon as we move into comparative analysis we have to add an historical dimension. We simply cannot make sense of variations in current alignments without detailed data on differences in the sequences of party formation and in the character of the alternatives presented to the electorates before and after the extension of the suffrage.[1] We have to carry out our comparative analyses in several steps: we first have to consider the initial developments toward competitive politics and the institutionalization of mass elections, we next must disentangle the constellation of cleavages and oppositions which produced the national system of mass organizations for electoral action, and then, and only then, can we make headway toward some understanding of the forces producing the current alignments of voters behind the historically given alternatives. In our Western democracies the voters are only rarely called upon to express their stands on single issues. They are typically faced with choices among historically given "packages" of programs, commitments, outlooks, and, sometimes, *Weltanschauungen,* and their current behavior cannot be understood without some knowledge of the sequences of events and the combinations of forces that produced these "packages." Our task is to develop realistic models to explain the formation of different systems of such "packages" under different conditions of national politics and socioeconomic development and to fit information on these variations in the character of the alternatives into our schemes for the analysis of current electoral behavior. This is why we have given this volume a double title. We hope to throw light on the origins and the "freezing" of different types of *party systems,* and we seek to assemble materials for comparative analyses of the *current alignments of voters* behind the historically given "packages" in the different systems.

In this introductory statement we shall limit ourselves to a few salient points of comparison. A full comparative treatment of the party systems and the voter alignments of the West, not to speak of the competitive systems in other regions of the world, must await the completion of a number of detailed sociological analyses of national political developments.[2] We shall first discuss a typology of possible cleavage bases within national political communities; we shall then move on to a consideration of the actual party systems in Western polities, and we shall finally point to differences between party systems in the voters' characteristic alignments behind the alternatives among which they are asked to choose. In this final section we shall give attention to alignments by such obvious sociocultural criteria as *region, class,* and *religious denomination,* but also to alignments by strictly political criteria of membership in "we" versus "they" groups. We shall consider the possibility that the *parties themselves* might establish themselves as significant poles of attraction and produce their own alignments independently of the geographical, the social, and the cultural underpinnings of the movements.

The Political Party: Agent of Conflict and Instrument of Integration

"Party" has throughout the history of Western government stood for division, conflict, opposition within a body politic.[3] "Party" is etymologically derived from "part" and since it first appeared in political discourse in the late Middle Ages has always retained this reference to one set of elements in competition or in controversy with another set of elements within some unified whole.[4]

It will be objected that since the twentieth century has given us an abundance of monolithic parties, totalitarian parties, and "one-party systems" these suggest another sense of the term, a divergent usage. This represents an old ambiguity in the use of the term. In his *Wirtschaft und Gesellschaft* Max Weber discussed the use of the term "party" in descriptions of medieval Italian city politics and asserted that the Florentine Guelfs "ceased to be a party" in the sociological sense once they had been incorporated as part of the governing bureaucracy of the city.[5] Weber explicitly refused to accept any equivalence between "party" as used in descriptions of competitive voluntary politics and "party" as used of monolithic systems. The distinction is of obvious analytical importance, but there is still a latent unity of usage. The totalitarian party does not function through *freie Werbung*—through free competition in the political market—but it is still a *part* of a much larger whole and it is still in *opposition* to other forces within that whole. The typical totalitarian party is composed of the active, mobilizing part of the national system: it does not compete with other parties for offices and favors, but it still seeks to mobilize the populace *against* something—against conspiratorial counter-forces within the national community or against the threatening pressures from foreign enemies. Totalitarian elections may not make much sense from a Western perspective, but they nevertheless serve important legitimizing functions: they are "rituals of confirmation" in a continuous campaign against the "hidden" opposition, the illegitimate opponents of the established regime.

Whatever the structure of the polity, parties have served as essential agencies of mobilization and as such have helped to integrate local communities into the nation or the broader federation. This was true of the earliest competitive party systems, and it is eminently true of the single-party nations of the post-colonial era. In his insightful analysis of the formation of the American party system, William Chambers has assembled a wide range of indications of the integrative role of the first national parties, the Federalists and the Democratic-Republicans: they were the first genuinely national organizations; they represented the first successful efforts to pull Americans out of their local community and their state and to give them roles in the national polity.[6] Analyses of parties in the new nations of the twentieth century arrive at similar conclusions. Ruth Schachter has shown how the African single-party organizations have been used by the political leaders to "awaken a wider national sense of community" and to create ties of communication and cooperation across territorial and ethnic populations.[7]

In competitive party systems this process of integration can be analyzed at two levels: on the one hand, each party establishes a network of cross-local communication channels and in that way helps to strengthen national identities; on the other, its very competiveness helps to set the national system of government *above* any particular set of officeholders. This cuts both ways: the citizens are encouraged to distinguish between their loyalty to the total political system and their attitudes to the sets of competing politicians, and the contenders for power will, at least if they have some chance of gaining office, have some interest in maintaining this attachment of all citizens to the polity and its rules of alternation. In a monolithic polity citizens are not encouraged to distinguish between the system and current officeholders. The citizenry tends to identify the polity with the policies of particular leaders, and the power-holders habitually exploit the established national loyalties to rally support for themselves. In such societies any attack on the political leaders or on the dominant party tends to turn into an attack on the political system itself. Quarrels over particular policies or particular incumbencies immediately raise fundamental issues of system survival. In a competitive party system opponents of the current governing team may well be accused of weakening the state or betraying the traditions of the nation, but the continued existence of the political system is not in jeopardy. A competitive party system protects the nation against the discontents of its citizens: grievances and attacks are deflected from the overall system and directed toward the current set of power-holders.[8]

Sociologists such as E. A. Ross[9] and Georg Simmel[10] have analyzed the integrative role of institutionalized conflicts within political systems. The establishment of regular channels for the expression of conflicting interests has helped to stabilize the structure of a great number of nation-states. The effective equalization of the status of different denominations has helped to take much of the brunt off the earlier conflicts over religious issues. The extension of the suffrage and the enforcement of the freedom of political expression also helped to strengthen the legitimacy of the nation-state. The opening up of channels for the expression of manifest or latent conflicts between the established and the underprivileged classes may have brought many systems out of equilibrium in the earlier phase but tended to strengthen the body politic over time.

This conflict-integration dialectic is of central concern in current research on the comparative sociology of political parties. In this volume the emphasis will be on *conflicts and their translation into party systems*. This does not mean that we shall neglect the integrative functions of parties. We have simply chosen to start out from the latent or manifest strains and cleavages and will deal with trends toward compromise and reconciliation against the background of the initial conflicts. Our concern in this introductory discussion as well as in the chapters on particular systems is with parties as *alliances in conflicts over policies and value commitments within the larger body politic*. For the sociologist, parties exert a double fascination. They help to crystallize and make explicit the conflicting interests, the latent strains and contrasts in the existing social structure, and they force subjects and citizens to ally themselves across structural cleavage lines and to set up priorities among their commitments to established or prospective roles in the system. Parties have an *expressive* function; they develop a rhetoric for the translation of contrasts in the social and the cultural structure into demands and pressures for action or inaction. But they also have *instrumental* and *representative* functions: they force the spokesmen for the many contrasting interests and outlooks to strike bargains, to stagger demands, and to aggregate pressures. Small parties may content themselves with expressive functions, but no party can hope to gain decisive influence on the affairs of a community without some willingness to cut across existing cleavages to establish common fronts with potential enemies and opponents. This was true at the early stage of embryonic party formations around cliques and clubs of *notables* and legislators, but the need for such broad alliances became even more pronounced with the extension of the rights of participation to new strata of the citizenry.

No one has given us a more concise literary analysis of this process of aggregation during the early phase of mass mobilization than H. G. Wells in *The New Machiavelli*:[11]

> . . . multitudinousness had always been the Liberal characteristic. Liberalism never has been nor even can be anything but a diversified crowd. Essentially it is the party of criticism, the "Anti" party. It is a system of hostilities and objections that somehow achieves at times an elusive common soul. It is a gathering together of all the smaller interests which find themselves at a disadvantage against the big established classes, the leasehold tenant as against the landowner, the retail tradesman as against the merchant and money-lender, the Non-conformist as against the Churchman, the smaller employer as against the demoralising hospitable publican, the man without introductions and broad connections against the man who has these things. . . . It has no more essential reason for lov-

ing the Collectivist state than the Conservatives; the smaller dealer is doomed to absorption in that just as much as the large one; but it resorts to the state against its antagonists as in the middle ages common men pitted themselves against the barons by siding with the king. The Liberal Party is the party against "class privilege" because it represents no class advantages, but it is also the party that is on the whole most set against Collective control because it represents no established responsibility. It is constructive only as far as its antagonism to the great owner is more powerful than its jealousy of the state. It organizes only because organization is forced upon it by the organization of its adversaries. It lapses in and out of alliance with Labour as it sways between hostility to wealth and hostility to public expenditure. . . .

Similar, if less vivid, descriptions could be given of most of the parties aspiring to majority positions in the West: they are conglomerates of groups differing on wide ranges of issues, but still united in their greater hostility to their competitors in the other camps. Conflicts and controversies can arise out of a great variety of relationships in the social structure, but only a few of these tend to polarize the politics of any given system. There is a *hierarchy of cleavage bases* in each system and these orders of political primacy not only vary among polities, but also tend to undergo changes over time. Such differences and changes in the political weight of sociocultural cleavages set fundamental problems for comparative research: When is region, language, or ethnicity most likely to prove polarizing? When will class take the primacy and when will denominational commitments and religious identities prove equally important cleavage bases? Which sets of circumstances are most likely to favor accommodations of such oppositions *within* parties and in which circumstances are they more apt to constitute issues *between* the parties? Which types of alliances tend to maximize the strain on the polity and which ones help to integrate it? Questions such as these will be on the agenda of comparative political sociology for years to come. There is no dearth of hypotheses, but so far very little in the way of systematic analysis across several systems. It has often been suggested that systems will come under much heavier strain if the main lines of cleavage are over morals and the nature of human destiny than if they concern such mundane and negotiable matters as the prices of commodities, the rights of debtors and creditors, wages and profits, and the ownership of property. However, this does not take us very far; what we want to know is when the one type of cleavage will prove more salient than the other, what kind of alliances they have produced and what consequences these constellations of forces have had for consensus-building within the nation-state. We do not pretend to find clear-cut answers, but we have tried to move the analysis one step further. We shall start out with a review of a variety of *logically possible* sources of strains and oppositions in social structures and shall then proceed to an inventory of the *empirically extant examples of political expressions of each set of conflicts*. We have not tried to present a comprehensive scheme of analysis in this context but would like to point to one possible line of approach.

Dimensions of Cleavage: A Possible Model

The much-debated fourfold schema devised by Talcott Parsons for the classification of the functions of a social system offers a convenient point of departure for an inventory of potential cleavage bases.

The four-function scheme was originally developed in *Working Papers in the Theory of Action*[12] and was derived from a cross-classification of four basic dilemmas of orientation in the roles taken by actors in social systems:

Categorization of situational objects	Attitudes to objects	Corresponding functions for the system
I. Universalism *vs.* Particularism	III. Specificity *vs.* Diffuseness	*A*daptation Integration
II. Performance *vs.* Quality	IV. Affectivity *vs.* Neutrality	*G*oal attainment *L*atency: pattern maintenance and tension release

This abstract schema came to serve as a basic paradigm in a series of successive attempts[13] to map the flows and the media of interchange among the actors and the collectivities within social systems or within total territorial societies. The paradigm posited four "functional subsystems" of every society and six lines of interchange between each pair:

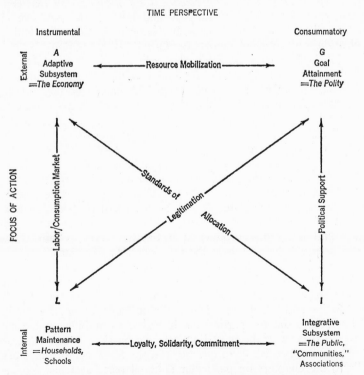

Figure 1—The Parsonian Paradigm of Societal Interchanges.

Three of these sets of interchanges are of crucial concern to the political sociologist:

He wants to know how the solidary collectivities, the latent communalities of interests and prospects, and the manifest associations and movements within a given territorial society limit the alternatives and influence the decisions of governmental leaders and their executive agencies—these are all processes of interchange between the *I* and *G* subsystems.[14]

He wants to know how ready or how reluctant individual subjects and households in the society are to be mobilized for action by the different associations and movements and how they make up their minds in cases of competition and conflict between different mobilizing agencies—these are all questions about interchanges between the *L* and *I* subsystems.

He is concerned finally to find out about regularities in the behavior of individual subjects and households in their direct interchanges (*L* to *G, G* to *L*) with the territorial agencies of government, be it as observers of legal regulations, as taxpayers and conscripted manpower, or as voters in institutionalized elections and consultations.

However, our task in this volume is narrower. We do not intend to deal with *all* the interchanges between *I* and *G,* between *I* and *L,* or between *L* and *G.* We are only concerned with the *I–G* interchanges insofar as they press forward the development of *systems of competing parties.* We are only interested in the *I–L* interchanges insofar as they help to establish *distinct links of membership, identification, and readiness for mobilization* between given parties and given categories of subjects and households. And we are not interested in *all* the *L–G* interchanges, but only in the ones that find expression in *elections* and in arrangements for *formal representation.*

In terms of the Parsonian paradigm our tasks are in fact fourfold:

1. We first have to examine the *internal structure* of the *I* quadrant in a range of territorial societies: What cleavages had manifested themselves in the national community in the early phases of consolidation, and what cleavages emerged in the subsequent phases of centralization and economic growth? Questions of this type will be dealt with in the next section.

2. Our next job is to compare *sequences of I–G interchanges* to trace regularities in the processes of *party formation.* How did the inherited cleavages find political expression, and how did the territorial organization of the nation-state, the division of powers between governors and representatives, and the broadening of the rights of participation and consultation affect the development of alliances and oppositions among political tendencies and movements and eventually produce a distinctive party system? Questions along these lines will occupy us in the two succeeding sections.

3. Our third job is to study the consequences of these developments for the *I–L interchanges.* Which identities, which solidarities, which communalities of experience and fate could be reinforced and made use of by the emerging parties and which ones had to be softened or ignored? Where in the social structure did the parties find it easiest to mobilize stable support, and where did they meet the most impenetrable barriers of suspicion and rejection? We shall touch on these questions in the final section but must refer for details to the chapters on particular national party systems.

4. And our final task is to bring all these diverse data to bear on the analysis of the *L–G interchanges* in the operation of *elections and the recruitment of representatives*. How far do electoral distributions reflect structural cleavages in the given society; how is electoral behavior affected by the narrowing of alternatives brought about by the party system; and how far are the efforts of indoctrination and mobilization hampered through the development of a politically neutral electoral machinery, the formalizing and the standardization of procedures, and the introduction of secret voting?[15]

Underlying this interpretation of the Parsonian scheme is a simple three-phase model of the process of nation-building:

In the first phase the thrusts of penetration and standardization from the national center increase territorial resistances and raise issues of cultural identity. Robert E. Lee's "am I a Virginian or an American?" is a typical expression of the *G–L* strains generated through the processes of nation-building.

In the second phase these local oppositions to centralization produce a *variety of alliances* across the communities of the nation: the commonalities of family fates in the *L* quadrangle generate associations and organizations in the *I* quadrangle. In some cases these alliances will pit one part of the national territory against another. This is typically the case in countries where a number of counterestablishment loyalties converge: ethnicity, religion, and class in Ireland under the raj, language and class in Belgium, Finland, Spain, and Canada. In other cases the alliances will tend to spread throughout the nation and pit opponents against each other in all localities.

In the third phase the alliances in the *I* quadrangle will enter the *G* quadrangle and gain some measure of control, not only over the use of central national resources (*G–A* interchanges) but also over the channeling of the flows of legitimation from *L* to *G*. This may find expression in franchise reforms, in changes in the procedures of registration and polling, in new rules of electoral aggregation, and in extensions of the domains of legislative intervention.

This model can be developed in several directions. We have chosen to focus initial attention on the possible differentiations within the *I* quadrangle—the locus for the formation of parties and party constellations in mass democracies.

DIMENSIONS OF CLEAVAGE AND ALLIANCE

Two Dimensions of Cleavage: The Territorial-Cultural and the Functional

Talcott Parsons has so far given surprisingly little attention to the possibilities of internal differentiation within the *I* quadrant. Among his collaborators, Smelser has devoted much ingenuity to the development of an abstract schema for the explanation of collective reactions and movements,[16] but this elaborate level-by-level procedure of analysis bears essentially on the emergence of single manifestations and offers no direct clues to the classification and comparison of *systems* of social movements and political parties within historically given societies. We cannot hope to fill this lacuna in the theoretical literature but feel tempted to suggest one line of conceptual development from the basic A–G–I–L paradigm. Our suggestion is that the crucial cleavages and their political expressions can be ordered within the two-dimensional space generated by the two diagonals of the double dichotomy:

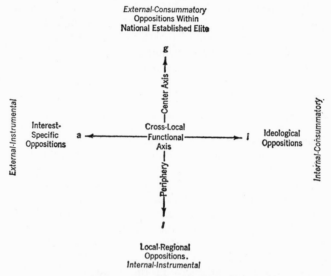

Figure 2—A Possible Interpretation of the Internal Structure of the I Quadrant.

In this model the Parsonian dichotomies have been transformed into continuous coordinates: the *l–g* line represents a *territorial* dimension of the national cleavage structure and the *a–i* line a *functional* dimension.[17]

At the *l* end of the territorial axis we would find strictly local oppositions to encroachments of the aspiring or the dominant national elites and their bureaucracies: the typical reactions of peripheral regions, linguistic minorities, and culturally threatened populations to the pressures of the centralizing, standardizing, and "rationalizing" machinery of the nation-state. At the *g* end of the axis we would find conflicts not between territorial units *within* the system but over the control, the organization, the goals, and the policy options of the system *as a whole*. These might be nothing more than direct struggles among competing elites for central power, but they might also reflect deeper differences in conceptions of nationhood, over domestic priorities and over external strategies.

Conflicts along the *a–i* axis *cut across* the territorial units of the nation. They produce alliances of similarly situated or similarly oriented subjects and households over wide ranges of localities and tend to undermine the inherited solidarity of the established territorial communities. At the *a* end of this dimension we would find the typical conflict over short-term or long-term allocations of resources, products, and benefits in the economy: conflicts between producers and buyers, between workers and employers, between borrowers and lenders, between tenants and owners, between contributors and beneficiaries. At this end the alignments are specific and the conflicts tend to be solved through rational bargaining and the establishment of universalistic rules of allocation. The farther we move toward the *i* end of the axis, the more diffuse the criteria of alignment, the more intensive the identification with the "we" group, and the more uncompromising the rejection of the "they" group. At the *i* end of the dimension we find the typical "friend-foe" oppositions of tight-knit religious or ideological movements to the surrounding community. The conflict is no longer over specific gains or losses but over conceptions of moral right and over the interpretation of history and human destiny; membership is no longer a matter of multiple affiliation in many directions, but a diffuse "24-hour" commitment incompatible with other ties within the community; and communication is no longer kept flowing freely over the cleavage lines but restricted and regulated to protect the movement against impurities and the seeds of compromise.

Historically documented cleavages rarely fall at the poles of the two axes: a concrete conflict is rarely exclusively territorial or exclusively functional but will feed on strains in both directions. The model essentially serves as a *grid* in the comparative analysis of political systems: the task is to locate the alliances behind given parties at given times within this two-dimensional space. The axes are not easily quantifiable, and they may not satisfy any criteria of strict scalability; nevertheless, they seem heuristically useful in attempts such as ours at linking up empirical variations in political structures with current conceptualizations in sociological theory.

A few concrete illustrations of party developments may help to clarify the distinctions in our model.

In Britain, the first nation-state to recognize the legitimacy of party oppositions, the initial conflicts were essentially of the types we have located at the *l* end of the vertical axis. The heads of independent landed families in the counties opposed the powers and the decisions of the government and the administration in London. The opposition between the "Country party" of knights and squires and the "Court and Treasury party" of the Whig magnates and the "placemen" was primarily territorial. The animosities of the Tories were not necessarily directed against the predominance of London in the affairs of the nation, but they were certainly aroused by the high-handed manipulations of the influential officeholders in the administration and their powerful allies in the boroughs. The conflict was not over general policies but over patronage and places. The gentry did not get their share of the *quid pro quo* exchanges of local influence against governmental offices and never established a clear-cut common front against the central power-holders. "Toryism about 1750 was primarily the opposition of the local rulers to central authority and vanished wherever members of that class entered the orbit of Government."[18]

Such particularistic, kin-centered, "ins-outs" oppositions are common in the early phases of nation-building: the electoral clienteles are small, undifferentiated, and easily controlled, and the stakes to be gained or lost in public life tend to be personal and concrete rather than collective and general.

Purely territorial oppositions rarely survive extensions of the suffrage. Much will depend, of course, on the timing of the crucial steps in the building of the nation: territorial unification, the establishment of legitimate government and the monopolization of the agencies of violence, the takeoff toward industrialization and economic growth, the development of popular education, and the entry of the lower classes into organized politics. Early democratization will not necessarily generate clear-cut divisions on functional lines. The initial result of a widening of the suffrage will often be an accentuation of the contrasts between the countryside and the urban centers and between the orthodox-fundamentalist beliefs of the peasantry and the small-town citizens and the secularism fostered in the larger cities and the metropolis. In the United States, the cleavages were typically cultural and religious. The struggles between the Jeffersonians and the Federalists, the Jacksonians and the Whigs, the Democrats and the Republicans centered on contrasting conceptions of public morality and pitted Puritans and other Protestants against Deists, Freemasons, and immigrant Catholics and Jews.[19] The accelerating influx of lower-class immigrants into the metropolitan areas and the centers of industry accentuated the contrasts between the rural and the urban cultural environments and between the backward and the advanced states of the Union. Such cumulations of territorial and cultural cleavages in the early phases of democratization can be documented for country after country. In Norway, all freehold and most leasehold peasants were given the vote as early as in 1814, but took several decades to mobilize in opposition to the King's officials and the dominance of the cities in the national economy. The crucial cleavages brought out into the open in the seventies were essentially territorial and cultural: the provinces were pitted against the capital; the increasingly estate-conscious peasants defended their traditions and their culture against the standards forced on them by the bureaucracy and the urban bourgeoisie. Interestingly, the extension of the suffrage to the landless laborers in the countryside and the propertyless workers in the cities did not bring about an immediate polarization of the polity on class lines. Issues of language, religion, and morality kept up the territorial oppositions in the system and cut across issues between the poorer and the better-off strata of the population. There were significant variations, however, between localities and between religions: the initial "politics of cultural defense" survived the extension of the suffrage in the egalitarian communities of the South and the West, but lost to straight class politics in the economically backward, hierarchically organized communities of the North.[20] The developments in the South and West of Norway find interesting parallels in the "Celtic fringe" of Britain. In these areas, particularly in Wales, opposition to the territorial, cultural, and economic dominance of the English offered a basis for communitywide support for the Liberals and retarded the development of straight class politics, even in the coalfields.[21] The sudden upsurge of Socialist strength in the northern periphery of Norway parallels the spectacular victory of the Finnish working-class party at the first election under universal suffrage: the fishermen and the crofters of the Norwegian North backed a distinct lower-class party as soon as they got the vote, and so did the Finnish rural proletariat.[22] In terms of our abstract model the politics of the western peripheries of Norway and Britain has its focus at the lower end of the l–g axis, whereas the politics of the backward districts of Finland and the Norwegian North represent alliance formations closer to g and at varying points of the a–i axis. In the one case the decisive criterion of alignment is *commitment to the locality and its dominant culture:* you vote with your community and its leaders irrespective of your economic position. In the other the criterion is *commitment to a class and its collective interests:* you vote with others in the same position as yourself whatever their localities, and you are willing to do so even if this brings you into opposition with members of your community. We rarely find one criterion of alignment completely dominant. There will be deviants from straight territorial voting just as often as from straight class voting. But we often find marked differences between regions in the *weight* of the one or the other criterion of alignment. Here ecological analyses of electoral records and census data for the early phases of mobilization may help us to map such variations in greater detail and to pinpoint factors strengthening the dominance of territorial politics and factors accelerating the process of class polarization.[23]

The Two Revolutions: The National and the Industrial

Territorial oppositions set limits to the process of nation-building; pushed to their extreme they lead to war, secession, possibly even population transfers. Functional oppositions can only develop after some initial consolidation of the national territory. They emerge with increasing interaction and communication across the localities and the regions, and they spread through a process of "social mobilization."[24] The growing nation-state developed a wide range of agencies of unification and standardization and gradually penetrated the bastions of "primordial" local culture.[25] So did the organizations of the Church, sometimes in close cooperation with the secular administrators, often in opposition to and competition with the officers of the state. And so did the many autonomous agencies of economic development and growth, the networks of traders and merchants, of bankers and financiers, of artisans and industrial entrepreneurs.

The early growth of the national bureaucracy tended to produce essentially territorial oppositions, but the subsequent widening of the scope of governmental activities and the acceleration of cross-local interactions gradually made for much more complex systems of alignments, some of them *between* localities, and others *across* and *within* localities.

The early waves of countermobilization often threatened the territorial unity of the nation, the federation, or the empire. The mobilization of the peasantry in Norway and in Sweden made it gradually impossible to keep up the union; the mobilization of the subject peoples of the Hapsburg territories broke up the empire; the mobilization of the Irish Catholics led to civil war and secession. The current strains of nation-building in the new states of Africa and Asia reflect similar conflicts between dominant and subject cultures; the recent histories of the Congo, India, Indonesia, Malaysia, Nigeria, and the Sudan can all be written in such terms. In some cases the early waves of mobilization may not have brought the territorial system to the brink of disruption but left an intractable heritage of territorial-cultural conflict: the Catalan-Basque-Castilian oppositions in Spain, the conflict between Flemings and Walloons in Belgium, and the English-French cleavages in Canada. The conditions for the softening or hardening of such cleavage lines in fully mobilized polities have been poorly studied. The multiple ethnic-religious cleavages of Switzerland and the language conflicts in Finland and Norway have proved much more manageable than the recently aggravated conflict between *Nederlands*-speakers and *francophones* in Belgium and between Quebec and the English-speaking provinces of Canada.

To account for such variations we clearly cannot proceed cleavage by cleavage but must analyze *constellations* of conflict lines within each polity.

To account for the variations in such constellations we have found it illuminating to distinguish *four critical lines of cleavage:*

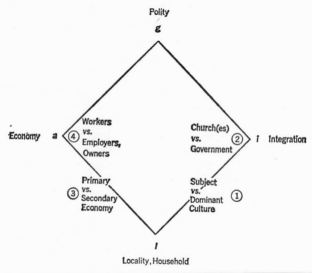

Figure 3—Suggested Locations of Four Critical Cleavages in the a-g-i-l Paradigm.

Two of these cleavages are direct products of what we might call the *National* Revolution: the conflict between *the central nation-building culture* and the increasing resistance of the ethnically, linguistically, or religiously distinct *subject populations* in the provinces and the peripheries (*1* in Fig. 3): the conflict between the centralizing, standardizing, and mobilizing *Nation-State* and the historically established corporate privileges of the *Church* (2).

Two of them are products of the *Industrial* Revolution: the conflict between the *landed interests* and the rising class of *industrial entrepreneurs* (3): the conflict between *owners and employers* on the one side and *tenants, laborers, and workers* on the other (4).

Much of the history of Europe since the beginning of the nineteenth century can be described in terms of the interaction between these two processes of revolutionary change: the one triggered in France and the other originating in Britain. Both had consequences for the cleavage structure of each nation, but the French Revolution produced the deepest and the bitterest oppositions. The decisive battle came to stand between *the aspirations of the mobilizing nation-state and the corporate claims of the churches.* This was far more than a matter of economics. It is true that the status of church properties and the financing of religious activities were the subjects of violent controversy, but the fundamental issue was one of morals, of the control of community norms. This found reflection in fights over such matters as the solemnization of marriage and the granting of divorces, the organization of charities and the handling of deviants, the functions of medical versus religious officers, and the arrangements for funerals. However, the fundamental issue between Church and State focused on the *control of education.*

The Church, whether Roman Catholic, Lutheran, or Reformed, had for centuries claimed the right to represent man's "spiritual estate" and to control the education of children in the right faith. In the Lutheran countries, steps were taken as early as in the seventeenth century to enforce elementary education in the vernacular for all children. The established national churches simply became agents of the state and had no reason to oppose such measures. In the religiously mixed countries and in purely Catholic ones, however, the ideas of the French Revolution proved highly divisive. The development of compulsory education under centralized secular control for all children of the nation came into direct conflict with the established rights of the religious *pouvoirs intermédiaires* and triggered waves of mass mobilization into nationwide parties of protest. To the radicals and liberals inspired by the French Revolution, the introduction of compulsory education was only one among several measures in a systematic effort to create direct links of influence and control between the nation-state and the individual citizen, but their attempt to penetrate directly to the children without consulting the parents and their spiritual authorities aroused widespread opposition and bitter fights.[26]

The parties of religious defense generated through this process grew into broad mass movements after the introduction of manhood suffrage and were able to claim the loyalties of remarkably high proportions of the churchgoers in the working class. These proportions increased even more, of course, as the franchise was extended to women on a par with men. Through a process very similar to the one to be described for the Socialist parties, these church movements tended to isolate their supporters from outside influence through the development of a wide variety of parallel organizations and agencies: they not only built up schools and youth movements of their own, but also developed confessionally distinct trade unions, sports clubs, leisure associations, publishing houses, magazines, newspapers, in one or two cases even radio and television stations.[27]

Perhaps the best example of institutionalized segmentation is found in the Netherlands; in fact, the Dutch word *Verzuiling* has recently become a standard term for tendencies to develop vertical networks (*zuilen,* columns or pillars) of associations and institutions to ensure maximum loyalty to each church and to protect the supporters from cross cutting communications and pressures. Dutch society has for close to a century been divided into three distinct subcultures: the national-liberal-secular, frequently referred to as the *algemene,* the "general" sector; the orthodox Protestant column; and the Roman Catholic column.[28]

The orthodox Protestant column developed through a series of violent conflicts over doctrinal issues within the established National Church. The *Nederlands Hervormde Kerk* came under heavy pressure in the decades after the French Revolution and the Napoleonic upheavals. With the spread of secularism and rationalism, the fundamentalists were increasingly pushed into a minority position, both within the Church and in the field of education. Originally, the orthodox protests against these developments restricted themselves to intellectual evangelical movements within the Establishment and to an isolationist walkout of pietistic lower-class elements in the separation (*Afscheiding*) of 1843. But from the 1860's onward, the movement achieved massive momentum under the organizational inspiration of Abraham Kuyper. This fundamentalist clergyman organized an Anti-School-Law League in 1872 and in 1879 succeeded in bringing together a variety of orthodox groups in a party explicitly directed against the ideas of the French Revolution, the *Anti-Revolutionary* party. This vigorous mass movement soon split up, however, over issues of doctrine and of cultural identification. Kuyper led his followers out of the Mother Church in 1886 and defended the rights of the *Kerkvolk,* the committed Calvinist Christians, to establish their own cultural community, free of any ties to the state and the nation. The very extremism of this anti-establishment posture produced several countermovements within the *Hervormde Kerk.* Important groups of orthodox Calvinists did *not* want to leave the Mother Church but wanted to reform it from within; they wanted a broad *Volkskerk* rather than an isolated *Kerkvolk.* The conflict between these two conceptions of the Christian community led to the breakup of the Anti-Revolutionary party in 1894 and the gradual formation of a second Calvinist party, the *Christian Historical Union,* formally consolidated in 1908. These two parties became the core organizations of the two wings of the orthodox Protestant front in Dutch society: the Anti-Revolutionaries deriving their essential strength from *Gereformeerden,* whether in separate dissenter churches or in *Hervormde* congregations controlled by clergymen of the same persuasion; the Christian Historicals deriving practically all their support from other orthodox segments *within* the Mother Church.

The Roman Catholic minority had at first found it to their advantage to work with the Liberal majority, but from the sixties onward took steps to form distinct political and social organizations. This was a slow process, however; the first federation of Catholic voters' associations was not formed until 1904 and a formally organized national party was not established until the twenties.[29]

Both the Protestant and the Catholic movements eventually developed large networks of associations and institutions for their members and were able to establish remarkably stable bases of support even within the working class. A nationwide survey carried out in 1956[30] tells a great deal about the importance of religious commitments for political choice in the Dutch system:

**Table 1—Denomination, Church Attendance, and Party Choice
in the Netherlands: Survey Evidence for 1956**

Denomination: Attendance:	NONE	HERVORMD		GEREFORMEERD		ROMAN CATH.	
		Yes	No	Yes	No	Yes	No
Party							
KPN (Communist)	7%	—	—	—	—	—	—
PvdA (Socialist)	75	22%	51%	2%	27%	3%	30%
VVD (Liberals)	11	7	18	—	—	—	9
Christian Historical	—	45	19	3	—	—	—
Anti-Revolutionary	—	17	6	90	63	—	6
Calvinist Extremist	—	5	3	1	5	—	—
KVP (Catholic)	1	—	—	—	—	94	52
Other	6	4	3	4	5	2	3
N = 100%	(218)	(134)	(236)	(101)	(22)	(329)	(33)

The segmentation is most complete within the active and intransigent minority movements: the *Gereformeerden,* the religiously active *Hervormden,* and the Catholics.

The passive members of the traditional National Church and the *onkerkelijken* tend to be aligned by class rather than by religious commitment: this was for long the only segment in which there was effective crosscutting of influences in the Dutch electorate.

In terms of our paradigm the orthodox Protestants and the Catholics form political fronts near the *i* pole of the cross-local axis. If all *three* of the subcultures had developed such strong barriers against each other, the system might conceivably have exploded, much in the way the Austrian polity did in 1934. The lower level of *Verzuiling* in the "national" sector and the greater possibilities of compromises and accommodation in a triangular system of oppositions may go far to explain the successful operation of corporate pluralism in the Dutch polity.

Analysts of the Dutch data on the three subcultures have tried to establish a variety of indicators of *changes over time* in the degree of insulation of each of the vertical segments: they use the term *Ontzuiling* for reductions in the distinctiveness of each segment and *Verzuiling* for increases.[31] In our paradigm these correspond to movements along the *a–i* axis: the more *ontzuild* a given opposition, the more crisscrossing of multiple memberships in the system and, in general, the less intolerance and distrust of citizens on the "other" side; the more *verzuild* the opposition, the fewer the crosspressures and the rarer the memberships across the cleavages. In a highly *ontzuild* system there is *low membership crystallization;* most of the participants tend to be tied to organizations and environments exposing them to *divergent* political pressures. By contrast in a highly *verzuild* system there is *high* membership crystallization; most of the participants tend to be exposed to messages and persuasive efforts in the *same* general direction in *all* their "24-hour–7-day" environments.[32]

This dimension cuts across the whole range of functional cleavages in our paradigm, whether economic, social, or religious. The symmetric representation of the four basic cleavage lines in Fig. 3 refers to *average tendencies* only and does not exclude wide variations in location along the *a–i* axis. Conflicts over the civic integration of recalcitrant regional cultures (1) or religious organizations (2) need not always lead to *Verzuiling*. An analysis of the contrasts between Switzerland and the Netherlands would tell us a great deal about differences in the conditions for the development of pluralist insulation. Conflicts between primary producers and the urban-industrial interests have *normally* tended towards the *a* pole of the axis, but there are many examples of highly ideologized peasant oppositions to officials and burghers. Conflicts between workers and employers have always contained elements of economic bargaining, but there have also often been strong elements of cultural opposition and ideological insulation. Working-class parties in opposition and without power have tended to be more *verzuild*, more wrapped up in their own distinct mythology, more insulated against the rest of the society. By contrast the victorious Labor parties have tended to become *ontzuild*, domesticated, more open to influence from all segments within the national society.

Similar variations will occur at a wide range of points on the *territorial* axis of our schema. In our initial discussion of the *l* pole we gave examples of *cultural* and *religious* resistances to the domination of the central national elite, but such oppositions are not always *purely* territorial. The movements may be completely dominant in their provincial strongholds but may also find allies in the central areas and thus contribute to the development of *cross-local* and *cross-regional* fronts.

The opposition of the Old Left in Norway was essentially of this character. It was from the outset a movement of territorial protest against the dominance of the central elite of officials and patricians but gradually broadened into a mass movement of cultural opposition to the dominant urban strata. As the suffrage was extended and the mobilization efforts proceeded it was also able to entrench itself in the central cities and even gain control in some of them.[33] This very broadening of the movement made the Old Left increasingly vulnerable to fragmentation. One wing moved toward the *a* pole and set itself up as an *Agrarian* party (3 in Fig. 3); another wing moved toward the *i* pole and after a long history of strains within the mother party established itself as the *Christian People's Party* (1 in Fig. 3). The Scandinavian countries have seen the formation of several such moralist-evangelist parties opposed to the tolerant pragmatism of the Established Lutheran Church.[34] They differ from the Christian parties on the Continent: they have not opposed national education as such and have not built up extensive networks of functional organizations around their followers; they have been primarily concerned to defend the traditions of orthodox evangelism against the onslaught of urban secularism and to use the legislative and the executive machinery of the state to protect the young against the evils of modern life. In their rejection of the lukewarm latitudinarianism of the national Mother Church they resemble the nonconformists in Great Britain and the Anti-Revolutionaries in the Netherlands, but the contexts of their efforts have been very different. In the British case the religious activists could work *within* the Liberal Party (later, of course, also within Labour) and found it possible to advance their views without establishing a party of their own. In the Dutch case, the orthodox dissidents not only set up their own party but built up a strong column of vertical organizations around it.

The National Revolution forced ever-widening circles of the territorial population to chose sides in conflicts over *values* and *cultural identities.* The Industrial Revolution also triggered a variety of cultural countermovements, but in the longer run tended to cut across the value communities within the nation and to force the enfranchised citizenry to choose sides in terms of their *economic interests,* their shares in the increased wealth generated through the spread of the new technologies and the widening markets.

In our *a–g–i–l* paradigm we have distinguished two types of such interest cleavages: cleavages between rural and urban interests (3) and cleavages between worker and employer interests (4).

The spectacular growth of world trade and industrial production generated increasing strains between the primary producers in the countryside and the merchants and the entrepreneurs in the towns and the cities. On the continent, the conflicting interests of the rural and the urban areas had been recognized since the Middle Ages in the separate representation of the estates: the nobility and, in exceptional cases, the freehold peasants spoke for the land, and the burghers spoke for the cities. The Industrial Revolution deepened these conflicts and in country after country produced distinct rural-urban alignments in the national legislatures. Often the old divisions between estates were simply carried over into the unified parliaments and found expression in oppositions between Conservative-Agrarian and Liberal-Radical parties. The conflicts between rural and urban interests had been much less marked in Great Britain than on the continent. The House of Commons was not an assembly of the burgher estate but a body of legislators representing the constituent localities of the realm, the counties and the boroughs.[35] Yet even there the Industrial Revolution produced deep and bitter cleavages between the landed interests and the urban; in England, if not in Wales and Scotland, the opposition between Conservatives and Liberals fed largely on these strains until the 1880's.[36]

There was a hard core of economic conflict in these oppositions, but what made them so deep and bitter was the struggle for the maintenance of acquired status and the recognition of achievement. In England, the landed elite ruled the country, and the rising class of industrial entrepreneurs, many of them religiously at odds with the established church, for decades aligned themselves in opposition both to defend their economic interests and to assert their claims to status. It would be a misunderstanding, says the historian George Kitson Clark,[37] to think of agriculture "as an industry organized like any other industry—primarily for the purposes of efficient production. *It was . . . rather organized to ensure the survival intact of a caste.* The proprietors of the great estates were not just very rich men whose capital happened to be invested in land, they were rather the life tenants of very considerable positions which it was their duty to leave intact to their successors. In a way it was the estate that mattered and not the holder of the estate. . . ." The conflict between Conservatives and Liberals reflected an opposition between two value orientations: the recognition of status through *ascription and kin connections* versus the claims for status through *achievement and enterprise.*

These are typical strains in all transitional societies; they tend to be most intensive in the early phases of industrialization and to soften as the rising elite establishes itself in the community. In England, this process of reconciliation proceeded quite rapidly. In a society open to extensive mobility and intermarriage, urban and industrial wealth could gradually be translated into full recognition within the traditional hierarchy of the landed families. More and more mergers took place between the agricultural and the business interests, and this consolidation of the national elite soon changed the character of the Conservative-Liberal conflict. As James Cornford has shown through his detailed ecological studies, the movement of the business owners into the countryside and the suburbs divorced them from their workers and brought them into close relations with the landed gentry. The result was a softening of the rural-urban conflict in the system and a rapidly increasing class polarization of the widened electorate.[38]

A similar *rapprochement* took place between the east Elbian agricultural interests and the western business bourgeoisie in Germany, but there, significantly, the bulk of the Liberals sided with the Conservatives and did not try to rally the working-class electorate on their side in the way the British party did during the period up to World War I. The result was a deepening of the chasm between burghers and workers and a variety of desperate attempts to bridge it through appeals to national and military values.[39]

In other countries of the European continent the rural-urban cleavage continued to assert itself in national politics far into the twentieth century, but the political expressions of the cleavage varied widely. Much depended on the concentrations of wealth and political control in the cities and on the ownership structure in the rural economy. In the Low Countries, France, Italy, and Spain, rural-urban cleavages rarely found direct expression in the development of party oppositions. Other cleavages, particularly between the state and the churches and between owners and tenants, had greater impact on the alignments of the electorates. By contrast, in the five Nordic countries the cities had traditionally dominated national political life, and the struggle for democracy and parliamentary rule was triggered off through a broad process of mobilization within the peasantry.[40] This was essentially an expression of protest against the central elite of officials and patricians (a cleavage on the *l–g* axis in our model), but there were also elements of economic opposition in the movement: the peasants felt exploited in their dealings with city folk and wanted to shift the tax burdens to the expanding urban economies. These economic cleavages became more and more pronounced as the primary-producing communities entered into the national money and market economy. The result was the formation of a broad front of interest organizations and cooperatives and the development of distinctive Agrarian parties. Even after the rise of the working-class parties to national dominance, these Agrarian parties did not find it possible to establish common fronts with the Conservative defenders of the business community. The cultural contrasts between the countryside and the cities were still strong, and the strict market controls favored by the Agrarians could not easily be reconciled with the philosophy of free competition espoused by many Conservatives.

The current conflicts over the prices of primary products between developed and underdeveloped countries can be seen as projections of these cleavages at the level of world economy. The Chinese Communists have for a long time seen the struggles of the emerging nations of Asia and Africa in these terms: as a fight of the peasantry against the city interests. As Lin

Piao put it in a recent policy statement: "The countryside, and the country-side alone, can offer the revolutionary bases from which the Revolution can go forward to final victory. . . . In a sense, the contemporary world revolution also presents the picture of the encirclement of the cities by the rural areas."[41]

The conflict between landed and urban interests was centered in the *commodity* market. The peasants wanted to sell their wares at the best possible prices and to buy what they needed from the industrial and urban producers at low cost. Such conflicts did not invariably prove party-forming. They could be dealt with within broad party fronts or could be channeled through interest organizations into narrower arenas of functional representation and bargaining. Distinctly agrarian parties have only emerged where strong cultural oppositions have deepened and embittered the strictly economic conflicts.

Conflicts in the *labor* market proved much more uniformly divisive. Working-class parties emerged in every country of Europe in the wake of the early waves of industrialization. The rising masses of wage earners, whether in large-scale farming, in forestry, or in industry, resented their conditions of work and the insecurity of their contracts, and many of them felt socially and culturally alienated from the owners and the employers. The result was the formation of a variety of labor unions and the development of nationwide Socialist parties. The success of such movements depended on a variety of factors: the strength of the paternalist traditions of ascriptive recognition of the worker status, the size of the work unit and the local ties of the workers, the level of prosperity and the stability of employment in the given industry, and the chances of improvements and promotion through loyal devotion or through education and achievement.

A crucial factor in the development of distinct working-class movements was the *openness* of the given society: Was the worker status a lifetime predicament or were there openings for advancement? How easy was it to get an education qualifying for a change in status? What prospects were there for striking out on one's own, for establishing independent work units? The contrasts between American and European developments must clearly be analyzed in these terms; the American workers were not only given the vote much earlier than their comrades in Europe; but they also found their way into the national system so much more easily because of the greater stress on equality and achievement, because of the many openings to better education, and, last but not least, because the established workers could advance to better positions as new waves of immigrants took over the lower-status jobs.[42] A similar process is currently under way in the advanced countries of Western Europe. The immigrant proletariats from the Mediterranean countries and from the West Indies allow the children of the established national working class to move into the middle class, and these new waves of mobility tend to drain off traditional sources of resentment.

In nineteenth and early twentieth century Europe the status barriers were markedly higher. The traditions from the estate-divided society kept the workers in their place, and the narrowness of the educational channels of mobility also made it difficult for sons and daughters to rise above their fathers. There were, however, important variations among the countries of Europe in the attitudes of the established and the rising elites to the claims of the workers, and these differences clearly affected the development of the unions and the Socialist parties. In Britain and the Scandinavian countries the attitudes of the elites tended to be open and pragmatic. As in all other countries there was active resistance to the claims of the workers, but little or no direct repression. These are today the countries with the largest and the most domesticated Labor parties in Europe. In Germany and Austria, France, Italy, and Spain the cleavages went much deeper. A number of attempts were made to repress the unions and the Socialists, and the working-class organizations consequently tended to isolate themselves from the national culture and to develop *soziale Ghettoparteien*,[43] strongly ideological movements seeking to isolate their members and their supporters from influences from the encompassing social environments. In terms of our paradigm, these parties were just as close to the *i* pole as their opponents in the religious camp. This "anti-system" orientation of large sections of the European working class was brought to a climax in the aftermath of the Russian Revolution. The Communist movement did not just speak for an alienated stratum of the territorial community but came to be seen as an external conspiracy against the nation. These developments brought a number of European countries to the point of civil war in the twenties and the thirties. The greater the numbers of citizens caught in such direct "friend-foe" oppositions to each other the greater the danger of total disruption of the body politic.

Developments since World War II have pointed toward a reduction of such pitched oppositions and some softening of ideological tensions: a movement from the *i* toward the *a* pole in our paradigm.[44] A variety of factors contributed to this development: the experience of national cooperation during the war, the improvements in the standard of living in the fifties, the rapid growth of a "new middle class" bridging the gaps between the traditional working class and the bourgeoisie. But the most important factor was possibly the *entrenchment of the working-class parties in local and national governmental structures* and their consequent "domestication" within the established system. The developments in Austria offer a particularly revealing example. The extreme opposition between Socialists and Catholics had ended in civil war in 1934, but after the experience of National Socialist domination, war, and occupation, the two parties settled down to share government responsibilities under a *Proporz* system, a settlement still based on mutual distrust between the two camps but at least one that recognized the necessity for coexistence.[45] Comparisons of the positions taken by the two leading Communist parties in Western Europe, the Italian and the French, also point to the importance of entrenchments in the national system of government. The French party has been much less involved in the running of local communities and has remained much more isolated within the national system, while the Italian party has responded much more dynamically to the exigencies of community decision-making.[46] Erik Allardt has implicitly demonstrated the importance of similar factors in a comparison of levels of class polarization in the Nordic countries. He points out that while the percentage of working-class voters siding with the Left (Communists and Social Democrats) is roughly the same in Finland as in Norway and Sweden, the percentage of middle-class leftists used to be much lower in Finland than in the two other countries. This difference appears to be related to a contrast in the chances of upward mobility from the working class: very low in Finland, markedly higher in the other countries.[47] The continued isolation of the Finnish working-class parties may reflect a lower level of participation in responsible decision-making in the local communities and in the nation. This has not yet been investigated in detail, but studies of working class mobility and political changes carried out in Norway[48] suggest that the principal channels of advancement were in the public sector and that the decisive wave of "bourgeoisification" came in the wake of the accession of the Labor party to a position of dominance in the system. In Finland the protracted period of underground Communism until 1944 and the deep split in the working-class movement during the next decades tended to keep the two parties from decisive influence on the public sector and maintained the old barriers against mobility; in the other Scandinavian countries the victories of the Social Democrat Labor parties had opened up new channels of mobility and helped to break down the isolation of the working class.

Cleavages in Fully Mobilized Polities

The four critical cleavages described in terms of our paradigm were all movements of protest against the *established* national elite and its cultural standards and were parts of a broad wave of emancipation and mobilization. Quite different types of protest alignments have tended to occur in *fully mobilized nation states*. In these the focus of protest has no longer been the traditional central culture but the rising networks of new elites, such as the leaders of the new large bureaucracies of industry and government, those who control the various sectors of the communications industry, the heads of mass organizations, the leaders in some countries of once weak or low-status minority ethnic or religious groups, and the like. Protest against these new elites and the institutions which foster them has often taken "anti-system" form, though the ideology has varied from country to country: Fascism in Italy, National Socialism in Germany, Poujadism in France, "radical rightism" in the United States. In our paradigm such protest movements would cut across the territorial axis very near the *g* pole; the conflict is no longer between constituent territorial units of the nation, but between different conceptions of the constitution and the organization of the national polity. These have all been *nationalist* movements: they not only accept, they venerate the historically given nation and its culture, but they reject the system of decision-making and control developed through the process of democratic mobilization and bargaining. Their aim is not just to gain recognition for a particular set of interests within a pluralist system of give and take but to *replace* this system by more authoritarian procedures of allocation.

In one way or another they all express deeply felt convictions about the destiny and the mission of the nation, some quite inchoate, others highly systematized; and they all endeavor to develop networks of organizations to keep their supporters loyal to the cause. They aim at *Verzuiling* but want only one column in the nation.

In our *a–g–i–l* schema, therefore, a fully *verzuild* nationalist movement would have to be placed at the *g–i* intersection outside what we might call the "competitive politics" diamond:

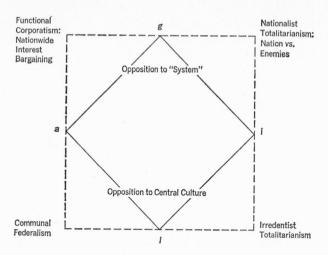

Figure 4—Suggested Locations of Four "Extremes" in the a-g-i-l Schema.

In its early varieties such nationalist movements essentially reflected the reactions of the lower-class strata of the dominant culture against the rising tides of mobilization within subject populations. In Hapsburg Austria the rise of the intransigent Pan-Germans was decisively accelerated through the alliance between the university *Burschenschaften* and Schönerer's nationalist workers' associations; these essentially recruited support among German-speaking craftsmen and workers threatened by the invasion of Czechs into the new centers of industry.[49] The xenophobia of the Austrian working class proved contagious. There are clear historical links between the early working-class nationalism of the eighties and nineties and the National Socialist movement after the defeat in 1918.[50] Hitler inherited his hatred of the Slavs and the Jews from the Austrian working-class nationalists. In our terminology, the National Socialist movement was an alliance at the *g* end of the territorial-cultural axis, the counterpart within the *dominant* national culture to an *l* opposition within some subject population at the periphery.

A variety of attempts have been made to determine the conditions for the emergence of such conflicts at the *g* pole of the political system. Contrasts in the continuity and regularity of nation-building have certainly counted. Austria, Germany, France, Italy, Spain, and the United States have all gone through extremely painful crises of nation-building and have still to contend with legacies of conflicts over national integration. Ralf Dahrendorf has recently interpreted the rise of National Socialism as the final breakthrough toward political modernization in Germany. It broke down the local pockets of insulation and established "*die traditionsfreie Gleichheit der Ausgangsstellung aller Menschen,*" an achievement-oriented society unfettered by diffuse status barriers.[51] The statistical histories of a number of "anti-system" movements of this type suggest that they made their greatest electoral gains through appeals to the "kleine Mann," the isolated "unit citizen" threatened by the rise of strong and complex corporations within a pluralist body politic. The "small man" came out not only against the great financial interests, the corporations, and the entrenched bureaucracies but also against the power of the churches, the trade unions, and the cooperatives. Studies of the crucial German elections of 1930, 1932, and 1933 show beyond doubt that the decisive thrust of mass support for the National Socialists came from owners of small and medium-sized farms, from artisans, shopkeepers, and other independents in the lower rungs of the middle class, most of them Protestants, all of them in more or less direct opposition to the giant cartels and the financial networks, to the unions, and to the forbidding column of Catholic organizations around the *Zentrum*.[52] Similar alignments have been documented for Italy, Norway, France, and the United States. There are obvious contextual variations, but the findings suggest important invariances in the conditions for the growth of such "anti-system" movements.[53]

We have come to the end of a cursory review of the typical cleavages generated in Western polities during the early phases of national consolidation and the later phases of suffrage extension and organizational growth. We have proceeded by way of exemplification rather than rigorous developmental comparison. Our purpose has not been to give an exhaustive account of differences and similarities country by country but to explore the potentialities of a scheme of classification developed from central concepts in current sociological theory. We hope to go further in this direction in other contexts; here we have simply wanted to initiate discussion of these possibilities and to point to new ways of analyzing the historical experience of these very different countries.

Whatever the shortcomings of the empirical applications, we feel confident that the Parsonian *A–G–I–L* schema can generate a set of analytical tools of great value in developmental comparisons of political systems. We have no doubt departed on several points from the standard interpretations of the Parsonian model and perhaps done violence to it in transforming it into a two-dimensional system of coordinates. To us this is of minor importance. We have simply used the original schema as a springboard for an attempt to bring some order into the comparative analysis of party-political developments. We might no doubt have come up with a very similar paradigm without recourse to the Parsonian core model, but we see great intellectual advantages in the unification of conceptualizations across several sectors of social life. The very fact that the same abstract schema has inspired analytical developments in such disparate fields as the family, the professions, religion, and politics seem to us to promise definite payoffs in the future.

Our use of the Parsonian categories is novel in two respects. First of all we have used them to bring some order into the comparative analysis of *conflicts, cleavages, and oppositions*. We think we have shown that they do not just serve to describe the functional requirements of viable social systems and the conditions of consensus and integration, but can be equally fruitful in analyses of sources of disequilibrium and disruption. Second, we have used the categories for purposes of *distinctly developmental* analysis. We have shown how the basic scheme of double dichotomies can be transformed into a model of step-by-step shifts in cleavage dimensions, from *l* to *i*, from *i* to *a*, and from *i* or *a* toward *g*.

We are aware that some of these innovations may prove to be purely terminological. We hope to show in our further development of these lines of analysis that they open up possibilities of direct gains in the intellectual control of the vast masses of information about party developments across the countries of the world.

THE TRANSFORMATION OF CLEAVAGE STRUCTURES INTO PARTY SYSTEMS

Conditions for the Channeling of Opposition

Thus far, we have focused on the emergence of *one cleavage at a time* and only incidentally concerned ourselves with the growth of *cleavage systems* and their translations into *constellations of political parties*. In terms of our schema we have limited ourselves to the analysis of the *internal differentiations* of the *I* quadrant and only by implication touched on *interchanges* between *I* and *G*, *I* and *L*, and *L* and *G*. But cleavages do not translate themselves into party oppositions as a matter of course: there are considerations of organizational and electoral strategy; there is the weighing of payoffs of alliances against losses through split-offs; and there is the successive narrowing of the "mobilization market" through the time sequences of organizational efforts. Here we enter into an area of crucial concern in current theorizing and research, an area of great fascination crying out for detailed cooperative research. Very much needs to be done in reanalyzing the evidence for each national party system and even more in exploring the possibilities of fitting such findings into a wider framework of developmental theory. We cannot hope to deal exhaustively with such possibilities of comparison in this volume and shall limit ourselves to a discussion of a few characteristic developments and suggest a rough typology.

How does a sociocultural conflict get translated into an opposition between parties? To approach an understanding of the variations in such processes of translation we have to sift out a great deal of information about the *conditions for the expression of protest and the representation of interests* in each society.

First, we must know about the *traditions of decision-making* in the polity: the prevalence of conciliar versus autocratic procedures of central government, the rules established for the handling of grievances and protests, the measures taken to control or to protect political associations, the freedom of communication, and the organization of demonstrations.[54]

Second, we must know about the *channels for the expression and mobilization of protest:* Was there a system of representation and if so how accessible were the representatives, who had a right to choose them, and how were they chosen? Was the conflict primarily expressed through direct demonstrations, through strikes, sabotage, or open violence, or could it be channeled through regular elections and through pressures on legitimately established representatives?

Third, we need information about *the opportunities, the payoffs, and the costs of alliances* in the system: How ready or reluctant were the old movements to broaden their bases of support and how easy or difficult was it for new movements to gain representation on their own?

Fourth and finally, we must know about *the possibilities, the implications, and the limitations of majority rule* in the system: What alliances would be most likely to bring about majority control of the organs of representation and how much influence could such majorities in fact exert on the basic structuring of the institutions and the allocations within the system?

The Four Thresholds

These series of questions suggest a *sequence of thresholds* in the path of any movement pressing forward new sets of demands within a political system.

First, the threshold of *legitimation:* Are all protests rejected as conspiratorial, or is there some recognition of the right of petition, criticism, and opposition?

Second, the threshold of *incorporation:* Are all or most of the supporters of the movement denied status as participants in the choice of representatives or are they given political citizenship rights on a par with their opponents?

Third, the threshold of *representation:* Must the new movement join larger and older movements to ensure access to representative organs or can it gain representation on its own?

Fourth, the threshold of *majority power:* Are there built-in checks and counterforces against numerical majority rule in the system or will a victory at the polls give a party or an alliance power to bring about major structural changes in the national system?

This gives us a crude four-variable typology of conditions for the development of party systems.

Level of each threshold				*Resulting party system*
Legiti-mation	Incorpo-ration	Represen-tation	Majority power	
High	H	H	H	Autocratic or oligarchic regimes, *Verfemung* of all parties:[55] protests and grievances either channeled through the field administration or through estate representation.
Medium	H	H	H	Embryonic internal party system: cliques of representatives, clubs of *notables*. Examples: Britain before 1832, Sweden during the quarrels between "Hats" and "Caps."[56]

Level of each threshold				Resulting party system
Legiti-mation	Incorpo-ration	Represen-tation	Majority power	
M	M	H	H or M	Internal party systems generating rudimentary outside support through registration association but safeguards introduced organizations: predominant in Western Europe during period between the breakdown of monarchic absolutism and the introduction of parliamentary rule under manhood suffrage.
Low	M	H	H	Initial phase in development of external party system: lower-class movements free to develop, but suffrage still limited and/or unequal. Example: Sweden before 1909.
L	M	H	M	Same but with parliamentary rule: Belgium before 1899; Norway, 1884–1900.
M	L	H	H	Isolation of lower-class or religious minority parties from the national system: restrictive measures against political organizations but full manhood suffrage. Examples: the Wilhelmine *Reich* during the period of the *Sozialistengesetze*, 1878–1890; France during the Second Empire and early decades of the Third Republic.
L	L	H	H	Competitive party system under universal and equal manhood suffrage but with high payoffs for alliances and with a clear separation of legislative and executive powers. The best example would be the United States if it were not for the restrictions on Communist Party activities and the low *de facto* enfranchisement of Negroes in the South. France under the Fifth Republic may be a better example.
L	L	H	M	Same but with parliamentary rule. Examples: France under later decades of the Third Republic and most of the Fourth; Great Britain since 1918.

Level of each threshold				*Resulting party system*
Legiti-mation	Incorpo-ration	Represen-tation	Majority power	
L	L	M	M	Same but with medium threshold PR (Proportional Representation): little need for alliances to achieve representation but safeguards introduced against fragmentation through explicit or implicit electoral minima. Examples: the Nordic countries, Belgium, the Netherlands, and Switzerland since 1918–20.
L	L	L	L	Same but with maximal PR and fewer restraints against majority power: the fragmented, centrifugal parliament and the plebiscitarian presidency of the Weimar Republic.

Empirically, changes in one such threshold sooner or later generated pressures to change one or more others, but there were many variations in the sequences of change. There is no "scalable" dimension of political development from a condition of four "high" thresholds to one of four "low" thresholds.

Clear-cut progressions toward lower thresholds are generally observed at the early stages of change: the recognition of freedoms of association, the extension of the suffrage. Much greater variations in the paths of development can be observed at the later stages. In fact there is no single terminal stage in the series of changes but several alternative ones:

LLHH—high-threshold majoritarian representation and separation of powers
LLHM—high-threshold majoritarian parliamentarism
LLMM—medium-threshold PR parliamentarism
LLLL—low-threshold PR and plebiscitarian majority rule

The early comparative literature on the growth of parties and party systems focused on the consequences of the lowering of the two first thresholds: the emergence of parliamentary opposition and a free press and the extension of the franchise. Tocqueville and Ostrogorski, Weber and Michels, all in their various ways, sought to gain insight into that central institution of the modern polity, the competitive mass party.[57] The later literature, particularly since the 1920's, changed its focus to the third and the fourth threshold: the consequences of the electoral system and the structure of the decision-making arena for the formation and the functioning of party systems. The fierce debates over the pros and cons of electoral systems stimulated a great variety of efforts at comparative analysis, but the heavy emotional commitments on the one or the other side often led to questionable interpretations of the data and to overhasty generalizations from meager evidence.

Few of the writers could content themselves with comparisons of sequences of change in different countries. They wanted to influence the future course of events, and they tended to be highly optimistic about the possibilities of bringing about changes in established party systems through electoral engineering. What they tended to forget was that parties once established develop their own internal structure and build up long-term commitments among core supporters. The electoral arrangements may prevent or delay the formation of a party, but once it has been established and entrenched, it will prove difficult to change its character simply through variations in the conditions of electoral aggregation. In fact, in most cases it makes little sense to treat electoral systems as independent variables and party systems as dependent. The party strategists will generally have decisive influence on electoral legislation and opt for the systems of aggregation most likely to consolidate their position, whether through increases in their representation, through the strengthening of the preferred alliances, or through safeguards against splinter movements. In abstract theoretical terms it may well make sense to hypothesize that simple majority systems will produce two-party oppositions within the culturally more homogeneous areas of a polity and only generate further parties through territorial cleavages, but the only convincing evidence for such a generalization comes from countries with a continuous history of simple majority aggregations from the beginnings of democratic mass politics. There is little hard evidence and much uncertainty about the effects of *later changes* in election laws on the national party system: one simple reason is that the parties already entrenched in the polity will exert a great deal of influence on the extent and the direction of any such changes and at least prove reluctant to see themselves voted out of existence.

Any attempt at systematic analysis of variations in the conditions and the strategies of party competition must start out from such differentiations of developmental phases. We cannot, in this context, proceed to detailed country-by-country comparisons but have to limit ourselves to a review of evidence for two distinct sequences of change: the rise of *lower-class* movements and parties and the decline of *régime censitaire* parties.

The Rules of the Electoral Game

The early electoral systems all set a high threshold for rising parties. It was everywhere very difficult for working-class movements to gain representation on their own, but there were significant variations in the openness of the systems to pressures from the new strata. The second ballot systems so well known from the Wilhelmine *Reich* and from the Third and the Fifth French Republics set the highest possible barrier, absolute majority, but at the same time made possible a variety of local alliances among the opponents of the Socialists: the system kept the new entrants underrepresented, yet did not force the old parties to merge or to ally themselves nationally. The blatant injustices of the electoral system added further to the alienation of the working classes from the national institutions and generated what Giovanni Sartori has described as systems of "centrifugal pluralism":[58] one major movement *outside* the established political arena and several opposed parties *within* it.

Simple majority systems of the British-American type also set high barriers against rising movements of new entrants into the political arena; however, the initial level is not standardized at 50 percent of the votes cast in each constituency but *varies from the outset with the strategies adopted by the established parties*. If they join together in defence of their common interests, the threshold is high; if each competes on its own, it is low. In the early phases of working-class mobilization, these systems have encouraged alliances of the "Lib-Lab" type. The new entrants into the electorate have seen their only chances of representation as lying in joint candidatures with the more reformist of the established parties. In later phases distinctly Socialist parties were able to gain representation on their own in areas of high industrial concentration and high class segregation, but this did not invariably bring about counteralliances of the older parties. In Britain, the decisive lower-class breakthrough came in the elections of 1918 and 1922. Before World War I the Labour Party had presented its own candidates in a few constituencies only and had not won more than 42 out of 670 seats; in 1918 they suddenly brought forth candidates in 388 constituencies and won 63 of them and then in 1922 advanced to 411 constituencies and 142 seats. The simple-majority system did not force an immediate restructuring of the party system, however. The Liberals continued to fight on their own and did not give way to the Conservatives until the emergency election of 1931. The inveterate hostilities between the two established parties helped to keep the average threshold for the newcomers tolerably low, but the very ease of this process of incorporation produced a split within the ranks of Labour. The currency crisis forced the leaders to opt between their loyalty to the historical nation and their solidarity with the finally mobilized working class.

Not all the simple-majority polities developed such strong and distinct working-class parties, however. Canada and the United States stayed at what we might call the "Lib-Lab" stage. Analysts of these two "deviant" nations have given prominence to factors such as early enfranchisement, high mobility, entrenched federalism, and marked regional, ethnic, and religious diversity.[59] There are important differences between the two cases, however, and these tell us a great deal about the importance of the *fourth* of our thresholds: the safeguards against direct majority power. In a recent comparison of the Canadian and the American party systems, Leon D. Epstein has argued with admirable cogency that the crucial differences reflect contrasts in the constitutionally set procedures of central decision-making: in Canada cabinet responsibility to a parliamentary majority, in the United States separate powers acquired through two distinct channels of representation.[60] The parliamentary system lowers the power threshold for numerical majorities, but the government depends for its existence on disciplined voting within the party or the parties supporting it in the legislature. The separation-of-powers system makes it more difficult to translate numerical victories into distinct changes of policy but also allows for much more flexible alliances within each of the parties. The Canadian party tends to be united in its legislative behavior and to maintain strict control over the recruitment of candidates. The American party tends to be a loose federation with a minimum of internal structure and is forced by the system of primaries to leave decisions on recruitment to a wider electoral market. As a result the Canadian system has tended to encourage regional and cultural protest parties, while the American parties have proved remarkably open to factional or local demands from a variety of movements and interests. The straight two-party system prevalent in the United States cannot be taken as a normal outcome of simple majority elections. American parties differ markedly in structure and in character from other parties produced under this system of elections and can best be explained through an analysis of the constitutionally established separation of the two arenas of decision-making, the Congress and the Presidential Executive.

This brings us to a crucial point in our discussion of the translation of cleavage structure into party systems: *the costs and the payoffs of mergers, alliances, and coalitions.* The height of the representation threshold and the rules of central decision-making may increase or decrease the net returns of joint action, but the intensity of inherited hostilities and the openness of communications across the cleavage lines will decide whether mergers or alliances are actually workable. There must be some minimum of trust among the leaders, and there must be some justification for expecting that the channels to the decision-makers will be kept open whoever wins the election. The British electoral system can only be understood against the background of the long-established traditions of territorial representation; the M.P. represents *all* his constituents, not just those who voted him in. But this system makes heavy demands on the loyalty of the constituents: in two-party contests up to 49 percent of them may have to abide by the decisions of a representative they did not want; in three-cornered fights, as much as 66 percent.

Such demands are bound to produce strains in ethnically, culturally, or religiously divided communities: the deeper the cleavages the less the likelihood of loyal acceptance of decisions by representatives of the other side. It was no accident that the earliest moves toward Proportional Representation came in the ethnically most heterogeneous of the European countries, Denmark (to accommodate Schleswig-Holstein), as early as 1855, the Swiss cantons from 1891 onward, Belgium from 1899, Moravia from 1905, and Finland from 1906.[61] The great historian of electoral systems, Karl Braunias, distinguishes two phases in the spread of PR: the "minority protection" phase before World War I and the "anti-socialist" phase in the years immediately after the armistice.[62] In linguistically and religiously divided societies majority elections could clearly threaten the continued existence of the political system. The introduction of some element of minority representation came to be seen as an essential step in a strategy of territorial consolidation.

As the pressures mounted for extensions of the suffrage, demands for proportionality were also heard in the culturally more homogeneous nation-states. In most cases the victory of the new principle of representation came about through a convergence of pressures from below and from above. The rising working class wanted to lower the threshold of representation to gain access to the legislatures, and the most threatened of the old-established parties demanded PR to protect their positions against the new waves of mobilized voters under universal suffrage. In Belgium the introduction of graduated manhood suffrage in 1893 brought about an increasing polarization between Labor and Catholics and threatened the continued existence of the Liberals; the introduction of PR restored some equilibrium to the system.[63] The history of the struggles over electoral procedures in Sweden and in Norway tells us a great deal about the consequences of the lowering of one threshold for the bargaining over the level of the next. In Sweden, the Liberals and the Social Democrats fought a long fight for universal and equal suffrage and at first also advocated PR to ensure easier access to the legislature. The remarkable success of their mobilization efforts made them change their strategy, however. From 1904 onward they advocated majority elections in single-member constituencies. This aroused fears among the farmers and the urban Conservatives, and to protect their interests they made the introduction of PR a condition for their acceptance of manhood suffrage. As a result the two barriers fell together: it became easier to enter the electorate and easier to gain representation.[64] In Norway there was a much longer lag between the waves of mobilization. The franchise was much wider from the outset, and the first wave of peasant mobilization brought down the old regime as early as in 1884. As a result the suffrage was extended well before the final mobilization of the rural proletariat and the industrial workers under the impact of rapid economic change. The victorious radical-agrarian "Left" felt no need to lower the threshold of representation and in fact helped to increase it through the introduction of a two-ballot system of the French type in 1906. There is little doubt that this contributed heavily to the radicalization and the alienation of the Norwegian Labor Party. By 1915 it had gained 32 percent of all the votes cast but was given barely 15 percent of the seats. The "Left" did not give in until 1921. The decisive motive was clearly not just a sense of equalitarian justice but the fear of rapid decline with further advances of the Labor Party across the majority threshold.

In all these cases high thresholds might have been kept up if the parties of the property-owning classes had been able to make common cause against the rising working-class movements. But the inheritance of hostility and distrust was too strong. The Belgian Liberals could not face the possibility of a merger with the Catholics, and the cleavages between the rural and the urban interests went too deep in the Nordic countries to make it possible to build up any joint antisocialist front. By contrast, the higher level of industrialization and the progressive merger of rural and urban interests in Britain made it possible to withstand the demand for a change in the system of representation. Labor was seriously underrepresented only during a brief initial period, and the Conservatives were able to establish broad enough alliances in the counties and the suburbs to keep their votes well above the critical point.

A MODEL FOR THE GENERATION OF THE EUROPEAN PARTY SYSTEM

Four Decisive Dimensions of Opposition

This review of the conditions for the translation of sociocultural cleavages into political oppositions suggests three conclusions.

First, the constitutive contrasts in the national system of party constellations generally tended to manifest themselves *before* any lowering of the threshold of representation. The decisive sequences of party formation took place at the early stage of competitive politics, in some cases well before the extension of the franchise, in other cases on the very eve of the rush to mobilize the finally enfranchised masses.

Second, the high thresholds of representation during the phase of mass politicization set severe tests for the rising political organizations. The surviving formations tended to be firmly entrenched in the inherited social structure and could not easily be dislodged through changes in the rules of the electoral game.

Third, the decisive moves to lower the threshold of representation reflected divisions among the established *régime censitaire* parties rather than pressures from the new mass movements. The introduction of PR added a few additional splinters but essentially served to ensure the separate survival of parties unable to come together in common defense against the rising contenders for majority power.

What happened at the decisive party-forming phase in each national society? Which of the many contrasts and conflicts were translated into party oppositions, and how were these oppositions built into stable systems?

This is not the place to enter into detailed comparisons of developmental sequences nation by nation. Our task is to suggest a framework for the explanation of variations in cleavage bases and party constellations.

In the abstract schema set out in Fig. 3 we distinguished four decisive dimensions of opposition in Western politics:

two of them were products of what we called the *National* Revolution (1 and 2);

and two of them were generated through the *Industrial* Revolution (3 and 4).

In their basic characteristics the party systems that emerged in the Western European politics during the early phase of competition and mobilization can be interpreted as products of *sequential interactions between these two fundamental processes of change.*

Differences in the timing and character of the *National* Revolution set the stage for striking divergencies in the European party system. In the Protestant countries the conflicts between the claims of the State and the Church had been temporarily settled by royal *fiats* at the time of the Reformation, and the processes of centralization and standardization triggered off after 1789 did not immediately bring about a conflict between the two. The temporal and the spiritual establishments were at one in the defense of the central nation-building culture but came increasingly under attack by the leaders and ideologists of countermovements in the provinces, in the peripheries and within the underprivileged strata of peasants, craftsmen and workers. The other countries of Western Europe were all split to the core in the wake of the secularizing French Revolution and without exception developed strong parties for the defense of the Church, either explicitly as in Germany, the Low Countries, Switzerland, Austria, Italy, and Spain or implicitly as in the case of the Right in France.[65]

Differences in the timing and character of the *Industrial* Revolution also made for contrasts among the national party systems in Europe.

Conflicts in the *commodity* market tended to produce highly divergent party alliances in Europe. In some countries the majority of the market farmers found it possible to join with the owner interests in the secondary sector of the economy; in others the two remained in opposition to each other and developed parties of their own. Conflicts in the *labor* market, by contrast, proved much more uniformly divisive: all countries of Western Europe developed lower-class mass parties at some point or other before World War I. These were rarely unified into one single working-class party. In Latin Europe the lower-class movements were sharply divided among revolutionary anarchist, anarchosyndicalist and Marxist factions on the one hand and revisionist socialists on the other. The Russian Revolution of 1917 split the working-class organizations throughout Europe. Today we find in practically all countries of the West divisions between Communists, left Socialist splinters, and revisionist Social Democrat parties.

Our task, however, is not just to account for the emergence of single parties but to analyze the processes of alliance formation that led to the development of stable *systems* of political organizations in country after country. To approach some understanding of these alliance formations, we have to study the *interactions* between the two revolutionary processes of change in each polity: How far had the National Revolution proceeded at the point of the industrial "takeoff" and how did the two processes of mobilization, the cultural and the economic, affect each other, positively by producing common fronts or negatively by maintaining divisions?

The decisive contrasts among the Western party systems clearly reflect differences in the *national histories of conflict and compromise across the first three of the four cleavage lines* distinguished in our analytical schema: the "center-periphery," the state-church, and the land-industry cleavages generated national developments in *divergent* directions, while the owner-worker cleavage tended to bring the party systems *closer to each other* in their basic structure. The crucial differences among the party systems emerged in the early phases of competitive politics, before the final phase of mass mobilization. They reflected basic contrasts in the conditions and sequences of nation-building and in the structure of the economy at the point of take-off toward sustained growth. This, to be sure, does not mean that the systems vary exclusively on the "Right" and at the center, but are much more alike on the "Left" of the political spectrum. There are working-class movements throughout the West, but they differ conspicuously in size, in cohesion, in ideological orientation, and in the extent of their integration into, or alienation from, the historically given national policy. Our point is simply that the factors generating these differences on the left are *secondary*. The decisive contrasts among the systems had emerged before the entry of the working-class parties into the political arena, and the character of these mass parties was heavily influenced by the constellations of ideologies, movements, and organizations they had to confront in that arena.

A Model in Three Steps

To understand the differences among the Western party systems we have to start out from an analysis of the *situation of the active nation-building elite on the eve of the breakthrough to democratization and mass mobilization:* What had they achieved and where had they met most resistance? What were their resources, who were their nearest allies, and where could they hope to find further support? Who were their enemies, what were their resources, and where could they recruit allies and rally reinforcement?

Any attempt at comparative analysis across so many divergent national histories is fraught with grave risks. It is easy to get lost in the wealth of fascinating detail, and it is equally easy to succumb to facile generalities and irresponsible abstractions. Scholarly prudence prompts us to proceed case by case, but intellectual impatience urges us to go beyond the analysis of concrete contrasts and try out alternative schemes of systematization across the known cases.

To clarify the logic of our approach to the comparative analysis of party systems, we have developed a *model of alternative alliances and oppositions.* We have posited several sets of actors, have set up a series of rules of alliance and opposition among these, and have tested the resultant typology of potential party systems against a range of empirically known cases.

Our model bears on relationships of alliance, neutrality or opposition among seven sets of actors. To underscore the abstract character of our exercise we shall refer to each set by a shorthand symbol:

N—a central core of cooperating "nation-builders" controlling major elements of the machinery of the "state";

C—an ecclesiastical body established within the national territory and given a large measure of control over education;

R—the supranationally established ecclesiastical body organized under the Roman Curia and the Pope;

D—a dissident, nonconformist body of religious activists opposed to C and R;

L—a cooperating body of established landowners controlling a substantial share of the total primary production of the national territory;

U—a cooperating body of urban commercial and industrial entrepreneurs controlling the advancing secondary sectors of the national economy;

P—a movement of resistance in the subject periphery against central national control.

The model sets these *restrictions on alliance formation:*

(1) N and D and N and P will invariably be opposed, never in any joint alliance;

(2) N must decide on alliances on two fronts: the *religious* and the *economic;*

   (3) on the religious front, N is faced with three options:
     —alliance with C,
     —a secular posture S,
     —alliance with R;

   (4) on the economic front, N is restricted to two alliance options:
     —with L,
     —with U;

   (5) N's alliances determine P's choice of alliances but with these restric-

tions: (a) if N is allied to C, the model allows two contingent outcomes: (aa) if C is dominant, the only P option on the religious front is D, (bb) if R still constitutes a strong minority, P will be split in two alliance-groups: the response to N–C–L will be P_1–S–U and P_2–R, the response to N–C–U will be P_1–D–L and P_2–R–L: (b) if N chooses S or R, the only possible P alliances are P–S–U and P–R–L or simply P–U and P–L; P–R–U and P–S–L do not occur.

These various elements and restrictions combine to produce an eightfold typology of basic political oppositions:

TYPE	N'S COMMITMENTS			P'S RESPONSE	CLOSEST EMPIRICAL EXAMPLES		
	Religious front	Economic front			Country	"N" party (parties)	"P" parties
	Option	Conditions					
I	C	C dominant	L	P–D–U	Britain	CONS. vs.	LIB: { Celtic fringe / Dissenters / Industry
II	C	C dominant	U	P–D–L	Scandinavia	CONS. vs.	"LEFT" { AGRARIANS / CHRISTIANS / RADICALS
III	C	R strong minority	L	{ $\dfrac{P_1\text{–}S\text{–}U}{P_2\text{–}R}$	Prussia/ Reich	CONS. vs.	{ BAVARIANS / LIB. / ZENTRUM
IV	C	R strong minority	U	{ $\dfrac{P_1\text{–}D\text{–}L}{P_2\text{–}R\text{–}L}$	Netherlands	LIB. vs.	{ Calvinists: CHU, AR / Catholics: KVP
V	S		L	{ $\dfrac{P_1\text{–}U}{P_2\text{–}R}$	Spain	LIB. vs.	{ Catalan LLIGA / Carlists
VI	S		U	P–R–L	France Italy	LIB./RAD. vs.	CONS.–CATH.–CHR.
VII	R		L	P–S–U	Austria	CHR. vs. LIB.	{ Pan-Germans / Industry
VIII	R		U	P–L	Belgium	CHR./LIB. vs.	Flemish separatists

This typological exercise may appear excessively abstract and unnecessarily mechanical. To us the gains in analytical perspective outweigh the loss in historical immediacy: the model not only offers a grid for the mapping of parallels and contrasts among national developments, it also represents an attempt to establish an explanatory paradigm of the simplest possible structure to account for a wide range of empirical variations. The literature on democratic politics is replete with examples of isolated discussions of parallels and contrasts among national party systems: ours, we believe, is the first attempt to develop a general typology of such variations from a unified set of postulates and hypotheses.

Our model seeks to reduce the bewildering variety of empirical party systems *to a set of ordered consequences of decisions and developments at three crucial junctures in the history of each nation:*

first, during the *Reformation*—the struggle for the control of the ecclesiastical organizations within the national territory;

second, in the wake of the *"Democratic Revolution"* after 1789—the conflict over the control of the vast machineries of mass education to be built up by the mobilizing nation-states;

finally, during the early phases of the *Industrial Revolution*—the opposition between landed interests and the claims of the rising commercial and industrial leadership in cities and towns.

Our eight types of alliance-opposition structure are in fact the simple combinatorial products of three successive dichotomies:

FIRST DICHOTOMY: THE REFORMATION

I–IV	V–VIII
State Controls National Church	State Allied to Roman Catholic Church

SECOND DICHOTOMY: THE "DEMOCRATIC REVOLUTION"

I–II	III–IV	V–VI	VII–VIII
National Church Dominant	Strong Roman Minority	Secularizing Revolution	State Allied to Roman Church

THIRD DICHOTOMY: THE INDUSTRIAL REVOLUTION

Commitment to		Commitment to		Commitment to		Commitment to	
Landed	Urban	Landed	Urban	Landed	Urban	Landed	Urban
Interests		Interests		Interests		Interests	

Type: I   II   III   IV   V   VI   VII   VIII

The model spells out the consequences of the fateful division of Europe brought about through Reformation and the Counter-Reformation. The outcomes of the early struggles between State and Church determined the structure of national politics in the era of democratization and mass mobilization three hundred years later. In Southern and Central Europe the Counter-Reformation had consolidated the position of the Church and tied its fate to the privileged bodies of the *ancien régime*. The result was a polarization of politics between a national-radical-secular movement and a Catholic-traditionalists one. In Northwest Europe, in Britain, and in Scandinavia, the settlement of the sixteenth century gave a very different structure to the cleavages of the nineteenth. The established churches did not stand in opposition to the nation-builders in the way the Roman Catholic Church did on the continent, and the "Left" movements opposed to the religious establishment found most of their support among newly enfranchised dissenters, nonconformists, and fundamentalists in the peripheries and within the rising urban strata. In Southern and Central Europe the bourgeois opposition to the *ancien régime* tended to be indifferent if not hostile to the teachings of the Church: the cultural integration of the nation came first and the Church had to find whatever place it could within the new political order. In Northwest Europe the opposition to the *ancien régime* was far from indifferent to religious values. The broad "Left" coalitions against the established powers recruited decisive support among orthodox Protestants in a variety of sectarian movements outside and inside the national churches.

The distinction between these two types of "Left" alliances against the inherited political structure is fundamental for an understanding of European political developments in the age of mass elections. It is of particular importance in the analysis of the religiously most divided of the European polities: types III and IV in our 2 x 2 x 2 schema. The religious frontiers of Europe went straight through the territories of the Low Countries, the old German *Reich,* and Switzerland; in each of these the clash between the nation-builders and the strong Roman Catholic minorities produced lasting divisions of the bodies politic and determined the structure of their party systems. The Dutch system came closest to a direct merger of the Southern-Central type (VI–VIII) and the Northwestern: on the one hand a nation-building party of increasingly secularized Liberals, on the other hand a Protestant "Left" recruited from orthodox milieus of the same type as those behind the old opposition parties in England and Scandinavia.

The difference between England and the Netherlands is indeed instructive. Both countries had their strong peripheral concentrations of Catholics opposed to central authority: the English in Ireland, the Dutch in the south. In Ireland, the cumulation of ethnic, social, and religious conflicts could not be resolved within the old system; the result was a history of intermittent violence and finally territorial separation. In the Netherlands the secession of the Belgians still left a sizable Catholic minority, but the inherited tradition of corporate pluralism helped to ease them into the system. The Catholics established their own broad column of associations and a strong political party and gradually found acceptance within a markedly segmented but still cohesive national polity.

A comparison of the Dutch and the Swiss cases would add further depth to this analysis of the conditions for the differentiation of parties within national systems. Both countries come close to our type IV: Protestant national leadership, strong Catholic minorities, predominance of the cities in the national economy. In setting the assumption of our model we predicted a split in the peripheral opposition to the nation-builders: one orthodox Protestant opposition (P–D–L) and one Roman Catholic (P–R–L). This clearly fits the Dutch case but not so well the Swiss. How is this to be accounted for? Contrasts of this type open up fascinating possibilities of comparative historical analysis; all we can do here is to suggest a simple hypothesis. Our model not only simplifies complex historical developments through its strict selection of conditioning variables, it also reduces empirical continuities to crude dichotomies. The difference between the Dutch and the Swiss cases can possibly be accounted for through further differentiation in the center-periphery axis. The drive for national centralization was stronger in the Netherlands and had been slowed down in Switzerland through the experiences of the war between the Protestant cantons and the Catholic *Sonderbund*. In the Netherlands the Liberal drive for centralization produced resistance both among the Protestants and the Catholics. In Switzerland the Radicals had few difficulties on the Protestant side and needed support in their opposition to the Catholics. The result was a party system of essentially the same structure as in the typical Southern-Central cases.[66]

Further differentiations of the "N–P" axis in our model will also make it easier to fit the extraordinary case of *France* into this system of controlled dimension-by-dimension comparisons.

In our model we have placed France with Italy as an example of an alliance-opposition system of type VI: Catholic dominance through the Counter-Reformation, secularization and religious conflict during the next phase of nation-building in the nineteenth century, clear predominance of the cities in national politics. But this is an analytical juxtaposition of polities with diametrically opposed histories of development and consolidation—France one of the oldest and most centralized nation-states in Europe, Italy a territory unified long after the French revolutions had paved the way for the "participant nation," the integrated political structure committing the entire territorial population to the same historical destiny. To us this is not a weakness in our model, however. The party systems of the countries *are* curiously similar, and any scheme of comparative analysis must somehow or other bring this out. The point is that our distinction between "nation-builder" alliances and "periphery" alliances must take on very different meanings in the two contexts. In France the distinction between "center" and "periphery" was far more than a matter of geography; it reflected long-standing historical commitments for or against the Revolution. As spelt out in detail in Siegfried's classic *Tableau,* the *Droite* had its strongholds in the districts which had most stubbornly resisted the revolutionary drive for centralization and equalization,[67] but it was far more than a movement of peripheral protest—it was a broad alliance of alienated elite groups, of frustrated nation-builders who felt that their rightful powers had been usurped by men without faith and without roots. In Italy there was no basis for such a broad alliance against the secular nation-builders, since the established local elites offered little resistance to the lures of *trasformismo,* and the Church kept its faithful followers out of national politics for nearly two generations.

These contrasts during the initial phases of mass mobilization had far-reaching consequences for each party system. With the broadening of the electorates and the strengthening of the working-class parties, the Church felt impelled to defend its position through its own resources. In France, the result was an attempt to divorce the defense of the Catholic schools from the defense of the established rural hierarchy. This trend had first found expression through the establishment of Christian trade unions and in 1944 finally led to the formation of the MRP. The burden of historic commitments was too strong, however; the young party was unable to establish itself as a broad mass party defending the principles of Christian democracy. By contrast, in Italy, history had left the Church with only insignificant rivals to the right of the working class parties. The result was the formation of a broad alliance of a variety of interests and movements, frequently at loggerheads with each other, but united in their defense of the rights of the central institution of the fragmented *ancien régime,* the Roman Catholic Church. In both cases there was a clear-cut tendency toward religious polarization, but differences in the histories of nation-building made for differences in the resultant systems of party alliances and oppositions.

We could go into further detail on every one of the eight types distinguished in our model, but this would take us too far into single-country histories. We are less concerned with the specifics of the degrees of fit in each national case than with the overall structure of the model. There is clearly nothing final about any such scheme; it simply sets a series of themes for detailed comparisons and suggests ways of organizing the results within a manageable conceptual framework. The model is a tool and its utility can be tested only through continuous development: through the addition of further variables to account for observed differences as well as through refinements in the definition and grading of the variables already included.

Two developments from the model require immediate detailed consideration:

(1) What variables have to be added to account for the formation of *distinctly territorial* parties?

(2) What criteria should count in differentiating between N–L and N–U alliances, and what conditional variables can be entered into the model to account for the emergence of *explicitly agrarian parties?*

Developments and Deviations: Parties for Territorial Defense

Nation-building invariably generates territorial resistances and cultural strains. There will be competition between potential centers of political control; there may be conflict between the capital and the areas of growth in the provinces; and there will be unavoidable tension between the culturally and economically advanced areas and the backward periphery.[68] Some of these territorial-cultural conflicts were solved through secession or boundary changes, but others were intensified through unification movements. To take one obvious example, the dismemberment of the Hapsburg Empire certainly settled a great number of hopelessly entangled conflicts, but it also led to the political unification of such culturally and economically heterogeneous entities as Italy, Yugoslavia, and Czechoslovakia. Territorial-cultural conflicts do not just find political expression in secessionist and irredentist movements, however; they feed into the overall cleavage structure in the national community and help to condition the development not only of each nationwide party organization but even more of the entire system of party oppositions and alignments.

The contrast between the British and the Scandinavian party systems stands out with great clarity in our step-by-step accounting scheme. The countries of Northwest Europe had all opted for national religious solutions at the time of the Reformation, but they nevertheless developed markedly different party systems during the early phases of democratization and mobilization. This contrast in political development clearly did not reflect a difference in the salience of *any single* line of cleavage but a difference in the *joint* operation of two sets of cleavages: the opposition between the central nation-building culture and the traditions of the periphery, and the opposition between the primary and the secondary sectors of the economy. In Britain the central culture was upheld and reinforced by a vast network of *landed* families, in the Nordic countries by an essentially *urban* elite of officials and patricians. In Britain the two cleavage lines *cut across* each other; in Scandinavia they *reinforced* each other. The British structure encouraged a gradual merger of urban and rural interests, while the Scandinavian made for division and opposition.[69] The British Conservative Party was able to establish a joint front of landed and industrial owner interests, while the

Scandinavian "Right" remained essentially urban and proved unable to establish any durable alliance with the Agrarians and the peripheral "Left."

Similar processes of interaction can be observed at work in the development of the continental party system. Conflicts between mobilizing elites and peripheral cultures have in some cases been reinforced, in some cases dampened, by conflicts between the State and the Church and by oppositions between urban and rural interests. Belgium offers a striking example of cleavage reinforcement. The "Union of Oppositions" of the early years of nation-building broke up over the schools issue, but this was only the first step in a gradual deepening of cleavages. The continuing processes of economic, social, and cultural mobilization brought the country closer to a polarization between French-speaking, secular and industrial Wallonia and Nederlands-speaking, Catholic and agricultural Flanders.[70] This polarizing cleavage structure contrasts dramatically with the crisscrossing of religious and linguistic oppositions in Switzerland. Of the five French-speaking cantons three are Protestant and two Catholic, and of the nineteen Alemannic cantons or half-cantons ten are Protestant and nine Catholic: "this creates loyalties and affinities which counterbalance the linguistic inter-relationships."[71]

Conditions for the emergence and consolidation of territorial counter-cultures have varied significantly within Europe. Organized resistance against the centralizing apparatus of the mobilizing nation-state appears to have been most likely to develop in three sets of situations:

—heavy concentration of the counter-culture within one clear-cut territory;

—few ties of communication, alliance, and bargaining experience toward the national center and more toward external centers of cultural or economic influence;

—minimal economic dependence on the political metropolis.

Federalist, autonomist, and separatist movements and parties are most likely to occur through a cumulation of such conditions. A comparison of Spain and Italy tells us a great deal about such processes of cleavage cumulation. Both countries have for centuries been heavily dominated by the Catholic Church. Both were caught in a violent conflict between secular power and ecclesiastical privileges in the wake of the National Revolution, and both have remained highly heterogeneous in their ethnic structure, in cultural traditions, and in historical commitments. Yet they differed markedly in the character of the party systems they developed in the phase of initial mass mobilization. Spanish politics was dominated by territorial oppositions; Italy developed a national party system, fragmented but with irredentist-separatist parties only in such extreme cases as the South Tyrol and the Val d'Aosta.

In Spain, the opposition of the Pyrennean periphery to the centralizing Castilian regime first found expression in the mobilization of the Carlist peasantry in defense of the Church and their local liberties against the Liberals and the Freemasons in the army and government bureaucracy during the second half of the nineteenth century. Around 1900, the Catalan industrial bourgeoisie and significant parts of the Basque middle classes and peasantry turned to regionalist and separatist parties to fight the parasitic central administration identified with the economically backward center of the nation. In the Basque areas, strong religious loyalties contributed to increase the hostility toward an anticlerical central government. In Catalonia, separatist sentiments could not repress cleavages along class lines. The conflicts between businessmen and workers, landowners and tenant-farmers divided the regionalist forces into a right (the *Lliga*) and a left (the *Esquerra*).[72]

In Italy, the thrust of national mobilization came from the economically advanced North. The impoverished provinces to the South and on the islands resisted the new administrators as alien usurpers but did not develop parties of regional resistance: the prefects ruled through varying mixtures of *combinazione* and force and proved as efficient instruments of centralization in the backward areas of Italy as the *caciques* in the regions of Spain controlled from Madrid.[73] There was an obvious element of territorial protest in the papal repudiation of the new nation-state, but it took several decades before this conflict found expression in the formation of a distinctly Catholic party. The loyal Catholics did not just oppose the Piedmontese administration as a threat to the established privileges of the Church; Rome fought the Liberal nation-builders as the conquerors of the Papal territories. But these resentments were not channeled into national politics. The intransigent policy of *non expedit* kept the Catholics out of the give and take of electoral bargaining and discouraged the eager advocates of a mass party for the defense of the Church. This policy of isolation divided the communities throughout the Italian territory. When the Pope finally gave in on the eve of the introduction of mass suffrage, these cross-local cleavages produced a nationwide system of oppositions among Liberals, Catholics, and Socialists. There were marked regional variations in the strength of each camp. Dogan's work on regional variations in the stratification of the Italian vote tells us a great deal about the factors at work.[74] But in contrast to the development in Spain, the territorial conflict within Italy found no direct expression in the party system. This was not a sign of national integration, however; the country was torn by irreconcilable conflicts among ideologically distinct camps, but the conflict cut across the communities and the regions. There were still unsettled and unsettling territorial problems, but these were at the frontiers. The irredentist claims against France and the Hapsburgs generated a nationalist-imperialist ideology and prepared the ground for the rise of Fascism.[75]

Such comparisons can be multiplied throughout Europe. In the multicentered German Reich the contrasts between East and West, North and South generated a variety of territorial tensions. The conflict between the Hamburg Liberals and the East Elbian Conservatives went far beyond the tariff issue—it reflected an important cultural opposition. The Bavarian particularists again and again set up parties of their own and have to this day found it difficult to fit into a nationwide system of party oppositions.[76] By contrast, in hydrocephalic France conflicts between the capital and the provincial "desert"[77] had been endemic since the sixteenth century but did *not* generate distinct regional parties. Paris was without serious competitors for political, economic, and cultural power—there was no basis for durable alliances against the center. "Paris was not only comparable to New York and Washington, as was London, but also to Chicago in transport, Detroit and Cincinnati in manufacturing, and Boston in letters and education."[78]

Developments and Deviations: Parties for Agrarian Defense

We distinguished in our initial paradigm (Fig. 3) between two "typical" cleavages at the *l* end of the territorial-cultural axis: on the *i* side the opposition of ethnic-linguistic minorities against the upholders of the dominant national culture (1), on the *a* side the opposition of the peasantry against economic exploitation by the financial, commercial, and industrial interests in the cities (3).

Our discussion of the "party formation" model brought out a few hypotheses about the transformation of cleavages of type 1 into a distinct parties for territorial defense. We shall now proceed to a parallel discussion for cleavages of type 3 in Fig. 3.

Our model predicts that agrarian interests are most likely to find direct political expression in systems of close alliance between nation-builders and the urban economic leadership—the four N–U cases in our eightfold typology. But in three of the four cases the opposition of the peasantry to the dominance of the cities tended to be closely linked up with a rejection of the moral and religious standards of the nation-builders. This produced D–L alliances in Scandinavia (type II) and the Netherlands (type IV) and R–L alliances in the secularizing southern countries (type VI). In the fourth N–U case (type VIII) there was no basis for explicit mergers of agrarian with religious opposition movements: the Belgian Roman Catholics were strong both in the urban "establishment" and among the farmers but, as it happened, were themselves torn between the *l* and the *g* poles over issues of ethnic-linguistic identity between Flemings and Walloons.

In only one of these four cases did distinctly agrarian parties emerge as stable elements of the national systems of electoral constellations—in the five countries of the North. A peasant party also established itself in the Protestant cantons of Switzerland. In the other countries of the West there may have been peasant lists at a few elections, but the interests of agriculture were generally aggregated into broader party fronts: the Conservative parties in Britain, in Prussia, and in France, the Christian parties elsewhere.

Why these differences? This raises a number of difficult questions about the economics of nation-building. In our three-step model we brutally reduced the options of the central elite to a choice between an alliance with the *landed* interests and an alliance with the *urban-financial-commercial-industrial*. This, of course, was never a matter of either/or but of continuing adjustment to changes in the overall equilibrium of forces in each territory. Our dichotomy does not help the description of any single case but simply serves to bring out contrasts among systems in the *relative* openness to alliances in the one direction or the other at the decisive stages of partisan mobilization.

To understand the conditions for alliance options in the one direction or the other it is essential to go into details of the *organization of rural society* at the time of the extensions of the suffrage. What counted more than anything else was the *concentration of resources for the control of the process of mobilization,* and in the countryside the *size of the units of production* and the *hierarchies of dependence* expressed in the tenure systems counted more than any other factors: the greater the concentration of economic power and social prestige the easier it was to control the rural votes and the greater the political payoffs of alliances with landowners. It was no accident that Conservative leaders such as Bismarck and Disraeli took a lead in the extension of the suffrage; they counted on the loyalty and obedience of the dependent tenants and the agricultural workers.[79] To measure the political potentialities of the land-owning classes it would be essential to assemble comparative statistics on the proportions of the arable land and the agricultural manpower under the control of the large estate owners in each country. Unfortunately there are many lacunae in the historical statistics and comparisons are fraught with many hazards. The data at hand suggest that the countries we identified as typical "N–L cases" (types I, III, V, and VII in our eightfold model) all tended to be dominated by large estates, at least in their central territories. This was the case in most of England and Scotland, in Prussia east of the Elbe, in the *Reconquista* provinces of Spain, and in lowland Austria.[80] There were, to be sure, large estates in many of the countries we have identified as "N–U cases" (types II, IV, VI, and VIII), but such alliances as there were between urban and rural elites still left large groups of self-owning peasants free to join counter-alliances on their own. In Belgium and the Netherlands the holdings tended to be small and closely tied in with the urban economy. In France and Italy there were always marked regional variations in the size of holdings and the systems of land tenure, and the peasantry was deeply divided over cultural, religious, and economic issues. There were large estates in Jutland, in southern Sweden, and in southwestern Finland, and the owners of these helped to consolidate the conservative establishments in the early phases of competitive politics, but the broad masses of the Nordic peasantry could not be brought into any such alliances with the established urban elites. The traditions of independent peasant representation were strong and there was widespread rejection of the cultural influences from the encroaching cities. In Denmark, Norway, and Sweden the decisive "Left" fronts against the old regime were coalitions of urban radicals and increasingly estate-conscious peasants, but these coalitions broke up as soon as the new parties entered government. In Denmark the urban Radicals left the agrarian *Venstre*; in Norway and Sweden the old "Left" was split in several directions on moralist-religious as well as on economic lines. Distinctly agrarian parties also emerged in the two still "colonial" countries of the North, Finland and Iceland. In these predominantly primary-producing countries the struggle for external independence dominated political life in the decades after the introduction of universal suffrage, and there was not the same need for broad opposition fronts against the establishments *within* each nation.

Typically, agrarian parties appear to have emerged in countries or provinces

(1) where the cities and the industrial centers were still numerically weak at the time of the decisive extensions of the suffrage;

(2) where the bulk of the agricultural populations were active in family-size farming and either owned their farms themselves or were legally protected lease-holders largely independent of socially superior landowners;

(3) where there were important cultural barriers between the countryside and the cities and much resistance to the incorporation of farm production in the capitalist economy of the cities; and

(4) where the Catholic Church was without significant influence.

These criteria fit not only the Nordic countries but also the Protestant cantons of Switzerland and even some areas of German Austria. A *Bauern-, Gewerbe- und Bürgerpartei* emerged in Berne, Zurich, and other heavily Alemannic-Protestant cantons after the introduction of PR in Switzerland in 1919. This was essentially a splinter from the old Radical-Liberal Party and recruited most of its support in the countryside. In the Catholic cantons the peasants remained loyal to their old party even after PR. Similarly in the Austrian First Republic the Nationalist *Lager* was split in a middle-class *Grossdeutsche Volkspartei* and a *Landbund* recruited among the anti-clerical peasants in Carinthia and Styria. The Christian Social Party recruited the bulk of its support among the Catholic peasantry but was able to keep the rural-urban tensions within bounds through elaborate organizational differentiations within the party.

The Fourth Step: Variations in the Strength and Structure of the Working-Class Movements

Our three-step model stops short at a point before the decisive thrust toward universal suffrage. It pinpoints sources of variations in the systems of division within the "independent" strata of the European national electorates, among the owners of property and the holders of professional or educational privileges qualifying them for the vote during the *régime censitaire*.

But this is hardly more than half the story. The extension of the suffrage to the lower classes changed the character of each national political system, generated new cleavages, and brought about a restructuring of the old alignments.

Why did we not bring these important developments into our model of European party systems? Clearly not because the three first cleavage lines were more important than the fourth in the explanation of *any one national party system*. On the contrary, in sheer statistical terms the fourth cleavage lines will in at least half of the cases under consideration explain much more of the variance in the distributions of full-suffrage votes than any one of the others.[81] We focused on the three first cleavage lines because these were the ones that appeared to account for most of the variance *among systems:* the interactions of the "center-periphery," state-church, and land-industry cleavages tended to produce much more marked, and apparently much more stubborn, differences among the national party systems than any of the cleavages brought about through the rise of the working-class movements.

We could of course have gone on to present a four-step model immediately (in fact, we did in an earlier draft), but this proved very cumbersome and produced a variety of uncomfortable redundancies. Clearly what had to be explained was not the emergence of a distinctive working-class movement at some point or other before or after the extension of the suffrage but the *strength and solidarity* of any such movement, its capacity to mobilize the underprivileged classes for action and its ability to maintain unity in the face of the many forces making for division and fragmentation. All the European polities developed some sort of working-class movement at some point between the first extensions of the suffrage and the various "post-democratic" attempts at the repression of partisan pluralism. To predict the *presence* of such movements was simple; to predict which ones would be strong and which ones weak, which ones unified and which ones split down the middle, required much more knowledge of national conditions and developments and a much more elaborate model of the historical interaction process. Our three-step model does not go this far for *any* party; it predicts the presence of such-and-such parties in polities characterized by such-and-such cleavages, but it does not give any formula for accounting for the strength or the cohesion of any one party. This *could* be built into the model through the introduction of various population parameters (percent speaking each language or dialect, percent committed to each of the churches or dissenting bodies, ratios of concentrations of wealth and dependent labor in industry versus landed estates), and possibly of some indicators of the cleavage "distance" (differences in the chances of interaction across the cleavage line, whether physically determined or normatively regulated), but any attempt in this direction would take us much too far in this all-too-long introductory essay. At this point we limit ourselves to an elementary discussion of the between-system variations which would have to be explained through such an extension of our model. We shall suggest a "fourth step" and point to a possible scheme for the explanation of differences in the formation of national party systems under the impact of universal suffrage.

Our initial scheme of analysis posited four decisive dimensions of cleavage in Western polities. Our model for the generation of party systems pinpointed three crucial junctures in national history corresponding to the first three of these dimensions:

Cleavage	Critical juncture	Issues
Center-Periphery	Reformation–Counter-Reformation: 16th-17th centuries	National vs. supranational religion National language vs. Latin
State-Church	National Revolution: 1789 and after	Secular vs. religious control of mass education
Land-Industry	Industrial Revolution: 19th century	Tariff levels for agricultural products; control vs. freedom for industrial enterprise

It is tempting to add to this a fourth dimension and a fourth juncture:

Cleavage	Critical juncture	Issues
Owner-Worker	The Russian Revolution: 1917 and after	Integration into national polity vs. commitment to international revolutionary movement

There is an intriguing cyclical movement in this scheme. The process gets under way with the breakdown of one supranational order and the establishment of strong territorial bureaucracies legitimizing themselves through the standardizing of nationally distinct religions and languages, and it ends with a conflict over national versus international loyalties within the last of the strata to be formally integrated into the nation-state, the rural and the industrial workers.

The conditions for the development of distinctive working-class parties varied markedly from country to country within Europe. These differences emerged well before World War I. The Russian Revolution did not generate new cleavages but simply accentuated long-established lines of division within the working-class elite.

Our three-step model does not produce clear-cut predictions of these developments. True enough, the most unified and the most "domesticable" working-class movements emerged in the Protestant-dominated countries with the smoothest histories of nation-building: Britain, Denmark, and Sweden (types I and II in our model). Equally true, the Catholic-dominated countries with difficult or very recent histories of nation-building also produced deeply divided, largely alienated working-class movements—France, Italy, Spain (types V and VI). But other variables clearly have to be brought into account for variations in the intermediary zone between the Protestant Northwest and the Latin South (types III and IV, VII and VIII). Both the Austrian and the German working-class movements developed their distinctive counter-cultures against the dominant national elites. The Austrian Socialist *Lager,* heavily concentrated as it was in Vienna, was able to maintain its unity in the face of the clerical-conservatives and the pan-German nationalists after the dissolution of the Hapsburg Empire.[82] By contrast, the German working-class movement was deeply divided after the defeat in 1918. Sharply contrasted conceptions of the rules of the political game stood opposed to each other and were to prove fatal in the fight against the wave of mass nationalism of the early thirties.[83] In Switzerland and the Netherlands (both type IV in our scheme), the Russian and the German revolutions produced a few disturbances, but the leftward split-offs from the main working class by parties were of little significance. The marked cultural and religious cleavages reduced the potentials for the Socialist parties, but the traditions of pluralism were gradually to help their entry into national politics.

Of all the intermediary countries Belgium (type VIII in our model) presents perhaps the most interesting case. By our overall rule, the Belgian working class should be deeply divided: a thoroughly Catholic country with a particularly difficult history of nation-building across two distinct language communities. In this case the smallness and the international dependence of the nation may well have created restraints on the internal forces of division and fragmentation. Val Lorwin has pointed to such factors in his analysis of Belgian-French contrasts:[84]

> The reconciliation of the Belgian working class to the political and social order, divided though the workers are by language and religion and the Flemish-Walloon question, makes a vivid contrast with the experience of France. The differences did not arise from the material fruits of economic growth, for both long were rather low-wage countries, and Belgian wages were the lower. In some ways the two countries had similar economic development. But Belgium's industrialization began earlier; it was more dependent on international commerce, both for markets and for its transit trade; it had a faster growing population; and it became much more urbanized than France. The small new nation,

"the cockpit of Europe," could not permit itself social and political conflict to the breaking point. Perhaps France could not either, but it was harder for the bigger nation to realize it.

The contrast between France, Italy, and Spain on the one hand and Austria and Belgium on the other suggests a possible generalization: the working-class movement tended to be much more divided in the countries where the "nation-builders" and the Church were openly or latently opposed to each other during the crucial phases of educational development and mass mobilization (our "S" cases, types V and VI) than in the countries where the Church had, at least initially, sided with the nation-builders against some common enemy outside (our "R" cases, an alliance against Protestant Prussia and the dependent Hapsburg peoples in the case of Austria; against the Calvinist Dutch in the case of Belgium). This fits the Irish case as well. The Catholic Church was no less hostile to the English than the secular nationalists, and the union of the two forces not only reduced the possibilities of a polarization of Irish politics on class lines but made the likelihood of a Communist splinter of any importance very small indeed.

It is tempting to apply a similar generalization to the Protestant North: the greater the internal division during the struggle for nationhood, the greater the impact of the Russian Revolution on the divisions within the working class. We have already pointed to the profound split within the German working class. The German Reich was a late-comer among European nations, and none of the territorial and religious conflicts within the nation was anywhere near settlement by the time the working-class parties entered the political arena. Among the northern countries the two oldest nations, Denmark and Sweden, were least affected by the Communist-Socialist division. The three countries emerging from colonial status were much more directly affected: Norway (domestically independent from 1814, a sovereign state from 1905) for only a brief period in the early 1920's; Finland (independent in 1917) and Iceland (domestically independent in 1916 and a sovereign state from 1944) for a much longer period. These differences among the northern countries have been frequently commented on in the literature of comparative politics. The radicalization of the Norwegian Labor Party has been interpreted within several alternative models, one emphasizing the alliance options of the party leaders, another the grass-roots reactions to sudden industrialization in the peripheral countryside, and a third the openness of the party structure and the possibilities of quick feedback from the mobilized voters. There is no doubt that the early mobilization of the peasantry and the quick victory over the old regime of the officials had left the emerging Norwegian working-class party much more isolated, much less important as a coalition partner, than its Danish and Swedish counterparts.[85] There is also a great deal of evidence to support the old Bull hypothesis of the radicalizing effects of sudden industrialization, but recent research suggests that this was only one element in a broad process of political change. The Labour Party recruited many more of its voters in the established cities and in the forestry and the fisheries districts, but the openness of the party structure allowed the radicals to establish themselves very quickly and to take over the majority wing of the party during the crucial years just after the Russian

Revolution.[86] This very openness to rank-and-file influences made the alliance with Moscow very short-lived; the Communists split off in 1924 and the old majority party "joined the nation" step by step until it took power in 1935.[87]

Only two of the Scandinavian countries retained strong Communist parties after World War II—Finland and Iceland. Superficially these countries have two features in common: prolonged struggles for cultural and political independence, and late industrialization. In fact the two countries went through very different processes of political change from the initial phase of nationalist mobilization to the final formation of the full-suffrage party system. One obvious source of variation was the distance from Russia. The sudden upsurge of the Socialist Party in Finland in 1906 (the party gained 37 percent of the votes cast at the first election under universal suffrage) was part of a general wave of mobilization against the Tsarist regime. The Russian Revolution of 1917 split Finland down the middle; the working-class voters were torn between their loyalty to their national culture and its social hierarchy and their solidarity with their class and its revolutionary defenders.[88] The victory of the "Whites" and the subsequent suppression of the Communist Party (1919–21, 1923–25, 1930–44) left deep scars; the upsurge of the leftist SKDL after the Soviet victory in 1945 reflected deep-seated resentments not only against the "lords" and the employers of labor but generally against the upholders of the central national culture. The split in the Icelandic labor movement was much less dramatic; in the oldest and smallest of the European democracies there was little basis for mass conflicts, and the oppositions between Communist sympathizers and Socialists appeared to reflect essentially personal antagonisms among groups of activists.[89]

IMPLICATIONS FOR COMPARATIVE POLITICAL SOCIOLOGY

We have pushed our attempt at a systematization of the comparative history of partisan oppositions in European polities up to some point in the 1920's, to the freezing of the major party alternatives in the wake of the extension of the suffrage and the mobilization of major sections of the new reservoirs of potential supporters. Why stop there? Why not pursue this exercise in comparative cleavage analysis right up to the 1960's? The reason is deceptively simple: *the party systems of the 1960's reflect, with few but significant exceptions, the cleavage structures of the 1920's.* This is a crucial characteristic of Western competitive politics in the age of "high mass consumption": *the party alternatives, and in remarkably many cases the party organizations, are older than the majorities of the national electorates.* To most of the citizens of the West the currently active parties have been part of the political landscape since their childhood or at least since they were first faced with the choice between alternative "packages" on election day.

This continuity is often taken as a matter of course; in fact it poses an intriguing set of problems for comparative sociological research. An amazing number of the parties which had established themselves by the end of World

War I survived not only the onslaughts of Fascism and National Socialism but also another world war and a series of profound changes in the social and cultural structure of the polities they were part of. How was this possible? How were these parties able to survive so many changes in the political, social, and economic conditions of their operation? How could they keep such large bodies of citizens identifying with them over such long periods of time, and how could they renew their core clienteles from generation to generation?

There is no straightforward answer to any of these questions. We know much less about the internal management and the organizational functioning of political parties than we do about their sociocultural base and their external history of participation in public decision-making.[90]

To get closer to an answer we would clearly have to start out from a comparative analysis of the "old" and the "new" parties: the early mass parties formed during the final phase of suffrage extension, and the later attempts to launch new parties during the first decades of universal suffrage. It is difficult to see any significant exceptions to the rule that the parties which were able to establish mass organizations and entrench themselves in the local government structures *before* the final drive toward maximal mobilization have proved the most viable. The narrowing of the "support market" brought about through the growth of mass parties during this final thrust toward full-suffrage democracy clearly left very few openings for new movements. Where the challenge of the emerging working-class parties had been met by concerted efforts of countermobilization through nationwide mass organizations on the liberal and the conservative fronts, the leeway for new party formations was particularly small; this was the case whether the threshold of representation was low, as in Scandinavia, or quite high, as in Britain.[91] Correspondingly the "post-democratic" party systems proved markedly more fragile and open to newcomers in the countries where the privileged strata had relied on their local power resources rather than on nationwide mass organizations in their efforts of mobilization.

France was one of the first countries to bring a maximal electorate into the political arena, but the mobilization efforts of the established strata tended to be local and personal. A mass organization corresponding to the Conservative Party in Britain was never developed. There was very little "narrowing of the support market" to the right of the PCF and the SFIO and consequently a great deal of leeway for innovation in the party system even in the later phases of democratization.

There was a similar asymmetry in Germany: strong mass organizations on the left but marked fragmentation on the right. The contrast between Germany and Britain has been rubbed in at several points in our analysis of cleavage structures. The contrast with Austria is equally revealing; there the three-*Lager* constellation established itself very early in the mobilization process, and the party system changed astoundingly little from the Empire to the First Republic, and from the First to the Second. The consolidation of conservative support around the mass organizations of the Catholic Church clearly soaked up a great deal of the mobilization potential for new parties. In Wilhelmine and Weimar Germany the only genuine mass organization to the right of the Social Democrats was the Catholic *Zentrum;* this still left a great deal of leeway for "post-democratic" party formations on the Protestant right. Ironically, it was the defeat of the National Socialist regime and the loss of the Protestant East which opened up an opportunity for some stabilization of the German party system. With the establishment of the regionally divided CDU/CSU the Germans were for the first time able to approximate a broad conservative party of the British type. It was not able to establish as solid a membership organization but proved, at least until the debacle of 1966, amazingly effective in aggregating interests across a wide range of strata and sectors of the federal community.

Two other countries of the West have experienced spectacular changes in their party systems since the introduction of universal suffrage and deserve some comment in this context—Italy and Spain. The *Italian* case comes close to the *German:* both went through a painful process of belated unification; both were deeply divided within their privileged strata between "nation-builders" (Prussians, Piedmontese) and Catholics; both had been slow to recognize the rights of the working-class organizations. The essential difference lay in the *timing* of the party developments. In the Reich a differentiated party structure had been allowed to develop during the initial mobilization phase and had been given another fifteen years of functioning during the Weimar Republic. In Italy, by contrast, the State-Church split was so profound that a structurally responsive party system did not see the light before 1919—three years before the March on Rome. There had simply been no time for the "freezing" of any party system before the post-democratic revolution, and there was very little in the way of a traditional party system to fall back on after the defeat of the Fascist regime in 1944. True, the Socialists and the *Popolari* had had their brief spell of experience of electoral mobilization, and this certainly counted when the PCI and the DC established themselves in the wake of the war. But the other political forces had never been organized for concerted electoral politics and left a great deal of leeway for irregularities in the mobilization market. The *Spanish* case has a great deal in common with the *French:* early unification but deep resentments against central power in some of the provinces and early universalization of the suffrage but weak and divided party organizations. The Spanish system of sham parliamentarianism and *caciquismo* had not produced electoral mass parties of any importance by the time the double threat of secessionist mobilization and working-class militancy triggered off nationalist counterrevolutions, first under Primo de Rivera in 1923, then with the Civil War in 1936. The entire history of Spanish electoral mass politics is contained in the five years of the Republic from 1931 to 1936; this is not much to go on and it is significant that a lucid and realistic analyst like Juan Linz does not base his projections about the possible structuring of a future Spanish party system on the experiences of those five years but on a projection from Italian voting alignments.[92]

These four spectacular cases of disruptions in the development of national party systems do not in themselves invalidate our initial formulation. The most important of the party alternatives got set for each national citizenry during the phases of mobilization just before or just after the final extension of the suffrage and have remained roughly the same through decades of subsequent changes in the structural conditions of partisan choice. Even in the three cases of France, Germany, and Italy the continuities in the alternatives are as striking as the disruptions in their organizational expressions. On this score the French case is in many ways the most intriguing. There was no period of internally generated disruption of electoral politics (the Petain-Laval phase would clearly not have occurred if the Germans had not won in 1940), but there have been a number of violent oscillations between plebiscitarian and representative models of democracy and marked organizational fragmentation both at the level of interest articulation and at the level of parties. In spite of these frequent upheavals no analyst of French politics is in much doubt about the underlying continuities of sentiment and identification on the right no less than on the left of the political spectrum. The voter does not just react to immediate issues but is caught in an historically given constellation of diffuse options for the system as a whole.

This "historicity" of the party alternatives is of crucial importance not only in the study of differences and similarities *across* nations but also *within* nations. The party alternatives vary in "age" and dominance not only from one overall system to another but equally from one locality to another within the same polity. To gain any detailed understanding of the processes of mobilization and alignment within any single nation we clearly need information not just about turnout and the division of votes but about the *timing of the formation of local party organizations*. This process of local entrenchment can be pinpointed in several ways: through organizational records, through membership registers, and through information about the lists presented at local elections. Representation in localities will in most countries of the West open up much more direct access to power resources than representation at the national level. The local officeholders tend to form the backbone of the party organization and are able to attract nuclei of active supporters through the distribution of whatever rewards their positions may command. To the parties of the underprivileged, access to the local machineries of government has tended to be of crucial importance for the development and maintenance of their organizational networks. They may have survived on their trade union strength, but the additional resource potentials inherent in local offices have meant much more to them than to the parties deriving their essential strength from the networks of economic power-holders or from the organizations of the Church.

The study of these processes of local entrenchment is still in its infancy in most countries, and serious comparative studies have so far never been attempted.[93] This is one of the great lacunae in empirical political sociology. There is an unfortunate asymmetry in our knowledge and our efforts at systematization: we know very little of the processes through which political alternatives *get set* for different local electorates, but we have a great deal of information about the circumstances in which one alternative or the other *gets chosen*. This, obviously, reflects differences in the access to data. It is a time-consuming and frustrating job to assemble data locality by locality on the formation, development, and, possibly, stagnation or disappearance, of party organizations. It is vastly easier to find out about choices among the alternatives once they are set; the machineries of electoral bookkeeping have for decade after decade heaped up data about mass choices and so have, at least since World War II, the mushrooming organizations of pollsters and surveyors. What is needed now are systematic efforts to bring together information about the timing of local party entrenchments to pin down their consequences for voter alignments.[94] With the development of ecological data archives[95] in historical depth such analyses are bound to multiply. What is needed now is an international effort to maximize the coordination of such efforts.

With the development of such archives the *time dimension* is bound to gain prominence in the comparative study of mass politics. The early school of French electoral geographers were deeply conscious of the importance of local entrenchments and their perpetuation through time. Statistical ecologists such as Tingsten were less concerned with diachronic stability than with rates of change, particularly through the mobilization of the latest entrants into the national electorates, the workers and the women. The introduction of the sample survey as a technique of data gathering and analysis shortened the time perspective and brought about a concentration on synchronic variations; the panel technique focused attention on short-term fluctuations, and even the questions about past voting and family political traditions did not help to make surveys an adequate tool of developmental research. The last few years have seen an important reversal in this trend. There is not only a marked increase in scholarly interest in historical *time series data* for elections and other mass data[96] but also a greater concentration of work on *organizational developments and the freezing of political alternatives*. These are essential prerequisites for the growth of a truly comparative sociology of Western mass politics. To understand the current alignments of voters in our different countries it is not enough to analyze the contemporary issues and the contemporary sociocultural structure; it is even more important to go back to the initial formation of party alternatives and to analyze the interaction between the historically established foci of identification and the subsequent changes in the structural conditions of choice.

This joining of diachronic and synchronic analysis strategies is of particular importance for an understanding of the mass politics of the organizationally saturated "high mass consumption" societies of the sixties. Decades of structural change and economic growth have made the old, established alternatives increasingly irrelevant, but the high level of organizational mobilization of most sectors of the community has left very little leeway for a decisive breakthrough of new party alternatives. It is not an accident that situations of this type generate a great deal of frustration, alienation, and protestation within the organizationally least committed sections of the community, the *young* and, quite particularly, the *students*. The "revolt of the young" has found many varieties of expression in the sixties: new types of criminality and new styles of living but also new types of politics. The rejection of the old alternatives, of the politics of party representation, has perhaps found its most spectacular expression in the civil rights struggle and the student protest movement in the United States,[97] but the disaffection of the young from the established parties, particularly the parties in power, is a widespread phenomenon even in Europe. The widespread disagreements with the national powers-that-be over foreign and military policy constitute only one among several sources of such disillusionment; the distance between levels of aspiration and levels of achievement in the welfare state has clearly also been of importance.

The probability that such resentments will coalesce into movements broad enough to form viable new parties is on the whole low, but the processes of socialization and recruitment within the old ones will clearly be affected. Much, of course, depends on local concentrations and the height of the thresholds of representation. In the low-threshold Scandinavian system the waves of disaffection have already disrupted the equilibrium of the old parties: there have been important splinter movements on the Socialist Left, and these have sapped some of the strategic strength of the old Social Democratic parties. This happened first in Denmark: the split-up of the Communist party led to the development of a remarkably vigorous national-Titoist party on the Socialist Left and brought about serious losses for the Social Democrats, most spectacularly in the autumn of 1966. Much the same sort of development has taken place in Norway since 1961. A splinter movement within the governing Labor Party suddenly broke through and gained two seats in 1961; for the first time since the war Labor was brought into a minority position. This was the beginning of a series of crises. By 1965 the Left splinter had grown to 6 percent of the votes cast and the Labor Party was finally out of power. Recent results for Sweden show similar developments there; the CP has switched to a "national" line close to the Danish model and has gained ground.

There is a crucial consideration in any comparative analysis of such changes in party strength: Which parties have been in power, which ones have been in opposition? In the fifties many observers feared the development of permanent majority parties. It was argued that the parties in government had all the advantages and could mobilize so many strategic resources on their side that the opposition might be left powerless forever more. It is heartening to see how quickly these observers had to change their minds. In the sixties the mounting "revolutions of rising expectations" clearly tend to place governing parties at a terrifying disadvantage: they have to take the responsibility for predicaments they can no longer control; they become the targets of continuous waves of demands, grievances, criticisms, and no longer command the resources needed to meet them. The troubles of the governing Labor parties in Scandinavia and in Great Britain can be understood only in this light. The welfare state, the spread of the "car and TV" culture, the educational explosion—all these developments have placed the governing authorities under increasing strains and made it very difficult for the old working-class parties to retain the loyalties of the younger generation. Even the Swedish Social Democrats, the most intelligent and the most farsighted of the Labor rulers in Europe, seem finally to have reached the end of their era. They met the demands for an extension of the welfare state with innovative skill through the development of the supplementary pensions scheme after 1956, but they could not live on that forever. Their recent troubles center on the *"queuing society"*: queues in front of the vocational schools and the universities, queues for housing, queues for health services. Swedish workers enjoy perhaps the highest standard of living in the world, but this does not help the Swedish Social Democratic government. The working-class youngsters see others get more education, better housing, better services than they do, and they develop signs of frustration and alienation. It is significant that in all the three Scandinavian countries the Social Democratic losses have been

most marked in the cities and quite small in the rural periphery; the governing parties run into the greatest difficulties in the areas where the "revolution
of expectations" has run the furthest.

It is still too early to say what kinds of politics this will engender. There
will clearly be greater fluctuations than before. This may increase the chances
of government by regular alternation, but it may also trigger off new varieties
of coalition-mongering: politicians are naturally tempted to "spread the
blame," to escape electoral retaliation through the sharing of responsibilities
with competing parties. Developments in Denmark suggest a trend toward
open negotiations across all established party barriers. Norway is experienc-
ing a four-party coalition of the non-Socialist front; there are strains among
the four but it seems to work because each party finds it easy to blame its
failure to perform on electoral promises on the need for unity within the government. In Sweden this alternative has not yet been tried, but there is much
talk about a "Norwegian solution." The events in the German *Bundesrepublik* during the summer and autumn of 1966 show similar processes at work
in quite a different political setting: an increasing disenchantment with the
top political leadership and with the established system of decision-making,
whatever the party coloring of the current incumbents.

To understand these developments and to gauge the probabilities of the
possible projections into the future it will be essential to build up, monograph
by monograph, analysis by analysis, a comparative sociology of competitive
mass politics. If this lengthy introduction to a volume of widely differing national analyses has helped to suggest new themes and new perspectives for
such research and such systematization, it will have served its purpose.

NOTES

1. Single-nation analysts sometimes reveal extraordinarily little awareness of this
historical dimension of political research: in their final theoretical chapter of *Voting*
(Chicago: University of Chicago Press, 1954), Bernard Berelson and his colleagues ask
themselves why "democracies have survived *through the centuries*" (p. 311, our italics).
What is problematic about this loose formulation is not the error of historical fact (only
the United States had had competitive politics and near-universal suffrage, although for
white males only, for more than a hundred years, and most Western polities did not
reach the stage of full-suffrage democracy before the end of World War I) but the assumption that mass democracy had had such a long history that events at the early stages
of political mobilization no longer had any impact on current electoral alignments. In
fact in most of the Western polities the decisive party-forming developments took place
in the decades immediately before and after the extension of the suffrage, and even in the
1950's these very events were still alive in the personal memories of large proportions of
the electorates.

2. For a review of current efforts to establish "statistical histories of national political developments" see S. Rokkan, "Electoral Mobilization, Party Competition and National Integration," a chapter in J. LaPalombara and Myron Weiner (eds.), *Political
Parties and Political Development* (Princeton: Princeton Univ. Press, 1966).

3. For a highly illuminating analysis of the place of the theory of parties in the his-
tory of political thought see Erwin Faul, "Verfemung, Duldung und Anerkennung des
Parteiwesens in der Geschichte des politischen Denkens," *Pol. Viertelj.schr.* 5(1)
(March, 1964), pp. 60–80.

4. For a general discussion of current usages of the term "party" in the context of a
comparative analysis of pluralistic vs. monolithic political systems, see Giovanni Sartori,
Parties and Party Systems (New York: Harper & Row, 1967).

5. "Wenn eine Partei eine geschlossene, durch die Verbandsordnung dem Verwalt-

ungsstab eingegliederte Vergesellschaftung wird—wie z.B. die "parte Guelfa". . . —, *so ist sie keine Partei mehr sondern ein Teilverband des politischen Verbandes*" (our italics), *Wirtschaft und Gesellschaft* (4th ed.; Tübingen: Mohr, 1956), I, p. 168; see the attempted translation in *The Theory of Social and Economic Organization* (New York: The Free Press, 1947), pp. 409–10.

6. W. Chambers, *Parties in a New Nation* (New York: Oxford Univ. Press, 1963), p. 80.

7. Ruth Schachter, "Single-Party Systems in West Africa," *Amer. Pol. Sci. Rev.*, 55 (1961), p. 301.

8. For a general analysis of this process see S. M. Lipset *et al.*, *Union Democracy* (New York: The Free Press, 1956), pp. 268–9.

9. E. A. Ross, *The Principles of Sociology* (New York: Century, 1920), pp. 164–5. ("Society is sewn together by its inner conflicts.")

10. G. Simmel, *Soziologie* (Berlin: Duncker & Humblot, 1923 and 1958), Chap. IV; see the translation in *Conflict and the Web of Group Affiliations* (New York: The Free Press, 1964).

11. First published in London, The Bodley Head, 1911; quoted from Penguin ed., 1946, p. 238.

12. T. Parsons, R. F. Bales, and E. A. Shils, *Working Papers in the Theory of Action* (New York: The Free Press, 1953), Chaps. III and V.

13. The first extensive development of the schema is found in T. Parsons and N. J. Smelser, *Economy and Society* (London: Routledge, 1956). A simplified restatement is found in T. Parsons, "General Theory in Sociology," in R. K. Merton *et al.* (eds.), *Sociology Today* (New York, Basic Books, 1959), pp. 39–78. Extensive revisions in the schema were adumbrated in T. Parsons "Pattern Variables Revisited," *Am. Sociol. Rev.*, 25 (1960), pp. 467–83, and have been presented in further detail in "On the Concept of Political Power," *Proc. Amer. Philos. Soc.*, 107 (1963), pp. 232–62. For an attempt to use the Parsonian schema in political analysis see William Mitchell, *The Polity* (New York: The Free Press, 1962); see also his recent *Sociological Analysis and Politics: The Theories of Talcott Parsons* (Englewood Cliffs, N.J.: Prentice-Hall, 1967).

14. Parsons has specified the "inputs" and "outputs" of the I–G interchange in these terms:

$$
\begin{array}{ccc}
 & \text{Generalized Support} & \\
 & \longleftarrow & \\
 & \text{Effective Leadership} & \\
G\text{: POLITY} & \longrightarrow & \text{PUBLIC: } I \\
 & \text{Advocacy of Policies} & \\
 & \longleftarrow & \\
 & \text{Binding Decisions} & \\
 & \longrightarrow & \\
\end{array}
$$

See "Voting and the Equilibrium of the American Political System," in E. Burdick and A. Brodbeck (eds.), *American Voting Behavior* (New York: The Free Press, 1959), pp. 80–120.

15. Talcott Parsons, in a private communication, has pointed out a number of difficulties in these formulations: we have singled out the dominant functional attributes of a series of concrete political acts without considering their many secondary functions. Clearly a vote can be treated as an act of support of a particular movement (L–I) or a particular set of leaders (I–G) as well as a counter in the direct interaction between households and constituted territorial authorities (L–G). Our point is that in the study of electoral mass politics in the competitive systems of the West a crucial distinction has to be made between the vote as formal act of legitimation (the elected representative is legitimated through the votes cast, *even* by those of his opponents) and the vote as an expression of party loyalty. The standardization of electoral procedures and the formalization of the act of preference underscored this distinction between legitimation (L–G) and support (L–I). For further discussion of these developments see S. Rokkan, "Mass Suffrage, Secret Voting and Political Participation," *Arch. Eur. Sociol.*, 2 (1961), pp. 132–52, and T. Parsons, "Evolutionary Universals in Society," *Amer. Sociol. Rev.*, 29 (June, 1964), pp. 339–57, particularly the discussion of Rokkan's article, pp. 354–6.

16. Neil J. Smelser, *Theory of Collective Behaviour*, (London: Routledge, 1962).

17. In conformity with Parsonian conventions we use *lower-case* symbols for the parts of *sub*systems and *capitals* for the parts of *total* systems.

18. Sir Lewis Namier, *England in the Age of the American Revolution* (London: Macmillan, 1930), quoted from second ed. (1961), p. 183.

19. For detailed discussion of the linkage between religious cleavages and political alliances in the United States see Seymour Martin Lipset, *The First New Nation* (New York: Basic Books, 1963), Chap. 4, and "Religion and Politics in the American Past and Present" in R. Lee and M. Martin, *Religion and Social Conflict* (New York: Oxford Univ. Press, 1964), pp. 69–126.

20. For details see S. Rokkan and H. Valen, "Regional Contrasts in Norwegian Politics" in E. Allardt and Y. Littunen (eds.), *Cleavages, Ideologies and Party Systems* (Helsinki: Westermarck Society, 1964), pp. 162–238, and the chapter by S. Rokkan below.

21. See Kenneth O. Morgan, *Wales in British Politics 1868–1922* (Cardiff: Univ. of Wales Press, 1963), pp. 245–55. For a detailed ecological analysis of vote distributions in Wales 1861–1951 see K. R. Cox, *Regional Anomalies in the Voting Behavior of the Population of England and Wales: 1921–1951*, diss., Univ. of Illinois, 1966. Cox explains the strength of the Liberals in Wales in much the same terms as Rokkan and Valen explain the strength of the Left "counterculture" in the south and west of Norway: the predominance of small farms, the egalitarian class structure, linguistic opposition, and religious nonconformity.

22. For Norway see the writings of S. Rokkan already cited. For Finland see Pirkko Rommi, "Finland" in *Problemer i nordisk historie-forskning*. II. Framveksten av de politiske partier i de nordiske land på 1800–tallet (Bergen: Universitetsforlaget, 1964), pp. 103–30; E. Allardt, "Patterns of Class Conflict and Working Class Consciousness in Finnish Politics" in E. Allardt and Y. Littunen, *Cleavages, Ideologies and Party Systems*, pp. 97–131; and the chapter by E. Allardt and Pesonen below.

23. See S. Rokkan, "Electoral mobilization . . . ," *op. cit.*

24. For a definition of this concept and a specification of possible indicators see Karl Deutsch, "Social Mobilization and Political Development," *Am. Pol. Sci. Rev.*, 55 (1961), pp. 493–514.

25. The contrast between "primordial attachment" to the "givens" of social existence (contiguity, kinship, local languages, and religious customs—all at our *l* pole) and "national identification" (our *g* pole) has been described with great acumen by Clifford Geertz in "The Integrative Revolution," in C. Geertz (ed.), *Old Societies and New States* (New York: The Free Press, 1963), pp. 105–57; see Edward Shils, "Primordial, Personal, Sacred and Civil Ties," *Brit. J. Sociol.*, 7 (1957), pp. 130–45.

26. For an analysis of steps in the extension of citizenship rights and duties to all accountable adults see S. Rokkan "Mass Suffrage, Secret Voting and Political Participation," *Arch. Eur. de Sociol.*, 2 (1961), pp. 132–52, and the chapter by R. Bendix and S. Rokkan, "The Extension of Citizenship to the Lower Classes," in R. Bendix, *Nation-Building and Citizenship* (New York: Wiley, 1964). For a review of the politics of educational developments see R. Ulich, *The Education of Nations* (Cambridge: Harvard Univ. Press, 1961).

27. This, of course, was not a peculiarity of Catholic–Calvinist countries; it can be observed in a number of polities with geographically dispersed if locally segregated ethnic minorities. For an insightful discussion of a similar development in Russia, see C. E. Woodhouse and H. J. Tobias, "Primordial Ties and Political Process in Pre-Revolutionary Russia: The Case of the Jewish Bund," *Comp. Stud. Soc. Hist.*, 8 (1966), pp. 331–60.

28. For detailed statistics see J. P. Kruijt, *Verzuiling* (Zaandijk: Heijnis, 1959) and J. P. Kruijt and W. Goddijn, "Verzuiling en ontzuiling als sociologisch proces" in A. J. den Hollander *et al.* (eds.), *Drift en Koers* (Assen: Van Gorcum, 1962), pp. 227–63. For an attempt at a broader interpretation of *Verzuiling* and its consequences for the theory of democracy, see Arend Lijphart, *The Politics of Accommodation: Pluralism and Democracy in the Netherlands,* manuscript, 1967. For comparative interpretations of data on religious segmentation see David O. Moberg, "Religion and Society in the Netherlands and in America," *Am. Quart.*, 13 (1961), pp. 172–78, and G. Lenski, *The Religious Factor* (rev. ed.; Garden City: Doubleday Anchor Books,

1963), pp. 359–66; see also J. Mathes (ed.), *Religiöser Pluralismus und Gesellschaftsstruktur* (Cologne: Westdeutscher Verlag, 1965).

29. For general accounts of the development of party oppositions and segmented politics in the Netherlands, see H. Daalder, "Parties and Politics in the Netherlands," *Pol. Studies,* 3 (1955), pp. 1–16 and his chapter in R. A. Dahl (ed.), *Political Oppositions in Western Democracies* (New Haven: Yale Univ. Press, 1966). Detailed party chronologies and "pedigrees" are given in H. Daalder "Nederland: het politieke stelsel" in L. van der Land (ed.), *Repertorium van de Sociale Wetenschappen,* I (Amsterdam: Elsevier, 1958), pp. 213–38.

30. Cited in S. M. Lipset, *Political Man,* op. cit., p. 258; for further breakdowns from a sample of a suburb of Amsterdam see L. van der Land, *et al., Kiezer en verkiezing* (Amsterdam: Nederlandse Kring voor Wetenschap der Politiek, 1963), mimeo. For analyses of a nationwide survey from 1964 see Lijphart, *op. cit.,* Chap. II.

31. Kruijt and Goddijn, *op. cit.*

32. The concept of "membership crystallization" has been formulated by analogy with the concept *status* crystallization developed by Gerhard Lenski in "Social Participation and Status Crystallization," *Amer. Sociol. Rev.,* 21 (1956), pp. 458–64; see Erik Allardt, "Community Activity, Leisure Use and Social Structure," and Ulf Himmelstrand, "A Theoretical and Empirical Approach to Depoliticization and Political Involvement," both in S. Rokkan (ed.), *Approaches to the Study of Political Participation* (Bergen: Chr. Michelsen Institute, 1962), pp. 67–110.

33. For an analysis of this process see Ulf Torgersen, "The Structure of Urban Parties in Norway During the First Period of Extended Suffrage 1884–1898," in E. Allardt and Y. Littunen (eds.), *Cleavages . . . , op. cit.,* pp. 377–99.

34. The Swedish Liberals split into two parties over alcohol policies in 1923 but these merged again in 1934. A new party, the Christian Democrat Union, was set up by Free Church leaders in 1964, but failed in the election that year.

35. For a comparative analysis of differences in the organization of estate assemblies, see especially Otto Hintze, "Typologie der ständischen Verfassung des Abendlandes," *Hist. Zs.,* 141 (1930), pp. 229–48; F. Hartung and R. Mousnier, "Quelques problèmes concernant la monarchie absolue," *Relazioni X Congr. Int. Sci. Storiche,* IV (Florence, 1955); and R. R. Palmer, *The Age of Democratic Revolution: The Challenge* (Princeton: Princeton Univ. Press, 1959), Ch. II.

36. The critical issue between the two sectors of the economy concerned foreign trade: Should domestic agriculture be protected against the cheaper grain produced overseas or should the manufacturing industry be supported through the supply of cheaper food for their workers? For a comparative review of the politics of the grain tariffs see Alexander Gerschenkron, *Bread and Democracy in Germany* (Berkeley: Univ. of California Press, 1943).

37. *The Making of Victorian England* (London: Methuen, 1962), p. 218, our italics. For a broader treatment see F. M. L. Thompson, *English Landed Society in the Nineteenth Century* (London: Routledge, 1963).

38. James Cornford, "The Transformation of Conservatism in the Late 19th Century," *Victorian Studies,* 7 (1963), pp. 35–66.

39. On the unsuccessful attempts of the Progressive Liberals to broaden their working-class base, see especially Thomas Niperdey, *Die Organisation der deutschen Parteien vor 1918* (Düsseldorf: Droste, 1963), pp. 187–92, and W. Link "Das Nationalverein für das liberale Deutschland," *Pol. Vierteliahreschr.,* 5 (1964), pp. 422–44. On the "plebiscitarian nationalism" of Friedrich Naumann and Max Weber, see Theodor Heuss, *Friedrich Naumann* (Stuttgart: Deutsche Verlagsanstalt 1957), W. Mommsen, *Max Weber und die deutsche Politik 1890–1920* (Tübingen: Mohr, 1959), and the discussions at the Weber centenary conference at Heidelberg reported in O. Stammer (ed.), *Max Weber und die Soziologie heute* (Tübingen: Mohr, 1965).

40. For a detailed presentation of the background of these developments see Bryn J. Hovde, *The Scandinavian Countries 1720–1865* (Ithaca: Cornell Univ. Press, 1948), particularly Chaps. VIII–IX and XIII.

41. Lin Piao, "Long Live the Victory of the People's War," *Peking Review,* 8 (Sept. 3, 1965), p. 24.

42. See S. M. Lipset, *The First New Nation, op. cit.,* Chaps. 5, 6, and 7.

43. This is the phrase used by Ernest Fraenkel, "Parlament und öffentliche Meinung,"

in *Zur Geschichte und Problematik der Demokratie: Festgabe für H. Herzfeld* (Berlin: Duncker & Humblot, 1958), p. 178. For further details on German developments, see the recent study by Günther Roth, *The Social Democrats in Imperial Germany* (Totowa: Bedminster Press, 1963), Chaps. VII–X.

44. One of the first political analysts to call attention to these developments was Herbert Tingsten, then editor-in-chief of the leading Swedish newspaper *Dagens Nyheter,* see his autobiography, *Mitt Liv: Tidningen* (Stockholm: Norstedts, 1963), pp. 224–31. For further details see S. M. Lipset, "The Changing Class Structure and Contemporary European Politics." *Daedalus,* 93 (1964), pp. 271–303.

45. On Austrian politics since 1945 see A. Vodopivec, *Wer regiert in Österreich?* (Vienna: Verlag für Geschichte und Politik, 1961), and the chapter by F. C. Engelmann on Austria in R. A. Dahl (ed.), *Political Oppositions in Western Democracies, op. cit.*

46. See Walter Laqueur and Leopold Labedz (eds.), *Polycentrism: The New Factor in International Communism* (New York: Praeger, 1962); L. Labedz (ed.), *Revisionism* (New York: Praeger, 1962), and S. M. Lipset, "The Changing Class Structure . . .", *op. cit.*

47. Erik Allardt, "Patterns of Class Conflict and Working Class Consciousness in Finnish Politics" in E. Allardt and Y. Littunen (eds.), *Cleavages, Ideologies and Party Systems, op. cit.,* pp. 97–131.

48. See chapter by S. Rokkan in this volume and the recent study of Egil Fivelsdal of unionization and politics among white-collar workers in Norway, *Funksjonærenes syn på faglige og politiske spørsmål* (Olso: Universitetsforlaget, 1964).

49. See Andrew G. Whiteside, *Austrian National Socialism before 1918* (The Hague: Nijhoff, 1962), and his article on Austria in T. Rogger and E. Weber (eds.), *The European Right* (London: Weidenfeld, 1965), pp. 328–63.

50. For a detailed analysis of the Austrian "invention" of mass anti-Semitism see Peter Pulzer, *The Rise of Political Anti-Semitism in Germany and Austria* (New York: Wiley, 1964).

51. R. Dahrendorf, *Gesellschaft und Demokratie in Deutschland* (Munich: Piper, 1965), esp. Chap. 26.

52. On the electoral support for the NSDAP, see especially Sten S. Nilson, "Wahlsoziologische Probleme des Nationalsozialismus" *Zs. Ges Staatswiss,* 110 (1954), pp. 229–311; K. D. Bracher, *Die Auflösung der Weimarer Republik* (3d ed.; Villingen: Ring-Verlag, 1960), Chap. VI; and Alfred Milatz. "Das Ende der Parteien im Spiegel der Wahlen 1930 bis 1933," in E. Matthias and R. Morsey (eds.), *Das Ende der Parteien 1933* (Düsseldorf: Droste, 1960), pp. 741–93. A summary of evidence from electoral analyses is given in S. M. Lipset, *Political Man, op. cit.,* pp. 140–51. The best analysis of the rural strength of the NSDAP is still Rudolf Heberle's *From Democracy to Nazism* (Baton Rouge: Louisiana State Univ. Press, 1945). The fuller German manuscript from 1932 has recently been published as *Landbevölkerung und Nationalsozialismus* (Stuttgart: Deutsche Verlagsanstalt, 1963).

53. Such similarities in social bases and in attitudes to national authority obviously do not necessarily imply similarities in organizational tactics and in actual behavior toward opponents. There is no implication that all such movements would conform to the Fascist or the National Socialist *ethos* if victorious. For a discussion of the evidence for Italy, France, and the United States see S. M. Lipset, *Political Man, op. cit.,* Chap. V, as well as "Radical Rightists of Three Decades—Coughlinites, McCarthyites and Birchers," in Daniel Bell (ed.), *The Radical Right* (New York: Doubleday, 1963), and "Beyond the Backlash," *Encounter,* 23 (Nov., 1964), pp. 11–24. For Norway, see Nilson, *op. cit.* For an interesting analysis of the Social Credit Movement in Canada in similar terms see Donald Smiley. "Canada's Poujadists: a New Look at Social Credit," *The Canadian Forum,* 42 (Sept., 1962), pp. 121–23: the Socreds are anti-metropolitan and anti-institutional and they advocate pure plebiscitarian politics against organized group interests and established elites.

54. In a recent review of Western European developments Hans Daalder has argued this point with great force. It is impossible to understand the development, structure, and operation of party systems without a study of the extent of elite competition *before* the industrial and the democratic revolutions. He singles out Britain, the Low Countries, Switzerland, and Sweden as the countries with the strongest traditions of conciliar

pluralism and points to the consequences of these preconditions for the development of integrated party systems. See H. Daalder, "Parties, Elites and Political Development(s) in Western Europe" in J. LaPalombara and M. Weiner (eds.), *Political Parties and Political Development, op. cit.* For a fuller discussion of contrasts in the character of the nation-building process, see S. P. Huntington, "Political Modernization: America vs. Europe," *World Politics,* 18 (1966), pp. 378–414.

55. This is Faul's term for the initial phase in the growth of parties, *op. cit.,* pp. 62–9.

56. See especially Gunnar Olsson, *Hattar och mössor: Studier over partiväsendet i Sverige 1751–1762* (Gothenburg: Akademi-förlaget, 1963).

57. For a review of this literature see S. M. Lipset, "Introduction: Ostrogorski and the Analytical Approach to the Comparative Study of Political Parties," in M. I. Ostrogorski, *Democracy and the Organization of Political Parties* (abridged ed.; New York: Doubleday, 1964), pp. IX–LXV.

58. "European Political Parties: The Case of Polarized Pluralism" in J. La-Palombara and M. Weiner (eds.), *Political Parties and Political Development, op. cit.*

59. For reviews of similarities and differences among two English-speaking democracies, see the chapter by R. Alford and A. D. Robinson in this volume and also L. Lipson, "Party Systems in the United Kingdom and the Older Commonwealth," *Pol. Studies,* 7 (1959), pp. 12–31; S. M. Lipset, *The First New Nation,* Chaps. 5, 6, and 7; and R. Alford, *Party and Society: The Anglo-American Democracies* (Chicago: Rand McNally, 1963), esp. Chap. XII.

60. Leon D. Epstein, "A Comparative Study of Canadian Parties," *Amer. Pol. Sci. Rev.,* 63 (March, 1964), pp. 46–59.

61. The basic reference work on the history of PR in Europe is still Karl Braunias, *Das parlamentarische Wahlrecht* (Berlin: de Gruyter, 1932) I–II. Polemical works such as F. A. Hermens, *Democracy or Anarchy?* (Notre Dame: Univ. of Notre Dame Press, 1941); E. Lakeman and J. D. Lambert, *Voting in Democracies* (London: Faber, 1955); and H. Unkelbach, *Grundlagen der Wahlsystematik* (Göttingen: Vandenhoeck u. Rupprecht, 1956) offer a great wealth of information but do not contribute much to the understanding of the *sociocultural conditions* for the success of the one or the other procedure of electoral aggregation. See S. Rokkan, "Electoral Systems," article in *International Encyclopedia of the Social Sciences* (forthcoming).

62. Braunias, *op. cit.,* II, pp. 201–4.

63. See J. Gilissen, *Le régime représentatif en Belgique depuis 1790* (Brussels: Renaissance du Livre, 1958), pp. 126–30.

64. The rise of the nationwide movement for universal suffrage and the parallel mobilization of support for the Liberals and the Social Democrats has been described in great detail by S. Carlsson, *Lantmannapolitiken och industrialismen* (Lund: Gleerup, 1952), and T. Vallinder, *I kamp för demokratien* (Stockholm: Natur o. kultur, 1962). For a convenient account of the bargaining over suffrage extension and PR see Douglas V. Verney, *Parliamentary Reform in Sweden 1866–1921* (Oxford: Clarendon, 1957), Chap. VII.

65. On the ties between the Church and the Right in France, see René Rémond, *La droite en France de 1815 à nos jours* (Paris: Aubier, 1954), pp. 239–45.

66. Types VI to VII in our typology, the deviant type V is discussed in detail below.

67. For an illuminating analysis of the sociocultural characteristics of the classic region of counterrevolutionary resistance, see Charles Tilly, *The Vendée* (London: Arnold, 1965).

68. For an interesting approach to the analysis of the political consequences of "monocephality" vs. "polycephality" see Juan Linz and A. de Miguel, "Within-Nation Differences and Comparisons: The Eight Spains," in R. L. Merritt and S. Rokkan (eds.), *Comparing Nations* (New Haven: Yale Univ. Press, 1966), pp. 267–319.

69. This point has been developed in further detail in S. Rokkan, "Electoral Mobilization, Party Competition and National Integration," *op. cit.*

70. For an analysis of the three decisive cleavage lines in Belgian politics, the language conflict, the church-school issue, and the owner-worker opposition, see Val Lorwin's chapter on Belgium in R. A. Dahl (ed.), *Political Oppositions in Western Democracies, op. cit.,* It is interesting to note that the same factors disrupted Belgian Fascism during the 1930s and made it impossible to build a single major nationalist-Fascist party; see

Jean Stengers, "Belgium," in Rogger and Weber (eds.), *The European Right, op. cit.,* pp. 128–67.

71. Herbert Luethy, "Has Switzerland a Future? The Dilemma of a Small Nation," *Encounter,* 19 (Dec., 1962), p. 25.

72. For sociological analyses of the system of cleavages in Spanish society after 1815 see Gerald Brenan, *The Spanish Labyrinth* (London: Cambridge Univ. Press, 1943; 2d ed., 1950; paperback, 1960); Carlos A. Rama, *La crise espagnole au XXe siècle* (Paris: Fischbacher, 1962); Juan Linz, *op. cit.,* and "Spain: an Authoritarian Regime" in E. Allardt and Y. Littunen (eds.), *Cleavages, Ideologies and Party Systems, op. cit.,* pp. 290–341. See also the analysis of the elections of 1931, 1933, and 1936 in J. Becarud, *La Deuxième République Espagnole* (Paris: Centre d'Etude des Relations Internationales, 1962), mimeo.

73. On the function of the *cacique* as the controller or rural support in the initial phase of mass mobilization, see Brenan, *op. cit.,* pp. 5–8; Raymond Carr, *Spain, 1908–1939* (Oxford: Clarendon, 1966), pp. 366–79; and the classic analyses in Joaquín Costa (ed.), *Oligarquía y caciquismo como el forma actual de gobierno en España* (Madrid: Hernández, 1902).

74. See Mattei Dogan, "La stratificazione sociale dei suffragi," pp. 407–74, in A. Spreafico and J. LaPalombara (eds.), *Elezioni e comportamento politico in Italia* (Milan: Ed. di Comunita, 1963), and his chapter in the present volume.

75. See R. A. Webster, *The Cross and the Fasces* (Stanford: Stanford Univ. Press, 1960).

76. On the origin of particularist movements in Germany see especially W. Conze (ed.), *Staat und Gesellschaft im deutschen Vormärz 1815–1848* (Stuttgart: Klett, 1962).

77. The vivid expression coined by Jean-François Gravier in *Paris et le désert français* (2d ed.; Paris: Flammarion, 1958).

78. Charles P. Kindleberger, *Economic Growth in France and Britain 1851–1950* (Cambridge, Harvard Univ. Press, 1964), p. 255.

79. For details see S. Rokkan, "Mass Suffrage, Secret Voting, and Political Participation," *op. cit.*

80. For a detailed evaluation of the comparative statistics of agricultural holdings see F. Dovring, *Land and Labour in Europe 1900–1950* (2d ed.; The Hague: Nijhoff, 1960), Chap. 3 and appendices. The standard source on nineteenth-century statistics of landholdings in Britain is J. Bateman, *The Great Landowners of Great Britain and Ireland* (London: 1883); see F. M. L. Thompson, *English Landed Society, op. cit.,* Chap. V. On *latifundia* and *minimifundia* in Spain see G. Brenan, *The Spanish Labyrinth, op. cit.,* Chap. 6.

81. Recent advances in the techniques of electoral analysis make it possible to test such statements about the weight of the different cleavage dimensions in conditioning the alignments of voters. For data from *sample surveys* the development of *"tree analysis"* procedures opens up interesting possibilities of comparison. A "tree analysis" of data for the *Bundesrepublik* for 1957, 1961, and 1965 gives interesting evidence of the interaction of two major cleavage dimensions in that setting:

Owner-worker cleavage: status of head of household	Church-state commitment of respondent	Percent voting SPD in total electrate		
		1957	1961	1965
Worker, unionized	None	56	61	64
Worker, not unionized	None	37	41	43
Worker, middle-class aspirations	—	18	28	28
Worker, unionized	Committed Catholic	14	24	33
Worker, not unionized	Committed Catholic	15	10	15
Middle class, of working-class origins	—	27	24	41
Salaried, civil servants, unionized	—	25	39	52
Middle class	Committed Catholic	6	5	9

Source: K. Liepelt, "Wählerbewegungen in der Bundesrepublik," Paper, Arbeitstagung 21, July 1966, Institut für angewandte Sozialforschung, Bad Godesberg.

For periods before the advent of the sample survey similar analyses can be produced through ecological regression analysis. So far very few statistically sophisticated analyses have been carried out for European electoral time series before the 1950's: an exception is K. Cox, *Regional Anomalies in the Voting Behavior of the Population of England and Wales, op. cit.;* this includes a factor analysis of the rural vote in Wales from 1861 to 1921. For an illuminating example of a possible procedure, see the analysis of the French rural cantons by Mattei Dogan, "Les contextes politiques in France," Paper, Symposium on Quantitative Ecological Analysis, Evian, Sept. 1966. His Tables 11 and 13 give these correlation coefficients for the electoral strengths of the two left parties in 1956:

	PCF				SFIO			
	Rural France	West	Center	North	Rural France	West	Center	North
Percent industrial workers:								
—direct correlation	.28	.26	.16	.55	.33	.19	.05	.03
—partial correlation	.25	.12	.08	.39	.01	.09	.03	.19
Percent attending mass								
—direct correlation	−.60	−.62	−.48	−.67	−.21	−.39	−.10	.30
—partial correlation	−.59	−.59	−.47	−.58	−.21	−.36	−.09	.35
Multiple correlation	.64	.62	.49	.73	.21	.40	.10	.35

Within rural France the traditions of anticlericalism clearly count heavier than class in the generation of votes for the Left. If the Parisian suburbs and the other urban areas had been included in the analysis class they would obviously have weighed much heavier in the equation; see Dogan's chapter in the present volume. To test the implications of our model, analyses along the lines suggested by Cox and Dogan ought to be carried out for the elections just before and just after the extensions of the suffrage in a number of different countries; see the contrasted maps for 1849 and 1936 in Georges Dupeux, *Le Front Populaire et les élections de 1936* (Paris: Colin, 1959), pp. 169–70 and discussion pp. 157–71.

82. For an insightful analysis of the conditions for the development of these three *Lager* see A. Wandruszka, "Österreichs politische Struktur" in H. Benedikt (Hg.) *Geschichte der Republik Österreich* (Vienna: Verl. für Geschichte und Politik, 1952), pp. 298–485, 618–21.

83. See K. Bracher, *Die Auflösung der Weimarer Republik* (3d ed.; Villingen: Ring, 1960), Chaps. III-IV., and E. Matthias and R. Morsey (Hg.) *Das Ende der Parteien 1933* (Düsseldorf: Droste, 1960), pp. 154–58, 655–739.

84. Val R. Lorwin, "Working Class Politics and Economic Development in Western Europe," *Amer. Hist. Rev.*, 63 (1958), pp. 338–51.

85. This was a major point in the classic article by the elder Edvard Bull in "Die Entwicklung der Arbeiterbewegung in den drei skandinavischen Ländern," *Arch. f. Geschichte des Sozialismus*, 10 (1922), pp. 329–61.

86. This has been brought out in an important paper by Ulf Torgersen, *Landsmøtet i norsk partistruktur 1884–1940* (Oslo: Institute for Social Research, 1966), mimeo, pp. 39–46, 73–98.

87. For an account of the period from 1924 to 1935 see I. Roset, *Det Norske Arbeiderparti og Hornsruds regjeringsdannelse i 1928* (Oslo: Universitetsförlaget, 1964), and the summary in S. Rokkan, "Norway: Numerical Democracy and Corporate Pluralism" in R. A. Dahl (ed.), *Political Oppositions in Western Democracies* (New Haven: Yale Univ. Press, 1966), pp. 81–84.

88. See especially John H. Hodgson, *Communism in Finland* (Princeton: Princeton Univ. Press, 1966).

89. On Icelandic parties see Mary S. Olmsted, "Communism in Iceland," *Foreign Affairs*, 36 (1958), pp. 340–7, and Donald E. Nuechterlein, *Iceland: Reluctant Ally* (Ithaca: Cornell Univ. Press, 1961), Chap. I.

90. A book such as Samuel J. Eldersveld's *Political Parties: a Behavioral Analysis* (Chicago: Rand McNally, 1964), suggests important themes for new research, but its utility for comparative analysis is severely limited by its overconcentration on perhaps the most atypical of all existing party organizations, the American.

91. To substantiate such generalization it will clearly be necessary to proceed to a comparative census of "ephemeral" parties in Europe. Hans Daalder has made a useful beginning through his inventory of small parties in the Netherlands since 1918, the country with the longest record of minimal-threshold PR; see "De kleine politieke partijen—een voorlopige poging tot inventarisatie," *Acta politica*, 1 (1965–66), pp. 172–96.

92. See Chapter 5 by Linz.

93. This is a major theme in the Norwegian program of electoral research; see especially S. Rokkan and H. Valen, "The Mobilization of the Periphery," pp. 111–58 of S. Rokkan (ed.), *Approaches to the Study of Political Participation* (Bergen: Chr. Michelsen Institute, 1962), and T. Hjellum, *Partiene i lokalpolitikken* (Oslo: Gyldendal, 1967). The possibilities of comparative research on the "politicization" of local government are discussed in S. Rokkan, "Electoral Mobilization, Party Competition and National Integration" in J. LaPalombara and M. Weiner, *op. cit.*, pp. 241–65.

94. For a general statement of the need for such controls for the character of the local party alternatives see S. Rokkan, "The Comparative Study of Political Participation" in A. Ranney (ed.), *Essays on the Behavioral Study of Politics* (Urbana: Univ. of Illinois Press, 1962), pp. 45–90.

95. On the development of this type of data files for computer processing see S. Rokkan (ed.), *Data Archives for the Social Sciences* (Paris: Mouton, 1966), and the forthcoming report by Mattei Dogan and S. Rokkan on the Symposium on Quantitative Ecological Analysis held at Evian, France, in September, 1966.

96. In the United States the central figures in this movement were V. O. Key and Lee Benson. It is interesting to note, however, that their work has in recent years been vigorously followed up by such experts on survey analysis as Angus Campbell and his colleagues Philip Converse, Warren Miller, and Donald Stokes; see *Elections and the Political Order* (New York: Wiley, 1966), Chaps. 1–3 and 9.

97. For a detailed effort to integrate the findings of various studies of American student activism see S. M. Lipset and Philip Altbach, "Student Politics and Higher Education in the United States," *Comparative Education Rev.*, 10 (1966), pp. 320–49. This article appears also in revised and expanded form in S. M. Lipset (ed.), *Students and Politics* (New York: Basic Books, 1967). The Lipset-Altbach article, as well as other essays in this volume contain extensive bibliographic references. Another comprehensive discussion of the relevant literature may be found in Jeanne Block, Norma Haan, and M. Brewster Smith, "Activism and Apathy in Contemporary Adolescents," in James F. Adams (ed.), *Contributions to the Understanding of Adolescence* (Boston: Allyn and Bacon, in press). A special issue of the *Journal of Social Issues* to be published late in 1967 will contain a number of articles dealing with "Protest on the American Campus."

One

The English-Speaking Democracies

Class Voting in the Anglo-American Political Systems

Robert R. Alford

Are the political parties in the Anglo-American countries actually based upon
distinctive social strata? If there is a pervasive tendency in wealthy and industrialized countries for class issues to become blurred and the parties to resemble each other, and if these changes have the consequence of reducing
the distinctive class character of the support for political parties, such tendencies should be more evident in the Anglo-American countries than in most
other nations of the world today.

An important point of view in modern political thought holds that parties
need not be representatives of social classes. Parties can constitute competing
bodies of men seeking political power, but need not represent any given set
of interests or coalition of such interests. This is the economist Joseph
Schumpeter's view of the essence of democracy. Democracy is a political
form that need not have any class content.[1] The competing political factions need not represent *any* set of interests consistently, but need only be
alternative sets of leaders for the given political unit, be it organization, party,
or nation.

If social classes in the Western democracies become so shifting and blurred that no social interests with a degree of stability can be distinguished, then we might expect that democracy in these countries will come to resemble Schumpeter's model. Support for a party would not be predictable from either an assessment of the legislative behavior of its representatives or an analysis of stratification among the electorate. The Anglo-American countries may be closest to the state of affairs where neither parties nor electorate can be divided sharply into Left and Right, have-nots and haves.

In the research report following, public opinion surveys of the electorates of four Anglo-American countries are utilized to answer the question: what are the differences in the relationship between social class and voting behavior in these countries?

Most of the following pages are taken from a study by the author published in 1963.[2] However, an attempt has been made to bring the data and the references up to date insofar as possible.

CLASS AND VOTING BEHAVIOR

Studies of voting behavior have routinely found a correlation between the social class position of voters and the party they typically vote for. Persons in professional and business occupations, persons at upper-income levels, persons with more than a high-school education are more likely to vote for a party that stands for protection of business interests and little welfare legislation than persons in low-prestige occupations, with low incomes, or with little education. A growing body of voting studies has amply documented this generalization, both for the United States and Great Britain.[3] That class position and voting behavior are correlated is by now commonplace.

It is possible that the relation of class and voting is declining, however. Continuing prosperity and the opportunities for education, middle-class incomes, and styles of life available to workers may be eroding the connection between class position and voting. The American political scientist V. O. Key, for example, suggests that "perhaps in the election of 1936 [in the United States] the party division most nearly coincided with differences of income and occupation. That coincidence declined, as class relevant questions faded from the forefront, and in 1952 and 1956 Republicans won substantial support from the lower-income groups."[4] A study of American voters has actually found that the correlation of the occupational status of voters with their party preferences dropped in the three successive Presidential elections from 1948 to 1956. Although no studies of changes in the relation of class and vote have been done in England, a study of the 1959 general election in Great Britain suggested that the prosperity and social mobility in Britain during the 1950's might be reducing the bases for class politics.[5]

WHY EXPECT CLASS VOTING?

A relation between class position and voting behavior is a natural and expected association in the Western democracies, for a number of reasons: the existence of class interests, the representation of these interests by political parties, and the regular association of certain parties with certain interests. Given the character of the stratification order and the way political parties act as representatives of different class interests, it would be remarkable if such a relation were not found.

Class interests compete for advantage in many ways in the Western democracies. James Madison's classic essay on factions in American society summarizes a state of affairs which exists in all of these societies even now: "Those who hold and those who are without property have ever formed distinct interests in society. Those who are creditors, and those who are debtors, fall under a like discrimination. A landed interest, a manufacturing interest, a mercantile interest, a moneyed interest, with many lesser interests, grow up of necessity in civilized nations, and divide them into different classes, actuated by different sentiments and views."[6]

Although class interests are universal in these societies, they are not completely homogeneous. Precisely because of this, class interests form a crucially important but not sole basis for political action. Income, occupation, religion, education, ethnicity, and the other components of life chances do not divide the population into two huge camps of privileged and oppressed. Persons in the same economic position may more or less permanently unite for a common political or economic purpose, but such class-based solidarities do not constitute a permanent majority of the population. Although some minority economic interests are usually dominant in a given society, the degree to which economic elites tend to coalesce is an important but not relevant problem.

Class interests are politically relevant to different degrees in the Western democracies. Group interests based upon incentives as strong and stable as economic ones are constantly struggling for *political* advantage. In the modern democratic state the political parties have developed largely as instruments of various class interests. But partly because of the lack of monolithic unity among groups sharing common economic interests, and partly because of the character of the party system itself as a device for straddling many kinds of social conflicts, "the party system is the democratic translation of the class struggle. It postulates national unity beneath the divisions of class. It postulates the rationalization of class interests so that these can make appeal on the grounds of their service to or compatibility with the national interest."[7] Thus, political parties usually have a dual and conflicting role: to represent group interests and to unite group interests. The intensity, scope, and direction of class interests at a given time and the extent to which they are crosscut or reinforced by other social cleavages will determine the degree to which those interests become or remain politically relevant.

Political parties historically have come to represent specific coalitions of class interests. Parties adopt programs, encourage legislation, and appeal to voters in a way that tends to make them the representatives of specific sets of class interests. And it is probably justified to infer that this representation is consistent with the class composition of the support for a given party. The sociologist S. M. Lipset asserts that "even though many parties renounce the principle of class conflict or loyalty, an analysis of their appeals and their support suggests that they do represent the interests of different classes."[8] And R. M. MacIver concludes that "[w]herever parties divide on serious issues, and above all on economic issues, the more advantaged or well-to-do are certain to show preference for one party or group of parties and the less advantaged for the other."[9]

For these several reasons—the existence of class interests, the representation by political parties of those interests, and the association of certain parties with certain interests—we may expect a consistent relation of social class position to voting behavior.

Few studies, however, have investigated the variations in the relation of class and vote in a number of countries. The voting studies already cited— and others—have almost without exception focused upon the one community, one constituency, or one nation. Furthermore, few attempts have been made to compare patterns of class voting between different communities or areas within a single nation.[10] Yet comparative analysis can clarify the way in which different national and community contexts affect the relevance of class membership for political behavior.

HOW HAS CLASS VOTING BEEN STUDIED?

Where direct evidence on the class position of voters has not been available, studies of the relation of class and vote have been based on inferences from other kinds of evidence. The "ecological" type of study draws inferences as to the character of party support from a correlation between the party strength in an area and such demographic characteristics of the area as religious or occupational composition. The classic study of this type was done by the French political scientist André Siegfried, in his study of voting patterns in France from 1871 to 1912.[11] A study of Southern politics in the United States relies heavily on this method to infer characteristics of voters.[12] A more recent study of the South uses the ecological method to infer the extent of urban Republicanism among different income groups.[13]

Another method of studying the relation of class and vote has been to make inferences from the occupational positions of a party's representatives in the legislature. The political scientist Alexander Brady concludes plausibly that the Labour Party in England was based on the working class because of the election of fifty-three working-class members of Parliament in 1906 and from other changes in the composition of the British governing elite in the nineteenth century.[14] The nature of party programs and the content of party appeals for support have also been used to infer the characteristics of party supporters. None of these methods guarantees the discovery of the real class composition of the support for a party. It is easy to assume that voters are likely to vote for candidates in occupations similar to theirs or for parties supporting legislation congruent with their class interests. But just because class interests are cut across by many other group interests, such assumptions may be contrary to fact. A party may have historically derived bonds to certain ideologies, pressure groups, and programs which do not at all reflect the needs and desires of its actual constituency. Particularly in the present period, when the class bases of politics may be dwindling, it is dangerous to infer anything concerning the social bases of the parties from such indirect evidence as ecological correlations (especially since geographic mobility is high), the occupational composition of parliamentary delegations, or the content of platforms and speeches. Where public opinion surveys have been taken, the relation of class and vote can be studied by means of direct information on the class position of voters.

POLITICAL SYSTEMS OF THE ANGLO-AMERICAN COUNTRIES

The Anglo-American countries are alike in the important respect that they have what may be termed "pluralist" political systems. In such systems, political parties are free to organize and compete for power, and pressure groups and interest groups of many kinds may also compete for influence upon political decision-makers.[15] Voters are not tightly integrated into enclaves of traditionalism which reinforce ancestral political loyalties. Instead, voters change fairly freely from one party to another. Parties must therefore compete for support; they are not guaranteed a reliable national majority, although they can count on many constituencies for consistent support.

The Anglo-American countries have a common heritage in British political culture and traditions. Where a common political culture exists—widespread values unifying a political system—specific political institutions may differ, but the "spirit" or "climate" of politics may be remarkably similar. In spite of the parliamentary system and cabinet government in the Commonwealth and the Presidential system in the United States, the countries share a common set of underlying political values: liberalism, individualism, and a pragmatic, nonideological sense of compromise. There is a high level of consensus in these countries upon these values. The American political scientist Gabriel Almond has described the political culture of these Anglo-American countries as "secular and homogeneous," referring in another way to the same characteristics.[16] Alexander Brady, in his comparative study of several Commonwealth countries, makes the same point. Although he is referring specifically to the overseas Dominions, his point applies to the United States as well. "The overseas Dominions . . . share two common socio-political elements: first, extensive and sparsely peopled territories, situated chiefly within the temperate latitudes, where politics and social life have been penetrated in various degrees with the spirit of a frontier; and secondly, political institutions, mainly derivative, rooted ultimately in the law, culture, and liberal philosophy of the British people."[17] A Canadian historian adds that although the United States, unlike the Dominions of the British Commonwealth, "shut [the] doorway to the past," by its Revolution, it "locked the stable door after the steed—that is, the traditional English institutions—had been securely tied inside. No one needs to be reminded that today, after nearly two centuries of separation, the institutions of the entire English-speaking world have tremendous areas in common."[18]

The Anglo-American political systems enjoy a high level of consensus on political procedures and on the political framework itself. More specifically, no social group feels itself so severely deprived by the operations of the system that it moves outside of the framework of existing political institutions to struggle for its demands. Also, no social groups are completely isolated from similar reactions to events affecting the nation.[19]

Since the Anglo-American countries share a common political culture, a comparative study of the association of class and vote is not complicated by widely varying political values and traditions. Also, such a political culture reinforces their pluralist political institutions with appropriate values and traditions.

Although a common political culture may exist without similar political institutions, in fact, these countries do share institutions relevant to the understanding of the association of class and vote. Their political parties fall along the classic Left-Right continuum, without the complications introduced by strong totalitarian parties cutting across the Left-Right dimension. Unlike continental Europe, political parties and issues are not polarized along religious lines. Instead, a secular norm is dominant in politics. The issues which dominate politics in these countries are mainly those relating to distribution of the national wealth. The degree of centralization of government necessary or desirable to accomplish a variety of social goals, the level of regulation of private business, and the level of public ownership necessary or desirable are explicit issues serving as sources for political division. These are Left-Right issues related to the basic divisions of class interests in these societies. The parties in the Anglo-American countries differ in their stands on these issues and in their "distance" apart, but these political systems are not torn by conflict over the existence of pluralist political institutions. The existence of parties primarily battling over Left-Right economic issues is in part a consequence of the moderate and compromising values of British political culture already mentioned, but the character of the parties also shapes and reinforces a particular political culture.

Each of the Anglo-American countries tends toward a two-party system, although three of the four have more than two parties actually running candidates for national office. (All of these countries have many truly minor parties springing up over a temporary issue, or representing some particular aggrieved public, but I am only referring here to those parties which are recognized as having some national importance.) Whether these countries "really" have two-party systems or not depends on the problem of interest, but both the legitimate way in which they constitute two-party systems and the reason for the existence of more than two parties are important for the understanding of the association of class and vote in these countries.

Political scientists, when distinguishing the Anglo-American countries from others, commonly consider them to have "two-party" systems, a theoretical rather than an empirical term referring to certain structural pressures and institutional imperatives common to all of these countries. According to the English political scientist D. W. Brogan, countries which have had "British political training . . . fall naturally back to the two-party system, even a two-party system with little intellectual consistency."[20] Maurice Duverger refers to the "Anglo-Saxon two-party systems," contrasting them with the single- and multi-party systems of continental Europe.[21] Such a description is most meaningful when these countries are contrasted with others more clearly of a multi-party or single-party type. The countries within the British Commonwealth share a system of parliamentary government. Power is not divided between the executive and legislative branches in the American manner, but must necessarily be exercised across the board by one or the other of the two major parties. Power in Great Britain is transferred back and forth from the Labour Party to the Conservative Party, with the Liberal Party playing a minor role. (Whether the Liberals would replace Labour as the major "Left" party was a matter of debate in the early 1960's.) Power in Australia shifts from Labor to a coalition of the Liberal and Country parties. Power in Canada shifts from the Liberal to Conservative parties, with the C.C.F. (and its successor—the "New Democratic Party") and the Social Credit parties having had no realistic hopes of gaining national governmental power. The parties which form a government or the opposition in these parliamentary systems may change, and the third or fourth parties may play crucial roles in influencing policies, but power is exercised by one of two major parties or coalitions. In the United States, which lacks a parliamentary system, a two-party system has become stable partly because of the party primary, allowing flexible coalitions within the framework of both parties. The Presidential and gubernatorial systems in the United States also encourage a two-party division, because these offices cannot be divided and coalitions tend to form around two candidates.[22]

Thus, although technically and actually more than two parties run candidates for national office in these countries, the realistic alternative governments presented to the electorate—the main concern here—are only two. This is another factor which these countries have in common, and which makes comparative generalizations more valid. The electorate is not fragmented into supporters of one or another small party hoping to gain a few seats and a voice in a coalition government.[23]

Considering only aspects of their political systems, the Anglo-American countries have been shown to be similar in major respects affecting the alternatives available to the electorate; they share a moderate, compromising political culture deriving from the British tradition; they have freely competitive parties battling along economic Left-Right lines; they have governmental and electoral systems which encourage the persistence of two major parties.

STRATIFICATION SYSTEMS OF THE ANGLO-AMERICAN COUNTRIES

Comparative generalizations about the relation of class and vote in the Anglo-American countries depend not only upon a similarity of political institutions and traditions, but also upon a similarity of the stratification systems in these countries. Certain characteristics—their wealth relative to most other countries, the extent of mobility, the prestige attached to different occupations, and the range of stratification positions available—are all roughly similar in the four countries. However, the relative proportions of persons in different strata, the degree of class consciousness, and the status structure differ somewhat, with Great Britain probably more sharply split into strata with differing prestige and honor than the other societies.

The range of stratification positions available is roughly the same in each of these societies. Professionals, skilled craftsmen, small businessmen, executives, civil servants, salesmen, laborers all exist in each of these societies. No important feudal segments remain in any of these countries.

Since these are all advanced industrial societies, the occupational composition of the labor force is also similar. Table 1 shows that the proportions of nonagriculturally employed males engaged in different nonagricultural occupations are similar in the four countries.

In addition to similar occupational structures, these countries have similar levels of occupational mobility. A major conclusion of a recent study of social mobility in a number of industrial societies was that the level of intergenerational mobility from a manual occupation to a nonmanual one (or back) is substantially the same in all industrial societies. Undoubtedly the level of mobility is even more similar for the Anglo-American countries than for countries just emerging from feudalism, or rapidly industrializing.[24] Since the occupational composition of these countries is similar, then similarity of levels of mobility also means roughly equal opportunities.[25]

Not only actual levels of mobility are similar in these countries, but also the prestige of different occupations is similar. A study comparing occupational prestige in a number of countries found that three English-speaking nations correlated more with each other than with the Soviet Union and Japan (but no more than with Germany) in the degree to which a sample of respondents in each country agreed upon prestige ranking of different occupations.[26]

An additional characteristic of the class structure of these societies for which no comparative data are available is the degree of "status crystallization," or the extent persons in these countries have inconsistent social statuses:

Table 1—Of the Economically Active Population, Percent in Various Occupations

Occupation	(Circa 1950) United Kingdom (1951)	Australia (1947)	United States (1950)	Canada (1951)
Professional, technical and related occupations	6%	5%	8%	7%
Managerial, administrative, clerical and related occupations	12	18	21	20
Sales workers	10	8	7	6
Farming, fishing, hunting, lumbering, and related occupations	5	15	12	19
Workers in mines, quarries, and related occupations	3 ⎫	– ⎫	1 ⎫	2 ⎫
Workers in operating transport	8 ⎬ 42	– ⎬ 42*	4 ⎬ 38	5 ⎬ 38
Craftsmen, production process workers, and others not elsewhere classified	31 ⎭	– ⎭	33 ⎭	31 ⎭
Service workers	14	7	10	8
Armed Forces	2	1	2	1
Not classifiable	9	4	2	1
	100%	100%	100%	100%
Total (thousands)	(22,578)	(3,196)	(60,037)	(5,330)

Source: United Nations, Demographic Yearbook (New York, 1956), Table 15, pp. 458–99.
* Certain Australian occupational categories were not tabulated separately.

high income and low-status occupation, low education but a high-status occupation, and so forth. This is obviously related to the extent and level of social mobility. Presumably if the level of social mobility is high, then many persons will possess contradictory status attributes. Yet two countries can probably have roughly similar rates of intergenerational mobility from manual to nonmanual occupations (as already shown) and yet the proportions of persons in inconsistent status positions may differ considerably. Studies of Detroit and Minneapolis in the United States have shown that a large proportion of the population has inconsistent status attributes (or, in terms of the city itself, a low level of "status crystallization" exists).[27] Less status crystallization was found in large cities than in smaller cities, in a comparison of Detroit and Minneapolis with Lloyd Warner's "Jonesville."

One might expect therefore that status inconsistency will increase as a country becomes urbanized. Because of greater social and geographic mobility in large cities or urbanized countries, a lower correlation between income, education, and occupation than in towns or less-urbanized countries will exist. Replications of these studies have not been done for other countries, but they would fill an important gap in our knowledge of variables affecting social mobility, class consciousness, and presumably the association of class and vote. Aside from any question of class consciousness, the "visibility" of the class structure is far higher in a country with a high level of status crystallization, since few workers are in contact with anyone with higher incomes or education than themselves.

The nature of the stratification systems in these countries is important for an understanding of the phenomenon of class voting. It has been shown that in a number of important respects they are similar: the shape and content of the occupational structure, the amount of occupational mobility, and the prestige attaching to different occupations. Differences in class voting can, therefore, not be ascribed to gross differences in the structural features of their stratification systems.

I have hitherto dealt with the class and political structures of these countries as if they were separable entities. Although it is possible to analyze the institutional structure of social classes and political parties separately, their mutual connection are vital for a study of class voting. Both the class structure and the nature of the party system are independent variables affecting the relation of social class and vote. For the Anglo-American countries, however, we may regard them as constants, at least for purposes of preliminary investigation. Although people more or less advantaged by the economic system exist, and press their respective demands upon the parties and the government, the essence of politics in these countries lies in devising a strategy of gaining majority support without either endangering the stable social base of a party, losing the chance of winning over part of another stratum, or moving too far away from the issues which are legitimately in the political arena at a given time.

This feature of Anglo-American politics I have called its moderate, compromising political culture, and it obviously is highly important in assessing the significance of differences in class voting in these countries. Moderation and compromise are undoubtedly sustained by the relatively high prosperity of these countries, which reduces the intensity of political and class struggles.[28]

Nothing that has been said thus far implies that the association of class and vote need be identical in the Anglo-American countries, although such an association of class position and voting behavior is to be expected from the character of both their class structures and their party systems. The following sections are devoted to, first, a discussion of what differences in the level of class voting we might expect from historical and institutional features of these societies, and second, a presentation of the evidence on class voting from a great number of public opinion surveys taken in those countries.

WHY SHOULD CLASS VOTING BE HIGHER IN GREAT BRITAIN AND AUSTRALIA?

Considerable historical and institutional evidence indicates that the association of class and vote should be higher in Great Britain and Australia than in the United States and Canada. In particular, the explicit links of the trade unions with the labor parties of Great Britain and Australia might seem to be prima facie evidence that manual workers are far more likely to support a labor party than nonmanual workers. But let me emphasize that this is no necessary connection. The links of a class organization with a party bearing the name of "Labor" are no guarantee that the actual character of the support of the party is actually sharply differentiated from that of the other party. *Particularly* in this historical period, when, according to authors already cited, class lines are blurring and the working class in advanced industrial societies is losing its distinctive identity and consciousness as it takes on middle-class values and aspirations, there is no reason to assume from historic links of class organizations to class parties that working-class and middle-class persons are still sharply divided in their political loyalties.

Before presenting the actual evidence, I want to spell out more specifically the views of political scientists on a few of the historical differences between these four political systems which probably affect the level of class voting. Clearly this is a large topic in itself, so only a few representative and current works will be cited. The point is an obvious one—class organizations and class ideologies have been much more explicitly linked to the political parties in Great Britain and Australia than in the United States and Canada.

The Labour Party of Great Britain was from the first an instrument of class organizations—the trade unions.

> The Labour Party was founded by the trade unions to secure Labour representation in Parliament and to support by political action the objectives sought by the trade unions in the interests of their members. . . . What produced that party was the discovery by the urban workers that they could secure better conditions of service by combinations among themselves, and the threat by the employers to seize the initiative by employers' federations which could also act as pressure groups in Parliament.[29]

Even today, the trade unions raise most of the money for the Labour Party, and are officially represented in the "National Council of Labour," composed of representatives of the Labour Party, the Trades Union Congress, and the Cooperative Party.[30] Although in practice the Labour Party has a high degree of independence, the "constitutional law" of the Labour Party holds that it is bound by the decisions of the Annual Party Conference, in which the unions are officially represented.

The point here is not the actual relationship between the trade unions and the Labour Party in Great Britain; they are complicated, often strained, and in no sense do the unions dictate to the Labour Party. The party is not the creature of working-class organizations; the very moderation of British political culture prevents any coincidence of class and party views. But clearly the trade unions—unquestioned instruments of working-class interests —and the Labour Party are historically and publicly linked. On this ground alone, we might expect that political loyalties in Great Britain might be explicitly class-linked.[31] On the other hand, Leon Epstein has documented the "sharp drop in the working-class character of the party's top parliamentary leadership" in the 1950's, which might seem to be linked to a decline of the traditional class base of the party among the electorate as well.[32]

The Labor Party in Australia is equally solidly linked to working-class organizations.

> The Labour Party was created by the trade unions and their Trades and Labour Councils. The solid core and majority of its membership, as of its electoral support, came and have ever since come from trade unionists and their families. Most of its Parliamentarians, Federal and State, have risen through the trade union ranks. For many years, it was little more than the trade-unions-in-politics—in earlier times, in some States at least, it was known as the "Labour-in-politics" movement, implying just that.[33]

Since the class structure of Australia is similar to that of the other countries, we might therefore expect that the level of class voting in Australia is close to that of Britain.[34]

But one feature of Australian history might lead to a different level of class voting than in Great Britain—whether lower or higher could either be plausibly predicted. The Australian Labor Party has always had higher prestige and authority than the British Labour Party. From the very beginning of Australia as a nation in 1901, the Labor Party has existed as a political force and has therefore shaped the political traditions of Australia far more than the Labour Party of Great Britain has shaped the traditions of that country. The British Labour Party arose partly as a means of breaking the dominance of the industrial and owning classes of Parliament; as a means of gaining recognition for the legitimacy of class organizations. The Australian Labor Party arose partly as an instrument for the unification of Australia as an independent nation and partly as a representative of strongly organized and militant unions, mainly in "rural" occupations such as sheepshearing. Its dominant role from the beginning of Australian political history is stated by the American political scientist Louise Overacker: "The position of the Labor Party, both as to program and actual strength in Parliament, is a determining factor from which the politicians calculate their course, right or left. . . . The matrix of Australian politics is the Labor Party, and Australian politics reflects working-class rather than middle-class thinking."[35]

The dominant role of the Labor Party in Australia might produce either higher or lower levels of class voting in Australia than Great Britain. Where the Right party has the halo of tradition and of the defender of the nation, and is supported by widespread values of deference toward the aristocracy, as in Great Britain, we might expect that a large minority of the workers would vote Conservative for nonclass reasons. Even if middle-class persons voted consistently Conservative in accordance with *their* class interests, the effect of the Conservative "deferential voting" among workers would be to reduce the level of class voting. On the other hand, it could be argued that the middle class in Australia is *more* likely to vote Labor because of the legitimacy and nationalism associated with the Labor Party in that country, thus reducing the level of class voting.

Both of these arguments are plausible, and both may be wrong. Actually, the greater legitimacy of the Right in Great Britain and the greater legitimacy of the Left in Australia may negligibly affect the voting of either social class. This point has been raised not to present a specific hypothesis but to underline the difficulty of predicting the level of class voting from information on only the historic links of class organizations to political parties in either country.

But regardless of the differences likely to be found between Australia and Great Britain, there seems to be little doubt from historical and institutional evidence that class voting is likely to be higher in both of these countries than in the United States and Canada.

The Left political parties in the United States and Canada do not have those public and historic links with trade unions and other class organizations which might be expected to repel the middle class and attract the working class, and therefore produce a high level of class voting. As R. M. MacIver has put it:

> . . . [P]arty government can under certain conditions operate with considerable indifference to class stratification. Thus for long periods and over large areas in the United States and in Canada there was little relation between class and party, the struggle between parties being essentially a contest of the "ins" and the "outs" for the spoils of office. When this happens, however, parties are hardly distinguishable from one another with respect to principles or to objectives.

MacIver notes that when, as in the 1930's, "both in Canada and the United States, one or another party came to propose important economic changes," the tendency of the more well-to-do to support one party and the poorer to support another showed again.[36]

That the political parties in the United States and Canada historically have been competing political elites—the "ins" and the "outs"—and not the direct representatives of class organizations does not clearly distinguish them from the parties of Australia and Great Britain, however. In all four societies, regardless whether class and party have been publicly linked, each party has in practice consented to whatever legislation has been passed and has even adopted some policies likely to be favored by the class base of the other party, in order to win over support. In Australia, "Labor's political opponents have accepted many of Labor's policies," and in Great Britain, most markedly in recent years, the policies of the parties have been well-nigh indistinguish-able.[37] Thus it cannot be maintained that the actual policies of the parties in Australia and Great Britain as compared to the other two countries *neces-sarily* are so different—aside from historic traditions and organizational links —that we may expect sharp differences in the level of class voting.

On another ground also, class voting may not be expected to be sharply higher in Australia and Great Britain than in the United States, at least. The public images of the two parties in the United States sharply define them as representatives of distinctive class bases.

> . . . [A] consistent majority—at times as high as two-thirds to three-quarters—of the adult population of the United States perceives a clear distinction in ideological and interest-group propensity between the two major parties. The polls tend to verify the commonly accepted carica-ture that the Democratic Party is the party of the poor and of labor and the Republican Party is the party of business and of the rich. . . . These stereotypes may be less important as accurate descriptions of party differences than as reflections of the public's belief that the parties actually provide meaningful alternatives in many areas of policy, even though there are important areas of consensus.[38]

Thus, even though there are no explicit links of class organizations to par-ticular parties, and regardless of the degree to which the parties *actually* represent distinctive class interests, American political parties are viewed by voters as representing different social classes. A much higher level of class voting in Australia and Great Britain than in the United States may not therefore exist.

In Canada, on the other hand, none of these factors favoring a high level of class voting exists. Except for the Cooperative Commonwealth Federation, one of the minor parties, no political party has any explicit links with class organizations, and such links are in fact sedulously avoided. The parties are not ideologically linked with any distinctive class interests historically, and are not identified at present with specific class bases. Therefore we might expect on these grounds alone that class voting might be low. But let me emphasize again that this need not be true. Class interests exist in Canada as they do in the United States, and certainly the political parties to some degree represent them. A complete absence of class voting is not therefore to be expected, but neither need the class bases of Canadian politics be much different from those of other countries in the British tradition. The origins of much of Canada's population in Great Britain might produce similar expectations and loyalties among the Canadians themselves and serve to shape the parties around specific class bases.

The Liberal Party in Canada has not historically been linked to class or-ganizations in the way that the labor parties in Australia and Great Britain have. This is partly due to the frontier character of Canada (and the frontier has had similar effects upon American politics), since class struggles were vitiated by the availability of land to the West to dissatisfied workers. The continual expansion of Canada and the domination of certain regions by agriculture has accentuated sectional conflicts of East and West based on urban-financial versus rural-agricultural conflicts rather than the classic form of class struggle between industrialists and workers. Therefore, working-class organizations have been relatively weak and relatively irrelevant politically.

The Conservative Party of Canada took the lead in the policy of national development and in the unification of Canada, in contrast to the lead of the Labor Party in those matters in Australia, and therefore has historically benefited from this identification with the national interest. The Liberal Party has been the defender of provincial autonomy, mainly due to its long association with the French-Catholic minority in Quebec, and this link has further deterred its identification as the party of the working class.[39]

The parties in Canada have therefore not been identified as class parties, but not for the reason that class interests do not exist in Canada, or are not politically expressed and politically relevant. Class interests have been cross-cut by so many other politically relevant cleavages—sectional, religious, ethnic—that they have not emerged as the chief basis for political loyalties. We may expect to find that class voting is lower in Canada than in the other Anglo-American countries here analyzed—but not necessarily any lower than in the United States, where so many diverse cleavages have also determined the strategies and appeals of the political parties.

We may now turn to the evidence for the relation of social class position and voting in these four countries, derived from a large number of public opinion surveys and summarized by means of an index of class voting.

A crude measure of class voting is afforded by subtracting the percentage of persons in nonmanual occupations voting for "Left" parties from the percentage of manual workers voting for such parties. For Great Britain, the Labour Party vote in each stratum was used; for Australia, votes for the Australian Labor Party; for the United States, the Democratic Party; for Canada, the combined vote for the CCF (or New Democratic) and Liberal parties. The percentage-point difference that results is given in Tables 3, 4, and 5, to be discussed later.[40]

This particular index does leave aside two important aspects of the relation of social classes to parties: the degree of political distinctiveness of the working class (the absolute level of Left voting by workers) and the degree of class distinctiveness of the Left party (the proportion of support for the Left party drawn from workers).[41] Table 2 illustrates this distinction by giving four limiting cases. Type I illustrates the case where the Left party draws almost exclusively from the working class *and* the working class supports no other party. Party and class lines are sharply drawn. Such a state of affairs might well constitute a revolutionary situation, and we need not expect that the Anglo-American countries will exhibit this pattern in the historical period dealt with here. Type II illustrates the case where the working class divides its support between the two parties but the Left party subsists almost entirely on its working class votes, and type III the opposite case, where the workers vote almost exclusively for the Left party, but the middle class divides its support between the two parties. The index of class voting does not differentiate these two types. Britain approximates type II while Norway, for example, is close to type III.[42] Type IV illustrates the case where neither party nor class can be sharply distinguished by their support or composition.

The United States and Canada are less polarized in both respects than Great Britain, as will be shown.

A comparative study of a wider range of political cultures and social structures would need to take into account these dimensions of the class-party relationship—the political distinctiveness of the working class and the class distinctiveness of the Left parties. For present purposes this inadequacy of the index of class voting can be neglected.

Table 2—Hypothetical Dimensions of Class-Party Relationships

Type I

High Political Distinctiveness of the Working Class
High Class Distinctiveness of the Left Party

PERCENT VOTING:	OCCUPATION	
	Manual	Nonmanual
Left	90%	10%
Right	10%	90%
Total	100%	100%
Index of Class Voting: 80		

Type III

High Political Distinctiveness of the Working Class
Low Class Distinctiveness of the Left Party

PERCENT VOTING:	OCCUPATION	
	Manual	Nonmanual
Left	90%	40%
Right	10%	60%
Total	100%	100%
Index of Class Voting: 50		

Type II

Low Political Distinctiveness of the Working Class
High Class Distinctiveness of the Left Party

PERCENT VOTING:	OCCUPATION	
	Manual	Nonmanual
Left	60%	10%
Right	40%	90%
Total	100%	100%
Index of Class Voting: 50		

Type IV

Low Political Distinctiveness of the Working Class
Low Class Distinctiveness of the Left Party

PERCENT VOTING:	OCCUPATION	
	Manual	Nonmanual
Left	60%	40%
Right	40%	60%
Total	100%	100%
Index of Class Voting: 20		

In these four countries, the working-class vote for the Left party varies between 50 and 70 percent, and the working-class segment of the Left party's support is usually no higher. The main exception is in Britain, where the working class supplies roughly three quarters of the Labour Party's support. But the situation in Britain may still be quite different from that in Norway, for example, where workers give heavy support to the Socialists (over 80 percent) but the middle-class support for that party is also relatively high.

DIFFERENCES IN CLASS VOTING IN THE ANGLO-AMERICAN COUNTRIES

Class voting is consistently higher in Australia and Great Britain than in Canada and the United States, as indicated by a number of public opinion surveys taken in each country between 1952 and 1962. It seems justified, further, to rank the countries in the following order: Great Britain, Australia, the United States, and Canada. Table 3 summarizes these results.

Class voting is almost always above zero, with only one Canadian survey falling below that mark. Great Britain is consistently higher than Australia for the 1952–62 period, with a mean index of 40 and a range of 35 to 44. Australia is consistently higher than the United States and has a mean index of 33 and a range of 27 to 37 for the same period. The United States is consistently higher than Canada, except for one 1958 Canadian survey, and has a mean index of 16 and a range of 13 to 23. Canada is always the lowest in its level of class voting, with the single exception mentioned.[43]

Table 3—Class Voting in Four Anglo-American Countries, 1952–1962*

INDEX OF CLASS VOTING

Country	Mean	Lowest	Highest	Based on No. of Surveys
Great Britain	40	35	44	8
Australia	33	27	37	10
United States	16	13	23	5
Canada	8	−1	17	10

* The index of class voting was computed by subtracting the percentage of nonmanual workers voting for "Left" parties from the percentage of manual workers voting for such parties. As stated, for Great Britain, the Labour Party was used, for Australia, the Australian Labor Party, for the United States, the Democratic Party, for Canada, the CCF and Liberal parties. Where two parties were classified as "Left," their votes within each stratum were combined. See Robert R. Alford, *Party and Society*, op. cit., Appendix A, for the exact questions asked in each survey, the occupational divisions used, the dates of polls, and the numbers of cases in manual and nonmanual occupations. The surveys were taken at various times between 1946 and 1962. Questions referred in most cases to voting intention in a national election, but past vote was used in a few instances.

Given the lack of tight integration of social groups, whether social class or others, and the lack of close correspondence of class and party, we would expect a rather high level of shifting of the social bases of the parties back and forth, as different issues—both class and nonclass—become salient, and as the parties jockey for support from various groups. But what is striking here is not the variation within the countries, but that, regardless of that variation, the differences in class voting between the countries are so sharp and consistent.

But before these results are accepted, we must consider the possibility that they are due to particular social groups within each country. It is possible, for example, that the solid Democratic loyalties in the South account for the lower level of class voting in the United States than in Australia. It is possible that the solid Liberal loyalties of Quebec (until 1958) account for the lower level of class voting in Canada than in the United States. It is possible that class voting is mainly manifested in Great Britain and Australia among older persons, in whom class loyalties are more deeply felt and depressions and oppression more bitterly remembered, on one side, or callously forgotten, on the other. If we find that the differences between the four Anglo-American nations disappear when certain subgroups of the population are examined, then we are not dealing with a true difference between political systems, but with a statistical artifact, produced by strong antipathies among certain segments of the population, and equally strong ties overriding those of class among other segments.

As Table 4 shows, the differences between the four Anglo-American countries in the level of class voting do not disappear when class voting is examined within different age groups, within two religious groups (Protestants and Catholics), within the regions highest and lowest in their respective countries in their level of class voting, and in large cities. By and large, the rank order of class voting is not affected. Within each age group, among either Protestants or Catholics, Great Britain has the highest class voting of any of these countries, Australia next, followed by the United States and then Canada. It may be noted that the difference between Britain and Australia disappears when the regions highest and lowest in class voting are considered. (To some extent the figures are artifacts of extremely high or low single index figures, so that here, as before, no particular number has any great significance.)

It is clear from Table 4 that the effect of regionalism and religion upon class voting is marked in each country, in the sense that class voting is consistently higher among Protestants than among Catholics, and that a considerable difference appears between the regions with the highest and the lowest levels of class voting. The differences between the countries remain, however, when class voting in cities of over 100,000 population is considered. Urbanization does not (or has not yet) reduce the international differences in class voting.

As a final check on the validity of the differences between these political systems in their level of class voting (and as a check on the adequacy of the manual-nonmanual distinction as a measure of class), it is possible to define social class more narrowly in terms of *two* criteria of class position instead of one, and compute a more refined measure of class voting. It seems reasonable to predict that the principal finding of the differences in class voting will be reinforced if the rank order remains when social class is

Table 4—Class Voting Within Selected Demographic Groups, Four Anglo-American Countries, Surveys Between 1952–1962 (Means)*

COUNTRY	AGE GROUPS				RELIGION		REGION		CITIES
	20–30	30–40	40–50	50–60	Protestants	Catholics	Highest	Lowest	over 100,000
Great Britain	39	36	37	42	46	44	47	23	41
Australia	30	28	35	39	36	29	47	22	36
United States	13	13	22	13	21	16	31	4	20
Canada	5	9	13	9	10	2	26	—12	11

* Figures given here are means of a number of index figures for each country, 5 in Britain and Australia, 4 in the United States, and 6 in Canada. See Robert R. Alford, *Party and Society*, op. cit., Appendix C, for the definition of regions used.

defined in terms of either education, income, subjective class identification, or trade-union membership in *addition* to occupation. Table 5 shows that the rank order of class voting in the four countries remains the same even when a more narrow (one should say more rigorous) definition of the social-class position of the respondents is used. The level of class voting is indeed higher in each country when social classes are defined more narrowly than simply by manual and nonmanual occupations, but the differences between the four countries remain the same.

Table 5—Class Voting Within Strata Defined by Two
Class Characteristics, Four Anglo-American Countries,
Surveys Between 1952–1962 (Means)*

Country	Education and occupation	Income and occupation	Subjective social class and occupation	Trade union membership and occupation
Great Britain	57	52	53	51
Australia	43	46	47	46
United States	26	31	35	22
Canada	10	11	12	16

* Figures given are means. In Australia, education and class identification were asked only in one survey. In Canada and the United States class identification was asked only in one survey. Otherwise the figures are derived from at least two surveys in each country. All figures are +. The figures are based upon a definition of "working class" and "middle class" defined by two class characteristics, as follows:

Great Britain: Manual workers were included who (a) either left school before the age of fifteen, (b) were judged to be in one of the lower two positions on a four-point socioeconomic status scale by interviewers, (c) identified themselves as "working class" when asked: "What social class would you say you are in?", or (d) had a member of a trade union in their family. Nonmanual persons were included who (a) remained in school past fifteen, (b) were judged to belong in one of the higher two positions on a socioeconomic status scale by interviewers, (c) identified themselves as "lower middle class" or higher, or (d) did not have a trade union member in the family.

Australia: Manual workers were included who (a) had primary, secondary, some technical or commercial education, or who finished technical or commercial school or who had an intermediate certificate, (b) were judged to be in one of the lower two positions on a four-point socioeconomic status scale by interviewers, (c) identified themselves as "working class" or (d) had a trade union member in the family. Nonmanual persons were included who (a) had some university training or a university degree, or either a leaving or a matriculation certificate, (b) were judged to belong in one of the upper two positions on a four-point socioeconomic scale by interviewers, (c) identified themselves as middle class or higher, or (d) did not have a trade union member in the family.

United States: Criteria in the United States surveys varied considerably. For education, the division was into high school or less for manual workers, and some college or more for persons in nonmanual occupations. The income criteria for Gallup and Roper surveys are parallel to the British and Australian surveys, but for a Michigan 1952 study manual workers were included who earned less than $3,000 per year, and nonmanuals earning more than $7,500.

Canada: The educational criteria were the same as the United States; the others the same as for Britain and Australia.

MORE RECENT EMPIRICAL
EVIDENCE

In order to check on the stability of these cross-national differences, surveys were reanalyzed that were conducted in each country since the time of the last survey reported in *Party and Society*. The results are given in Table 6 for selected surveys between 1962 and 1965. These include the last surveys received from each country by the Roper Public Opinion Research Center up to June 1966 and the 1964 election survey conducted by the Survey Research Center, University of Michigan. As Table 6 indicates, there has been no change in the relative position of the countries with respect to their levels of class voting, and this remains true when Protestants and Catholics are analyzed separately.[44] Class voting is almost always lower among Catholics, however.

The attempt made here to summarize the pattern of association of class and party in each country into a single numerical figure is useful for comparative studies, but clearly is not adequate for case studies of individual parties and countries.[45] Table 7 separates the two parties of Canada and

Australia that were grouped together in Table 6 for purposes of computation of an index of class voting.

Table 6—Class Voting in the Four Anglo-American Countries, by Religion, 1962–1965*

		CLASS VOTING	
Country and Date	Total	Protestants	Catholics
Great Britain			
August 1963 (CQ 315)	+34	+34	+32
December 1963 (CQ 350)	+43	+43	+40
Australia			
February 1963 (APOP #161)	+29	+33	+21
November 1963 (#167)	+28	+29	+27
November 1964 (#174)	+26	+28	+17
United States			
October 1962 (AIPO #664)	+10	+12	+ 4
October 1964 (#669)	+16	+14	+19
November 1964 (SRC)	+17		
Canada			
May 1962 (CIPO #295)	− 4	0	−11
March 1963 (#301)	− 4	− 8	− 5
November 1965 (#315)	+ 6	+ 7	+ 2

* The data were obtained from the Roper Public Opinion Research Center. I am indebted to Philip K. Hastings and Richard Rosch of the Center for their immediate response to my request for tabulations. The numbers and letters in parentheses refer to the original study numbers of the Gallup agencies which conducted the surveys, respectively Social Surveys, Limited, in England, Australian Public Opinion Polls, American Public Opinion Polls, and Canadian Public Opinion Polls. For purposes of comparability with previous data, the New Democratic Party is included with the Liberal Party in Canada, and the Democratic Labor Party with the Australian Labor Party, as "Left" parties. The mean for the region highest in class voting in the ten surveys was Britain +49, Australia +44, United States +19, Canada +10; for the region lowest in class voting Britain +29, Australia +11, United States +1, Canada −1. Data from the 1964 United States national election survey conducted by the Survey Research Center were obtained from the Inter-University Consortium for Political Behavior Research. The question referred to voting intention for President, and those who did not know their preferred candidate even when pressed are eliminated from the totals. "Leaners" are included with those who responded more positively.

The cross-national results do not change if the "third" parties in Canada and Australia are examined separately. The support of nonmanual Catholics for the Democratic Labor Party in Australia and of manual Protestants for the New Democratic Party in Canada does not alter these cross-national differences appreciably, although obviously they have considerable consequences for the internal politics of these countries. The New Democratic Party clearly has some tinge of a distinctive class base, while the Democratic Labor Party does not.

Another deficiency of the comparative indices used here is the excessive simplicity of the division into manual and nonmanual occupational strata as the measure of "class." It is possible that a more detailed and differentiated measure of class would uncover considerably more variation within these broad and heterogeneous strata than is visible from a dichotomy. But some grounds for confidence, in the British figures at least, that this measure probably does describe a true cross-national difference is given by a recent national survey in Britain.

The most careful and elaborate study of British voting behavior yet done has examined the problem of classifying persons into social classes in detail, and found that the index of class voting does not change appreciably whether lower nonmanual persons were classified as "working class" or as "middle class." The index was + 48 if the former procedure was used, + 50 if the latter.[46] Cross-class voting (the proportion of working-class Conservatives and of middle-class Labourites) is more affected by the alternative classifications than is the index of class voting.

Table 7—Class Voting in Canada and Australia, by Region and Party, 1964 and 1965*

Canada (November 1965)

| Province or Region | PARTY | | |
	Liberal	New Democratic	Total
Atlantic	− 2	+ 4	+ 2
Quebec	0	+ 2	+ 2
Ontario	− 4	+10	+ 6
Prairies	− 8	+ 9	+ 1
British Columbia	− 8	+30	+22
Total	− 2	+ 8	+ 6

Australia (November 1964)

State	Australian Labor Party	Democratic Labor Party	Total
Western Australia	+27	− 5	+22
South Australia	+17	0	+17
Queensland	+37	− 6	+31
New South Wales	+26	+ 2	+24
Victoria	+19	+ 4	+23
Tasmania	+28	+10	+38
Total	+25	+ 1	+26

* The surveys are Australian Public Opinion Poll #174 and Canadian Institute of Public Opinion #315, obtained from the Roper Public Opinion Research Center. The totals are included in the ten surveys summarized in Table 6. The figures entered are the percentage-point differences in the preferences given to each party by persons in manual and nonmanual occupations. The "totals" column is the sum of the two separate figures for each party, under the assumption that the two parties can be classed together as "Left" parties for purposes of international comparisons.

Perhaps just as important a finding for our purposes here is that the difference of Labour voting was far greater between the lower nonmanual stratum and the skilled manual stratum (32 percentage points) than between any other two "adjacent" occupational strata. Although the dichotomy into two social classes has theoretical and empirical deficiencies, this is another piece of evidence justifying its use for broadly comparative studies, although probably not for focused case studies.

Also, regardless of the procedure used, class voting in this 1963 British study was found to be considerably higher than in any Australian survey. In fact, both index figures of + 48 and + 50 are higher than that level found in any other survey in any of the Anglo-American countries. There seems to be little reason to suspect therefore that these cross-national differences are due to methodological or theoretical errors of classification. Class voting was actually slightly *higher* when these lower nonmanual persons were assigned to the middle class than when they were assigned to the working class, although a majority of the group favored the Conservatives.

Additional empirical support for the finding of a higher level of class voting in Britain than in the United States is given by a reanalysis of still more surveys done in those two countries between 1961 and 1964. Four national surveys conducted by Research Services, Limited, prior to the general election of 1964 in Britain, and eight national surveys conducted by the Survey Research Center at the University of Michigan and by the National Opinion Research Center were aggregated, and the association between stratification (as measured by a combination of occupation and income) and party affiliation was computed. Cramer's V, the statistic, showed the association to be .171 for the United States and .372 for Great Britain.[47]

The relatively great importance of class in Britain is supported by ecological studies of voting. A study of population, economic, health, voting, and household characteristics of the 157 British towns of over 50,000 population in 1951 found that the set of variables with the highest average correlations with all other variables included concerned social class, specifically the proportions of persons in higher nonmanual or lower manual occupations.[48]

The authors performed a factor analysis, and found that the variables most highly correlated with the first factor extracted were social class (as measured by occupational composition) and the proportion voting Left in the 1951 and 1955 general elections. (The correlations of these variables with the factor were all over .85.)[49] The first factor accounted for 30 percent of the total variance. The product-moment correlations of the occupational status of the towns' populations with the proportion voting Left in the 1951 and 1955 elections were over .75 (Table 26, facing p. 58, in the work cited). These findings document the importance of class in the social and political structure of Great Britain.

A review of the literature on social cleavages and voting in Britain concludes that a number of nonclass influences on voting, such as religion, have been waning in significance, leaving class as the main social base of party support, although by no means uniform.[50] Surveys prior to the British election of 1964 found that class voting dropped slightly, since the Labour vote rose a bit among both middle- and lower-middle-class groups, and dropped among both skilled and unskilled working-class groups.[51]

At the other extreme, the Canadian political parties have "resolutely avoided class symbols," particularly "King Liberalism," according to Gad Horowitz. Horowitz' explanation of the nonclass character of the Canadian parties is in terms of the triumph of the Center over the Left and the Right.

> In Canada, the classless appeal of King centrism is the winning strategy, drawing lower-class support to the Liberals away from the left parties, and higher-class support away from the right parties. This forces the left and right parties themselves to emulate (to a certain extent) the Liberals' classless strategy. The Conservatives transform themselves into Progressive Conservatives. The CCF transforms itself from a "farmer-labour" party into an NDP calling for the support of "all liberally minded Canadians." The Liberal refusal to appear as a class party forces both right and left to mitigate their class appeals and to become themselves, in a sense, centre parties.[52]

A recent study of Canada's social and political structure also asserts that Canada's "two major political parties do not focus to the right and the left. In the sense that both are closely linked with corporate enterprise the dominant focus has been to the right."[53] According to the author, "[t]he political dialogue, if it can be called such, in which the [Liberal and Progressive-Conservative parties] participate is not related to any basic class differences in the society. . . ."[54] One of Porter's major concerns is with documenting the existence and nature of the class structure of Canada, and he concludes that the obsession with national unity has produced a situation in which Canada "must be one of the few major industrial societies in which the right and left polarization has become deflected into disputes over regionalism and national unity."[55] Porter explicitly distinguishes Canada from the United States in this respect, hypothesizing that "the moderate polarization which had taken place between Republican and Democratic parties in the United States had not taken place between the two major parties in Canada despite the fact that World War I and the depression had created a new class structure."[56]

The most detailed study of public opinion in Canada yet done, by Mildred Schwartz, focuses upon the basis of party support as one of several themes related to the functions (and dysfunctions) of parties and public opinion for the national integration of Canada. While her study finds also that social class is not related to national party support, she discovers that it *is* related to a number of opinions that can be considered "Left-Right" in their nature. Thus social class does correlate in the "expected" way with public opinion in Canada, showing that its political system differs more sharply from that of the other Anglo-American countries than does its stratification system. To put the point another way, her study found that "class differences, instead of being accentuated between political parties, exist within parties."[57]

Canadian sociologist S. D. Clark stresses the weakness of *all* "orthodox" group bases of voting behavior in Canada—nationality, religion, social class— in his discussion of recent elections in the context of Canadian history. He suggests that Marxist views, which "fit everyone into an interest grouping," and the conventional sociological view, concentrating upon the "group determinants of behaviour," are both inadequate to explain Canadian voting patterns. Professor Clark is more aware than most American students of voting behavior of the instability and volatility of voting behavior in a country like Canada, where national integration, almost by definition implying a firm structure of group affiliations, has not yet been achieved.[58]

CONCLUSIONS

Survey data from the four Anglo-American countries have shown that clear and consistent differences between the countries exist, regardless of whether class voting is examined for the total electorate divided into manual and nonmanual occupations, for the same division within various demographic groups, for a more rigorous definition of classes, or for the parties taken separately. Great Britain and Australia have higher levels of class voting than the United States and Canada.

Although the supporting data cannot be given here in detail, there is no tendency for the class bases of politics to change drastically in this historical period in any of these countries. The differences between these countries in class voting, according to surveys available from 1940 to 1965, have remained fairly stable.

An important point to emphasize is that in none of these countries is the voting of one stratum for "its" party unanimous. Political consensus in these countries is shown by the constant shifting back and forth from Right to Left, but the vote by manual workers for the Right party, or nonmanual workers for the Left party, never drops below about 20 percent. Never does the index of class voting rise above 60 percentage points (80 percent of the manual workers voting Left, 20 percent of the nonmanual workers voting Left, for example), even when, as in Table 5, classes are defined more narrowly than only by occupation. This narrower definition leaves out so much of the potential electorate that it is meaningless as an overall measure of class voting. The imperfect "status crystallization" of these four countries produces a high level of "cross-class" voting, no matter how class is defined.[59] The fairly even impact of politically relevant events upon the classes is also shown clearly by the parallel moves to the Right or Left in most election periods.

A search for political and social differences between the Anglo-American countries which parallel the differences in class voting and which might account for them suggests four possibilities, none of which can be explored here.[60] The parties in countries where class voting is higher might more consistently *represent* class interests, or might more consistently *appeal* to class interests—and the two need not be synonymous. Or, where class voting is higher the parties might simply command the historical loyalties of certain classes, regardless of how they appealed to or represented class interests. A fourth possibility is that, regardless of historical loyalties or the actions of the parties, the social classes in these societies might be differently exposed to situations in which the political relevance of class interests becomes apparent: i.e., the social structure of these countries might be sufficiently different (despite such crude similarities as the range and number of class positions, the prestige of different occupations, and the gross level of social mobility) that a higher level of class voting is produced in one country than in another.

NOTES

1. See Joseph A. Schumpeter, *Capitalism, Socialism, and Democracy* (New York: Harper & Row, 1947), p. 269.

2. See Robert R. Alford, *Party and Society* (Chicago: Rand McNally, 1963). Material is taken from Chaps. 1, 2, and 5 of that book, and the reader is referred to it for a more detailed treatment of the regional and religious, as well as social class, bases of voting behavior in the Anglo-American countries. Separate chapters on each country consider the historical factors contributing to their present party and class systems.

3. For the United States, Gallup Polls of national samples have consistently found that middle-class people vote more Republican than working-class people. Studies with similar results of single communities include: P. Lazarsfeld, B. Berelson, and H. Gaudet, *The People's Choice* (2nd ed.; New York: Duell, Sloan and Pearce, 1948), and B. Berelson, P. Lazarsfeld, and W. McPhee, *Voting* (Chicago: Univ. of Chicago Press, 1954). For Great Britain, Social Surveys, Inc. (formerly the British Institute of Public Opinion) has consistently found that middle-class people vote more Conservative than do workers. Studies with similar results of single constituencies include M. Benney, A. P. Gray, and R. H. Pear, *How People Vote* (London: Routledge, 1956), and R. S.

Milne and H. C. McKenzie, *Marginal Seat, 1955* (London: Hansard Society for Parliamentary Government, 1958). A summary of the voting studies bearing on this point is presented in S. M. Lipset, *Political Man* (New York: Doubleday, 1960), Chap. VII.

4. V. O. Key, Jr., *Politics, Parties and Pressure Groups* (4th ed.; New York: Crowell, 1958), p. 274.

5. For the United States, see A. Campbell, P. E. Converse, W. E. Miller, and Donald E. Stokes, *The American Voter* (New York: Wiley, 1960), p. 347, and also P. E. Converse, "The Shifting Role of Class in Political Attitudes and Behavior," in E. Maccoby, T. Newcomb, and E. Hartley (eds.), *Readings in Social Psychology* (3d ed.; New York: Holt, Rinehart & Winston, 1958), pp. 388–99. For Great Britain, see D. E. Butler and Richard Rose, *The British General Election of 1959* (London: Macmillan, 1960), pp. 14–16.

6. Saul K. Padover (ed.), *The Complete Madison* (New York: Harper & Row, 1953), p. 52.

7. R. M. MacIver, *The Web of Government* (New York: Macmillan, 1947), p. 217. The phrase "democratic class struggle," referring to the party system, is an enticing one, uniting as it does Jeffersonian democracy and Marxism. It was used in the title of a work in political sociology by D. Anderson and P. Davidson, *Ballots and the Democratic Class Struggle* (Stanford: Stanford Univ. Press, 1943), and as a chapter heading in S. M. Lipset, *op. cit.* See also Max Lerner, *America as a Civilization* (New York: Simon & Schuster, 1957), pp. 536–41.

8. S. M. Lipset, *op. cit.,* p. 220.

9. R. M. MacIver, *op. cit.,* p. 123.

10. One United States study compares the Presidential voting patterns in a predominantly Republican community, Elmira, New York, in 1940 with those in a predominantly Democratic community, Sandusky, Ohio, in 1948. The authors' chief comparative finding was that the political climate of the Republican community affected Democratic lower class voters mainly when the latter were not surrounded by friends and relatives who agreed with them politically (and vice versa for the Republicans in the Democratic community). This effect they called the "breakage effect," implying that until the primary-group environment of the voter "broke," he was insulated from the political atmosphere of the community. The particular finding was one of the first results from the use of comparative voting data to investigate the effect of a different social context upon voting behavior. See B. Berelson, *et al., op. cit.,* pp. 98–101.

11. André Siegfried, *Tableau Politique de la France de l'Ouest sous la Troisième République* (Paris: Librairie Armand Colin, 1913).

12. V. O. Key, Jr., *Southern Politics* (New York: Knopf, 1949).

13. Donald S. Strong, *Urban Republicanism in the South* (Birmingham: Univ. of Alabama, Bureau of Public Administration, 1960).

14. A. Brady, "The British Governing Class and Democracy," *Canadian Journal of Economics and Political Science,* 20 (1954), pp. 405–20.

15. See William Kornhauser, *The Politics of Mass Society* (New York: The Free Press, 1959), for a recent discussion of political pluralism, and Alexis de Tocqueville, *Democracy in America* (New York: Vintage Books, 1954), for the classic statement of the preconditions of pluralism.

16. Gabriel A. Almond, "Comparative Political Systems," in H. Eulau, S. J. Eldersveld, and M. Janowitz (eds.), *Political Behavior: A Reader in Theory and Research* (New York: The Free Press, 1956), p. 36.

17. Alexander Brady, *Democracy in the Dominions* (Toronto: Univ. of Toronto Press, 1947), p. 1.

18. A. R. M. Lower, "Theories of Canadian Federalism—Yesterday and Today," in A. R. M. Lower, F. R. Scott, *et al., Evolving Canadian Federalism* (Durham: Duke Univ. Press, 1958), pp. 5–6.

19. Consensus may be distinguished from legitimacy—the acceptance of the nation (or any institution) as right and proper. Political consensus, in this sense, is not a fundamental requirement for the continued existence of a political system. Political systems may exist without either consensus or legitimacy, and the conditions under which such stabilizing factors are lost or gained are an important problem for further research.

20. In Lord Campion, *et al., Parliament, A Survey* (London: Allen & Unwin, 1952), p. 75.

21. Maurice Duverger, *Political Parties* (London: Methuen, 1954), p. 203.

22. See S. M. Lipset, "Party Systems and the Representation of Social Groups," *European Journal of Sociology*, 1 (1960), pp. 50–85. See Leon P. Epstein, "A Comparative Study of Canadian Parties," *American Political Science Review*, 58 (March 1964), pp. 46–59, for a discussion of the possible causes and consequences for government of the Canadian party system. Epstein emphasizes the consequences of the British-style parliamentary system for party cohesion, which is not, however, accompanied by "programmatic or policy cohesion" (p. 56).

23. Variations in the electoral system account for differences in the numbers of parties to some extent. All of these countries have the single-ballot, simple-majority system except Australia, and the "preferential ballot" in use there may account for the rise of small parties, which can thereby gain influence without weakening the major party to which they are linked. The role of the "third" parties in these countries is evaluated in R. Alford, *op. cit.*, Chap. 10.

24. S. M. Lipset and R. Bendix, *Social Mobility in Industrial Society* (Berkeley: Univ. of California Press, 1959), pp. 13–25. In a footnote on p. 29 the authors specifically dispute data from a Melbourne study which found that Australia has less mobility of this kind than other Western countries.

25. *Ibid.*, p. 27. The authors note that if a country is 90 percent peasant, "even with completely equal opportunity most children of peasants must remain peasants."

26. A. Inkeles and P. H. Rossi, "National Comparisons of Occupational Prestige," *American Journal of Sociology*, 61 (January 1956), p. 332. The countries considered in this study were Great Britain, the United States, New Zealand, Japan, and Germany. A parallel study, done in Canada, found equally high correlations. See Bernard A. Blishen, "The Construction and Use of an Occupational Class Scale," *Canadian Journal of Economics and Political Science*, 24 (November 1958), pp. 521–31. The same British data are analyzed in more detail in C. A. Moser and J. R. Hall, "The Social Grading of Occupations," in David Glass (ed.), *Social Mobility in Great Britain* (London: Routledge, 1953). Similar results are reported for Australia in Ronald Taft, "The Social Grading of Occupations in Australia," *British Journal of Sociology*, 4 (June 1953), pp. 181–88.

27. Gerhard E. Lenski, "Status Crystallization: A Nonvertical Dimension of Social Status," *American Sociological Review*, 19 (August 1954), pp. 405–13. This study of Detroit was repeated for Minneapolis, and the latter is reported in G. Hochbaum, J. G. Darley, E. D. Monachesi, and C. Bird, "Socioeconomic Variables in a Large City," *American Journal of Sociology*, 61 (July 1955), pp. 31–8.

28. Certain problems are outside the scope of this study. Since the basic data of the study concern only party and class divisions within the electorate, the extent to which class organizations directly influence party programs and policies cannot be clarified. A study of the influence of interest groups upon the policies and personnel of political parties would be important to study comparatively, but is beyond the range of the present work.

29. Sir Ivor Jennings, *Party Politics II: The Growth of Parties* (Cambridge: Cambridge Univ. Press, 1961), pp. 235, 237.

30. *Ibid.*, pp. 356–57; R. T. McKenzie, *British Political Parties* (London: Heinemann, 1955), p. 529. The trade unions in Britain "provide more than seven-eighths of the members of the Labour Party and more than three-quarters of its income." See Richard Rose, *Politics in England* (Boston: Little-Brown, 1964), p. 16.

31. A common Conservative accusation against Labour is that it is dominated by "special interest," and therefore cannot represent the nation as well as the Conservative Party. McKenzie devotes much of his book on British political parties to a demonstration that the Labour Party is no more (and no less) bound to outside pressure groups than the Conservative Party. See McKenzie, *op. cit.*, Chap. 1.

32. See Leon D. Epstein, "British Class Consciousness and the Labour Party," *Journal of British Studies*, 1 (May 1962), p. 147.

33. L. F. Crisp, *The Australian Federal Labour Party: 1901–1951* (Melbourne: Longmans, Green, 1955), p. 182. See also D. W. Rawson, *Australia Votes: The 1958 Federal Election* (Melbourne: Melbourne Univ. Press, 1961), p. 2.

34. See A. F. Davies and S. Encel, "Class and Status," in A. F. Davies and S. Encel (eds.), *Australian Society: A Sociological Introduction* (New York: Atherton, 1965), pp. 18–42, for an analysis of the nature and correlates of social class in Australian

society. For a discussion of the similarities and differences between the American and Australian class systems, see Kurt B. Mayer, "Social Stratification in Two Equalitarian Societies: Australia and the United States," *Social Research,* 31 (Winter 1964), pp. 435–65.

35. Louise Overacker, *The Australian Party System* (New Haven: Yale Univ. Press, 1952), p. 81. Here, as is the case with the British Labour Party, such origins and such a political role do not imply a consistent ideological position or unwillingness to compromise.

36. R. M. MacIver, *The Web of Government* (New York: Macmillan, 1947), p. 123. MacIver offers no evidence for his assertion that when the parties differ in their objectives class voting is likely to increase, although it is certainly a plausible inference.

37. Overacker, *op. cit.,* p. 81, and Jennings, *op. cit.,* Chap. 9 ("Sham Fight").

38. Stephen K. Bailey, *The Condition of Our National Political Parties* (An Occasional Paper of the Fund for the Republic, New York, 1959), p. 22. Evidence for this statement was provided by the Roper Public Opinion Research Center, Williamstown, Massachusetts, which tabulated every question in American public opinion polls since 1946 that dealt with public images of the two parties.

39. For general descriptions of the links of the Canadian political parties to sectional, class, and urban-rural interests, see R. McGregor Dawson, *The Government of Canada* (Toronto: 4th ed. rev. by N. Ward; Univ. of Toronto Press, 1963), pp. 453–472, and H. McD. Clokie, *Canadian Government and Politics* (Toronto: Longmans Green, 1944), pp. 75–95.

40. See R. Alford, *Party and Society, op. cit.,* for a discussion of the advantages and limitations of such a measure of class voting.

41. I am indebted to Stein Rokkan for calling this defect of the index to my attention.

42. Stein Rokkan and Angus Campbell, "Citizen Participation in Political Life: Norway and the United States of America," *International Social Science Journal,* 12 (1960), pp. 69–99. I have computed an index of class voting from their data given in Table 9, and the figure for the United States is +14, for Norway +47 (combining the Socialist and Communist parties). Norway's class voting level is thus close to Britain's, but the political distinctiveness of the working class in Norway is much greater.

43. Table 4 includes only the 1952–62 period for summary purposes. The data prior to that are more unreliable for the various countries, because of greater sampling variability in the early Gallup Polls and the unavailability of really comparable British data prior to 1955.

44. Parallel findings for Australia are reported in Leonard Broom and Richard J. Hill, "Opinion Polls and Social Rank in Australia: Method and First Findings," *Australian and New Zealand Journal of Sociology,* 1 (October 1965), pp. 97–106, which reports on the correlation of voting with five different measures of social class in three different surveys. A review of the correlates of voting with social characteristics of Australian voters also appears in A. F. Davies and S. Encel, "Politics," in A. F. Davies and S. Encel, *op. cit.,* pp. 96–113.

45. This point has been made by, among others, Frederick Engelmann and Robert R. Gilsdorf, "Recent Behavioural Political Science in Canada: An Assessment of Voting Behaviour Studies," unpublished paper, 1966.

46. See Michael Kahan, David Butler, Donald Stokes, "On the Analytical Division of Social Class," *British Journal of Sociology,* 17 (June 1966), p. 129. They do not actually compute the index of class voting, but the relevant figures are given in Table 5. This lower nonmanual stratum included shop salesmen and assistants, policemen, caretakers, lodging-house keepers, street vendors, factory guards, waiters, telephone operators, nonsupervisory clerks, and transport inspectors. The group contributes a sizable fraction of those who identify themselves as working class but vote Conservative.

47. Morris Janowitz, Klaus Liepelt, and David R. Segal, "An Approach to the Comparative Analysis of Political Partisanship," unpublished paper, 1966. The total number of cases was 5,628 for Britain, 11,146 for the United States. The results were essentially the same whether four or eight social strata were used in the computation. In a further "tree analysis" of the relative importance of several variables, social class was found to be the most important single variable for voting in Britain, religion in the United States. Germany was also included in the study.

48. See C. A. Moser and Wolf Scott, *British Towns* (Edinburgh: Oliver & Boyd, 1961), p. 63.

49. *Ibid.,* p. 71. See also A. J. Allen, *The English Voter* (London: English Universities Press, 1964) for a detailed description of the voting patterns of individual constituencies as related to their industrial and occupational composition.

50. Richard Rose, "Social and Party Cleavages in Britain," *Revue Française de Sociologie,* forthcoming. Rose notes that "the 1966 victory of Labour did not reflect a tendency towards class polarization, for shifts occurred relatively evenly within all strata of the electorate" (p. 21). See Jean Blondel, *Voters, Parties, and Leaders* (Baltimore: Penguin Books, 1963), for a comprehensive discussion of the politics and social structure of Britain. A view of the social bases of voting parallel to that presented here appears on pp. 56–68. See also Mark Abrams, "Social Class and Politics," *Twentieth Century,* 173 (Spring 1965), pp. 35–48, for a brief exploration of the interrelations of subjective and objective class as they affect voting patterns in Great Britain.

51. See D. E. Butler and Anthony King, *The British General Election of 1964* (London: Macmillan, 1965), pp. 296–7. Five pre-election polls with a total of 12,000 interviews conducted by National Opinion Polls were combined, and the class voting index (recomputed from a table on p. 296) was approximately +31.

52. G. Horowitz, "Conservatism, Liberalism and Socialism in Canada: An Interpretation," *Canadian Journal of Economics and Political Science,* 29 (May 1966), p. 170.

53. John Porter, *The Vertical Mosaic* (Toronto: Univ. of Toronto Press, 1965), p. 368.

54. *Ibid.,* p. 373.

55. *Ibid.,* p. 369.

56. *Ibid.,* p. 377.

57. See Mildred Schwartz, *Public Opinion and Canadian Identity* (Berkeley: Univ. of California Press, 1967), Chap. 10. See also Peter Regenstreif. *The Diefenbaker Interlude: Parties and Voting in Canada* (Toronto: Longmans Canada, 1965) for another reanalysis of Canadian surveys that finds the same pattern of party support discussed here, and Robert R. Alford, "The Social Bases of Political Cleavage in 1962," in John Meisel (ed.), *Papers on the 1962 Election* (Toronto: Univ. of Toronto Press, 1964). Both of the above papers deal with the four parties separately, a procedure not used here because of the broader comparative approach.

58. See S. D. Clark, "Group Interests in Canadian Politics," in J. H. Aitchison (ed.), *The Political Process in Canada* (Toronto: Univ. of Toronto Press, 1963), pp. 76–7, and Chap. 9 of R. Alford, *Party and Society, op. cit.* The large switches of Canadian suburbanites, which Clark points to as evidence, may be more pronounced in Canada than in the other Anglo-American countries precisely because of the weakness of the association of voting with group affiliations, except for upper-class Protestants.

59. See the article by Robert McKenzie and Allan Silver in this volume for a discussion of the implications of Tory voting among the British working class. A reanalysis of the data contained in *Party and Society, op. cit.,* found that persons with inconsistent statuses were more likely to be Left voters in all four of the Anglo-American countries. See Gerhard Lenski, "Status Inconsistency and the Vote: A Four Nation Test," unpublished paper, 1966.

60. For a detailed analysis of the causes and consequences of varying levels of class polarization in the Anglo-American systems, see R. Alford, *Party and Society, op. cit.,* Chap. 5 and 10.

Two

Class Voting in New Zealand: A Comment on Alford's Comparison of Class Voting in the Anglo-American Political Systems

Alan D. Robinson

In the comparative study of voting behavior one approach, exemplified by Robert Alford's chapter, is the systematic gathering of data to make international comparisons. A complementary approach, reflected in the following pages, is the discussion, investigation, and explanation of national patterns of voting behavior in the light of the growing international framework of concepts and hypotheses. The writer hopes to put class voting in New Zealand into international perspective by applying concepts and hypotheses derived from work in other countries. In particular, the various categories employed by Alford will be adopted here as a framework for analysis. At the same time this article is a statement of hypotheses currently under investigation at the Victoria University of Wellington[1] and also an interpretation of New Zealand political history that only several more years' research can confirm or modify.

With its two-and-a-half million people of predominantly British origin, a unitary and parliamentary system of government on the British model, a disciplined two-party system, and political culture and social structure most like those of Australia, New Zealand falls clearly into the category of Anglo-American political systems. As such it has some striking contrasts to offer the student of class voting. On the one hand is the moderation of its politics and a stratification system apparently devoid of marked differences between strata in regard to most aspects of human behavior, for example, in speech, type of education, levels of material consumption, and leisure activities. On the other hand a marked distinctiveness in voting behavior exists between upper and lower strata of society irrespective of whether the criterion of class is occupation, income, wealth, duration of education, or subjective social status.

Investigation of the relationship between class and vote is still at an early stage in New Zealand. Preliminary evidence suggests that there is a high political distinctiveness of the professionals, businessmen, and farmers who vote mainly for the National Party; and of "blue-collar" workers, both skilled and unskilled, who vote mainly for the Labour Party. In between "comes the 'buffer-zone' formed by the 'white-collar' workers, who are, on the economic side, little if at all better off than the workers, but whose status aspirations are to the groups above them rather than to those below."[2] Their votes tend to be fairly evenly divided between the two main parties. Comparison with English studies suggests that in New Zealand the working class may be more solidly pro-Labour than in Britain (perhaps due to the absence of the "deference vote" among New Zealand manual workers), and that the intermediate group may be more evenly divided. This pattern of voting prevails throughout the seventy-six electoral districts in which non-Maoris vote. The remaining four electoral districts, reserved for the Maori minority, exhibit a political behavior all their own. Tribal ties and the strong influence of the minority Ratana sect with its commitment in the nineteen-thirties to support the Labour Party have combined to make Labour dominance of the four Maori seats unchallenged since 1943. Little research has been carried out on Maori politics which can throw much light on Maori political behavior. For this reason discussion in this article will concentrate on behavior within the seventy-six non-Maori electoral districts.

Research into the relationship between class and vote has been carried out in the course of three interview surveys of urban electorates, Wellington Central in 1957, Dunedin Central in 1960,[3] and Miramar, Karori, Palmerston North, and the Palmerston North city portion of the Manawatu electorate in 1963. Accompanying the latter survey in December 1963 were also an interview survey of farmers in part of the Manawatu electorate and a large postal survey of electors in thirteen widely varying electorates throughout the country, several of which were predominantly rural. Analysis of the 1963 surveys at the time of writing is still incomplete and cannot be referred to here at length. In addition to these surveys of individual behavior much useful information has been provided by ecological studies based on the analysis of detailed electoral statistics.[4] The following pages will refer to some of the findings from these varieties of research.

The following table, compiled by A. V. Mitchell,[5] shows the relation between vote and occupational group in Dunedin Central.

In Wellington Central R. S. Milne asked voters which of a number of classes they belonged to.[6] In spite of the myth widespread in New Zealand that this country has a classless society, nearly 70 percent were ready to place themselves in a particular social class. Twice as many opted for the middle class as for the working class. Working-class identifiers mostly voted Labour, but there were nearly as many middle-class as working-class identifiers among Labour voters. Just under two-thirds of those identifying with the middle class or above voted for the National Party.

Occupation and Vote: Percentage of Each Major Group Voting for Each Party in Dunedin Central Electorate, 1960

GROUP	PARTY			
	Labour	National	Social Credit	No.
1. Upper professional and company directors	12%	86%	2%	59
2. Lower professional, self-employed, and business people	25	67	8	161
3. "White-collar" and "uniform" workers	44	55	1	91
4. Skilled and semiskilled "blue-collar" workers	74	15	11	142
5. Unskilled "blue-collar" workers	87	8	5	60
Totals	244	236	33	513

The 1963 interview survey of two electorates in Wellington and one and one-third in Palmerston North city, in addition to asking questions about occupation, education, and income—the answers to which showed a strong relationship between these attributes and the direction of voting behavior—also asked electors in which class they would put themselves. They were given three classes to choose from: working class, middle class, and upper middle class. Those placing themselves in the middle class were then asked whether they were closer to the working class or to the upper middle class. The following table of responses to these questions in Palmerston North electorate, put to slightly over half of the respondents in this particular area, is representative of the pattern in the other areas surveyed; it is probably representative also of the pattern in urban areas throughout New Zealand since Palmerston North both by general repute and by analysis of census statistics is in most demographic aspects highly typical of New Zealand urban areas. Politically the electorate of Palmerston North, which occupies about two-thirds of the city, has for many years been finely balanced between the Labour and National parties.

The table reveals the strong support of the working class for the Labour Party and the progressive fall in support for the Labour Party and rise in support for the National Party as one glances in turn at the middle class but closer to working, the middle class undifferentiated, the middle class closer to upper middle, and the upper middle class, where the National Party enjoys the support of all. Moreover, if the figures in parentheses are examined as a proportion of each party's total it can be observed that the Labour Party draws most of its support from the working class and the National Party from the middle and upper middle classes.

Not surprisingly, subjective class is also related to the intensity of party support. Thus in the same sample strong Labour supporters comprised 27 percent of the working class, 3 percent of the middle class, and none of the upper middle class; on the other hand strong National supporters comprised 5 percent of the working class, 25 percent of the middle class, and 100 percent of the upper middle class.

Subjective Class and Vote: Percentage of Each Class Voting for Each Party in Palmerston North Electorate, 1963

			1	2	3	4	5	6
Voting choice	%	No.	Working class	Middle class closer to working class	Middle class undiffer-entiated $=(2+4)$	Middle class closer to upper middle	Upper middle	Don't know
Did not vote	5	(11)	5 (6)	2 (1)	2 (2)	2 (1)		30(3)
Labour	42	(99)	63(72)	34(19)	25(25)	13 (6)		20(2)
National	45	(104)	25(28)	50(28)	61(61)	75(33)	100(10)	50(5)
Social Credit	4	(10)	3 (3)	9 (5)	7 (7)	5 (2)		
Liberal	1	(2)	2 (2)					
No answer	3	(7)	2 (2)	5 (3)	5 (5)	5 (2)		
Totals	100	(233)	100	100	100	100	100	100
	No.:	233	113	56	100 $=(2+4)$	44	10	10

Note: Numbers are given in parentheses alongside percentages.

Ecological studies based on electoral statistics have provided further evidence of class voting in New Zealand, especially of its nationwide coverage. Recent work in this area, particularly in the hands of R. M. Chapman, has involved the detailed examination of statistics from local polling places and their matching with census data. For example, in an analysis of the 1960 election results Chapman devised an index consisting of the proportion of managers, professional people, and employers, and the proportion of washing machines, refrigerators, and hot water services in each of the sixty-one census districts of Auckland, New Zealand's largest city. The ranking derived from these six factors was matched with the ranking derived from the percentage voting Labour in each of the census districts in the 1957 and 1960 elections. A coefficient of correlation (Spearman) of a very high order appeared for both elections: .801 for 1957 and .781 for 1960. Chapman concludes that "the voters discriminate with the utmost nicety and a district is National, for example, not just when it is well up on the status and possessions index but also to the degree in which it is so."[7]

The study of electoral statistics has been of considerable value in the investigation of trends in New Zealand history, but it has also been useful in the study of rural or small town political behavior in the absence of national voting surveys. In this respect it has furnished evidence for the general observation that farmers vote overwhelmingly for the National Party. In the last two elections, for example, the National Party, which won with slightly less than half the total votes, appeared to have about three-quarters of the farmers' votes. The remaining farmers' votes split between the Labour Party and the small minority party, the Social Credit Political League, whose strength is greatest in rural and mixed rural/small-town constituencies. Furthermore, it appears that outside the four main cities and the towns over 20,000 in population, the cutting point between the National and Labour parties in non-farmer occupations favors the National, presumably because the prevailing climate of opinion in rural areas and in towns servicing these areas is profarmer and anti-trade-union. In 1963, for example, the National Party had a large majority of voters in small towns and an overwhelming majority in rural areas. Which occupations are affected most by the different cutting points is currently under investigation.

Given the present high degree of class voting in New Zealand, the question arises: has class voting increased or declined in recent years? Alford's suggested index of class voting, computed by subtracting the percentage of persons in nonmanual occupations voting for a "Left" party from the percentage of persons in manual occupations voting for such a party, is as yet difficult to apply in the case of New Zealand conditions, although it does suggest lines for future research. Difficulties in application arise from the lack of research into occupational trends in New Zealand (although abundant census data appear to exist), from the fact that only one study of a New Zealand constituency can be easily broken down into the manual-nonmanual distinction (an index figure of 40 was computed by Alford[8] for Dunedin Central), and from the existence in New Zealand of farmers as a major class-conscious occupational category not readily placed in a manual-nonmanual dichotomy. It is hoped, however, to apply the Alford index to the data from the 1963 surveys as soon as this is possible.

If meanwhile we look at the political distinctiveness of different classes and the class distinctiveness of different parties, certain trends in the last generation seem perceptible. Thus there appears to be a growing political distinctiveness among farmers, the bulk of whom vote National or Social Credit, and a stable or declining distinctiveness among other occupational groups.[9] This is suggested by the fact that voting shifts among rural and mixed rural/urban constituencies have taken place at a different rate from voting shifts in city and large-town constituencies. In the former there has been a fairly steady decline in Labour support since its peak in 1938 and in the latter there has been considerable stability. As for changes in class distinctiveness of the parties, it might be suggested that this has been declining slightly in the case of the National Party as a consequence of the reduction (perhaps partly offset by increasing National identification among farmers) in the proportion of farmers in the population (expressed in the decline in percentage of persons engaged in agriculture from 24 percent of the labour force in the 1936 census to 14 percent in 1961), and the need of the party to make up for this loss in the rapidly growing cities. In the case of the Labour Party, class distinctiveness may have been increasing with the decline in its support among farmers and the addition of a higher proportion of manual workers to the labor force as a consequence of the continued expansion of manufacturing in New Zealand.

Why does such a high level of class voting exist in New Zealand today? Alford offers four possible factors: (1) the parties might *represent* class interests; (2) the parties might consistently *appeal* to class interests; (3) the parties might simply command the historical loyalties of certain classes; and (4) classes might be exposed to situations in which the political relevance of class interests becomes strongly apparent. While in Alford's analysis these factors are presented as scales on which the Anglo-American systems could be systematically compared, it is proposed here rather to discuss the relevance of the factors as generalizations about New Zealand politics and to use comparison to illustrate the discussion.

New Zealand experience provides evidence of the importance of all four factors. It is proposed to look at each of these in turn.

PARTIES MIGHT REPRESENT CLASS INTERESTS

Major parties in New Zealand have always been class-based. They have all risen to power on the basis of the support of class-conscious occupational groups. New Zealand's first party, the Liberal Party, came to power in 1890 with the support of urban manual workers, small farmers, and the landless, who had become class conscious during the long depression of the eighteen eighties. Before this time there had been dominance by a landed oligarchy since the establishment of responsible government in 1856, and parliamentary factions were based on sectional or issue differences rather than class differences. The Liberal Party proceeded to enact measures for the benefit of its urban and rural supporters and was only seriously threatened with loss of its dominance when tensions between farmers and urban manual workers could no longer be contained within the same party framework. On its right grew up the Reform Party, which took office in 1912 on the basis of support from class-conscious small farmers in the North Island allied with urban businessmen. On the left of the Liberal Party developed the Labour Party, supported by trade unionists. Between these two extremes the Liberal Party was almost completely wiped out of existence. It had a brief revival under the name "United" in 1928 on the basis of non-Labour protest votes in a period of increasing economic stress, and became a minority government for two years until it eventually joined in a Reform-dominated coalition government. The severity of the depression and the government's inept handling of it led to an overwhelming Labour victory in 1935. With the creation in the following year of the National Party as a new party designed to unite all those in the community opposed to the Labour Government, the present two-party system was established.

Both parties when out of office have expressed class interests and when in office have enacted legislation in accordance with their class-based support. The Labour Party has emphasized the interest of the manual worker and the lower-income clerical worker. Schemes such as the introduction of the present social security system in 1938, compulsory unionism, the construction of low-rent state housing for lower-income people, food subsidies, price control, higher family benefits, and low-interest housing loans for those with lower incomes are policies reflecting the representation of class interests. On the other hand, the representation of class interests has had to be modified in practice by the need to seek the cooperation of those groups upon whose welfare depends the welfare of Labour supporters, namely the farmers and the manufacturers. Manufacturers in particular have received generous treatment from Labour Governments, because the development of secondary industry in New Zealand is in line with manual worker interests.

Whereas the class basis of the Labour Party is fairly homogeneous, the National Party rests on a combination of classes. The diversity of interests involved means that the representation of interests by the National Party tends to be the representation of aggregated interests. In other words, National Party policy reflects compromises between its diverse supporting groups, especially between farmers and businessmen, often by maximizing common elements or by inaction where there are differences. An example of a common element is the practice of National Party Ministers of Finance to reduce rates of income tax in almost every budget. At the same time, the National Party, which in the nineteen thirties was concerned virtually only with representing the interests of businessmen and farmers, has had to modify its class representation for electoral reasons by continuing (and sometimes extending) most of Labour's class-representing policies and by seeking to avoid measures which might antagonize people with lower incomes.

It is easy, however, to exaggerate the extent of class representation in New Zealand today. Most actions of governments in New Zealand are limited by the economic and political environment, which often provides little room for class-relevant decisions. There is, indeed, far less scope for such decisions than formerly, since the major needs of the various occupational classes have already been satisfied. The complexity of the welfare state and the fine balance of the two-party system have developed in both parties a remarkable similarity of attitude even on economic questions, and the class content in decision-making is small, though perceptible to a class-oriented individual. Nevertheless, the class bias of the parties, small though it now is, seems likely to help preserve existing patterns of class voting until New Zealand society develops some cleavage around which parties could develop, other than the present one concerning distribution of the national income.

PARTIES MIGHT APPEAL TO CLASS INTERESTS

Both main parties appeal to class interests, though to a different degree. The Labour Party has the more explicit and obvious appeal to class interests. Not only is the name "Labour" a symbol that attracts or repels voters according to their attitudes to the trade unions, which are formally integrated into the Labour Party's structure, and to the interests of manual workers, but also the party in its propaganda holds up the business and farmer elements in the community as negative reference groups, often referring to members of these occupations as "the National Party's wealthy friends." Labour's strongest appeal is to manual workers and lower-income salaried people in terms of such symbols as "the working man" and "fair shares" or "just distribution"; an example is the aim stated in the party's constitution as part of its "purpose": ". . . to ensure the just distribution of the production and services of New Zealand."[10]

The National Party's appeal is more a residual one, as befitting a party originally welded together mainly by opposition to the Labour Party and to its trade union supporters. Its appeal is thus to "all sections of the community." One of the objects in its constitution is "to formulate and carry out policies designed to benefit the community as a whole, irrespective of sectional interests, particularly to bring about co-operation between country and city interests, and between employers and employees."[11] Normally its appeals are on ideological lines, stressing the virtues of free enterprise, lower taxation rates as an incentive to high productivity, sound leadership, and industrial peace—ideals appealing to a wide variety of interests in the community. Compared with nonlabor parties in other countries the National Party may be at a disadvantage in that New Zealand conditions do not provide many issues which can strengthen its nonclass appeals. Foreign policy issues, for example, play no part in electoral appeals and defense issues are probably less important than in most other countries. Partly as a consequence of this the National Party's course in the last twenty years has often been to try to reduce the effects of Labour's appeals by offering similar policies and by maintaining Labour policies, which it claims to administer more soundly.

An important element in the appeals of the parties to class interests is the composition of their parliamentary members.[12] The Labour Party draws most of its parliamentarians from lower-income groups, such as manual workers, teachers, and civil servants, while the National Party draws most of its parliamentarians from higher-income groups, such as farmers (usually about half), lawyers, and accountants. The class differences between the two sides of the House of Representatives are less marked today than they were thirty years ago but they are probably still obvious to most voters. Given the existence of class consciousness among various groups in the community, the class differences in Parliament itself have probably made many people aware of the political relevance of their own position. As Angus Campbell *et al.* express it: "Political salience of the group is high . . . when a candidate for the election is recognized as a member of the group.[13]

PARTIES MIGHT COMMAND
THE HISTORICAL LOYALTIES
OF CERTAIN CLASSES

Historical loyalties have varied in importance at different stages of New Zealand's political history. When class issues first seriously invaded New Zealand politics there were no parties with deep historical loyalties, as in the United States. The first party, the Liberal, was thus able to come to power on a class basis without obstruction from long-standing loyalties to parties on the part of manual workers and small farmers. The Liberal Party, in its turn, was unable to generate sufficient strength of party identification among its rural and urban worker wings to prevent the rise of class-based rivals, although it did hold the historical loyalties of parts of the population not identifying with the trade unions or with business and dairy-farming interests. One of the factors delaying the rise of the Labour Party to power in the nineteen twenties was the strength of historical loyalties to one or the other of the two main nonlabor parties and it was only after the full severity of the depression had hit New Zealand that the Labour Party was able to overcome voter resistance in nonmanual workers and attain power.

The intensity of political conflict in the nineteen thirties is still largely reflected in the New Zealand party system and in voting behavior. The party-class alignment today is similar to that in 1931 when Labour opposed a coalition of the nonlabor parties, although the bitterness has disappeared after twenty years of overfull employment.

Evidence for the strength of historical loyalties was provided in the Dunedin Central survey.[14] Not only had nine-tenths of those who voted in 1957 voted the same way in 1960, while three-quarters of major party voters had never voted for any other party, but also two-thirds of major party voters fifty years and under clearly still voted for the same party as their parents. Furthermore, half of those voting for a different party from their parents were married women, who may have changed their vote on marriage. Voting habits in New Zealand, as this evidence indicates, are tradition bound. The relationship of these habits and class voting is uncertain. Perhaps parental influence determines the scope of children's choice of occupation, and hence produces occupational interests similar to those of the parents. Perhaps the meager differences between the parties place little strain on traditional party loyalties and enable many voters to vote against their occupational tide. Perhaps the strength of party loyalties partly depends on the continued alignment of certain major economic organizations, which are important reference groups for many voters, with particular parties. Much research needs to be undertaken on these problems, especially concerning parental transmission of party and class loyalties to the generation now entering the electorate.

CLASSES ARE EXPOSED TO CONDITIONS IN WHICH THE POLITICAL RELEVANCE OF CLASS INTERESTS BECOMES STRONGLY APPARENT

In his analysis Alford stresses the similarity of the Anglo-American systems as to political culture, party systems, and governmental and electoral systems. He argues that "because of this great similarity, correlations between class voting and other social characteristics are more plausible as causal relationships." The following discussion concerns both several of the "other social characteristics" mentioned by Alford and certain aspects of political culture, party systems, and governmental and electoral systems which appear on the basis of New Zealand experience to be related to class voting.

Political Culture

Alford himself discusses differences between the Anglo-American countries in their regional, religious, and ethnic loyalties, which especially in Canada and to some extent in the United States and Australia cut across class interests and may inhibit class voting. The New Zealand pattern of class voting provides evidence for the greater political relevance of class interests in a relatively homogeneous political culture. In New Zealand regional loyalties have existed since the early days of scattered settlements but have been diluted by continuous immigration and internal population movements. Religious and ethnic loyalties are also of little political importance and surveys have revealed only a slight tendency on the part of Catholics to vote for the Labour Party. One reason for this lack of importance is the high proportion of population of Protestant and British background. Catholics, for example, according to the 1961 census comprise only 15.1 percent of the population. Another reason may be the relatively late expansion of rural settlement in New Zealand which enabled many Irish Catholic immigrants to become integrated into the rural and small-town social structure instead of remaining in the main centers as part of the urban working class.

Besides differences as to extent and strength of such loyalties in the Anglo-American systems, there are other attitudes according to which these systems may be contrasted. It is possible, for instance, to contrast attitudes toward the state. Thus in the United States, "if a man wants housing, lower prices, or other material satisfactions, he generally tries to gratify these needs individually by shopping around in the existing market, rather than through political organization."[15] The New Zealander or Australian in a similar position would be likely to seek political solutions to his problems. Explanation of these attitudes may be very complex. Walter Adams explains the American attitude as a consequence of settler attitudes: "In colonial America, individualism meant—in the negative sense—a distrust of government. To the early settlers, the state was an instrument of privilege, a creator of monopolies, an oppressor of individual liberties.[16] A contrasting explanation of New Zealand attitudes is provided by J. B. Condliffe: "The New Zealand colonists departed early from the *laissez-faire* theory of the State. They had little option but to undertake activities that in other countries were the agenda of private enterprise; but they embarked on these activities in an empirical, opportunist spirit without any doctrinaire belief in state socialism."[17] Whatever the origins of these different attitudes toward the state, they have probably had some effect on the extent of class voting, since favorable attitudes toward the state obviously increase the political relevance of class interests.

A counterpart of such attitudes is the relative strength of the "rags-to-riches" myth in the United States and New Zealand. New Zealanders generally prefer economic security and moderate material comfort to the risks involved in the search for rapid upward mobility. The state in New Zealand is the principal satisfier of the desire for economic security, which makes control of the machinery of government a prize to be fought over by rival groups actively competing in the search for security. New Zealanders appear to have a high level of expectation of government performance, perhaps encouraged by the triennial competitive bidding for votes. High expectations are often disappointed, however, since New Zealand is too dependent on world trade for any New Zealand government to prevent fluctuations in economic life. The observations of V. O. Key may be highly relevant in the New Zealand context: "Since one set of expectations tends to be fulfilled except in a rapidly expanding economy) at the expense of others, it might plausibly be expected that a sustained high level of expectation associated with a focus upon government for fulfillment would tend to generate high stresses within a society."[18]

Evidence of the difference in salience of politics in the United States and New Zealand is provided in the Survey Research Center's study of the 1958 congressional elections and in Mitchell's study of Dunedin Central. In the United States, conclude Donald E. Stokes and Warren E. Miller, "the electorate sees very little altogether of what goes on in the national legislature. Few judgments of legislative performance are associated with the parties, and much of the public is unaware even of which party has control in Congress."[19] In New Zealand, on the other hand, Mitchell found that the majority of major-party supporters were able to attribute correctly most items on a list of policy statements in an election where policy differences between the parties were few.[20]

While these differences in level of information are probably related to attitudes to the state and to a high level of expectation, they may also be related to a further aspect of political culture in which the United States and New Zealand appear to differ, namely, political participation. New Zealanders have a high rate of political participation. There is a fairly strong general inclination for participation in clubs and associations of all kinds, an inclination which seems to be present in all strata of society. Not only is group cohesion strong in the sense that organizational splits are rare but also such groups tend, if they are occupational ones, to include most of their potential membership. A similar tendency is reflected in the high percentage of dues-paying members of parties to party voters. The National Party, for example, has in an election year about 250,000 members or roughly 40 percent of its voters. Furthermore, at general elections the national participation rate normally exceeds 90 percent of registered electors, and rates of 95 percent in individual electorates are not uncommon. These examples illustrate a high level of political efficacy, a factor reflected also in the disagreement of 77 percent of a sample of Palmerston North electors with the statement: "I don't think politicians care much what people like me think." Some of these examples of participation, especially in elections, may also demonstrate a strong sense of citizen duty, reflected in the disagreement of 95 percent of the same sample of Palmerston North electors with the statement: "So many other people vote in a general election that it doesn't matter much whether I vote or not."

High levels of political efficacy and citizen duty have a similar influence to that of a high rate of urbanization in that they increase the effective number of lower-status individuals in the electorate, since it is normally from the lower strata that most nonvoters are drawn. One consequence, then, of these characteristics is that in a country like New Zealand with a homogeneous political culture more voters are available toward whom class appeals may successfully be directed.

Another effect of a high rate of political efficacy is brought about by group enhancement of class sensitivity. Widespread participation in occupational associations extends occupational consciousness. The generalization of Campbell *et al.* appears to apply in New Zealand as well as in the United States: "Thus we find that groups somewhat more formal than the social class can, when interests are incorporated as group goals, serve to heighten status polarization. Since the labor and management groupings are current points of heightened class sensitivity within the total society, they bear particularly close attention."[21] In New Zealand the points of heightened class sensitivity have been the trade unions of skilled and unskilled workers at the one end, now organized in the Federation of Labour; the Associated Chambers of Commerce and the Employers' Federation at the other end of the urban scale; and the Federated Farmers in the countryside. The two main points of class sensitivity on the nonlabor side are held together in an alliance mainly by a common interest in opposition to wage increases, which tend to increase the costs and reduce the profit margins of both businessmen and farmers. Tensions between the unions and the business and farming communities have since early in this century been stimulated by the activities of the Court of Arbitration, which since 1895 has fixed wage rates and conditions of work for about half of New Zealand's wage and salary earners. The court has acted as a focus for wage demands of unions and has fostered the growth of trade unionism and class consciousness among manual workers. It may also have fostered class consciousness on the part of farmers and businessmen. The three groups mentioned form today an important basis of the present party system by being reference groups for voting behavior.

Another aspect of the attitudes of New Zealanders to associations is the high degree of toleration shown toward pressure group activity. Groups are treated as legitimate elements in the formation and expression of public opinion. An extension of these attitudes is the toleration of interest representation in Parliament. In this regard ideas of interest representation are especially strong among the more class-sensitive elements of society, the unions and the farmers, both of whom seek to have their own kind in Parliament. Such ideas of group representation, strong in British political culture, have been passed on to New Zealand. They are a modern manifestation of what S. H. Beer calls the "Old Whig" theory of representation, according to which members of Parliament represented "interests" or classes, but not individuals.[22] In Beer's view the Old Whig theory has been weak or nonexistent in American politics, where the main theories of representation are derived from Liberal and Radical traditions. An example of the important place of interest representation ideas in the New Zealand political culture is provided by the assertion in the 1963 budget statement of the National Government that "this Budget again expresses the Government's determination to seek solutions to our various problems in co-operation with all interested groups, and not to impose decisions based on outmoded dogmas."[23]

In addition to a strong infusion of interest representation ideas, New Zealand also appears to exhibit strong elements of the Radical tradition, perhaps even more than the United States. Certainly radical assumptions are embedded in New Zealand political institutions, for example, in the electoral system, where boundaries are frequently altered to ensure virtually equal population in all electoral districts, in the practice of three-yearly elections, and in the great strength of the attitude that election promises must be carried out. The importance of these attitudes is that in combination with attitudes supporting or tolerating interest representation they legitimize a class-based political system.

The Party System

Although both the United States and New Zealand have two-party systems, the New Zealand system is much more disciplined and programmatic. These characteristics tend to increase what Anthony Downs calls "the expected differential.[24] The power and intention to implement a program increases the meaning for the voter of his decision. Given the existence of class tensions it can be expected that voters will relate their class attitudes to their party choice with much less effort in a country with a disciplined two-party system than in the United States, where partly because of the looseness of party discipline there is usually a considerable gap between promise and performance. However, where there are cleavages in society other than class cleavages, such as the ethnic and religious cleavage in Canada, a disciplined two-party system could not be expected to be as class relevant as in a more homogeneous society like New Zealand, Britain, or Australia.

The Governmental and Electoral System

The governmental and electoral aspects, though interwoven, can be discussed as separate influences on the level of class voting. If we first look at the influence of governmental structure we can note differences between the various Anglo-American systems in the efficiency of the machinery of government in transforming demands into decisions. David Easton observes that "in all societies one fact dominates political life: scarcity prevails with regard to most of the valued things. Some of the claims for these relatively scarce things never find their way into the political system but are satisfied through the private negotiations of or settlements by the persons involved."[25] The tripartite division of branches of government in combination with the federal system has made the American machinery of government less efficient in transforming demands into decisions than the machinery in the other Anglo-American countries. A consequence of this inefficiency is that groups and individuals have concentrated on other devices in society, like collective bargaining, for satisfying their demands. In this situation politics tends to become less relevant to class interests than in countries where decision-making machinery is more efficient. New Zealand perhaps provides in this regard the most striking contrast to the United States. Both the parliamentary system (unicameral since 1950 but effectively unicameral for the previous fifty years) and the unitary system of government, which is even more highly centralized than that of Britain, provide a great concentration of power in the hands of the parliamentary majority. This machinery has proved to be very efficient in satisfying group demands, with the result that groups and individuals have often used the political mechanisms in preference to other mechanisms in society.

Regarding the influence of the electoral system, the elements relevant to class voting include the number of votes electors are expected to cast, the methods of voting, and the methods of redistricting. An example of the influence of the first of these is the apparent reduction in the interest of working-class electors in the United States because of the sheer number of votes electors are expected to cast. Concerning voting methods, all of the Anglo-American countries except Australia have the plurality system of selecting representatives. The effect of this system is to penalize third parties and to discourage them from competing. By itself it has probably not contributed significantly to the relative extent of class voting in these countries. It may, however, have been of some importance in the United States and Canada through its reinforcement of the influence of the system of redistricting.

Methods of drawing boundaries of electoral districts can have profound effects on political life. In particular, the drawing of boundaries to favor rural interests tends to reduce the impact of urban class issues on party strategies and on voting behavior. Such distorted representation has been very considerable in the United States and Canada, and relatively slight in Britain, Australia, and New Zealand. New Zealand experience indicates the influence of distorted representation in the past. From 1887 to 1945 a mild form of distorted representation existed, the so-called "country-quota," under which rural areas were given a fictitious quota of population, fixed at 28 percent in 1889, when the Representation Commission carried out its redistricting after each population census. Although a mild distortion, it slowed the Labour Party's rise to power and delayed the fusion of Labour's rivals, the Reform and Liberal parties, which could afford to compete for each other's votes in over-franchised rural and mixed rural/small-town areas without fear of a Labour victory. Since 1945 the New Zealand system of redistricting has been organized on the basis of "one vote–one value." Under the 1956 Electoral Act the two main islands of New Zealand must have equal proportions of districts to total population, and no electoral district may exceed 5 percent above or below the average population of electoral districts for its particular island, while boundaries are altered by a nonpartisan Representation Commission after every five-yearly census.[26]

The electoral system, then, is an important factor in adding weight to one side or other of the balance of forces in a community. If the system is genuinely representative, it can enable trends in class consciousness in urban areas to be reflected in politics, but if it distorts representation, it adds weight to other forces in society.

Urbanization

New Zealand has developed class voting without the assistance of large cities. Even today the largest city, Auckland, has only half a million inhabitants, and at the time patterns of class voting were being established it had only half that number. It is likely that the state of urbanization in the first decade of this century was unpropitious for the rise of a class-based Labour Party, since in 1901 the rural population of New Zealand was 56.9 percent as against the urban (boroughs and town districts with over 1,000 population) figure of 43.1 percent. Only 10.1 percent lived in towns of 25,000 and over.[27] Labour fortunes, however, improved with the rise in urbanization over the next generation. By 1926 the urban population had increased to 59.2 percent and 25.2 percent now lived in towns of 25,000 and over. The rise of the Labour Party in New Zealand appears to be closely related to trends in urbanization. It was able to win power in the thirties, however, only by making inroads into rural areas.

The statistics of distribution of population are rather misleading in that they do not indicate the extent to which urban ways of thinking have extended into rural areas in New Zealand. Rural dwellers in New Zealand, unlike their counterparts in the United States,[28] exhibit few differences in outlook from city dwellers. This is not surprising since most New Zealanders are descended from migrants from a highly industrialized Britain and there has been considerable mobility in and out of farming. Class consciousness among farmers probably springs from these urban roots. The New Zealand farmer in many ways resembles the class-conscious Saskatchewan farmer described by S. M. Lipset,[29] both in his high level of political efficacy and his urban origins.

The Educational System

Alford suggests that the greater opportunities for education in the United States and Canada may affect the character of social mobility and thus tend to less class voting than in the other Anglo-American countries. This suggestion is probably more relevant to the upper end of the educational scale than to the lower end. Concerning the lower end it can be argued that the higher the minimum level of education the greater is the degree of class voting. There is some evidence in support of this in voting studies. Campbell *et al.* say of the American farmer and urban laborer: "Both are poorly educated, and one consequence of this fact is a lowered capacity to organize a steady input of political information. With restricted information goes a reduced sense of involvement in the outcome of political events."[30] In a study of Wellington Central in New Zealand, R. S. Milne noted that the most interested Labour voters were in the lowest socioeconomic status groups, a contrast with British results. "In Britain the worse-off sections of the population are markedly inferior in status and in education. But in New Zealand there are no such wide gaps which would cut voters off from taking an interest in politics, because they felt that they were too ignorant or that they lacked 'a stake in the country.' "[31] If education and political involvement are related and if as Campbell *et al.* say, "the more involved the individual is in politics, the more likely he is to cast his vote according to class lines,"[32] then further investigation of educational opportunities at the lower end of the educational scale may throw more light on differences in class voting in the Anglo-American countries.

Economic Development

New Zealand is similar to Australia in its per-capita income and levels of consumption. Thus it is a poorer country than the United States or Canada, though a rich country in comparison with most others. While it does seem likely, as Alford's analysis suggests, that high levels of consumption in Canada and the United States have been a factor inhibiting the development of class consciousness, one can ask why this factor should have been so much less important in the other Anglo-American countries, which, after all, are not poor. Perhaps in the latter, economic fluctuations may be more common, more intense, or more widely felt. It may be expected that economic fluctuations in a country with a materialist emphasis in its political culture and with a favorable attitude to government action will intensify class sensitivities and bring them into the political process. This has been the case in New Zealand. Its economy has always been a highly dependent one because of a high ratio of value of external trade to national income and a high ratio of imports essential for production to total imports. Its economy has always been subject to vacillation arising from fluctuations in demand on the British market for New Zealand's three main exports, wool, meat, and butter. Such fluctuations, whether upward or down, have produced sharpened tensions in New Zealand society, especially between urban manual workers and farmers. The pattern seems to have been that large downward fluctuations have increased urban class consciousness, especially when unemployment has occurred, as in the eighteen eighties, the early nineteen twenties, and the early nineteen thirties, and that they have reduced farmer class consciousness by stressing differences between rich farmers and poor farmers. At elections near the conclusion of the most serious depressions, in 1890 and in 1935, urban manual workers have been joined by other low-income workers and by poorer farmers to give political power to the Liberal Party and the Labour Party respectively, and party identification appears to have had an independent influence on the subsequent voting behavior of those not developing strong occupational class identification in conditions of prosperity. When economic fluctuations have been moderate or in an upward direction, tensions have increased between manual and white-collar workers and farmers because of divergences of economic interest. In particular, inflationary pressures resulting from increases in overseas prices suit farmers' pockets but hit the urban manual or white-collar workers. Thus the rise of the Reform Party to power and the breakaway of manual workers from the Liberal Party to join Labour were given considerable stimulus by the tensions set in force by inflationary pressures. Even today, in an economy with many built-in stabilizers, similar tensions arising from fluctuations in agricultural export prices provide the present parties with differences in outlook corresponding with the interests of their strongest supporters.

An important aspect in any comparison of economic fluctuations between countries is the degree to which such fluctuations are national or only sectional. If they are national they will tend to produce a nationwide impact on class awareness and on voting alignments. Britain, Australia, and New Zealand all have homogeneous economies in this sense, whereas Canada and the United States represent combinations of sectional economies which have fluctuations at different times and with different intensities; party-class alignments are perhaps fostered in the latter two countries only to the extent to which economic fluctuations are extreme and nationwide.[33]

SOME CONSEQUENCES OF CLASS POLARIZATION

New Zealand provides evidence in support of Alford's suggestions concerning the differences in the consequences of class polarization. Indeed, some of the evidence is very striking, possibly because the simple system of government and the homogeneity of political culture enable social forces to be felt rapidly in politics.

Parties in New Zealand are mass parties. Alford's suggestion that "the rise of a working-class party organized along disciplined lines forces the more conservative party in each country to organize likewise in self-defense," is an accurate description of the circumstances surrounding the establishment of the National Party in 1936. Until the election in 1935 both of the main nonlabor parties were "cadre" parties led by "notables" in conjunction with members of Parliament. The massive Labour victory of 1935 led in 1936 to the creation of a new party out of the remnants of the other parties. The National Party's structure reflected the view that the paramount need was to build up a permanent party organization with a large membership both in order to compete with the Labour Party's organization and to unite everyone in the community opposed to the Labour Government under the banner of a single party. The considerable degree of internal democracy within the party and the activities of professional organizers have undoubtedly contributed to a membership of about 40 percent of the party's vote, but of greater importance would be the strong antipathies among farmers, businessmen, and professional people to the demands of organized labor.

Alford's suggestion that "the effect of parties strongly organized on a class basis is to spread party organization to every political level" has a limited application in New Zealand, where local government performs few important functions. The Labour Party contests local elections in the four main urban areas and in some of the larger towns, normally opposed by a local "citizens' association" with aims and membership similar to those of the National Party but not officially linked with it.

The dominance in New Zealand elections of mass parties linked with occupational interests is reflected in the unimportance of local personalities and issues in determining election results. Both aggregate data and survey data suggest that local issues or candidate personalities are seldom responsible for more than about 2 percent of the votes, though this may be sufficient to gain, lose, or retain individual marginal electorates.[34]

There is some evidence in New Zealand in support of Alford's suggestion that there is a relationship between the extent of class voting and the smallness of difference between high- and low-status groups in political participation and sense of political efficacy. While it is likely that the smallness of such differences in New Zealand may have contributed to the extent of party-class alignments, it is also highly probable that the existence of the Labour Party has intensified political interest and activity on the part of individuals of lower status, both in union and Labour Party affairs and at election time. For example, Milne found in Wellington Central in 1957 that the most interested Labour voters were in the lowest socioeconomic status groups, as were also those who gave their party the highest degree of support.[35]

Alford suggests that political shifts may take place more readily in the more class-polarized systems. Perhaps postwar New Zealand provides a good example of this. There was a change from Labour to National in 1949, from National to Labour in 1957, and from Labour to National in 1960. One reason for a more rapid change in New Zealand than elsewhere may lie in the fact of "massive stability" in voting behavior. Neither the National nor the Labour Party has fallen below 40 percent of the total vote since the present party system was established in 1936. Since 1946 the parties have been finely balanced in a situation where 2 percent of the voters could remove the government by changing their vote. The highest swing (defined as the average of one party's loss plus the other party's gain expressed in terms of a percentage of the two-party vote) since the war has been 4 percent between 1957 and 1960. In New Zealand, as in Britain, a small change in voting support is greatly magnified, roughly according to the "cube law"; that is, if votes are divided between the parties in the ratio A : B, parliamentary seats will be divided in the ratio $A^3 : B^3$.[36] In this situation it can be argued that governments find it difficult to prevent the slow erosion of support that eventually results in defeat. On the other hand, it can be argued to the contrary that voting stability provides the basis for the dominance of one party over a long period. According to this interpretation—which derives much of its persuasiveness from the National Party's retention of power in 1963 with the loss of only one seat—the National Party has been the dominant one in New Zealand politics for most of the postwar period, and electoral defeats, like that of 1957, are the exception in the midst of a series of electoral successes.[37]

Concerning the legislative and administrative consequences of a high level of class voting, New Zealand's highly developed welfare state reflects a long history of legislation and administration in favor of the classes supporting the government of the day, although as indicated earlier this tendency has apparently diminished with the development of the welfare state. In the class-oriented politics of New Zealand, both parties have moved to the left of the major parties in the United States; the National Party, for example, holds views about the need for full employment which the most ardent American trade unionist would advocate. Thus a situation of overfull employment has existed since the war which no government will reassess without caution for fear of creating unemployment. This climate of opinion has probably been conducive to the high degree of industrial peace experienced, with the exception of a major dock strike in 1951, since the war, though the system of compulsory arbitration of disputes and the existence of the Labour Party may have been equally or more important.

In New Zealand both major parties share a high degree of consensus on policy. The National Party has accepted the welfare state and the Labour Party the system of enterprise. A reflection of this consensus can be seen in the 95 percent agreement of a sample of 478 Palmerston North electors with the statement: "The government has a definite duty to see that everybody has a job and a decent standard of living." However, such consensus does not imply that there will not continue to be differences between the parties perceptible to the class-oriented voter. Admittedly, the welfare state has modified tensions between occupational interests, but it may also have contributed to the continuance of such tensions through the increasing role of government in the management of economic life. The welfare state, if this is true, will maintain, not reduce, class voting in New Zealand. On the other hand, class voting will become less important as a predictor of the actions of a government. More and more of the issues facing New Zealand governments concern problems of economic and educational development for a rapidly expanding population, and the allocation of the national income for such purposes to particular sectors of the economy and to particular geographical areas; such problems are either not relevant to class interests or involve delicate compromises to secure general cooperation. At the same time a highly developed system of interest groups has been evolving and reducing the importance of parties in the representation of interests. A result of these trends is that class voting is tending to become less related to the actual substance of government decisions, and that its importance in politics in New Zealand is being increasingly confined to the function of providing the base for a stable two-party system.

NOTES

1. Following the general election in November 1963 the School of Political Science and Public Administration at the Victoria University of Wellington carried out an election survey in the course of which some 1,700 persons were interviewed. These were divided fairly evenly among four electorates of varying social composition. Respondents were selected at random from the electoral roll in three of these, the urban electorates of Miramar, Karori, and Palmerston North; while in the fourth electorate, Manawatu, respondents were selected at random from the Palmerston North city portion; in the latter electorate there was a random sample of farmers only in rural Kairanga County adjoining Palmerston North. A supplementary postal survey involving over 5,000 questionnaires was also used to produce a broader coverage of electorates, especially of those containing small towns and rural areas.

Results published or in course of publication appear in A. D. Robinson and A. H. Ashenden, "Mass Communications and the 1963 Election: A Preliminary Report," *Political Science* (Wellington), 16 (2) (Sept. 1964); A. H. Ashenden, R. H. Brookes, and A. D. Robinson, "Attitudes Towards Liquor Among New Zealand Voters," *Political Science,* 18 (1) (March 1966); and R. H. Brookes and A. H. Ashenden, "The Floating Vote in Wellington and Palmerston North 1960–63," *Political Science,* 19 (1) (July 1967). Further articles are in course of preparation on class voting, participation, party identification, and parental influence.

2. A. V. Mitchell, Chap. X of R. M. Chapman, W. K. Jackson, and A. V. Mitchell, *New Zealand Politics in Action: The 1960 General Election* (London: Oxford Univ. Press, 1962), p. 175.

3. R. S. Milne, "Voting in Wellington Central, 1957," *Political Science,* 10 (2) (Sept. 1958); Austin Mitchell, "Dunedin Central," *Political Science,* 14 (1) (March 1962).

4. Most of this work is in the form of unpublished M.A. theses. Notable among these are R. M. Chapman, "The Significance of the 1928 General Election," Auckland Univ. College, 1948, and J. R. S. Daniels, "The General Election of 1943," Victoria Univ. of Wellington, 1961. The most important work published in this field is R. M. Chapman Chaps. XI and XII of *New Zealand Politics in Action, op. cit.* For a critique of Chapman's analysis see A. D. Robinson, "Why Did Labour Lose?", *Political Science,* 15 (1) (March 1963). The contribution of ecological studies is also discussed in R. S. Milne, *Political Parties in New Zealand* (Oxford: Oxford Univ. Press, 1966), Chap. 3.

5. A. V. Mitchell, *op. cit.,* p. 176. The scale is based on a modified and contracted version of a social-status scale devised by A. A. Congalton [see R. J. Havighurst *Studies of Children and Society in New Zealand* (Christchurch, 1954), Appendix A. 1].

6. R. S. Milne, "Voting in Wellington Central, 1957," *op. cit.,* pp. 32–4.

7. R. M. Chapman *et al., New Zealand Politics in Action, op. cit.,* p. 257.

8. R. Alford, *Party and Society* (Chicago: Rand McNally, 1963), p. 105.

9. Constitution and Rules of the New Zealand Labour Party, 1955, p. 3.

10. Constitution and Rules of the New Zealand National Party, 1960, p. 1.

11. However, in the 1966 election campaign, after this was written, the National Government's Vietnam policy was a major issue.

12. For details see Austin Mitchell, "The New Zealand Parliaments of 1935–60," *Political Science,* 13 (1) (March 1961).

13. Angus Campbell, Philip E. Converse, Warren E. Miller, and Donald E. Stokes, *The American Voter* (New York: Wiley, 1960), p. 318.

14. A. V. Mitchell, "Dunedin Central," *op. cit.,* pp. 67–72.

15. Robert E. Lane, *Political Life* (New York: The Free Press, 1959), p. 103.

16. Walter Adams, "Economics, Ideology and American Politics," *Diogenes,* 36 (Winter 1961), p. 59.

17. J. B. Condliffe, *The Welfare State in New Zealand* (London: Allen & Unwin, 1959), p. 211.

18. V. O. Key, *Public Opinion and American Democracy* (New York: Knopf, 1961), p. 551.

19. Donald E. Stokes and Warren E. Miller, "Party Government and the Saliency of Congress," *Public Opinion Quarterly,* 26 (4) (Winter 1962), p. 545.

20. A. V. Mitchell, "Dunedin Central," *op. cit.,* pp. 57–61.

21. A. Campbell *et al., op. cit.,* p. 380.

22. Samuel H. Beer, "The Representation of Interests in British Government: Historical Background," *American Political Science Review,* 51 (3) (Sept. 1957).

23. Financial Statement 1963, *Appendices to the Journals of the House of Representatives,* 1963, B.6., p. 26.

24. Anthony Downs, *An Economic Theory of Democracy* (New York: Harper & Row, 1957), Chap. 3.

25. David Easton, "An Approach to the Analysis of Political Systems," *World Politics,* 9 (3) (April 1957), p. 387.

26. The Electoral Amendment Act of 1965 made a change in the operation of this system. It fixed the number of European electorates in the South Island at twenty-five and provided for the number of North Island electorates to be ascertained by the Representation Commission after each census on the basis of the quota fixed for the South Island. The changes took place after the 1966 census.

27. Population Census, 1961, Vol. I, p. 14. The figures exclude Maoris.

28. See A. Campbell *et al., op. cit.,* Chap. 15, for an analysis of American agrarian political behavior.

29. S. M. Lipset, *Agrarian Socialism* (Berkeley: Univ. of California Press, 1950).

30. A. Campbell *et al., op. cit.,* p. 425.

31. R. S. Milne, "Voting in Wellington Central, 1957," *op. cit.,* pp. 36–7.

32. A. Campbell *et al., op. cit.,* p. 354.

33. For a general discussion of the effects of economic insecurity on voting behavior see S. M. Lipset, *Political Man: The Social Bases of Politics* (London: Heinemann, 1960), pp. 232–6.

34. Local issues and personalities, however, were more important than usual in the 1963 election, in several cases being worth more than 5 percent of the votes in an electorate.

35. R. S. Milne, "Voting in Wellington Central, 1957," *op. cit.,* pp. 36, 40.

36. For a mathematical explanation of the "cube law" see M. G. Kendall and A. Stuart, "The Law of Cubic Proportion in Election Results," *British Journal of Sociology,* 1 (3), pp. 183–96. Its application in New Zealand is discussed in R. H. Brookes, "Seats and Votes in New Zealand," *Political Science,* 6 (2) (Sept. 1953).

37. Further evidence for this interpretation was provided in 1966 when the National Party won its sixth election out of the last seven.

Three

The Delicate Experiment:
Industrialism, Conservatism,
and Working-Class Tories in England

Robert T. McKenzie
and
Allan Silver

THE HISTORICAL CONTEXT

Between 1886[1] and 1964 there were thirteen British elections that produced a House of Commons in which a single party held a "working majority" of seats; and on eleven of these thirteen occasions it was the Conservative Party which found itself in this position. The most heavily—and
longest—urbanized and industrialized electorate of any democracy only twice
returned a Parliament in which a party of the Left had a working majority.

The Conservative achievement is particularly striking if it is recalled that
the modern party was born (after 1832) specifically of resistance to the idea
of political equality and that it was, in its beginnings, largely lacking in sympathy with industrialism. In addition its leadership, always drawn overwhelmingly from the upper and upper-middle classes, has faced a preponderantly
working-class electorate without the advantage of explicit religious support
of the sort that has bolstered the Right in the preponderantly Catholic countries of continental Europe.

What accounts for the Conservatives' success in holding power alone (or
in Conservative-dominated coalitions) for three-quarters of the period since
Britain became a political democracy? In part the answer lies in the fragmentation of the non-Conservative vote. At the beginning of the period the
Liberals split (in 1886) over Gladstone's proposals for Irish Home Rule
and an important wing of the party entered what was to be a permanent

alliance with the Conservatives. Meanwhile after 1900 the emergent Labour Party drained off working-class support for the Liberals; and when the latter were again wracked by bitter quarrels during and after World War I, Labour was able to supplant the Liberals as the second party in the state. The Socialists, in turn, virtually fell apart in 1931; again, twenty years later, after its only period of majority rule, Labour became absorbed in internecine conflict which was to last for almost a decade. Meanwhile the Liberals, who had continued to poll a small but significant share of the electoral vote, began to regain marked public support (in by-elections at least) during the early 1960's. The Conservatives, although often deeply divided during the years since 1886, were a far more cohesive political force than their opponents on the Left. Undoubtedly this was a major factor in enabling them to retain their parliamentary ascendency even though their share of the total votes cast in elections during the period 1886–1959 was no more than 47 percent.

But Conservative electoral success in Britain is not solely or even primarily the consequence of the fissiparous tendencies of the British Left (or of its political ineptitude, striking though that has been). A much more important consideration is the fact that the Conservatives have been one of the most successful of all Right-wing parties in coming to terms with the political implications of industrialism and the "age of democratic revolution."[2] It can be argued that the true forerunners of modern sociology are those European Conservatives (like Burke in England, Bonald, de Maistre, and others on the Continent) who were profoundly concerned about "the poison of social disintegration" which they saw flowing from the French Revolution and the break-up of the old preindustrial society.[3] They became deeply concerned with the concept of order; they saw society as an organic whole, not as a mere aggregate of individuals; they stressed the interdependence of institutions, customs, and habits; they argued that religion (and even folk beliefs and "prejudices," in Burke's terminology) acted as an "emotional cement" within society. Above all they insisted on the importance of a structured group life, and an hierarchical social order in which each is assured of his status.

Certain of the more pessimistic (and frightened) Continental Conservatives concluded that the answer to the problem of social disorganization raised by the industrial and democratic revolutions lay with "the Pope and the executioner." But British Conservatives (which in any case could not rely on the Pope) were wise enough for the most part to eschew the assistance of the executioner; they perceived that the answer lay with the reinforcement of those institutions in British society which would help to maintain cohesion and strengthen consensus in that society.[4]

The greatest of nineteenth-century British Conservative leaders, Benjamin Disraeli, recognized as vividly as did his contemporary, Karl Marx, the existence of "the two nations" in nineteenth-century industrial Britain. Disraeli and his followers of course rejected the Marxist view that this division was the inevitable precursor of a revolution out of which a new consensus would be established in a classless society. But they also rejected the view of those Liberal advocates of laissez faire who were prepared to depend on the self-regulating mechanisms of the market automatically to produce a harmony of interests. Nor were they in the least attracted by the doctrines of Social Darwinism.

The Conservatives accepted the inevitability of the class system, for they believed that it reflected the innate inequality of men. They realized however that conflict was immanent in the worker-owner relationship, and they therefore tried to redress the balance of interests when it shifted too far in the direction of the owners of industry; hence, their willingness to sponsor legislation recognizing trade unions and governing the condition of work in factories. In addition they, rather than the Liberals, took the initiative in bringing the urban masses within the pale of the constitution by the first major extension of the franchise to the urban working classes in 1867. But above all else the Conservatives, under Disraeli's inspiration, attempted to ally themselves with the forces of social cohesion within British society; they championed the monarchy and the system of "orders" reflected in the peerage, religion, nationalism (and toward the end of the century, imperialism)— indeed all the institutions and forces likely to eliminate domestic strife, to ensure stability, and to override sectional interests.

In what was perhaps the most important address ever made by a British Conservative leader, Disraeli, in his Crystal Palace speech in 1872, declared that the fundamental purposes of Conservatism were to "maintain the institutions of the country; to uphold the empire of England; and to elevate the condition of the people."[5] With characteristic audacity Disraeli hereby claimed for his party a unique role as custodian of the national interest (as a contemporary Conservative publication puts it "there is no textbook of Conservatism, except the history of Britain"); but Disraeli also demonstrated the wisdom of British Conservatism by coupling with the national appeal a concern for the welfare of the masses. This program was to prove attractive, not merely to the upper strata of British society, but also to a large section of the working class which had remained unmoved by appeals to class solidarity even though, by sheer weight of electoral numbers, the working class has been in a position to control the levers of political power for the past eighty years.

From their earliest beginnings the Conservatives had been able to rely on the support of the "squirarchy" and of a large part of "the landed interest"; in addition, by the turn of the century they had become the acknowledged champions of the business community; and, with the decline of the Liberals, they were to inherit the preponderant part of the middle-class vote. But these sources of electoral support would not have enabled the Conservatives to maintain their parliamentary ascendancy had they not also been able to win and retain the support of a very considerable proportion of the working class, which from 1884 onward represented two-thirds of the electorate. It would appear that at most elections the Conservatives have won about one-third of the working-class vote, and that this working-class element has constituted about one-half the party's total electoral support.

The phenomenon of working-class Conservatism has long been a source of exasperation to the Left in Britain. After the general election of 1868 (following the passage of the Second Reform Act of 1867, which enfranchised a large proportion of the urban working class), Engels wrote to Marx:

> What do you say to the elections in the factory districts? Once again
> the proletariat has discredited itself terribly. . . . It cannot be denied
> that the increase of working class voters has brought the Tories more
> than their simple percentage increase; it has improved their relative
> position.[6]

Ninety years and thirty-three elections later a considerable section of the
proletariat was, in the view of the Left, still "discrediting itself terribly." After
the Labour Party's ejection from office in 1951, an official party publication
brooded over the failure of universal suffrage to produce the expected result:

> Once the mass of the people have the vote, Socialists were convinced
> that Conservatism and all that it stood for would be swept away. Their
> victory seemed certain for Conservatism which was based on privilege
> and wealth was inevitably a minority creed, whereas socialism, with
> its appeal to social justice and economic self-interest, would recruit
> the big battalions of the poor and under-privileged, whom the vote
> would make the masters of political democracy. . . . Yet it is clear that
> events have falsified these predictions. . . . The question which must
> now be asked is why the fruits of universal suffrage have taken so long
> to ripen. How is it that so large a proportion of the electorate, many of
> whom are neither wealthy nor privileged, have been recruited for a
> cause which is not their own?[7]

One need not accept the assumptions underlying either of these quotations
to recognize that working-class Conservatism has been a major factor in determining the distinctive pattern of modern British politics.

THE TORY WORKER TODAY

This section provides a very brief account of some findings from research
undertaken by the present writers into the nature of contemporary working-
class Conservative allegiance in England. A sample survey undertaken in six
urban constituencies—in London, Manchester, Halifax, and Coventry—
yielded 604 working class voters, including 178 Conservatives. The research
was not concerned with the social psychological mechanisms of particular
voting choices, nor with the effects of an electoral campaign, but rather with
the relatively enduring conditions out of which party affiliations emerge under
the pressures of events, issues, and propaganda.[8]

Two kinds of approaches to the material were taken: straightforward comparisons of working-class Labour and Conservative voters, and internal analyses of the population of working-class Conservatives. According to the former
procedure, we ask what characteristics are associated with the frequency with
which working-class electors vote Conservative. In the latter, we are less interested in the frequency of working-class Conservative voting, and more in
the conditions and consequences of the social and ideological bases out of
which this behavior emerges.

The most general impression one gets from a comparison of Labour and
Conservative working-class voters in this sample is of a prevailing homogeneity between the two groups. There is little difference between them in
terms of sex, income, or occupational skill level, and only a moderate differ-

ence in terms of age. No comparable studies exist to provide a base line, but previous research does suggest that an earlier tendency for working-class Conservatives to be older and have lower incomes than Labour voters is disappearing, though the Conservatives are still somewhat older.

These aggregate results conceal some diverging trends: among the lower-income group, older voters more frequently vote Conservative than younger (Table 1); and, while age and sex separately are either moderately related

Table 1—Among Working-Class Voters with Below-Average Incomes, the Older Are More Often Conservative than the Younger

| | BELOW AVERAGE INCOMES | | ABOVE AVERAGE INCOMES | |
| | Below age 44 | Above age 44 | Below age 44 | Above age 44 |
	(percent)		(percent)	
Labour	83	63	71	70
Conservative	17	37	29	30
N (= 100%)	72	162	150	102

or unrelated to voting Conservative, older working-class women vote Conservative with considerably more frequency than do other groups. We shall return to these findings later, in another context.

The political and social perspectives of Labour and Conservative working-class voters differ where one would expect them to—with respect to objects of partisan concern like the issue of nationalization, key power sources such as the trade unions, big business and the upper classes, and the parties themselves. Yet the differences are not such as to override an impression that Conservative values pervade much of the urban working class, including many Labour voters. There is, for example, a widespread dislike or distrust of trade unions: more than half of the entire sample agrees that unions have too much power. The unions are often perceived—even by working-class Labour voters—as unduly disruptive or officious; and there is a good deal of feeling that strikes are called too frequently, despite the far lower strike rate of Britain compared to that of the United States. The organic view of society, promulgated by the great Conservative spokesmen, Burke and Disraeli, finds a responsive echo in the contemporary urban working class. For such reasons, it is hard to think of working-class Conservatives in Britain as normatively deviant from working-class political culture; on the contrary, they seem to express aspects of a wide national consensus.

It is also difficult to think of working-class Conservatives as apathetic, ignorant, or alienated people—a kind of psychological *lumpenproletariat*. Working-class Conservatism cannot, apparently, be ascribed to political pathology in ways analogous to the alleged link between the "authoritarian personality" and clinical pathology. In fact, the working-class Conservatives in our sample tend to be better informed than the Labour voters in terms of political knowledge; somewhat more of them (to take but one example) knew the name of the leader of the Labour Party. Furthermore, Conservative voters show no signs of a greater sense of political futility. In short, the Conservatives appear to be as well integrated as Labour voters into the political process in contemporary Britain.

Conservative working-class voters proved to be much more committed to their party in terms of a range of criteria than Labour voters. While Labour is widely perceived as more concerned with the interests of the common man, it is often seen as more solicitous than efficacious, while the Conservatives are widely seen as more efficacious than solicitous. In short, many working-class voters believe that the Conservatives have a capacity to get things done —a superior executive ability—which appears to offset their lesser concern with the class interests of manual workers.

"Concern for the interests of the common man" is almost the only criterion on which Labour is consistently ranked higher than the Conservatives. With respect to foreign policy, Commonwealth relations, national prosperity, and the sense of patriotism, the Conservatives are evaluated as far superior by Tory voters, and as almost the equal of (or superior to) Labour by Labour voters. In fact, Conservative voters in the working class appear to enjoy greater congruence between voting behavior and broad perceptions of the parties than do Labour voters, who seem to be linked to Labour almost entirely in terms of class interest. In a political culture which values so highly the Burkean themes of consensus and national community, this suggests that working-class Conservatives may be under less ideological cross-pressure than Labour voters.

Let us turn, for the moment, from the analysis of working-class Conservative and Labour voters, to focus on the population of working-class Conservatives. Here, we can no longer rely upon the dichotomous choice situation imposed by a two-party system to provide the categories of analysis. Rather, it is necessary to develop analytic categories derived from the historical origins of working-class Conservatism in Britain.

Both Marx and Disraeli conceived working-class Conservatism to be based on what Walter Bagehot, in *The English Constitution,* called "deference": the voluntary abnegation of power by the working class in favor of an hereditary, or quasi-hereditary elite. A reading both of Bagehot and of Conservative propaganda directed at the working class suggests the following set of definitions of "deferential" Conservatism. Deferentials

(1) prefer ascribed, socially superior political leadership;

(2) prefer power to originate from the elite, rather than from the mass franchise;

(3) form and express political judgments in terms of the intrinsic characteristics of leaders, not pragmatically in terms of issues or the outcome of policy;

(4) view political outcomes benefiting the working class as indulgent or paternalistic acts by the elite, not as flowing from the machinery of government or the economy;

(5) prefer continuity to abrupt change;

(6) view the Conservative Party as more patriotic than the opposition.

We have also used a typological opposite to deference—perspectives which run counter to these traditional values; we called working-class voters with such outlooks "seculars." The question then becomes: are all, or almost all, working-class Conservatives "deferentials"—as envisioned by observers so diversely committed as Marx, Bagehot, and Disraeli? If not, what are the conditions and consequences of these two kinds of working-class Conservatism?

It is necessary to illustrate at least the single most important criterion used to define deference and secularism. We asked respondents to explain their choice for Prime Minister as between two men—one of them the son of a banker and MP, a graduate of Eton and Oxford, and an officer in the Guards; the other, the son of a lorry (truck) driver who went to a grammar school, won a scholarship to a provincial university, entered the Army as a private and was promoted to officer rank. We have, then, caricatured but not unrealistic pictures of ascribed, elitist leadership and of achieved leadership of working-class origin. A few quotations will give the flavor of the distinctions made possible by this procedure.

> *Deferential responses:* [Respondent prefers son of MP.] "Because he should have the brains or instincts of parents. The qualities to make a prime minister are in the breeding. When it comes to critical questions like whether the country should go to war you want someone with a good headpiece who knows what he's doing. It's born in you."
>
> "The MP's son. Breeding counts every time. I like to be set an example and have someone I can look up to. I know the other man has got a long way on his own merits, and I do admire that, but breeding shows and is most important in that position."
>
> *Secular responses:* [Respondent prefers lorry (truck) driver's son.] "He has struggled in life. He knows more about the working troubles of the ordinary person. Those who inherit money rarely know anything about real life. This man has proved he is clever and can achieve something without any help from others."
>
> "Either of them because it depends upon their individual ruling ability."

Using this criterion alone, it was possible to compare working-class voters for the two parties. Deference is considerably more common among Conservative than Labour voters. Half of the Conservatives, but only one-fifth of the Labour voters, preferred the Prime Minister of elite social origin. It seems that deferential perspectives continue to sustain the Conservatism of very many working-class voters in contemporary urban England.

Among working-class Conservatives, it was possible to classify individuals on the basis of more of the six criteria defining deference and secularism. When we look for social differences between these two ideological kinds of working-class Conservatives, the factors of age, sex, and income that failed to discriminate (or do so decreasingly) between Labour and Conservative voters, come to life: deferentials tend strongly to be older than seculars and to have lower incomes; and there is a marked, but lesser tendency for fewer women than men to be seculars.

Insofar as youth and higher incomes are linked to postwar social change—to which women can be thought of as socially less exposed than men—secularism may be displacing deference as an ideological basis of working-class Conservatism in Britain. It is not possible, however, definitively to establish this conclusion by means of observations at one point in time. Moreover, the themes and motifs of traditional, hierarchical Conservatism—so richly available in British culture—may well be available for resuscitation under the impact of future events.

Some political attitudes of deferentials and seculars diverge. Seculars, for example, are less often unconditionally committed to the Conservative Party: almost all the deferentials, but only half the seculars, said that they would definitely vote Conservative in an imminent hypothetical election—a result obtained long before the pressures of the campaign, and of the necessity for choice, precipitated long-standing loyalties. There is a moderate, but consistent tendency for seculars to be more frequently "leftist" on a variety of issues and judgments. There is considerable evidence to suggest that seculars are more concerned with social mobility: many more of them than deferentials endorse a complaint that it is "too hard for a man with ambition to get ahead in Britain." Finally, seculars seem to be more sensitized to economic deprivation: among low-income working-class Conservatives (but not those with high incomes), seculars are much more likely to identify with the working class than are deferentials (Table 2).

Table 2—Among Working-Class Conservatives with Below-Average Incomes, Seculars Are More Likely than Deferentials to Identify with the Working Class*

Class Identification	BELOW-AVERAGE INCOMES			ABOVE-AVERAGE INCOMES		
	Deferential	Mixed (percent)	Secular	Deferential	Mixed (percent)	Secular
Working class	58	70	89	77	73	73
Middle class	34	21	11	23	13	21
Other, don't know	8	9	—	—	14	6
N (= 100%)	26	24	18	13	15	34

* The income of the chief wage earners of forty-eight respondents could not be ascertained.

Keeping in mind that deferentials are considerably older than seculars, we can now suggest why, as we have reported, low income has a conservatizing effect among older working-class voters, but seems to move younger ones in the direction of Labour. Low income may be tolerated by deferential Conservatives and, indeed, experienced as calling for increased reliance upon the traditional elite. But for seculars, low income may represent a severe strain upon their commitment to the Conservative Party—a commitment based upon pragmatic rather than traditional grounds. The political impact of low income, then, depends on the values and perspectives upon which party loyalty is based. Analogous reasoning may account for the uniquely high level of Conservative voting among older, working-class women: both their age and sex combine to leave them relatively unexposed to "secularization" among Conservative voters; hence, they are less able to withdraw support from the traditional elite.

We can also suggest why the typical correlates of working-class rightist voting—age, sex, and income—do not obtain, or are decreasing, in contemporary Britain. We are, perhaps, witnessing a shift from the politicized ethos of earlier working-class protest to what has been called the "post-political" age. In the earlier context, traditionalist ideologies like deference were linked, in the working class, to low income (among unskilled rural migrants from traditional backgrounds), to women (relatively insulated from change), and to the older (who had been socialized into traditional values); hence, these characteristics in turn were often linked to rightist voting. But as working-class Conservatism is stabilized in Britain on the basis of ideologies more appropriate to industrial culture, like secular Conservatism, the earlier empirical correlations between working-class rightist voting and these attributes begin to diminish.

Does this mean that something like Jacksonian, or more generally egalitarian, perspectives are emerging in the working-class electorate? Not necessarily. Even in the United States, as Robert Lane has suggested, inegalitarian values have important functions for the industrial working class.[9] And, as Gabriel Almond has argued, traditional elements in modern political culture can be seen not as deviant, anachronistic, or atavistic, but as serving critically important expressive and symbolic purposes.[10] Where would these things be more likely to persist than in the peculiarly and triumphantly mixed political culture of Britain, in which traditional themes bear so close a relationship to the very sense of nationality?

The data contain other suggestions as to the future of working-class deference. For example, as younger working-class Conservative voters appear to move away from deference—at least for the present—younger Labour voters are not; indeed, they may be moving toward it. Thus, proportionately more younger than older Conservatives prefer the lorry driver's son as Prime Minister, but somewhat more younger than older Labour voters prefer the candidate of elite social origin (Table 3). It is possible that, while secularism

Table 3—Older Working-Class Voters Are More Likely than Younger to Prefer a Prime Minister of Elite Social Origin Among Conservative Voters, but Not Among Labour Voters

	LABOUR VOTERS		CONSERVATIVE VOTERS	
	Below age 44	Abover age 44	Below age 44	Above age 44
	(percent)		(percent)	
Prefers Prime Minister of:				
Working class origin	70	80	54	39
Elite origin	27	17	40	53
Neither, don't know	3	3	6	8
N (= 100%)	207	218	65	113

is "modern" for working-class Conservatives it is less so for Labour voters. It is as if deferential predispositions among working-class voters for both major parties are converging toward a common level.

It may be, then, that as recent social change in Britain—expanded working-class horizons, improved access to education, higher incomes, the slow erosion of class boundaries—is diluting deference among Conservatives, the resulting greater integration of the working class into British society is confronting Labour voters with traditional themes to which they had previously been unexposed or hostile. Such themes, deference among them, may, in the Britain to come, begin to lose their intimate connection with the Conservative Party and become more than ever norms for the good citizen, regardless of party loyalty. Indeed, the data show that the connection between deference and Conservative voting is far stronger among older than among younger workers (Table 4). Thus, deference may be declining among Conservative

Table 4—Deference Is More Closely Linked to Conservative Voting Among Older than Younger Working-Class Voters, Regardless of Income

Prefers Prime Minister of:	BELOW-AVERAGE INCOME				ABOVE-AVERAGE INCOME			
	Below age 44		Above age 44		Below age 44		Above age 44	
	Elite origin (deferential)	Working-class origin (secular)	Elite origin (deferential)	Working-class origin (secular)	Elite origin (deferential)	Working-class origin (secular)	Elite origin (deferential)	Working-class origin (secular)
	(percent)				(percent)			
Labour	70	86	36	76	64	75	48	81
Conservative	30	14	64	24	36	25	52	19
N (= 100%)	19	51	47	105	44	95	33	63

working-class voters, increasing or maintaining itself among Labour voters, and thus becoming less factional and more consensual among the working-class electorate.

At least until 1964, however, it appeared that postwar social change in urban Britain had acted less dramatically to change the frequency with which working-class electors voted Conservative than to shift the social and ideological basis of working-class Conservative allegiance from the older and poorer to the younger and better paid, from deferentials to seculars. The Conservative Party is well prepared by its history to cope with this change. But one hundred years after the Reform of 1867, the decline of deference among working-class Conservatives sharpens the party's need to attract the increasingly prosperous descendants of the Victorian working men whom Disraeli and his followers enfranchised.

Five years after that reform, Bagehot, fearing the domination of the "poor ignorant people," saw deference as crucial to "the happy working of a delicate experiment."[11] As working-class Conservatives come to include fewer of the poor and the deferential, the shape of the party's relationship to its working-class voters remains to be clarified by time, research, and the course of events.

NOTES

1. 1886 marks the beginning of modern electoral history in Britain since the Third Reform Act of 1884 and the redistribution of seats in 1885 carried the country almost the whole way to "one *man* one vote" and "one vote one value." The Liberal Party won its only clear-cut victory in 1906, although it was able to rule with the support of other parties after the election of 1892 and the two elections of 1910; Labour won its first working majority in 1945, although it formed minority governments in 1924 and 1929–31 and ruled briefly without a working majority in 1950–51.

2. For a perceptive analysis of the problems involved in the adjustment of western European political societies to these social and political changes see R. Bendix, "The Lower Classes and the Democratic Revolution," *Industrial Relations,* 1 (1) (Oct. 1961), pp. 91–116.

3. The most recent exposition of this view is to be found in Leon Bramson, *The Political Context of Sociology* (Princeton; Princeton Univ. Press, 1961), Chap. 1.

4. It is not intended to suggest that the British Conservative Party was monolithic

in its reactions to the political problems of industrialism; at many critical periods there were acute internal tensions within the party between the advocates of differing political strategies.

5. T. E. Kebbel (ed.), *Selected Speeches of the Earl of Beaconsfield,* (London, 1882) II, pp. 530 ff.

6. *Karl Marx and Frederick Engels on Britain* (Moscow, 1953), pp. 499–500.

7. Peter Shore, *The Real Nature of Conservatism,* Labour Party Educational Series, No. 3, Sept. 1952.

8. Field work was carried out during May-June 1958, a time of political quiescence in Britain, and eighteen months before the subsequent general election.

9. R. E. Lane, "The Fear of Equality," *American Political Science Review,* 53 (1) (March 1959), pp. 35–51. See also his *Political Ideology* (New York: The Free Press, 1962), pp. 57–81.

10. G. Almond and J. Coleman, *The Politics of the Developing Areas* (Princeton: Princeton Univ. Press, 1960), pp. 20–25.

11. *The English Constitution* (intro. to 2d ed., 1872; London: Fontana Library, 1963), p. 275.

Two

Continental Europe

Four

Political Cleavage and Social Stratification in France and Italy

Mattei Dogan

INTRODUCTION

France and Italy, alike in their Latin and Catholic heritage, offer many similarities from the point of view of economic structure, social morphology, and psychosocial stratification. These two old countries are characterized by great regional diversity, and the impact of history has been heavy. Their multiparty political systems and ideologically divided labor movements reflect the whole range of the political spectrum. They are also the only two Western countries, with the exception of Finland, which have powerful Communist

129

parties. Together with Finland, they have undergone swift economic development during the last twenty years. Besides Germany and Japan, few countries have shown faster rates of economic growth. And finally, France (until 1958) and Italy share with Finland the record for the greatest cabinet turnover among the democratic governments of the world today.

This means that comparisons between the political attitudes of Frenchmen and Italians can be carried out within largely similar contexts. But I shall not seek analogies at all costs. I have tried to go beyond the mere juxtaposition of two parallel studies and have emphasized comparisons: whenever possible, I have dealt simultaneously with the two countries. However, in some cases, where contrasts exist, I have considered each country separately for the sake of clarity.

The voting behavior of the various social strata is presented first. Next, other variables are considered—sex, age, level of education, social identification, and so forth. All these data lead us to trace an outline of a political typology. Extending the analysis further, we shall examine electoral behavior in the light of its regional diversity and historical dimension. We shall then return to the present in order to observe the political parties in their recent dynamic aspects.

Any sociological study of voting behavior is inevitably caught in a vicious circle. A thorough analysis should not be limited to such gross categories as working class and middle class. One must consider the complexity of the economic and psychosocial stratification in urban and rural milieus. Nevertheless, the more one takes into account the actual social diversity, the more one is limited to rough guesses and surmises. What one gains in following the shape of social diversity more closely, one loses in attempting to ramify the political cleavages of the social categories. Indeed, the greater the number of social strata differentiated, the less reliable the results of opinion surveys become, because the number of cases in each analytic category is reduced. It is much easier to determine the relationship between the working-class vote and the socialist tendency than to estimate the variations of this tendency among skilled, semiskilled, and unskilled workers. Similarly, it is easier to look for the relationship between the rural population as a whole and the conservative tendency than to calculate the correlation between the diverse social categories of the agricultural population and party vote. Thus, paradoxically, the more one looks for precision in the social infrastructure, the more one risks being imprecise in analyzing the social bases of each party.

It is more difficult to analyze voting behavior in a multiparty system than in a two-party system, because political diversity is then added to social diversity. Finally, all these difficulties are compounded when, without oversimplifying social structures, one attempts international comparisons.

The regional diversity of France and Italy from the economic, social, religious, cultural, and political viewpoint facilitates the analysis of the social composition of the various parties by means of the ecological method. It is hardly necessary to emphasize that, contrary to the traditional method of electoral geography, which uses the technique of relating characteristics presented on maps, ecological analysis deals with the spatial distribution of phenomena by statistical correlations which permit the direct search for causal relationships and aims to go beyond the geographical framework.

The ecological method seems particularly relevant for France and Italy, since opinion surveys are carried out there under much more difficult conditions than in countries like the United States or Great Britain. Many factors such as the greater regional diversity, multiparty systems, a peasant class that is in many respects psychologically impenetrable, and the reluctance of some voters, particularly Communists, to indicate their voting choice, make polling very difficult in France and Italy. These difficulties must not be underestimated, although they can be overcome. The French and Italian institutes specializing in opinion surveys based on stratified samples deserve particular credit for successfully resolving some of these problems. Thus, they have been able to demonstrate that most of the "recalcitrants" who refuse to state their political choice are potentially Communist voters who fear to declare themselves as such, despite the guarantees of secrecy given by the interviewers. Techniques have been worked out to remedy this. Of course, a margin of error may persist in opinion surveys, but it is no larger than the margin of approximation that necessarily intervenes in the interpretation of the correlations and indices obtained by ecological methods.

For these reasons, it would appear that the best way to analyze voting in France and Italy, and perhaps in some other countries as well, is by means of a combination of the results obtained by ecological analysis with the findings of opinion surveys based on stratified samples.

THE POLITICAL DIVISION OF
THE "WORKING CLASS"

Both France and Italy are characterized by a strong regional concentration of industry. The proportion of workers in the active male population[1] varies considerably: 65 percent in the Moselle as against only 10 percent in the Gers; 66 percent in the province of Varese, as compared to 15 percent in Nuoro (Sardinia). The strength of the different parties is just as varied. Thus, in France, in the 1956 elections, Communist votes rose to 47 percent in Creuse and fell to 7 percent in Vendée; in Italy, in the 1953 elections, from 43 percent in the province of Livorno, to 4 percent in the province of Bolzano.[2] The same holds true for the Socialist Party as well.

Is there some relation between this double diversity in each of these countries? We shall look for such a relationship first in the cities, then at the level of the *départements* and the provinces.

The Workers' Vote in Large Cities

In the urban setting, the number of people employed in agriculture is negligible, and the proportion of industrial workers is far higher than in the total electorate. We have carried out such an analysis, based on seventy-one French and seventy-seven Italian cities of over fifty thousand inhabitants.

In the case of a "macrocephalic" country such as France, the situation in the Paris cluster should be analyzed first. For the city of Paris itself in the 1956 elections, the ratio between the percentage of Communist votes and that of the workers' votes was .77, which means that if we arbitrarily postulate that all Communist voters are workers, then at the maximum 77 percent of the workers voted Communist. But in Paris there live many clerks and lower civil servants, of whom at least a fifth, according to some surveys, are Communists. To these should be added some other social categories from which Communist voters are drawn. If, on the basis of various indices, we assume that a fourth of the Communist voters are not workers, we find that 55 percent of the Parisian workers voted Communist.

Paris suburbs present a very different picture, particularly fifteen satellite towns, where the electorate is mainly composed of workers living in a proletarian subculture and working in big enterprises where trade unions are influential. Thus, in 1956, the Communist Party received more than half of the valid ballots cast in these working-class communities. The ratio between Communist votes and workers' votes is .85. It is substantially higher than that found in Paris itself. On the other hand, because the proportion of workers in the active male population is much higher in these working-class suburbs than it is in Paris (64 percent as compared to 38 percent), one may assume without the least hesitation that the proportion of nonworkers among Communist voters is lower in the Paris suburbs than it is in Paris proper. We might even venture to estimate that in the 1956 elections, in the "red belt" of Paris, two-thirds of the working class voted Communist, and that four-fifths of the Communist voters belonged to the working class.[3] But as we shall see from the following, the political behavior of the Parisian workers is not representative of workers in other cities.

Let us consider the twenty-four French cities with over a hundred thousand. The ratio of Communist votes to workers' votes varies greatly from one city to the next: .30 in Strasbourg, .28 in Metz, .24 in Mulhouse, as compared with .62 for Le Havre and .87 for Toulon. In these twenty-four cities, where on the average almost half the male and female voters are from the working class, the Communist Party obtained only 25.8 percent of the votes in 1956.[4] Under the absurd hypothesis that all the Communists were workers, half of the workers did not vote Communist. If we assume that 10 percent of the Communists were not workers, then 45 percent of the workers appear to be Communists. Such an hypothesis implies that 5 percent of the voters from other social categories voted for the Communist Party, an obviously insufficient proportion. But if we were to increase this proportion, we should have to diminish correspondingly the number of Communist workers.

In the seventy-one major French cities, nearly five million votes were cast in the 1956 elections, of which 2,175,000 were from the industrial working class (*Table 1*). The Communist Party obtained 1,418,000 votes—not all of them from workers, of course. A certain number must have come from clerks, lower civil servants, artisans, shopkeepers, and so on. The results of opinion surveys, as well as of elections within the white-collar unions and the civil service associations, suggest that approximately one quarter of the Communist votes in these cities came from nonmanual strata. In other words, out of a total of 1,418,000 Communist votes, about one million appear to have been cast by workers. If this assumption is valid, one must conclude that half (49 percent) of the workers residing in the major French cities, Paris included, voted Communist. If one reduces the estimate of nonworkers among Communist voters from 25 percent to 20 percent, then the number of workers voting Communist would rise slightly, to 52 percent, while that of the nonworkers voting Communist would drop to 9 percent.

Table 1—Workers' Suffrage and Communist Vote in the Main Cities of France and Italy

France: 71 cities with more than 50,000 inhabitants (including Paris)
Italy: 77 cities with more than 50,000 inhabitants

France 1956 Elections (in thousands)		Italy 1953 Elections (in thousands)
4,963	Total votes cast in the elections	7,972
2,175	Industrial workers' votes	3,810
1,418	Communist votes	1,925
2,788	Votes of other social categories	4,162
757	Minimum number of industrial workers who did not vote Communist, assuming all Communist voters were industrial workers	1,885
44.3	Percent of industrial workers	48.0
28.9	Percent of Communist votes	24.2
65.0	Highest possible percent of industrial workers voting Communist	50.0
	Hypothesis { France: if 25% of the Communists are not workers: Italy: if 15% of the Communists are not workers:	
355	—number of Communist nonworkers	289
1,063	—number of Communist industrial workers	1,636
1,112	—number of non-Communist industrial workers	2,174
49.0	Percent of industrial workers voting Communist	43.0
13.0	Percent of other social categories voting Communist	7.0

In Italy, at the time of the 1951 census, there were seventy-seven cities with a population over 50,000. In the 1953 elections, nearly eight million votes were cast in these cities, 3,810,000 of which came from the industrial working class. The Communist Party received 1,925,000 votes. Even if all the Communist votes had come from the working class, nevertheless, half of that class did not vote Communist (*see Table 1*).

If we assume that a third of the 210,000 agricultural laborers living in these cities voted Communist, then there would remain 220,000 Communist votes that were cast neither by the industrial workers nor by agricultural laborers, which would represent 5 percent of the votes cast by all other social categories (a bit less than four million). Most of these votes should be attributed to clerks and lower civil servants, whose electoral potential may be evaluated at 1,400,000. According to various indices, 10 percent of the clerks and civil servants would have voted Communist, as against 2 percent of the independent lower and middle bourgeoisie. If the latter percentage seems too low, then the proportion of nonworkers among the Communists should be increased (20 instead of 15 percent). The proportion of workers voting Communist would then diminish: 40 instead of 43 percent.

But, as in France, this average cloaks a strong diversity. The proportion of industrial workers varies considerably from one city to the next: 76 percent in Carrara, as compared to 15 percent in Andria. The same holds true for the Communist votes: 52 percent in Cerignola, as against 7.5 percent in Trapani. Nevertheless, there is no relation between the two curves:

in cities with hardly any industry the Communist Party receives an impressive number of votes, while in workers' towns, it gets very few (*Table 2*).

Table 2—Worker Conservatism in a Predominantly Working-Class Context in Italy

Cities	% of industrial workers	% for PCI[a]	% for PCI + PSI[b]	Index % PCI/ % Industrial workers	Index (% PCI + PSI)/ % industrial workers
Massa	71	20.4	39.0	29	54
Monza	68	13.7	30.4	20	45
Busto Arsizio	62	14.7	33.7	24	54
Bolzano	57	8.7	22.7	14	37
Varese	56	9.4	28.5	17	51
Vicenza	55	14.3	26.8	26	49
Bergamo	53	8.3	20.6	16	40
Verona	52	13.7	31.9	26	60
Como	52	10.5	27.8	20	53
Trento	50	8.2	18.1	16	36
Salerno	50	11.7	30.4	21	55
Treviso	44	12.2	23.5	28	53
Averages	56	13.2	28.0	24	50

[a] PCI = Partito Comunista Italiano (Italian Communist Party).
[b] PSI = Partito Socialista Italiano (Italian Socialist Party).

In the five leading cities of Italy (Rome, Milan, Turin, Genoa, and Naples) where 1,885,000 workers' votes were cast in the 1953 elections, the Communist Party received only 791,000 votes. If we arbitrarily assume that all the Communist votes came from the industrial working class, the conclusion would have to be that, at most, 42 percent of the workers voted Communist. In all likelihood, only a third of the workers voted for the Communists.

Analysis of the Workers' Vote at the Level of the Départements and Provinces

If, on a scattergram, we place along the X-axis the percentage of industrial workers for each French *département,* and along the Y-axis the percentage of Communist votes, we do not observe any relation between these two variables, whatever the date of the elections—1946, 1951, 1956, 1958, or 1962. If we add together the percentage of industrial workers and that of agricultural laborers, the dispersion is hardly modified. An analysis at the level of the cantons shows a significant correlation for certain regions (Brittany, Normandy, Alsace-Lorraine, Nord, Pas-de-Calais, and so on), but not for the whole of France.

If we add the Communist and Socialist votes together, we again observe a great dispersion. In *Fig. 1* we can see that fifty-three *départements* lie above the diagonal, which means that the proportion of workers there is higher than that of the Socialist-Communist vote, whereas the contrary is true in the other thirty-seven *départements*. If we add together the percentage of industrial workers and that of agricultural laborers, some *départements* move closer to the diagonal, while others move farther away. The absence of a

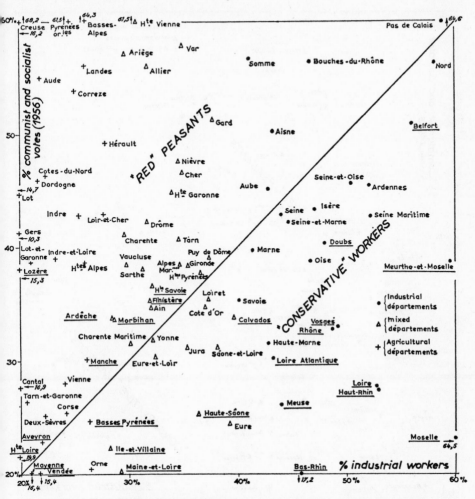

Figure 1—"Conservative" Workers and "Red" Peasants in France.

relation between the strength of the working class and the strength of the Communist and Socialist parties is clearly apparent. The essential factor accounting for it could be the Catholic influence on the workers in certain regions. Communism and Socialism find it difficult to penetrate them. In order to stress this Catholic resistance, we have, in the graph, underlined those *départements* which stand out for their strong religious observance.[5]

The picture is the same for Italy: *Fig. 2,* indicating the ninety provinces, shows clearly the absence of a relation between the percentages of industrial workers and Communist-Socialist votes. However, if we include agricultural laborers, a few clusters of dots appear, several cumulus clouds show up on both sides of the diagonal, and some stratus clouds can be observed along it. But if the wide dispersion is absorbed into clumps it better emphasizes regional diversity.[6]

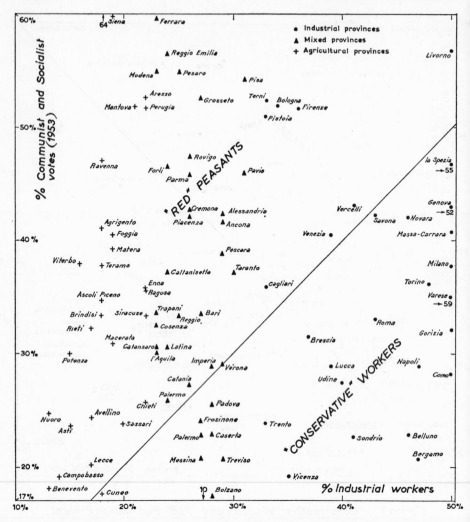

Figure 2—"Conservative" Workers and "Red" Peasants in Italy.

In Search of "Conservative" and "Traditionalist" Workers

In the graph, each *département* or province is represented by one dot, whatever its demographic weight. We should therefore take the analysis a step further by considering the *départements* and provinces from the viewpoint of the size of their population, and particularly, of the working class. The regional concentration of the working class allows us to isolate, for our analysis, a great number of workers within a small number of administrative units.

In Italy, according to the 1951 census, the province of Milan alone contains as many industrial workers as twenty-five other provinces combined.

The two biggest industrial centers of Italy, Milan and Turin, include as many workers as a third of all the provinces. If we add Rome, we reach a number of workers equal to that in half the provinces, and if we then add Naples, we attain a figure higher than for fifty-four provinces.

In these four great provinces, 46 percent of the electorate is composed of workers. Now, in the 1953 elections, the Communist Party only obtained 22 percent of the votes (and nearly as much in the succeeding elections of 1958 and 1963). If for a moment we accept the absurd hypothesis that all these Communist votes came from the working class, then it will be obvious that more than half of the workers did not vote for the Communist Party. As for the Socialist Party, it received 12 percent of the votes. Even if all the Communist or Socialist voters had been workers, this would mean that one out of every four workers was a "conservative."

We can push the analysis further by adding six other provinces (Genova, Como, Udine, Varese, Brescia, and Bergamo) to the four mentioned above. We then reach a total of 3,570,000 working-class votes, out of a total of 8,800,000 for the whole of Italy. In 1953, in these ten provinces, although 47 percent of the voters were workers, the Communist Party obtained only 20 percent of the votes, and the Socialist Party 13.4 percent, that is, for the two parties together 33.4 percent. Thus, under the assumption that all of these votes were cast by workers, a minimum of 29 percent of the workers voted neither Communist nor Socialist.

We might go further still, this time considering twenty provinces which aggregate nearly half the Italian working class, and where 45 percent of the voters are workers. Yet, the PCI received only 17 percent of the votes. A simple confrontation of these two percentages demonstrates that at least three-fifths of the workers were not Communists. But local monographs, public opinion surveys, results of trade union elections, socioprofessional distribution of the membership of the Communist Party, and the like, show that it drew the votes of a great many agricultural laborers, tenant farmers, clerks, and lower civil servants. If, on the basis of these indices, we accept the hypothesis that at least 20 percent of the Communist votes did not come from the working class, then it follows that 70 percent of the workers did not vote for the Communist Party. This hypothesis implies, besides, that 6 percent of the other voters chose this party.

If we add the Socialist vote (14.3 percent), we reach a total of 31.3 percent of the votes for the PCI and the PSI, a proportion which, divided by that of industrial workers, gives us a ratio of 66. This means that even if all the Communist and Socialist votes had come from the working class— hypothesis which is even more absurd for both than for the PCI alone— there would remain a third of the workers who voted neither Communist nor Socialist. The proportion of nonworkers among the Socialists is certainly higher than among the Communists. Ecological analyses and public opinion surveys leave no doubt about that. Various calculations lead us to estimate that only half of the workers in these twenty provinces voted Communist or Socialist. As for the other half of the workers' vote, according to certain indices, the Italian Social Democratic Party obtained one out of five, and the Liberals, Monarchists, and Neo-Fascists 5 percent at most. Thus, according to our estimates, the remaining third of the working-class in these twenty provinces would have voted for the Christian Democratic Party.

In France, more than a third of the workers can be found in twelve highly industrialized *départements,*[7] where 54 percent of the voters belong to the working class on the average but where the Communist Party obtained only 23 percent of the votes in 1956. If we arbitrarily suppose that the only source of all the Communist votes is the working class, it would appear that, at most, 42 percent of the workers voted Communist. But this hypothesis is clearly absurd, for all Communist voters are surely not workers. Without doubt a certain number of agricultural laborers, clerks, lower civil servants, artisans, and other "little people" voted Communist, although we are unable to determine in what precise proportions. In all likelihood, only a third of the workers in these twelve *départements* voted Communist.

In some heavily populated *départements,* such as Moselle, Haut-Rhin, Bas-Rhin, and others, the numbers of working-class voters is three times higher than the number of Communists and Socialists. In other words, at least two-thirds of the workers voted "conservative" or "traditionalist."

Ecology of Communism: a Typological Outline of the Départements and Provinces

In view of this discrepancy between the distributions of workers and of Communist voters, a typological outline of French *départements* and Italian provinces might give a better picture of the spread of Communism in the various social categories.

First of all, we have classified the *départements* and provinces according to their degree of industrialization. We thus obtain three categories: industrialized, mixed, and agricultural.[8] Then, within each category there has been a further classification, according to the ratio resulting from the division of the percentage of Communist votes by that of workers' votes. This ratio (multiplied by 100) varies in Italy from 16 for Bergamo to 257 for Siena; in France from 23 for Haut-Rhin to 290 for Creuse. Finally, the *départements* and provinces have been reclassified into three categories: "red" (ratio higher than 100); "pink" (ratio between 50 and 100 for Italy, between 60 and 100 for France); "blue" (ratio less than 50 for Italy, less than 60 for France). On the basis of these two criteria (degree of industrialization and ratio), we obtain eight types of *départements* or provinces (*Tables 3 and 4*).[9]

The criteria chosen might appear too rigid for a reality so diverse and complex. Certainly, this typological classification is not satisfactory in every respect. It would be possible to improve it, by making it more subtle, provided we increase the number of types, but this would present some disadvantages. Nevertheless, we should not lose sight of the fact that any typology is by definition more or less arbitrary, because it sacrifices details in order to emphasize essential features.

As such, this classification permits an analysis of the diffusion of Communism in the working class. As a matter of fact, the ratio between the percentage of Communist votes and that of workers' votes determines, for most of the *départements* or provinces, the maximum percentage of Com-

Table 3—Typology of French Départements
Workers' Votes and Communist Votes

	Type	Elections of 1956	Votes cast (in thousands)	% of industrial workers	% Communist votes	Index % Communist votes/ % workers
blue	A 12	industrialized départements	4,556	50.0	23.1	40
	B 20	mixed départements	4,316	31.8	19.1	60
	C 9	agricultural départements	1,462	22.6	11.8	52
		Total and averages	10,334	38.7	20.0	52
pink	A 15	industrialized départements	6,503	42.9	32.1	75
	B 8	mixed départements	1,305	32.4	30.4	94
	C 4	agricultural départements	380	22.4	22.2	99
		Total and averages	8,188	40.4	33.7	83
red	A 6	Mixed départements	876	30.8	34.2	111
	B 6	Agricultural départements	2,092	21.2	28.9	136
		Total and averages	2,968	24.1	30.5	125
		France	21,490	37.2	25.7	—

munist workers, according to the theoretical hypothesis that all Communist votes are cast by the working class. For other *départements* or provinces, this classification highlights the minimum number of Communist voters who do not belong to the industrial working class.

Table 4—Typology of Italian Provinces
Workers' Votes and Communist Votes

	Type	Elections of 1953	Votes cast (in thousands)	% of industrial workers	% of agricultural workers	% Communist votes	Index % PCI/ % industrial workers
blue	A 17	industrialized provinces	7,769	47	4	18.0	38
	B 3	mixed provinces	923	29	12	8.7	30
		Total and averages	8,692	45	5	17.0	36
pink	C 8	industrialized provinces	2,930	41	9	25.2	61
	D 20	mixed provinces	6,011	27	19	20.5	76
	E 8	agricultural provinces	1,713	18	14	14.4	80
		Total and averages	10,654	28	14	20.8	74
red	F 3	industrialized provinces	1,283	35	6	37.9	108
	G 12	mixed provinces	2,567	27	18	34.3	127
	H 19	agricultural provinces	3,842	19	19	27.1	143
		Total and averages	7,692	23	16	37.3	134
		Italy	27,038	33	12	22.6	—

On the basis of this typology, it is possible to estimate the proportion of workers voting Communist. The least hazardous method consists in formulating, for each type of *département* or province, a series of hypotheses as to the proportion of nonworker voters among the Communists. Using various indices and local studies, one is able to appreciate the reliability of such estimates from the resulting proportion of Communists among voters from other social categories. It is obvious that the percentage of workers who vote Communist is a function of the percentage of nonworker voters among the Communists.

Aside from the indication provided by the ecological analysis upon which the typology is based, various data are available for the formulation of these hypotheses: public opinion surveys, local monographs, socioprofessional distribution of the members of the various parties, the returns of union elections, and so on.[10]

We cannot enter here into the details of the calculations undertaken for each type of *département* or province. We limit ourselves to presenting, in *Table 5,* a global and comparative estimate of the distribution of the workers' votes between the political parties. Naturally, these are conjectural figures.

To sum up, we may estimate that in France, half the working class voted Communist in 1956 (nearly as many as in 1951), as against less than two-fifths of the Italian workers in 1958 (a bit less than in 1953). But the Italian Socialist and Social Democratic Parties drew more ballots from workers than their French counterpart. Finally, in both countries, two-thirds of the working class voted for Marxist-inspired parties (*Fig. 3*). But it is the final third—composed of Catholic, Conservative, Gaullist, radical, or Neo-Fascist workers—which is the most interesting from a sociological viewpoint.

Political Stratification of the Industrial Working Class

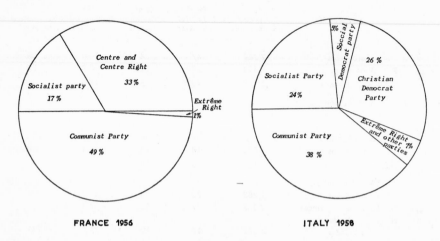

FRANCE 1956   ITALY 1958

Figure 3

Table 5—Political Cleavage of the Industrial Working Class in France and Italy

THE ENTIRE ELECTORATE			THE WORKERS' ELECTORATE	
Conjectural Estimate (in thousands)			Conjectural Estimate (in thousands)	
France 1956	Italy 1958		France 1956	Italy 1958
26,775	31,888	Voters	10,300	10,460
		Abstentions, nullified		
5,285	2,328	ballots	2,300	700
21,490	29,560	Valid votes	8,000	9,760
5,530	6,700	Communists	3,900	3,700
3,270	5,560	Socialists[a]	1,370	2,810
2,370	12,520	Christian-Democrats[b]	900	2,520
		Conservatives, Liberals,		
7,580	1,940	Radicals[c]	1,730	200
2,740	2,840	Extreme Right[d]	100	530
(percent)			(percent)	
25.7	22.7	Communists	49 ⎱66	38 ⎱67
15.2	18.7	Socialists	17 ⎰	29 ⎰
11.1	42.4	Christian-Democrats	11	26
		Conservatives, Liberals,		
35.2	6.6	Radicals	22	2
12.8	9.6	Extreme Right	1	5
100.0	100.0	Total	100	100
% of workers among the		Communists	71	55
		Socialists	42	52
		Christian-Democrats	38	20
		Conservatives, Liberals,		
		Radicals, etc.	22	10
		Extreme Right	4	19
			37.2	33.0

[a] For France, SFIO; for Italy, PSI (Italian Socialist Party) and PSDI (Italian Democratic Socialist Party).
[b] France, MRP (Popular Republican Movement); Italy, DC (Christian Democrats).
[c] France: Moderates, Radicals, Social Republicans; Italy: PLI (Italian Liberal Party), PRI (Italian Republican Party), Comunità (Community), PPT (Tyrolian Popular Party), and several local groups.
[d] France, classical Extreme Right and Poujade's movement; Italy, Monarchists and Neo-Fascists (MSI, Italian Social Movement).

THE MOSAIC OF THE AGRICULTURAL ELECTORATE

The diversity of the French countryside is great: experts distinguish at least six hundred distinct rural territories. Italy, too, presents an extremely varied conglomerate. Thus, half the Italian tenant-farmers are concentrated in three regions—Emilia, Tuscany, and Marche—which contain 18 percent of the electorate. If this regional diversity creates complex problems for opinion surveys in the rural areas, it permits an ecological analysis of the political cleavages of the various categories of farmers.

Italy is more of an agricultural country than France. In 1954, 26 percent of the French active population was employed in agriculture, as against 37 percent of the Italian active population. On the other hand, France is more rural than Italy. Still, the notion of rural habitat is not the same in the two countries, because it reflects in a way a different reality. As a matter of fact, in France, where 37,000 communes exist, a locality with fewer than 2,000 inhabitants is considered, administratively, as a rural locality. In Italy, where there are 8,000 communes, many official statistics set the threshold at 10,000 inhabitants.

In view of this discrepancy between the rural population and the agricultural electorate, we must have recourse to different methods for each country.

Political Cleavages of the French Agricultural Electorate

Several documentary sources, of unequal reliability, and reflecting the situation at different times, can be used for breaking down the French agricultural electorate into its various political tendencies.

The first one consists of a document compiled by the Ministry of Interior on the 1947 municipal elections. It has no official character and is unpublished. It indicates the distribution of the votes in the rural communes (under 2,000 inhabitants) where 95 percent of the population employed in agriculture was living. The electoral system for these municipal elections in most communes favored a coalition of two and even three parties on a single list, such as the frequent alliance between the Moderates and the *Rassemblement du Peuple Français* (Gaullist). These statistics have to be considered with caution, since many electors in the rural communes are employed in the industrial or tertiary sector. On the other hand, and this is a greater source of uncertainty, local factors without political significance intervene in the municipal elections. They provide, however, useful indicators.

Our second source of information comes from statistics on the returns of the 1956 legislative elections in rural communes of fifteen *départements,* where 80 percent of the votes recorded are agricultural. These data outline the implantation of Communism and Socialism in areas of small peasant landownership, as well as permitting observation of the differences in the voting behavior of small peasants and agricultural laborers.[11]

Public opinion polls periodically conducted by IFOP supply us with data pertaining not only to the distribution of the agricultural votes between the various parties, but to the motivations for the vote as well. *Table 6* presents the average of three polls taken between 1947 and 1951.

Finally, a precise and thorough analysis of 600 cantons where more than 70 percent of the active population works in agriculture, has been done by J. Klatzmann for the 1956 elections.[12] Obviously, the proportion of non-agricultural people in these cantons cannot be neglected, but as Klaztmann rightly pointed out "the distribution of the votes in a canton where three fourths of the voters are peasants approximates that for the peasants. The electoral behavior of the non-agricultural people would have to be strikingly different from that of the peasants to influence the outcome in a significant manner."[13] He extrapolated to the level of the *départements* from the data gathered for these 600 cantons,[14] and then reckoned the distribution of the agricultural votes between the various parties at the national scale.

Between these documentary sources, one can notice some discrepancies partially caused by trends in the political forces between 1947 and 1956.

One can nevertheless estimate that the Communists and Socialists together at the 1956 elections gathered less than a third of the total agricultural vote, although they won two-thirds of the suffrage of the industrial working-class.

Table 6—Political Behavior
of the French Agricultural Electorate (in percentages)*

	Communists	Socialists	Radicals	(MRP) Popular-Republicans	Moderates	(RPF) Gaullists	Extreme Right[a]
Municipal elections (1947)	13	11	20	10	47		—
Rural communes in 15 agricultural departements—elections of 1956	19	17	14	8	42		
French Institute of Public Opinion (IFOP) surveys. Average of three surveys 1947–1951	17	12	16	12	24	19	—
Analysis on 600 rural cantons—elections of 1956	17.5	14	14	12.5	15.5		16.5

* All social strata: small peasants, big and middle landowners, tenant farmers, agricultural laborers.
a Poujadist movement and traditional Extreme Right.

Political Cleavages of the Italian Agricultural Electorate

Our first methodological step for the study of political cleavages in the Italian peasantry is to delimit the agricultural electorate. In the 1958 elections, its size was 10,000,000 out of a total of 29,560,000 votes. For most of the provinces, the distribution of votes among the various parties, in communes of less than 10,000 inhabitants, is a good indication of the distribution of the agricultural ballots themselves, since the great majority of the inhabitants of these communes are occupied in agriculture.

But in some provinces, the population of the small communes is more heterogeneous. In particular, it includes many industrial workers. Elsewhere, in Puglia, Sicily, and Calabria, we find the opposite situation: large towns populated by many laborers who work in the surrounding countryside.[15]

Thus, the heavily industrialized Piedmont in one sense appears as a more "rural" region than Puglia, which is essentially agricultural. Strange as it may seem, there are proportionally more "rural" people in Lombardy, the principal industrial region of Italy, than in Sicily, primarily agricultural. Indeed, 31 percent of the inhabitants of Piedmont and 22 percent of the inhabitants of Lombardy live in communes of fewer than 3,000 inhabitants, while only 2 percent of the population of Puglia and 3 percent in Sicily live in communes of the same size. Despite these regional differences, Italy as a whole is a more urban than industrial country, less rural than agricultural, while the contrary is true of some other Western countries.

Consequently, in our analysis, we can provisionally leave out those provinces inhabited by many *city-dwelling farmers* and *rural industrial workers*. In this manner, we are able to focus on more than three-quarters of the agricultural population, living in communes of less than 10,000 inhabitants. The results thus obtained have been extrapolated to the other provinces. The margin of error involved in this extrapolation is relatively low. Of course, in different psychosocial contexts, the political behavior of a particular social category may not be identical. But in reality, the city-dwelling agricultural electorate does not exhibit the same social characteristics as the agricultural electorate of the small communes. In the agro-towns of Puglia (Andria, Cerignola, Barletta, Molfetta) for instance, we find unskilled farm laborers, while in the small communes of the same region, small landowners. Before extrapolating, we have had to resort to certain operations of weighting for some of the provinces. It turns out that these calculations balance one another at the national level.

Table 7—Demarcation of the Agricultural Electorate in Italy

1958 Elections		PCI	PSI	DC	PSDI	Other parties	Total
Total votes		6,704	4,207	12,520	1,345	4,784	29,560
Votes obtained by the various parties in communes of ... (official statistics)	more than 10,000 inhabitants	4,227	2,516	6,459	810	3,457	17,469
		24.2%	14.4%	37.0%	4.6%	19.8%	100%
	fewer than 10,000 inhabitants	2,477	1,691	6,061	535	1,327	12,091
		20.5%	14.0%	50.1%	4.4%	11.0%	100%
Agricultural vote (estimation)		2,300	1,150	5,200	300	1,050	10,000
		23%	11.5%	52%	3%	10.5%	100%

Remarks: Out of a total of 12,091,000 ballots cast in communes under 10,000 inhabitants, more than 9,500,000 were agricultural votes (from all social categories engaged in agriculture). In cities of over 10,000 inhabitants, half a million male and female voters were occupied in agriculture.

One basic fact, revealed by official statistics, cannot be strongly enough emphasized: the Christian Democratic Party received in the 1958 election half the votes cast in communes of under 10,000 inhabitants—i.e., 6,061,000 out of a total of 12,091,000 (*Table* 7), while in the big cities, this same

Table 8—Christian-Democrat Votes Related to Size of Community (in percentages)

Community Size	1946	1948	1953	1958	1963
Less than 1,000	44.3	57.9	48.8	52.4	46.0
1,000 to 3,000	42.6	55.1			
3,000 to 5,000	41.1	52.6	46.0	49.7	
5,000 to 10,000	37.8	49.9	43.0	46.2	
10,000 to 30,000	33.6	46.1	38.1	41.3	38.3
30,000 to 100,000	31.9	44.4	35.9	37.7	34.8
100,000 to 250,000	29.3	41.8	35.5	37.5	32.5
250,000 to 500,000	28.4	45.1	33.7	36.4	24.0
More than 500,000	27.0	46.3	32.7	32.0	26.9
National Average	35.1	48.5	40.1	42.4	38.3

party collected only a third of the votes. The proportion of Christian Democratic votes increases as the size of the commune diminishes. This phenomenon also occurred in the 1946, 1948, 1953, and 1963 elections (*Table* 8).

Of course, the Christian Democratic ballots cast in communes of less than 10,000 inhabitants are not all drawn from voters occupied in agriculture. According to opinion surveys in rural areas, the workers, craftsmen, small

Table 9—Regional Contrasts of the Agricultural Electorate in Italy (Results in communes where more than three-quarters of the active population are employed in agriculture) (in percentages)

1960 "Administrative" Elections	Christian Democrats	Communists and Socialists	Communists (PCI)	Socialists (PSI)
Veneto	66.9	23.6	10.0	13.6
Friuli	63.1	26.2	8.2	18.0
Liguria	55.6	24.6	16.0	8.6
Toscana	29.6	60.7	43.2	17.5
Emilia	29.3	56.4	40.2	16.2
Umbria	35.2	52.6	33.9	18.7

Source: Barberis, Dall-Oglio, and Schepis, "Il voto rurale," *Rivista Italiana di Sociologia Rurale*, 1961.

shopkeepers, and lower civil servants living in these communes backed the Christian Democratic Party less than farmers. Although the difference in voting behavior between the various social categories is relatively low, sometimes negligible, nevertheless one may estimate that the percentage of farmers who voted for the Christian Democratic Party was slightly higher than for the whole electorate of these communes.

In communes of under 10,000 population, the minor parties (Social Democratic, Liberal, Monarchist, Neo-Fascist, Republican, and so on) together collected 15 percent of the votes (see *Table 7*). In the cities, where society is more diversified, these parties found a wider audience. Even in the small communes, they draw support from the secondary or tertiary economic sectors. It is quite probable that in the 1958 election these minor parties may have received about 13 percent of the agricultural votes.[16]

Thus, if we assume that the Christian-Democratic Party in the 1958 elections gathered a bit more than half of the agricultural votes, and the minor parties less than a seventh, then the remaining third went to the Communist and Socialist parties. Incidentally, this third also represents a third of the total of the 10,911,000 Communist and Socialist votes.

Finally, for the whole of Italy, the gap between the distribution per party of the votes in communes of less than 10,000 population, and the estimate of the distribution of agricultural votes, appears very small (see *Table 7*).

Social and Political Contrasts in the Agricultural Milieu

We ought now to push the investigation a step further, by differentiating several social categories within the agricultural population because profound economic and political conflicts exist among them; they are small farmers, great and middle-class landowners, tenant farmers, and hired hands.

Social contrasts in the agricultural setting are more striking in Italy. Let us therefore begin with that country. The most numerous category is that of the small farmers. Legislation concerning social security and subventions to agriculture favors their membership in para-political organizations, so that the number of the rank and file of these organizations gives us some clues as to the political orientations of that social category. Three para-political organizations claim representativity for this class:

1. The *Confederazione dei Coltivatori Diretti*, with Christian-Democratic

ties. At its twelfth national congress, held in April 1958, it claimed a membership of 1,683,000 families, totaling 3,385,000 economically active individuals (the latter figure includes young people under twenty-one years of age, who consequently do not vote, but whose number is roughly equivalent to that of the very aged inactive peasants who do vote).[17]

2. The *Confederazione Generale dell' Agricoltura Italiana,* including small farmers as well as great and middle-class landowners. In 1957, it consisted of 417,000 families, i.e., 900,000 male and female voters, the owners of 9,140,000 acres of land—nearly a third of the agricultural surface of Italy. Its members are divided among several parties, Christian-Democratic, Liberal, Monarchist, Neo-Fascist.

3. The *Alleanza Contadina,* whose membership is low (about 200,000 families), and which is linked with the Communist Party and the Socialist Party.

In the March 1958 elections for the administrative boards of the communal social security funds, the candidates of the *Coltivatori Diretti* received 90 percent of the votes, the *Alleanza Contadina,* 9 percent, and the other lists 1 percent. The *Confederazione dell' Agricoltura Italiana* did not participate directly in these union elections. We must nonetheless take this organization into account, since more than half of its members would support the Liberal, Monarchist, or Neo-Fascist parties.

Various surveys of the Doxa Institute and of the *Centro Italiano Studi e Ricerche* show that over three-quarters of the farmer-landowners back the Christian Democratic Party. An ecological analysis stresses a strong correlation between the proportion of small and middle cultivators and that of the Christian Democratic ballots. By confronting indices of diverse nature, we can suggest conjectural estimates, with an acceptable margin of error (see *Table 15*).

If the Christian Democratic Party is the largest Italian party, this is first of all due to its support among small- and middle-income farmers, thanks to the influence of the clergy and Catholic Action, through the powerful para-political organization of the *Coltivatori Diretti.* At a higher socio-economic level, among great landowners, the Liberals, Monarchists, and Neo-Fascists form the majority.

But while the small- and middle-income landowners vote massively for the Christian Democratic Party, to the contrary the majority of tenant farmers and agricultural workers support the Communist and Socialist Parties.

Figure 4 illustrates the diffusion of Communism among tenant farmers and farm laborers. Indeed, the provinces in which Communist votes far outnumber workers are characterized by the presence of large numbers of tenant farmers and farm laborers. In most of the other provinces, small farmers predominate in the rural population.

Two-thirds of the tenant farmers are concentrated in three regions—Emilia, Tuscany, and Umbria—and this fact calls forth an ecological analysis.[18] In these three regions, the Communist and Socialist Parties obtained more than half the votes (*Table 9*). It is remarkable that the rural zones of Tuscany and Emilia are among the reddest of all western Europe today.

Even in the other regions of Italy, with the exception of Catholic Venetia,

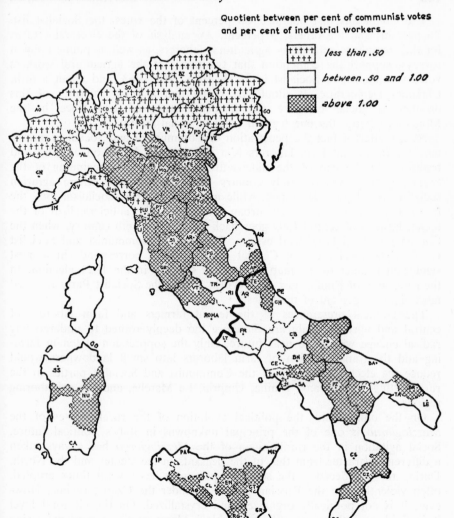

Quotient between per cent of communist votes
and per cent of industrial workers.

⁺⁺⁺⁺⁺ ⁺⁺⁺⁺	*less than .50*
(blank)	*between .50 and 1.00*
(hatched)	*above 1.00*

**Figure 4—Ecology of Italian Communism. Elections of 1953,
Census of 1951.**

most of the tenant farmers have Communist or Socialist preferences. Opinion
surveys leave us in no doubt about that.

We may find a first indicator of the attitudes of farm laborers in the
political distribution of the delegates to the congress of the *Federazzione dei
Braccianti* held in 1948. At the time, this union organization represented
most of the Italian farm-laborers (afterwards, the nomination of delegates to
the congress followed other criteria that did not reflect political tendencies).
Delegations to this congress were elected on the basis of politically colored
lists.

The Communist list obtained 68 percent of the votes; the Socialist list, 26 percent; and the others, 5 percent. An analysis of the electoral returns for the communes with many agricultural laborers, as well as public opinion surveys, support the contention that two-thirds of the agricultural workers voted Communist or Socialist in 1953, 1958, and 1963, and about a fifth, Christian Democratic. It should be noted that a small minority of this disinherited social category paradoxically expressed confidence in the Monarchist Party, the one least in favor of social reforms.

As a matter of fact the penetration of Communism and Socialism among tenant farmers and farm laborers is a phenomenon based on a rather old tradition. At the end of the nineteenth century and the beginning of the twentieth, Italy was the only country in western Europe where agrarian socialism was highly developed, while in other countries, socialism took the form of an almost exclusively urban movement. The anticlericalism of the tenant farmers of central Italy goes back to the eighteenth century, when the Church possessed large land estates. The map of Communist and Socialist votes in the rural areas of Central Italy for 1958 corresponds in a most significant manner to the map of Socialist strength in the 1921 election. In the rural area of Emilia, just after World War I, the Socialist Party received more than 60 percent of the votes.

The political preferences of the tenant farmers and farm laborers of central and northern Italy are therefore too deeply rooted to undergo any radical change within the near future. Only the suppression of tenant farming and the transformation of farm laborers into small landowners would reduce the electoral strength of the Communist and Socialist parties in the rural settings of Tuscany, Emilia, Umbria, Le Marche, and the neighboring regions.

On the other hand, the political evolution of the rural masses of the *Mezziogiorno* is one of the principal unknowns in Italy's political future. Social agitation in the rural milieu of the *Mezziogiorno* has always taken a different character from that of the peasants in the Center and the North. During the last decades, the southern peasantry has several times erupted, often violently, like the Russian peasantry under the Czarist regime. However, it is not politically organized and crystallized. On the electoral level it is fluid, and therefore still "available." Many southern peasants swing easily from one extreme to the other, from Monarchism to Communism (we shall have an opportunity to emphasize this aspect further on). Nevertheless, they remain closely tied to Christian tradition, and until recently, the clergy quite often influenced their electoral behavior. But the Catholic impact might weaken. Modern propaganda techniques are able to reach even the ignorant and illiterate. It would be relatively easy to start a process of political extremism among this peasantry. The electoral equilibrium of Italy depends on the future political orientation of these peasants, for their votes could acquire a decisive marginal weight if the electoral forces of the rural and urban milieus of northern and central Italy remains relatively stable.

If we now look at the problem from a different angle, that of the social composition of the agricultural electorate of the various parties, we can observe that in 1958, four-fifths of the agricultural voters for the Communist and Socialist parties were tenant farmers or hired hands, and that, to the contrary, four-fifths of the agricultural voters for the Christian Democrat Party were small, middle, or large landowners. In short, the political struggle in an agricultural milieu reflected the conflicts between the social classes.

The situation in France is quite different. The tenant farmers, much less numerous than in Italy, vote Catholic. And this is so because Brittany has remained traditionalist, while Tuscany and Emilia became strongholds of anticlericalism. The majority of laborers working on the big farms of northeastern France vote Communist. To the contrary, in other regions of France, laborers are employed on middle-sized farms and in a way are socially integrated into the owner's family—a situation which favors paternalism and therefore preserves them from Communist or Socialist propaganda. Accord-

Figure 5—Agrarian Communism in the Underdeveloped Areas of France.

In the 30 *départements* whose names are underlined, the proportion of small farmers and agricultural workers who vote Communist is high. All these *départements* are characterized by a low religious observance; some of them are even "dechristianized."

ing to estimates for the 1956 elections, in all of France, one-third of the farm laborers voted Communist, and one-fifth, Socialist (see *Tables 13* and *14*).

In France nearly a third of the small farmers would vote Socialist or Communist; in Italy only a tenth would do so (see *Tables 14* and *15*). The most plausible explanation for this is the overlapping of poverty and de-Christianization in some areas of the Center and South, the "inner desert" shown on the map (*Fig. 5*).[19] Moreover, these small farmers face tough competition from the big mechanized farms which are able to produce in more efficient conditions.

Thus, paradoxically, Socialism and Communism have taken root and developed in the French agricultural milieu mainly among small farmers (see *Table 10*), who remain poor although they own land; in Italy, they grew either among tenant farmers who enjoyed a relatively high standard of living, but who demanded the expropriation of the big proprietors, or else, among farm laborers who were exploited by great landowners. On one side of the Alps they vote Communist or Socialist because they aspire to the possession of the rich lands they plough; on the other side, in order to protest against the great poverty of their small farms. What they share is their anticlericalism, which, however, came about through different historical circumstances.

Table 10—Small Peasant Property Voting
Communist or Socialist:
Some Examples from the 1956 Election (percentages)

Rural Communes (less than 2,000 inhabitants)	Workers and White-Collar Employees in Industry	Agricultural Workers	Total	Communist and Socialist Votes	Difference
Creuse	10	6	16	69	53
Aude	12	22	24	59	35
Landes	16	8	24	59	35
Lot	11	3	14	44	30
Gers	8	8	16	42	26
Côtes-du-Nord	13	6	19	40	21

Remarks: According to the hypothesis that all workers or white-collar employees in industry and all agricultural workers voted Communist or Socialist, the last column indicates approximately the minimum proportion of Communist or Socialist votes from the category of small farmers (shopkeepers and craftsmen not being very numerous).

THE TWO FACES OF THE
PETTY BOURGEOISIE

At least one-third of the French and Italian voters belong to the urban middle classes. The diversity in these strata is such that the usual distinction among upper, middle, and lower-middle classes seems inadequate. The lower-middle class should be divided between employed clerks and civil servants, whose income is often below that of skilled workers, and self-employed, small shopkeepers, small contractors, and craftsmen, even if their socioeconomic position is modest. This distinction between the salaried and self-employed lower-middle classes is all the more necessary since, as we shall see, their political attitudes vary to a striking degree.

Salaried Lower-Middle Class

The differences between the standard of living and way of life of white- and blue-collar workers were rather important only a short time ago. White-collar workers were relatively better paid, they often had other sources of income which supplemented their wages, and they enjoyed a relatively good social status. In the space of one generation their situation has deteriorated. Today one-third of them receive a salary lower than that of the average skilled worker, although their way of life requires greater expenditures on certain items (clothing, for example). They now experience the same insecurity of employment as manual workers and often formulate the same wage demands as the latter; the lesser civil servants and clerks in the nationalized industries often resort to strikes. Mechanization and rationalization of work in the offices of large companies place many clerks in work conditions similar to those of manual workers, e.g., having fixed working hours, punching time clocks, and so forth.

However, the two employed strata should not be confused with one another. The one does manual work; the other keeps its hands white. As R. Girod[20] accurately noted, important psychosocial differences exist between white- and blue-collar workers. "Exploited but aggressive as workers" and at the same time "respectable and conformist as middle-class," notes M. Crozier,[21] the white-collar workers find themselves in an ambivalent social situation, which cannot but affect their political behavior.

While the *Confédération Générale du Travail* (CGT), a French trade union federation dominated by the Communist Party, obtained, in the union

Social Structure of the Communist Electorate

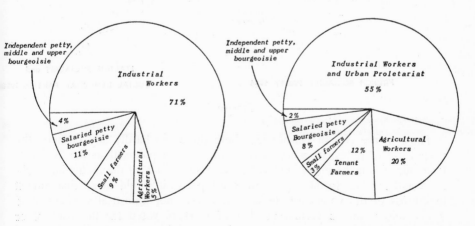

FRENCH COMMUNIST PARTY 1956   ITALIAN COMMUNIST PARTY 1958

Figure 6

elections held during the 1950's, two-thirds of the manual workers' vote, it received less than one-fourth of the vote of the white-collar workers. On the other hand, *Force Ouvrière* (FO), ideologically close to the Socialists, and the French Confederation of Christian Workers (CFTC), both minority unions among the workers, are supported by the majority of the clerks and lower civil servants.

In urban centers there is a significant relationship between the strength of the Communist Party and the proportion of clerks and lower civil servants voting Communist. Where the Communist Party is very weak, its electoral base is almost exclusively composed of manual workers (90 percent). Where it is strong, its electoral base is more heterogeneous, including at times one-fourth of the nonworkers. Since the contribution of the upper or middle strata to the Communist electorate is negligible, outside of the working class Communist votes in the cities come largely from clerks and lower civil servants. There are some cities with a relatively low proportion of manual workers where, however, the leftist vote is very high, a fact that means many white-collar workers vote left.

Social Structure of the Socialist Electorate

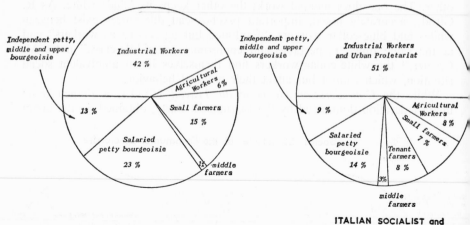

FRENCH SOCIALIST PARTY 1956

ITALIAN SOCIALIST and
SOCIAL DEMOCRAT PARTIES 1958

Figure 7

Thus, in the city of Narbonne, where there are hardly any farmers, the proportion of industrial workers is smaller by 40 points than the Socialist-Communist vote (*Table 11*). Even if we assume that all the industrial workers voted for the Socialist or Communist party, it would mean that almost two-thirds of the voters for these parties were not industrial workers. And if one allows that a certain number of workers voted for the Radical or Conservative tickets, the proportion of nonworkers among the Socialists and Communists would rise to 70 percent or more. In this city, the Socialist vote clearly extends well beyond the category of manual wage earners.

**Table 11—Socialist or Communist Petty Bourgeoisie
in Some Southern Cities of France (in percentages)**

Legislative Elections 1956	Communists	Socialists and Communists	Industrial Workers	Difference Between % Workers and % Communist-Socialist Votes
Narbonne	26.3	62.7	23.0	39.7
Carcassonne	24.8	48.8	20.8	28.0
Aurillac	22.1	48.8	23.7	25.1
Mont de Marsan	10.6	46.2	21.6	24.6
Cahors	27.6	46.4	22.8	23.6
Dax	11.1	42.5	22.1	21.4

The returns of trade union elections in the white-collar sections, as well as the surveys of the French Institute for Public Opinion (IFOP), indicate that the political attitudes of white-collar workers in private enterprise are different from those of civil servants and white-collar workers in nationalized industries, where the boss is the state, and where any demand necessarily has a political undertone, especially when the government has a conservative leadership. Without going into details, it should be noted that in France the Socialist vote is stronger among lower-level civil servants than among white-collar workers in private enterprise; the latter are more prone to support the Popular Republican Movement (MRP: Christian Democrats), the conservative "Moderates," or the "Gaullists."

In Italy, the Italian General Confederation of Labor (CGIL), linked to the Communist and Socialist parties, has obtained 17 to 19 percent of the votes of white-collar employees as compared to 54 percent among manual workers in trade union elections between 1950 and 1960.[22] These averages cover important regional disparities, confirming the existence of a relationship between political and trade union voting.

According to a survey of the Italian Doxa Institute, undertaken in January and February 1958, there would be, in absolute numbers, as many white-collar workers and lesser civil servants among the Socialists as among the Communists, but because the Communist Party is larger than the Socialist Party, the proportion of white-collar workers would be higher in the Socialist electorate and still higher in the Social Democratic electorate. The Communist Party is five times as large as the Italian Social Democratic party, but the proportion of Communist white-collar workers is hardly twice as high as that of Social Democratic white-collar workers. According to the same survey this social category should be among the most favorable to the Christian Democratic Party. Another survey of the Doxa Institute, undertaken in November 1957, found the same results.

The three Italian Left parties receive approximately 40 percent of the vote of this salaried lower-middle class, whereas in France Socialists and Communists secure nearly 50 percent. The Extreme-Right and the Conservatives secure the same amount of support from these strata in both countries (one-sixth of the vote); yet in France, such voters are largely clerks in private enterprise, while in Italy they are lower-level civil servants. In Rome, where many civil servants live, the Neo-Fascist movement (MSI) in 1958 obtained 12.6 percent of the vote, as against 4.7 percent in Italy as a whole. Union leaders, who know the civil service personnel, estimate that the supporters of the Neo-Fascist movement have been proportionally four or five times more numerous among civil servants than among other voters in the capital. Similar patterns are reported for other localities (Trieste, Bari, Palermo).

There are a number of factors which explain these variations in political attitudes among lower civil servants and clerks in private enterprise in the two countries: first of all, the old lay and republican tradition of the French public administration, and particularly the civic role played by the teachers, who have been Left-wing for a long time (the majority were Radicals at the turn of the century, and then became Socialists or Communists). In Italy, on the contrary, almost all contemporary civil servants joined the government service under Fascism, or under the reign of Christian Democracy. On a different level, it should be noted that many lower civil servants in both countries come from the less developed South; this geographical origin is tinged with a Jacobin tradition in France, but with conservatism in Italy.

Although the pay of lesser French civil servants is relatively higher than that of their Italian colleagues, the education of the former is higher, and consequently more may feel frustrated—feelings which, in a republican environment, should dispose them to vote for leftist parties.

Among clerks and lower civil servants, women are proportionally more numerous than among workers. This should be kept in mind when considering political cleavages in that social category. We shall deal with that aspect further on.

Independent Lower-Middle Class

Composed of small shopkeepers, and small entrepreneurs and craftsmen, both urban and rural, the stratum of independent petty bourgeoisie took part in the Revolution of 1789, and during the next century continued to declare itself in favor of democratic reforms. They supported the Second Republic in 1848, and helped by their votes the Third Republic in its gestation period, the years 1870–80. At the beginning of the twentieth century, their support went largely to the Radical Party. In Italy for a long time this class had liberal tendencies. However, the economic consequences of the war of 1914–18 marked a turning point in its political orientation; in Italy, it adapted itself quite well to the Fascist regime, and in France, it slid progressively toward social conservatism.

Today, handicapped by technical progress and the development of large-scale industry and commerce, producing at non-competitive prices, or for a reduced clientele, a good part of this self-employed lower-middle class is economically and socially "reactionary" and, consequently, politically discontented. Hostile to the "financial feudality," fearful of falling into a proletarian condition, they feel that neither liberalism nor socialism defends their interests. Incapable of understanding their own political Malthusianism, they find a scapegoat in the political system, the "impotent parties and Parliamentary system." The ideology that they find most attractive is a kind of neo-corporatism. Poujadism and the *Uomo Qualunque* movement found their main electoral support among small shopkeepers and craftsmen. One might even estimate that nearly half the vote obtained in 1956 by Poujadism came from this social class and that half the votes of this class were absorbed by the Extreme Right. Poujadism was just a flash in the pan, but the cause of the discontent that it expressed remains: the plethora of small shopkeepers, which is one of the principal ailments from which French society suffers.

In Italy, the Neo-Fascists and the Monarchists collected one-tenth of the vote of the entire electorate in 1958. But in all probability, one-fourth of the independent petty bourgeois electorate voted Neo-Fascist or Monarchist. No other social group has been more sensitive to the appeal of the Extreme-Right in both Latin countries.

Thus, the lower-middle strata present a double political face, as we have tried to outline in *Table 12*. In France, during the Fourth Republic, according to our estimates, nearly half of the white-collar workers were of Socialist or Communist tendencies, and a good third, Radical, Catholic, or Moderate, whereas approximately half the independent petty bourgeoisie manifested antidemocratic tendencies, at least in the election of 1956.

Table 12—The Two Faces of the French Petty Bourgeoisie*

Attitude toward the Church	Position in the Political Spectrum	Vote in 1956	Attitude Toward the Economic and Social Regime	Potential Identification in the Prospect of a Bipolar System of Social Classes	Petty Bourgeoisie (percent) Salaried	Inde-pendent	Together
Anticlerical	Extreme left	Communist	Protesting against social inequalities	Turns toward the "workers' class"	47	11	33
	Left	Socialist	Reformist				
	Center left	Radical	Liberal	Turns toward the "middle bourgeoisie"	37	39	38
	Center	Christian Democrat (MRP)	Reformist				
Tradi-tionalist	Right	Moderate	Conservative				
	Extreme right	Anti-Republican or Poujadist	Refractory to economic progress	Against the "nobs" but at the same time "anti-proletarian"	16	50ª	29

Source: Figures derived from the data of the 1954 census.
* Salaried petty bourgeoisie: 2,850,000 votes in 1956; Independent petty bourgeoisie: 1,800,000 votes in 1956; Total: 4,650,000.
ª This estimate refers only to the 1956 elections marked by the "Poujadist" flash in the pan.

POLITICAL CONFORMISM OF THE "TRUE" BOURGEOISIE

Analytic necessities oblige us to group under the heading of "middle bourgeoisie" voters belonging to some twenty socioeconomic categories, ranging from middle-class merchants to middle-level military officers, from high-school teachers to industrial engineers, from a good part of the clergy to most stage actors. Any attempt to explain the political behavior of the middle bourgeoisie should begin with an examination of each of the subcategories which compose it.[23] The main reason for its political polyvalence must be found in its social heterogeneity. Indeed, however "middle" this bourgeoisie may be, its vote nevertheless is distributed through the whole political spectrum. According to several indices, flimsy if considered separately, but more significant when compared and combined, the center and center-right parties share two-thirds of the vote of this stratum. Socialists, Social-Democrats, and Communists in France, as in Italy, receive about one-sixth of the votes, while the Extreme Right gets approximately one-fifth. These estimates ignore some

Table 13—Stratification of the Vote by Large Economic Sectors in France (conjectural estimates: to be interpreted as a scale of magnitude)

Legislative Elections of 1956	Communist	Socialist SFIO	Center and Right Center	Extreme Right	Total
			(thousands)		
I Industrial working class	3,900	1,370	2,630	100	8,000
agricultural workers	300	200	500	50	1,050
small farmers	500	500	1,850	500	3,350
middle farmers	—	30	820	150	1,000
great landowners	—	—	150	40	190
II Total agricultural sector	800	730	3,320	740	5,590
Bourgeoisie:					
petty—salaried	600	750	1,050	450	2,850
petty—independent	100	100	700	900	1,800
middle	120	250	1,380	400	2,150
upper	10	70	870	150	1,100
III Total middle class	830	1,170	4,000	1,900	7,900
France as a whole	5,530	3,270	9,950	2,740	21,490
			(percent)		
I Industrial working class	70.5	41.9	26.4	3.6	37.2
agricultural workers	5.5	6.1	5.0	1.8	5.4
small farmers	9.0	15.3	18.6	18.2	15.1
middle-class farmers	—	0.9	8.2	5.5	4.7
great landowners	—	—	1.5	1.5	0.9
II Total agricultural sector	14.5	22.3	33.3	27.0	26.1
Bourgeoisie:					
petty—salaried	10.8	22.9	10.6	16.4	13.2
petty—independent	1.8	3.1	7.0	32.9	8.4
middle	2.2	7.7	13.9	14.6	10.0
upper	0.2	2.1	8.8	5.5	5.1
III Total middle class	15.0	35.8	40.3	69.4	36.7
Grand total	100	100	100	100	100

rather important differences among the several socioprofessional subcategories.

The leftist votes in this social category may be attributed to a variety of factors: anticlericalism, involvement in the resistance against German occupation or against Fascism, the defense of certain acquired positions linked to leftist strength (high position in nationalized industries), the desire to achieve certain social reforms advocated by the Left (for example, legalizing divorce in Italy), the philosophical outlook of some intellectuals and artists, and so forth.

As for the upper bourgeoisie, its own votes have little weight on the electoral scale—5 percent. Nevertheless, it is not submerged, drowned in the universal suffrage. Its influence remains considerable in the political as well as the economic domain.

Table 14—Social Classes and Political Parties in France (in thousands)
(conjectural estimates: to be interpreted as a scale of magnitude)

Vote Cast in the 1956 Elections	Communist Party	Socialist SFIO	Center and Right Center	Extreme Right	Total	General Total
Industrial workers	3,900	1,370	2,630	100	8,000	
Agricultural workers	300	200	500	50	1,050	9,050
Salaried petty bourgeoisie	600	750	1,050	450	2.850	
Independent petty bourgeoisie	100	100	700	900	1,800	
Small farmers	500	500	1,850	500	3,350	8,000
Urban middle bourgeoisie	120	250	1,380	400	2,150	
Middle-class farmers	—	30	820	150	1,000	3,150
Great urban bourgeoisie	10	70	870	150	1,100	
Great landowners	—	—	150	40	190	1,290
Total Votes	5,530	3,270	9,950	2,740	21,490	21,490

It is obvious that Communism and Socialism can attract but a negligible number of its votes. Marxists and anti-Marxists may easily agree on this point. To distribute this social stratum, privileged in the share of the national revenue, among the tendencies of economic liberalism, traditional conservatism, and the Extreme Right is a difficult problem. One fact impresses any impartial observer: contrary to a certain doctrine, the owners of capital, the big industrialists, and the summit of the social scale, in the foreground of the national scene, are able to adapt themselves very well to the democratic regime (with the exception of some high-ranking Army officers, some Church dignitaries, and a few industrialists seeking a political springboard). For a century now, most of the "true" bourgeoisie has played the democratic game well, much like the old nobility in Great Britain. In France they vote preferably for the moderate Conservatives, Gaullists, or Christian Democrats (MRP); in Italy, for the Liberal Party or the Right wing of the Christian Democratic Party. Only one out of ten or twelve of these upper bourgeois would back the classical Extreme Right (*Tables 13, 14,* and *15*).

Opinion surveys, voting returns in the residential districts of the large cities, membership of the General Confederation of the Italian Industry

Table 15—Social Classes and Political Parties in Italy (in thousands)
(conjectural estimate: to be interpreted as a scale of magnitude)

Vote Cast in the 1958 Elections	Communist	Socialist PSI	Social Democrat PSDI	Christian Democrat	Liberal, Republican, and Others	Monarchist and Fascists	Total	General Total
Industrial workers	3,700	2,360	450	2,520	200	530	9,760	
Agricultural workers	1,300	400	50	300	20	130	2,200	
Tenant farmers	800	450	50	250	30	120	1,700	13,660
Salaried petty bourgeoisie	550	500	300	1,450	180	370	3,350	
Independent petty bourgeoisie	80	50	70	1,250	300	500	2,250	
Small farmers	200	250	150	3,000	100	100	3,800	9,500
Urban middle bourgeoisie	70	130	200	1,400	500	500	2,800	
Middle-class farmers	—	50	50	1,500	50	150	1,800	4,600
Great urban bourgeoisie	—	20	30	700	500	150	1,400	
Great landowners	—	—	—	150	50	300	500	
Total Votes	6,700	4,210	1,350	12,520	1,930	2,850	29,560	1,900
								29,560

(CGII), and other sources, tend to show that the Italian Liberal Party has probably reached in the industrial and business bourgeoisie a proportion of votes ten to fifteen times superior to that it obtained in the whole Italian electorate. There is nothing more natural, considering its attachment to economic liberalism and its opposition to state monopolies and to *"dirigisme"* (state control). This hypothesis will be confirmed further on by the analysis of political cleavage according to levels of education.

The political attitudes of the captains of industry or finance contrast with those of the landowning nobility, which adapted badly to economic development. Everywhere in Europe, long after the establishment of a republican regime, the great landowners, in contrast to the great urban bourgeoisie, held out nostalgically for the monarchy, and many of them swung toward the Extreme Right.

If Karl Marx were still alive, he would disapprove of his epigones, who do not observe with sufficient attention the changes that have occurred for more than half a century. He would draw their attention to the fact that in France and Italy the possessors of great capital are not antirepublican or antidemocratic and that, on the electoral level at least, Neo-Fascism, Poujadism, and the "activism" of Extreme Rightists are—as were German Nazism, Belgian Rexism, French *Croix de Feu,* Romanian Iron Guard of the 1930's —the expression of the petty bourgeoisie rather than that of the upper bourgeoisie.

Surveys on the most diverse problems—economic, social, cultural, religious, and moral—show that the so-called independent petty bourgeoisie manifest more sectarian, more "misoneistic" (anti-novelty) opinions than the middle bourgeoisie, who in turn appear somewhat less liberal, less tolerant, than the upper bourgeoisie. And this is a fact not only in France and Italy, but in many other countries as well.

OLD WOMEN AND YOUNG MEN AS ELECTORAL COMPETITORS

In most Western countries, more women than men vote for conservative and traditionalist parties. In Catholic countries the difference between the electoral behavior of men and women is much greater than in Protestant countries. When analyzing electoral cleavages in Anglo-Saxon or Scandinavian countries it is not usually necessary to stress the political divergencies between men and women, while it is an important factor in Italy and France.

Disparity Between the Votes of Men and Women

Various data sources, particularly opinion surveys and the electoral results in some cities where women and men placed their ballots in separate boxes,[24] point up the variations in the way in which men and women distribute their votes among the various parties (*Tables 16* and *17*). In Italy, a dozen surveys, between 1952 and 1963, support the same conclusion: more than three-fifths of those voting Communist and Socialist (considered together) are men; by contrast, nearly two-thirds of those voting Christian Democratic are women. In other words, the preponderance of males in the Marxist parties is nearly as strong as the preponderance of females in the Christian Democratic Party, and this independently of the gains or losses registered by the three largest Italian parties in the elections of 1953, 1958, and 1963.

Whatever the margin of error in our evaluation, it may be safely affirmed that, in 1958, had men alone voted, the "Marxist bloc" would have obtained more votes than the Christian Democratic, whereas, thanks to the female suffrage, the Catholic electoral strength is superior to that of the two Marxist parties.

In 1958, the Christian Democratic votes exceeded by 1,600,000 the Socialist-Communist votes. But this advantage was obtained primarily because of female suffrage. From the male electors Communist and Socialist parties gathered two million votes more than the Christian Democratic Party. Yet female electors gave the Christian Democrats an advantage of more than three-and-a-half million votes over their Marxist adversaries. The differences between male and female suffrages in the Christian-Democratic electorate is therefore more than twice as high as the difference between the total votes gathered by the Christian Democrats and the "Marxist" votes.

The consequences of female suffrage bear heavily on the relation between Catholic and Marxist forces. Nevertheless, even with an exclusively male suffrage, the Communist and Socialist parties could not have obtained, in 1958, an absolute majority. They would probably have reached about 47 percent of the male votes. Whereas, before and after—at the 1953 and 1963 elections, when the Christian Democrats got less votes than in 1958—the Marxist bloc would have exceeded the absolute majority of the male electorate, and, therefore, achieved a parliamentary majority. The marginal value of the female suffrage would have been decisive: one can easily figure out the consequences for Italy, western Europe, and the Atlantic Alliance.

In France, as in Italy, the Left parties are more "masculine" than those of the Right. In the elections of 1946, an estimated 65 percent of the men voted for the left (Communist, Socialist, Radical) as against 53 percent of the women; in 1951, 58 percent compared to 47 percent. This gap has remained in the elections of 1956, 1958, and 1962. Gaullism has always had more support from women than from men. However, the Popular Republican Movement—MRP (Christian Democratic) is the most "feminine" party. The proportion of men among the Communist voters has remained remarkably stable since the war, 60 percent; among the Socialists, 53 percent.

In the October 1962 referendum, according to a survey of the French Institute for Public Opinion (IFOP), 42 percent of the men voted "no" (anti–de Gaulle) compared to 25 percent of the women.[25] The marginal value of the feminine vote was decisive in the referendum of May 1946: the projected constitution was rejected by the women. The male vote was indecisive; 50 percent voted "yes" and 50 percent "no." However, only 36 percent of the women voted for the projected constitution. Thus it was actually the feminine vote which accounted for its rejection. Many women voters may have voted "no" as a consequence of Church intervention in the campaign (the proposed constitution represented an indirect threat to parochial schools).

Everywhere in western Europe Christian Democratic parties are favored, and Communist and Socialist parties disadvantaged, by female suffrage. This was true in previous decades as well. In Austria, in the 1920 elections, where men and women voted with different colored ballots, women strongly backed

Table 16—Men and Women's Choice
Between Catholicism and Marxism in Italy

1958 Elections Parties	Doxa Surveys a Men (percent)	Women	Total	Men (in thousands)	Women	Total	Men (percent)	Women
Communist and Socialist	61	39	10,910	6,650	4,260	36.9	47	27
Christian Democratic	37	63	12,520	4,640	7,880	42.4	32.5	51.5
Others	47	53	6,130	2,870	3,260	20.7	20.5	21.5
Total vote	47.9	52.1	29,560	14,160	15,400	100	100	100

a "Secondary" analysis of the raw data provided by Doxa Institute.

the Christian Social Party against the Socialists. In Germany, in the elections of 1953 and 1957, where the voting papers of men and women were counted separately in one thousand precincts (a sample of the entire electorate), 58

Table 17—Men and Women's Choice
Between Left and Right in France

1951 Elections Parties		IFOP Surveys a Men (percent)	Women	Total	Men (in thousands)	Women	Total	Men (percent)	Women
Left	Communist	60	40	5,056	3,034	2,022			
	Socialist	53	47	2,745	1,455	1,290	52.3	57.5	46.8
	Radical	51	49	2,111	1,076	1,035			
Right	MRP (Christian Democrats)	39	61	2,370	924	1,446			
	Moderates	47	53	2,434	1,144	1,290	47.7	42.5	53.2
	RPF (Gaullists)	48	52	4,125	1,982	2,143			
	Others	—	—	126	63	63			
	Total turnout	51	49	18,967	9,678	9,289	100	100	100
	Nonvoters	35	65	4,860	1,700	3,160			
	Invalid ballots	—	—	704	352	352			
	Registered electors	47	53	24,531	11,730	12,801			
	Adult population			26,500					

a "Secondary" analysis of the data provided by IFOP.

percent of the Christian Democratic Union voters were women. The preference of women for traditionalist parties, Christian or conservative, has also been established for Finland, Great Britain, Norway, and Denmark. By contrast, all Socialist parties of Europe have been harmed by the female vote, with the exception of Sweden in 1960. But there, as in Denmark, two-thirds of the Communists are men. In Weimar Republican Germany, in 1920, 63 percent of the Communist votes came from men; the same was true in Austria in the same year.[26]

It is important to note that the feminine suffrage, while disadvantaging the Extreme Left, unfavorably affects the Extreme Right as well. Indeed, the Italian Neo-Fascist movement in 1953 and 1958 counted fewer women than men in its ranks,[27] as did the Poujade movement in 1956. In Germany, the Nazi Party received fewer votes from women than from men in the years 1928–33.

In order to interpret the political orientation of women, it is necessary to consider other factors which influence political behavior, especially religious attitudes, social conditions, age, and civil status.

The Religious Motivation of the Female Vote

The political differences between sexes are not essentially related to class conflict. The standard of living of the economically inactive wife depends on that of her husband. The wage of the working wife usually constitutes an additional salary which does not change the family's social position; besides, in economic life, women generally occupy a lower position than that of the men. As for young girls, they are in the same social class as their brothers. Widows quite often live in very difficult material conditions; yet from the psychosocial point of view, they remain attached to the socioeconomic milieu in which their late husband belonged. One must not, therefore, search in the economic field for an explanation of the difference between men's and women's political behavior.

On the other hand, as several studies show, important differences exist between the religious attitudes of the two sexes (*Table 18*). In view of the very significant relationship between religious feeling and political opinion, it is normal that women, who compared to men are more religious, more sympathetic to the recommendations of the Church, and more subject to the clergy's influence, should tend to vote for the parties which directly or indirectly, openly or discreetly, are backed by the Church.[28]

This religious influence has also affected women's turnout. Everywhere in European countries, when we refer to the national level, we find that a higher percentage of women than men fail to vote. Yet, in Italy in the 1953 and 1958 elections a larger proportion of women voted than men. And, unique phenomenon in the European electoral annals, female absenteeism was less accentuated in the rural areas than in the cities; and in communities under 30,000 inhabitants, it was even lower than male absenteeism. The Catholic influence on women is stronger in the countryside than in large cities. What should be emphasized here is the relation between the variations in female abstentions and the variations in the electoral strength of the various parties. The rate of abstention and the percentage of the Christian Democratic vote varies inversely. In other words, the higher the proportion of women that go to the polls, the more votes for the Christian Democratic party, and vice versa. In France the difference between feminine and masculine abstention is much less noticeable in strongly Catholic areas than in areas with low religious observance.[29]

If it is true that the primary reason for the discrepancy between feminine and masculine voting behavior is due to religious reasons, we should try now to find in which social strata religious motivation most effectively affects voting behavior.

The Vote of Women in Lower Social Strata

Women belonging to the bourgeoisie or to the upper strata of the middle bourgeoisie have sufficient socioeconomic reasons not to vote Communist or Socialist. It is difficult to determine which of the two variables, religious feeling or socioeconomic factor, most influences their vote, because men in the same social condition also vote "conservative." In fact, no important discrepancy between feminine and masculine voting patterns appears in this social class.

Table 18—Difference in Religious Behavior of Men and Women, Particularly Among the Working Class (in percentages)

Sample of 2,432 Persons		CATHOLICS		WITHOUT RELIGION	OTHER RELIGIONS	Total
		Active	Nonactive			
Industrial workers	Men	16	61	20	3	100
	Women	40	47	10	3	100
Agricultural workers	Men	26	59	13	2	100
	Women	50	42	6	2	100
Small clerks and civil servants	Men	31	52	15	2	100
	Women	36	47	14	3	100
Shopkeepers and craftsmen	Men	27	53	14	6	100
	Women	44	44	6	6	100
Industrialists, professionals, upper civil servants, and managers	Men	39	39	17	5	100
	Women	42	36	17	5	100
Farmers	Men	52	39	5	4	100
	Women	64	29	3	4	100
Retired people (all categories)	Men	30	55	12	3	100
	Women	56	34	7	3	100
Total	Men	32	51	14	3	100
	Women	47	42	8	3	100

Source: Based on an unpublished document of M. A. Girard, National Institute for Demographic Studies (INED). The survey was taken in 1956. Women were classified according to the profession of the head of the family, i.e., in most cases the profession of the husband.

It is among peasant and working-class women that an ambivalence of feelings may occur; that a conflict may arise between their feeling of belonging to the Catholic community and their identification with a disfavored social class (better defended in some respects by the "anticlerical" parties); that religious motivation supersedes socioeconomic motivation; and that a discrepancy occurs between the male and female vote.[30]

The excess of women that we observe in the electorate of the Christian Democratic Party is necessarily composed, in large measure, by women working in industry, and wives, mothers, or daughters of industrial workers, or by peasants' wives.

There is no doubt that the difference between masculine and feminine suffrage is greatest among industrial workers, tenant farmers, agricultural workers, and small farmers, than in the bourgeoisie and middle classes. Since, as we have already noted, the Christian Democratic Party collects many more votes in rural areas than among industrial workers, it follows that farm women weigh heavily in the Christian Democratic electorate. This party collected 5,600,000 agricultural votes in 1958; we might estimate that three-and-a-half millions, approximately, represent the feminine contribution.

Is the Feminine Vote Traditionalist or Conservative?

Given its religious motivation, the vote of these economically underprivileged women must not be interpreted as a conservative vote. It should rather be seen merely as a traditionalist vote. If the wife of a tenant farmer or an agricultural or industrial worker does not vote Communist or Socialist as her husband does, it is because Catholic tradition warns her against political ideologies condemned by the Church, and not because she wishes to maintain the capitalistic economy or to safeguard the large landowners' interests. Morally and logically, Catholicism is not tied to industrial or agrarian capitalism. But Socialism and Communism, by reason of circumstances present in everybody's mind, have always been anticlerical and even antireligious. For—it is not superfluous to record here—there is a basic incompatibility between Christian conceptions (or those of any other religion or deist ethic), and dialectical materialism. Women are more often conscious of this incompatibility than men. To the question posed by the Doxa Institute in November 1953, "Do you think that one can be at the same time a good Communist and a good Catholic?" many more women than men answered in the negative. Socialism is not as often considered as irreconcilable with Catholicism as is Communism: 44 percent of men and 30 percent of women judge them to be conciliable. The relationship between such answers and the sympathy shown by the respondents toward the parties is highly significant; most of those who think that there is no contradiction between voting Communist or Socialist and being Catholic favor the Communist or Socialist parties. It is highly probable that these persons are lukewarm Catholics, if not agnostics. By contrast, believers think that Marxism and Catholicism are radically opposed. The believers, and particularly the women among them, cannot take into account, when they vote, only their economic and socioprofessional interests—assuming that they clearly perceive them, which is certainly not always the case; they must "act as good Catholics," i.e., "vote against the enemies of the Church."

The religious motivation of the vote and its socioeconomic component are not easily dissociable—except for the good Catholics who are also "good bourgeois," and who thus have a double reason for voting against the Marxist parties. There are, however, good bourgeois who are bad Catholics, and who nevertheless vote Christian Democratic, Moderate, or Gaullist, because they think, and not without reason, that these political tendencies can combat Communism more efficiently than the Extreme Right.

Summing up, the Catholic vote of the lower social strata may be interpreted as a traditionalist vote even by leftists who think that such a vote is exploited in the end by economic and social conservatism. It is obvious that a vote so defined, and which results from such a conflicting allegiance, is much more frequent among women than among men, particularly among poor farmers and the industrial workers. Hence, the religious factor is more often decisive in affecting the vote of economically underprivileged women than that of upper-class women.

Identity of the Votes of the Husband and Wife

Women, especially those who are not employed, are less interested than men in politics. Poorly informed about public affairs, most of them adopt their husband's point of view, even if they remain more faithful to Christian traditions. They do not concern themselves with political ideology. They give no symbolic value to their vote, and this allows them to accept the lead of their husband who, involved in economic and trade union activities, may better grasp the interests of the social class to which he and his family belong.

As a consequence of this influence of the husband on his wife, or less frequently of the wife on her husband, the proportion of married couples who vote in an identical manner is very high. It is difficult to determine the exact proportion because some of those interviewed said that they did not know how their spouse voted. If we consider only those who gave a precise answer, the proportion of those voting as their mates did reached 85 percent for France in 1954. However, it is possible that split family voting is more frequent among those who say they are not aware of how their spouse voted (or prefer to declare that they do not know). The available data for France indicate that the discrepancy between male and female votes must be attributed only to a limited extent to married voters.[31]

Identical voting by husband and wife is probably less frequent in Italy than in France, particularly in lower social classes, since a Communist or Socialist vote is more severely and more openly condemned by the ecclesiastic hierarchy in Italy. The Italian Socialist Party remained more faithful to Marxist ideology than the French SFIO, at least until the years 1956–58. However, in case of a difference of opinion between a Communist husband and his wife, it may happen that she lets the parish priest believe that she votes Christian Democratic, and makes what one might call an intuitive compromise, by slipping into the ballot box, without anyone being the wiser, a Social Democratic or Socialist voting paper. In most cases there are seldom any political discussions in the family; the husband makes no attempt to convince his wife.

There is no contradiction, as might at first sight appear, between the fact that most wives normally vote as do their husbands and the fact of a large discrepancy between feminine and masculine voting patterns: married women only constitute about three-fourths of the feminine electorate, and married men form approximately seven-tenths of the male voters.

Political Contrasts Between Young Single Men and Old Women

The data concerning political variations in relation to sex and age considered together, indirectly confirm the frequency of identity of vote among spouses.

The relation among vote, age, and sex presented in the results of opinion surveys indicates that the difference between feminine and masculine voting is much less in the middle-age categories which contain a high proportion of married people, than among young voters among whom single people are very numerous, or among the aged, in high proportion widowers. Several French and Italian surveys point to the predominance of men among the young Communists or Socialists, while females abound within the more youthful segments of the Christian Democratic or Popular Republican (MRP) electorate. Thus, during the years 1946–51, two-thirds of the French Communists under thirty years of age were men; above this age the imbalance between sexes was much lower.

It would be ideal to present a triple correlation among voting, sex, and marital status. Unfortunately, documentation is lacking. But the distribution of marital status varies according to age; thus we can indirectly deduce from the actually observed correlation (voting, sex, and age) the general outline of the triple correlation that we lack (vote, sex, and marital status).

A confirmation of this distortion may be found in Italy by contrasting the voting in precincts reserved for young men in military service with the results from some villages of the South (*Mezzogiorno*) where voters under twenty-five years old are largely young single women (since most of the men have emigrated). Voters under twenty-five may be identified by comparing results in those villages of the election for the Chamber of Deputies with those for the Senate. These statistics are too detailed and too varied to be reproduced here. But their examination shows that a relatively high proportion of single young women vote for the Christian Democratic Party, while on the contrary, single young men vote in larger proportion for the Communist and Socialist parties. The difference between the feminine and masculine voting behavior in these villages is much greater than that observed for the electorate as a whole.

In the 1958 elections, the Christian Democratic Party and the Italian Communist Party were both favored by the voters between twenty-one and twenty-five years of age. But it is important to note that the success of the Christian Democratic Party with the new generation is essentially due to the vote of the young women, whereas the success of the Italian Communist Party among this generation must be credited to the young men.

The Vote of Widows

Any analysis of female voting must consider the large number of the very aged—especially widows—among them. In the 1954 French census, in an adult female population of fourteen million there were six million women without husbands, half of whom were widows or single women over fifty-five years of age. In Italy, at the time of the 1958 elections, in an adult female population of sixteen million the number of women without husbands was more than six million, of whom one-third were elderly widows or single women. Single aged women were more numerous in France because of the loss of 1,700,000 men during World War I.

Censuses of religious observance and opinion surveys clearly point out the attachment of elderly women to religious values, as well as their traditionalist tendencies in social and cultural matters. Greater age seemingly stimulates increased religious commitment among elderly widows, and thus affects their political opinions. But age itself may exercise a direct influence on political orientation by emphasizing differences in generational experiences. A life turned toward the past tends to reject "advanced" political positions and to support those rooted in past events. Many widows are obliged, after their husband's death, to make a living by work which does not correspond to their previous social status. They often lose status as a result. Their political opinions, however, remain more traditionalist, more "bourgeois," than one would expect given their current socioeconomic status. Their precarious situation leads them to view social or political disturbances as dangers which could further jeopardize their insecure position. There is a political conservatism of the powerful, who seek to defend their privileged position, and a political conservatism of the weak, who want to defend their meager pittance in a period of change. Thus it is not surprising that the proportion of single aged women who vote Christian Democratic, Popular Republican, Moderate, or Gaullist, is very high, much greater than among young or middle-aged women. Nevertheless, the latter, much more numerous in the population, still form the majority among the female followers of traditional parties.

If we compare the demographic pyramid of the Communist and Socialist electorate with that of the Christian Democratic or Popular Republican parties, a striking contrast appears between the vote of old women and young men. Political differences among the sexes therefore conceal, to a certain extent, differences among age groupings. The uneven distribution of women without husbands, and of men without wives, between Marxist-tinged parties and Catholic parties, leads us to the problem of age of voters, and age, in turn, leads us to religious behavior and psychological components.

In conclusion, if we assume that the large majority of married men and women vote identically, we have also to admit that the surplus of young men voting for leftist parties is mainly composed of bachelors, that the surplus of young women voting for traditionalist parties of all shades is mainly formed of single women, and finally, that the excess of aged women, so numerous in the Christian Democratic Party, is constituted, in a large majority, by widows.

France and Italy were among the last major democracies to grant women their rights as citizens, a reform long advocated by the Left and opposed by the Right. Twenty years after gaining access to the Republic of Men, their political culture is still inferior, as is their political participation. But in certain circumstances, their vote is decisive in keeping conservatives in power.

LEVEL OF EDUCATION, POLITICAL PARTICIPATION, AND VOTING BEHAVIOR

In many countries in the days of limited suffrage, the number of citizens who could read and write determined the size of the electorate. In France today, illiteracy is reduced to a negligible fraction of the population

(2 percent); yet in Italy, according to the 1951 census, illiteracy is still large: 18 percent of the adult population.[32] As the social physiognomy of the Italian parties achieves sharper features, the analysis of political cleavage according to the educational level is more relevant for Italy than for France.

For Italy, a survey of the Doxa Institute undertaken in November 1957 and two surveys of the Italian Institute of Public Opinion in April and July 1958 are available. By combining the results of these surveys, we present in *Table 19* conjectural estimates.

Table 19—Level of Education and Political Preference in Italy
(conjectural estimate—in thousands)

Elections of 1958	LEVEL OF EDUCATION				
	Elementary or illiterate	Lower secondary	Upper secondary	University	Total
PCI[a]	6,000	550	100	50	6,700
PSI	3,300	600	200	100	4,200
PSDI	800	250	200	100	1,350
DC	8,250	2,400	1,500	350	12,500
PLI	250	250	400	150	1,050
MSI, Monarchist	1,350	800	500	200	2,850
Other (PRI, etc.)	550	150	100	50	850
Total	20,500	5,000	3,000	1,000	29,500
PCI	90%	8	1	1	100%
PSI	78%	15	5	2	100%
PSDI	61%	19	15	7	100%
DC	66%	19	12	3	100%
PLI	24%	23	38	14	100%
MSI Monarchist	47%	28	18	7	100%
Other (PRI, etc.)	64%	18	12	6	100%
Total	70%	17%	10%	3%	100%
PCI	30%	11%	3%	5%	22.7%
PSI	16	12	7	10	14.2
PSDI	4	5	7	10	4.5
DC	40	48	50	35	42.4
PLI	1	5	13	15	3.5
MSI, Monarchist	7	16	17	20	9.6
Other (PRI, etc.)	2	3	3	5	3.1
Total	100%	100%	100%	100%	100%

[a] PCI, Italian Communist Party; PSI, Italian Socialist Party; PSDI, Italian Social-Democratic Party; DC, Christian-Democratic Party; PLI, Italian Liberal Party; MSI, Italian Social Movement (Neo-Fascist); PRI, Italian Republican Party.

A few facts are immediately apparent. Nine out of ten Communists have attended only elementary school or are illiterate, as compared to only one out of four Liberal voters. The Liberal Party is characterized by the support it receives from those with an upper-secondary or university education, who amount to half of the Liberal electorate. This observation takes on a particular significance if one considers that only 13 percent of Italian adults have continued their studies beyond the age of fifteen (see *Table 19*).

A clear difference can also be observed between the levels of education of the Communist and Socialist electorates, which bears out our previous remark that clerks, small civil servants, and skilled workers are relatively more numerous among voters supporting the Italian Socialist Party than among those backing the Italian Communist Party. The latter, conversely, includes more unskilled workers, agricultural workers, tenant farmers, and urban sub-proletarians. This difference becomes even more accentuated if we compare the Italian Communist Party with the Italian Social Democratic Party (PSDI).

Almost half the Monarchists and Neo-Fascists (grouped together, because the Italian Institute of Public Opinion did so) have a secondary education, which is typical of the urban petty bourgeoisie. If an analysis of Fascist voters were possible, it would reveal that an even higher proportion among them have a secondary education. At the same time, the proportion of illiterate voters or those with an elementary-school education would be greater among the Monarchist supporters, many of whom belong to what has been called *"la plèbe méridionale."*

For the Christian Democratic Party, the impression differs depending upon whether one analyzes its electoral strength or those in each educational category. Thus, out of one hundred Christian Democratic voters, only three have a university education, but among the voters with a university education, 35 percent vote Christian Democratic. For those who have an upper or lower secondary education a similar contrast appears. The reason is simple: the Christian Democratic electorate is twelve times greater than the number of Italians with a university degree and four times larger than the number of those who have a high-school education. In absolute numbers, the well-educated voters are much more numerous in the Christian Democratic Party than in the Liberal Party, although the latter is "the most educated party."

In brief, voters with a university education are divided into three equally important groups: approximately one-third supports the Christian Democracy; one-third backs the Left (Communist, Socialist, Social Democratic, Republican); and one-third votes for the Right (Liberals, Neo-Fascists and Monarchists). This distribution should be interpreted taking into account that the leftist parties reach 43 percent of the votes, while those of the Right, only 13 percent.

The picture looks somewhat different when comparing small and large parties. Whereas 86 percent of the voters, male and female, who are illiterate or have an elementary education concentrate their votes on the three large mass parties (Christian Democratic, Communist, Socialist), half of those with a university education are scattered among the minor parties. The support enjoyed by the (conservative) Liberal Party among the well educated, who hold positions of power in the economy, in public administration, or who are professionals, needs no comment. It has its own logic. The case is different with the well educated who, under a republican regime, show sympathy for the defunct monarchy or for Neo-Fascism. Despite their university education, their political attitude seems more emotional than rational. They are "nostalgics." As for leftist intellectuals, few of them feel at ease in the Communist or the Socialist parties; they, rather, vote for the Social Democratic Party or the Republican Party.

If the analysis of the relationship between the educational level and the political tendency is limited to the urban electorate, we would see, for all parties, a considerable decrease of persons without any education or with only an elementary education, and a corresponding increase of persons with a high-school or university education. However, this modification would be more apparent for the Christian Democratic Party, which has a solid rural foundation, particularly among small farmers with an elementary education only.

As men, on the whole, are better educated than women, it is obvious that if the analysis was confined only to men voters, the proportion of educated persons would rise, for all the parties. For ten persons with a university education, eight are males. This should be kept in mind when estimating the figures in *Table 19,* in which, as opposed to the other tables, women have not been classified according to the social situation of their husbands. The number of Communists or Liberals with a university education is probably not underestimated, as it concerns men in most cases, their wives being more often in the high-school-education categories.

A comparison between France and Italy is not easy, since the criteria for distinguishing the various levels of education are not the same in both countries. The French Institute of Public Opinion, in one survey, divided the population by the number of school years completed, while another survey used the divisions primary, technical, secondary, and so forth. In France where education is more widespread, the relationship of political preference to schooling is lower than in Italy.

Nevertheless, significant differences exist in France as well. In 1958 the proportion of voters having continued their education beyond the age of fourteen was slightly higher among the Radicals and Popular Republicans than among the Moderates and Gaullists. The proportion falls to 18 percent among the Communists and amounts to 31 percent among Conservative supporters.[33] The difference between the Communist and Socialist parties is also quite marked; it comes, as in Italy, from the broad support of the SFIO among clerks and civil servants. However, even considering the greater spread of education in France, the cultural level of the electorate of the SFIO seems higher than that of its Italian counterpart (Italian Socialist and Social Democratic parties considered together). Besides, the social basis of the SFIO is more heterogenous than that of the Italian Socialist parties. In the 1962 referendum, according to an IFOP survey, 54 percent of the voters with a university background voted "no," as compared with 36 percent of the voters with a secondary education, and 32 percent with only an elementary education.[34]

If the relationship between level of education and political preference is not higher, the reason for it is simple. Citizens with little education are generally either peasants or industrial workers; while the latter vote largely for leftist parties, the former back center or rightist parties, in both countries.

Level of education and degree of political maturity should not, however, be confused. An analysis of the results of opinion surveys carried out since the war in France and Italy clearly shows that the social category least informed about politics is the peasantry, whereas the level of political sophistication of the working class is relatively high, nearing the level of the better educated. This fact is easily explained: workers, as urban dwellers, are better organized into unions, and therefore more exposed to political propaganda than peasants are.

Contrary to American findings, in France, Italy, and some other European countries, the degree of political participation is hardly correlated with the level of education. Of course, the higher one goes in the political hierarchy, the greater the number of the well educated. But if one considers the mass of voters, it appears that the degree of political participation increases toward the two extremes of the political spectrum.

Whatever the indicator, party membership ratio (number of members in relation to voters), participation in election activities, capacity to mobilize demonstrators, and the like, the most active, the most engaged, are indisputably Communists. Although they are the least educated, they are the most dynamic partisans. By contrast, the better-educated citizens often participate half-heartedly and dislike becoming engaged in militant politics. Normally the better educated one is, the more eclectic one becomes. Eclecticism leads to hesitation and lack of commitment.

Finally, we observe a distortion between the three levels of education, of political knowledge, and of political participation, as the following diagram shows:

| | | CENTER | | |
Level	EXTREME LEFT	Peasants	Urban dwellers	EXTREME RIGHT
Of education	very low	very low	high	average
Of political knowledge	high	very low	high	average
Of participation	very high	very low	low	very high

Another discrepancy is worth pointing out. One can be well educated and have little wealth, or very wealthy although little educated. Level of education and level of income are not always related, and the divorce between the two levels engenders rather interesting behavior patterns.

In the old days of the apogee of radicalism, many French had their heart on the Left and their wallet on the Right. A similar pattern occurred in Italy in the old days of the *Risorgimento*.

This syncretism reveals itself today in a new form. Those whose level of income is relatively higher than their level of education tend to hold conservative ideas tinged with Malthusianism; on the other hand, a level of education greater than the level of income leads to reformist opinions tinged with altruism. Such is the case of the moderate shopkeeper—conservative rather than traditionalist—and of the socialist professor—liberal as well as collectivist. The latter is the more frustrated, since he must live modestly although he is highly educated.

Briefly, those whose income is higher than their education lean toward the Right; those better educated than they are paid lean toward the Left. This is true for a minority of citizens; for the majority, however, level of education and level of income are nearly balanced.

If level of education and political tendency are obviously linked, to the contrary, as we shall see now, a low level of education does not prevent the blossoming of a strong class consciousness.

SOCIAL CONDITION, SOCIAL
CONSCIOUSNESS, AND POLITICAL
TENDENCY

If two individuals of the same profession and rank do not identify themselves with the same social class, there is a strong probability—everything else being equal—that they will not vote for the same party. On the other hand, if two individuals of different professions and unequal incomes consider themselves as belonging to the same social class, they will be inclined to manifest similar political preferences. Various surveys carried out in France and Italy show that each socioeconomic category is itself divided according to psychological factors. Thus the influence of the socioeconomic status upon voting behavior occurs at the levels of class self-identification.

Several French surveys concerning the relationship between social condition and the perception of this condition reach the same conclusion: many workers do not identify with the working class but willingly connect themselves to the petty bourgeoisie. Some of these surveys inform us furthermore that self-identification with the working class does not always imply the existence of feelings of alienation, oppression, injustice, or nonintegration in the national community.

In 1947, only one-third of the workers interviewed by the French Institute of Public Opinion (IFOP) classified themselves in the "poor" class, 60 percent placed themselves in the "modest" class and 8 percent among the "well-off." Most of those who placed themselves in the "poor" class voted Communist, whereas the majority of those who ranked themselves in the "modest" class showed their preference for the Social Democratic Party (SFIO), the Christian Democratic Party (MRP), Gaullism, or the conservative "Moderates."

In 1950, according to a survey of the French National Institute of Demographic Studies, nearly half of those identifying their status as "working class" did not consider themselves to be in the most disinherited class (*Table 20*). Thus the consciousness of belonging to the working class is not necessarily equivalent to self-identification with the depressed proletariat. This distinction, perceived by the workers themselves, between "working class" and "poor class" has important psychological significance and may explain the political behavior of many workers.

Another IFOP survey carried out in 1951 reports that one-quarter of the workers who fully identify themselves with the working class believe that their position and standard of living depend on the wealth of France as a nation, rather than on the position of their social class inside France. What significance could the slogan "Workers of the world, unite!" have for these workers? Whatever the case, most of these workers who feel themselves integrated into the national community, declare themselves to be Socialist, Gaullist, Catholic, or Moderate, whereas those whose class consciousness prevails over their identification with the nation most often put their hope in the Communist Party.

Five years later, in 1956, IFOP asked a similar question: "Do you feel that, if France's prosperity increases, your own standard of living will increase proportionally, or do you believe that things will not change much for you?" One-third of the workers interviewed felt that their personal situation was linked to the general prosperity of the country. Such optimism prevents these workers from taking extremist political positions. Another third, mainly composed of workers who support the Communist Party or who are members of the General Confederation of Labor (CGT) stated that nothing would change for them if the national wealth were to increase. The remaining third did not have a clear opinion. This feeling that they would benefit from greater national prosperity varied, as it should, with income. The better-paid workers appeared to be better integrated in the national community.

Class consciousness and the feelings of frustration which are associated with it among the lowest-income groups may be reflected in the answers given to other questions, such as the following: "Do you feel that, in the present state of affairs, there is much or not too much injustice?" Two-thirds of the workers answered—"much injustice"—a feeling which cannot but influence political opinions and engender attitudes of protest.

Few data are available in France on the trifold relationship between vertical social mobility, social self-identification, and political affiliation. However, two points seem quite well established. The downwardly mobile—more numerous than is generally thought—as for example, workers who are sons of clerks, lower civil servants who are sons of landowners, rentiers who are victims of monetary devaluation, and the like, very often remain attached to the social status and the symbols of their former class but, strongly frustrated, express Extreme-Right tendencies. Among those ascending the social ladder one category deserves special attention: the sons of teachers who, thanks to their fathers' care and attention, benefit from a good education and thus may climb, by the springboard of the school, the rungs of the social hierarchy. Their fathers, longtime leftists, also give them a political education. In spite of their social success, often brilliant, they feel politically close to the "humble" and remain Radical, Socialist, or Communist like their fathers.

For Italy, we can refer first to a survey carried out in 1958, which indicates that, as in France, only a minority of industrial workers identify themselves with the "poor class," although half of the agricultural workers do so. More significant perhaps is the fact that more than one-third of the clerks identify themselves with the "working class."

Economic progress in Italy since the war has resulted in considerable geographical mobility. Hundreds of thousands of agricultural workers and sons of small farmers have found jobs in urban industry, generally as unskilled workers. These new workers from the traditionalist milieu of the *Mezzogiorno* have emigrated to the North, lacking skill and education and impregnated with the values of a strongly hierarchical society. Changing one's occupation does not necessarily result in a change in thinking. Mental structures are usually rather rigid; one does not acquire class consciousness overnight. One might have thought that Christian Democratic and Monarchist voting is more frequent among industrial workers who are sons of southern peasants than among workers born and raised in the northern industrial cities. The more so since many emigrants have found work in the North, thanks to Catholic recommendations. This hypothesis, although valid in the recent past, as we shall see further on, does not hold any longer.

A survey in 1960, by the *Centro Italiano Studi e Ricerche,* analyzes the relationship between social class identification and the image people had of the various parties through this identification. Unfortunately, a good number of persons refused to answer or gave an unclassifiable answer. Nevertheless the survey showed that no class of social self-identification designates en bloc one single party as its legitimate representative. In each class, opinions diverge. However, the image of each party varies significantly from one class to another.

Table 20—Working-Class Consciousness and Proletarian Consciousness

FRANCE: Survey of the National Institute of Demographic Studies, 1950	GIVEN THE FOLLOWING CLASSIFICATION, IN WHICH CLASS WOULD YOU PLACE YOURSELF?					
	Working class	Peasant class	Middle class	Bourge- oisie	Other	Number interviewed
And given this classification ...						
Rich class	0.1%	0.9%	0.4%	8.3%	2.6%	30
Upper-middle class	3.7	25.9	26.4	61.8	2.6	459
Lower-middle class	46.6	39.8	57.8	21.1	23.7	1,006
Poor class	43.2	23.5	2.9	3.1	34.2	510
Other answers	6.4	9.9	12.5	5.7	36.9	225
Total	100.0%	100.0%	100.0%	100.0%	100.0%	
Number interviewed	799	425	664	228	114	2,230

Another survey by the *Centro Italiano Studi e Ricerche,* based on interviews with youths from twenty-one to twenty-five years of age, but whose results, we believe, could be extrapolated to the whole of the Italian popula-

Table 21—Social Identification and Political Preference in Italy*

Social Self-identification	POLITICAL TENDENCY						
	Communist	Socialist	Social Democrat	Christian Democrat	Liberal, Right	Not Classifiable	Total
Upper class	0.3%	0.2%	0.9%	1.3%	5.3%	1.2%	1.4%
Middle class	18.5	22.7	38.5	37.4	47.7	32.8	33.3
Working class (ᵃ)	65.2	66.5	51.7	50.9	42.8	51.1	54.6
Poor class	12.8	10.2	6.1	5.9	3.5	6.3	7.3
No answer	3.2	0.4	2.8	4.5	0.7	8.6	3.4
Total	100.0%	100.0%	100.0%	100.0%	100.0%	100.0%	100.0%
Absolute numbers	345	411	213	1,037	285	174	2,465

* Survey carried out in January 1963 by the Italian Center for Study and Research (CISER) among youths between twenty-one and twenty-five years of age (mimeographed manuscript).
ᵃ The expression "*classe lavoratrice,*" used by the surveyors is somewhat ambiguous.

tion—indicates that the supporters of most of the political parties show a great heterogeneity at the level of social self-identification (*Table 21*). We also know through other surveys, too detailed for reproduction here, the results of which, however, are similar to those found for France, that the relation between social condition and social self-identification is far from close.

The phenomenon that we are trying to analyze is therefore complex, for it involves the interplay of four variables: objective social condition, perception of this condition, political party, and the subjective image of this party. Perhaps the inclusion of a fifth variable, for example, religious attitude, would help us to gain a clearer picture.

Let us conclude, provisionally, that the relationship between voting behavior and social-class perception appears to be more significant than the relationship between voting and objective class position. In any event, the essential reason for political cleavages should be sought at the sociopsychological level, as well as in terms of socioeconomic stratification.

We shall now use these elements to characterize the various types of voters.

OUTLINE OF A POLITICAL TYPOLOGY OF THE VOTERS

Any typology is necessarily more or less arbitrary. It is not easy to discover actual individuals who conform to an ideal type. The average worker just does not exist. However, the concept of the average worker greatly aids the economist, the sociologist, and the statistician. Any typology is necessarily rather schematic because it must bring to light essential characteristics and leave in the shadow secondary traits. Distinguishing several types nevertheless permits a better grasp of the actual diversity. From a political point of view, six types of French workers may be described:

REVOLUTIONARY WORKER. He is convinced that his social condition will be improved by a revolution rather than by slow changes. When asked by IFOP surveyors, "Do you think that under certain circumstances, your party should take power by force, that is, by non-constitutional means?" he replied in the affirmative. This worker identifies himself with the working class and agrees with the principal tenets of Marxist ideology. His class consciousness is well developed. For him, worker solidarity ranks first in the hierarchy of values. He keeps himself informed on political events by reading his newspaper daily. A union man, he is always favorable to strikes, whether they are strictly economic or political in character. His affiliation to a Marxist party has an emotional coloring as well as a rational component. Combative by temperament, he normally votes Communist.

PROTESTING WORKER. He votes for the Communist Party without adopting Marxist ideology. This worker accepts the tag but in fact rejects the content of the doctrine. He declares that he votes Communist, but when asked concrete questions on Marxist subjects, he proves to be ignorant about Marxism, or at least he does not accept many of its fundamental principles. Voting Communist is a way of protesting for him. He votes "against." He is the proletarian without savings who lives in a state of insecurity, who feels himself exploited, persecuted, and frustrated, who complains, yet without adopting Marxist ideology. In 1952, more than half the workers supporting the Communist Party said that the doctrine of this party was not an essential reason for their vote. To the question, "Does the party for which you have voted at the last election receive your complete confidence?", less than two-thirds of the Communist workers answered affirmatively. The answers that they gave to various questions show that in reality less than half of them were all-out supporters. The protesting worker votes for the Communist Party as a party of opposition, without necessarily desiring a Communist regime. He would perhaps stop voting Communist if such a possibility really presented itself. His continual discontent leads him to vote for the party of greatest opposition or, sometimes, for a new movement: Gaullist in 1947, for Mendès-France in 1956. Thus he is very often a switch voter. He tends to be pessimistic in his outlook, whereas the revolutionary worker is rather optimistic on the whole. His ideas are not consistent. In the psychological configuration of his personality, one perceives traits commonly found in extreme rightists. He votes for the Extreme Left, but he could become, under certain circumstances, an extreme rightist. He could easily pass from one extreme to the other, as occurred during the Weimar Republic, when many German voters who had backed the Extreme Left in the 1928 election supported the Nazis in 1932 and 1933.

The Communist voters who adhere to Marxist ideology are proportionally more numerous among skilled or specialized workers than among unskilled workers. In other words, the protesting type of worker is more likely to be found among the unskilled, especially among agricultural workers. The most exploited workers, i.e., the worst housed, the lowest paid, the least educated, are also those who most frequently vote Communist without adhering to Marxist ideology.

REFORMIST WORKER. He willingly identifies himself with the working class, approves of union action and thinks that the lot of workers will be improved by gradual change rather than by revolution. He is mainly interested in social reforms that can be achieved in the short run in contrast to the revolutionary worker who projects his ideals into a rather distant future. The reformist worker is indifferent to religious beliefs, and is often anticlerical. He normally votes Socialist, but he may also vote Communist. In the latter case, he attaches more weight to immediate reforms advocated by the Communist Party than to its long-range objectives. He may vote for the Extreme Left in a specific social and political context, because, paradoxically, in this context, the Communist Party appears to him as a reformist party. Indeed, during the Fourth Republic, when Parliament was the center of gravity of the regime, the Communist group weighed heavily in the polling on social reforms.

CATHOLIC WORKER. His vote is determined by religious commitment. His political orientation has a moral basis which is not necessarily tied to his socioeconomic status. He is to be found among skilled workers as well as unskilled, among workers with high or low income, in large as well as small businesses. Naturally, he generally votes for the MRP (Popular Republican Movement—Christian Democratic) or, when there is no candidate from this party, for a "right-minded" moderate. In trade union elections, he supports the CFTC (French Confederation of the Christian Workers). The Catholic worker may also be a reformist. Nevertheless, the religious motivation of his political orientation differentiates him from the preceding type.

CONSERVATIVE WORKER. He identifies himself with the petty bourgeoisie, and thinks that his socioeconomic condition depends on the wealth of France rather than on the fate of his class within the nation. He voted for the RPF (Gaullist) in the 1947 municipal elections and in the 1951 elections for the legislature; for moderate or rightist candidates in 1956, and for the UNR

(Union for the New Republic—Gaullist) in 1958 and 1962. He is often nationalist or at least jingoistic in his speech. He does not willingly join a trade union; he votes for independent candidates or autonomous tickets in the elections for factory committees. In the legislative elections he prefers to vote for a person rather than for a party. His father's family belonged to the urban petty bourgeoisie or to the peasantry; sometimes he is downwardly mobile, particularly if he is of urban origin. He usually works for a small company and has good skill qualifications. His salary is relatively high and he does not fear unemployment. Finally, and this is an essential characteristic, he is often a veteran who holds fond recollections of the war and of the years spent in the service, whereas the worker who participated in the *Résistance* is more apt to be a leftist.

INDIFFERENT WORKER. He is a nonvoter. He does not follow politics in the press and remains poorly informed about public affairs. He has no opinion and no preference; no interest in trade-union activity, even if he may support a strike; no political discussions with his workmates. He has neither sympathy nor deep-seated hostility toward any party. Without illusions about collective action, he seems to be secure from political disappointment of any kind. He lives withdrawn within his family. But, though he may be amorphous politically, he is not isolated socially; on the contrary, he may even be well integrated socially.

These same types of workers may be found in Italy. First of all the revolutionary worker. One out of five Italian workers is convinced that social injustices can be terminated by a revolution. He normally votes Communist. The majority of workers, however, believe in a gradual reduction of social injustice. They are reformists. They are spread among various political parties and this scattering occurs according to criteria that a secondary analysis readily reveals. Thus we may distinguish the Catholic reformist who votes for the Christian Democratic Party, and the anticlerical reformist who tends to vote Socialist or, if he is highly skilled, Social Democratic. This anticlerical reformist may even vote Communist, particularly if he firmly believes in the effectiveness of strikes, or if he participated in guerrilla warfare against the Germans.

But, as in France, many Italian Communists are neither revolutionaries nor reformists. They are instead protesters. Discontented with their situation like the revolutionaries, they seem less optimistic. They do not believe that social injustice can be eliminated even by revolution. But far from being resigned, they make a point of expressing their discontent. However, their protest vote, as surveys have shown, does not imply an adherence to Marxist ideology.

Catholic workers are more numerous in Italy, where Catholic action is better organized, and many industrial workers are closely tied to religious traditions. On the other hand, conservative workers are less common in Italy. Like his French counterpart, the Italian conservative worker remains apart from trade union activity. He is more favorable than other workers toward a law which requires union leaders to call a vote before a strike. His political opinions are more conservative than traditionalist, which, as in France, differentiates him from the Catholic worker.

Besides the six types of workers common to both countries, it is possible to add another one, peculiar to southern Italy, the "*clientèle* worker." In certain regions of the *Mezzogiorno,* there is a subtle system of *clientèles* with numerous ramifications. Unemployment being chronic, the worker without any skills considers himself rather privileged compared to the unemployed, when, after a long wait and thanks to recommendations, he finally finds a job. On election day, he will give his support quite naturally to his protector, who is himself only a link in a *clientèle* chain. In the 1946 referendum on the monarchy, most of the *clientèle* workers voted Monarchist. In the following elections their votes were determined by the particular *clientèle* they were tied to, from the Communists to the Neo-Fascists. No explanation of the political behavior of a part of the *popolino* (common people) of southern Italy is possible without taking into account the *clientèle* voter. The *clientèle* type of voter is less common today than ten or fifteen years ago.[35]

Although in part intuitive, this typology may help explain certain tendencies which do not appear in voting behavior, for the shade of the vote does not necessarily reflect coherent ideas, nor the entire range of the voter's opinions. One can support a party, while disapproving of the positions taken on certain issues by its leaders. To give only two examples, in 1951 one out of six French Communists interviewed expressed hostility toward the Soviet Union; in 1958, one Socialist in five approved of a reference to God in the preamble of the Constitution, and one Popular Republican (Christian Democrat) out of five disapproved of it.

According to a survey by the IFOP in 1956, already referred to, one-fifth of the French workers believed that they could achieve real improvement in their social condition but by a revolution. Admitting that such a conviction denotes a certain propensity, more or less latent, to revolutionary ideology, it would appear that in France, out of a total of nine million industrial workers and their wives, less than two million conceive of political action and class struggle in the perspective of a social revolution in the Marxist sense of the word. Let us also assume that almost all of these "revolutionaries" voted Communist. Since the number of workers (and members of their families) who voted Communist in the 1956 elections may be estimated at something less than four million, it follows that revolutionaries do not constitute a majority of the working-class supporters of the French Communist Party.

Similarly in Italy, the results of opinion surveys indicate that in 1958, out of a total of ten million industrial working class voters, male and female, two million at most entertained, more or less consciously, revolutionary hopes. In the same year, according to our estimates, the Italian Communist Party received 3.700,000 votes from this social category. In other words, approximately half of the Italian Communist workers do not express revolutionary sentiments. There is a striking similarity between both countries in this respect.

In short, while all revolutionaries may be Communists, not all Communists are revolutionaries. The proportion of revolutionaries is, of course, greater among male voters. It is certainly much greater among party militants and members than among Communist voters not registered in the party. In this connection it should be noted that in France, in 1956, nine out of ten Communist voters were not party members, while in Italy, in 1958, only three out of four were not.

In short, among workers particularly, three types of Communist voters can be distinguished: the revolutionary, the protester, and the reformist. The two latter types, while voting Communist, support the Atlantic Alliance, condemn both the Russian military intervention in Hungary in 1956, and the repression of the workers' strike in Berlin in 1953, may approve of subsidizing private (Catholic) schools, and may criticize many other policies of the Communist Party.

Is it possible for a party which appeals to such a diversified electorate to offer the same outlook everywhere, to be identical everywhere?

REGIONAL POLYMORPHISM
OF PARTIES

The laws of Lamarck and Darwin have been applied to human society for a long time. Political "species" vary from one socioeconomic environment to another, and the same "species" may give rise, in different cultural contexts, to different "varieties."

In France and Italy, political cleavages do not take on their complete meaning if they are not observed in regional contexts, varying with the focus peculiar to each region. Political problems are often seen from an altered perspective in different parts of the country. Thus, voting is influenced by local considerations. Parties try to adapt themselves to their milieu of implantation. Therefore, there is at the same time both symbiosis and polymorphism. In each type of party, we can discover at least two varieties.

TWO COMMUNISMS. One is industrial, the other agrarian (*Fig. 8*). The Communist vote does not respond to the same motivation for the tenant farmers of Ferrara as for the metal workers of Turin; for the small farmers of Creuse as for the lower-level civil servants of Paris; for the agricultural workers of Andria as for the clerks of Genoa. According to whether it is addressed to industrial workers, farmers with small plots, or agricultural workers, Communist ideology will advocate nationalization of large plants for the first, defense of peasant property for the second, and collective farms for the third.

The peasants of central Italy and of the Massif Central area in France, both "protesters" and anticlerical, belong to the same type of Communist voters; the workers in the Milan and Paris suburbs, to a completely different type.

TWO SOCIALISMS. In France Socialism for a long time has been divided according to several tendencies. Party unity, more apparent than real, occurred quite late in its history. In Italy in 1964, three parties called themselves socialist: PSI (Italian Socialist Party), PSDI (Italian Social Democratic Party), and PSIUP (Italian Socialist Party of Popular Union). This situation was due partially to rivalry among leaders but it resulted also from different social as well as political regional structures. As for Communism, it is necessary to distinguish urban Socialism from rural. In France the northern miner and the southern vine grower both vote Socialist. But the former is well paid and a union member; the latter, poor and unorganized. They do not belong to the same variety of Socialism. Neither do the skilled factory workers of the Fiat works and the illiterate unemployed of Matera.

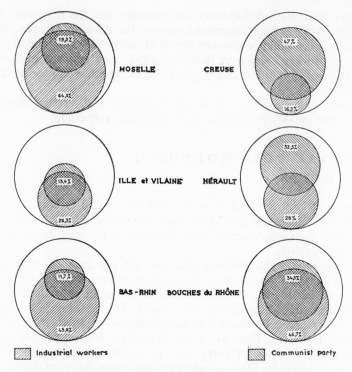

| Industrial workers | Communist party |

Figure 8—The Two Types of Communism in France.

MOSELLE: Highly industrialized department; Communist party weak. Two-thirds of the industrial workers vote Christian-Democrat or Socialist, but nearly all Communist voters are industrial workers.

CREUSE: Heavily agricultural department; Communist party strong. At least half of the industrial workers do not vote Communist, and three-quarters of the Communist voters are small farmers.

ILLE ET VILAINE: Half of the industrial workers are not Communists, but three-quarters of the Communist voters are industrial workers.

HÉRAULT: Same percentage of industrial workers as in Ille et Vilaine but note strength of the Communist party. Two-thirds of the industrial workers are not Communists and two-thirds of the Communists are not industrial workers.

BAS-RHIN: The majority of industrial workers are not Communists; among the Communist workers the majority are "reformist-type" voters.

BOUCHES DU RHÔNE: The majority of industrial workers vote Communist; of these, the majority are "protest-type" or "revolutionary-type" voters.

Furthermore, where Socialism is strong and Communism weak, the former appears as a bulwark against the latter, and Socialist propaganda denounces totalitarianism; where Communism constitutes the principal political power, Socialism figures as an "enemy brother" and allows itself to be swept into "popular front" alliances, particularly to win municipal elections with the aid of the Radicals. Finally, where both parties are weak, that is, in conservative areas, Socialism emphasizes anticlericalism and is polarized against the right. In short, from the point of view of electoral strategy, the physiognomy of Socialism varies, being at times on the Left, at times on the Right, in the directional rather than political sense of these words.

TWO RADICALISMS. In some regions, particularly in the North, Radicalism has changed its traditional electoral basis and lost its anticlerical character as well as its Socialist tone. It has become a moderate party. In other regions, for example in the Southwest, it has remained anticlerical and close to the Socialists. Here it is rural, there it is urban, and everywhere, a party of notables who are almost divided in parliament. The political split between the Parliament's Left and Right usually slices through the Radical ranks, cutting the party in two.

TWO CHRISTIAN DEMOCRACIES. The Christian Democratic Party is, in reality, a federation of parties, for it is composed of several factions which can be grouped into a Left wing and a Right wing. The former is reformist in social matters and liberal in the religious domain; the latter is liberal (laissez faire) in economic affairs and more or less "integrist" in religious matters. The one wing is strong in the poorer urban districts and leans toward the center Left; the other finds its support among peasantry or the bourgeoisie and leans toward the center Right. Considered on a national level, this party appears as a multi-class party; observed on a regional level, a polymorphous party. It shows a different physiognomy in Lombardy and in Basilicata, in Liguria and in Sardinia, in Rome of Andreotti and Florence of La Pira, at the top and at the bottom of society.

In Alsace, the only region in France where the concordat with the Vatican is still in effect, the MRP vote (Popular Republican Movement—Christian Democratic) has a religious meaning. In Burgundy, it means, in simple terms, social conservatism, without the backing of any strong religious tradition. In the east of France, the MRP electorate is working class and progressive; in Brittany, peasant and reactionary.

TWO GAULLISMS. One is rather charismatic, diffused in all social strata; the other rather eclectic, a mixture of neo-liberalism, old nationalism, technocratic reformism, civic virtue, and opportunism. The regional diversity of these two Gaullisms is not yet very accentuated.

TWO EXTREME RIGHTS: Fascists and Monarchists in Italy, Maurrassiens and Poujadists in France. The "activist" officer and the reactionary shopkeeper do not slip toward the Extreme Right for the same reason. The emulators of Maurras find a favorable climate mainly in large cities; the Poujadistic social epidemic spread particularly in the small sleepy towns. The Monarchist vote in Naples and the Fascist vote in Brindisi are both *clientèle* votes and are nourished by postwar unemployment, whereas in Rome or in Bari, both movements express a nostalgia for one or the other defunct regimes. In Trieste, Neo-Fascism is a consequence of anti-Yugoslav nationalism.

The vote for the same party clearly does not have the same meaning everywhere. It is differently colored from one region to another, according to the dominant social category or the balance of power of the opposing political forces. Moreover, the party leaders cultivate this polymorphism by adapting their programs to regional contexts.[36] Here they insist on one point, there on another. Among the regional variations of the campaign platform, some contradictions may exist. They matter little; the voter does not notice them because he generally knows only one version of the platform. The contradictions will not appear until later, in parliament. But at the following elections, after several cabinet crises, it is easy to place the responsibility on "the others."

In both countries the political "rainbow" refracts the seven colors of the solar spectrum, from violet to red, and the polymorphism of the parties widens the range of colors, which are all reflected, sometimes confusedly, in the "broken mirror" (as Gambetta put it) of the Chamber of Deputies. It is not so much that polymorphism of the parties tends to multiply parliamentary groups, but, and this is much more dangerous, it accentuates their incoherence, which is a source of ministerial instability.

Because of this regional polymorphism, the adoption in France and Italy of a uninominal electoral system, with only one ballot, as in Great Britain and in the United States, would probably not result in a two-party system, even in the absence of the Communist mortgage. Such an electoral system would, of course, favor the two-party system at the local level, but the two opposing parties would not be the same everywhere: Catholics against Radicals, Socialists against Catholics, Conservatives against Radicals, Socialists against Conservatives, and so on. A national multiparty system, based on local two-party systems, might result in a more stable political regime. Perhaps. But the existence of a Communist Party capable of securing a relative majority of the votes in numerous constituencies presented short- or long-term risks, which made government hesitate to adopt a uninominal electoral system with one ballot.

De Gaulle in 1945 or 1958 and de Gasperi in 1948–53 would have been able, if they had wanted, to adopt a simple majority system. Neither one decided to do so.[37]

For this polymorphism is not only subject to present-day realities. It has its roots in the distant past.

HISTORICAL ROOTS OF POLITICAL CLEAVAGES

Even if all the quantifiable data concerning the economic, social, cultural, and political structure of present-day France and Italy were processed by a computer, it would not produce an understanding of the political cleavages in these countries if their historical background were neglected. Certain findings are better understood if they are placed in historical perspective.

Seeking the reasons for the political difficulties of contemporary France, Charles Morazé concludes that "the responsibility belongs to the history of France."[38] "Without reference to history, the analysis of the Fourth Republic would be deprived of an essential dimension," writes Raymond Aron.[39] "In order to explain certain differences having consistently reoccurred in the electoral behavior of some cantons or communes, one has to go back to history," notes François Goguel.[40] The existence of two Italys, one in the north, the other south of Rome, is the fruit of history as well as of geography.

Political regimes follow one another, interrupted by revolutions or *coups d'état:* monarchy by divine right, revolutionary republic, charismatic empire, constitutional monarchy, liberal monarchy, presidential republic, plebiscitarian empire, parliamentary republic, military occupation, multiparty republic, charismatic republic. But, in their passing, they leave layers of opinion, analogous to geological sediments. In the year 2,000, there will still be Gaullists, as there were Orleanists, Legitimists, and Bonapartists in the 1880's.

The Revolution of 1789, by undertaking the partition of the large domains of the Church and nobility, transformed the peasants of some regions into allies of the Republic. The return of the Bourbon in 1815, with the support of the Church, renewed the question of land ownership. Thus the republicanism of many peasants was tinged with anticlericalism. The Radical, Socialist, and Communist parties still place themselves in the tradition of the Revolution and that of the Jacobins. The support given by the Church to the Bourbons made Bonapartist Corsicans anticlerical. In the fatherland of Napoleon, Radicalism is the grandchild of Bonapartism. In Brittany, Anjou, and Le Maine, conservatism has its roots in the *chouannerie,* a royalist insurrection under the First Republic. In the Vendée, even today, political cleavage is not defined in terms of Left and Right, or "reds" and conservatives; people rather use the terms Whites and Blues, which owe their origin to the opposition between the *chouans* and the republicans. The Dreyfus affair caused some eastern zones to move toward the Right because of the anticlericalism of the *Dreyfusards.* Some Basque districts ignore the border between France and Spain.

The roots of political cleavages sometimes go deep into the past. Consider the remarks of André Siegfried in his *Electoral Geography of Ardèche,* in which he underlines the political difference between Catholics and Protestants: "If one realizes that the present area of Protestantism coincides with the old diocesan boundaries, themselves traced from those of the Roman *civitates* and the Gallic *pagi,* one cannot help feeling awed by the persistence of this millenary influence."[41]

In the northwest of France "the granite soil votes for the Right and the chalky soil for the Left." Siegfried has erroneously been credited with this remark. This is of no significance. There is surely no direct causality, in the rigorous sense of the word, but there is some correspondence between nature of the soil, agrarian landscape, type of dwelling, distribution of land ownership, degree of stratification of society, the stronger persistence of traditions, and political orientation.

A comparison, doubtlessly audacious, might be made between Radicalism in the Toulouse region and the *Cathar* heresy of the twelfth century. Scandalized by the sumptuous life of the dukes of Toulouse, the Cathars or Albigenses undermined ownership, fought every form of authority, and suppressed Catholic religious services. Pope Innocent III waged a crusade against them in 1208. This heresy prepared the way for Protestantism and for hostility toward feudalism. Remnants of the Cathar spirit still persist. Anticlerical Radicalism found its favorite homeland in this area. The spread of the famous newspaper *La Dépêche de Toulouse* answered an historical need. This bold interpretation does not exclude other explanations.

In certain regions of Italy, vote varies according to altitude. Mountain areas are more conservative than the hills, and these more so than the plains: the nearer to heaven, the better preserved is Christian tradition, as is small landownership. Large landownership is more common in the rich plain and the low hills. Thus, geography leads back to economy, and this to history.

There is no spontaneous generation in politics. A map of Communist-

Socialist votes in 1946 coincides to a large extent with the map of Socialist support in 1919. They match almost perfectly for central Italy.

Of the four most "red" regions of Italy, three belonged once to the Pontifical State: Emilia-Romagna, the Marches, and Umbria. In order to understand the voting behavior of the citizens of these regions, it is necessary to go back to the time when the Church owned extensive lands and exploited the peasants. In 1831, representatives of the cities of these regions gathered in Bologna in order to protest against "the temporal power of the Pope." Today these cities have town councils with Communist-Socialist majorities. Bologna has a Communist mayor.

The fourth "red" region, Tuscany, did not belong to the Vatican, but its anticlericalism has a very long history, as attested by Tuscan folklore of the sixteenth and seventeenth centuries. There is one exceptional "white" spot in it which deserves some attention: the province of Lucca which overwhelmingly votes Christian Democratic. Small landownership is prevalent there, whereas in the rest of Tuscany, as well as in Emilia, Umbria, and the Marches a large part of the agricultural population is composed of tenant farmers and workers. But its present social structure does not explain everything because in some other regions small farmers vote for the Left, and in the province of Venice, tenant farmers and agricultural workers vote Christian Democratic. Lucca today is "white," even though the surrounding region is "red," because it was able to preserve its own individuality through the centuries (it was an independent duchy once), and because church attendance there is still high.

During the last war, the front settled for a long time in these "red" regions of central Italy: the Resistance took on Communist political overtones, much as in earlier times the *Risorgimento* became anticlerical, because Popes Gregory XVI and Pius IX opposed the unification of Italy and refused to intervene in favor of the liberation of the provinces occupied by Catholic Austria.

To simplify, it would appear that in most cases, everything else being equal, where the temporal power of the Church was strong in the past, contemporary parties with Christian orientation are weak and vice versa. In both of these Latin and Catholic countries, Communism is historically the spiritual heir of anticlericalism as much as it is an ideology generated by the economic conflict between social classes.

The collective memory of the past is preserved to the extent that a community, by its ties with the land, conserves a certain cohesiveness. What happens in the case of massive emigration, of population mixture due to economic development?

SOCIAL ATAXIA: ECONOMIC DEVELOPMENT IN THE NORTH, COMMUNIST RISE IN THE SOUTH, OF ITALY

Theorists, in the recent past, used to postulate that strong economic development should result in a drop in the Communist electorate. However, Italian events would seem to defy this hypothesis. Despite the considerable economic progress of the last twenty years, such that one may rightly speak of an "economic miracle," Communist strength has steadily increased from 19 percent of the vote in 1946 to 25.3 percent in 1963, a 30 percent increase. How to explain such a challenge to these widely accepted assumptions? A double analysis, on one hand, of the development of the society and, on the other hand, of the change in the social basis of Communism could throw some light on this paradox.

Economic Evolution of the Two Italys

The contrast between northern Italy, industrialized, with an intensive type of agriculture, and the *Mezzogiorno* (southern Italy), essentially agricultural, poor, and prey to chronic unemployment, is great. In 1951, the *Mezzogiorno* had 37 percent of the national population but only 12.6 percent of the automobiles, 13.1 percent of the tractors, 10.6 percent of the telephones, 9.9 percent of the total circulation of the daily and weekly press, 10 percent of the factories with more than one hundred employees, and the like. In the North only 4.4 percent of those over six years of age were illiterate, as compared to 24 percent in the *Mezzogiorno*. Income per capita was but 119,000 *lire* in the *Mezzogiorno,* in contrast to 278,000 in the North.[42]

Between 1951 and 1961 the Italian population increased by 6.2 percent, but in the capitals of the provinces the increase was 20 percent, and in other communes, only 0.7 percent. The process of urbanization was stronger in the North than in the South. In the same period, Italy rapidly industrialized, but the increase in the number of the industrial workers in the North was 40 percent compared to 16 percent in the South.

The economic disparity between the two Italys brought about a large emigration from the South to the North; 12 percent of the entire population of the *Mezzogiorno* has emigrated. Since the emigrants are mainly young men, the actual migratory movement of the work force is greater still, and the social and political consequences of the migration are actually even more important than the gross figures indicate.

The Mutation of Communism

The great changes that have occurred in Italian society could not help having important repercussions on the social composition of the Communist Party. Although the Communist strength has not fallen, its social base has undergone profound change.

Figure 9 clearly shows this. Italian provinces may be grouped into four areas: South, Center, Northeast, and Northwest, roughly corresponding to different economic, social, religious, and cultural realities. The star indicates the national average of Communist votes in 1946 and 1963. The political evolution of the various provinces must be interpreted in relation to this average. In 1946, the Communists were weakest in the poorest part of the country, the *Mezzogiorno,* but it is precisely there that the party has grown the most. Indeed, in every province of the *Mezzogiorno,* Communist gains between 1946 and 1963 have been greater than the national increase of the Communist vote (6.3 percent). The same phenomenon of great gains oc-

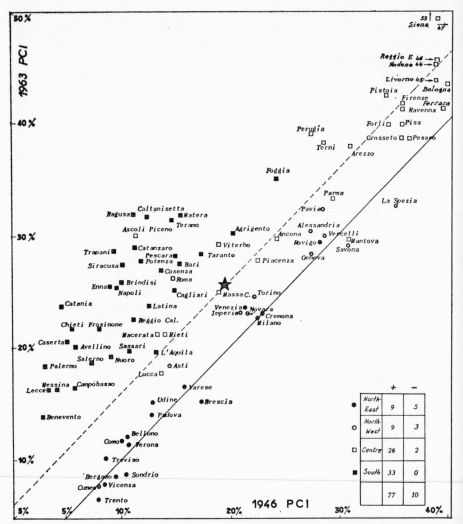

**Figure 9—The Italian Communist Party Slips Southward,
Becoming More Rural and Agrarian.**

curred in nine other provinces, but with one exception (Pistoia in Tuscany),
these are located in the southern part of central Italy. They are Rome,
Viterbo, Rieti, Perugia, Terni, Macerata, Ascoli, and Arezzo. So that of the
forty-two provinces showing the greatest increase in Communist strength,
forty-one form a compact block, constituting the southern half of Italy. By
contrast, in the most industrialized provinces, Milano, Torino, Genova,
Como, Varese, Vercelli, Brescia, and La Spezia, the Communist Party
marked time or actually lost ground.

Figure 10 illustrates the same phenomenon from a different outlook. The provinces are classified, on the one hand according to an index which measures standard of living and level of consumption, the Tagliacarne index,[43] and on the other hand according to the increase in the Communist votes, i.e., the difference between the percentage of Communist votes in 1946 and in 1963. For example, in the province of Ragusa, the Communist Party vote grew in this period from 11.2 percent to 31.9 percent, a gain of 20.7 percent. Thus, it tripled its electoral strength there. Conversely, in the province of Florence, where Communism was much more deeply entrenched than in Ragusa, the increase was only 5.7 percent. Comparing the two graphs indicates clearly that the Communist Party has grown most in the areas in which it was weakest.

In thirty-four provinces the Communist Party vote increased by more than 10 percent (in relation to the total number of votes). Except for one of them, all these provinces are poor, their standard of living is lower than the median of Tagliacarne index. Almost all of these are southern provinces. Of fifty-three provinces in which the Italian Communist Party gained less than it did nationally or actually lost votes, only thirteen are poorer than the national average.

What little industrialization has occurred in the *Mezzogiorno* is to be found in the cities. In other words, it was there that the proportion of industrial workers increased. Now, in many provinces of the *Mezzogiorno,* the Communist Party gained much more in small towns than in cities. On the other hand, local studies that we have undertaken, and too detailed for discussion here, show that if in a given zone the number of industrial workers doubles, that of Communist votes triples or quadruples. It appears that the Communist Party has been much more successful in the rural and agricultural milieu than in the urban industrial environment. The "agrarianization" of the Communist Party is perhaps even more striking than a simple comparison between extent of industrialization and Communist gains would indicate. The available evidence indicates that new industrial workers in the south consider themselves privileged relative to the unemployed remaining in the countryside; therefore they are less prone to voting Communist than the latter. Many new workers owe their jobs to *clientèle* protection, as was noted earlier. Communist growth, therefore, has not only been southern but also largely agrarian in character.

Various factors could account for the Communist advance in the *Mezzogiorno.* Two aspects seem particularly important: the psychological consequences of economic development, and migration as an ideological vector.

Economic Improvement and Psychological Dissatisfaction

In a country in which everybody is equally poor, nobody resents social injustice. In some societies, people live in misery, without knowing it. In India, some time ago, poverty was so widespread that it appeared "normal." The caste system represents an extreme case of an attitude of surrender to a fatality attributed to the nature of things or to a divine order. In other societies which have a certain level of well being, but a rigid status structure,

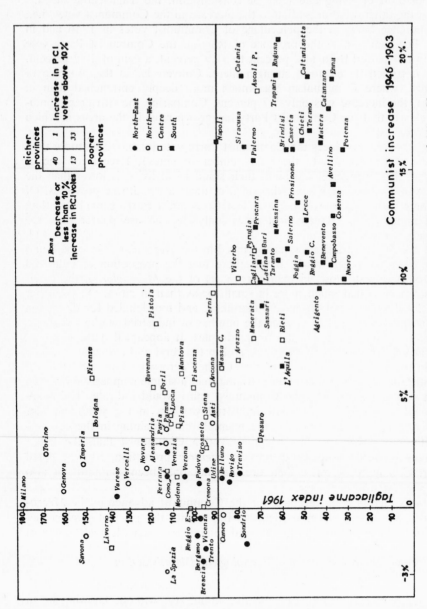

Figure 10—*Low Economic Level, Strong Communist Progress, and Vice Versa.*
The progress of Communism in the poorer provinces of Southern Italy between
1946 and 1963 elections.

men do not foresee the possibility of improving their fate. Their grandfathers were poor, so were their fathers. They resign themselves to believing that it is an inescapable necessity of life that there be rich and poor, powerful and weak; and religion often supports such fatalistic attitudes. Men do not fight for what appears to them inaccessible.

What happens in a country which experiences rapid economic development, social mobility, and cultural progress? Improvement in the standard of living, even slight, proves precisely that improvement is possible. As soon as the poor people see a chance, small though it may be, of extricating themselves from poverty, their resignation gives way to a feeling of frustration. Those who improve their social conditions somewhat are the very ones whose needs and aspirations grow more rapidly than the possibilities to satisfy them. For even when growth and prosperity benefit everybody, they cannot benefit everybody equally. Often growth throws existing social inequalities, both objective and subjective, into public focus.

In the end, what holds the attention of the man of modest means is not the improvement of his standard of living but the fact that he is still badly off as compared to others. The perception of social contrast can become sharper even when the standard of living is actually rising. One is less poor, but at the same time more discontent.

On this point, Communists and liberals agree. "Economic development has accentuated and made more evident a series of disequilibria, contrasts and social injustices from which the workers suffer," declared P. Togliatti in 1963.[44] "Economic progress creates as many demands as it satisfies," writes Raymond Aron.[45]

Emigration of People, Immigration of Ideologies

Many of the Italian emigrants to northern Italy, Germany, Switzerland, Belgium, and France remain, long after having emigrated, registered on the voting lists of their home towns, where their family has remained. On Election Day, many come to vote in their home village, all the more willingly as they are given railroad transportation at reduced rates. It is a good opportunity to see their family again at government expense. In spite of having migrated they, nevertheless, remain voters at home. At the time of the April 1963 elections, hundreds of thousands of migrants returned to their villages in the south.

Uprooted from their traditional milieu, thrust into the midst of industrial suburbs, with whose negative aspects they are well acquainted, influenced by political and union propaganda, these migrants, having changed their social milieu, very often modify their political opinions as well. They are not content with having switched their votes to Communism; once back in their villages for the elections, they often become strong advocates of their new political beliefs. The spread of political ideologies may be likened to the propagation of some contagious diseases. The implanting of Communism in some southern Italian regions is a good example of this process. Thus, curiously, the transfer of manpower from agriculture to industry has fostered the penetration of Communism in the countryside more than in the cities.

Ecological analyses in the northern industrial zones of Italy suggest a sig-

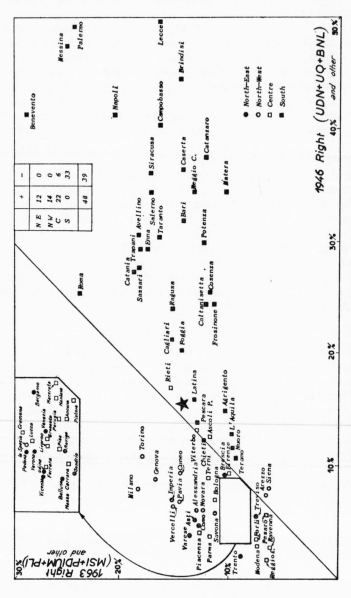

Figure 11—The Collapse of the Right in the South of Italy.

nificant relationship between the concentration of immigrants in the working-class suburbs of large cities and the increase in Communist support. But since Communist strength has remained relatively constant among the provinces of the "industrial triangle," it seems evident that many nonmigrants, old residents, deserted the Communist Party. Thus, the Communist Party has increasingly become southern even in the northern provinces! Although the strength of the Communist Party in the North has not varied much, the internal composition of its electorate has changed: less skilled workers (frequently of Lombardian or Piedmontese origin) and more unskilled workers (principally of southern origin).

Social Ataxia

Between 1951 and 1961, the rate of economic growth was almost the same for the *Mezzogiorno* (121 percent) as for the North (126 percent). However, it should be noted that the same rate of increase for unequal income strata means, in absolute terms, an aggravation of inequalities. If the income of two men, one receiving one hundred thousand *lire,* the other two hundred thousand *lire,* each double, the difference between them increases from one hundred thousand to two hundred thousand *lire.* The migration of people to the North has been much more important than the migration of capital to the South. The two Italys have undergone further distortion: economic miracle in the North; mirage in the South.

For two centuries Italian intellectuals—from economists to novelists—have denounced the misery in the South. The monarchy did nothing to remedy it; Fascism, by halting both internal and external migration, aggravated it; and the Republic, in spite of its good intentions (the Vanoni Plan) could not make up in a few years for a century-old backwardness. It is this backwardness which at the present time accelerates Communist growth.

To whose detriment? Of those who gave proof of inertia. The economic right (Liberals) and the political Extreme Right (Monarchists and Neo-Fascists) lost half of their votes in the *Mezzogiorno* between 1946 and 1963 (*Fig. 11*). As the Socialists (*Fig. 12*) and the Christian Democrats have gained some ground there, although in very modest proportions compared to the Communists, it would appear that the transfer of votes has occurred in part directly from one extreme to the other, in part by stages. Extreme Right votes shifted toward the Christian Democrats in 1948, but since then, were picked up by the Communist Party. In any event, the majority of new recruits of the Extreme Left come directly or indirectly from the Extreme Right, particularly the Monarchists. Among these new Communists, we observe mainly "protesters," rarely revolutionary Marxists. The Communist Party absorbs them very well by adapting itself to the surrounding milieu. This is one of the reasons for the ideological changes brought to the party program during recent years.

The various indicators of the improvement in the standard of living do not vary simultaneously, nor to the same extent. In the underdeveloped countries, the first sign of such an improvement is a decline in the death rate. In southern Italy this occurred together with another very noticeable consequence of

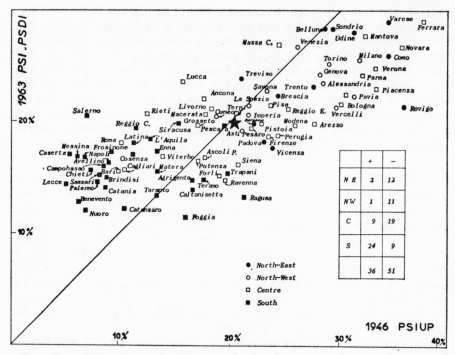

Figure 12—Decline of Socialism in the Industrial Areas of the Center and North, and Its Strengthening in the Agrarian Areas of the South of Italy.

economic development: the rise of Communism. Indeed, by 1963, for the first time, the death rate was lower in the South than in the North (must we put a bit of sunshine into our statistics for the standard of living?), and the proportion of electorate voting Communist, for the first time, was greater in the southernmost forty-two provinces than in the northernmost twenty-six provinces (26 percent as against 23 percent of the votes cast respectively, whereas in 1946 the proportions were 11 percent and 22 percent).

While the migratory movement pushed northward, Communism slipped southward; while the country became more and more urban, Communism became more and more *rural;* while Italy became increasingly industrialized, Communism became increasingly *agrarian.* Thus, Communism goes against the stream. Society goes in one direction; Communism in the other. The compass of economic development remains aimed at the polar star; Communism navigates toward the southern seas. This phenomenon is best conceptualized as social *ataxia,* to use a biological term, which designates the pathological noncoordination of movements of the body.

Finally, it would seem as if Communism has reached its high-water mark in the economically developed regions—recently it has been able to do no more than maintain its strength. Conversely, in the underdeveloped regions, especially in the *Mezzogiorno,* there subsists a reservoir of forces that could pour into the ranks of Communism.

In France, to the contrary, the Communist Party lost from 1956 to 1958 a third of its electoral strength, passing from 25 percent to 19 percent of the national vote (in the 1962 elections it recouped some of its losses). This phenomenon is due to the political conjuncture rather than to economic factors. It should be accounted for mainly by the charismatic influence of General de Gaulle in the dramatic circumstances which brought a new political regime.[46] The Republics may pass, but the deep cleavages of the French electorate among the Left, Center, and Right remain.

NOTES

1. The breakdown of the electorate into various socioprofessional categories poses a difficult problem. Economic and social statistics include foreigners, and young people under twenty-one years who aren't voters. In France, most of them belong to the industrial working class. Therefore, the percentage of industrial workers among the electors is less high than in the active population: in 1956, 37 against 40 percent. On the other hand, a significant part of the electorate is composed of women without a job (housewives) and of retired people. Since the social status of married women depends on their husbands', we consider only the statistics referring to the socioeconomic distribution of the active male population. So, by working-class electorate, we not only mean men employed in the industry, mines, transports, and such, but also their wives, working or not, as well as retired workers. The same procedure is adopted for all socioeconomic categories differentiated in this study. This applies to Italy too.

2. We have focused our analysis on the 1956 French elections, in order to make use of the socioeconomic data provided by the 1954 census. (The results of the 1962 census had not been fully published at the time of this analysis). For Italy, we focused on the 1953 elections, the closest to the 1951 census and on 1958 elections, evaluating the socioprofessional structure of the Italian electorate on the basis of more recent estimates published by the Istituto Centrale di Statistica.

3. J. Klatzmann, in his analysis of the Communist and Socialist vote in the Paris area, in Duverger, Goguel, and Touchard (eds.), *Les élections du 2 janvier 1956* (Paris: A. Colin, 1957), pp. 254–85, ends up with results somewhat different from ours: his percentages for the workers voting Communist, and the workers among the Communists are, the former superior, the latter inferior to our own estimates. This difference comes from a divergence at the start: his analysis is based upon the socioprofessional distribution of the whole labor force (men and women), while ours is derived from the socioprofessional structure of the male population only. Actually, there are more workers among men than women. As a result, our definition of the working class is much broader.

4. Official French documents published under the auspices of the Ministry of Interior do not show electoral returns for the cities. We had access to unpublished statistics at the Ministry itself, from which we derived the electoral data for the seventy cities. Election returns for Italian cities figure in the official handbooks published by the Istituto Centrale di Statistica.

5. See F. Boulard and G. Le Bras, *Carte religieuse de la France rurale* (Paris: Cahiers du clergé rural, 1952). Also F. Boulard, *Premiers itinéraires en sociologie religieuse* (Paris: Ed. Ouvrières, 1954).

6. G. Braga, in his study *Il Comunismo fra gli Italiani* (Milan: Comunità, 1956), 190 pp., undertook a thorough analysis of the diffusion of Communism across the various regions of Italy.

7. The twelve *départements* which group a third of the industrial workers are Moselle, Haut-Rhin, Bas-Rhin, Loire-Atlantique, Nord, Pas-de-Calais, Ardennes, Doubs, Meurthe-et-Moselle, Loire, Rhône, and Meuse.

8. The twenty-seven *départements* in which the proportion of industrial workers rises above the national average (37 percent) are considered "industrialized." The twenty-nine *départements* in which this percentage is inferior to 28 percent are classified as "agricultural." The thirty-four others, between these two limits, are labeled "mixed" *départements*. For Italy, the threshold is set respectively at 25 and 33 percent.

9. For further details concerning the manner in which we proceeded for setting up

this typology, see M. Dogan: "Le vote ouvrier en France: analyse écologique des élections de 1962," *Revue Française de Sociologie,* Oct.–Dec. 1965, pp. 435–71. The same criteria were adopted for the 1956 and the 1962 elections. However, because a change occurred in the electoral strength of the parties, the distribution of the *départements* among the different typological categories is not quite identical.

10. In these two countries, characterized by a multiparty system and by multiunionism, where each union is more or less linked to a party, and where union vote has a certain political significance, the returns of union elections provide useful indications as to the political preferences of workers. The same is true for white-collar employees, who constitute a separate electoral body at union elections. Many statistical data on these elections are available. We heavily rely upon them in our analysis, although we are unable to present them here in detail.

11. The electoral statistics on the rural communes of these fifteen *départements* are unpublished; we drew them from the archives of the Ministry of Interior.

12. J. Klatzmann, "Géographie électorale de l'agriculture française," in J. Fauvet and H. Mendras (eds.), *Les paysans et la politique dans la France contemporaine* (Paris: A. Colin, 1958), pp. 39–68.

13. *Ibid.,* p. 41. The 600 cantons considered do not represent an accurate sample of the whole agricultural population. As a matter of fact, in the northeastern part of France, few cantons have more than 70 percent of their population employed in agriculture; however, because these regions are characterized by a high demographic density, the absolute number of agricultural people might well reach that of certain southern regions, predominantly agricultural, but weakly populated.

14. There are 3,000 cantons in the 90 *départements.*

15. See *Classificazione dei comuni secondo le caratteristiche urbane e rurali* (Rome: Istituto Centrale di Statistica, 1963), 66 pp.

16. For more details on the distribution of the agricultural votes, see M. Dogan, "La stratificazione sociale dei suffragi," in A Spreafico and J. Palombara (eds.), *Elezioni e comportamento politico in Italia* (Milan: Comunità, 1962), pp. 407–74.

17. See Confederazione Nazionale Coltivatori Diretti, XII Congresso Nazionale, aprile 1958, *Relazione del Presidente Paolo Bonomi,* I, p. 10.

18. Tuscany has been analyzed in detail from an ecological point of view by Giorgio Braga, *Sociologia elettorale della Toscana* (Rome: Edizione Cinque Lune, 1963), 178 pp.

19. In order to provide a clearer picture of the diffusion of Communism in the underdeveloped areas, we chose as a background a demographic map drawn by Alain Girard and Jean Stoetzel for the National Institute of Demographic Studies and the French Institute of Public Opinion. In this map the size of each *département* represents its demographic weight.

20. See R. Girod, *Etudes sociologiques sur les couches salariées,* (Paris: Rivière et Cie, 1961).

21. M. Crozier, *Petits fonctionnaires au travail* (Paris: C.N.R.S., 1956).

22. See *Indagine sulle elezioni delle commissioni interne dal 1950 al 1961* (Rome: Confederazione Italiana Sindicati Lavoratori, 1962), 126 pp., mimeo.

23. See in my study "La stratificazione sociale dei suffrage," *op. cit.,* the passages referring to the vote of the middle class.

24. In the French towns where women voted separately, local official results confirmed the findings of public opinion surveys.

25. See *Sondages,* Revue Française de l'Opinion Publique, 1963, II, p. 92.

26. For more details, see M. Dogan, "Le comportement politique des femmes dans les pays de l'Europe Occidentale" in *La Condition sociale de la femme* (Brussels: Institut de Sociologie, 1956), pp. 147–86.

27. The Italian Monarchist Party appeared to be a conservative party at the local level, rather than an Extreme Right one, which would explain its slight superiority in female votes.

28. See M. Dogan, "Il voto delle donne in Italia e in altre democrazie," *Tempi Moderni,* Jan.–Feb. 1959, pp. 621–44; and "Unterschiede im Wahlverhalten der Männer und Frauen in Italien," *Kölner Zeitschrift für Soziologie und Sozialpsychologie,* 1965, 3, pp. 543–55.

29. M. Dogan and J. Narbonne, "L'abstentionnisme électoral en France," *Revue*

Française de Science Politique, Jan.-March, 1954, pp. 5–26, and April-June, 1954, pp. 301–25.

30. See M. Dogan, "Les attitudes politiques des femmes en Europe et aux Etats-Unis." in Boudon and Lazarsfeld (eds.), *Le vocabulaire des sciences sociales* (Paris: Mouton, 1965), pp. 283–302.

31. See M. Dogan and J. Narbonne, *Les françaises face à la politique. Comportement politique et condition sociale* (Paris: A. Colin, 1955), 192 pp.

32. In Italy the proportion of illiterates dropped sharply between the 1951 and the 1961 censuses.

33. See *Sondages,* Revue Française de l'Opinion Publique, 1960, IV, p. 18.

34. See *Sondages,* 1963, II, p. 93.

35. Some of the remarks in Joseph La Palombara's book *Interest groups in Italian Politics* (Princeton: Princeton Univ. Press, 1964) on *la clientela* and *la parentela* in the administration can be applied to the client voter.

36. In France, the adaptation of the party platform to the regional context clearly emerges from an analysis of the electoral addresses written by candidates for their home electors. In Italy, propaganda material aimed at the different social categories also reflects the regional adaptation of the parties.

37. In 1958, General de Gaulle revived the old electoral law of the Third Republic, the two-ballot uninominal system, which does not favor the two-party regime.

38. C. Morazé, *Les français et la République* (Paris: A. Colin, 1956), p. 21.

39. Raymond Aron, *Immuable et changeante. De la IVème à la Vème République* (Paris: Calmann-Lévy, 1959), p. 43.

40. François Goguel, *La politique des partis sous la IIIème République* (Paris: Seuil, 1946), p. 27.

41. André Siegfried, *Géographie électorale de l'Ardèche sous la IIIème République* (Paris: A. Colin, 1949), p. 57.

42. *Un secolo di statistiche italiane, Nord et Sud, 1861–1961* (Rome: Associazione per lo sviluppo dell' industria nel mezzogiorno (SVIMEZ), 1961, 1,809 pp.

43. See G. Tagliacarne, "Calcolo del reddito prodotto dal settore privato e dalla pubblica amministrazione nelle provincie e regioni d'Italia nel 1961," *Moneta e Credito,* Sept. 1962.

44. Statement made by P. Togliatti to the press after the legislative elections of April 28, 1963.

45. Raymond Aron, *op. cit.,* p. 72.

46. See M. Dogan, "Le personnel politique et la personnalité charismatique," *Revue Française de Sociologie,* July–Sept. 1965, pp. 305–24.

Five

The Party System of Spain: Past and Future*

Juan J. Linz

* This chapter was originally prepared as a paper for delivery in the Session on "Dimensions of Party Systems" organized by the Research Committee on Political Sociology at the Sixth World Congress of Sociology at Evian, September 4–11, 1966. The reader is also referred to subsequent publications under the author's continuing project on the structure of Spanish society. This larger project of research is supported by the John

INTRODUCTION

Spain, one of the first states of Europe, builder of an empire in the sixteenth and seventeenth centuries, was ushered into the liberal and democratic era by an internal crisis and the Napoleonic invasion of 1808. A large part of its elite accepted the ideas of constitutional government, enacted them into the 1812 Constitution, and fought for them against the absolutist and traditionalist reaction for almost a century. Liberalism and democracy did not come to Spain at a time of power and prosperity but in a time of defeat and economic backwardness. They were not, as in some nations, associated with an upsurge of nationalism and nation-building but coincided largely with the crisis of political unity challenged by minority nationalisms.

The liberal-democratic state is not the builder of a colonial empire like Britain or France, nor the hope of romantic nationalists as in Italy or some of the smaller new nations of Europe. It is a state in crisis, reminding one of the Austro-Hungarian Empire, Weimar Germany, or Italy after World War I. The gap between, on the one hand, political development arising from openness to all European ideological currents and a Western cultural and institutional tradition, and, on the other, economic, social and educational underdevelopment separates Spain from northcentral Europe and contributed—as in Italy —to the instability of new institutions.[1]

Spain in the nineteenth century was a country divided by civil wars between the liberals—generally supported by the elite—and the traditionalists, particularly the clergy, who mobilized important sectors of the people (notably some segments of the peasantry) in the defense of king, religion, and the old laws. After the liberal victory finally imposed peace with the Restoration constitutional monarchy (1874), and a number of legal enactments[2] seemed to open the way to democracy in the Western sense (earlier than in certain other countries), the "real country" was not or could not be mobilized and integrated into the "official country" created by the political class and its supporters.[3] The parliamentary two-party system created after the British model, with its Conservative and Liberal parties, was unable to assimilate some of the traditionalist opposition on the periphery, to use the talents of the growing industrial and commercial bourgeoisie, and to win the tolerance of the small but lively academic and nonacademic intelligentsia. The system was controlled by professional politicians, mostly lawyers, professionals and landowners, who relied on the largely apolitical and even illiterate mass electorate of the countryside and the provincial cities and towns—populations often brought to the polls by local notables or bosses (the *caciques*).[4] This "official Spain" became increasingly alien to emergent social forces. The years of internal peace between 1876, when the new constitution was ap-

Simon Guggenheim Foundation and the Council of Research in the Social Sciences of Columbia University. I am indebted to the Center for Advanced Study in the Behavioral Sciences and the Bureau of Applied Social Research, Columbia University, for assistance in the preparation of this paper, to Edward Malefakis of Columbia University, for his reading and suggestions on the manuscript, to Stein Rokkan for his help in getting it ready for publication, to Antonio Ugalde for research assistance and to Joan Warmbrun for assistance in typing the successive versions.

proved, and the coup of Primo de Rivera in 1923 witnessed considerable social change. The system may have more to its credit than its critics would admit; but obvious failures and the inevitable defeat overseas in 1898, plus the difficulties created by industrialization, led to its demise. The failure of what could have been a transition to stable liberal-democratic politics, such as that experienced by Britain, France, and other countries, deserves more analysis. It poses an interesting problem to those who assume that democratic rights inevitably will lead to an integration of masses of voters into the polity through increased mobilization due to competition between parties[5] and to the persistence of certain internally created parties when Proportional Representation is not introduced with universal suffrage.[6]

The Conservatives-versus-Liberals competition and alternation in power was largely reduced to a conflict between ins and outs, managed from the Ministry of Interior, with more or less electoral corruption and (according to the critics) without representing any real policy alternatives or distinctive social interests. Although there is much truth in this image, more careful research—as will be shown later—probably could prove that, particularly since 1900, the two parties were not faces of the same coin. It is a question why, with social change, they did not become more distinct, and why, failing this and failing to represent new social strata and currents of opinion, they were not increasingly displaced, around 1920, by powerful new anti-system parties like the Republicans and Socialists. The rise and importance of regionalist, nationalist, and separatist parties in some of the peripheral regions certainly was one factor accounting for this.

The fact that industrialization started and was most successful in two areas of distinctive history, legal traditions, culture, and language, and even different intensities of religiosity, led to a complex combination of territorial-cultural resistances to centralization in which the business bourgeoisie opposed the traditional interests of the landowners who had become allied with the large bureaucratic-military and professional class. This conflict between the business class of Catalonia, later, to a lesser extent, also of the Basque country, and the bureaucratic capital of Madrid and its supporters in the largely underdeveloped rural and provincial Spain is a unique characteristic of Spanish politics in the early twentieth century. The conflict between a bourgeois and a revolutionary conception of society takes place largely within this context. The struggle between the manufacturers of the *Lliga* and the anarchosyndicalist unionists in Barcelona acquires special dimensions due to the ambivalent relation of those employers to the central authorities, while the ethnic-linguistic differences between many of the immigrant workers and their Catalan employers must have intensified the conflicts over redistribution of wealth.

The importance of regional and intraregional politics differentiates Spain from many stable Western democracies where, with the passing of time, politics became more nationalized and peripheral opposition was assimilated or channeled through a generally conservative national party. In this respect Spain's problems resemble those of some eastern European countries, or Belgium (even though, in those countries, the national parties tended to bridge regional conflicts) more than they resemble the problems of France or even Germany. Another obstacle to the transformation of the party system, once the vitality of the two dynastic parties—Conservatives and Liberals—was in doubt, was the absence in a Catholic country of a Catholic or Christian Democratic Party like those appearing in Germany, Austria, Belgium, the Netherlands, and even Italy after World War I. The long-time weakness of the Socialist Party in a country with great class differences in wealth and style of life, both in the cities and in most of the countryside, poses another problem. The strength of the anarchosyndicalist trade union movement, with its antiparliamentary and apolitical stance, accounts for much of this, but does not seem to be the only explanation. The presence of the anarchosyndicalists and the Carlists in the twentieth century certainly distinguishes Spanish politics from that of all European countries.

The dictatorship of Primo de Rivera accelerated or perhaps precipitated the total disintegration of the dynastic parties, and with this the establishment of the Republic in 1931 and the almost complete disappearance of the political class that led those parties. The dictatorship did not come (in 1923) with the support of a new mass movement. Nor was it able to create a real single party, of the type appearing in Europe at the time, but only a patriotic association whose leaders were largely without ideology and apolitical, if not merely office-seekers. The opposition to the new regime divided the forces outside of the Restoration party system which had been pressing for its reform (such as the Reformists and the Catalan *Lliga*) or hoping to inherit it, such as the Republicans, particularly the Radicals. The Socialists, thanks to the tolerance of the dictatorship toward the party and its trade union federation, the *Unión General de Trabajadores* (UGT) had grown and could become a mass party at the advent of the Republic. In 1931, the Socialists were the only organized modern mass party. In the absence of a well-organized conservative bourgeois or clerical Right in 1931, this strength, which did not fully correspond to the Socialists' electoral appeal, and the fact that their Left bourgeois partners were organizationally weak and divided, made the Socialists the dominant party. This position, combined with lack of experience with power and administration (largely because of the centralized character of the state), the ideological ambivalences of Marxism, the developments in other European countries, the strains created by nonopposition to (or even collaboration with) Primo de Rivera, all contributed to the upsurge in the party of maximalism in 1933 and particularly from 1934 on. The maximalism versus reformism split of the party that could have been a basis for the Republic enhanced its crisis in a way reminiscent of similar situations in Italy at the time of the rise of Fascism, or in Austria before democracy was abandoned for a short-lived Austrian authoritarian regime. This internal split within the Socialist party, *Partido Socialista Obrero Español* (PSOE), pitted against each other the two polar alternatives of an economic interest conflict between classes and an ideological fight to reshape society. The addition of Socialist maximalism to the anarchosyndicalist opposition was decisive in the breakdown of democracy in 1936.

After the short-lived *alliance sacrée* of all Republican parties, from Socialists to the Radicals and Republican Conservatives, the shift toward the Right of the Radicals, the emergence of a clerical Center Right party (the CEDA), and of a small monarchist authoritarian party in the 1933 elections, Spain became one more example of what Giovanni Sartori has called polarized centrifugal multiparty systems.[7] Spain was in this sense like Weimar Germany, France, and postwar Italy, but with the added complexity of regional-nationalist parties, with the Catalans bitterly divided between Left and Right. The openness of Spain to foreign ideological influences added to the spectrum the Fascist and Communist parties, which were perhaps more important in exacerbating the conflicts and the distrust between the major parties, and in subverting them internally than on account of the number of their members and supporters. Our attempt to account for the weaknesses of the traditional Spanish parties before 1936 will help to shed further light upon the differences in social structure and political climate between Spain and other European countries. Perhaps the most illuminating comparison is with Italy in the early twenties, where the economic and social structure is otherwise relatively comparable to that of Spain.

The importance of institutional, symbolic, and ideological conflicts in the thirties makes the distinction between parties of the democratic system, those semiloyal to it, and those more or less explicitly disloyal, central to the understanding of the system. The problem is further complicated by the fact that the judgment of a more or less dispassionate scholar studying the facts decades later would not coincide with the perceptions the participants had at the time, that led them to speak of a "Republic for the republicans." They made a particular content more important than formal democracy, excluding any party questioning the anticlerical if not antireligious elements in the constitutional laws, and denying legitimacy to the Radicals for their alliance with the Catholic Conservatives, a tendency that later led to the general use of the term "fascist" to designate any opponent. The ambivalence of regional nationalisms toward the form of government under the Monarchy, the constitutional arrangements regarding the role of central and regional governments and, among their extremists, even about the integrity of the Spanish state, is another distinction between Spanish parties and those of the most stable democracies, with the exception of the extreme Flamingants in Belgium.

The multiple cleavages, the lack of overlapping cleavages, the increasing polarization between parties, all did not help to make the Spanish party system under the Republic the best instrument for creating stable and effective governments that might have consolidated democracy in Spain. Even without the difficulties created by the anarchosyndicalists (who never became a party nor part of the system), nor the great inherited and social problems accentuated by the world depression, nor the impact of the age of ideology, the Spanish party system and the type of elites it produced could not be up to the task.

In the last part of this paper we will explore tentatively some of the prospects for the future party system of Spain, should parties be allowed to compete for power. As in the earlier discussion, we will turn to a comparison with Italy, which, disregarding many differences, is the most useful point of reference for a comparative study of Spain. Our "futurible" will be based on the relative similarity of the social structure of present-day Spain and Italy of a few years back, and of the fact that they both are part of Catholic, centralistic, semideveloped Europe, with many similar institutional problems.

PARTY SYSTEM OF THE
RESTORATION MONARCHY

The Restoration period (1875–1923)[8] poses to the political scientist and historian some difficult problems. Here we have a country where the legitimacy of parties had been recognized, basic civil liberties—freedom of association (law of 1887), of speech, of the press, and so forth—were respected and there was even toleration of a wide (but not perfect) freedom for some of the trade union movements (right to strike, 1909), but where the party system did not go through the stages of the model presented by Lipset and Rokkan.[9] Nor did some of the hypotheses advanced by Sartori find a clear confirmation. The parties retained their registration association character and did not develop effective membership organizations; in fact even the caucus-disciplined organizations began to disintegrate almost as soon as the dominant leaders—Cánovas and Sagasta—retired. Universal male suffrage, enacted at almost the same time (June 26, 1890)—without popular pressure, but more thanks to the weakness of the Liberal Party, which wanted to expand its support on the "possibilist left" (Castelar)—did not mobilize mass support for the regime nor revitalize the party organizations. Parliament, the power of which could have been greatly expanded due to the ambiguities of the Restoration Constitution in the course of the years between 1876 and 1923, lost power to the king. The causes of this process are difficult to explain, but to the personality of Alphonso XIII, which contributed much to it, one has to add the lack of solid majorities, the incompatibilities and personal vendettas between politicians (even of the same party), the extraparliamentary pressures of the street, the small clubs (among them the Masons), and ultimately the army. None of the democratic forces was able to gain sufficient parliamentary strength to force a democratic revision of the constitution, by limiting royal authority, democratizing the senate, and restraining the growing veto power of the army (which initially had accepted the system). In contrast to Imperial Germany, where the power of the Emperor was securely anchored in the Bismarckian constitutional arrangements, even when the forces of democratization in the Reichstag and the electorate were making gains, in Spain the obstacles did not come from the strength, self-confidence, and legitimacy of the forces of tradition, but from the weaknesses of those who could and should have transformed the system.

Why was a system built on the ideal of Britain—without numerous and strong antagonists—unable to slowly integrate, if not the masses, at least the business and professional bourgeoisie, use the talents of the intellectuals, and continue the peaceful process of mobilization of increasingly larger segments of the population and particularly those with serious grievances against the social order? The same question incidentally can be asked about the *sinistra* and the *destra* in Italy and, in the twentieth century, about the Colombian two-party system. Without monographic research on the Conservative and Liberal parties of the time, their organization, their clientèle, their leadership, it will be difficult to answer that question, but at least we want to suggest some hypotheses to be explored. But before that, some additional questions may be raised. Why, in view of the failure of the system, did there not emerge (even to the degree of Italy) powerful new parties: a strong and numerous Republican-Radical Party, or a Socialist Party with the working-class masses behind it, or even something like the *Popolari* to represent progressive urban Catholic middle classes? Instead, the two-party system dominated the parliament and even the electorate until after World War I. Even during the Republic the modern mass parties did not dominate in the system, certainly not in the Government, a bit more in Parliament, but probably not in the electorate, even when they did so at the great mass rallies. The lack of mobilization for the parties of the system, but even more the concomitant lack of mobilization for its antagonists, is perhaps the most striking aspect of this period, particularly if we consider the lively and free press and the occasional bursts of activation outside the parties. In this, Spain is certainly different from Imperial Germany at the time, and, in the second aspect, even from Giolittian Italy. Was it only economic and educational underdevelopment? Probably not.

The great question that remains to be answered by historians and sociologists of the Restoration period is: Why did the Conservatives and Liberals remain so relatively undifferentiated and unable to compete for the expanding electorate, to assimilate new issues, and make a real and honest electoral fight? To say that *caciquismo* and electoral corruption, the agreement of the politicians to rotate in office (the so-called *Pacto del Pardo* of 1885), were the explanation is to mistake the description of some of the facts for an explanation. The question remains: Why were such arrangements possible or even necessary? Our guess is that multiple explanations must be sought:

1. Elements in the political situation forced both parties to expand their base broadly rather than by delimiting their appeals and ideology. Among them the primary one must have been a certain tiredness of the country after more than half a century of largely useless and devastating ideological and armed conflicts between Carlists, Catholics, and Liberals, and, later, within the liberal side, between various shades of moderation and radicalism, centralism and federalism, that led to the failure of the doctrinaire First Republic.[10] The agreement to institutionalize the new regime that developed between Cánovas and Sagasta has perhaps a parallel in the Austrian two-party *Proporz* system which also deprived the voters of a real choice from 1945 to 1966.

2. However, the most important cause must have been the social structure of Spain at the time: an overwhelmingly agrarian and underdeveloped country with few centers of modern industrial and commercial development. An expanded suffrage to start with and universal suffrage after 1889 made both parties dependent on the votes of the countryside and small agrarian towns. With a few exceptions, even the cities were inhabited by an upper and middle class dependent on agriculture, with little or no understanding of democratic processes and ideological issues. Now it might be argued that a cleavage could have developed between an aristocratic and conservative landowning class and a bourgeois middle-class urban stratum supported perhaps by a middle peasantry. A number of factors must have stood against this: on the one hand, compared to England, Prussia, and other countries, the aristocracy versus nonaristocracy struggle had lost its *raison d'être* in Spain because the aris-

tocracy had already lost much of its power and self-consciousness in the eighteenth century,[11] was further weakened by the collaborationist record of many of its members in the war against Napoleon, and had largely identified itself with the Liberals in the dynastic wars. The aristocracy had done so partly because of its higher level of education and its background in the Enlightenment, which contrasted it to the local clergy and peasantry who supported the Carlists, partly because it benefited much from the acquisition of Church, monastery, and communal lands sold by the Liberal reformers (Mendizábal, 1836 and afterward) for ideological reasons and through economic necessity. Ultimately the interests of aristocratic landowners, who had transformed feudal entailed property into free property, while adding to it disentailed Church property, and those of the bourgeoisie, professionals, and wealthy peasants, who also benefited from the liberal land reform, were not so different. It would be interesting to study the political evolution of nineteenth-century Andalusia from this angle: Where did the urban merchants and even the few industrialists, as well as the big landholding grandees, stand in the early nineteenth century? Where would we find them in the second half, particularly after the Restoration? To what extent—if any—could their changes in political outlook be attributed to the different relationship to the ownership of land? Certainly the expansion of the nonaristocratic landowning classes—partly absentee, partly local notables—linked with the professional, bureaucratic, and military middle classes, made the conflict between landowning aristocratic conservatives and bourgeois liberals in the European sense less likely. To this we have to add that the Monarchy in the course of the century ennobled innumerable upwardly mobile military leaders of the civil wars and pronunciamientos, as well as under Amadeo and Alfonso XII, of financiers, businessmen, and politicians.[12] In a sense we have a feudalization of the liberal bourgeoisie which made personal and family ties easier across status and objective class lines, weakening the antiaristocratic affect that characterized Liberals in other countries.

Another social-structural factor was the important reservoir of votes and—what is more important—political elites in the relatively large number of professionals (mainly lawyers, but also doctors, pharmacists, and so on), civil servants—multiplied by the spoils system—and, above all, bourgeois army officers corps overexpanded in the civil and colonial wars. Such groups constituted an important part of the middle classes, particularly in Madrid and the provincial capitals of agrarian Spain. They did not have distinctive economic interests like manufacturers and merchants, were closely linked by family ties and property to the landowning rentier sector, and did not have the proud independence of the bourgeoisie of north central Europe, Britain, or even France. Their livelihoods and careers were more dependent on government favoritism and patronage. They could serve both parties, while a minority among them became the basis for the more doctrinaire anticlerical Liberal and Republican parties. As Pi y Margall, the incorruptible ideological Federalist Republican, formulated it in the middle 1860's:

> I also felt that in a corrupt and immature society, the absence of highly developed and clearly marked group interests made ideas the only genuine touchstone for differententiating between parties. Only by

digging up ideological roots could politics escape from continually shifting party lines where loyalties were determined by whim, personal rivalry and private profit, enabling the monarch to be the ultimate political arbiter.[13]

Last, but not least, it has to be stressed that much of that electorate—particularly the rural, except in north central Spain—was illiterate. Spain, when it introduced universal male suffrage, did not include—as did Italy—any literacy requirement. In 1915, the voters on the electoral registry were classified by their ability to read and write. Of the 4,733,715 for which the information was available (it was not for 19,984 voters), those unable to do so were 1,874,786 (39.6 percent). The proportion of literate voters ranged widely from a maximum in peasant Burgos of 93.2 percent and other north central relatively poor but peasant owner areas like León, Palencia, Santander, Soria, Segovia, Valladolid, Zamora, and among the more industrial areas the two Basque provinces—Álava and Vizcaya—as well as Madrid and Oviedo. At the bottom of the list we find the Canaries, followed by Jaén—an olive-growing and latifundia area—together with eastern Andalusia (Málaga, Granada, Almería), and the adjacent southern Levante (Murcia and Alicante). Even in the great industrial center of Barcelona literates amounted to only 76 percent.[14]

In a sense the social structure favored a triple division in the political culture[15] not based strictly on interest cleavages:

a. A passive mass electorate existed, constituted largely by illiterate and poor farm laborers and peasants—either abstaining from voting or doing it as told by the local landlord or *cacique* in exchange for minor benefits or out of fear.

b. There were oligarchic rural and small-town strata who were interested in controlling the political machinery not so much to advance distinctive policies, but so as to share in power, prestige, patronage, the pork-barrel (since this a period of railroad expansion, road construction, and other internal developments), and to ensure the unequal application of the law in their conflicts with farm laborers, tenants, and neighbors on the use of land, water rights, and the like. The two-party system, whatever it might have meant at the top leadership level, in this sector represented only conflicts between cliques or, to a lesser extent, neighboring communities, not broadly based interest or ideological alignments.

c. In the more developed parts of the country, the two parties must have represented better-defined social class and ideological groupings, particularly in Madrid. However, the regionalist traditions reflected in Carlism, and later Integrism, in the Basque country, and by historical Republicanism, particularly in its Federalist variety in Catalonia and the Levante, weakened the two-party system from the beginning. Even so, there are indications that issues like the policy to be followed in overseas territories, the tariff, the naval-building program of Maura, and taxation, influenced the alignment with one or the other of the two parties of leading businessmen and their organizations.[16]

That the social composition of the two dynastic parties was by no means identical is often ignored, but there are sufficient data to suggest that this aspect of Restoration politics deserves more study. For example, in the

Liberal-dominated Cortes elected in 1910, among 213 Liberal deputies there were thirteen noble titles (6 percent), of which five dated from before 1808, that is 2.3 percent. In contrast, among the 106 Conservative deputies, there were eighteen noble titles (17 percent), six of them granted before 1808 (that is, 5.6 percent). An indication of how the Crown used titles to reward loyal politicians can be found in the fact that among the Liberals, twelve (5.6 percent), and eleven of the Conservatives (10.4 percent) were subsequently granted titles (in some cases the award was made posthumously to their widows). There were also legislators in both parties whose surnames indicate an extended family relationship with some of the nobility; again these were more numerous among the Conservatives (5.6 percent) than among the Liberals (3.3 percent).[17]

If we turn to the proportion of lawyers, particularly if we compare those elected by each party in the same region, we also find considerably more lawyers on the Conservative benches.

The differences between the parties in their parliamentary leadership, while important, probably were minor compared to those within the parties by region and level of development. Furthermore, the whole tone and political style of the system was ultimately determined by the weight of the agrarian—gentry and peasant—and small-town *clases medias* in the electorate, society, and economy of the country. This dead weight and the administrative inefficiency of the central government, its military defeat by the United States and its failures in Morocco, contributed to an increasing hostility in Catalonia (the most industrialized region at the time) to the parties of the system. This hostility crystallized in the great movement of the *Solidaridad Catalana,* a coalition of antisystem forces (1906), in the *Asamblea de Parliamentarios* (1917), in some of the support to the Republicans, and in the eager acceptance of Primo de Rivera's coup (1923), but could not find a nationwide party platform.[18] Ultimately the bourgeois and intellectual reactions to the failures of the system were weakened by indecision when faced by the growth of a radical labor movement, particularly the anarchosyndicalist *Confederación Nacional del Trabajo* (CNT), which coincided with the rapid industrialization and increased internal migrations of the 1910's and the upsurge of revolutionary sentiment throughout the world as an aftermath of World War I and the Russian Revolution.

3. However, the chances for an internal transformation of either of the two major parties would still have been there if the Catalan cultural revival, with its *Renaixenca,* and the fight about regional legal traditions inspired by the Historical School of Law of Savigny at the time of codification (1889), had not reawakened the love for the local language and history. This added to the inherited ideological distinctiveness of Carlism and Federalism and to the distinctive interests of an industrial-commercial economy in an underdeveloped and badly administered country, a new appeal represented by the *Lliga Regionalista* (1901), that turned an important part of the bourgeoisie to regionalism and even local nationalism. A decisive effort to win control of Spain was given up for the sake of increased local administrative, political, and cultural autonomy. Since the centralistic governments, particularly the

Castilian Liberals, were unwilling to grant any such autonomy, but thought · they could buy off discontent in Catalonia by economic advantages and by co-opting Catalan leaders by giving them control of finances, a strange relationship developed between the central and local power structure. Ramos Oliveira[19] in a Marxist interpretation argues that the Catalan textile industrialists used their regionalist nationalism as blackmail to obtain economic advantages, particularly in tariff matters, but without going that far we can say that a contradiction soon developed between the more aggressive nationalist Catalan statements made in Barcelona and the willingness of the *Lliga* to participate in the Madrid government coalitions of the disintegrating two-party system. This deprived the Catalan bourgeoisie of their chance to become the spearhead of a movement for national reform, particularly in 1917 with the *Asamblea de Parliamentarios,* and slowly weakened the hold of the *Lliga* on the Catalan petty bourgeoisie, as well as on some of the intelligentsia, who turned to leftist and more nationalistic Catalanist forces (growth of the *Esquerra* and *Estat Catalá* in the thirties).[20]

Outside of the two dynastic parties there were also the more clerical segments of Spanish Catholicism, particularly among the northern peasantry, who had never fully accepted the Liberal monarchy, and the emerging working class, divided between an ideological radical petty bourgeois Republicanism, the slowly growing Socialist Party, and a renewed and fighting anarchosyndicalist, antiparliamentary, revolutionary labor movement.[21] The division of the working class into these three forces, together with its numerical weakness, plus probably some of the ethnic cleavages in the Basque country (and even Barcelona), prevented it from becoming a third force within Restoration Spain, despite universal suffrage and considerable political freedoms. The working-class Left never appeared as a potential coalition partner or source of support for a Left liberal government to the extent that it could in France or even in Giolittian Italy. This lack of a cohesive, legitimate third force to appeal to, or to fend off, *on the parliamentary level* probably contributed to the lack of cohesion of the two major parties after 1910.

4. Another factor preventing the real crystallization of the two-party system was probably that religious fervor in the society did not find itself identified with the Conservatives—who were after all heirs to the nineteenth-century Liberalism—and that the Liberal Party under Sagasta trying as it did to disassociate itself from the anticlerical excesses of the First Republic and to contribute to the "pacification of the spirits," came to accept the 1851 concordat and the ambiguous religious provisions of the Constitution of 1876 which could satisfy the moderate Catholics. The occasional flaring-up of conflict on clerical-anticlerical lines between Conservatives and Liberals,[22] particularly the Democrats—a faction led by Canalejas (the *"ley del Candado,"* the aftermath of the *Semana trágica,* and such) was not sufficiently deep to differentiate the two parties along those lines.

5. The shared responsibility of both parties for the lack of military and diplomatic preparation for the Spanish-American War and the colonial conflict that led to it, as well as for the handling of the Moroccan problem, eliminated another basis for real cleavage.

The history of the two-party system in Spain suggests that the lack of social differentiation between the electoral and social basis of parties can be as detrimental to the development of real democracy as the excessive polarization, a point made already by Georges Lavau in his important essay on the French party system.[23]

SPAIN—AN UNDERDEVELOPED AND UNEVENLY DEVELOPED COUNTRY

To put the Spanish party system in comparative perspective, one should always keep in mind the economic underdevelopment of the country, even as compared with another Mediterranean country, Italy. The data available are neither fully comparable as to their classifications, nor as to date (since the censuses were taken at different times in both countries), but the fact that in Spain in 1877—early in the Restoration—72.3 percent of the active males were engaged in agriculture compared to 56.0 percent in Italy, shows the gap in economic development between the two countries. At the turn of the century the difference had been reduced, but remained appreciable: Spain was still at the 61.6 percent level as late as in 1920.

Even more notable than the greater agriculturalism of Spain compared to Italy is its much lower industrialization and development of commerce and transportation, particularly in the early decade of the twentieth century. The differences between the "nonmodern" middle classes—what we call *clases medias* in contrast to the bourgeoisie—are much smaller: Spain has a larger army, as many or more people in the professions, a similar proportion of clergymen (in fact, in the 1877 census, fewer), and a comparable number of rentiers. Its public administration started with a similar size, but does not seem to have kept pace with the Italian growth. This discrepancy between industrial—and commercial—economic development and the early existence and growth of a middle-class sector not linked to the growth of the economy, created many of the imbalances in Spanish society and politics and indirectly contributed much to the growing tension between the industrial or industrializing periphery and the capital of the centralistic state.

This cleavage is particularly visible in the "tale of two cities": Barcelona and Madrid—the industrial metropolis and the capital of the Monarchy. (Unfortunately, we cannot isolate the data for the city from those for the province, but since the proportion active in agriculture in both provinces is similar, a comparison can be made, without forgetting that the data for Barcelona include a number of industrial suburban communities.)

In the early Restoration, we find in Madrid 1.0 percent active in industry proper, compared to 18.4 percent in Barcelona, but even when we add to that group in both cities the artisans and craftsmen the proportions remain very different—18.4 and 36.7 percent. To this one might add the different proportions in transportation, 2.0 and 6.2 percent (mostly due to shipping), as an indicator of economic development. On the other extreme we find the noneconomic middle classes occupying a dominant position in the life of Madrid: civil servants (6.7 versus 1.1 percent for Barcelona), military personnel (10.8 as against 3.7 percent), liberal professions and education (4.0 compared to 1.8 percent). These three groups add to 21.5 percent in Madrid and only 6.6 percent in Barcelona. The different style of life is also reflected

Table 1—Occupational Structure of Spain in 1877 and 1920, and Italy in 1881 and 1921

Census data for active males: percentage distributions

OCCUPATIONAL GROUP	SPAIN		ITALY	
	1877	1920	1881	1921
Agriculture	72.3	61.6	56.0	53.8
Industry (including mining)	3.1	23.5	23.9	24.9
Artisans and craftsmen	10.2			
Commerce	2.4	5.2	}6.2	6.6
Transportation	2.8	.3		5.8
Public administration	1.5	1.3	1.7	1.5
Armed forces	2.8	3.1	1.6	1.7
Liberal professions (and teaching)	1.0	1.7	.8	1.8
Education	.4		.3	
Clergy	.4	.8	1.1	.5
Capitalists and rentiers		2.0	4.3	1.0
Domestic servants	1.6	.5	2.7	.5
Total	(5,690,240)	(6,825,876)	(9,776,420)	(13,286,916)

Note: In both countries those in ill-defined occupations, criminals, vagrants (in Italy, this category seems to include some peons) have been excluded from the active male population. In Spain in 1877 this group without occupation or non-classified includes 2,659,541 men and in Italy in 1881 it leaves out of our calculations 1,482,548. The Italian data refer to the population over age 9, and the Spanish to the total, a fact that may account for the different proportions in those excluded categories. In Italy the category "Domestic Servants" included private employees in 1881.

in the proportion of men active in personal service in both cities—5.1 and 1.1 percent respectively. The data for 1920 show similar patterns: even when in the years between 1877 and 1920, Madrid had industrialized considerably, Barcelona had almost one fourth more men in industry.

Table 2—Occupational Structure of the Provinces of Madrid and Barcelona in 1877 and 1910 (percent active males)

OCCUPATIONAL GROUP	PROVINCE			
	MADRID		BARCELONA	
	1877	1920	1877	1920
Agriculture	41.7	17.9	38.5	17.2
Industry	1.0 }	42.5	18.4 }	54.0
Artisans	17.4		18.3	
Commerce	9.4	12.6	7.8	14.4
Transport	2.0	2.2	6.2	1.1
Armed forces	10.8	8.9	3.7	3.0
Administration	6.7	4.5	1.1	1.3
Clergy	.8	.9	.7	1.0
Liberal professions	4.0	4.4	1.8	3.0
Rentiers	—	4.2	—	4.3
Domestic service	5.1	1.9	1.1	.7
Total	(218,347)	(306,565)	(295,974)	(464,251)

Table 3—Representation of Parties and Factions in the Lower House in the Last Decade of Constitutional Monarchy
(Number and percent of seats)

PARTIES AND FACTIONS	1910 No.	1910 %	1914 No.	1914 %	1916 No.	1916 %	1918 No.	1918 %	1919 No.	1919 %	1920 No.	1920 %
Liberals												
Liberal Democrats	210	54.6	35	8.9	218	57.1	68	17.8	59	15.1	43	10.9
Romanones Liberals			84	21.3			42	11.0	37	9.5	31	7.8
Liberal Left							37	9.7	34	8.7	27	6.8
Independent Liberals							7	1.8	2	0.5	10	2.5
Conservatives												
Liberal Conservatives	107	27.8	211	53.4	85	22.3	97	25.4	95	24.3	174	44.0
Mauristas					23	6.0	51	13.4	97	24.8	44	11.0
Total dynastic parties		82.4		74.7		85.4		79.1		82.9		83.0
Reformistas	37	9.6	12	3.0	12	3.1	9	2.4	6	1.5	9	2.3
Republicans (different groups)			21	5.3	17	4.5	15	3.9	18	4.6	15	3.8
Socialists					1	0.3	6	1.6	6	1.5	4	1.0
Regionalists and Nationalists	8	2.1	13	3.3	15	3.9	31	8.1	18	4.6	19	4.8
Jaimists, Integrists, Traditionalists	11	2.9	7	1.8	10	2.6	9	2.4	7	1.8	5	1.3
Catholics, Agrarians, Independent, and ill-defined	11	2.9	11	2.8	0	0	9	2.4	11	2.8	14	3.5
Total	384	99.9	394	99.8	381	99.8	381	99.9	390	99.7	395	99.7

LAST YEARS OF THE TWO-PARTY SYSTEM: DOMINANT, BUT FACTION-RIDDEN; WITH APATHY AND ALIENATION, BUT NO ALTERNATIVE

In 1910 the two-party system—before the major parties divided openly into personalistic factions—was able to obtain 318 seats out of 387 (82 percent). (There were seven contested results and five vacant seats, plus five districts where results were voided because of irregularities, for a total of 404.) This was also the first election in which a Socialist won a seat, and the first one after obligatory voting and other considerable reforms of the electoral procedure were inaugurated. If we turn to the sixty-three districts, most of which elected several deputies, in which the elections were contested, we find fifty (79 percent) in which the two parties combined had an absolute majority; in fact, in twenty-five districts they gained more than 80 percent of the vote. Only in thirteen (21 percent) constituencies did they win less than 50 percent. It is important to note that of those thirteen constituencies, four had sizable Carlist votes, a challenge to the system that did not come from emergent forces, but from the shadows of the past (63.6 percent of the vote in Navarre went to Carlists, 55.7 percent in Álava, and 21.3 percent in Gerona; in Guipúzcoa, Carlism already had been displaced by Integrists (19.4 percent) and Independents (nationalists: 26.1 percent), but even in industrial Vizcaya "Catholic" candidates got 15.7 percent. Only in the three largest urban centers, only one of them highly industrialized, did the Republicans, sometimes with the Socialists, obtain an important share in the vote: Barcelona (capital district), 38.7 percent (to which one would have to add the Federal nationalists with 19.7 percent); Madrid (capital), where 47.7 percent went to the Republican-Socialist "conjunction"; and Valencia (capital), 19.4 percent. Málaga (capital), without being industrialized, as a commercial harbor city was another stronghold of the Left (58.2 percent), as it had been in the nineteenth century and was soon to prove by producing the largest Communist vote in the Republic. Zaragoza (capital) could not bring out an absolute majority for the dynastic parties, but the Republicans obtained only 40.5 percent. Outside the capital districts just mentioned, three of the Catalan provinces, Barcelona Province, Lérida, and Tarragona denied their support to the parties of the regime, not in favor of a Spanish Republicanism (respectively 8.7, 0.1, and 2.7 percent) but rather in that of the Regionalists (29.3, 20.2, and 10.3 percent), and the Catalan Left of Federalist tradition (14.3, 34.9, and 15.5 percent).

The challenge to the system was not widespread. Only in twenty of the sixty-three contested districts for which we have information did the dynastic parties obtain less than 70 percent of the vote. But the gap in political culture between the developed part of the country and most of provincial and rural Spain was already gigantic: five of the six largest population centers were totally lost. Of the twenty-two districts above average in industry, eight did not give a majority to the two traditional parties, four gave less than 70 percent, and only ten (among them Seville, the fourth largest city) more than 70 percent. The conflict in Spain at this point cannot be called one of center versus periphery, but of national capital and peripheral capitals versus the countryside. However, in contrast to other countries, particularly Italy, the challenge to the *trasformismo-cacique* notable, electoral organization type of party system did not come from parties that could expand over the whole

Table 4—Vote in Catalonia and Madrid in the 1910 Lower Chamber Election

Party or Faction	Barcelona Capital	Barcelona Province	Gerona	Lerida	Tarragona	Madrid Capital
Liberals	—%	27.3%	24.1%	21.9%	48.8%	21.7%
Conservatives	4.6	9.3	—	—	—	21.0
Republicans	38.7	8.7	6.3	.1	2.7	47.7
Regionalists	19.7	29.3	17.1	20.2	12.3	
Federal nationalists	29.6	14.3	7.3	34.9	15.5	
Carlists		4.0	21.3			
Catholics	4.5				—	
Socialists	(6 votes)					9.3
Independents			11.0			
Minor party and void	2.7%	7.2%	12.9%	22.9%	22.6%	0.3%
Total	(396,006)	(105,305)	(56,378)	(40,728)	(37,065)	(437,663)
Percent participation		72.1%	78.0%	88.0%	76.0%	66.0%

countryside and thereby soon offer a massive electoral alternative to it. It came from shadows of the past (Carlism and its demonarchized Catholic successors) and regional nationalism, in itself already divided between Left and Right in Catalonia. The returns in Barcelona Province and its capital

Table 5—Legislative Election Results in the Basque Country in 1910

Party or Faction	Vizcaya[a]	Guipúzcoa	Álava	Navarre[b]
Liberals	—%	—%	19.1%	33.9%
Conservatives	55.5	26.7	—	
Republicans	16.7	.8	19.4	
Carlists	—		55.4	63.6
Integrists	—	19.4	—	
Catholics	15.7	—	—	
Socialists	1.1	—	—	
Independents		26.1	—	
Minor and void	11.0%	27.0%	5.7%	2.4%
Total	(48,610)	(23,398)	(12,225)	(17,928)
Percent Participation	70%	98%	80%	86%

a Without the district of Marquina.
b Without the district of Tudela.

symbolize the complexity of the challenge. In one of the most developed and politically conscious regions the dynastic parties had almost disappeared (except in Tarragona where even under the Republic the Spanish Conservatives would win some seats), but no single dominant party had displaced them. The working-class masses of Barcelona were still Republican, rather than abstentionist anarchosyndicalists or indirect supporters of the Left Catalans, and the Catalanists were split into Left and Right. The contrast between Madrid and Barcelona reveals how the regional-cultural cleavages prevented the transformation of the two-party system into a three-party system of Republicans, or perhaps a Republican-Socialist alliance, with the Socialists alone later displacing one (or both) of the dominant parties. The practical absence of the major parties in key regions like the metropolis of Barcelona and large parts of Catalonia was the greatest and most consequential failure of the two-party system. Neither of the two dynastic parties could absorb the discontent of the big-business bourgeoisie or of the lower bourgeoisie and peasantry of Catalonia. It contributed to the unique crisis of a system that otherwise had considerable achievements to its credit. In another increasingly industrial region, the Basque country, a similar process was going on, but much of the opposition came from the Carlists and their successors, the Integrists and "Catholic" candidates, who like the *Lliga,* professed indifference to the question of regime while focusing on the rights of the Church.

The comparison with the first Italian election under universal male suf-

Table 6—Electoral Participation in the Elections to the Lower Chamber, 1910 to 1923

Election Date	Voting in Districts Where Seats Were Contested (percent)	Change in Participation (percent)	Number of Uncontested Seats Where a Candidate Was Proclaimed According to Article 29
May 8, 1910	73.7		119
March 8, 1914	68.7	−5.0	93
April 9, 1916	68.1	− .6	145
February 24, 1918	66.6	−1.5	62
June 1, 1919	64.3	−2.3	82
December 19, 1920	60.0	−4.3	93
		(−13.7 from 1910 to 1920)	
April 29, 1923	65.0	+5.0	146
June 28, 1931 (Constituent Assembly)	70.1		
November 19, 1933 (First with female suffrage)	67.5		

frage (1919) in which neither Fascists nor Communists had yet made their appearance, is revealing.[25] Only in seven of the sixteen regions of that country did the parties of the system win an absolute majority, and all of these were south of Rome. In the other nine, the combined strength of two great challengers of the system, the official Socialists and the new *Popolari,* held an absolute majority. Nationally, these two parties respectively obtained 32.4 and 20.5 percent of the vote. In Lombardy, whose position as an industrial center could be compared to that of Barcelona, the Socialists obtained 46.0 percent of the votes, the *Popolari* 30.2 percent, while the old parties held on to 18.4 percent and a leftist bloc gained 5.4 percent of the popular vote.

We have focused on the Chamber elected in 1910 because this was a critical year in the history of the system. The major parties still had strong leaders and were not yet openly split into incompatible factions. Moreover, the recent events of the Tragic Week in Barcelona and the enactment of the obligatory vote in 1907 had brought electoral participation to a high of 73.7 percent, a figure that would not be surpassed again until 1936. The succeed-

Table 7—The Two-Party System in 1921 (Elections for Diputados Provinciales) by Region (in percentages)

Region	Conservatives	Liberals	Reformists	Republicans	Socialists	Regionalists	Unión Monárquica	Jaimists Integrists	Agrarians Independents
Murcia	77.0	15.4	7.7						
Madrid	66.7	28.6	4.8						
Extremadura	65.6	34.4	—						
Andalusia	56.0	42.4	.8						0.8
Asturias	53.0	5.9	35.4						
Baleares	50.0	50.0							
Canaries	50.0	37.5		6.3		6.3			
Castile and Leon	48.9	41.0	1.4						8.6
Galicia	44.8	48.3	1.7	1.7	3.4				
Levante	44.2	42.3	3.8	7.7			1.9		4.8
Aragon	42.8	47.6	2.4	2.4					
Castile and Albacete	41.0	55.7	1.6						1.6
Basque Provinces	30.0	5.0	—			15.0	25.0	15.0	10.0
Navarre	20.0	40.0		—		20.0	20.0		
Catalonia	5.5	18.2	—	16.4		50.9	3.6	5.5	
Total Spain	46.4	38.6	2.4	2.4	0.3	5.0	0.9	1.4	2.8

ing elections represent a period of disintegration of the two-party system with a three-way split among the Liberals in 1918 and a twofold division of the Conservatives after the 1916 election. However, the share in the seats of the two dynastic "parties" remained almost constant until 1923 (between 85 percent in 1916 and a low of 79 percent in 1918; *Table 3*). The feelings of alienation that led to more and more frequent crises, to terrorism in Catalonia, to the 1917 general strike, and a revolutionary situation in the countryside were not reflected so much in parliament (except for the rise of the regionalist-nationalist representation to 8 percent in 1918) as in a persistent drop in electoral participation.

In the last legislative election of the Restoration participation was particularly low in most of the provinces with large cities: Barcelona (with 48 percent), Guipúzcoa (49 percent), Madrid (55 percent), Cádiz (57 percent), Seville (59 percent), Zaragoza (60 percent), Málaga (60 percent), Valencia (61 percent), as well as in Tarragona (58 percent) and Pontevedra (57 percent). The great urban centers by their low voting rates already showed their alienation from the system, something they would once again show by quite different means eight years later when there was a massive turnout in favor of antiregime candidates in the municipal elections, except in some anarchist areas.

The drop in participation can also be found in the elections to *Diputados Provinciales:* 1915, 69 percent; 1917, 62 percent; 1919, 59 percent; and 1921, 58 percent.[26]

The crisis of the two-party system in 1923 that led to its overthrow by General Primo de Rivera was not caused by any rise on the national level of forceful new parties which challenged the system. As the data for the provincial assembly elections of June 12, 1921 (*Table 7*) show, the two parties still dominated the scene except where regionalism had displaced them. In such regions the monarchist pro-central government forces in fact turned to create a new party: *Unión Monárquica de Cataluña*. One of the most exciting attempts to challenge the nondemocratic and antiliberal aspects of the Restoration, Melquíades Álvarez' Reformista Party, was minoritarian in most regions except Asturias. It was the internal division of the two major parties, the increasing apathy of the electorate, and the popular challenges on the street that caused what might almost be called the sense of relief with which the downfall of the system was received.

The process we have just described poses for the political sociologist the interesting and difficult problem of the conditions—institutional, social, political, and cultural—under which a party system can become less and less effective as a channel for discontent and participation, without, at the same time—despite conditions of considerable political freedom—giving birth to any successor parties. The conditions of considerable political freedom must be stressed: even if Anarchosyndicalists often suffered illegal persecution, this was not the case with the Reformists, the Republicans, and normally the Socialists. In fact, the Socialist leaders, after having been sentenced to prison for a semirevolutionary general strike in 1917, were freed when elected to Parliament. The assumption of democratic political theory is that, given the vote and minimal political freedom, political parties will compete on the electoral market and the competition will displace inefficient parties and politicians (unless they use force to assure their monopoly). The situation in Spain and many other parts of the world (Argentina in the last decades) makes this hypothesis questionable.

To approach an answer to this question we will examine in more detail the following four features of the Spanish situation:

(1) The role and sources of failure of the Republican opposition.

(2) The importance of regionalist, autonomist, separatist politics.

(3) The reasons for the slow growth of the Spanish Socialist Party.

(4) The causes for the absence of an effective political presence of Catholicism in Spanish democratic politics.

REPUBLICANS UNDER
THE RESTORATION

The relative weakness of the Republicans under the Restoration poses a problem.[27] After all Spain had been a Republic, and the Monarchical regime had not been outstandingly successful. Why should the electorate not have turned back to Republican symbols and leaders?

One factor was the failure and disintegration of the Republic of 1873, but more important were the differences in ideology and the personal clashes between the former presidents of the 1873 Republic and their followers. Some of them, under the leadership of Ruiz Zorrilla and in a typically nineteenth-century Spanish way, put all their hopes for a return to power on a military *pronunciamiento,* and devoted their energies to conspiracy. On the other extreme, we find Castelar with his *posibilismo* ready to recognize and support (without accepting office) the monarchy in exchange for the concession of universal suffrage (1890) and the jury. Other Republicans, like Pi y Margall, who were concerned with an ideal constitution and inclined to basic social reforms, but opposed a change by violence, continued in a dignified opposition, occupying in the later years of the regime their parliamentary seats. The fourth leader with some egotistic tendencies—Salmerón—formed a party he called the *Partido Centralista.* There were several efforts at unification, particularly after the death of each of the great leaders, but they never produced a single strong organization. Sometimes Republicans elected to local office, in contrast to Socialists, compromised themselves in the corruption that characterized the dynastic parties. These parties and the Crown never consulted the Republicans during the Regency, even when they were not illegal parties. Their own doctrinaire rigidity contributed to their isolation. On the other side, the Liberals offered the bait of office to prominent Republic leaders (e.g., Canalejas in 1881), weakening their parties. Only in the early nineties was the *Unión Republicana,* which temporarily grouped most of the republican notables, able to defeat the monarchists in Madrid while holding on to Catalan districts conquered before. New leaders also slowly appeared on the scene: Esquerdo, his secretary, Alejandro Lerroux, and Melquíades Álvarez. The latter, elected in 1901, presented a moderate view on the political issues, placed a greater emphasis on social problems and education, took a less doctrinaire position on religious issues (leaving separation of State and Church for the future, while arguing for a secular state but not society), and soon would be looking for an opening toward the Socialists on the condition they would adopt a reformist (Bersteinian) position.

The great split in the Republican forces was provoked—like so many other splits in Spanish politics—by the Catalan question. An attack by army officers on a Catalanist humor magazine led the Liberal government under the pressure of the Army and with the intervention of the King to pass a law putting insults to "national symbols" under military jurisdiction. Lerroux, a Republican appealing to the Barcelona immigrant electorate which he had organized in co-ops, political clubs, newspapers, and so forth, supported the army, while Salmerón, his nominal leader, turned to an outspoken support of the Catalanist cause. A strange electoral coalition was formed by all opponents of the regime under Salmerón's name: the *Solidaridad Catalana* (1906), in which Catalan nationalist republicans, the regionalists of the *Lliga* (led by Cambó), the Federalists, the Carlists—all of whom felt threatened by the law and appealed to the emotions of Catalonia—obtained a resounding victory. An attempt on the life of the *Solidaridad* leaders, in which Cambó was wounded, contributed much to its success. Melquíades Álvarez, while fighting the law, and therefore disagreeing with Lerroux, nevertheless criticized Salmerón for his unconditional support of Catalanism and from the wings aimed to support a Reformist Liberal program under the leadership of Moret and the rising Liberal-Democrat leader Canalejas. The idea was to foster a progressive Liberal Party independent of the King's influence. Álvarez, Azcárate, and Esquerdo, with the support of Pérez Galdós, began constituting a group of non-Catalan Republicans (with bases in Madrid, Asturias, León, and later Salamanca and La Mancha, where the urban educated middle class, the working and lower middle-class voters, supported them). Their feeling was that the reform of Spain could not be done from Catalonia. The expulsion of Lerroux from the Republican Union (which had its stronghold in Barcelona and got much economic support from emigrants in Latin America that Lerroux visited during a short exile) gave origin to the Radical Party. The Cortes election of 1907 gave power to the Maura Conservatives, but the political scene was dominated by the demands of the *Solidaridad* group, which Maura attempted to satisfy with changes in Catalan local administration. Maura's attempt to introduce further legislation against terrorism brought about a temporary alliance of Liberal Monarchists, the Álvarez Republicans, and the Socialists in a Liberal bloc (1908–1909) with emphasis on constitutional revision and democratization of the Senate. The *Conjunción-Republicano-Socialista* formed in 1909 against the Conservative Maura offered opportunity for the left to expand its base. It gave the Socialists their first parliamentary seat, as well as conciliar seats in forty municipalities and access to two *Diputaciones provinciales*. One weakness of the alliance was that the main partners had safe bases of support in different regions—Asturias, Catalonia, Valencia, Madrid—and therefore could not add much to each other's strength. The embrace of Álvarez and Pablo Iglesias symbolized this period. The death of Esquerdo and the break with Lerroux and his Radicals on account of a scandal opened the way to a new party—a "governmental republican" or reformist party—with Azcárate more uncompromisingly republican and Álvarez more willing to work for constitutional reform within the monarchy. However, the Left Catalans withdrew from the *Conjunción* on the local autonomy bill project, and some of the Salamanca reformists (Giral was opposed to any collaboration) formed the *Unión Republicana Salamantina*. The Reformists had the support of many leading intellectuals, many of them members in the *Liga de Educación Política,* among them Ortega y Gasset, Madariaga, Azaña, de los Ríos, R. de Maeztu, García Morente, Hoyos Saínz, Américo Castro, González Posada, Salinas, F. de Onís, Simmaro, Pitaluga, *et al.* A new opportunity was presented by the *Asamblea de Parliamentarios* (1917), in which the Socialists, Republicans, and Catalanists displayed unity, but the desertion of Cambó (in face of a general strike that had been provoked by a premature railroaders strike) to the government put an end to that. The election of 1918 that followed, fought on the basis of the amnesty of the strike committee, brought eight reformists into a divided parliament.

The Reformist Party of Melquíades Álvarez would deserve more attention than it has received.[28] As a force that wanted the full constitutionalization of the monarchy, real democratic elections, and a modicum of administrative, social, and educational reform, it should have had a broad appeal to the more progressive middle classes and could and should have been effective within a monarchical (as well as a republican) framework. However, it failed to become an electorally important force, acting more as the conscience of the country, too advanced for much of the middle and upper classes of the early part of the century, and too conservative when the Republic finally was proclaimed. The tragedy of this party, in which many intellectuals participated and where Manuel Azaña gained his first political experience (as a defeated candidate in 1918) is symbolized in the life of its founder Melquíades Álvarez—an ally of the Socialists and Republicans in 1917—who was taken out of the Modelo Prison of Madrid in the summer of 1936 to be assassinated by the popular militias. If we look at the areas of strength of this middle-class reform party, we see its home constituency of Oviedo—an industrial capital of a Socialist mining district—some provincial cities like Zaragoza, Levante, areas of some modern economic development not tied to the latifundia structure and with no aspirations toward autonomy. Unfortunately for Spain those areas were not important enough to support in themselves a strong national party.

The Radical Party of Lerroux, whose demagogic flair and organizational abilities gave him considerable electoral support among the working class and the petty bourgeoisie of Barcelona, became an instrument of the central government in its fights with the autonomist bourgeoisie of Barcelona (or at least the *Lliga* and the Left Catalans were able to depict him as such). This, and the administrative immoralities of which he and his collaborators were accused weakened him as a national figure, until the nonclerical conservative bourgeoisie of Spain turned to him in the 1930's as a leader allied with Catholics and Monarchists against the Left Republicans and agrarian reform. In 1929 the Radical Socialists—who were to play a major role in the Constituent Assembly of the Second Republic split away from him under the leadership of Álvaro de Albornoz and Marcelino Domingo.[29] Around that time too Azaña separated from the Reformists.[30] Politics in opposition to a dictatorship probably encouraged the development of principled positions and personal rivalries, which would have been more difficult had the parties affected been in power, even if only locally, or represented in the legislature.

REGIONALISM AND LOCAL NATIONALISM AS ANOTHER DIMENSION OF THE PARTY SYSTEM

Regionalist, nationalist, and cultural autonomy movements are often characterized by a strong cohesion and a local dominance that converts their areas of support into one-party regions. However this was not the case in Spain. First of all, the working-class masses in Catalonia and the Basque country were immigrants from other regions. Also, particularly in the Basque country, a significant part of the native population did not identify with the romantic nationalist movement, nor use the local language. In Catalonia even those who identified with a Catalan regional personality were divided very early among different parties. A few were loyal to the Carlist version of anticentralism, but more important was the split between the regionalist *Lliga,* based mainly on the wealthy bourgeoisie of Barcelona and some rural districts, and the various groups generally called *Esquerra*—the Left—that represented an ideological continuity with the Federalist Republicans. The Left obtained strong support among the lower middle classes (particularly among commercial white-collar employees) and the tenant farmers of the *Unio de Rabassaires.* The class conflicts between the big textile mill owners who supported the *Lliga* (and its leader, the financier and creator of giant enterprises like the CHADE, Francisco Cambó) and other strata of the population of this highly developed industrial and commercial center became too great to permit any permanent coalition of Catalanist forces. The capitalistic and economically progressive landowners of the *Instituto Agrícola de San Isidro* could not be in the same party as the *rabassaires*—who wanted a change in the ancient and complex tenancy laws—organized by the Left Catalan lawyer, Companys. Llayret and Companys, both lawyers, also started to defend the Syndicalist labor leaders—often unjustly and cruelly persecuted by the central government with the approval of the employers federations supporting the *Lliga*—thus establishing contacts that occasionally would give them the votes of a working class that in principle believed in nonparticipation in bourgeois elections. The existence of a demagogic Radical Party appealing to the immigrant working class and petty bourgeois of non-Catalan origin on a platform of anticlericalism and Republicanism, as well as by organizing co-ops, political clubs, and schools, was an attraction to form coalitions or to compete for the same votes for a more popular Catalanism. In addition to this the *Lliga,* tightly controlled by a group of politicians, businessmen, and lawyers tied to entrepreneurial elements, which therefore often exchanged its more political and ideological demands for favorable economic legislation and control of the economic ministries, was unable to hold some of the activists of its youth organization. A group of intellectuals (Antonio Rovira y Virgili, Nicolau d'Olwer, Pi y Sunyer) called a conference (1922) to revitalize and democratize the *Lliga* but ended in the formation of a new party, *Acció Catala,* that attracted some of the youth. Its victory in the Barcelona provincial elections of June 1923 was a serious blow to the *Lliga* and led Cambó to present his temporary resignation from leadership.

Catalonia therefore reflects divisions similar to those we find in the rest of Spanish politics: conservative businessmen with a Catholic orientation, becoming increasingly willing to support the monarchy but outside of the traditional two parties (thus not so different in appeal from Maura's neo-Conservative dynamic following); a party of the intellectuals, *Acció Catala* (which has some parallels in Reformism); a party of a discontented petty bourgeoisie and peasantry attempting to gain also support of the non-Socialist workers: the Nationalist Republicans and other groups normally called *Esquerra* (probably at that time appealing among Catalans to the same groups that Lerroux and Blasco Ibáñez were appealing to as Radicals), and that later would follow Left Republican parties like Azaña's *Acción Republicana* and the Radical Socialists of Albornoz and Marcelino Domingo. The competition along class, ideological, and style lines within regional politics often took the form of a competition to prove oneself the most Catalan, thus making compromise solutions in Madrid much more difficult and using appeals that increased the hostility of Castilian nationalists. The businessmen of the *Lliga* were split between their nationalist sentiments and the economic interests that led them to support a central government repressive of labor and terrorism and then to welcome the Primo de Rivera dictatorship, which initially appeared sympathetic to Barcelona where it was born, but later turned anti-Catalan.

The Basque Nationalist Party (*Partido Nacionalisto Vasco,* PNV) was more able than the *Lliga* to hold on to supporters from all classes, partly because of its strong religious component (activated early in the Republic through resistance to the anticlerical policies of the Madrid government).[31] Another factor was that the financial and industrial bourgeoisie of Bilbao— with rare exceptions like the shipping magnate Sota and a few others (mostly of foreign origin)—did not identify with the nationalists and that the Basques had early organized their own trade union movement (the *Solidaridad de Obreros Vascos*). The relations between medium and small industrialists, often of working-class origin, in many of the well-to-do small industrial towns of the Basque country with their Basque skilled workers—who often were part-time peasants—were probably better than in any other part of Spain. The workers of Spanish origin joined the UGT and supported the Socialists: it is not probable that the PNV—in contrast to the *Esquerra*—made much effort to gain the votes of those immigrants. The relative unity of the Basque nationalists across class lines and the basically religious orientation of all Basque nationalists, made the PNV a focus of stability within the region. But this strength and its irremediable minority status within Spain facilitated an opportunism on the national scene to achieve its local objectives that could not contribute to national stability.

It is important to stress that in Spain, since the rise of the *Lliga* at the turn of the century, the national parties have not served to bridge the linguistic, social, and economic cleavage between Catalonia and the rest of Spain. In this the situation is quite different from Belgium, where all three parties, but particularly the Christian Social Party, aggregate interests across the linguistic borders.[32] Not only did the Conservatives and Liberals lose most of their support in Catalonia, but in the last year of the monarchy the pro-regime leaders felt the need to form a local pro-Spanish party: the *Unión Monárquica.* The great Republican parties, from the Socialists (PSOE) to the *Acción Republicana* (later *Izquierda Republicana*) on the Left, the Radicals in the Center, and the *Confederación Española de Derechas Autónomas* (CEDA) on the Right, did not have much support in Catalonia either, partly because the immigrant population was mostly anarchosyndicalist, and because the native Catalans overwhelmingly supported the regional parties. Undoubtedly the electoral system, which imposed coalitions to assure a disproportionate number of seats to those having a plurality, reinforced this tendency, while PR would have assured more seats to the Spanish parties. Even so, it is noteworthy that in the two main electoral coalitions the Spanish parties could not assure themselves a better position on the ballot lists. It is also significant that even the Communist Party ran its candidates as a separate party: the *Partido Socialista Unificado de Cataluña.*

The situation was quite different in the Basque country; even in the last elections under the Monarchy the dynastic parties held their own. When the coming of the Republic and the opportunity for regional autonomy encouraged the growth of the PNV (the religious question also led some nonnationalists to support it initially), the strength of the Socialists and Spanish Republicans (Azaña was a candidate for Bilbao) on the one side, and the Monarchist-Catholic conservative bloc, on the other, was sufficient to reduce the PNV in most of the Basque country to a strong minority. Even so, out of the seventeen available seats, the electoral system assured the PNV of eleven seats in 1933 and of nine in 1936, with respectively 46 and 35 percent of the popular vote. (In Catalonia the *Esquerra* and *Lliga* combined gained forty-five of the fifty-four seats in both elections.)

Would it have been possible for the various regional-nationalist parties to have become federated parties of national parties of similar ideological and class composition, acting within them as pressure groups for local interests, somewhat like the CSU within the CDU in the German Federal Republic after 1949? We feel that the most serious obstacle to such a development was the advanced economic development of Catalonia and the Basque country, the wealth of which enabled them to achieve things by local self-government, together with the strong feeling of Castilian nationalism pervading almost all national parties when faced with the autonomist demands. Only Maura's Conservatives, with their conception of decentralization and bourgeois reform from above, together with the personal sympathy between Cambó and Maura, could have led to some form of collaboration, but Maura could not even control his own Conservative Party. Another possibility was the cooperation between Azaña's party and Companys's *Esquerra,* but here the pressures of the anarchosyndicalists on Companys and of the Socialists on Azaña, probably would have made a closer collaboration impossible. The PNV—in view of its basically Catholic and even clerical middle-class orientation—should have worked with the CEDA of Gil Robles, but the basically Castilian and thus antiautonomist following of the CEDA was a serious obstacle. The CEDA electoral alliance with the Monarchists and Carlists in 1933 also obviously did not favor such an opening to the PNV (the

Carlists and the PNV competed largely for the same electorate), even when CEDA could work with the *Lliga* (perhaps because the conservative Catalan party was at that time in the opposition in the regional parliament). The regional party system did not establish permanent and stable ties with the national party system, though Azaña perhaps came closest to achieving these in his relationship with Companys, a relationship that in the fall of 1934 exacerbated the hostility of the centralist right to him.

THE SPANISH SOCIALIST WORKERS PARTY: SLOW INITIAL GROWTH AND SUDDEN EXPANSION

The politics of Spain in the twentieth century cannot be understood without a monographic study of the role played by the Socialist Party (PSOE) and its closely allied trade union federation (UGT) as well as of the internal struggles in these organizations that affected decisively the fate of democracy in Spain.[33] This is not the place to do so, particularly considering the lack of adequate research, and we shall limit ourselves to presenting some data in comparative perspective that should help to complete the overview of the party system. The PSOE was founded in 1879 and the UGT in 1889. Their control of the Spanish labor movement was almost always contested by the followers of Bakunin, anarchists and anarchosyndicalists, particularly by the *Confederación Nacional del Trabajo* (CNT) founded in 1910, rather than, like in other countries, by the Communists. The weakness, almost absence, of the PSOE and the UGT from the most industrialized region of the country, Catalonia, is a decisive difference from all western European countries and prevented the integration of a large part of the working class into politics through democratic elections. The party, as its name indicates, was essentially a workers' party, under the strong leadership of a printer—Pablo Iglesias (1850–1925), who was strongly influenced by Guesde—and, except at a later stage, intellectuals never played a role comparable to the one they had in the Italian party. For a long time the tactics of the party responded to those advocated by Kautsky—with its basic ambivalence—that became manifest when access to power became possible with the Republic and even when the dictatorship of Primo de Rivera opened access to a corporative structure to representatives of the UGT. The law-abiding character of the party, its commitment to political participation, in contrast to the anarchosyndicalists, made the party appear reformist; but a vague commitment to the Marxist conception of class politics, the difficulties in achieving concrete gains for the working class in a social and economic structure like that of Spain, and the ideological climate of Europe in the thirties brought out the maximalist tendency, latent in it, under the leadership of Largo Caballero and probably the influence of intellectuals, if not of the Communists. It is impossible to account here for this internal evolution, but some of the data on the strength of the party and the UGT over time and within different sectors of the Spanish working class will help to account for it, as well as for the difficulties encountered by Spain in its democratization process once democratic institutions had been enacted.

For many years Socialism experienced in Spain a very slow growth, it won few elective offices, its membership figures were small, its penetration in many parts of the country weak. It has been customary to attribute this to the fierce competition of the Bakunians, but it is our feeling that additional explanations are necessary. Electoral corruption and chicanery certainly helped to slow down the growth of the party and the weakness of local self-government probably deprived it of this platform to appeal to the workers and to develop its organization as in other countries, but these institutional factors would not seem to tell us the whole story. It is probable that the importance of petty bourgeois republicanism, particularly in Catalonia but also in Madrid and Levante, must have prevented many workers from turning to the party, an aspect that has not been stressed in the literature. The retarded industrialization should not be considered decisive since dominantly agricultural provinces contributed disproportionately to the membership of both the PSOE and the UGT, and highly industrial ones—like Catalonia— were closed to its appeal.

The slow growth becomes apparent when we compare the Spanish Socialist strength in votes, membership, and trade union affiliation with the Italian figures for the same dates. In 1896 the party obtained 14,000 votes, while the sister party in Italy polled 82,523. In 1901, it had reached 25,400; the Italians obtained 164,946. In comparing these figures we should take into account that the Italian suffrage laws were much more restrictive although the population was close to twice as large. By 1904, the Spanish party had elected fifty municipal councillors in twenty towns and villages, but only in 1910, and on a Republican-Socialist coalition ticket, could the party leader be elected to Parliament as the first representative of his party, while a similar coalition in Italy in 1900 brought thirty-three representatives to the Chamber. The election figures for Madrid—a city in which the Socialists were always strong—show the importance of the Republican-Socialist competition. In May 1910, Pablo Iglesias was elected on a coalition ticket with 40,589 votes, in 1914, however, only with 22,094 and similar figures in 1916 and 1918 and finally with 36,469 in 1919; but after the break of the Republican-Socialist *conjunción* he was able to obtain only 17,047 in 1920 and then 21,341 in April 1923. It is worth noting that in July 1921 the UGT had 45,402 members in Madrid, so that—even assuming that many members were under twenty-three and therefore not entitled to vote—it seems probable that not even all UGT members voted for the party.

The comparison with the Italian monarchy for the first decade of the century shows the lag of the PSOE behind the Italian party even more markedly than the figures for trade union membership. They also give us a cue for one explanation: the relative importance of the Republican opposition to the monarchy in both countries: in 1904, only 4.2 percent of the Italian voters supported the Republican party, while in Spain, Catalan and Non-Catalan republicans added up to 8.2 percent, and a few years later the proportions were 4.4 (1909) versus 10.6 percent in Spain (1910). Certainly the mixture of the Catalanist and the Republican appeal must have contributed to this difference in strength of political vs. more strictly social protest, particularly because the PSOE until 1917 refused to make a declaration of Republican principles.

The membership of the UGT—for which we have continuous official statistics—started with 3,355 in 1889 and experienced a sudden growth after the Spanish-American War and another one in the first years of the century, probably because of the relatively rapid industrialization of the period, to reach 56,900 in 1904. A slump began in 1905 that lasted until 1911, when in the aftermath of the *Semana Trágica* and with the rise to power of the less hostile Liberal party a new upsurge started which brought the membership to 147,729 in 1913. Despite social agitation, the discontent with rising prices, and the return of workers from France, the following period saw a drop to 76,304 in 1916 with an increase in 1917. The attempts to democratize the monarchy at the *Asamblea de Parlamentarios* (1917), the defeat of the general strike, and the revolutionary atmosphere provoked by the Russian Revolution and the end of World War I, the revolutionary atmosphere in the countryside led to a rise to 211,342. This figure slowly but continuously increased during the remaining years of the Restauratión and under the Primó de Rivera dictatorship to reach 258,203 by 1930. The coming of the Republic in 1931, provoked a spectacular jump to 958,451 (December), even though the acceleration had started shortly before. These figures, however, lose some of their impressiveness when compared to the membership figures of the *Confederazione Generale del Lavoro* (CGL) of Italy and the respective ratios to the population (*Table 8*). Even considering that the Spanish labor movement was divided between two hostile camps the mobilization of the Spanish working class was much slower than that of the Italian, even though in the thirties it might have been higher than in Italy in 1920.

Who were the members of the UGT—and thereby an important part of the Socialist electorate—and how do they compare with the members of the CGL?

In a country with a large rural proletariat—a large part of it seasonally unemployed and living in large agrotowns and villages—this group represents an important part of the membership. Before the Republic, however, this sector of the working class was less organized by the Socialists than in Italy where rural Socialism and, later, Communism were already strong in the early decades of the century. The UGT and with it the PSOE had their strongholds among the working class of mining districts, such as Oviedo and the Basque country, industrial districts of the North and in Madrid. Miners (17 percent of the non-agricultural members) and skilled and semiskilled workers constituted its main support, with the railroaders contributing at least as much as in Italy. The UGT weakness in the textile industry—located almost exclusively in Barcelona—contrasted with its strength in the metal trades, which then employed fewer workers. If we look at an electoral map of the Socialist vote in 1907 we see how the party had started to penetrate agricultural areas of North-Central Spain—some of which also had some Republican tradition—but not the latifundia South in which the political opposition to the Restoration was still limited to the Republicans and social protest was largely anarchosyndicalist.

Table 8—The Socialist and Republican Vote in Spain and Italy in Selected Legislative Elections

Spain 1907		Italy 1904	
Republicans		Republicans	4.2
Non Catalan	5.31		
Catalan	2.93		
PSOE	.24	Socialists	7.3
Number of voters	3,071,142		1,174,392
Spain 1910		Italy 1909	
Republicans		Republican party	4.4
Non Catalan	7.4		
Catalan	3.2		
PSOE	.6	Socialist party	11.2
Number of voters	2,451,776		3,081,897
(only districts with more than one candidate)			
Spain 1933		Italy 1921	
PSOE	19.9	Socialista Ufficiale	25.7
PSOE in coalition with Esquerra	5.7		
Other coalitions with PSOE	3.9		
Communists	2.2	PCI (Communists)	3.5
Dissident Communists	.1		
Number of voters	8,072,110	(only men)	6,308,995
(women were eligible to vote for the first time)			

The data on the 1907 election from Modesto Sanchez de los Santos and Juan de Onuba, *Las Cartes Españolas. Las de 1907* (Madrid, Tipografia Antonio Marzo, 1908) pp. 565–68, for 1910 from Modesto Sanchez de los Santos y Simón de la Redonela, *Las Cortes Espanolas. Las de 1910* (Madrid, Tipografia Antonio Marzo, 1910) Appendix. The data have been calculated adding the votes in single member districts and multimember constituencies taking into account for the second the number of votes that each voter had according to the law. This and the lack of information on the number of voters casting their ballots (but not on the votes cast) in Barcelona allow only rough estimates of party strength. The data for the 1933 election—the only one in the Republic in which it is possible to separate the popular vote for the PSOE from other Republican and Leftist parties—are from an appendix to Largo Caballero, *Discursos a los Trabajadores* (Madrid, publication ordered by the Comision Ejecutiva del PSOE, 1934). p. 165, based on the records of the voting registry.

The Italian data are from the chapter on elections of the publication by the SVIMEZ on comparative statistics of the South with the rest of Italy.

In Spain all males over 25 with minor exceptions were eligible to vote in 1907 and 1910. The difference in the number of voters in both elections is due to the enactment of art. 29 of the 1907 electoral law that did away with elections in districts with only one candidate running. In 1933 women had obtained the suffrage.

In Italy the 1904 and 1909 elections were held under laws that restricted the suffrage (basically of 1882) requiring a very low census—paying taxes or rent—and literacy. The age, however, was lower than in Spain, being set at 21 and not 25. In the 1919 election the illiterates, according to a 1913 law, were allowed to vote, as they had been in Spain since 1890. The difference was reflected in the fact that in 1909 the eligible voters were 8.3 percent of the total population and in 1919 27.3 percent. The earlier expansion of suffrage in Spain is reflected in the fact that in 1907 the eligible voters were 23.6 percent of the population.

The figures for the UGT membership in 1932 (those for the Socialist electorate in municipal and national elections in 1931 will be presented later) show how long it took the party and the union to mobilize in its favor the reservoir of proletarian protest in the countryside, particularly in Andalusia and Extremadura. Once mobilized in the newly created *Federación de Trabajadores de la Tierra* the importance of the traditional urban-industrial working class was considerably reduced since 42.8 percent of the UGT membership now came from the agricultural sector.

The history of the Federación de Trabajadores de la Tierra—the farm workers federation of the UGT—reveals the process of rapid mobilization under favorable circumstances of a group that before had proved difficult to reach for the Socialist labor movement. On April 7, 1930, various local groups created the organization at a Congress in which 235 delegates from 157 villages (there were 9,262 municipalities in Spain) representing 27,340 members participated. In June it counted 275 trade unions with 36,639 members, two years later the figures were 2,541 and 392,953, in addition some peasants were directly affiliated with the UGT, so that the total number of rural members in the Socialist unions in June 1932 was 445,414 in 2,429 organizations (plus 460 not giving information). If we take the reported membership figures in different provinces and relate them to the number of males active in agriculture, we find in Toledo an affiliation rate of 31 percent and of 22 percent in Badajoz, a province of Extremadura, and similar rates in two Andalusian provinces in the Guadalquivir valley, though only an 11 percent in Sevilla where it had to compete with the CNT. The national membership claimed would have been 10.7 percent of the active males in agriculture.

The membership of the party in the early twenties was largely concentrated in Madrid, Asturias and the Basque country—that added up to 35.9 percent—but in the 1930's shifted to the economically underdeveloped South (Andalusia and Extremadura, in 1932 added 44.6 percent of the membership, compared to 36 percent in 1928). All this certainly contributed

Table 9—Regional Distribution of the Spanish Socialist Party (PSOE) Membership in 1918 and in 1932 and the Ratio Between Membership and Population Distribution

Region	Population 1920	PSOE 1918	Ratio	Population 1930	PSOE 1932	Ratio
Andalusia	19.7	26.5	134	18.6	33.4	180
Extremadura	4.9	9.5	193	4.9	11.2	229
New Castile (incl. Madrid)	11.4	16.3	142	12.3	16.1	130
Old Castile	6.4	7.6	118	6.4	8.7	136
Asturias	3.2	14.2	445	3.4	.9	26
Basque country and Navarre	5.0	5.4	108	5.3	2.1	40
Catalonia	11.0	5.0	45	11.8	1.8	15
Aragon	4.4	4.8	109	4.4	2.3	52
Levante	12.6	7.9		12.2	12.6	102
Baleares	1.5	1.8	120	1.6	1.1	69
Leon	4.7	*	*	4.5	2.2	49
Galicia	9.0	5.6	57	9.5	4.8	51
Canaries	2.2	*	*	2.4	2.2	91
Morocco	—	—	—	—	.4	
Foreign countries	—	1.3	—	—	.1	
	(21,161,314)	(32,430)		(23,327,447)	(71,320)	

* No separate listing. In 1920 Leon was listed with Old Castile. In 1920 there were only two organizations in the Canaries.
Data from the Anuario Estadistico de España.

to the increased attention to the agrarian problem and to a new and even more bitter hostility of the conservative strata towards a labor movement that otherwise had gained a certain respect within the business classes and the State—by contrast with the CNT. These changes in membership and image together with the ideological climate of the thirties must have contributed to the turn toward maximalism initiated in 1933, that exploded in the Asturias revolution of 1934 and that in the spring of 1936 split the party.

Table 10—Occupational Composition of the Membership of the Spanish UGT and the Italian CGL

Occupational groups	UGT			CGL
	1923 December	1929 December	1932 June	1914 January
Primary sector				
Agriculture	32.1	26.5	42.8	41.5
Wine	.5	.7		
Mining	11.4	11.9	3.9	3.9
Fishing				.1
Secondary sector				
Textiles	1.2	2.0	.7	2.7
Clothing	.4	.7	.4	.5
Metal	6.3	5.5	3.2	5.2
Leather goods	1.9	1.7	1.1	1.0
Wood	.1	.9	1.4	2.1
Furniture	1.2	.9		
Printing	3.4	2.8	.9	2.9
Food industries	4.4	5.3	2.7	4.4
Construction	16.0	16.2	8.0	9.1
Tertiary sector				
Railroads and transport	6.5	7.2	4.7	6.1
Sea transport and harbors	1.0	1.8	2.5	2.7
Service occupations	2.0	3.9	5.2	2.6
Commerce	1.8	3.6	2.5	
Bank employees			2.6	
Other industries and occupations	8.7	7.9	13.0	10.2
Members	(210,617)	(258,203)	(970,072)	(682,002)
Sections or organizations	1,275	1,617	5,107	6,536

The Spanish data are from the Official Statistical Yearbook—*Anuario Estadistico de España*—for different years and the Italian from the *Anuario Statistico* II Serie, vol. IV Anno 1914, p. 297, for Organizzazione libera, as distinct from the Catholic and Independent organizations.

The data for the early twenties that give membership in the PSOE and in the UGT allow us to compare the relative strength of the trade union and party in different regions. In the strongholds of the party that coincide with industrial regions—such as Asturias and the Basque country—the unions had considerably more members than the party, while in less industrialized areas the number of Socialist trade unionists was only slightly larger than that of party members. In such areas it is not impossible that some of the Socialist constituency may not have been composed of workers or that farm laborers would have been activated politically while the resistance of the employers would have prevented their organization in unions. The peculiar position of the Socialist movement in Catalonia is also reflected in the fact that this is an industrial region in which party and union tend to coincide.

The same pattern is found in another region of strong CNT tradition: Aragon, where the UGT almost coincides in membership with the PSOE.

Table 11—Number of UGT Members Per PSOE Member in Different Regions of Spain: 1921

Asturias	33.5	Levante	7.6
Basque country and Navarre	26.7	Catalonia	6.7
Old Castile and Leon	15.4	Andalusia	4.8
Baleares	10.2	Aragon	1.6
Galicia	10.2	Canaries	.5
Extremadura	9.8		
New Castile (including Madrid)	7.9		
Nation: PSOE 23,010 UGT 246,113.			
Union members per party member:			10.7

Data from the *Anuario Estadistico de España.*

Let us stress that the PSOE was the only well-organized mass party in Spain, the strongest party in both the first and last legislatures of the Republic, almost the only party that with exception of Catalonia was able to present candidates all over the country and elect some in all regions. A party of which Ortega y Gasset could write on June 6, 1931:

> With the exception of the Socialist Party, all the other parties that engage in politics are not really parties nor anything worthy of it. Some are survivals of degenerate and ossified oppositions, others on the contrary improvisations created under the pretext to struggle against the monarchy.[34]

Only the CEDA based on the Catholic laity and improvised under the sponsorship of the Church became another mass party more than two years later.

The PSOE perhaps has attracted less interest of foreign scholars than other Spanish parties and social movements because it was the least originally Spanish, the most European of Spanish parties. At the same time, Spanish scholars, knowing little about the sociology and history of the labor movement in other countries, lacked the perspective to understand its problems that reflected in the Spanish context those of Marxist Socialist parties all over Europe. Without such monographic research our treatment of the PSOE in this paper has to remain necessarily sketchy and unsatisfactory.

THE ABSENCE OF A CATHOLIC DEMOCRATIC PARTY

One basic difference between Spain and Italy (and some other Catholic European countries) is that Spanish Catholicism was a latecomer to democratic-liberal politics and to populist mass organization. A number of complex circumstances account for this.

1. Carlism continued until the last quarter of the nineteenth century to hold the loyalty of much of the lower clergy, some of the religious orders, and much of the devout peasantry of northern and northeastern Spain. This

loyalty was partly transferred to Integrism—a fundamentalist political position indifferent to the dynastic question—once the Carlist cause was lost.[35] In the twentieth century one of the most Catholic regions—the Basque country —transferred its loyalty to the Basque nationalist cause. Significant segments of the lower clergy found nationalism an alternative to the secularizing tendencies of the central power structure, particularly in the first year of the Republic. To a lesser extent the same happened among some of the more religious segments of the Catalan bourgeoisie and perhaps in the Catalan countryside.

This attraction of the peripheral and sectional movements deprived Spanish Catholic politics of some of its potential mass and popular basis, of voluntary associations of Catholic inspiration, weakened the Catholic trade union movement, and in the twentieth century deprived political Catholics of a lay leadership emerging in regions of high education and economic development, and in the case of the Basque countryside and smaller industrial towns of a democratic social structure.[36]

The contrast with Italy becomes evident when we consider the hypothesis that the Veneto, Trentino, and Lombardian Catholic communities would not have supported first the *Unione Cattòlica* and later the *Popolari,* but autonomist parties.

2. The violence of anticlericalism at some points in the nineteenth century, particularly in the 1830's and 1840's, the civil strife caused by the Carlist wars and the need to end them (the 1851 Concordat), the demagogic anticlericalism of the first Republic—all led in the Restoration period to an agreement to accept a status quo between the Conservatives (who were closer to the Church) and the Liberals (the inheritors of some anticlerical traditions). The constitutional texts in which this compromise was embodied were sufficiently ambiguous to allow shifting interpretations by various prime ministers and a progressive liberalization, particularly by the Liberals early in the twentieth century (Canalejas). This meant that the non-ultramontan, non-Integrist Catholic masses of most of Spain did not feel the need to rally—as some of the Italians did—in opposition to a godless Liberal regime. It also facilitated the modus vivendi with the hierarchy, which through the Crown could still exercise considerable influence. There was less need for a "Catholic" party in view of the less violently anticlerical position of the dominant parties and the absence of anything comparable to the Roman Question. At the same time the extremism of the Integrists of Nocedal and the acceptance of the regime by the *mestizos* (halfbreeds) of Pidal, divided Spanish Catholicism politically and sterilized it in bitter polemics.

3. The Carlist or Integrist orientation of many of the devout Catholics, together with the desire of a large part of the hierarchy (appointed in agreement with the Alphonsine governments) and of the Vatican after Leo XIII, made the active involvement of laymen in public life more difficult. The hierarchy (and this should be investigated) seems to have felt ambivalent about encouraging such participation in the fear that it would provide a new platform for the Integrists. The Catholic Congress in Zaragoza in 1889—at a time of ascendancy of the Liberals and of the enactment of universal suffrage —made the cleavages among Catholics manifest.

4. The poverty of the country, the low level of education, the small number of priests and the weakness of Catholic educational institutions and religious orders until early in the twentieth century (due to disentailment) weakened Church impact on the population, particularly in densely populated areas with considerable political weight. Only the expulsion of religious orders from France, and a limited Catholic cultural revival, early in the twentieth century produced the sparks of a social mobilization of Catholic laymen (the founding of the *Acción Católica Nacional de Propagandistas* and of the newspaper *El Debate* [1911], and later the various branches of Catholic Action); some attempts to create a Catholic labor movement (the first white-collar union in 1903), a successful system of cooperatives (1912), and credit societies (*Confederación Católica Agraria;* CONCA [1913]) for the Catholic peasantry, also began at this time.[37] But the momentum was not yet there when the old party system disintegrated and some talk about a Catholic party did not crystallize (perhaps the dependence of the hierarchy on governmental favor and its gratitude for their appointment may have slowed down that process). The appeal of Maura as a conservative reformer from above—being a devout Catholic attacked for his hostility to the anticlerical Ferrer and to radicalism (after the *Semana Trágica*)—may have rallied some of the potential Catholic leadership to his Conservative faction. Furthermore we can speculate that the anti-*cacique* reform from above, and slightly corporative ideas of Primo de Rivera and his *Unión Patriótica,* as a movement of honest citizens and a party above parties, may have drawn some leadership potential just emerging in groups like the ACNDP (there are some data to support this).

5. The slow mobilization of the Catholics in the age of mass politics is reflected in this brief history of Catholic Action. Its embryo stage corresponds to the founding on January 29, 1881, of the *Unión de los Católicos de España* (it is not accidental that February 1881 was also the date that the Liberals first came to power). But in a few years it disappeared since, as Cardinal Reig put it: "It was difficult for many people not to identify, in the reality of our fatherland, Catholic unity and Spanish traditions, with certain political parties." And this despite the pressures of the Vatican in the encyclical *Cum Multa* (December 8, 1882) asking not only to distinguish but to separate and push politics completely away from religion "and not to consider as almost separate from Catholicism those who belong to another party." The year 1889 saw another attempt in the *Congreso Católico Nacional,* and in 1894 the organizing committee of these congresses was transformed into the *Junta Central de Acción Católica* and the *Consejo Nacional de Corporaciones Católicas Obreras* was organized. Women's Catholic Action was organized in 1919, the Catholic Youth in 1924, but the most extensive organizational effort came only in 1926 under Cardinal Reig and around 1929 under Segura with the first National Congress and the first *Semana Nacional de Consiliarios.*

A good indicator of how much the organizational mobilization of the Catholic laity was limited in the first decades to the advanced parts of the country and particularly the regions with a Carlist tradition and regionalist sentiments can be gleaned from the data on membership in Catholic organizations in the 1920's and a comparison with the figures for Catholic Action in the 1960's (*Table 12*).

**Table 12—Regional Composition of the Membership of Catholic
Lay Organizations in 1920 and 1960 (in percentages)**

Region	1920			1960		
	Congregaciones Marianas	Catholic Women Workers	Population 1930	Catholic Action		Population
				Male	Female	
Basque country and Navarre	33.4	10.2	4.8	10.6	10.4	5.8
Catalonia	17.0	6.5	11.8	14.1	10.1	12.9
	50.4	16.7	16.6	24.7	20.5	18.7
Baleares	9.0	4.4	1.6	1.7	4.3	1.5
Valencia and its region	12.6	50.0	8.0	17.1	11.5	8.2
	71.6	71.1	27.2	43.5	26.0	28.4

THE REPUBLIC
(APRIL 14, 1931–JULY 18, 1936)

The municipal elections of April 12, 1931, brought a victory for Republican candidates in almost all provincial capitals and, without waiting for a final count of the votes, particularly in the rural areas where one could still expect some monarchical strength, the Republic was proclaimed and the King left the country after renouncing his powers. Even before the proclamation of the Republic in Madrid, Catalonia made its own proclamation.

We do not have a final count of that election, nor do we have the number of votes cast for candidates of different parties, but the data on the number of municipal councillors elected by the different parties is easily accessible.[38] The election took place in 9,259 municipalities (divided into 18,969 election districts) to elect 81,099 councillors from among 117,895 candidates. The eligible voters according to the 1930 census were 5,440,103. In a number of districts candidates ran unopposed and, according to article 29 of the electoral law of 1907, no election took place. These districts comprised 1,101,644 inhabitants (20 percent of the electoral census) and involved 29,804 conciliar seats. Among the remaining 4,338,459 men eligible to vote, 67 percent or 2,916,193 cast their ballots, electing 50,668 councillors.

The provincial capitals plus the African cities of Ceuta and Melilla were to elect 1,729 councillors among 9,447 candidates (with only five for the Left unopposed in Melilla). Among the 1,104,159 eligible voters in these capitals 715,911, 65 percent, cast their votes. The victory of the anti-Monarchists was clear in those cities: 722 (45 percent) Republicans of a multitude of parties, 290 (17 percent) Socialists, three lonely Communists, 192 (11 percent) of different parties, largely regionalist. The Monarchists had to content themselves with 467 (27 percent) seats. Let us stress that the average participation in the cities was not higher than in the countryside where there were competing candidates (there are only a few important cities that are not provincial capitals).

The data by region for the provincial capitals are quite revealing of some basic tendencies that would persist throughout the Republic. The most outstanding is the relatively low electoral participation in Catalonia—a highly industrial and relatively highly educated region—with only 59.7 percent voting (even slightly lower in Barcelona—58.5 percent), probably due to the anarchists' refusal to participate. In contrast we have the highest participation in the Basque country (82.4 percent), followed closely by some relatively traditional areas like Aragon (80.5 percent), New Castile and Albacete (73.7 percent), and the provincial cities of Old Castile and León (70.3 percent). Madrid, despite its politicization as the capital did not have a high turnout (66.7 percent). The regions of high turnout gave an important minority vote to the Monarchists (above 33 percent), except in the Basque country. The lowest turnout (57.6 percent) was found in the provincial capitals of Andalusia, several of them large cities, which voted for Republican (43.5 percent) and Socialist (19.9 percent) candidates. In this, Andalusia set a pattern

Table 13—Participation in the Municipal Elections of
February 8, 1920, and of April 12, 1931—Which
Brought the Republic into Being
(by region, in percentages)

Region	1920	1931	Difference
Basque country	69.2	79.0	9.8
Navarre	66.0	73.0	7.0
Catalonia	54.8	65.1	10.3
Madrid	58.6	62.8	4.2
Old Castile and León	70.6	75.4	4.8
New Castile (including Albacete)	58.4	74.1	15.7
Levante	67.0	67.4	.4
Aragon	56.8	70.1	13.3
Andalusia	57.2	64.5	7.3
Extremadura	68.5	75.7	7.2
Galicia	55.5	54.1	− 1.4
Baleares	43.0	77.0	34.0
Canaries	78.0	44.5	−33.5
Murcia	60.0	63.0	3.0
Asturias	73.0	69.0	− 4.0
National average	61.0	67.0	6.0

of considerable leftism, but a leftism not sustained by high participation or effective organizational strength (as the rapid defeat of the Andalusian working-class masses by the pro-Franco army and bourgeoisie of the cities would prove in 1936). The Andalusian cities were also characterized by a large number of void and blank votes (2.0 percent) as was the other underdeveloped region, Extremadura (1.1 percent). The Republican candidates were strongest in Catalonia (69.5 percent) and south of it in the Levante, with its three prosperous commercial–semi-industrial capitals (59.7 percent) (that had already strongly supported the first Republic). The Socialists had some strength in the Basque capitals (particularly Bilbao—26 percent), but the regional nationalists had even greater strength (37.1 percent). The most striking fact, and one which represented a heavy mortgage for the Republican-Socialist–created regime, was that in the three Catalan capitals only 6.9 percent of the councillors were Socialists. The provincial capitals of central Spain south of Madrid, despite their low industrialization, were strongholds of Socialism, but even northern Castilian cities gave them a significant share of seats. How were the different regions outside the capital cities represented, ignoring for the moment the distinction between those elected unopposed and those elected by votes?

The Monarchists could hold on in the two regions of large estates, Extremadura (39.4 percent) and Andalusia (42.4 percent), and were weakest in Catalonia (4.5 percent) and Aragon (12.4 percent). The countryside of Old Castile and León (that later would give an important share of its votes to the center Right, CEDA and the *Agrarios*) was very weak in its support for the monarchy (19.7 percent). In fact in this region the number of monarchist councillors was larger in the provincial capitals (36.1 percent) than in the countryside as it was in the provincial capitals of Aragon (30.2 percent), in those of New Castile, and with a small difference in those of Galicia. Even in largely socially conservative areas the countryside was not more monarchical than the cities. It was markedly so only in the Basque country (15.5 versus 7.8 percent), Andalusia (42.4 versus 27.3 percent, and the Levante (28.7 percent). Only the difference in Andalusia might be attributed to *caciquismo.* Some evidence in support of this is the comparison of the results outside the capital cities when voting took place and when Article 29 was applied. Even so the Andalusian countryside, that was later so largely radical and where the Socialist trade unions were able to mobilize so much support (in addition to large areas of anarchist strength—reflected in low voting turnout), was still in 1931 susceptible to pressures by the landlords (particularly the districts under Article 29 of western Andalusia, giving 55 percent of their seats to the Monarchists). This incidentally was not the case in Levante where the districts in which no election took place were slightly more Republican, less Socialist, and gave only 4 percent more seats to the Monarchists.

Table 14—Political Affiliation of Municipal Councillors Elected on April 12, 1931, in Andalusia (in percentages)

	POLITICAL AFFILIATION					
	Republican	Socialist	Communist	Monarchist	Other	Unidentified
Provinces outside of capitals						
—Contested elections	24.0	16.6	.1	40.6	7.9	10.0
—Under Article 29	20.5	3.5	—	48.7	8.5	18.8
Total provinces without capitals	23.2	14.0	.1	42.4	8.1	12.2
Capital cities (all contested)	43.5	19.9	.3	27.3	9.0	—

It has often been asserted[39] that Article 29 of the electoral law of 1907 made possible vile *caciquismo* and thereby the election of Monarchist councillors. The data for the 1931 municipal election published in the *Anuario Estadístico* allow us to compare the proportion of seats won by the Republicans in Article 29 districts and in those where election took place. Certainly fewer Socialists were elected (2.9 versus 7.5 percent), but slightly more Republicans (46.5 versus 40.3 percent). The Monarchists identified as such, rather than having an advantage in the districts under Article 29, were stronger in those where an election took place. However, it may be argued that many of those running under other labels, or whose affiliation was not known, usually were Monarchists. Such lists indeed had some advantage under Article 29 (respectively 20.2 versus 18.1 percent and 9.7 versus 8.2 percent), with a difference of approximately 3.6 percent, but this factor did not account for much and did not compensate the greater weakness of the Monarchists.

The pattern becomes even more evident when we turn to the data by region, limiting our attention to the strength of the Republicans (not including the Socialists) where there was balloting and under Article 29 (and without distinguishing the rural areas from the provincial capitals in which there was always balloting). The differences are generally minor, and in Catalonia, Madrid, New and Old Castile, Extremadura, Levante, Asturias, Canaries, Article 29 actually favored the Republicans, sometimes by appreciable margins. Balloting favored them by a small margin in the Basque country, in Navarre, Aragon, and Galicia. But only in the Balearics and Andalusia was the difference more than 4.5 percent. Thus only in those two regions was there some support for the *caciquismo* interpretation. But even that is not so decisive, since Article 29 was not applied to many candidates in Andalusia. Certainly Article 29 did not favor the Conservatives that much and the *caciquismo* interpretataion may deserve reanalysis, unless we want to accept the thesis that there were also Republican *caciques,* or that in 1931 some *caciques* already had shifted their allegiances to the Republic. Certainly the last hypothesis cannot be fully discounted.

The Republicans—*stricto sensu*—were strong in the countryside of Catalonia (68.4 percent), Aragon (60.0 percent), and Levante (51.1 percent), less so in Old Castile and León (45.0 percent), and weakest in the Basque country, where the countryside and small towns overwhelmingly supported regionalist candidates (65.8 percent). The weakness in the Andalusian countryside (23.2 percent) is particularly striking compared to their strength in the cities.

The Socialists were everywhere weaker in the countryside than in the capital cities—a handicap they seem to have overcome in later elections. However, they already were able to muster appreciable strength in Extremadura (14.4 percent) and Andalusia (14.0 percent), both east and west. Their weakness in the countryside and small industrial towns of the two most industrial regions—the Basque country (3.7 percent) and Catalonia (1.4 percent)—is particularly striking.

Galicia is distinguished by the large number of candidates whose party identification remains unknown (21.1 percent) or who identified with "other" parties than regular Republicans, Socialists, or Monarchists (some of them perhaps regionalist: 22.6 percent). Its countryside remained still more Monarchist than that of most of the country. This and the continuous presence of Restoration politicians in the Republican parliament suggests that *caciquismo*—personalistic politics—had its stronghold there. Candidates that could not be identified with the major parties and were not regionalists could otherwise be found mainly in Old Castile and León (24 percent) and Aragon (21.4 percent), areas in which the non-Monarchist right would soon have considerable strength.

The differences between provinces and most of the urban centers was apparently less than generally assumed, as these percentages show:

Area	Republican	Socialist	Communist	Monarchist	Other	Unknown	Number of Councillors
Capitals	44.6	16.7	.2	26.9	11.2	—	1,724
Provinces without capitals							
Under Article 29	46.7	3.0	.03	20.4	20.2	9.6	29,804
Contested elections	40.3	7.5	.1	25.6	18.3	8.4	48,944

Only the Socialist strength was distinctly urban. The number of candidates of unknown political orientation—probably personalistic candidacies—was stronger in the rural areas (thanks particularly to Article 29). The proportions of "other-party" candidates, particularly due to the strong showing of the Basque nationalists, was also greater outside the capitals. Not so for the Monarchists, not even in the noncontested districts (in these they were generally weaker than where an election was held, except in Andalusia).

Table 15—Region and Republican Strength in the Elections of April, 1931, in the Municipios Where Balloting Took Place and Those in Which Article 29 Assured Their Seats to Unopposed Candidates (percentages)

Region (including capitals and remainder of the province)	REPUBLICAN COUNCILLORS DECLARED ELECTED:			Councillors Declared Elected by Article 29 Among Total Elected
	By Article 29	After balloting	Total	
Basque country	13.1%	17.1%	15.5%	40.6%
Catalonia	71.6	65.9	68.4	44.3
Madrid	68.5	52.8	57.7	31.2
New Castile and Albacete	45.3	34.3	38.8	40.6
Old Castile and Leon	50.0	41.9	44.9	37.0
Levante	55.5	50.0	51.3	23.1
Aragon	59.2	60.7	59.9	51.0
Andalucia	20.5	25.0	23.9	24.0
Extremadura	30.7	28.1	29.0	35.6
Galicia	24.7	26.0	25.5	38.0
Asturias	72.0	55.2	57.0	13.9
Navarre	26.7	29.6	28.0	52.2
Murcia and Albacete	40.9	32.2	34.7	28.2
Baleares	10.0	14.5	13.8	19.0
Canaries	38.5	31.4	36.4	58.0
Ceuta and Melilla	60.0	52.3	59.7	13.6
Total Spain	46.6	40.2	41.5	37.0

Data from: *Anuario Estadistico de España*, Vol. XVII, 1931, pp. 480–482.

The main conclusion that one can draw from the 1931 municipal elections —in which the number of councillors naturally was not fully proportional to the population, given the minimum representation in each municipality and the patterns of settlement in different regions, plus the electoral agreements that might have existed—was that the country was Republican, but not very Socialist, and that the Monarchy had even lost areas that would vote Conservative in the 1933 and 1936 elections. The change of regime was inevitable, and already this election sealed forever the fate of the parties of the Restoration.

The importance of the urban electorate in a parliamentary election as against one of municipal councillors becomes apparent, particularly in the Basque country. Otherwise the pattern of Socialist strength in both elections is parallel with the two areas of maximum strength in the latifundia Spain (Extremadura and Andalusia) together with Madrid.

Table 16—Socialist (PSOE) Vote in Selected Regions in the April Municipal Election (percentage of seats in municipal councils) and the June Constituent Assembly Election (percentage of deputies)

Region	April	June
Basque country	4.4	18
Catalonia	1.5	4
Madrid	12.7	37
New Castile and Albacete	6.8	33
Old Castile and Leon	3.3	17
Levante	5.9	22
Aragon	4.2	10
Andalusia	14.2	36
Extremadura	14.4	39
Galicia	2.7	24

THE PARTY SYSTEM OF THE REPUBLIC (1931–36)

When we look at the party system of the Republic we discover a curious mixture of old parties surviving from the Restoration period (and even from the early nineteenth century), together with the sudden growth of many small Republican groups. The most outstanding fact is the lack of continuity with the two-party system of the Monarchy, either in name or in personnel. The Primo de Rivera *coup* did not interrupt a constitutional regime and its parties, but swept them away, a fact that indicates how weak their roots were. The regionalist and local nationalist parties suddenly expanded their appeal— due to a changed electoral system and partly to the new climate of opinion favorable to local autonomy. The only mass party with continuity with the past was the strengthened PSOE. Among the Republican parties, the most important with a continuous history was the Radical, led by Lerroux, which however came to occupy a completely different position on the political spectrum. The strength of the PSOE and its trade union (*Unión General de Trabajadores*—UGT) on the one hand, and of the antielectoral and antiparliamentary anarchosyndicalist movement (*Confederación Nacional de Trabajadores*—CNT) on the other, accounts for the continuous weakness of the Communists, quite in contrast with most of Europe and even Italy a decade earlier. Unemployment, disappointed hopes for social change, fear of Fascism did not produce in Spain a strong Communist Party but pushed the PSOE into the maximalist positions that led to the October revolution of 1934 and to the internal dissension in the spring of 1936. Perhaps a different electoral system would have crystallized these social tensions in a formal split of the PSOE or a strengthening of the Communist Party, and who knows if that rather than the polarization and radicalization of the major democratic parties would not have served the country better, making possible coalitions in the Center. On the Right or Center we do not find the parallel to the Fascist upsurge in the Spanish electorate, perhaps because the emotions represented by it in other countries were channeled into a radical revolutionary turn of the Monarchist parties and even of some segments of the Catholic Center Right. Since there was little place for Communists there was also little for Fascists, even though in some ways the Left Socialists acted as we would expect Communists to act and the traditionalist and Alphonsine Monarchists in many ways acted like Fascists. In a sense, this phenomenon deserves to be stressed as evidence against those who see making the emergence of new or small parties difficult as the panacea against radicalization in electoral systems, for it shows that, when there are certain strains in the social structure, they will erupt either in the form of new parties or if prevented from doing so by changing the character of existing parties.

Table 17—Party Affiliation of Deputies of the Republic
Who Had Been Deputies in the Lower House Elected
in the 19th Legislature (1920–23)

Party Identification as Member of the Republican Legislature	LEGISLATURE ELECTED		
	1931	1933	1936
PSOE	3	3	2
Izquierda Republicana		2	2
Esquerra	2		1
Reformists		2	2
Radicals	3	4	1
Progressives			
Center	2	1	1
Agrarian		3	3
Lliga	1	3	2
CEDA		2	2
Traditionalists		1	
Independent		1	1
Monarchical Independent	1	1	1
Unidentified	16	11	2
Total	28	34	20

The lack of continuity with the past is not only evidenced in the number of new parties—among them such important ones like *Izquierda Republicana* (Azaña) and the CEDA (Gil Robles)—but in the few continuities in parliamentary personnel. If we compare the three legislatures of the Republic with the one sitting from 1920 to 1923 we find only forty-seven persons who sat in both. Certainly those forty-seven individuals occupied a total of eighty-two incumbencies (twenty-eight in the first legislature, thirty-four in the second, and twenty in the third). However, the low proportion becomes apparent when we consider that there were 1,219 incumbencies to be filled (that means 6.6 percent of the members had been in the legislature elected in 1920). To these we can add some eight legislators who undoubtedly were members of the same family as solons of 1920 to 1923. Of the forty-seven, only four would reappear in the Franco legislature, to which one might add one who must be a close relative of a 1923 legislator.

The initial dispersion of political forces and the relative weakness of the great mass parties in 1931 is reflected in the fact that the 473 deputies elected were representing forty-nine political groups. In 1933 their number was reduced to approximately eighteen, and in 1936 the same number appeared in the parliamentary list.

Electoral Law of the Republic and Its Impact on the Party System

To understand the party system under the Second Republic it is important to take into account the election system introduced by decree on May 8, 1931, by the provisional government. As the decree explains in a preamble, the (relatively) small single-member districts of the old law were to be superseded by districts identical to a whole province in order to weaken the dangers of *caciquismo*. Each district would elect one deputy for each 50,000 inhabitants and one for each additional 30,000 inhabitants. Madrid, Barcelona, and other cities of more than 100,000 inhabitants (Cordoba, Murcia, Málaga, Cartagena, Seville, Valencia, Bilbao, Zaragoza) constituted separate districts from the countryside. (However, the city was defined by the municipality, which, in the cases of Córdoba, Murcia, Cartagena, includes much rural territory.) Ceuta and Melilla, in Africa, were also each given a seat.

The difference in the structure of the election districts becomes apparent when we consider that in the Restoration (data for the December 19, 1920, Lower House elections) there were 311 uninominal electoral districts and 28 *circunscripciones* where several (95 in all) candidates could be elected. Under the new law the 50 provinces, plus Ceuta and Melilla and the 11 cities of over 100,000 inhabitants, formed a total of 63 districts.

The vote was by a system of lists with limited choice, so that where twenty deputies had to be elected the voter could vote for sixteen; where nineteen, for fifteen; and so on. This meant that in some districts the winning slate would obtain 80 percent of the seats, while in others it could get as few as 67 percent (four out of six). The minority, in turn, was assured of from 20 to 33 percent of the seats, with 25 percent as the approximate median. To be elected, a plurality was needed as long as the candidate obtained at least 20 percent of the votes cast. When he received less, a new election had to take place a week later, but seats still vacant could now be filled by simple plurality. These by-elections were often, particularly in 1936, a bone of contention, since they took place with the presumed winners in power. The system certainly favored party organizations as against individual candidates of local appeal. In view of this, the myriad of party labels voted into the Constituent Assembly on June twenty-eighth shows the weakness of the party organizations even more blatantly. The 20 percent clause and the advantage given to the winners in the number of seats made it more difficult for new parties to emerge (unless allied with others) and thus should have favored a two-party system. But the list system encouraged coalitions, and

Table 18—The Election System Introduced May 8, 1931

Number of Seats in the Constituency (One for Each 50,000 Voters or Fraction)	Number of Seats Given to Those Obtaining the Plurality	Representation Given to the Winning Plurality
18	14	78%
17	13	77
16	12	75
15	12	80
14	11	78
13	10	77
12	9	75
11	8	72
10	8	80
9	7	78
8	6	75
7	5	71
6	4	67
5	4	80
4	3	75
3	2	67
2	1	50
1	1	100%

therefore had some of the consequences of PR. Perhaps the favoring of a majority, however, without allowing—like PR—a test of the relative strength of the multiple parties wanting to be on the ballot encouraged small extremist or personalist parties to make demands on the leaders of the coalitions, thus weakening the dominant parties and, what is more important, forcing them to accept allies who compromised them and muddled their appeal, where different coalitions were necessary in different districts. Much of the ambivalence of the CEDA with respect to the Monarchy versus Republic issue, which caused the Republicans and Socialists to deny violently the party's "Republican legitimacy"—and therefore its right to form part of a government when its parliamentary strength fully justified it—was due to the compromises the CEDA made in the 1933 elections with the Monarchists—Alphonsine and Carlist (as it had made others with the Radicals and the Conservative Republicans).[40] The same situation favored the Communists in the Popular Front coalition. The real strength of each and everyone of the parties, particularly in Catalonia the strength of the non-Catalan versus the Catalan parties, will never be known due to the electoral system. Only the number of votes given to the different members of the same slate can serve as an indicator. In view of the weakness and the regional localization of the extremists participating in Parliament, it is not certain that PR would not have served Spanish democracy better than the hybrid system introduced in 1931. Certainly the parliamentary strength of the regional nationalisms would have been more proportional to their vote-getting ability (in the Basque case and among non-Catalan population in Barcelona). The relative unanimity of such regional parliamentary representations in favor of local autonomy may have given them a sense of power, representativeness, and capacity to withdraw as a group, the classic Spanish *retraimiento*,[41] beyond that desirable for compromise and national integration.

The 1931 Constituent Assembly

Once the Republic was proclaimed, a Constituent Assembly had to be elected on June 28, 1931. There were 2,411 candidates aspiring to 469 seats. Of these 448 were elected on that day and 45 were elected later in by-elections among 484 aspirants. The electoral participation was 70.1 percent, only slightly higher than in the municipal contest (67 percent).

The increase in participation was not evenly distributed. It was low in the Basque country, where participation had already reached a high level, nor did it change much in the traditionally Socialist areas. We find only one decrease, which seems difficult to explain, in Andalusia (− 2.7 percent). The most marked increase is in Galicia (8.6 percent), which even so remains an area of very low participation, something that would not seem surprising in view of the backwardness of its social structure.

Since the cities over 100,000 became separate election districts from the surrounding province—mostly rural except in Barcelona and Vizcaya—we can compare the rates of participation in city and countryside.

With the outstanding exception of Granada, and the lesser exceptions of Zaragoza and Córdoba, participation tended to be higher in the countryside than in the cities. This tendency in Barcelona and Vizcaya must have benefited the regionalist parties, stronger in the province than in the capitals, which have a larger number of immigrants.

Table 19—Participation in the 1931 Constituent Assembly Elections in the Capital City District and the Remainder of the Province (in percentages)

Area	Capital City	Province without Capital City
Madrid	53.2	71.3
Barcelona	62.1	66.5
Zaragoza	78.8	73.2
Vizcaya	76.9	80.1
Valencia	64.3	72.9
Murcia	68.7	67.7
Cartagena[a]	47.6	
Andalusian capitals:		
Seville	58.0	66.2
Córdoba	67.6	63.8
Málaga	47.2	65.3
Granada	72.1	53.2

[a] Cartagena, though populous enough to form a separate district, is not a capital city.

Anticlerical, Anti-Military, and Anti-Aristocratic Parties

It might appear strange to characterize a set of parties by a series of "anti" labels, by what they stood against rather than by what they stood for, but such an exaggerated characterization might give a better impression of their motives and style of politics than if we were to speak of secularist, pacifist, and "democratic" parties. Such a positive content would never sufficiently account for the intensity of the support they were able to mobilize and for the hostility they aroused among their opponents. The challenge to—the desire to weaken if not destroy—key institutions of Spanish society was more central to their policies and appeal than any desire and practical program to change the social structure, modernize the economy, and integrate the working class, even when the uneasy alliance with the PSOE led them to support the social legislation drafted by the Socialists.

The issues derived from the role of the Church in Spanish society had been bitterly fought over in the nineteenth century, beginning with the regalist conceptions of the royal ministers of the Enlightenment, the ideas of freedom derived from the French Revolution (*e.g.* suppression of the Inquisition) and the economic problems derived from the accumulation of land in the hands of the Church and the religious orders. The Liberals were able to win the first round of the battle and deprive the Church of its landed property and seriously weaken its organization, the defeat of the Carlists ended the dream of a society without heterodoxy, but the turn toward the moderates, which was provoked by increasing class conflict, imposed a compromise (the 1851 Concordat) that left the Catholic Church as an established church rather than introducing a separation of Church and State and absolute religious freedom. The Revolution of 1868 and the First Republic attempted to go further, but the Restoration turned back to the moderate compromise and the politicians of both dynastic parties attempted, outside of occasional flare-ups, to limit the impact of this most divisive issue. The growing strength of the religious orders, their importance in teaching, the slow but visible revitalization of the Church early in the century, the saliency of the anticlerical conflict in France and Portugal, and the increased self-consciousness of the secular intelligentsia, all led to the Liberals—under the leadership of Canalejas—to introduce legislation limiting the influence of the clergy guaranteeing more rights to the nonbelievers, strengthening secular education. This coincided with a more popular anticlericalism of the Radicals and the labor movement, particularly the anarchosyndicalists, who did not want just to redress the balance of power within the moderate compromise but to shift it decisively. It was a mixture of the intellectuals and the popular anticlericalism that converged in the policies of the Republican founding fathers, with Azaña—*Acción Republicana*—as their most articulate leader, the Radical-Socialists as the most passionate advocates and the Socialists, particularly the humanist Socialists as most effective even when not as enthusiastic supporters. The Lerroux Radicals having been displaced from power by the Left Republicans in collaboration with Socialists and the Catalan Left and in search of the middle-class electorate frightened by Agrarian and social reforms and the Socialist influence soon toned down opportunistically what had been their position. The fact that most of the urban working class as well as the lower rural strata, particularly in the South, was irreligious and/or anticlerical, and that the middle and upper classes, on the other hand, with the exceptions noted among the intelligentsia and petty bourgeoisie, tended to be religious, cumulated the religious conflict upon the class conflict. Outside of the Basque country and a few isolated areas there was almost no religious working class, and the simultaneous attack on the whole traditional social order and its symbols even reinforced the attachment to the Church of middle-class sectors who before had not been clerical. The disorganization of the conservative parties of the *ancien régime* and their lack of ties with important organized business interests (due to the regional issue) led to a great reliance on the Catholic lay community and the Church in organizing the mass party of the people who had something to lose, "*la gente de orden*," the CEDA. The class and religious conflicts became inseparable. The Radicals on their part, forced by the electoral system to unite with the Catholics and govern with their support, could not resist the strains of such a *volte-face* and split, while the Catholic and reactionary extremists had a field day denouncing the cooperation between a "religious" party and the now tamed anticlericals.

Typically, *Unión Republicana*—a party formed by the fusion in September 1934 by the Radical Socialists with *Partido Radical Democrata* (the anticlerical radicals that broke with Lerroux) and some minor splinter groups— had no provincial organizations in six of the eight provinces of Castile nor in any of the Basque provinces, all areas of considerable religiosity, but was represented in six of the eight Andalusian provinces which stand out for their low religious practice and the few religious vocations they produce. The absence of the party in Catalonia can easily be accounted for by the fact that the *Esquerra* competed for a comparable electorate in that region. Despite the importance of the Radical Socialists in the Constituent assembly—the third largest parliamentary party—its local organizations existed only in 504 localities (in a country with over 9,000 municipalities) and the new *Unión Republicana* had locals in only 1,153 places. This indicates how weak the penetration of this type of party was. The membership figures for *Unión Republicana* for 708 local organizations were 50,191, and a party leader calculates up to 80,000 for the total, including the other 445 locals.

To the anticlerical issue some of the Left Republicans, particularly Azaña, added the antimilitary issue: an area where reforms were certainly needed, but where the affect put into them and the style of their implementation, deeply affected the military elite. The military around 1931 had by no means been devoted monarchists and a significant number had welcomed and a majority accepted the Republic, but this attack and what they perceived as disorder (particularly after the Revolution of October 1934) brought them closer to the Right. While it cannot be proven, there is evidence to suggest that the Army had no strong sympathies for clericalism and that its social origins did not link it with the large landowners of the South or the nobility (in contrast to Germany); the fact that their enemies were also the enemies of the Church and the property owners brought these three social forces closer together.

In trying to understand the cleavages in the Republic it is important to stress that many, and some of the deepest, were not class-based, instrumental interest conflicts or even interest conflicts sublimated into ideological conflicts, but style or cultural conflicts. This was the main basis of division between the Left Republican *Acción Republicana* led by Azaña, the Radical Socialists of Domingo, Albornoz and Gordon Ordas in 1931 and the *Izquierda Republicana* (of Azaña) and *Unión Republicana* formed by some of the Radical Socialists and those Radicals (led by Martinez Barrio) who could not stomach the cooperation between their leader Lerroux and the clerical CEDA—and the Right Republicans like the Lerroux Radicals. There was probably much overlap between these parties in terms of social class, occupation, and regional strength and considerable shifting across party lines in

1933 and 1936. The strata more threatened by agrarian reform probably shifted to the Radicals in 1933, but after the disintegration of the party in 1935 may have turned toward Left Republicans on a mixture of anticlericalism, defense of "the Republic," sympathy of the "victims" of the repression of the Asturias revolution and disgust with the "corruption" of the Radicals. The boundaries between *Acción Republicana,* Independent Radical Socialists, Radical Socialists, and other minor parties of the same type or their regionalist parallels, were probably fluid and the positions taken by their leaders on specific issues, particularly the agrarian laws and the collaboration with the Socialists, would be difficult to relate to their electorate, but might reflect the composition and regional basis of their activists and local leaders. However these shades of opinion, added to personal conflicts among the leaders, contributed to the instability of politics. The main difference among such parties was often the degree of emphasis on the anticlerical and other ideological issues, and their support—besides personalistic and clientelistic elements—probably was based on such ideological differences. The more ideological character of Spanish Republican Left, probably, distinguished them from the much more pragmatic French Radicals, whom they otherwise tended to consider as models. Perhaps the emphasis in the Spanish culture on honor, dignity, loyalty to principle, contributed to weaken the tendency to compromise and to give a moral value to the intransigeance of leaders, the permanency of vetoes, and to sublimate or rationalize personal antagonisms. Unfortunately we have little information about the membership and the activists of such parties, about the ties that might have existed between them and masonic organizations, and what would be more revealing: the personal life experiences of their leaders that would account for their emotional involvement in certain issues like the role of the Church or the Army, or focusing the agrarian problem on the nobility rather than on all large landowners. Elements of personal *ressentiment* certainly played a great role in the form of handling problems, the style of politics, that often was more important than the substantive consequences for them and for those affected by their policies. Some elements of petty bourgeois mentality probably would account for much of that style. The weak development of interest groups—with a few exceptions—in Spain, particularly among the rural and small-town middle classes, made those strata particularly sensitive to ideological issues and allowed the politicians an independence for their personalistic feuds they would not have had if they had been more dependent on interest groups. Highly organized interest groups—as in Weimar Germany—can contribute to a fragmented party system, but their weakness or lack of link with the parties can also facilitate another type of fragmentation and rigidity—as Lavau suggests for France—and we suspect in the Spanish case.

Acción Nacional, Acción Popular, Confederación Española de Derechas Autónomas (CEDA)

While Fascism emerged in the thirties on the fringes of the political system, with a minority appeal, novelty, and noisiness, the support of most of the conservative but not fully reactionary middle classes went to the forces which, under the labels *Acción Nacional* (April 29, 1931–October 22, 1932), *Ac-*

ción Popular, and CEDA, were acting under the leadership of a lawyer in his early thirties by the name of Jose M. Gil Robles, behind whom stood the more experienced Catholic lay leader, Angel Herrera. The CEDA has never been studied,[42] and Monarchists, Republicans, and Fascists have done their best to ridicule and criticize it. Their hostility has paid off, and few Spaniards have a good word for a party that many of them or their fathers supported with so much enthusiasm between 1933 and 1936. The boastful demands and hopes of victory in the 1936 elections expressed in the slogan *a por los trescientos* (for the 300 seats among 473) contributed much (they in fact won only 88 seats) to the alienation from a party that so many hoped would peacefully protect the social order they cherished. Today Gil Robles, perhaps wiser than when he became the youngest cabinet member of the Republic at thirty-five, is an opponent of Franco, perhaps with the hope of becoming a De Gasperi or Adenauer of Spain. This hope and its potential importance in a Catholic country with a strong tradition of clericalism in politics make it even more important to understand the failure of a party that could be called a Christian Democratic party or a clerical-Fascist party, but which was really neither. The CEDA was too conservative to be a Christian Democratic party and too exclusively concerned with the rights of the Church (much like the German *Zentrum* during the *Kulturkampf*), despite its open attempts to link with the twentieth-century Demo-Christian tradition (as the adjective "popular" derived from Dom Sturzo's *Partito Popolare Italiano* suggests). Nor was it "clerical Fascism" in that it never made the decisive move toward dictatorship and never openly substituted corporativism for parliamentarism, even when the temptation was there (as the participation of CEDA leaders in the Vienna Congress of corporative studies suggest). However, some of the external features at CEDA mass meetings and some of the ideas spreading in the youth organization of the party conveyed to its enemies such an image. There was some equivocation that certainly contributed to the violent hostility of the Socialist Party (whose Austrian counterpart had just been defeated by Dollfuss) and its refusal to let the CEDA share in the government. During the period between December 16, 1933, and October 4, 1934, in which the CEDA supported the Radical party minority government with its votes, and between that date and December 15, 1935, when it left the cabinet, the party played a major role. Those two years have been called the *bienio negro*—the two black years—by both the Republican Left and the Fascists—black as a symbol of clericalism, reaction, and waste of political energies. Certainly the CEDA did not have a program, nor the cohesion to face and solve any of the great political, social, and economic problems of the thirties. It allowed itself to be pushed by a hostile Left and by pressures from its Right-wing allies into a purely defensive conservative policy, despite some significant attempts by ministers like Jiménez Fernández and Salmón to deal with the agrarian problem and unemployment, and to expand the education budget (even for those institutions most hated by the clerical Right). However, more than its failure to solve acute social problems—a point on which few democratic parties in the thirties have much to be proud of—it failed as a political movement. To explain this is not irrelevant to an understanding of Spanish politics ever since.

In 1931, Spanish Catholics found themselves without any institution or party that could protect them from the onslaught of anticlerical Republican politicians (like Azaña), the anticlerical extremism of the Socialists, and even the violence of the masses, particularly the anarchosyndicalists. The monarchy and the dynastic parties (even the slightly anticlerical Liberals) had always respected the role of the Church and granted it privileges in exchange for a certain subordination to state influence (in the appointment of bishops, and the like). The official religiosity of the state lulled it to the dangers of laic and areligious life, that were not fought by competition but by petty hostility and harassment. The presence of the Church hierarchy among the "authorities," in the Senate and later the *Asamblea Nacional* made it appear to the masses as part of the oligarchic establishment. It also limited its efforts to mobilize the Catholic laymen. The links of clergy with the people were underdeveloped, perhaps with the exception of some of the peasant organizations of the CONCA. As we have already noted, the Catholicity of the state, the fear inherited from the Carlist-Integrist versus Liberal Catholic conflicts of ideological cleavages within Catholic ranks, and the complications created by the importance of regionalist sentiment in two of the more Catholic regions probably contributed to that low effort of mobilization. However some of the Jesuits quite early realized the need for a more active Catholic lay organization and in 1909 inspired the founding of the ACNDP, that to this day constitutes the leadership group of "political" Catholicism, a group formed by higher civil servants, professionals, professors, and from which cabinet members, undersecretaries, and the like have been recruited.[43] The other attempt, also by Jesuits, was to sponsor working-class circles and later trade unions, but with much less success than with the ACNDP.

The leader of the ACNDP was D. Angel Herrera who, in collaboration with Cardinal Tedeschini, was to formulate the *ralliement* policy which the Vatican set at the advent of the Republic. The policy of the Republic, the positions of some of the bishops, the extremism of the ultra-Right Monarchists and Carlists would make such an endeavor an arduous task. Nor would it be always pursued without ambivalence. It happened that the ACNDP was holding a retreat on the day the Republic was proclaimed, and Angel Herrera immediately formulated the need for a mass organization that was launched on April 29, under the slogan: Religion, Family, Order, Work, and Property. "*Acción Nacional* is not a political party; it is an organization of social defense, that will act within the political regime de facto established in Spain, to defend institutions and principles not essentially tied to any specific form of government, but fundamental and basic to any society that does not turn its back to twenty centuries of Christian civilization." The great Catholic newspaper *El Debate,* founded in 1911 on April 15th expressed its recognition of the new regime. The growth of *Acción Nacional* was rapid, but it could not become an integrated party before the June elections to the Constituent Assembly, where the Catholic interests were defended by its thirty-nine deputies, the Traditionalists, the Basques—who at the time cooperated with them—the Agrarians, and the small group of nonclerical but Catholic Republicans who had promised a Republic acceptable to the Catholics. The latter, despite their role in bringing the regime into being, could not prevent the rampant anticlericalism in the Constitution. The solid Catholic tradition in the Basque country served as a platform of protest for such bizarre ideas as a separate concordat between Basconia and the Vatican. In 1932 (after the *putsch* of August), facing a consolidated Republic, *Acción Popular* held an assembly in which 610,000 members were represented and decided to sponsor the CEDA, a federation of parties that was to follow a possibilist line (or, as its enemies on the monarchical Right would say, the curve rather than the straight line) to achieve the nonapplication and ultimately the revision of the anticlerical provisions of the constitution, without, however, getting entangled in the dilemma of monarchy versus republic. The nonparty character of *Acción Nacional* and its main goal of defense of the Church made it possible for men of different ideologies and affiliations to join: those ready to accept the Republic as well as the Carlist and ultra-Monarchists. The creation of the CEDA led some of those close to *Acción Española* to leave, but others continued in its ranks. The 1933 election, because of the electoral system, led to a *Frente Unido de Derechas* (United Right Front) "which, respecting the particular goals and ideologies of the component groups, would pursue the revision of the laic and socializing legislation, defend the economic interests of the country and recognize to agriculture its legitimate preponderance as the basis of national wealth and gain an amnesty for political prisoners." But the union of the parliamentary and antiparliamentary Right was not enough and the CEDA turned to a coalition with the Conservative Republican and the Radicals of Lerroux, who, in the first years of the Republic, had turned toward the Right.[44] The latter coalition was to be labeled by the Monarchist Right an unholy alliance with laic positivism. Perhaps pragmatic interest-group parties can stand the strains created by such broad coalitions imposed by the electoral system, but certainly ideological parties are likely to suffer recriminations for treason and opportunism when they engage in them. The CEDA won a dominant position in the Right-Center coalition, particularly if we consider the regional parties close to it (of 380 seats on that side of the aisle it had 98, plus 51 of the Agrarians, 24 of the *Lliga*—but all these parties combined were short of the 237 needed for a majority, the Radicals of Lerroux with 100 seats and other center forces with 39 being short of it too). The Right-wing parties of the TYRE (*Tradicionalistas y Renovación Española*) with 43 seats, and without legitimacy to participate in the system, could not be the basis of any government but would be decisive in needling the CEDA. The only possibility was a Radical-CEDA government or Radical minority government with CEDA support, and this was the choice of Gil Robles to facilitate the transition without however renouncing his right to take a larger share in power at the earliest opportunity. Lerroux had conceived the idea of bringing the CEDA into the system and with it the Catholic middle class into a Republic that was born without its support. In this frightened, potentially—but not necessarily—monarchic sector of the society, the collaboration of the Radicals and CEDA was a strain for both parties: the Left of the Radicals led by Martinez Barrio and the Right of the CEDA worked with the antagonists of the pact and ultimately split away. If one reads a Right-wing interpretation of the events (like Galindo Herrero), the CEDA was acting with duplicity as a vanguard of the Monarchists. The same conclusion could be drawn from reading the leftists' versions. But a pro-CEDA source (like Casares) shows how often Gil Robles made statements recognizing the new regime, while insisting on the future need of a constitutional revision of the anti-Church legislation. The Radicals with some delay enacted the minimum program of the CEDA and this outraged the Left. A jurisdictional struggle between the regional *Esquerra* government of Catalonia and the central government, in which the landowners of the *Lliga* pressed for the support of Madrid, led to a crisis of the Radical government after a conflict between Lerroux and the President on the occasion of the amnesty. In October the CEDA was to claim a larger share in the government and this provoked the Asturias and Barcelona rebellions. Their aftermath could have been used constructively by the CEDA but it was not; the passions and hatred aroused by the Revolution, the crisis of the Radicals and the personal loss of prestige of Lerroux caused by the two scandals (rightly or wrongly put at his door)—the Stavisky affair of the Spanish Republic—the radicalization of the *Acción Española* group that touched some CEDA leaders, and the equivocations of the JAP youth—all contributed to make politics frustrating and sterile for the still unintegrated party. Economic crisis, revolutionary disorder, reactionary landlords and employers, made its weak government dependent on repression rather than any progressive program. While in December 1934, the CEDA broke clearly with Calvo Sotelo and those led by him on the issue of possibilism, parliamentarism versus principled opposition to the regime, a conflict which in the spring of 1935 affected the internal unity of Catholic Action, the discredit of the Radicals brought the party closer to the *Bloque Nacional*. The independent Center-Catholic politics was in crisis: the choice in 1936 became *Frente Nacional Antirevolucionario* versus Popular Front. The CEDA would still be the mass party on the Right with eighty-eight seats compared to twenty-two of the *Renovación y Tradicionalistas,* but its Radical former allies had only four seats and the spokesman of the fearful Catholic middle and upper classes became the passionate Calvo Sotelo.

Failures in leadership and policy certainly had much to do with the defeat of the CEDA, particularly in its slow and always reticent identification with the Republic (due to its desire to hold the monarchical voters), but perhaps one should look further into the structural factors. The party was not as strong as its bureaucracy and its campaign techniques would make one believe: its members and even leaders had not assimilated a Christian Democratic ideology, its labor and intellectual left-wing were weak, its dominantly agrarian base made it unresponsive to new problems, the worldwide climate of opinion was not favorable to an attempt parallel to the nineteenth-century *Zentrum,* the Low Country Catholic parties, or the twentieth-century *Popolari.* Democracy was in crisis everywhere and authoritarian, corporative solutions were in the air, and, as the writings of Fernando Martín Sánchez (the successor of Herrera at the head of the ACNDP) show, the Spanish Catholics could not escape their appeal, since its organizations could not avoid copying some of the style of the new mass movements. To this we must add that the two regions where a "democratic" Catholic party could have gained support with a progressive or slightly conservative focus—the Basque country and Catalonia—were identified with the *Lliga* and the PNV. The dominantly Castilian basis of the CEDA made concessions to the Basques difficult, and this contributed to another of the crisis of the *bienio,* when the PNV joined forces with the Socialists in a tax strike. The urban Catholic bourgeoisie that could have counterweighted the agrarian dominance in the party was not there. In this the CEDA failed like the parties of the Restoration. In most countries Christian Democratic parties have appeared as the standard-bearers of regionalism—even when in practice once in power they did not do much for it—but the Spanish party despite its federative character, did not even think of taking this issue away from the Left that had so often been centralist. Only its Valencian wing, the *Derecha Regional Valenciana,* led by Lucia, introduced an element of decentralization.

The CEDA did not participate very actively in the planning of the uprising in 1936, even when it did know of it and supported it. Its supporters became the mass basis for the apolitical military rebellion. Its youth even survived for a while as an organization, but the party was forced to dissolve, and its leader broke with Franco and went into exile. Many of its younger men turned to the *Falange,* some as early as the spring of 1936, and one of them (Serrano Suñer) became the master architect of the Franco regime's single party.[45] The CEDA, together with its ideology and tradition, was completely ostracized. However, the religious elite nucleus of the ACNDP survived; its newspaper chain, though put under government control, also survived; its functional organizations (like the CONCA) were *gleichgeschaltet;* but its men, as apolitical experts, still influenced policies. In 1945 when Fascism became untenable and Franco needed to establish contacts with the rest of the world to break the circle of isolation, Martin Artajo, a brother of a former CEDA deputy, the secretary-general of Catholic Action, and a member of the ACNDP, became minister of foreign affairs. Until the *Opus Dei* assumed the role of a Catholic elite group supplying the regime with cabinet members, the groups that once stood close to the CEDA provided many men for the regime. Some of them, like the minister of education, Ruíz Jiménez, who collaborated with the intellectual wing of the *Falange* to escape a narrow clerical point of view, even attempted a certain liberalization. But this participation divided the men of the *Santa Casa,* the "holy house," as the headquarters of this group are called in the Spanish political argot. Participation in a government committing support without responsibility to a constituency is a dangerous and thankless task.

Christian Democrats have been co-opted by the pluralistic dictatorship of Franco more than by any Fascist regime, for nowhere was the anticlericalism of the Left so brutal and the state more willing to grant the Church privileges. This and the failure in the thirties are a heavy mortgage, while the structural weaknesses of the mobilization of Catholic laymen continue, as does the lack of understanding between Madrid Catholics and those of the sectionalist Spain. However the extreme Right as well as the Fascists in the regime are sensitive to the danger that Christian Democracy represents. Their constant critique of the Italian *Democracia Christiana* and of such attempts at national integration as the *appertura a sinistra* show this clearly. A magazine like *Cuadernos para el Diálogo* and even some of the editorial policy of *Ecclesia* (the official publication of Catholic Action) show how groups that could someday constitute a Christian Democratic party are groping for expression. In the meantime the future Christian Democratic party voters are passive supporters of the regime, part of that *masa neutra, macizo de la raza,* just as they were passive Monarchists before 1931.[46] The emerging elite nuclei are small and not fully free from the temptation to take any opportunity to cooperate positively if offered a chance in a nondemocratic regime, as many of their predecessors were in the twenties under Primo de Rivera. Persecution could save them, but Franco would not make that mistake.

RENOVACIÓN ESPAÑOLA—FROM THE LIBERAL MONARCHY TO MONARCHICAL FASCISM

Today Spain is formally a monarchy without a king. This makes the study of the Monarchist Party under the Republic all the more interesting, particularly since this party provided much of the leadership and ideological support to the Franco regime through its influence on some sectors of the Army and the Church. *Renovación Española* or *Bloque Nacional,* as the party was called at one time or another, and its ideological magazine *Acción Española* was one more example (though it did not reach its ultimate conclusion) of the uneasy transition of European conservatism toward Fascism that was first exemplified by *Action Française,* later by the DNVP under Hugenberg in the Weimar Republic and by the *Heimwehr* in Austria.[47] All of these movements appeared in countries where the monarchy, unable to accept without reservations true constitutional parliamentarism and the process of democratization, had not been able to keep a pseudo-constitutional regime working. In all of them a republic—with a certain ambiguity about its legitimacy but accepted by large segments of the population—had come to power. The sectors of the Church—more concerned with the defense of the altar than the throne—were not hostile to a policy of *ralliement,* even when segments of the clergy and the religious orders resisted that Vatican-inspired solution. The business community in its opportunism was by no means unanimously willing to sacrifice itself for the monarchy and even less for a monarchy that would have crowned a regime whose content de facto would not have been different from a parliamentary republic. In addition the Catalan businessmen tended to support the *Lliga* that had declared itself "indifferent" to the issue of monarchy versus republic. Many Basque small businessmen and a few of the very important ones supported the PNV (the Basque nationalist party).

Only the aristocracy, particularly the landowning aristocracy, could feel bound to the crown. This led the monarchists to turn back to more romantic and preliberal, predemocratic notions, at the same time as they tried to mobilize a broader basis of support than the strictly aristocratic monarchists. This basis was sought in a counterrevolutionary intelligentsia with a mixture of extremist nationalism (not originally an ingredient of monarchism), the antilabor big-business circles using corporativist appeals, the Church by comparing its supposedly glorious past under the protection of the kings to its new dependence on the whims of an electorate. In Austria and to a lesser extent in Germany, the conservative peasantry was another target of the Monarchists, but in Spain (as in Prussia) the dominance of the latifundia owners in the party and the fact that the stable peasantry in the North was either organized in the Demo-Christian camp or with the Carlists, made this appeal less important. By dissociating itself from the old two-party system that had crumbled in 1923 and again in 1931, when it had been unable and even unwilling to defend a king that had broken with the constitution, *Renovación* was led inevitably to some identification and continuity with the collaborators of the Primo de Rivera dictatorship. At the same time the ideological weakness of commissary dictatorship became apparent, as did the need for a solid counterrevolutionary ideological basis that had been absent in the Conservative party of the Restoration and even in Maura. The political situation also led, almost inevitably, to some rapprochement with the Carlists and their antiliberalism.

The man who led this new political force was José Calvo Sotelo (1892–1936), of Galician background, whose father was a judge, and who thus represented the *clase media,* devoted to the service of the state. At age twenty-three. Calvo Sotelo was number one in the competition to the elite civil service class (*abogado del Estado,* the Spanish equivalent of the French *Inspection des Finances*). He turned to the Maurista Youth and wrote on the social question. In 1919 he was elected to parliament and shortly afterward became governor of Valencia. A week after the Primo de Rivera *coup,* he agreed to collaborate with the dictatorship even though he was not then an antiparliamentarian, but still favored female suffrage, proportional representation, municipal autonomy, and a kind of city-manager system. His main concern was with municipal reform, and with an attempt to give each region a certain administrative personality, issues on which he did not always get support from the Dictator. In the Civil Directory he was minister of finance, in which post he developed an interest in foreign trade, tried to create an income tax and increase existing tax yields, and made several attempts at economic stabilization. At that time he still was favorable to a parliament elected by PR and critical of a government party created from above, but his civil-servant sense of loyalty to his task kept him working with the regime. After the advent of the Republic he went into exile in Portugal and, being unable to return to Spain despite his election to parliament, went to France, where he had contacts with Maurras and conservative politicians. Before returning to Spain he visited Italy. His collaboration with Primo, his travels abroad, the hatred of the Left toward him, and the parliamentary weakness of his party compared to the CEDA, led him to favor a Right-wing authoritarianism with corporatist elements and strongly nationalistic. He spoke of *instauración* rather than *restauración,* and the idea of a strong state sometimes took precedence over monarchism.

The list of "protectors"—economic supporters with 500 pesetas a year— of the *Acción Española* magazine in June 1936 is revealing as to the character of the extreme Right in the Republic. Twenty of the fifty-nine persons listed had nobility titles. Despite the great interests of the Andalusian landowners in fighting the Republic and its agrarian legislation, only three were residents of that region, while twelve came from Bilbao (the great industrial center of the north whose wealth had become identified with the Bourbon Monarchy), two from San Sebastián, and fifteen from Barcelona. The list is likely to be exhaustive, since it was used to encourage other patrons to do the same, and it allowed those who wanted to remain anonymous to list only initials[48] and the name of a city. The small number of such sponsors, the limited representation of the great landholding aristocracy, is one more indicator of the low level of mobilization for continuous political action and the ideological efforts of much of the conservative upper classes of Spain, particularly in the less-developed regions.

The Absence of a Strong Agrarian Party

The absence of a distinctive agrarian party in the early periods of the party system and its relative weakness considering the agricultural character of the country and the rural economic crisis in the thirties is not difficult to account for. Under the Restoration the wealthy landowners, noble and bourgeois, resident or absentee, could control—as *caciques* or as administrators acting as *caciques*—the votes of the peasantry dependent on them in the areas of latifundia estates south of Madrid or in some of the northern minifundia regions like Galicia. Some of the areas with an independent peasantry on the northern and eastern periphery were attracted to Carlism as a defender of religion, the traditional law and the social order, challenged by the centralizing tendencies of the Liberal governments and the desamortización of public and church lands. It is not surprising that it was in some parts of Castile and the Ebro valley, where there are wealthier peasant owners that the anti-tax protest movements around 1900 had some echo, as the early Agrarian wing of the Liberal party and later the Agrarian party itself would have. Without a regional linguistic and legal autonomy tradition to defend and without such loyalty to a local clergy they were much freer to articulate these interests. Once awakened most of the discontented peasantry found itself supporting the various Republican parties also supported by urban middle classes hostile to the Establishment of the Restoration, or the Left-oriented regionalist movements in the periphery (*Esquerra,* ORGA in Galicia, and even the autonomist radicals in Valencia), while the poorest a-religious peasants and farm laborers had either turned early to the anarchosyndicalist protest or the new Socialist federation of farm laborers. With the challenge of secularization and economic crisis in the thirties much of the Castilian-Leonese peasantry turned to the CEDA which could count on the organizational base built up years before by the CONCA. In Spain the cities were too important, the ties between the urban power structure and the landed wealth too close, and religion as a national issue too salient to make the rural-urban conflict more important than the class and religious conflicts.

TWO SMALL MINORITIES

Spain in the thirties was well aware of and informed upon the great political tensions of western Europe; this contributed much to increase the accumulated tensions produced by underdevelopment, ideological rigidity, and rapid political mobilization in Spain itself. In view of such exposure, it is significant that neither the Communists nor the Fascists, which elsewhere fed on the depression and the crisis of the existing major parties, became mass movements in Spain until after the Civil War had started, though both (particularly the Fascists) rapidly gained strength after the February 1936 elections. Until 1936 both ideologies were more important for their impact on other parties than their own numerical strength. How can we account for this?

Fascism—A Latecomer

Fascism as a political ideology sweeping Europe in the twenties and thirties and appealing to men in all classes, particularly among youth, to a greater or lesser extent in different countries and times, is only beginning to be studied comparatively.[49] The distinctive racist version of Nazism with all its evil consequences and the simplistic Marxist interpretations have contributed much to our lack of knowledge and understanding of this ideological force and of the parties that incarnated it. The Fascist parties or movements that appeared after the founding by Benito Mussolini of the *Partito Nazionale Fascista* had much in common ideologically, but also exhibited interesting national variations in their ideology resulting from the different cultural and intellectual traditions and the problems faced in each country: anti-Semitism, for example, could not be important in Italy with its small Jewish population and even less so in Spain with practically no Jews, but could become significant or central in eastern Europe. The political alignments at the time of Fascism's appearance in each country contributed to defining its position on a Left-Right continuum, and thus its enemies and allies. The social structure of each country and nature of its peculiar "crisis strata" determined its social bases—due to its basically emotional rather than pragmatic character and its potential for opportunism—and its success or failure to become a mass party. The moment of its appearance in turn reflected the political problems of each country, its greater or lesser originality and its chances of independent success. Spanish Fascism has to be seen in this international context and a certain neglect of such a perspective is the only weakness of the excellent monograph by Stanley Payne on the *Falange*.[50]

The first Fascist groups in Spain appeared shortly before the proclamation of the Republic in 1931, at a time when Mussolini had already been in power for eight years, and Hitler had obtained 18.3 percent of the German electorate (1930). This late emergence would be decisive in making the development of the party extremely difficult and would contribute to its numerical weakness in 1936 (in February 1936 it had some 8,000 members). This numerical weakness in turn accounts in large part for limited effectiveness of "pure" Falangism in the fusionist single party created by Franco to neutralize the Fascist ideology and rhetoric and its talk of National-Syndicalist revolution. Being a latecomer, its adversaries on the Left (particularly the Socialist Party) as well as on the Right had good reason to take it seriously. The violence of the Socialists, the lack of trust of the oligarchic Right that did not finance it, the hostility of the bourgeois center—both laic and clerical —that used the power of government, censorship, and preventive detention to make its proselytizing difficult are better understood if we keep that fact in mind. Why did it make its appearance so late? We can only list some reasons: because Spain did not participate in World War I, there was no nationalistic youth coming back from the front unintegrated into bourgeois society and alienated by a lost war or a lost peace. Because of Spain's early national unification, romantic nationalism never had the strength of, say, the *Risorgimento* feelings. The postwar revolutionary attempts of the proletariat (the 1917 general strike and anarchosyndicalist violence) were checked by the Army and the dictatorship of Primo de Rivera, which gave the bourgeoisie a respite without obliging it to become politically active. Under Primo de Rivera the younger middle class, though increasingly alienated from its conservative and liberal elders, without dynamic ideas for the nation's future, could still put its hopes in a bourgeois democratic—that is to say a Republican—revolution against the monarchy, and the "oligarchy." Characteristically early in the Republic we find some transitions between the small Fascist nuclei and the Republicans; nor would José Antonio and Ramiro Ledesma ever question the legitimacy and significance of April 14, 1931. The religiosity of significant segments of the middle classes and peasantry proved another obstacle, when groups like *Acción Popular* and later the CEDA appeared as new antirevolutionary but not purely reactionary parties. The late emergence of political Catholicism in Spain made the critique of its semiparliamentarian position more difficult than that of the German *Zentrum,* while its corporativist fringe and some pseudo-Fascist trappings in its youth organization (*Juventudes de Acción Popular*—JAP) made the competition more difficult. To this we must add that the strong anarchosyndicalist tradition with its belief in direct action offered a more idealistic and activist alternative to those revolutionary segments of the working class alienated from the more bureaucratic Socialist Party. The weakness of the landowning peasantry in many parts of Spain, the attachment of significant parts of it to other antiparliamentary, traditionalist, and antiurban movements—the Carlists and, in the Basque country and Catalonia, to the regional nationalisms (which also embodied much of the criticism of the centralist, oligarchic, bureaucratic, capitalist state)—made those groups— which in other European countries became an important base for the Fascist demagogues—resistant to the appeal of the *Falange.*

The task of Ledesma Ramos[51] and his *Conquista del Estado* group was difficult. The idea of a National-Syndicalist movement appealing to the petty bourgeoisie, intelligentsia, and working class, for a nationalist social revolution, for "Fatherland, Bread and Justice" met with little success. He interpreted the national weakness in terms which make the nation a proletarian victim of foreign capitalism, developing a historicist nationalism of secular rather than religious and clerical emphasis, trying to nationalize and discipline the anarchosyndicalist proletariat. After the working class had been freed of the restraints of the dictatorship, and the intelligentsia was triumphant in the Republic, there was little room for a leftist Fascism. The only appeal could be to Castilian sentiment against the dangers to national unity coming from the autonomy granted to the Catalans and Basques. This sentiment was shared by many of the leading intellectuals, who were often quoted by the Fascists and unsuccessfully courted for their support. It is not surprising that another group, the *Juntas Castellanas de Actuación Hispánica,* whose slogan was "One Great and Free [Spain]" should appear with a more

Catholic outlook, a clear back-to-the-country theme, in Valladolid, in the core of Castile (whose leading politician had been forever an extreme anti-Catalanist), and should succeed in organizing beet growers against the sugar mills. Nor is it strange that the *Falange Española,* the more educated literary and esthetist group, should appeal most strongly to the nonclerical bourgeois students and find some of its supporters among the writers, technicians, and businessmen of Bilbao, hostile to Basque nationalism and the Republic.

The leader's biography reflects very well the elements that were to join in Spanish Fascism. Ramiro Ledesma, son of a schoolteacher born in a village of Zamora, had studied philosophy and physics, collaborated in Ortega's *Revista de Occidente,* and thereby had become an admirer of Germany, where he studied at Heidelberg (1930). In the thirties he was making a meager living as a postal employee. Onésimo Redondo came from a peasant family, had studied with the Jesuits, and had gone as a teacher of Spanish to a business school in Germany (1928). In their social mobility, their youth (twenty-five and twenty-six years), their semi-intellectual position, their foreign contacts, they shared some of the characteristics of other Fascist leaders. The content and style of their appeal was a Spanish adaptation of the foreign models, from which they would get no support until after the Civil War had started. In fact the ardent nationalism prevented the new party from participating in the weak attempts to create a Fascist international. Even the modernistic writer and secondary-school professor Giménez Caballero, whose main contribution was ideological and literary, without much active participation during the Republic, fits the early Italian type of Fascist-Futurist.

However important the contributions of these men to the party founded by the fusion of the *Juntas de Ofensiva Nacional Sindicalista* (JONS) of Ramiro and Onésimo and the *Falange Española,* its limited success was due mainly to the personality of José Antonio Primo de Rivera.[52] There is general agreement that the latter was an intelligent, educated, charming, eloquent, and courageous young man. His father was the Dictator Miguel Primo de Rivera. In the process of building a successful law practice, he was drawn into politics on a Monarchist ticket to defend the memory of his father against the Republicans, even when he recognized the final fall of the monarchy. His analysis of the failure of his father to create a real party and to appeal to the intellectuals, whose influence, particularly that of Ortega, he felt strongly, together with a critical attitude toward regional nationalism, brought him to formulate on October 29, 1933, a nationalist, antiliberal, antisocialist appeal to his own class: "We come to fight so that hard and just sacrifices may be imposed on many of our own class, and we come to struggle for a totalitarian state that can reach the humble as well as the powerful with its benefits." "May political parties disappear. No one was ever born a member of a political party; on the other hand, we are all born members of a family, we are neighbors in a municipality; we all labor in the exercise of a profession." "We want less liberal word-mongering and more respect for the deeper liberty of man." But his main appeal was its romantic idealism eloquently expressed in phrases like: "We are not going to argue with habitués over the disordered remains of a dirty banquet. Our place is outside. . . . Our place is in the fresh air, under the cloudless heavens, weapons in our hands, with the stars above us." The talk of direct action and readiness to fight for a new Spain soon was put to a test by the Left that tried to prevent the circulation of the *Falange*'s newspaper, while the Right cheered the fight. The need to maintain the loyalty of its few followers in face of violence led the party—with serious misgivings on the part of José Antonio—into continuous violence and counterviolence, by which it contributed its share to the climate of tension that preceded the Civil War. In 1933, José Antonio, due to his family connections, managed to get elected to parliament, where he criticized the Radical-CEDA governments for the *straperlo* (*straperlo* was a gambling device which was authorized for a few hours presumably due to influences close to Lerroux, the word entered the Spanish language as *estraperlo* and has since the Civil War been used to refer to the black market and all unsavoury deals) scandal and the incapacity to carry out an agrarian reform. The outcome of the 1933 elections, the *Falange*'s lack of monarchical faith, and its acceptance of the separation of Church and State, limited its appeal to the conservative strata. Isolation and ideological purity went together. José Antonio's personality made him the undisputed leader, and some of the more monarchist activists, as well as Ramiro, left the party. It fought the election of 1936 alone, despite attempts to find some honorable part in a coalition to gain at least one seat. On March 14th, the leader and many of the party's heads were arrested—and José Antonio would never be free again after the outbreak of the Civil War. He was shot in Alicante. The spring of 1936 brought a radicalization of the Spanish youth: electoral defeat had alienated the Catholic middle-class students and youth from their organizations (Catholic Students Association and JAP), while their proletarian peers were moving to unification of the Socialist and Communist youth. The *Falange* grew without absorbing its new sympathizers, but the leadership of the opposition to the Republic was in the hands of Calvo Sotelo—who sometimes declared himself a Fascist. The Republican persecution forced the party to act: contacts with the Carlists—who were less tied to the oligarchic self-interest the *Falange* so often criticized—and to the Army were tried. The Army, however, wanted no political compromises, even when it wanted the Falangist volunteers. In the course of the Civil War the party would become part of the *Movimiento*—the single party—of what Nellessen titled his book: *Die verbotene Revolution*.[53] Another great European movement present, and influential, but without mass appeal, was that of the Spanish Communists.

Communism—A Small Minority

The Spanish Communist Party was founded in 1921 when the PSOE refused (by 59 percent of the 14,823 votes cast at an extraordinary congress) to accept the Twenty-one Conditions set by the Comintern.[54] The split was two-way, with the majority joining the Second International. No maximalist intermediary position like that of Serrati in Italy (who got 57 percent of the votes at the Leghorn Congress in 1921) emerged even when the pro-Communist vote in Spain was larger than that received by the Bordiga group in Italy (34 percent). This was an auspicious beginning, and the new party attracted six members of the executive committee of the Socialists (among them prominent founders Facundo Perezagua and García Quejido), two of the six city councillors of Madrid, and others. However, its main efforts soon were directed to gain influence within the CNT, which was invited to attend the Red Trade Union International Congress in Moscow in July 1921. An underground CNT meeting in Lérida, where alternate members substituted for those in jail, decided to send a delegation, but a later meeting of the regular leadership rejected the Lérida Congress leaders, two Catalans of middle-class background, Andrés Nin and Joaquín Maurín, and decided instead to join the International Association of Workers of Berlin. The new party had appeal mainly in Asturias (coal mining), Vizcaya (heavy industry), and Madrid. Initially two parties appeared: the *Partido Comunista Español* (PCE) founded by a group of young Socialists in 1920 and the *Partido Comunista Obrero* (Workers Communist Party) constituted mainly by split leaders of the Socialists and trade unionists. The two were fused in Moscow in November 1921, and Maurín and Nin also joined. The first period was mostly one of competition and conflict with the Socialists, and soon the police persecution of the Primo de Rivera dictatorship made Communist activities difficult. After the fall of the dictator, Joaquín Maurín, who favored a policy of collaboration with other forces to establish the Republic and gain Catalan autonomy, broke with the party to found the *Bloc Obrer i Camperol* (BOC). This group would soon fuse with the Trotskyite secession of Nin called *Izquierda Comunista* to form, in February 1936, the *Partido Obrero de Unificación Marxista* (POUM). Apparently in most of Catalonia the BOC did not allow the regular Communist Party to make any gains, though it itself obtained only 17,536 votes among 466,316 voters (3.3 percent), apparently mainly in Lérida (9.0 percent) and less so in Barcelona city (2.1 percent), something that may indicate that the *camperol* (farmer) element might have been important. After Moscow failed to convince Maurín to return to the fold it supported the founding of the *Partido Communista de Catalunya.* Maurín conceived the idea of the *Alianza Obrera,* which would encompass some of the small splinter Communist parties as well as some of the CNT members tired of the dominance of the FAI. The idea would soon be influential on grass-roots moves in 1934, particularly in Asturias, for collaboration between the CNT and the UGT, now in a revolutionary mood.

The PCE in 1931 obtained 4.4 percent (190,605) of the vote for the Constituent Assembly, but its strength varied widely, from a maximum in Córdoba province and Asturias (probably on a joint list or for several candidates). The districts where its strength was above average were in the Guadalquivir Valley (Jaén, Córdoba, Seville) and in Málaga capital (15.8 percent) and province, as well as Cadiz. The Andalusian average was 13.6 percent. Outside of these two main centers it seems to have made some inroads in Vizcaya (20.8 percent) and Zaragoza (10.9 percent). Certainly the underprivileged farm laborers and workers of an underprivileged region (particularly the harbor city of Málaga that would elect the first PCE deputy in 1933) constituted the main basis of the party, together with some of the working class elite, not unlike other countries, particularly Italy. At the time of the Fourth National Party Congress (March 1932) the 276 delegates claimed to represent some one hundred thousand persons. Of them 201 represented 8,547 members and 20 youth delegates 3,570 members, a figure that suggests the youthful character of the party, with 55 delegates representing factories and organizations and presumably 90,000 workers and farmers. The party newspaper *Mundo Obrero* claimed a circulation of 35,000 but this was probably exaggerated. However, in comparative perspective at that advanced date the party was and continued being weak. Splinters, regional tensions, and police persecution under Primo do not seem sufficient explanation. We would suggest that the strong revolutionary tradition of anarchosyndicalism was the main factor. The fact that the reformist Socialist had not had a share in central power in the period preceding the depression, nor even many local offices (which anyhow would not have had the importance as a source of *embourgeoisement* given their limited power in Spain) freed them from blame for social conditions. The short period they participated in the Republican government (1931–32) was not sufficient to disillusion their followers, particularly since the party quickly—under the leadership of Largo Caballero—turned to a maximalist position that crystallized in the ill-fated and ill-advised October 1934 revolution. The Communists could not appear as a radical competitor to the CNT, nor even to the PSOE, particularly after Stalin turned to support Popular Fronts. On the other side the maximalism of the PSOE could attract some of the middle-class intellectuals that otherwise might have turned Communists, while the party held its reformist wing, which would not have turned to Moscow. Furthermore, the initiative to organize the underprivileged farm laborers—who could have become a mainstay of the PCE—was taken by the *Federación de Trabajadores de la Tierra* of the UGT, mobilizing a new base for the Socialists and this was largely made possible by the immediate advantages Largo Caballero could grant them as Minister of Labor (1931–32). The historical delay in the Spanish political and social evolution benefited the Socialists—even when contributing to their radicalization so dysfunctional to Spanish democracy—rather than the Communist Party much as it did strengthen the CEDA when strata similar to its supporters had already turned to the Fascists.

CATALONIA: RIGHT AND LEFT CATALANISM, LOW PARTICIPATION (1933), AND MOBILIZATION (1936)

The elections in a highly industrialized metropolis and its surrounding industrial cities and relatively industrial provinces with regionalist politics and an anarchosyndicalist labor movement have a special interest. The election system does not allow us to estimate the electoral strength that the non-Catalanist candidates would have had running alone, since their seats were determined by the agreements with the Catalanists of the Right or the Left on the Antirevolutionary Front or the Popular Front. The strength of the CNT proletariat, obviously, was never tested in elections due to the antiparliamentarism of the syndicalist labor movement. However, the appeal of the Popular Front on the issue of amnesty and the less decisive campaign of the CNT in favor of nonparticipation in 1936 suggests that some of the increased turnout must have been due to a vote for the *Esquerra*-led candidature by the CNT workers. Certainly the low participation in 1933 must to a significant extent be attributed to the CNT.

Table 20—Party Alignment of the Parliamentary Representation of Catalonia and the Basque Country in the Republic

Region and Year	Total Seats	Lliga	Esquerra	Other Regionalist	NATIONAL (SPANISH) PARTIES Right	NATIONAL (SPANISH) PARTIES Center	NATIONAL (SPANISH) PARTIES Left
Catalonia							
1931	54	2	32[a]	4		13	2
1933	54	23	22		5		4
1936	54	12	33	1			8
		Defensores del Estatuto de Estella					
Basque Country			PNV				
1931	17	4	5		2		6
1933	17		11		4		2
1936	17		9		1		7

[a] Not all those classified ran under the label "*Esquerra*," but as "*Izquierda Catalana*" or similar names.

The returns of the Catalan elections of 1933 and 1936 allow some interesting comparisons.[55] The most striking fact is that the poll increased 13.4 percent—if we compare the official figure of those voting with the sum of both blocs in 1936 (since we do not have the total participation)—and 15.2 percent if only the votes for the two great blocs are compared. This higher turnout allowed the Right to gain 2.7 percent more votes but increased the Left vote from 537,329 to 706,079, or a 23.9 percent gain. The Right made absolute gains in all four provinces, but not in Barcelona capital; it was able to gain only 7.4 percent of the increased participation. In the provinces there probably was not much transfer of votes from the Right to the Left, but in Barcelona city some of the voters might have changed parties, since the gain of 84,674 votes for the Left over the 177,996 it had received in 1933 could not be fully accounted for by the net increase in participation of 65,482; some of the 19,292 voters lost to the Right may have turned into nonvoters; others may have been attracted by the *Esquerra* after the *Lliga* had turned to the Central authorities to fight a decision of the Regional Parliament (*Generalitat*) and the CEDA had suspended the autonomic regime after the October 1934 rebellion. The changes in participation between the two elections, the greater gains made by the Left in Barcelona city and province and the slight ones in Lérida, compared to Tarragona and Gerona, suggests that many of the nonvoting CNT workers must have gone to the polls, even when one cannot discount shifts in the lower middle class aroused by Catalanist sentiments. With rates of participation between 60.1 in Barcelona city, 61.3 in Gerona and Lérida, and 65.6 percent in Barcelona Province in 1933, there was certainly room for the mobilization of additional voters.

Table 21—The Elections of 1933 and 1936 in Catalonia

Region	1933 Left	1933 Right	% voting of those eligible	1936 Left	1936 Right
Barcelona Capital					
Votes	177,996	173,045	60.15	262,670	153,751
% of voters	48.7	47.3			
% of sum of both blocs number of seats	50.7	49.3		63.1	36.9
Barcelona Province					
Votes	155,384	138,514	65.6	196,928	145,572
% of voters	52.9	47.1			
% of sum of both blocs number of seats	52.9	47.1		57.5	42.5
Gerona					
Votes	68,058	50,229	61.3	82,597	60,719
% of voters	56.3	41.5			
% of sum of both blocs number of seats	57.5	42.5		57.6	42.4
Tarragona					
Votes	78,837	60,492	65.3	93,647	69,596
% of voters	55.4	42.5			
% of sum of both blocs number of seats	56.6	43.4		57.4	42.6
Lérida					
Votes	57,054	52,830	61.3	70,237	58,875
% of voters	51.2	47.5			
% of sum of both blocs number of seats	51.9	48.1		54.4	45.6
Total Catalonia					
Votes	537,329	475,110	62.6	706,079	488,513
% of voters	51.9	45.9			
% of sum of both blocs number of seats	53.1	46.9		59.1	40.9
Seats:	22 Esquerra 4 Spanish Left	23 Lliga 5 Spanish Right		33 Esquerra 8 Spanish Left	12 Lliga 1 Regionalist

THE TRANSITION FROM EXTREME MULTIPARTISM TO POLARIZED CONFLICT AND CIVIL WAR

If we look at the Spanish party system in the Republican years—particularly as it found expressions at the electoral and even more at the parliamentary level (the two are almost inseparable due to the election law)—we see three main stages:

1931–1933. The destruction by its own crisis and by the Primo de Rivera dictatorship of the old two-party system left a vacuum that except for the PSOE was filled by a very large number of small parties or groups that almost did not deserve the name but were closer to factions or personalist cliques. The sudden turn to democracy, the indecision of the old political leaders in abandoning the monarchy together with their unwillingness to

Table 22—Party Composition of the Spanish Legislature During the Second Republic (1931–1936)

	Constituent Assembly elected June 1931	Legislature elected November 1933	Legislature elected February 1936
Sindicalista	—	—	1
Bloque Unificación Marxista	—	—	1
Partido Comunista	—	1	17
PSOE	105	61	99
maximalists			49
other			50
Esquerra (Catalan Left)	34	22	36
Acción Republicana (Azaña)	24	5	—
Izquierda Republicana (I.R.)	—	—	87
Organiz. Regional Gallega Autonoma (ORGA)	14	6	in I.R.
Radical Socialista Independiente	—	2	—
Radical Socialista	50	2	—
Unión Republicana	—	—	39
Republicans on different coalitions	62	—	—
Partido Federal	10	1	—
Progresistas	8	3	6
Intelectuales al Servicio de la República (Ortega y Gasset)	10	—	—
Derecha Republicana	13	—	—
Republicano Liberal Demócrata	2	9	1
Derecha Liberal Republicana	6	—	—
Republicanos Conservadores	—	17	3
Partido Radical (Lerroux)	70	100	4
Centro	—	—	16
Lliga Regionalista (Catalan Right)	2	24	12
Partido Nacionalista Vasco etc.	13	12	10
Independents of the Center-Right and the Right	13	10	4
Agrarios	24	49	12
Acción Nacional	3	—	—
Acción Popular, CEDA, Derecha Regiónal Valenciana (Gil Robles)	—	105	88
Renovación Española (C.Sotelo)	2	13	—
Bloque Nacional (same)	—	—	13
Tradicionalistas (Carlists)	2	25	9
Nacionalista (Fascist)	—	1	—
Falange	—	1	—
Unidentified	3	5	5
	470	474	474

The data for 1931 have been taken from the *Anuario Estadistico de España*, published by the Presidencia del Consejo de Ministros, Dirección General del Instituto Geografico Catastral y de Estadistica, Año XVII, 1931, pp. 487 and 489, giving the party affiliations of candidates to the Constituent Assembly elected on June 28, 1931 and in successive by-election until November of that year. The parliamentory manual *Cortes Constituyentes de 1931, Lista de los Señores Diputados*, December 1932, does not provide information on party affiliation. The data of the statistical yearbook have the disadvantage that they do not allow to distinguish the party identification of those elected on coalition lists of Republican unity and this accounts for some discrepancies with data that the reader may find elsewhere.

The data for the Legislature elected 1933 are derived from those published in the *Anuario Estadistico de España*, p. 653. Since some were elected on coalition lists or under the label of minor parties allied with some of the major parties and in by-elections for which the statistical yearbook does not give party affiliation the information was completed from additional sources: Santiago Galindo Herrero, *Los partidos monárquicos bajo la Segunda República* (Madrid: Rialp, 1956), Francisco Largo Caballero, *Discursos* (published by the Comision Ejecutiva of the PSOE) Apendix, pp. 163–165. In case of coincidence of these three sources there was no problem, in case of discrepancy we made a judgment of the reliability of the data and chose those that seemed best.

Those for the legislature elected in 1936 were taken from the official *Lista de los Señores Diputados* published by the Cortes in 1936 which lists the parliamentary groups. This list is dated June 1936 and therefore takes into account the results of the "second round" elections that took place in districts where none of the candidates had obtained the required minimum or where the first election was voided. Since those elections were held after the left had taken power in February 1936 they were specially controversial. Some of the discrepancy between these figures and those given in other source are due to this.

It is extremely difficult not to say impossible to group the parties on some continuum of Left-Right nor to distinguish clearly those loyal to the Constitution enacted in 1931 and those whose aim were revisionist, nor those we can consider democratic—that is willing to abide by the will of the electorate whatever turn it might take—and those openly anti- or a-democratic.

We can briefly add for each legislative period parties in some approximation of such groupings:

	Constituent Assembly 1931–33	I Legislature 1933–1936	II Legislature 1936
Extreme Left	isolated deputies	1 PCE	19 PCE et al.
			49 maximalists
Moderate Left	105 PSOE	61 PSOE	50 moderate PSOE
Bourgeois Left	194 Azaña	38 Azaña	162 Izquierda Rep. or Unión Rep.
Bourgeois Left tending toward the Right	70 Lerroux		
Republican Center-Right	39 minor groups Miguel Maura	129 Lerroux	40 minor groups Radicals, PNV
Center Right		95 Agrarians Lliga	
Right willing to accept Republic but not the Constitution of 1931	42 Agrarios	105 Gil Robles	116 CEDA
Extreme Right	17 Monarchists, extreme Catholics	40 Calvo Sotelo et al.	22 Calvo Sotelo
Other	3	5	5
Total:	470	474	474
Regional parties			
Left—*Esquerra*, ORGA	48	28	36 (ORGA in I.R.)
Right—Lliga	2	24	12
Basques et al.	13	12	10
Aggregate strength of regional parties (never united):	63	64	58
Required Majority	236	238	238

fight for it had left them without followers, the weakness of most interest groups except the UGT, the reliance of the Church on the State rather than on the laity, made the appearance of new electoral mass parties extremely difficult. Only the Radicals who had played a considerable role at the local level over a few decades represented a larger parliamentary force. However, the veto of many of the conspirators to overthrow the dictatorship against Lerroux and the hostility of the Socialists did not allow the party to become the basis of the new regime. A new and unexpected leader—Manuel Azaña— was able to bring together many of the dispersed factions, with the flanking support of the PSOE and of the *Esquerra* (in exchange of regional autonomy) on a basically negative program of rejection of traditional institutions, but could barely bring it to enact an agrarian reform (and this only thanks to the emotional unity provoked by a feeble and outdated *pronunciamiento*). The fragmented left-bourgeois parties were unable to accept the dominant role of the PSOE which in turn was not fully willing or able to assume the task to govern, an ambivalence that led it to run alone in the November, 1933, elections

1933–1935. The election law, the bourgeois fear of the Socialists, the inherent organizational weakness of most left bourgeois parties, the exhaustion of much of their program with the enactment of the Constitution, contributed to a basic shift in the 1933 election. Except for the *Esquerra,* left republicanism was reduced to a minority representation and the PSOE, while loosing many seats due to its going alone and to the electoral system, consolidated its position. A new and major force emerged in this situation of extreme pluralism: the CEDA, which could not be a government party under the Constitution enacted in 1931 and which on account of its size, the weight of the interests it represented (the Church and many economic interests), could not resign itself to be a permanent and sterile opposition. Being in the periphery of the Center both politically and socially—representing large part of the *clases medias,* the landowning peasantry and collaborating with the *Lliga* businessmen, it was forced into a semiresponsible opposition. The Fascisticized Monarchists and antiparliamentary Carlists remained in their position of irresponsible opposition outbidding on the religious issue the Catholic moderates. On the Left the Socialists, disillusioned with the achievements in the first *bienio* moved toward irresponsible opposition. The hope for a workable system hinged on the capacity of a center around the Radical party to unite some of the right-of-center bourgeois groups, particularly the Agrarians, and on its capacity to act centripetally on the CEDA. This was the course on which Lerroux set out with considerable skill, but rather than finding any benevolence within the Left bourgeois center—Azaña, the Radical Socialists, and the Republican Catholics (the President Alcala Zamora and Miguel Maura)—personal hostility and ideological rigidity led them to deny any legitimacy to that attempt, thus contributing to split his party (the secession of the Radical Democrats led by Martinez Barrio). This turn to semi-responsible opposition, reflected in the withdrawal from parliament upon the vote of subsidies to the older clergy, contributed to a divisive centrifugal trend that was reinforced with the rigid opposition of the PNV on a local tax autonomy issue and the *Esquerra's* unwillingness to accept a decision of the Constitutional court in a conflict between central and regional government on legislative competence. The decision of the maximalist wing of the PSOE to support a revolutionary uprising in Asturias and a general strike, when the weakness of the Radical-led coalitions forced them to call on the CEDA to participate in the government, left the center reduced to a minimum and dependent on the strength of the Radicals. Even so the added strength of Radicals, Agrarians, *Lliga* and CEDA could have governed against the extremism of the PSOE, the semi-illegal attitude of the bourgeois Left and the Extreme Right, with which the centripetal turn of Gil Robles in 1935 had led to a complete break. The Center did not just have to face unilateral opposition; it was torn apart under pressure from two sides.

February 16, 1936–July 17, 1936. An untimely and obscure, premature dissolution of the Chamber in December 1935 (when it could have gone on until late 1937) combined with an internal crisis of the Radical party led in February 1936 to a complete realignment of which the main beneficiaries would be the extremes: the PSOE and the radicalized and divided CEDA now freed of its ties with the now nonexistent Center on the other. The Center Right parties: Radicals, Agrarians, *Lliga,* had been reduced from 173 seats in 1933 to 28. The centrifugal tendencies on the Right fed on those of the Left-wing PSOE—which refused to enter the government in coalition with the Left Republicans (with whom it had joined to win the election as a Popular Front)—and the strengthened Communist Party. Outside of parliament the unfair competition of the CNT with the UGT and the new appeal of Falangism introduced a further divisive and centrifugal element in the extreme multipartism. The new Left center around the *Izquierda Republicana* (with 87 seats) and *Unión Republicana* (with 39) to which we can add the 36 of the *Esquerra,* made a total of 157 in a parliament of 474. Any attempt to add the Center Right to this Center Left, turning it away from a semiresponsible and even disloyal opposition—even when made in the Spring of 1936—could not overcome the hatred developed between them after October 1934, the ideological denial of legitimacy to a clerical party in a "Republic for the Republicans" and the ties of the Center Left with the PSOE created in the opposition to the "black two-years." The bourgeois Left unwillingly was drawn into a centrifugal semiresponsible policy to which the Right responded in kind. The crystallization of the Right around Calvo Sotelo on his program of anti-Marxism and antiregional nationalism and in the defense of traditional values, ultimately led to a confrontation that turned into a civil war. The weak attempts of a few splinter groups to which the real center had been reduced to prevent the extreme polarization were condemned to defeat. Only a split of the PSOE led by Prieto or his taking over the party could have reinforced the Center Left and maintained an uneasy equilibrium, of the kind the Radical-CEDA coalition had managed to keep after October 1934, in face of an open threat by the extreme Right. The military uprising and the emotional polarization provoked by the assassination of Calvo Sotelo precluded that last possibility to save democracy in 1936.

The saliency of the class conflict in the cities as well as the countryside and within one of the two regions with linguistic-minority nationalism and the dominance of the Socialist Party after 1934 and particularly in 1936, pushed the Spanish party system closer to the class based politics of other countries: with the *Lliga* becoming allied with the non-Catalan conservatives and the *Esquerra* working closely with the other Popular Front parties and trying to attract the anarchosyndicalist "apolitical" workers. The crosspressures between nationalism and religious and to a lesser extent social conservatism of the Basque were finally decided by the anti-constitutional military rising; they decided in favor of the Left which was willing to satisfy their nationalist aspirations. The deep-seated hostility that had developed between the non-Basque Monarchist Right, particularly the Carlists who were really warring brothers, and the PNV, added another element of bitterness to the polarization that tore apart the country in a civil war. In Spain, the regional conflicts which in other countries cross-cut and weaken the intensity of the class and ideological conflicts, added further strength to them. In the same way the anticlericalism of the proletarian Left, reinforced by the bourgeois Left allied to it, had cumulated socioeconomic and religious conflicts. For many on the Right and Center Right the conflict became a crusade against the red-separatists, and for the Left and much of the Center Left a struggle against clerical, reactionary, centralist, and Fascist Spaniards. Those who did not agree with one or the other elements in the resulting alliances could only hope to moderate their allies or emigrate. The fight was won by the alliance of the centralists, with the Catalan bourgeoisie forced to sacrifice its local autonomy to its class interests, the middle-class intellectuals, including the Fascists, accepting clerical dominance, and the ideological conservatives—Monarchists and conservative enemies of social change and social reform—having to see the Fascists and reformist bureaucrats imposing more changes then they ever would have expected.

The dominance of the Army, and of Franco as a politically largely uncommitted leader, as a "neutral party" kept the coalition together, something that certainly was important for victory. The coalition of Socialists, Left Republicans, anarchosyndicalists, Communists, the Catalan Left and the Catholic Basques, within which ideological differences were much greater, was much less able to avoid internal dissension and perhaps only the moderate cynicism of the Communists was able to consolidate the Republican resistance. On both sides the legitimate pluralism of parties was threatened, on the Republican side by the dominance of the trade unions and their militias and particularly of the anarchosyndicalists who rejected bourgeois democracy, and on the Franco side by the institutionalization in the spring of 1937 of a single party which fused the Falangists and Traditionalists (Carlists).

THE FUTURE

The last election in which multiple parties competed in Spain was in February, 1936. Those eligible to vote then (they had to be at least twenty-three years old) now are fifty-three or older. In 1960 the population over forty-five—that would include those voters and those younger but old enough to sympathize with parties at that time—was only 28 percent and even less among the males. How much continuity could we expect if in the future—either in a constitutional monarchy or a republic—a multiparty system would emerge? At first sight the thirty or more years that have passed, the deep social and economic changes in Spain, the ideological changes in the world, together with these hard facts about the change of generations would suggest little continuity. However, we know how in Italy after over twenty years of Fascism and in Germany after twelve years of Nazism, the party system, voter loyalties, and even much of the political elite had some continuity with the past. Obviously, thirty years are not twenty and, even with important continuities, new and different types of parties emerged in those two countries. Furthermore Italy did not experience as many (or as favorable) social changes as Spain in the last decade. In addition the Civil War and its aftermath discredited many of the parties and dispersed or suppressed their leaders more seriously than in Italy. However, the continuity in the areas and strata of support in those countries that a correlation between the first postwar elections and the last ones with multiple parties shows suggests the usefulness of thinking in terms of continuities. Furthermore it should not be forgotten than many of the forces of the Right and the Center never so completely submerged their identity in Franco's Spain as they were forced to do under the dominance of real ideological and bureaucratic single parties. The *Movimiento* had after all been a coalition that recognizes the distinct origin of many of its components, and the limited pluralism of the regime has allowed the survival of organizational nuclei, particularly among the Catholics, that contributed much to creation and support of parties in the past. Certainly the Carlists, Alphonsine Monarchists, conservative Catholics, and wealthy businessmen of the *Lliga* have never lost contact with their "party friends" nor stopped talking politics, even sometimes publishing a manifesto and organizing some meetings. On the Right the opportunities for continuity have been and are much greater than they were in Italy and Germany.

Certainly the discontinuities in Spanish party politics between the periods of ideological seething and democratic optimism and their interruption by more stable periods or dictatorships suggest caution. The First Republic found little continuity even after the Restoration moved toward universal suffrage, more honest counting of ballots, and so forth. Nor did the parties of the Restoration reappear after eight years of dictatorship (except for the Socialists and the *Lliga*). Why should the post-Franco period be different? In many respects most parties of the Republic are dead. Unless a very liberal Proportional Representation law guarantees every vote representation, the key bourgeois national republican parties will not appear again: the *Izquierda Republicana, Acción Republicana, Partido Radical Socialista,* and the Lerroux Radicals are not likely to reemerge with the same names, ideologies, or leaders (who were already aged when the Republic came). Where will their former clientèle go? Some could go to a not overly proletarian and revolutionary Socialist Party, some to a not too clerical Christian Democratic Party (at least the sons of some supporters of such parties who have received a religious education and whose parents have not transmitted their own anticlericalism in the years of Franco rule. Some minority party of the non-Socialist, nonreligious middle classes will have to emerge, but the importance of regionalism in the most bourgeois areas of Spain will limit its appeal. A party of intellectuals that wanted to be Socialist without however assuming all the heritage and symbols of the PSOE, or its proletarian tone, was created by Dionisio Ridruejo—an ex-Falangist turned democratic—but such a new party has some of the difficulties of the Italian Action party. The growth of the industrial working class, the changed outlook of the Church in the world and even in Spain, the weakening of anticlericalism in other countries, the growing interest in economic and social questions—all have weakened bourgeois liberal Radicalism. Only a protracted struggle over the question of monarchy versus republic, with a Socialist acceptance of the monarchy and support for it from the Christian Democrats, could revive a "Republican Party." Another victim of discontinuity and change would be the CNT and its political arm, the FAI. The anarcho-syndicalists have had neither the support of Moscow nor of the West, the constant anti-Communism of Franco has not allowed them to become a symbol of opposition, the news from foreign countries and the experience of working in them has not reinforced the old Libertarian ideology among any of the younger generation. The more passive attitude of labor in the old syndicalist strongholds as compared with those of former Socialist strength may be an indication of this weakening. Even so, the small number of faithful—freed of the control of the activists of the FAI—might be tempted to follow the path initiated during the Republic by A. Pestaña toward participation—rather than rejection—of elections by creating a "syndicalist party." Such a party would deprive the Communists of some of their potential support.

In contrast to Germany, where the continuity on the Right was weak due to the aging of their cadres, the loss of prestige of the monarchy, the share of the DNVP in the responsibility for Hitler's takeover of power, the social changes produced by the Nazi revolution after the 20th of July, and the Russian occupation and agrarian reforms, the persistence of monarchist parties under Franco and their ambivalent role as part of the regime and as potential opposition will assure their survival. Given the localized strength in Navarre and parts of the Basque country and only the absence of PR or a requirement to obtain at least three seats in provinces, or a minimum of votes in them to share in the distribution of seats would eliminate the Carlists from parliament. The monarchical form of government seen in the present constitution, indirectly, gives life to the two competing dynastic-ideological monarchic parties and forces any potential Christian Democratic leadership to accept a monarchy, something that in the future may divide it. If Franco would have considered a republic—like the Portuguese or the Fifth in France—as the constitutional alternative, the emergence of a more integrated party system on the Right of the Center would have been facilitated. The pretender also could contribute to such a process by denying to his followers the right to form a party of their own and forcing them to join other parties. The extent to which, in contrast to postwar Italy, the Christian Democrats will be ambivalent or even split on the monarchy versus republic issue introduces another big "if."

Certainly, unless outlawed, the small pre–Civil War Communist Party will reemerge much strengthened by years of propaganda against it, by the appeal of the Soviet Union of Sputniks and imagined economic as well as social achievements, by the support the sister parties can give it, by the growth of a new industrial working class with little continuity with the non-Communist parties and trade unions of 1936, even by its appeals to moderation and national reconciliation. Against its achieving a strength comparable to that presently held in France and Italy stand the lack of a high-quality leadership (there was no Spanish Gramsci or Togliatti), the hostility of many of those who suffered from the Communists in the internal Civil War in Republican Spain—particularly the Anarchists, some Trotskyites, and even many Socialists, who in exile have maintained a strong anti-Communist line. The weakness in the twenties and thirties—there was no Spanish equivalent to the Congress of Tours and not even an early success as in Italy—deprives the party of traditional loyalties. A probable split between a legalistic Moscow-oriented wing and a "Chinese" revolutionary wing probably will add to the weakness, but even so, the Moscow-oriented party is likely to play a much greater role than in the thirties. Certainly a democratic Left would benefit much from an initial outlawing—at least from electoral participation—of the CP as an antidemocratic party, before it wins a strong hold of the masses.

Inevitably any party system in Spain will turn around two dominant tendencies, Socialism and Christian Democracy, even when at this stage it is difficult to say what these labels will cover or what their degree of unity or cohesion will be. In the early post-Civil War period a split would have been inevitable between a "Nenni Socialism"—led by Negrín—and a Saragat Socialism—led by Prieto—(probably with the second as the stronger). Today with the death of both men, it is not so likely, even when the splits between an anti-Communist bureaucratic exile faction and more tolerant intellectual and youth groups in the interior does not bode well for the unity of the party (ignoring for the moment the regional tensions). Its electoral strength will depend greatly upon the competition that the Communists and, to a lesser degree, the Syndicalists (as a party or as abstentionists) offer them in competing for the proletarian vote, as well as on their capacity to appeal to white-collar strata in competition with Christian Democrats. Certainly, in order to appeal to, or at least gain the benevolent neutrality of, the middle classes, the party would have to disavow much of the ideology that led to the Asturias revolution in 1934.

Just as the Socialists would limit unduly their base and legitimacy by running on their record during the Republic, the Christian Democrats could not stand for the basically conservative social and economic policies of the CEDA, even when some of the progressive legislation of the latter in the so-called *bienio negro* is not to be ignored. Whatever continuity in leadership the two major parties may have, they cannot stand on their record during the Republic but must attempt to expand their electoral base considerably. However, the hard core of ideological sympathizers, sons of former supporters, and interest groups once linked with them (UGT and CONCA) will serve them well.

If there is to be multiparty politics in Spain it will be between Socialists and Demo-Christians, with a fairly strong Communist Party cutting into the strength of the Socialists. Much will depend on the cohesion that the different Socialist tendencies will be able to muster if there is to be a single party. The same can be said about the Christian Democrats, even though here Church pressure may achieve some unity among otherwise divided groups. The openness or closure to persons who have played a preeminent role in the Franco regime will pose some problems for the Demo-Christians, but the most difficult still will be the decision to give the party a federative structure that would include the moderate bourgeois regionalists of Catalonia and the Basque country. In this attempt, a Spanish party would face much more serious difficulties than did the CDU with the CSU, or the DC with the Sicilian branch of the party. Certainly it would be in the interest of Spain if the party could serve—like its Belgian counterpart—as a cross-cutting loyalty uniting the country.

While the national party system—with odd survivals on the extremes like the Carlists, perhaps the Monarchists, some neo-Fascists groups, the Anarchists—would tend toward the Italian pattern of three or three-and-a-half parties, the regional-nationalist sentiments are likely to complicate it much more than the Italian. How much more? Some data on the demography of

Catalonia and the Basque country will allow us some hypothetical conclusions. However, the electoral system chosen may play a decisive role in
shaping a future parliament.

Some reader may ask why we turn to the Italian case as a model and not
consider the German and North-Central European experience as a possibility. This would assume that the Communists have no place in Spain,
something that would surprise us considering the large number (still) of
underprivileged farm laborers, the number of new industrial workers with a
rural background of discontent, and the pro-Communist sentiments founded
on a distorted image of the Soviet Union, among sectors of the intelligentsia.
Only an immediate outlawing without persecution could limit Communist
strength. A two-party system of Socialists and Demo-Christians allowed to
emerge under Franco, or a transition regime—with a policy like that used
in Turkey or planned in Brazil to transform a one- or no-party system—
could initially strengthen the tendency toward a two-party dominance system.
The fact that the *Movimiento* never destroyed the various tendencies and
groups on the Right certainly gives them more a chance of survival than in
Germany. Another alternative that we have not considered is a system like
the French, with the presence of a large non-Christian democratic party like
the UNR on the Center-Right. The fact that the UNR is a very personal
creation of de Gaulle makes it difficult to imagine it in Spain. In a sense
many of the men who now run Spain with Franco could fit into such a
party—particularly the higher civil servants and technocratic elements, as
well as the business community, satisfied with peace and order and not
hostile to some social progress. It would seem unlikely, however, that such
elites would be capable of creating, during the lifetime of Franco or afterward, a party of continuity with the present regime capable of competing in
multiparty elections. If Franco should—something not likely, but given his
political flexibility, not impossible—decide to allow other parties to compete
and himself head a party of this type (let us say in a competition for a
presidency à la the Fifth Republic), such a system would not be excluded.
However it is doubtful whether the Socialists would agree to participate in
such an election, which could give a new legitimacy to the regime.

This forces us again to center our speculations on a future party system
along Italian lines. Our effort will gain some sociological sense if we apply
to the Spanish social structure the patterns of support to different parties
found in Italy. We are going to undertake the intellectual experiment of
finding out what the outcome—in terms of popular votes not of seats—
would be if the Spanish electorate were to vote like the Italian (considering
the different social structure of both countries). The only major difficulty
for the experiment would be to estimate the behavior of the Basque and
Catalan electorate, particularly since we have no up-to-date data on the
region of origin of immigrants, and even less of region of origin, residence,
and occupation combined.

If Spaniards Were to Vote Like Italians

Using the data from the 1964 labor force survey *Población activa en 1964*
and the estimates of Mattei Dogan[56] on the electoral behavior of different
strata in the Italian population, we have attempted to make some hypothetical

Table 23—Political Behavior of a Hypothetical Spanish Electorate If the Different Social Strata Would Behave Like Their Italian Equivalents*

SOCIAL STRATA	PARTY PREFERENCE				Total	
	Communists–Left Socialists	Democratic Socialists	Demo-Christians	Other, mostly Conservatives, Monarchists and a few neo-Fascists		(percent)
The rural electorate:						
Farmers who employ others	—	—	24,870 (30%)	58,030 (70%)	82,900	.9
Farmers not employing others and self-employed rural workers (including family members)	471,714 (23%)	82,024 (4%)	1,312,384 (64%)	184,554 (9%)	2,050,600	23.0
Farm laborers and unemployed	818,823 (69%)	23,734 (2%)	225,473 (19%)	118,670 (10%)	1,186,700	13.6
Total rural	1,290,537	105,758	1,562,727	361,254	3,320,200	37.5
% of vote in Spain	39.0	3.2	47.2	10.9	100.3	
% of vote in Italy (Dogan)	34.0	3.0	51.0	12.0	100.0	
The nonrural electorate:						
Employers in the nonagricultural sector	—	—	141,132 (57%)	106,468 (43%)	247,600	2.8
Self-employed without employees in industry, commerce					(621,900)	
Self-employed workers					(181,300)	
(Family members of above)					(208,000)	
					1,011,200	
White-collar employees (public and private)					(1,097,800)	
Unemployed white-collar					(9,300)	
					1,107,100	
Upper and middle class	320,922 (15%)	149,763 (7%)	1,048,560 (49%)	599,055 (28%)	2,118,300	24.2
Blue-collar workers (including personal services 220,500)	1,976,640 (64%)	154,425 (5%)	803,010 (26%)	154,425 (5%)	3,088,500	35.2
Total nonrural	2,297,562	304,188	1,992,702	859,948	5,454,400	62.2
% of vote in Spain	42.1	5.6	36.5	15.8	100.0	
% of vote in Italy	38.1	5.4	37.4	19.1	100.0	
Total electorate	3,588,099	409,946	3,555,429	1,221,202	8,774,676	99.7
% of vote in Spain	40.9	4.7	40.5	13.9	100.0	
% vote Italy (1958)	36.9	4.5	42.4	16.2	100.0	

* The percentage figures in parentheses are based on Mattei Dogan's estimates for Italy and are used to calculate the figures above them on the basis of the occupational distribution from the *Encuesta Sobre la Poblacion activa en 1964* (given under the total column).

estimate of the outcome of Spanish elections if Spanish workers, businessmen, farm laborers, and such voted like their Italian peers. The attempt made here is very crude and deserves refinement but can be indicative. Some of the criticism we will make shows in what direction the refinement would be needed if the data could be obtained.

The *Población activa* figures used will be those for the active males, irrespective of age. It naturally excludes retired males (738,000). The latter group is likely to have a larger proportion of nonvoters, and so is unlikely to change our estimates substantially. The young included in the active population, but not in the potential electorate, are more numerous (1,028,500 under twenty years, to which we would have to add those twenty to twenty-one, also ineligible to vote).

Their inclusion into our "hypothetical electorate" affects our predictions. Since they are more likely to be urban and to be manual workers (the middle-class youth is likely still to be studying at that age) their inclusion should favor the Left. However, survey data indicating the high level of satisfaction with life, the future, their work, and the involvement in a mass-consumption and mass-culture society would suggest that the young nonvoters might well be a reservoir for depoliticization and perhaps a support for the moderate Left and even the Center. The young also have fewer memories of the Civil War, less hatred for the Franco regime and, in all likelihood, are slightly more religious, so that their exclusion from the electorate should, on the whole, benefit rather than harm the Left.

In our calculations we have ignored the differential rates of electoral participation of different classes, but it is not unlikely that the working-class abstention would be higher, particularly among the Andalusian farm laborers (as the figures for the Republic show) and consequently some of our figures for the Left would have to be reduced on account of this. We ignore completely the possibility of an anarchosyndicalist revival.

The greatest difficulty—which I plan to discuss later in transferring the Italian patterns to Spain—is to predict the electoral impact of regional dissidence. Even so, the importance of this factor should not be overestimated —in electoral terms—since only 4.5 percent of the Spanish population lives in the Basque country and 12.9 percent in Catalonia. Of the former— according to the 1950 census figures (and since then the figures must have increased with migration) a third are not Basque-born and, of the latter, a fifth—leaving only 3 percent and 10.3 percent as a potential constituency for those parties. That 10 percent—more or less—of the electorate could affect the relative strength of parties decisively, especially since the opportunism which often characterizes such autonomist movements would be an additional factor of instability and unpredictability.

We have made no attempt to distinguish—since some of the estimates of Dogan used do not allow us to do so—the share of Communists and Left Socialists. Such an attempt would be futile in any case considering the organizational, ideological, and factional problems within the Socialist camp that would decisively influence the relative strength of the Communists and Socialists. However, using the calculations of Dogan about the relative strength of the PCI and the PSI in different strata we can arrive at a figure of 2,185,000 votes for the Spanish Communist Party—equal to 25 percent of the hypothetical electorate—and that would leave the Left Socialists reduced to 15.9 percent. This Communist vote would come largely from farm laborers and rural unemployed (552,000) but even more from blue-collar workers (1,172,000) even assuming that fewer among them (38 percent) would vote Communist than among the farm laborers (47 percent). The share of the party of the independent farmers, by applying the Italian proportion of 14 percent may be exaggerated, but that of the blue-collar workers might be underestimated given the Spanish situation of a recent rapid industrialization without political continuity with non-Communist working class parties, as it might be in the case of the 8 percent attributed to the party in the middle sectors (169,500 votes). On historical grounds we would expect the Spanish Communists to be weaker than the Italian, since the party never had such strength as the Italian before Mussolini and its leadership was not comparable as to intellectual and moral quality.

Future of the Regional Parties

In the course of Spanish political history, regionalism and local nationalism have played a decisive role. What are the prospects for such parties in the future and to what extent do they force us to modify our analysis based on similarities with the Italian social structure?

Let us begin by noting once again that the two regions with autonomic sentiments, to which Valencia and Galicia may perhaps be added in the future, do not represent a large proportion of the total population. Certainly the share of the three autonomistic Basque provinces (we exclude Navarre) has been increasing over the last decades because of accelerated industrialization: from 3.7 percent in 1940 to 4.5 percent in 1960, a gain of 1.2 percent of the total national population. But that gain has been largely due to immigration from the rest of Spain. This change has been noticeable in Álava, which already in the thirties was the least Basque province (maximum PNV vote 29 percent), and therefore the one least able to absorb the recent immigrants into its local political culture. The rate of immigration is even higher in Vizcaya, not only in Bilbao, the capital, but also in the province— which in 1936 was the only district that gave a majority (51 percent) of its vote to the PNV. Only in Guipúzcoa has the change been moderate particularly in the city of San Sebastián. Therefore, while in the past the main base of the PNV was in Vizcaya (the party was born in Bilbao), in the future San Sebastián will probably become one of its centers. If we turn to the place of birth of the population in the Basque provinces in 1950 and compare it to similar data for males in 1920, we see that in thirty years the proportion of those born outside the province had increased appreciably in Álava and Guipúzcoa, but not so much in Vizcaya. Data from a recent national sample survey (1966)[57] found 38 percent of the heads of households and their wives born outside the Basque province in which they resided. Unless we assume a capacity to assimilate the immigrants to the local subculture, an ability not generally recognized for the Basque country, at least not so far as the language is concerned, these figures limit the electoral base for a regionalist movement more than in the 1930's. The high voting rates at that time suggest that there was not a great reservoir of non-mobilized supporters of Basque nationalism, since probably quite a few of the then-nonvoters were immigrant workers (the increase of 8 percent in voting between 1933 and 1936 was accompanied by a drop in PNV vote of 11 percent and an increase in the Spanish Left of 4 percent and the Right of 7 percent). Only the higher rate of intermarriage of Basques with non-Basques, compared to Catalans with non-Catalans, discovered in the 1966 survey, might lead us to assume some assimilation, but it might be in either direction. In addition, the immigrant population is more likely to have a larger proportion in those of voting age.

The patterns in Catalonia also suggest a further de-Catalanization by those whom a recent book called *Les altres Catalans,* at least in Barcelona. If we compare the figures for the proportion of males born outside Barcelona Province in 1920 (and at that time probably quite a few "immigrants" were really native to other Catalan provinces) to those of 1950, we find an even greater change than in the Basque country (probably due to the much lower birth rate in less religious Catalonia): from 28.7 percent of the males (1920) to 37.9 percent of the population (1950). The changes in the other provinces reflect the depopulation of the countryside and of the smaller towns, which goes together with a certain growth—likely to be accelerated in the case of Tarragona by new industrial plants there—of the capital cities. Undoubtedly the immigrants in rural areas might be more easily absorbed into the local culture and language, whereas they are likely to form sub-communities in the larger population centers. There are also indications that the Catalan countryside felt its local nationalism quite deeply, perhaps more so than some of the cities. The proportion of foreign born in 1950 in Gerona and Tarragona has almost doubled; in Lérida it has grown even more. The sample survey of 1966 already mentioned found only 23 percent of the population born outside the Catalan provinces, perhaps because it corrected for the inclusion in the census data of the non-province born of the intra-Catalan migrations, more important than the intra-Basque, due to the greater inequalities of economic development and the larger population of Catalonia. Since the immigrants to Catalonia come from the poorer parts of Spain and thus have less education and less "Castilian" national consciousness than those migrating to the Basque country, and because the Catalan language—as a Romance language—is easier to learn, Catalonia may assimilate more of its immigrants. Even so, the demographic trends work against Catalan nationalism, particularly if that nationalism were to mean any direct or indirect disadvantage for the non-Catalan-speaking citizens of Barcelona. Another consideration in estimating the political significance of these figures is that if—as we tend to assume—the CNT and the anarchosyndicalist ideology will have lost much of its appeal, being replaced by Socialism and Communism as the great working-class parties, we would not expect the low rates of electoral participation of the 1930's, particularly 1933. The increase of participation in this case would not benefit parties similar to those dominant among the more restricted bourgeois and petty bourgeois electorate of that period—the *Lliga* and the *Esquerra.* On the other hand, increased immigration of non-Catalans and a greater electoral participation (than in the 1930's) on their part may be perceived as a threat to Catalan national identity and therefore intensify their nationalist sentiments. The impact of

Table 24—Population Increase Due to Migration of Selected
Provinces and Their Capital Cities Between 1955 and 1960
(in percentages)*

	Province, Including Capital	Capital Only
Álava	14.83	5.76
Guipúzcoa	6.08	0.53ᵃ
Vizcaya	9.76	8.18
Barcelona	8.57	5.31
Gerona	2.35	2.16
Lérida	− 2.45	1.22
Tarragona	− 1.46	2.67
Madrid	11.03	11.51

* Data based on calculations by Alfonso G. Barbancho of the difference between expected population—on the basis of births and deaths—and actual population figures in 1960.
ᵃ San Sebastián is not an industrial city compared to the rest of the province.

shifting demographic balances on the politics of Ulster, South Africa, and Belgium, would suggest the latter hypothesis.

Certainly any prediction about the strength of regional parties will depend decisively on the electoral system introduced. Representation by majority vote or by a plurality in single-member districts, particularly smaller districts,

Table 25—Proportion of the Male Population of Catalonia and the
Basque Country Not Born in the Same Province of Residence
(in percentages)*

Province	1920	1950
Basque country:		
Álava	17.3	21.7
Guipúzcoa	18.3	23.7
Vizcaya	27.4	26.2
All three provinces	23.0	24.8
Catalonia		
Barcelona	28.7	36.5
Gerona	8.3	17.8
Lérida	6.8	19.6
Tarragona	8.6	18.0
All four provinces	19.7	30.7

* 1920 males only; 1950 total population.

would benefit the regionalist parties, while PR would benefit the non-regionalist parties, and if combined with limits on splinter parties (minimum vote, election in a minimum number of constituencies and/or in more than one province), the major national and mass parties.

However, whatever election system Spain may have, even assuming that regionalist parties may emerge in parts of the country with little previous tradition of that type (Valencia, Galicia), such parties would not constitute a majority or be able to determine the new constitution of Spain unless they found support in one or the other of the major national parties. This permanent-minority status of the 4.5 percent Basque and 12.8 percent Catalan electorates creates special problems for Spanish democracy: elections cannot by a majority principle solve the problem of local autonomy and nationalistic demands.

Establishment of a Party System and the Electoral Law

The shape of any future party system will depend much on the conditions prevailing during the transition from the present regime to one tolerating a multiparty system, particularly with the electoral system used in the first elections. If you will permit a paradox, the chances for a two-party system would be greatest if Franco himself would establish it. He could condition free elections so as to exclude the Communists as an antidemocratic party and—this would be more difficult to do—exclude parties appealing openly for regional secession or a federal structure (while allowing parties to advocate "administrative" autonomy, and the like). Under such conditions, with full freedom for licensed Christian Democratic and Social Democratic parties, together with a revitalized *Movimiento* playing the role of a UNR by supporting a presidential candidacy of Franco, the initial loyalties of the voters could be directed toward such major parties, rather than to a myriad of minor parties, and the working-class support for the Communists might be drastically reduced. But such a "controlled" transition along the lines of Turkey in 1947 and the present Brazilian attempt is most unlikely, since the Socialists probably would not accept it and Franco would not think of it. The usefulness of such a licensed creation of a party system was shown by the decision of all four allied powers in Germany, and particularly the Russians, to encourage the creation of a Liberal, a Christian Democratic, a Socialist and a Communist party, making the revival of many of the smaller bourgeois and conservative parties, as well as of the local parties beyond state boundaries, difficult. A decision of Franco in favor of a Presidential Republic would also weaken the initial appeal of monarchist parties.

The great dilemma of single-member majority or plurality systems versus proportional representation is particularly difficult in Spain. Certainly PR would encourage the fractionalization of the party system, the survival of historical relics, and the class and ideological splits within the regional parties, but it would also have the advantage that the regions with autonomist sentiments would in no case be represented by a homogeneous bloc of deputies that could use—in view of its permanent minority status—the classic Spanish *retraimiento* (withdrawal from parliament) if its demands were not granted by the majority. The parliamentary delegation of such regions under PR would be composed by representatives of the regional parties and those of national Spanish parties elected by the immigrants and would in no case "speak for the whole region."

In view of the modern history of Spain, it also seems likely that the polarization between two major parties or blocs (in a second ballot election), which a single-member district system would produce, would heighten the political tensions and weaken the role of the minor center parties in working out compromises. Such a system would give the extremists on each side a considerable lever against the great mass parties closer to the center, since their small number of votes could decide (in a *politique du pire*) who would win. Perhaps a mixed system with a strong component of PR and with stringent requirements of a minimum of votes in more than one province could serve the country best. It would allow the representation of relatively strong parties, exclude local and notable candidacies, allow the representation of the non-Basque and non-Catalan inhabitants of the autonomist regions, and force a nationalization of the party system. The requirement of a minimum of votes (5 or even 10 percent) in more than one province would not exclude the regionalist parties, since each of the regions with serious autonomist sentiments comprises three or more provinces. (To make the requirement 10 percent of the total number of provinces [that is, five] would be a way to force a federation of the autonomist parties of different regions, that may have advantages and disadvantages.) A decision to outlaw antidemocratic parties in the constitution, as in West Germany, would be difficult to uphold (in view of the ideological-intellectual belief in democracy, rather than a pragmatic conception of it, dominant in Spain), considering the potential for Communism in the Spanish social structure. It also would pose the difficult problem of the legal status of the Carlists whose devotion to "inorganic democracy" is at least as dubious as that of the Communists, but whose localized strength in Navarre would make any enforcement of a decision to outlaw them impossible. Furthermore, it may be argued that a Communist Party like the Italian could negatively integrate—to use the expression of Guenther Roth[58]—into the society a sector of the working class that otherwise might be of an anarchosyndicalist or simply anomic political outlook. The initial outlawing of the Communists, even if they were legalized subsequently, could give the democratic Socialists a head start.

Another, utopian, possibility to avoid hopeless debates in parliament would be to declare unconstitutional parties explicitly advocating secession from the Spanish state—not federalism or autonomy—but the declaration of independence by any region. This obviously would be a norm of difficult enforcement, and would require a respected constitutional court to ascertain the facts in case some of the Castilian nationalists unfairly accused a regional autonomist party of such designs or appeals. Even so the provision could, if accepted by the regionalist parties, be a show of consensus on national unity denying legitimacy *ab initio* to a cleavage on that issue. Secession from a nation-state by minority nationalities, particularly if they do not belong to another nation-state across the border, is something neither democratic theory nor international law has been able to solve satisfactorily, and in the case of Spain is absolutely undesirable given the historical, cultural, economic, and social integration achieved. To outlaw such secession would only be to recognize facts that only the most romantic nationalist dreamer would deny. In any case it seems out of the question that, legal or not, this solution could be realized without a civil war. Nevertheless, a carefully worked out agreement to exclude any cleavage in separatist terms at the same time as legitimate concessions were made in cultural and local self-government, could set the boundaries of which cleavages the society wants to consider legitimate. Sociologists, when they study the cleavage and consensus within a polity, often forget that in any system there must be limits to the activation of cleavages in the democratic process if it is to be stable.

NOTES

1. There is no work on the social and economic history of the late nineteenth and early twentieth centuries and its politics, particularly *caciquismo,* that would satisfy modern scholarship. The dissertation of Robert W. Kern (*Caciquismo vs. Self-government; The Crisis of Liberalism and Local Government in Spain, 1858–1910,* Univ. of Chicago, 1966) is a good summary of the contemporary discussion and allegations, particularly of the critics of the Cánovas-Sagasta period, but is not based on the necessary study of electoral ecology (of the two parties as well as of cases of electoral fraud) and of the political elite and its ties and background. There is even less research on the period of transformation or disintegration of the *caciquismo* in its traditional forms with the emergence of new leaders like Maura and Canalejas in the first decade of the century, and the divisions and factions within the two dynastic parties. A study like A. William Salomone's *Italy in the Giolittian Era: Italian Democracy in the Making, 1900–1914* (Pittsburgh: Univ. of Pennsylvania Press, 1960) remains to be written, perhaps using his study as a comparative frame of reference. The reappraisal of the Italian critics of *trasformismo* by Salomone, and by Salvemini in the foreword to his book, could lead historians of Spain to give some second thoughts to the work of Costa and the Regenerationists, while a comparative analysis of social and economic change in both countries in selected regions and cities during this period would probably prove most revealing.

2. The basic constitutional texts and electoral laws can be found in: Ramón Sáinz de Varanda in collaboration with F. Laguna and T. Sánchez Casajús (eds.), *Colección de leyes fundamentales* (Zaragoza: Acribia, 1957). For the universal suffrage law (June 26, 1890) see pp. 425–453, and the electoral law (August 8, 1907) regulating election procedures (to whose Article 29 we refer frequently), still largely in force, see pp. 453–479.

3. Spain became unified early under a single crown, even while maintaining much of the distinctive legislation of the component kingdoms until the eighteenth century. The late nineteenth century saw the completion of administrative and economic unification. In contrast to Italy and Germany, the unification was not carried out under the signs of nationalism but mostly before its upsurge, something that may help to account for the importance of minority nationalism, the lack of enthusiasm for national and colonial expansion, and even the weakness of true Fascism in contrast to those two countries.

4. On *caciquismo* the *locus classicus* is the *Ateneo* public inquest organized and published by Joaquín Costa on the basis of his "discussion paper": *Oligarquía y caciquismo como la forma actual de gobierno en España. Urgencia y modo de cambiarla. Información en el Ateneo Científico y Literario de Madrid sobre dicho tema, publícalo la Sección de Ciencias Históricas del Ateneo* (Madrid: Imprenta de los hijos de M. G. Hernández, 1902). There is an extensive literature on Costa, trying to interpret his basically ambivalent political thought as a precursor of the Primo de Rivera dictatorship, the 1931 Republic, or as proto-Fascist. In English there is Gabriel Jackson, "Joaquín Costa, Prophet of Spanish National Recovery," *South Atlantic Quarterly,* 53 (1954), pp. 182–92. For two recent books on Costa and other critics of the 1874–1923 political system, see Enrique Tierno Galván, *Costa y el Regeneracionismo* (Barcelona: Editorial Barba, 1961) and Rafael Pérez de la Dehesa, *El pensamiento de Costa y su influencia en la generación del 98* (Madrid, 1966). Kern's dissertation, *op. cit.,* summarizes much of the material of the Ateneo inquest and even publishes some of the materials submitted that at the time seemed too hot for publication, available in the Ateneo archives. He also has an interesting analysis of how the inquest made apparent disagreements in the interpretation of the phenomenon, and even greater ones on the remedies advocated, something that together with the social and probably political changes in subsequent years led to different perspectives, even when the label *caciquismo,* deprived of its specificity, remained part of the political language and polemics.

5. For a discussion of differences in strategies of democratization, from "below" and from "above," see S. Rokkan, "The Comparative Study of Political Participation," in A. Ranney (ed.), *Essays on the Behavioral Study of Politics* (Urbana: Univ. of Illinois Press, 1962), also the same author's "Electoral Mobilization, Party Competition and National Integration," in J. LaPalombara and M. Weiner (eds.), *Political Parties and Political Development* (Princeton: Princeton Univ. Press, 1966).

6. That great compilation of arguments against PR, F. Hermens's *Democracy and*

Anarchy (Notre Dame: Univ. of Notre Dame, 1941) is strangely silent on the Spanish case. The influence of the Spanish electoral system is discussed in a comparative perspective by S. S. Nilson, "Wahlsoziologische Probleme des Nationalsozialismus," *Z. ges. Staatswiss.* 110 (1954), pp. 279–311; see the rejoinder in H. Unkelbach, *Grundlagen der Wahlsystematik* (Göttingen: Vandenhoeck, 1956), pp. 74–5 and 174.

7. G. Sartori, *Parties and Party Systems* (New York: Harper & Row, 1967).

8. For a general history of Spain paying special attention to the period, see Raymond Carr, *Spain 1808–1939* (Oxford: Clarendon Press, 1966). This excellent scholarly study should provide the necessary historical background for this chapter. The work by Gerald Brenan, *The Spanish Labyrinth, an Account of the Social and Political Background of the Civil War* (Cambridge: Cambridge Univ. Press, 1950) is an earlier source still indispensable to gaining a feeling for the mentality of the participants, particularly the Carlists, anarchists, and anarchosyndicalists. But it also is valuable for an understanding of the social and economic conditions and the agrarian question. In Spanish the *Historia social y económica de España y América,* edited by Jaime Vicens Vives, *Vol. IV: Burguesía, Industrialización, Obrerismo* by Jorge Nadal Oller, J. Vicens Vives, R. Ortega Canadell, M. Hernández Sánchez-Barba (Barcelona: Editorial Teide, 1959) is a standard source.

9. See the discussion of the deviant Spanish case in the introduction by S. M. Lipset and S. Rokkan, this volume, pp. 42–43.

10. On the First Spanish Republic and the party and ideological divisions that contributed to its demise, see C. A. Hennessy, *The Federal Republic in Spain. Pi y Margall and the Federal Republican Movement, 1868–1874* (Oxford: Clarendon Press, 1962).

11. On the weakening of the role of the aristocracy at the national level in the eighteenth century, see R. Carr, "Spain," in A. Goodwin (ed.), *The European Nobility in the Eighteenth Century,* (London: A. and C. Black, 1953). And on the ennobling of military, politicians, bureaucrats, and businessmen in the late nineteenth and early twentieth centuries, see Jorge Nadal *et al., Historia social y económica de España y América, op. cit.,* IV, pp. 131–40.

12. On the Spanish army, see Stanley Payne, *Politics and the Military in Modern Spain* (Stanford: Stanford Univ. Press, 1967).

13. Francisco Pi y Margall, *La Réacción y la Revolución,* pp. 30–32, quoted by Hennessy *op. cit.* p. 10.

14. The *Anuario Estadístico de España, 1915* (Madrid: Instituto Nacional de Estadística, 1916).

15. José Ortega y Gasset, *La Redencion de las Provincias* (Madrid: Rev. de Occidente, 1931), pp. 71–80, describes the different "political cultures" of Madrid, a number of provincial capitals, and the vast countryside. In his analysis he considers *caciquismo* as a logical and inevitable form of organizing political life under a broad suffrage, given the social structure and cultural level of the country. See also his distinction between "official" and "vital" Spain in *Vieja y nueva politica* (Madrid: Rev. de Occidente, 1965), pp. 3–63.

16. Studies on the politics of particular areas suggest the need to study more carefully the link between the parties and interest groups. The book by Javier de Ybarra, *Política nacional en Vizcaya; de la Restauración a la República* (Madrid: Instituto de Estudios Políticos, 1947) has brought together much information on elections and politicians in Vizcaya that suggest that the shift from the Liberals dominant in nineteenth-century Bilbao to the Conservatives is not unrelated to policy differences.

17. Modesto Sánchez de los Santos, *Las Cortes Españolas. Las de 1907* (Madrid: the author, 1907) and Modesto Sánchez de los Santos in collaboration with Simón de la Redondela, *Las Cortes Españolas. Las de 1910* (Madrid: Establecimiento Tipográfico de A. Marzo, 1929) have brought together invaluable information on the political elites and elections of the period: voting statistics, electoral district maps, biographies of Senators and Deputies, controverted elections, some tables with biographical background data, and much more. The data presented here on elections and elites, unless stated otherwise, come from this source. I am in the process of carrying out a more detailed analysis of these data. A similar volume exists for the first legislature of the *Regencia:* Modesto Sánchez Ortiz and Fermín Merástegui, *Las Primeras Cámaras de la Regencia* (Madrid: Imprenta de Enrique Rubiños, 1887).

18. On Catalanism, besides the work of Brenan, Carr, *et al.*, already mentioned, there are Maximiano García Venero, *Historia del nacionalismo Catalán, 1793–1936* (Madrid: Editora Nacional, 1944) and the excellent little volume by Jaime Vicens Vives, *Cataluña en el siglo XIX* (Madrid, Ed. Rialp, 1961); the biographies of Cambó, the leader of the *Lliga:* Josep Pla, *Cambó, Materials per una Història d'Aquests Ultims Anys* (Barcelona: Liberia Catalónia, 1930) 3 vols.; Jesús Pabón, *Cambó 1876–1918* (Barcelona: Alpha, 1952). There is no biography of comparable quality of the Left Catalanist leaders, Maciá and Companys. An important sourcebook for Catalanist thought and the biographies of the authors: J. Ruiz i Calonja, *Panorama del pensament català contemporani* (Barcelona: Vicens Vives, 1963). For the *Lliga Catalana* in the 1930's, see the official publications of the party: *Un partit. Una politica 1933* (February), edited by the Assemblea General de la Lliga Regionalista, and the volume: *Dos anys d'actuacio. Primera assemblea ordinaria de Lliga Catalana* (Barcelona: Biblioteca Política, 1935). Nothing can be substituted for reading of the Catalanist thinkers and leaders themselves, particularly Almirall, Prat de la Riba, and Rovira Virgili. The introduction to Pierre Vilar, *La Catalogne dans l'Espagne Moderne. Recherches sur les fondements économiques des structures nationales* (Paris: S.E.V.P.E.N., 1962, 3 vols.), I, pp. 131–65, gives us a fascinating glimpse of the climate of opinion among Catalan intellectuals in the twenties as seen by a scholar doing research in Barcelona.

19. Antonio Ramos-Oliveira, *Historia de España* (Mexico City: Cía. General de Ediciones, 1952) of which there is an earlier English edition: *Politics, Economics and Men of Modern Spain* (London: Gollancz, 1946).

20. There is no study of the *Esquerra* and the *Estat Catalá* parties. The basic sources are some biographies of Companys, and some books published after the October 6, 1934, events. On the Catalan labor movement, besides Brenan, *op. cit.*, the reader is referred to the classics of Spanish syndicalism: Anselmo de Lorenzo, *El proletariado militante* (Barcelona, 1901); Manuel Buenacasa, *El movimiento obrero español 1886–1928* (Barcelona: Impresos Costa, 1928), and the history of the CNT by José Peirats, *La CNT en la Revolución Española* (Toulouse: Ediciones C.N.T., 1958), 3 vols. For an overview of the history of Spanish labor: Maximiano García Venero, *Las Internacionales en España* (Madrid: Editora Nacional, 1956–7), 3 vols. In recent years there has been some monographic research that is challenging many assertions made in the basic literature: Casimiro Marti, *Origenes del anarquismo en Barcelona* (Barcelona: Publicaciones de la Cátedra de Historia General de España, 1965).

21. There is no good history of Republican politics and the working class, particularly of the role and organization of the Radical party of Lerroux in Barcelona. The writings of Lerroux are useful but obviously unsatisfactory to the scholar. One of the best studies to give a sense of the complexity of working-class and petty-bourgeois radicalism in Barcelona—trade unions, anarchists, socialists, republicans, Catalanists, and free-thinkers competing for leadership of the masses, is Joan Connelly, *The Tragic Week. A Study of Anticlericalism in Spain,* Ph.D. diss. Bryn Mawr College, 1964 (to be published by Harvard Univ. Press).

22. The best sources on the anticlericalism versus clericalism issue between the Liberals, particularly the Democrats, and the Conservatives, mainly Maura, are the biographies of these two leaders. The one by the friend and follower of Canalejas, José Francos Rodríguez, *La vida de Canalejas* (Madrid: Tipografía de la Revista de Archivos, Bibliotecas y Museos, 1918) reprints most of the programmatic statements and the parliamentary speeches. For the popular anticlericalism and its most violent manifestation, see J. Connelly, *op. cit.*

23. Georges Lavau, *Partis politiques et réalités sociales* (Paris: Colin, 1953).

24. For these figures and other data on the social structure of Spain, see Juan J. Linz and Amando de Miguel, "Within-Nation Differences and Comparisons: The Eight Spains," in Richard L. Merritt and Stein Rokkan (eds.), *Comparing Nations* (New Haven: Yale Univ. Press, 1966), pp. 267–319; see pp. 291–2 and the sources quoted there.

25. For information on the election laws, participation, and so on in Italy for this period, see Istituto Centrale de Statistica e Ministero per la Constituente, *Compendio delle Statistiche Elettorale Italiane dal 1848 al 1934, vol. I: Elettori Politici e Circoscrizioni Elettorali* (Rome, 1946).

26. Data from the election to the Provincial Councils (*Diputaciones Provinciales*).

27. For the history of Republicanism early in the twentieth century, in addition to the sources quoted, see the biographies of the leaders, like Salmerón, Lerroux (also his own writings and autobiographical memoirs), Azcárate, Melquíades Álvarez, and the commemorative volume of the Catalan Left by Emilio Navarro, *Historia crítica de los hombres del republicanismo catalán en la ultima década* (*1905-1914*) (Barcelona: Ortega y Artis, 1915).

28. On the *Partido Reformista,* see the biography by Maximiano García Venero, *Melquíades Alvarez. Historia de un liberal* (Madrid: Editorial Alhambra, 1954).

29. On the Radical Socialists the best source is the three volumes of memoirs and speeches by Félix Gordón Ordás, *Mi politica en España* (Mexico City: Impr. Fígero, 1961), and the writings of Marcelino Domingo, who split with the party to form the Independent Radical Socialists.

30. The biography by Frank Sedwick, *The Tragedy of Manuel Azaña and the Fate of the Spanish Republic* (Columbus: Ohio State Univ. Press, 1963) is a sympathetic portrait of the man and very good on his early years as a writer, but not a study of the politician, and gives us little information on the party he created—*Acción Republicana* and later *Izquierda Republicana*. On his military policies, see Stanley Payne, *op. cit.*; José Mariano Sánchez, *Reform and reaction. The politico-religious background of the Spanish Civil War* (Chapel Hill: Univ. of North Carolina Press, 1964) is useful on the religious issue. Nothing can be substituted for his collected speeches, both in parliament, in his defense, and on the hustings, as well as his "Platonic" political dialogue: *La Velada en Benicarló* (Buenos Aires: Losada, 1939); there is a French translation published by Gallimard.

31. On Basque nationalism the main sources are the writings of Sabino de Arana Goiri, the founding father, and of José Antonio de Aguirre, particularly his memoirs: *Entre la libertad y la revolución 1930-1935; la verdad de un lustro en el país vasco* (Bilboa: Verdes, n.d.), Maximiano García Venero, *Historia del nacionalismo vasco (1793-1936)* (Madrid: Editorial Nacional, 1945). Fernando Sarrailh de Ihartza, *Vasconia* (Buenos Aires: Editorial Norbait, 1962) includes the party platforms of the different Basque parties. One of the best sources to get a feeling for the milieu and mentality of the early nationalists is *Pedro de Basaldúa, El libertador Vasco. Sabino de Arana Goiri* (Buenos Aires: Editorial Vasca Ekin, 1953) with a foreward by José Antonio de Aguirre.

32. See the chapter by Val Lorwin on Belgium in R. A. Dahl (ed.), *Political Oppositions in Western Democracies* (New Haven: Yale Univ. Press, 1966).

33. The Spanish Socialist movement can only be understood in contraposition with the anarchosyndicalist labor movement, for a brief summary see: R. Carr, *op. cit., pp.* 439-455. The classic work of G. Brenan: *Spanish Labyrinth,* is indispensable. A bibliography can be found in R. Lamberet, *Mouvements ouvriers et socialistes. Chronologie et bibliographie* (Paris, 1953). There is however no scholarly or even official history of the Socialist party and the UGT, except the memoirs of some of the leaders and the biography of Pablo Iglesias by Juan J. Morato (Madrid, 1931), cf. *El partido socialista* (Madrid, 1931) by the same author, and the *Historia del socialismo obrero español* (Madrid, 1902) by Francisco Mora. However the Socialist press can provide much of the necessary information. The excellent unpublished Ph.D. dissertation in history of Edward Malefakis on the *Agrarian Reform and Agrarian Unrest under the Second Republic* (Columbia University, 1965) is today the best study of the role of the party in the Second Republic and of the change in its social basis and the conflicts between reformists, centrists and maximalists that split the party.

34. Jose Ortega y Gasset "Las Provincias deben rebelarse contra toda candidatura de indeseables," reprinted in *Rectificación a la Republica* (Madrid, Revista de Occidente, 1934), p. 34.

35. John N. Schumacher, "Integrism: A Study in Nineteenth-Century Spanish Politico-Religious Thought," *Catholic Historical Review* 48 (3) (Oct. 1962), pp. 343-64.

36. On the Catholic trade union movement and social Catholicism in general see Juan N. García-Nieto, *El sindicalismo cristiano en España; notes sobre su origen y evolución hasta 1936* (Bilbao: Universidad de Deusto, Instituto de Estudios Economicos-Sociales, 1960).

37. For the evolution of "liberal" and "social" Catholicism, the writings of Angel Herrera (now Cardinal), *Obras selectas de Mons. Angel Herrera Oria* (Madrid: Biblioteca

de Autores Cristianos, 1963) and of his successor as head of the ACNDP, Fernando Martín-Sánchez Juliá, *Ideas Claras. Reflexiones de un español actual* (Madrid: A.C.-N.D.P., 1959) are essential; however, the best source would still be the reading of *El Debate* and of the *Boletin del A.C.N.D.P.* and the writings of different bishops. For a sociological interpretation of Catholic Action as an organization and its relations to Catholic parties, see Gianfranco Poggi, *Catholic Action in Italy. The Sociology of a Sponsored Organization* (Stanford: Stanford Univ. Press, 1967) and Joseph La-Palombara, *Interest Group Politics in Italy* (Princeton: Princeton Univ. Press, 1964) and the literature on Christian Democratic parties, particularly Michael Fogarty, *Christian Democracy in Western Europe, 1820–1953* (Notre Dame: Univ. of Notre Dame Press, 1957).

38. The data on the 1931 municipal and Constituent Assembly elections are taken from the *Anuario Estadístico de España, 1931* (Madrid: Instituto Nacional de Estadística, 1932).

39. The link between *Caciquismo* and art. 29 is made in Raymond Carr, *Spain, 1808–1939, op. cit.,* p. 268–9, footnote 3. The Decree of May 8, 1931, that established the election system for the Constituent Assembly expressly derogated art. 29. For this important decree, see R. Sáinz de Varanda (ed.), *Colección de leyes fundamentales, op. cit.,* pp. 628–32.

40. For the list of the CEDA coalitions with Radicals and Republicanos Conservadores, see Francisco Casares, *La C.E.D.A. va a gobernar (notas y glosas de un auo de vida pública nacional)* (Madrid: Gráfia administrativa, 1934).

41. In this they followed the traditional pattern of the *retraimiento*, or withdrawal from parliament, that became so frequent in the nineteenth century and often served as a prelude to the use of force (see C. A. Hennessy, *op. cit.,* p. 4 and passim).

42. There is no monographic study of the CEDA nor a collection of the speeches of its leaders. The book by Casares contains much material even when slanted to prove the "democratic," "constitutional," and "republican" character of the party, scorning the contrary statements. The program of the *Juventud de Acción Popular,* that, like so many party youth organizations, was a source of trouble for the parent party, with corporativist-authoritarian points but with a style that is far from that of real Fascists, can be found in Casares. The work of Santiago Galindo Herrero, *Los partidos monárquicos bajo la Segunda República* (Madrid: Ed. Rialp, 1956), while focused on *Renovación Española* and the Traditionalists, presents much material to accuse the CEDA of ambivalence or double talk, aimed at discrediting the Christian Democrats before the Right as unreliable and dangerous, before the Left as not to be trusted either. The younger Spanish generations have derived much of their image of the CEDA and its policies from the biting Fascist attack of José Antonio that in blaming it for a reactionary social policy coincided with the Popular Front attacks, while another sector accepted Calvo Sotelo's criticism of the weakness of the party and its ambivalence. An adequate study of the CEDA and the policies of the so-called "*bienio negro*" is badly needed. Interesting data on the agrarian policies that are not so "black" can be found in Malefakis, *op. cit.*

43. There is no study of this most successful of all the Catholic social organizations. This was also the last large-scale interest organization that was "*gleichgeschaltet*" by the official *Sindicatos* in Franco Spain; see Antonio Bouthelier, *Legislación sindical española desde el 18 de julio 1936 hasta el 31 de diciembre de 1944* (Madrid: Instituto de Estudios Politicos, 1945) 2 vols.

44. On the *ralliement* policy and its ideological justification, see José M. Sánchez, *op. cit.;* Angel Herrera, *op. cit.*

45. For the presence of men coming from the CEDA or groups close to it in the Franco cabinets, see Juan J. Linz, "An Authoritarian Regime: The Case of Spain," in Erik Allardt and Yrjö Littunen (eds.), *Cleavages, Ideologies and Party Systems* (Helsinki: Transactions of the Westermarck Society, 1964) pp. 291–341; see especially p. 330.

46. For a brilliant description of this section of Spanish society see the pages on *el macizo de la raza* in the political essay on the politics of Spain, past and future, by Dionisio Ridruejo, *Escrito en España* (Buenos Aires: Losada, 1962). The term *masa neutra* was used by the regenerationists and by Antonio Maura, the conservative who

attempted to rally the citizens for a revolution from above, ignoring the old *cacique* party leaders.

47. On the difficult problems of delimiting the Right, particularly the radical or revolutionary Right, from Fascism, see articles by Eugene Weber, Ernst Nolte, and Andrew Whiteside, in H. Rogger and E. Weber (eds.), *The European Right* (London: Weidenfeld, 1965). Also S. M. Lipset, "Fascism, Left, Right and Center," in *Political Man* (Garden City: Doubleday, 1960).

48. Stanley Payne, "Spain" in H. Rogger and E. Weber (eds.), *op. cit.*, traces the history of Carlism up to the present and discusses the Renovación group, with a useful bibliography. The writings of Calvo Sotelo, Eugenio Vegas Latapié, and the magazine *Acción Española* are fundamental for the study of the authoritarian monarchist Right. The data on sponsorship are from the covers of *Acción Española* and the sales figures of Maurras are from an ad inserted in a summer issue of 1936.

49. See especially H. Rogger and E. Weber (eds.), *op. cit.*, and E. Nolte, *Der Faschismus in seiner Epoche* (Munich: Piper, 1963) and *Die faschistischen Bewegungen* (Munich: Deutscher Taschenbuch Verlag, 1966); see also the collection of articles in the *Journal of Contemporary History* 1 (Jan. 1966) now published in W. Laqueur and G. L. Mosse (eds.), *International Fascism 1920–1945* (New York: Harper Torchbooks, 1966).

50. The literature on Spanish Fascism, *stricto sensu,* is abundant. The basic texts are easily available and there are two excellent scholarly studies: Stanley G. Payne, *Falange. A History of Spanish Fascism* (Stanford: Stanford Univ. Press, 1961), and Bernd Nellessen, *Die verbotene Revolution. Aufstieg und Niedergang der Falange* (Hamburg: Leibniz Verlag, 1963). There is also an anthology of writings by José Antonio Primo de Rivera, edited by Gonzalo Torrente (Madrid: Ed. Almena, 1947). The biography by Felipe Ximénez de Sandoval, *José Antonio* (Barcelona: Ed. Juventud, 1941), together with the official party history of Francisco Bravo Martínez, *Historia de F.E.T. y de las J.O.N.S.* (Madrid: Editora Nacional, 1940), are the main sources in Spanish. Nothing can be substituted for the reading of the writings of José Antonio Primo de Rivera, Ramiro Ledesma Ramos, particularly his *Discurso a las Juventudes de España* (3d printing; Barcelona: Ed. Fe, 1939), the much flimsier speeches by Onésimo Redondo, and the marginal intellectual essay by Ernesto Giménez Caballero, *El genio de España; exaltaciones a una resurrección nacional y del mundo* (Madrid: Ed. de "La Gaceta Literaria," 1931).

51. Ramiro Ledesma Ramos, *Fascismo en España?* (Madrid: Ed. La Conquista del Estado, 1935).

52. See Payne, *op. cit.,* Chaps. III–VII.

53. Bernd Nellessen, *op. cit.*

54. On the Communist Party, in English: David T. Cattell, *Communism and the Civil War* (Berkeley: Univ. of California Press, 1956) which, as the title indicates focuses on the party after 1936. A number of party leaders, both loyal and dissident, have published memoirs and polemics. Among them we may mention José Diaz, Dolores Ibarruri, Jesús Hernandez, El Campesino, Hidalgo de Cisneros (an air force officer that joined the party in the war). The writings on the Socialist Party and the anarchosyndicalists contain important references to the party, as all the literature on the labor movement does. There is an official *Historia del Partido Comunista de España,* redactada por una comisión del Comité Central formada por Dolores Ibarruri, presidenta, y Manuel Arcárate, Luis Balaguer, Antonio Cordón, Irene Falcón y José Sandoval (Paris: Éditions Sociales, 1960). Eduardo Comin Colomer, *Historia del Partido Comunista de España* (Madrid: Editora Nacional, 1967) contains much useful information.

55. The data for the 1933 elections have not been subject to much controversy. The party affiliation is taken from the *Anuario Estadístico de España 1933* (Madrid: Instituto Nacional de Estadística, 1934). Some of the seats gained by coalitions, without distinction of party according to the *Anuario,* have been allocated, using different sources; thus, for the PSOE Francisco Largo Caballero, *Discursos a los trabajadores; una crítica de la República, una doctrina socialista, un programa de acción* (Madrid: Gráfica Socialista, 1934). To complete the data on the Monarchist groups, we have used, with some caution, the data in Galindo Herrero, *op. cit.* The returns for 1936 are disputed between the pro- and anti-Franco sources. The differences between the José Venegas exile publication, *Las elecciones del frente popular* (Buenos Aires: Patronato Hispano-Argentino de Cul-

tura, 1942) and the semiofficial *Historia de la cruzada española* (Madrid: Ediciones Españolas, S.A., 1934–1944, 8 vols.) edited by Joaquín Arraraś, are appreciable: thus the *Cruzada* has 100 votes less for the Right in Gerona, 315 less in Barcelona Province, and 95 more for it in Lérida.

56. See Mattei Dogan, "La stratificazione sociale dei suffragi," in A. Spreafico and J. LaPalombara (eds.), *Elezioni e comportamento politico in Italia* (Milan: Ed. di Comunitá, 1963), pp. 407–74 and his chapter in the present volume. For a further analysis of the structure of the Spanish population see J. Linz and A. de Miguel (eds.), *op. cit.* There has been little sociological research on Spanish elections. Among the first studies two articles by Joaquín Tomás Villaroya deserve to be mentioned: "Las primeras elecciones directas en España," *Anales de la Universidad de Valencia,* 38 (1964–1965), pp. 7–56, and "El cuerpo electoral en la ley de 1837", *Revista del Instituto Ciencias Sociales de la Diputación Provincial de Barcelona,* 1965, pp. 157–205. See also: Miguel M. Cuadrado, "La elección general para Cortes Constituyentes de 1869," *Revista de Estudios Politicos,* 132, (1963), pp. 65–102. For the Republican period see: Jean Becarud, *La deuxième République Espagnole (1931–1936),* (Paris: Centre d'Etudes des Relations internationales 1962, mimeo).

57. Carried out by DATA S. A., Madrid.

58. G. Roth, *The Social Democrats in Imperial Germany* (Totowa: Bedminster, 1963).

Six

Cleavage and Consensus in West German Politics: The Early Fifties*

Juan J. Linz

INTRODUCTION

The expression of the social cleavages through political parties, and their articulation by them, has been and is central to the interests of political sociology. On the other side, the problem of how consensus is achieved in a society despite all the cleavages is a problem that has been gaining the attention of social scientists. In this chapter we shall present some hypotheses and data on these problems for West Germany. The interest of social scientists lies in the fact that here is a European society where the conflicts created by industrialization were acute; where preindustrial and predemocratic institutions, and the values linked to them, retained their strength until quite late and even persist to a certain extent in some strata; but a society where the

*Unless otherwise stated all the data presented in the text are from tabulations made from a national random sample survey of the West German population by the *UNESCO Institut für Sozialforschung* under the direction of Dr. Erich Reigrotzki, originally published under the title *Soziale Verflechtungen in der Bundesrepublik* (Tübingen: J. C. Mohr [Paul Siebeck], 1956). There were 3,246 interviews executed by the Institut für Demoskopie and DIVO.

My gratitude cannot be great enough for the UNESCO Institut and to Dr. Reigrotzki for their making these data available to me for secondary analysis.

The absolute figures on which the percentages are based, the exact wording of the questions, complete tables, and so forth can be found in my study *The Social Bases of West German Politics*. Ph.D. diss., Columbia University, 1959. Microfilm Publication #59–4075, University Microfilms, Inc., Ann Arbor, Mich., 945 pp.

I wish to express my indebtedness to S. M. Lipset, who directed the Ph.D. dissertation class conflict seems to have been finally institutionalized. Here is a society in which religious cleavages are important, where secularization has made important inroads, but where religious politics do not have the same bitterness as in other European countries. Industrialization, prosperity, and a competent, universalistic bureaucracy have transformed problems that in other societies are political into administrative ones, with the consequent lowering of political temperature.[1]

By its industrialization, it belongs together with the Anglo-Saxon democracies and the Scandinavian and Benelux countries, but because of the importance of organized religion in public life it is distinct from the Protestant Anglo-Saxon and Scandinavian countries and closer to the Benelux and Latin ones. It, however, differentiates itself from France and Italy and even the Benelux by slow changes toward secularization without violent democratic conflict and the consequent tolerant coexistence between Protestants and Catholics. The survival of a landowning nobility linked with the army and the bureaucracy, an artisan tradition maintained by guild-type organizations, the *"Stand"* consciousness of large parts of the old middle classes, a traditional peasantry finding it difficult to adapt to a new commercial agriculture supported by romantic ideologies—all made the adaptation to the values of industrial, equalitarian, secularized, pragmatic society more difficult than in most European countries, perhaps with the exception of Austria. Only the economic crisis, Nazi demogogic equalitarianism, war and defeat, the disintegration of Prussia, and the changes in the agrarian structure of the East, have weakened those elements of German social structure to the point that they have been submerged and largely assimilated to a new industrialized society. The elements it shares with the nations mentioned make it possible to generalize certain of the findings about German politics and social structure, while the unique combination of the various characteristics should not be forgotten and makes it a particularly interesting case.

Looking at the party system we find that the present modified three-party system grew out of a long history of politico-ideological cleavages closely linked with sociostructural cleavages. One has only to look at the "genealogical tree" of West German parties to see how a previously complex multiparty system has been simplified—in essence, reduced to Christian Democracy, Democratic Socialism, and Liberalism.[2] The appeal of avowed Conservatism has been weakened by its support of the Nazi rise to power, the changes in the social structure, the greater unity of interest groups, the ideological

---

on which this paper is based, and also to Stein Rokkan, Renate Mayntz, Sidney Verba, and Dietrich Bracher for their many useful suggestions.

Abbreviations used to designate parties: BHE, Block der Heimatvertriebenen und Entrechteten (Refugee party); BP, Bayernpartei (Bavarian Party); CDU, Christlich-Demokratische Union (Christian Democratic Union) (more exactly we should use the abbreviation CDU–CSU since we will refer to the federated parties CDU and CSU—its Bavarian wing called officially Christlich-Soziale Union, but for reasons of brevity we use CDU referring to both); DP, Deutsche Partei (German Party); FDP, Freie Demokratische Partei (Free Democratic Party); KPD, Kommunistische Partei Deutschlands (German Communist Party); SPD, Sozialdemokratische Partei Deutschlands (German Socialdemocratic Party); Z, Zentrum (a small Catholic splinter party after World War II).

climate of the early postwar period, and changes of outlook among the Protestant clergy. Preindustrial Conservatism, after having dominated German political life after unification and been a radical opposition, has become absorbed by a Christian party and bourgeois liberalism. At the other extreme of the spectrum, Communism was reduced (even before being outlawed) to an insignificant minority, and this was done without another leftist party taking its place or a radicalization of the SPD itself; the SPD, on the contrary, has turned from reformist Marxism to mere reformism. The dismissal of the KPD, a mass party growing out of the ideological response to the frustrations of a working class isolated from a nationalistic half-feudal, half-capitalist society,[3] and strengthened by the impact of the depression and changes in the industrial structure, would deserve more study. The usual explanation in terms of the Russian occupation and annexations, the influx of refugees, and the record of the East German regime—while important—may not be sufficient if one considers that in the elections between 1946 and 1948, and even in the federal election of 1949, the Communists had a larger share of the vote than in 1953. It should also be considered that in another country with free elections and somewhat similar experiences—Finland—the Communists, since the war, had been able to hold over 20 percent of the vote. The changes in West German social structure have to be taken into account: the emergence of a prosperous welfare state, the fact that many of the least privileged jobs were left to the refugees recruited from a traditionalist background, and last, but not least, that during the difficult postwar years the SPD was in opposition to, rather than sharing the responsibilities of, the government, as did other European reformist Socialist parties.

The total defeat of Nazism, the onus attached to Fascism, to some extent the flexibility—for some people's taste excessive—in allowing the reintegration of former Nazis into the democratic parties, together with prosperity have kept the attempts of neo-Fascism below the Italian level. Historical survivals of divisions within the bourgeoisie weakening the democratic center which existed during the Weimar Republic have been smoothed by a changed approach to politics of many interest groups and by the extension of the integrative conception of Christian Democratic politics to the Protestant middle classes. In the postwar years the CDU has been able to hold together much of the heterogeneous middle class, upper class, and rural support that the MRP could not hold together. As a catch-all aggregate acting as a vast interest market, united by the prestige of the chief and the magic of prosperity, it has done well as a party of "democratic integration."

It would be interesting to outline the processes by which the strife-torn multiparty system of Weimar and the conflict-laden social structure created by uneven industrialization in an autocratic-bureaucratic setting were transformed into the politics of a Federal Republic where interest groups work with the professional politicians within a framework of reasonably well-enforced constitutional restrictions, in a political climate free of destructive and rigid ideologies. Our focus is on the social structure making this system possible, but the importance of institutional arrangements: constitutional provisions; the electoral system; the constitutional court; and the state governments, allowing the opposition to hold a share of power; and so forth, should not be forgotten. Nor should the increasing acceptance of those institutions—expressed in part by the support to the three major parties—be neglected. But it is impossible to do all this here and consequently we limit ourselves to describing some of the characteristics of the bases of political diversity in the early years of the Adenauer era.

The main cleavages of West German politics run along class lines, but, in contrast to the United Kingdom and with different intensity and visibility than in Scandinavia, the religious cleavages affect the political loyalties of important segments of the population. These two cleavages tend to overlap considerably less than in some of the Catholic Latin countries, and cross-cut each other and the political alignments in a way that is particularly interesting to the sociologist. A third minor line of cleavage, between urban and rural Germany—not unimportant in the past—has been losing importance on the ideological and political level, even when it persists as interest conflict. On the other side, the urban class conflict, institutionalized[4] through the trade unions and the SPD, does not penetrate rural society. Religion in turn has contributed to bridge the urban-rural value conflicts and the small survivals of romantic regionalism, particularly in Bavaria. Therefore, we will focus on the socioeconomic cleavages and the religious cleavages.

The generational cleavages that under Weimar contributed to the appeal of the extremists—Nazis and Communists—seem to have almost disappeared and are not reflected in politics. There are indications that, among the younger generation, the class and status lines underlying politics are less rigid: young workers independent of income, skill, size of place of employment, social origin, and region in 1953 were somewhat less SPD and more CDU than their active elders, while among their white-collar counterparts, we found the opposite pattern. On the other side, the changed image of the SPD seems to have facilitated its attractiveness to the young religious Protestants, while the young religious Catholics have remained attached to the CDU even when religious motives or issues appeared to them as less relevant. The changes in the social structure provoked by the Nazis, war and defeat, and the socialization of the younger generations under those conditions, seem to have weakened the rigidity of the lines of cleavage underlying German politics and facilitated among the younger generation the acceptance of the changed images presented by the major political contenders.

The interest and social cleavage between the various categories of refugees, that came to constitute a large and underprivileged sector of the population, and the old residents, was seen with concern in the early postwar years. Despite the limitations imposed on the creation of refugee parties, political groups representing them emerged, and the BHE appeared as a national party appealing to them. However, the successful integration into the West German economy and society of the refugees, the ties with the churches, and even party traditions reduced the support for this party to isolated pockets, particularly in smaller communities and among the poorer and older refugees, as well as among those of agricultural background. In 1953 the BHE—more a pressure group than a real party—was able to gain only one-fourth of its potential constituency.

THE SOCIAL BASES OF POLITICS

The Class Basis of West German Politics

West Germany is a highly industrialized country with slightly less than half the people coming from households headed by manual workers, an increasing proportion of the population white-collar employees, close to one-fifth in private employment, plus close to one-tenth civil servants—many without the traditional status conscience, in public services rather than in the authority structure of the government. The farmers and farm laborers represent only a small part of the population, even though slightly larger than in the United Kingdom.[5] A party able to win all the votes of the workers could not obtain a majority; but the SPD is far from this, with only 50 per-cent of the votes of the urban workers (*Table 3*) and around 30 percent of the farm laborers. Its success among the salaried middle class and other strata—farmers, small-business and professional people—would have to be extraordinary to overcome this weakness at its natural base. In fact the SPD in 1953 derived some 70 percent of its total strength from the working class: this can be read out of *Tables 1 and 2,* both derived from a nationwide

Table 1—Occupation of the Respondent or Head of Household and Political Preference

OCCUPATION	KPD	SPD	Z	CDU/CSU	FDP	BP	DP	Other	BHE	None	Total
Skilled workers	1	39	1	23	3	1	2	1	3	24	(662)
Semiskilled workers	1	36	2	26	3	.7	2	2	5	26	(567)
Unskilled workers	.6	32	1	23	2	3	2	2	7	25	(320)
Subtotal workers	1	36	2	23	3	2	2	2	5	25	(1571)
Lower white collar	.3	23	.8	38	8	1	2	2	3	20	(399)
Upper white collar	—	14	—	42	11	1	6	4	3	19	(154)
Civil servant	—	20	1	41	9	2	2	2	4	18	(279)
Businessman	—	13	5	29	16	3	6	2	4	22	(239)
Artisan	—	12	2	36	13	3	2	2	5	25	(235)
Free profession	—	5	2	47	18	—	7	3	—	18	(61)
Subtotal middle class	—	17	2	37	11	2	5	2	4	21	(1367)
Farmer	.4	4	1	46	8	9	5	2	2	22	(413)
Farm laborer	—	21	—	25	—	9	—	2	5	38	(63)
Total Sample	.5	24	1.5	32	7	3	3	2	4	23	(3466)

Source: UNESCO Institute Survey, 1953.
Remarks: We have omitted forty-four students and ten apprentices from the Table, but not from the totals and subtotals.

survey of the *Bundesrepublik* electorate that year. This figure is lower than for the Scandinavian, the British and the Belgian Social Democratic Labor parties and also lower than for the combined Communist-Socialist voting blocs in France and Italy.[6] Having less working-class support than the northern European Socialist parties (except the Dutch and Finnish), its electorate was more homogeneously working class than British Labour (where industrial workers constitute 60 percent of the population). It was clearly *a working-class party, but not the party of the working class.* Many of its problems came from this fact; with limited hopes to increase its strength sufficiently

Table 2—Social Composition—Occupation of the Respondent or the Head of the Household—of the Support of West German Parties

OCCUPATION	PARTY PREFERENCE										
	KPD	SPD	Z	CDU/CSU	FDP	BP	DP	Other	BHE	None	Total
Skilled workers	42	31	19	14	9	8	15	12	14	20	19
Semiskilled workers	37	25	23	11	7	4	9	17	21	18	16
Unskilled workers	10	12	7	7	3	12	.7	8	17	10	9
Subtotal workers[a]	89	70	49	32	20	27	31	37	55	49	45
Lower white collar	5	11	6	14	14	5	8	12	10	10	11
Upper white collar	—	3	—	6	7	2	9	8	3	4	4
Civil servant	—	7	6	10	10	5	7	10	8	6	8
Businessman	—	4	23	6	15	8	14	7	7	7	7
Artisan	—	3	7	8	13	7	4	7	8	7	7
Free profession	—	.4	2	3	5	—	4	3	—	1	2
Subtotal middle class	5	28	43	47	65	28	73	47	36	35	39
Farmer	5	2	8	18	13	41	22	11	7	11	12
Farm laborer	—	2	—	1	—	6	—	1	2	3	2
Total	(19)	(836)	(53)	(1096)	(239)	(95)	(100)	(72)	(142)	(814)	(3466)

Source: UNESCO Institute Survey, 1953.
[a] Students, apprentices and workers without information are left out of the Table, but included in the total and the last two categories in the subtotal of workers.

among the workers, it would still be defined by a large part of the population as a workers' party.[7] However, if we look at its support we may also characterize it as an *Arbeiter- und Angestelltenpartei* (workers' and employees'

Table 3—Party Preferences of the Major Divisions of the West German Population (Men and Women) by Occupation of the Respondent or the Head of Household (1953)

	WORKING CLASS	URBAN MIDDLE CLASS			URBAN OCCUPATIONS	FARMERS AND FARM LABORERS
		Salaried middle class	Independents	Total		
SPD-KPD	50%	25%	15%	21%	36%	8%
CDU-Z	32	51	49	49	40	58
Bourgeois	9	16	29	21	14	28
Other	2	3	3	3	3	3
BHE	7	5	5	5	6	4
Total	100%	100%	100%	100%	100%	100%
	(1172)	(669)	(414)	(1083)	(2297)[a]	(365)
No preference	26%	19%	23%	21%	23%	24%
Total	(1579)	(829)	(538)	(1367)	(2983)[a]	(481)

Source: UNESCO Institute Survey, 1953.
[a] Including students.

party), since almost 90 percent of its votes come from workers—urban or rural—and white-collar employees. Given the expansion of the tertiary sector, the hopes of the party lie in making this image dominant while holding and expanding its present industrial-worker base.

All parties naturally depend heavily on the workers and their families, who constitute close to half of the population and slightly less of the electorate. Even the bourgeois party par excellence, the FDP, got 20 percent of its vote from them (other surveys make it less). The CDU can count on one-third of the preferences of the working class—a figure close to that of the British Conservatives, but considerably more than the Italian and, particularly, the French Christian Democrats,[8] though perhaps less than the Belgian and certainly less than the combined vote for the three main Christian parties in the Netherlands. The CDU also depends more on that industrial working class vote than those in the two Latin republics (32 percent of its support compared to 18 percent in Italy). The problem of how this advantageous position of the CDU among the workers comes about will concern us later. The question is to some extent parallel to the problem of the Tory worker in Britain, with the difference here being that religion plays an important part and—in contrast to across the Channel—CDU and SPD workers are quite different in terms of sex, income, occupational skill level, and other social characteristics.[9]

The salaried middle class—belying the Marxist hope and the sociological interpretations of the thirties that nationalism and style issues kept it from the SPD—gives around 50 percent of its preferences to the CDU and only one-fourth to the SPD.[10] The appeal of the CDU to this class is comparable to that of the SPD to the workers (see *Table 3*).

If we consider the cleavage between "independent"—self-employed—and "dependents"—employed in the modern industrial and commercial sector of the economy—the differences between CDU and SPD—while not negligible —are not very great. The workers and employees that constitute 89 percent of the SPD strength represent 64 percent of that of the CDU (and only 52 percent of the FDP). The CDU depends more heavily (29 percent) on the salaried middle class than the SPD (18 percent). But this obviously ignores internal differentiation in terms of skill, income, social origin, and so on, and above all the religious composition.

A CDU-SPD coalition—that was and may again be possible—would have more than three-fourths of the salaried population behind it: 82 percent of the working and 76 percent of the salaried middle class, which would mean three-fourths of the coalition support coming from these strata. It should not be surprising that when asked (May 1952 and April 1953) to choose between a CDU, an SPD, and a CDU-SPD government, the latter was approved by almost half (43 percent and 38 percent) of the population.[11]

With around one-half of the workers supporting nonworking-class parties, and one-fifth of the middle class and up to one-fourth of the salaried middle class supporting the "working class party," we see that class and status lines cannot be the only basis of cleavage.

A salient fact of German politics is that the dominant party—the CDU— is to a large extent what the Germans call a *Volkspartei* (people's party). It realizes an ideal of class integration, which contributed much to the anti-democratic sentiments in the Weimar Republic, when a more divisive social structure found almost exact replication in parties attempting to represent specific classes and interests (with the exception of the *Zentrum*).[12] A large party of democratic integration brings the conflicts of interests of socio-economic groupings from the level of the electorate to that of the inner cleavages within the party and the conflicts of interest groups in their efforts toward influencing the party leadership. In a sense, with what is known about the social bases of West German parties (with the exception of interesting monographic problems), our focus of attention should shift to the study of the internal politics of the CDU. The party derives 47 percent of its electoral support from the upper and middle classes, 32 percent from the working class, and 19 percent from the agricultural sector: the welding together of such divergent forces raises a series of problems, well worth detailed sociological research.

The SPD on the other hand is not fully wrong when it also claims to be more than a workers' party, with 29 percent of its urban support from nonmanual groups. It has more right to be considered more than a class-opposition party than the Labor party in 1951, when that party received between 14 and 22 percent of its votes from nonmanuals, depending on the estimates.[13] The German social structure with a smaller industrial working class than the United Kingdom makes the SPD even more dependent than Labor on the salaried middle class: to maximize the working-class support—even if it were possible—would not get the SPD out of its minority position. The limits to its expansion among the small peasant population seems too difficult to overcome; consequently, all the effort has to be directed to winning more middle-class votes and holding the loyalties of the workers. The "me-tooism" of the SPD in the postwar modified two-party system is not unrelated to these social structural facts.

The Non-Socialist Working Class

It appears to be easier to account for the "class deviance" of the German worker than for the Tory loyalty of the British workingman. If we look at the data, we see that 64 percent or more of the workers and their families not supporting the SPD (themselves 50 percent of the working-class vote) turned out for the CDU or Z. The deviation in favor of bourgeois and other minor parties was only 11 percent. In 1953 still 7 percent of the workers vote went to the refugee party, the BHE (with 26 percent expressing no preference). The share of the nonreligious bourgeois liberal or conservative parties is smaller than in France (where the added RGR, Independent, URAS, and Poujade—UDCA—1956 support was 22 percent, and in 1952 25 percent) where in turn the Christian Democrats are considerably weaker (8 or 10 percent in the 1956 and 1952 studies.)[14] In Italy, the share of the non-Socialist and Demo-Christian parties has been found similarly low, if not lower, even including the "Lumpenproletariat." The crosscutting of class and religious cleavages plays a decisive role in keeping many workers from the SPD, even when not all those supporting the CDU would favor the SPD. This occurs even in the absence of religious loyalties, as the data about the conservative vote of workers in other countries suggest.

Franz Neumann formulated the problem in these terms:

> It is exceedingly unlikely that, no matter what the political situation in Germany is, the Social Democratic Party can substantially increase its vote and its control, primarily in view of the religious stratification in Germany and the tight control exercised by the Catholic political party over Catholic labor. Consequently, the Social Democratic party, in contrast to the British Labor party, must expect to remain a minority party for the near future, and consequently it will be able to carry out its policies solely in coalition with other parties.

Let us explore in more detail the impact of the religious factor. If the German population were only Protestant, the SPD could count on some 60 percent of the vote of workers and their dependents; in this hypothetical electorate, it would be around 30 percent of the vote. In an all-Protestant electorate, assuming wrongly that none of the Protestant workers and salaried employees is inclined to the CDU for religious reasons, the SPD would be close to 40 percent. Since a purely Protestant Lutheran country would not have produced a strong religious party, in such a hypothetical dream world, the SPD strength would be perhaps even greater. But let us turn back to reality! Let us compare Protestant and Catholic workers and their families (*Tables 4 and 5*). We find that the advantage of the CDU comes from 14

Table 4—Political Preferences of Workers by Sex and Religion: 1953

	MEN				WOMEN			
	Protestants	Catholics	Other	None	Protestants	Catholics	Other	None
SPD	67%	47%	50%	84%	51%	28%	50%	78%
KPD	1	1		4	2	1		11
CDU/Z	16	36	25		24	54	50	11
Bourgeois	9	8	12.5	8	11	7		
Other	3	3	12.5	4	2	1		
BHE	4%	5%			10%	9%		
	(226)	(253)	(8)	(24)	(265)	(298)	(4)	(9)
No preference	19%	16%	20%	11%	34%	30%	50%	44%
	(280)	(302)	(10)	(27)	(401)	(423)	(8)	(16)

percent of the Catholics who, if they were Protestants, would support the SPD, and from 5 percent of those who in that case would not express a preference.

Table 5—Origin of the CDU/Z Advantage Among the Catholic Working-Class in Comparison with the Protestant: 1953

	All	Men	Women
SPD	−14%[a]	−14%	−14%
KPD		0	
Bourgeois	−3	−2	−2
Other	1	1	
BHE	1	1	−1
No preference	−5	−3	−4
CDU/Z advantage	20%	17%	21%

[a] The minus sign indicates that the difference between the proportions of support the party has among Protestants and Catholics is unfavorable to the party.

In view of the greater religious allegiance of women, it is interesting to note that the advantage to the CDU at the cost of the SPD, among the Catholics (that we assume would support the Socialists if they were Protestants), is almost the same among men and women. The larger CDU advantage among Catholic working-class women is due to the mobilization of those who among the Protestants remain apathetic or support other parties. The difference in SPD support among Protestant men and women with a political preference (67 versus 51 percent) is 16 percent, that between Catholic men and women (47 versus 28 percent) is 19 percent, only slightly larger.

Are the workers who follow the religious loyalties differently located in the social structure? Only to a certain extent. Protestants and Catholics are equally likely to be union members, but Catholics are also more prone to be members of other voluntary associations. The difference in SPD support between the two religious groups becomes smaller among male union members (69 percent among Protestant men and 56 percent among Catholics) than among non-members (43 and 27 percent respectively). (The corresponding CDU figures are 21, 10, and 32, 15 percent; with all percentages including those with no preference). The impact of the Catholic subculture is reflected in the greater weakness of the SPD among union members who are also members of voluntary associations, something that is not the case among Protestants.

Among both Catholics and Protestants who are not union members, identification with the church weakens the SPD appeal in favor of the CDU among the Catholics, and leads to increased apathy and support for bourgeois parties among the Protestants. Among church-going Catholic trade unionists, the SPD has a strength similar to the church-going Protestant nonunion workers and this loss benefits the CDU exclusively; however, there are also more undecided among them, reflecting a certain cross-pressure between union and Church. Among Protestant union members, church-going does not affect much the SPD appeal, but has mobilized in favor of the CDU some who otherwise would have remained apathetic. The impact of the Catholic subculture is reflected in the fact that non-church-going Catholic trade unionists behave almost like their fellow Protestants who go to church.

To what extent are these CDU voters motivated by religious issues or even loyalties (*Table 6*)? The CDU support among nonpracticing Protestants is

Table 6—Religious Practice Among Working-Class Supporters of the SPD and CDU: 1953

| Religion | Men | | | | Women | | | |
| | Protestants | | Catholics | | Protestants | | Catholics | |
Party supporters of the	SPD	CDU	SPD	CDU	SPD	CDU	SPD	CDU
Church attendance								
Regular	8%	16%	27%	57%	13%	32%	37%	77%
Irregular	19	27	33	16	31	28	35	15
Seldom	43	41	16	15	42	29	21	6
Never	30%	16%	24%	12%	14%	11%	7%	2%
	(152)	(37)	(119)	(85)	(139)	(62)	(84)	(142)

an indication that such support is due not only to religious factors, but probably to some of those described by McKenzie for the Tory worker. The non-religious base of a religious party obviously limits its ability to follow a decidedly clerical course. There is also a CDU vote coming from nonpracticing Catholics. They form part of a Catholic subculture that extends to those not practicing, something that we would not find in France or even Italy. Even so, the majority of the Catholic CDU supporters are Catholics attending church regularly.[16] The religious Protestants—going regularly or irregularly to church—are a less significant part of the working-class CDU support. The lower proportion of support for the CDU coming from religious Protestants is a result of their greater secularization and indicates that factors other than religious loyalties account for such support. The fact that the SPD could get considerable support from religious Protestants shows that, at the same level of practice among them, the inclination to the CDU—while existing—is less intensive than among Catholics. The favorable position of the CDU among the Catholic working class is largely due to greater religiosity, but not alone to that factor, since among those never going to church the difference between Protestants and Catholics persists (9 versus 19 percent among men, 15 versus 17 percent among women, supporting the CDU).

The comparison between the workers supporting the SPD, CDU, and the bourgeois parties—FDP, DP, and BP—shows how the latter are clearly different in terms of social characteristics, while the religious base of the CDU allows it to penetrate to a greater or lesser extent into all segments of the German working class. Changes between 1953 and 1957 may have modified this, increasing SPD appeal to the more privileged core of the industrial working class—the skilled workers.[17]

Data about political involvement (e.g., intention to vote, talking politics, concern about the outcome of the election, general information, understanding the democratic party system, and so on) show that the differences between workers supporting the SPD and the CDU are minor—slightly in favor of the SPD supporters. On the contrary, the differences in "quality of the electorate" between both SPD and CDU and the bourgeois workers are quite marked, to the disadvantage of the deviants from appropriate class-voting. The religious subculture, the ideological and political versatility, and to some extent the regional diversity in the party organization, of the CDU indicate its working-class electorate should not be subject to cross-pressures, that in the case of the bourgeois-party supporters lead to some withdrawal from politics. The CDU working-class vote is not a traditionalist vote, and it might be argued that it is not an inadequate vote in terms of class and in view of the position of the party—or at least its perception by part of its working class constituency.

Other Bases of Differentiation Within the Working Class

We cannot discuss in detail the interesting internal differentiation within the German working class—by skill, income, size of plant, place of residence, unemployment experiences and feelings of job security, work satisfaction, social origin—and the overlapping of these bases of differentiation with each other and with the religious cleavages, as well as with their organizational activation through the trade unions.[18] We shall limit ourselves to noting that the difference between SPD and CDU workers—among men—is only to a small degree related to such social and positional factors, which often are in turn correlated with religious differences.

The male skilled workers in 1953 represented 47 percent of the SPD support (among male workers) and 44 percent among the CDU, and up to 51 percent among the bourgeois-party sympathizers. (The proportions of unskilled were 16, 19, and 19 percent). Among the SPD supporters 13 percent earned over 400 Deutsche Mark, and among those of the CDU close to 10 percent; yet the underprivileged (under 150 Mark) were respectively 13 and 20 percent. The proportions working in small and large plants differentiate the two parties considerably more: 18 percent of the SPD workers were in plants employing fewer than twenty persons, compared with 27 percent of the CDU; and the largest plants—over 1,000 workers—employed 28 percent SPD and 16 percent CDU members. Here the difference between the two major parties is in the same direction as that between them and the bourgeois parties, but considerably less markedly so, since these find almost half their supporters in the small shops and only 5 percent in the giant plants employing 24 percent of the male industrial labor force (in the sample). CDU workers are more likely to live in small towns (47 percent in those under 5,000 persons, compared with 38 percent of the SPD), but we also find them in the big industrial cities of over 100,000 (24 versus 36 percent).

Upper- and Middle-Class Politics

In previous pages we already stressed how socioeconomic cleavages were central to the German party system, with around 50 percent of the workers favoring the Socialist parties and only 21 percent of the urban middle and upper classes supporting them, while they gave around 50 percent of their support to the CDU. Now we can point to a few internal differences within this group, defined as Bonham,[19] analyzing British surveys, put it: "With universal suffrage, only numbers count. The votes of the 'upper class' are too few to count. It is the working class and all the rest. For better or worse, or for want of a better name, the 'rest' are called the middle class."

All those who are neither workers nor farmers are even a more heterogeneous aggregate, and many internal differences and cleavages in their interests, mentality, and ideology can be found that are reflected in political cleavages. Distinctions like salaried middle class versus independents, new versus old middle class, have a sociological tradition behind them. Occupational distinctions like upper and lower white-collar employees, civil servants, free professionals, businessmen and industrialists, and artisans to some extent overlap with those more theoretical distinctions, even when a careful sociological analysis would have to allocate different sectors of such groups to one or another, rather than equate the first two with the salaried middle class and the last two with the independents.[20] The free professions—contrary to what their own name says—are today largely salaried rather than independent, but, because of their traditional place in the *Bildung und Besitz* (education and property) status order, they probably are closer to the "old" middle class. There is no place to refer here to the important sociological efforts of the early thirties—particularly of Theodore Geiger—[21] to give meaning to these classifications and to explore their political implications in face of the rise of Nazism. Sigmund Neumann's characterization of the different bourgeois parties in relation to the complex status and interest differentiation of middle and upper classes is also significant.[22] The greater homogeneity of these strata in the postwar era is reflected in the dominance of the CDU among both salaried and independents, with approximately one-half of their preferences. The different orientation of the salaried and the independents could not be better shown than by the opposite position they take toward the SPD and the bourgeois parties (FDP, DP, BP): one-fourth of the salaried for the SPD and less than a sixth for the bourgeois, while one-third of the independents favors the bourgeois and one-sixth supports the SPD (*Table 7*).

To the extent that the SPD, as a "people's party," can speak for the middle classes, it can also do so for the "salaried," from whom it receives almost

Table 7—Proportion of the Support of the "Salaried" and "Independent" Middle Class Going to Various Parties: 1953

Party Preference	"Salaried" Middle Class	Independent Middle Class
SPD	25%	15%
CDU	49	44
FDP	11	19
DP, BP	6	9
Other	4	8
BHE	4	5
Total preferences	100%	100%
	(671)	(412)
No preference	19%	23%
TOTAL	(831)	(534)

three-quarters of the urban nonmanual preferences (*Table 8*). The CDU's share of the two middle classes is fairly close to their respective position in the society (61 versus 39 percent in the sample, 64 versus 36 percent in the CDU constituency). The FDP, DP, and particularly, the BP depend for their urban middle-class support on the independents to a larger extent than their

Table 8—Proportion of the Support of Various Parties Coming from the "Salaried" and "Independent" Middle Class

	SUPPORT WITHIN THE URBAN MIDDLE CLASS COMING FROM		
	"Salaried"	"Independent"	
SPD	73%	27%	(232)
CDU	64	36	(514)
FDP	49	51	(155)
DP, BP	48	52	(73)
Other	65	35	(34)
BHE	59	41	(51)
No preference	57	43	(282)
Sample	61%	39%	(1341)

presence in the population would indicate. That the CDU is the "positionally adequate" choice for the "salaried" can be deduced from the fact that between Bundestag elections (1949, 1953, and 1957) there were fewer shifts among them from the CDU to the bourgeois parties or to indecision, than the number of shifts among salaried supporters of the bourgeois parties. On the other side, despite the general trend toward the CDU, the independents were more loyal to the bourgeois parties than to the CDU (*Table 9*).

"White-Collar" Politics

In 1931 Theodor Geiger wrote:

> The ideological disorientation of the middle strata is closely connected with the self-imposed isolation of "party socialism" . . . . I maintain that

Socialism is the adequate and necessary social movement of the non-owners (proletarian stratum). But this stratum changes in size and internal composition. This has to lead to new shades in class awareness and to changes in the socialist conception of society, and finally even to the formulation of new socialist doctrines.[23]

Thoughts like this and a lively discussion of the topic, plus the awareness that "Success or defeat, mainly of the Social-Democratic order, will depend upon the results of this influence upon the middle strata," as Adenauer himself put it in 1946,[24] led the SPD to make great efforts to change its image from a Marxist, working-class, nonnationalistic party, just to appeal to these strata. In the absence of survey data for the Weimar Republic comparable with those for the present, it is impossible to judge the success of such efforts.

Table 9—"Party Loyalty" (That Is, 1953 Preferences of
Those Who in 1949 Voted for a Party) Among "Salaried"
and "Independent" Middle-Class Men

PREFERENCE, 1949:	SALARIED MIDDLE CLASS BP/DP/FDP	CDU	INDEPENDENT MIDDLE CLASS BP/DP/FDP	CDU
Preference, 1953:				
BP, DP, FDP	64%	8%	76%	12%
CDU	10	82	7	73
SPD	8	3	3	9
All Other	5	3	3	6
No preference	13	4	10	6
	100%	100%	100%	100%
	(39)	(91)	(25)	(66)

Source: UNESCO Institute Survey, 1953.

At this point we might discuss some changes in the social composition of the new middle class, its relative social position, and its cultural and ideological climate, which should be kept in mind in trying to apply the ideas of the thirties to the present, but that would take too much space.[25] A more practical alternative is to discuss a few empirical findings on the politics of lesser white-collar workers compared to that of manual workers.

The main point of departure for any consideration of the politics of the salaried middle class is its social and economic heterogeneity, as seen in the following polarities: public as against private employment; civil-service status versus government employment without such status; highly qualified managerial functions versus routine office work; salaries below those of manual workers and above those of many independents; work in small offices and in giant enterprises like banks; work within industrial or commercial organizations; being union members, members of professional associations, or unorganized. Crosscutting these structural differences there are often great differences in background: social origin, and education, as well as ideological traditions. And all this in turn may be cut by the religious cleavages, whose importance we have already stressed. Furthermore, the existence of a large number of employed women and their relative position on all these variables has to be kept in mind in any careful analysis. Let us apply the tools of multivariate survey analysis to one segment of this stratum: the lower white-collar employees, the *"nichtleitende Angestellte."*

An obvious but often neglected fact is that women constitute a large proportion of the lower white-collar force and that they generally take jobs where the "status and skill proletarization" proceeds fastest.[26] Those positions where work alienation and consequent political protest would be greatest are to a large extent held by persons for whom the occupational world is only a transitional phase before or after marriage and whose social status is largely derived from the male family heads. White-collar employed women, particularly when single, give less support to the SPD and more to the CDU than men, even when this advantage gets partly lost in their greater political apathy. Interestingly enough, the bourgeois parties receive the same proportion among men and women.

Within the urban middle class the correlation of income and conservative party preference is generally high. The question can be asked: Is the lesser appeal of the SPD to persons who in some respects are in the same situation of dependency toward an employer as workers due to a different economic position? A comparison of the income distribution for male manual and lower white-collar workers shows that while 33 percent of the manuals made less than 250 DM a month and only 18 percent of the white collar, not more than 14 percent of the manuals reported over 400 DM and 31 percent of the *Angestellten*. Even limiting the comparison to skilled workers, 24 percent earned under 250 DM and only 19 percent above.[27] The civil servants tend to be, on the average, in higher-income groups than those in private employment. At the same level of income, blue-collar workers are more leftist than their colleagues wearing white collars, who in turn are considerably less likely to support the bourgeois parties than independents—mainly businessmen and artisans—of the same income level. Since the dispersion of incomes within broadly defined classifications makes comparisons risky, it is best to take those earning between 150 and 399 DM in the shop and the office: among the shop workers the SPD receives 49 percent of the preferences, the CDU 20 percent, and the bourgeois parties 7 percent, and 18 percent express no preference; while among the office employees the proportions are 37, 35, 18, and 9 percent. That means that SPD and CDU are almost equally strong, and that the conservative parties receive almost half the support of the Socialists, rather than one-seventh, as among the workers.

If an equalization of incomes between the "black coated" workers and those in "overalls" does not eliminate the difference in politics, what other factors in the work situation may account for it? One important privilege of employees was their greater job security. However, the difference in feeling of job security between them and the workers, particularly skilled workers and those of the same income, is not great. Both among men and women those feeling insecure are more favorable to the SPD.

The relation between work satisfaction and political behavior is still an unexplored area. Using a number of questions about the job, we developed an index of satisfaction,[28] and we found that among blue-collar workers those satisfied and dissatisfied were almost equally favorable to the SPD, with those most satisfied slightly more so *(Table 10)*. Among office workers, however, those dissatisfied are considerably more in favor of the opposition, particularly among the men. Since a somewhat larger proportion of white- than blue-collar employees are among the satisfied—even limiting the comparison to the skilled, and particularly among women—this contributes to the overall lesser opposition to the existing order. Comparing groups of the same income, particularly in the medium- and upper-income groups, the employees give more favorable responses about their work (for example, among those making over 400 DM, 15 percent of the manuals are dissatisfied, but only 3 percent of the nonmanuals), and this contributes somewhat to the political position of the group. However, the differences in satisfaction are not marked enough—particularly among men—to account for it. Furthermore, even among those of the same income and the same level of satisfaction, the SPD appeal among employees is still significantly lower.

Table 10—Percentage SPD and KPD Support Among Employed Male "Blue" Collar and Percentage SPD Among "White" Collar Workers of the Same Income Level and Similar Satisfaction with Their Work

	INCOME						
	250–399 DM				Over 400 DM		
	"White"		"Blue"		"White"		"Blue"
Satisfied	23%	(22)	64%	(96)	17%	(18)	61%	(33)
Less satisfied	47%	(19)	65%	(81)	29%	(7)	57%	(28)

Incidentally, the sensitivity to dissatisfaction among the middle-class strata and not among workers was also found by Centers in his study of the United States.[29] Dahlström in Sweden also found that income made little difference in the political preferences of workers but affected those of white-collar employees considerably.[30] The greater political heterogeneity of this stratum is not only due to its greater internal differentiation but also to the greater sensitivity to differences in position among white-collar employees than among manual workers.

The social relations growing out of the work situation—the rates of interaction with fellow workers and superiors and the communication channels between personal and employers—are closely related to political behavior.[31] The whole literature on the new middle class has focused on this aspect to stress how different the relations between boss and employee are from those in a factory. The more similar both situations, the more similar should the politics be. The size of the enterprise of employment is a good indicator of different types of social relations on the job. The larger the enterprise the more impersonal the contacts with superiors, the greater the need for trade union representation, the greater the chances for informal political communication among colleagues rather than with superiors (we have data to prove all these points) and consequently the likelihood of supporting the SPD. It is interesting to note that the bourgeois support comes from those employed in small enterprises; the CDU makes great gains in those of from ten to one hundred employees; and the SPD is strongest in the even larger ones. These differences in politics according to size become quite small among those affiliated with a trade union, but are quite remarkable among nonmembers, who naturally are found more often in small work places. Some may be tempted, following C. W. Mills,[32] to blame the alienating conditions of modern work in the large offices and salesrooms, but our data—tentative as they are—do not seem to support such an interpretation. Even so, with similar feelings about work, the larger employers create a climate of opinion in favor of the SPD.

THE HANDWERK. For an analysis like this there are in most countries groups deserving special attention because of their numbers, special position in the social structure, ideological traditions, degree of organization—be it the Italian *braccianti,* the French civil servants, Norwegian fishermen—something that has to be taken into account in planning cross-national studies. Among the independents in the old German middle class, the self-employed craftsmen or artisans for several of these reasons occupy a distinctive position. In most societies they are considered and consider themselves either skilled workers or small businessmen, i.e., little fellows with more or less income and skill but without a specific status consciousness, ideology, or organization. Complex historical and political circumstances have made this group, a distinctive survival of preindustrial society, quite well adapted to modern society, even to assimilating some new groups of the industrial order. We have no space to describe in detail its social position, changes in it, organizational mobilization, the strong religious traditions, particularly among Catholics, its satisfaction with work conditions compared to small business, and so forth. Here we can only note that the members are very reluctant to support the SPD, giving it much less support than skilled workers with the same income (13 versus 56 percent among those making 150 to 339 DM and 11 and 56 percent among those with over 400 DM), and even less than small businessmen (26 percent among those making under 400 DM as against 10 percent). On the other hand, they are less pro-bourgeois parties than small businessmen of the same income and position, giving their strong support to the CDU and strongly supporting its policies.

"Upper Stratum" Politics

In our analysis we have attempted to define an upper stratum, including free professionals, businessmen, civil servants, and upper white-collar employees, who had at least completed the *mittlere Reife* (approximately socially equivalent to a United States high-school diploma) and had a monthly personal income of over 250 DM. This group was the upper fifth of the urban middle class as defined above. Its members manifested—as we could expect—a higher level of information, political self-interest, concern about the election outcome, sense of political efficacy, and political participation than the remainder of their class. Politically the group was considerably more inclined to support the FDP (28 percent) almost as much as the CDU (29 percent) and gave little (13 percent) support to the SPD, a few (9 percent) expressing no party preference. This was true for both Catholics and Protestants, with the Catholics naturally more heavily CDU and the Protestants more FDP (up to 35 percent). Within this minority upper stratum, in turn socioeconomic differences were related to politics, with those making over 600 DM giving 37 percent of their support to the FDP compared to 10 percent among those making 250–399. The different nature of the FDP and the DP–BP is reflected in the strength of these parties in the two income subgroups just mentioned: 4

and 10 percent respectively. The upper bourgeoisie in Germany, while giving one third or more of its support to the Demo-Christians, gives considerable support to the Liberal-Conservative party, the FDP, and not to the more petty bourgeois, rural, regional, reactionary parties (which get among them the same share as among the remaining middle class). Our data confirm the conclusions of Dogan for the same group in Italy and France.[33]

The Rural Vote

One of the characteristics Germany shares with other advanced industrial societies is a decreasing proportion of the labor force engaged in agriculture. Like other northern and central European countries, its rural population is largely composed of independent farmers, rather than by a large number of farm laborers or even tenants. This, together with historical factors, explains the weakness of class politics among the rural population in contrast to western and southern Europe (see *Table 11* for a comparison with France

Table 11—Party Preferences of the Rural Sector in Germany (1953), France (1952), and Italy (1958)

	GERMANY			FRANCE			ITALY	
	Farmers	Farm Laborers		Farmers	Farm Laborers		Farmers	Farm Laborers
KPD	0.5%	—	PCF	9%	47%	PCI } PSI }	22%	69%
SPD	5	34%	SFIO	7	19	PSDI	4	2
FDP	10		RGR	19	9			
Z	1	—						
CDU/CSU	59	40	MRP	14	5	DC	62	19
BP	12	15	Modérés	28	6			
DP	6	—	RPF	23%	14%			
OTHER	3	3				Other	12%	10%
BHE	3 %	8%						
	(325)	(39)		(2,874,000)	(859,000)		(8,100,000)	(2,900,000)

The German data are from the UNESCO Institute Survey, the French from estimates made on the basis of a sample survey of 1952 applied to the rural electorate of 1951 in the chapter on "Le monde paysan et la politique" in Jacques Fauvet and Henri Mendras, *Les paysans et la politique dans la France contemporaine* (Paris: A. Colin, 1958), p. 18, and those for Italy from Mattei Dogan, "Interpretazione del voto agricolo," *Politica Agraria* (September 1962, Table 3, p. 9).

and Italy). On the other side, religious loyalties of the Catholics (in the case of the *Zentrum* and now the CDU), regionalistic politics in Bavaria and Hannover, and in the past the dominance of the Junker-led Conservative parties, have made the appearance of "peasant" or "farmers' " parties of the Scandinavian or eastern European type impossible, despite sporadic attempts in this direction. The increased awareness of the conflict of interest between east Elbian large-scale farming and peasant agriculture and the incapacity of the SPD to channel agrarian protest led many farmers—in the early thirties—to the Nazis who appealed to them with a romantic peasantist antiurban ideology.[34] This was particularly true for the Protestant peasant-farmers. The postwar period has brought important changes: the disappearance of the Junker-dominated East, the unification of agricultural pressure groups, the weakening by the electoral system of regional parties—and all have contributed to consolidation of the rural support behind the CDU. The farmers are in a sense the politically most homogeneous group in the German electorate; however, all the indicators of political involvement, information, commitment to the party system, and so on suggest that this CDU identification is based largely—except for some of the Catholic farmers—on interest politics: the awareness that the support for splinter parties is likely to be ineffective in a highly industrialized world and that access to power is best assured by ties with the dominant party. The farm laborers, isolated as farmhands in mostly peasant-owned farms, despite their dissatisfactions, cannot be easily reached by the SPD, and anyway their number makes them insignificant. Hence, it is not surprising that they should be the most apathetic occupational group in the electorate.

RELIGION AND POLITICS

West Germany is numerically a dominantly Protestant country (52 percent in 1950) with a very self-conscious and organized Catholic minority (44 percent), dominant in part of the country. The secularized minority is not negligible (11 percent never going to church and 24 percent rarely), is found largely among Protestants (13 and 36 percent respectively, compared with 8 and 12 percent among Catholics), but has not been aggressively laic or anticlerical, compared with France or Italy. There are appreciable differences in religious practice between workers and the bourgeoisie (among male workers 33 percent of the Protestants and 40 percent of the Catholics are church-goers, compared to 50 and 59 percent respectively of the urban middle-class men). Although the gap between classes in Germany is similar to the gap between classes in France, the absolute level of religiosity is greater in Germany.[35] Owing to a number of historical circumstances—among them the minority status in parts of the country and in the Hohenzollern Reich—the Catholic Church did not become identified with the alliance of throne and altar, the wealthy and powerful, and relatively early gave up many of the romantic corporativist illusions for a more pragmatic and democratic social action program. The antireligious element in Nazi totalitarianism put the churches in the opposition, and this and their organizational strength made them one of the few legitimate social forces in the postwar era, a situation quite different from that in other European countries where anti-Communism contributed to the identifying of the Church with authoritarian solutions.

Due to all this, religious cleavages are neither deep, nor rigidly institutionalized (as in the Netherlands), nor overlapping with the class structure, and secularism-clericalism cannot amount to a dominant rift between parties. The "parity"—*Parität*—between Protestants and Catholics in allocating offices is a compromise fostered by an interconfessional party. The long tradition of a powerful Catholic party—the *Zentrum*—and the high degree of organization of social Catholicism make it a powerful force with strong loyalties among its members, but one that is still aware of its minority status. This leads to a certain restraint and tolerance (compared with countries like Italy and Spain). At the same time it has a "majority vocation"—due to a higher degree of activation—that once the postwar crisis allowed it to realize the long-sought breakout from isolation (*aus dem Turm heraus*),[36] led to the fusion with the few politically conscious Protestant leaders of the *Christlich-soziale Volksdienst* and Christian trade union leaders to form the CDU.

Table 12—Party Preference of Protestants and Catholics by Occupation (of the Respondent or the Head of the Household): 1953

	Urban workers Protes. Cath.		Salaried P.	C.	Independ. P.	C.	Total Middle cl. P.	C.	Farmers P.	C.	Total sample P.	C.
SPD	43%	29%	22%	17%	14%	10%	19%	14%	5%	1%	28%	19%
Z	—	3	—	1	a	6	a	3	—	2	—	3
CDU	14	31	31	52	24	44	29	49	34	60	23	42
FDP	4	3	13	5	19	11	15	8	12	3	10	4
BP	1	2	a	3	a	5	4	3	6	13	1	5
DP	3	1	3	3	5	2	—	3	11	—	4	2
Other, incl. KPD	3	3	3	1	4	1	4	1	2	3	3	2
BHE	5	5	3	4	5	3	4	4	5	—	4	4
None	27%	23%	24%	18%	28%	18%	25%	15%	26%	18%	27%	20%
	(730)	(779)	(429)	(353)	(245)	(276)	(674)	(629)	(209)	(204)	(1681)	(1649)

Source: UNESCO Institute Survey, 1953.
a Less than 1%.
b Includes student apprentices and farm laborers.

That collaboration has helped to tone down clericalism, so that religion can serve as a force of social integration, while at the same time institutional loyalties, latent tensions, and occasional conflicts, from patronage to school issues, do not allow the religious cleavages to disappear from politics. The

Table 13—Religious Composition of the Support of German Parties in 1953: Men and Women

	Z	BP	CDU	BHE	SPD	KPD	Other	DP	FDP	No Preference	Sample
Catholics	92%	81%	63%	45%	38%	37%	35%	29%	28%	39%	48%
Protestants	6	19	35	51	55	53	56	67	69	56	48%
Other			1	3	1		3		2	1	1
No religion	2%		1%	1%	6%	10%	7%	4%	1%	4%	3%
	(53)	(95)	(1096)	(142)	(836)	(19)	(72)	(100)	(239)	(814)	(3472)

open support by the Catholic Church of the CDU as a factor in the mobilization of many voters should not be forgotten. It would not be practical politics for a "Christian" party to renounce the mobilization of some its followers, many quite apolitical, in the name of the defense of Christianity, nor for the other parties—particularly the Liberals—to give up fully one of their bases of distinctiveness. In fact, the cultural policies have formed a convenient issue for the FDP to differentiate itself from the dominant coalition partner in Bonn—without making cooperation impossible, since, fortunately, cultural issues are not the competence of the federal government—and to appeal to the Protestant secularized educated classes.[37]

Religious loyalties are a source of moderate cleavage among parties and at the same time facilitate, as we will see, consensus across party and class lines.

The CDU is an interdenominational Christian Democratic party whose supporters (as of 1953) were around 63 percent Catholic and 35 percent Protestant,[38] with the most loyal voters being slightly more Catholic and its party members even more so (73 percent in one estimate and 83 percent in another),[39] but which, for the sake of unity, makes an effort to give a proportional share in offices and candidacies to both (62 percent of the members of the Bundestag were Catholics). However, the unique interdenominational character should not obscure the importance of the Catholics and the old *Zentrum* tradition for the party.

The SPD has almost the inverse denominational composition: among its supporters 38 percent are Catholics, 55 percent Protestants, and a significant proportion (6 percent) report no affiliation; among the party members[40] respectively 31, 48, and 21 percent.

It could be argued, however, that many SPD supporters, while identifying themselves as either Protestants or Catholics, are actually nonpracticing. Actually, the SPD support from Catholics seldom or never going to church (13 percent) and Protestants never going (11 percent) plus the 6 percent with no religion, constitutes only 30 percent of its total, while Catholics attending regularly (12 percent) and Protestants attending at least irregularly (20 percent) add up to 32 percent (the remainder being irregular Catholics, 12 percent, and seldom-going Protestants, 24 percent).[41]

The FDP is a dominantly Protestant party (67 percent of its supporters). Most of these Protestants are secularized, with 44 percent of them going to church only infrequently or never. Here the FDP plays an important role in the system as an alternative to the CDU and as a competition that can indirectly protect the CDU from one-sided pressures, e.g., from Catholic clerical elements. Incidentally, the same would be said for the FDP as an alternative to the CDU in class politics, particularly for the independent middle class.

Religion and Politics in Comparative Perspective

To put these data into proper perspective we can compare them with the Dutch parties, where the KVP receives practically all of its support from Catholics, and the Anti-Revolutionary and Christian Historical Parties similarly from Protestants of greater or lesser orthodoxy, while the Socialists (PvdA) receive 8 percent from Catholics and 61 percent from Protestants—almost all *Hervormden*—and 31 percent from those with no religion.[42]

A comparison between the Catholic support of the SPD and that for the French Left—PCF (Communists) and SFIO (Socialists)—also shows that the clericalism-secularism cleavage can never be as deep as in Latin Europe. Among the PCF supporters 33 percent admit no religion and of the 64 percent who admit being Catholics only 11 percent—that is 7 percent of the total support of the party—are practicing. Among the SFIO supporters 11 percent declare no affiliation and only 14 percent admit being *pratiquants*. In contrast, 33 percent of the Catholic SPD supporters are regular church-goers.[43] The differences in religiosity and, at the same time, in the political climate between the two countries becomes even more apparent: if we compare only workers, 41 percent of West German Catholic men go regularly to church, compared with 25 percent of the French (among women 60 and 39 percent). Turning to the politics of French and German Catholic male workers, we find west of the border a much closer relation between religiosity and politics (*Table 14*). Among Germans never going to church (17 percent),

Table 14—Party Preferences of West German and French Catholic Male Workers of Comparable Religiosity

	Regularly	Irregularly	Seldom	Never	Total
WEST GERMANY					
SPD	34%	56%	46%	63%	47%
KPD	1	—	2	2	1
CDU-Z	54	21	29	19	36
Other	11	23	23	16	16
TOTAL	100%	100%	100%	100%	100%
	(95)	(70)	(41)	(46)	(252)
FRANCE					
PCF	—		22%	44%	24%
SFIO	15		48	38	33
MRP	54		—	5	21
Other	31		26	10	20
TOTAL	100%		100%	100%	100%
	(26)		(23)	(39)	(99)

Notes: A great deal of caution is needed in interpreting this table. It is based only on those giving information on their religious practice and on their party preference. The questions were phrased quite differently and consequently different categories had to be combined to make the levels of religious practice roughly comparable. Furthermore, it should be kept in mind that the French data refer only to the baptized population—and a certain proportion of the second-generation working class unreligious may not be baptized—(in another survey among French male workers, 17 percent answered "without religion" rather than "Catholic but not practicing"). This would account—among things—for the low PCF support compared to the SFIO.

The French data were kindly made available by the IFOP through the courtesy of Prof. Jean Stoetzel. I want to express here my most sincere gratitude to him and the IFOP staff for their cooperation in secondary analysis of their data.

more than half support the SPD and 19 percent the CDU or Z; among the French (40 percent of baptized Catholic male workers) almost one-half support the PCF and more than one-third the SFIO (in a sample that underestimates the working-class support for the Left). Among those attending "seldom," the proportions showed similar differences. On the other side the minority of religious French workers gave no support to the PCF and very little to the SFIO, while their German counterparts gave one-third of their preferences to the CDU or Z.

The bitterness of the clerical-laicist conflict due to the overlap in social bases of the major parties in Germany has to be much less intensive. The conflict of interests between the bourgeoisie and the working class is not intensified by religious tensions that contributed so much to the crisis of Spanish and even Italian democracy.

CONSENSUS ACROSS LINES
OF CLEAVAGE

Introduction

We have already noted how the overlapping social bases of parties—good Catholic Socialists and not too religious CDU supporters—limited logically the freedom of the parties to follow radical policies consistent with their dominant ideological traditions. This is one of the ways in which consensus in the society becomes possible. In the following pages we want to present somewhat more direct and systematic evidence on the importance of the "web of group affiliations," the *Krezung sozialer Kreise,* of which Simmel wrote, for stable democratic politics.[44]

Political democracy implies the expression of the conflict of the self-interests of different groups—of the cleavages in the society—but also requires that those conflicts take place within an institutional framework and in a way that would not make impossible a process of consent to authoritative decisions. Whatever the cleavages, there must be, for at least a limited time, an acceptance of the government resulting from the election as the legitimate authority.[45]

Consensus has many aspects: (1) Consensus on basic institutional arrangements—the "agreement on fundamentals" or "legitimacy," a certain trust in those contending for power however much one may disagree with their policies; within the system of legal democratic authority this legitimacy is based on the belief that they will accept "the rules of the game." (2) Consensus on certain minimum qualifications of the political leadership, despite disagreement on specific policies. Finally, (3) some consensus on issues that have been decided and closed. Outside the political consensus—and to some extent underlying it—there has to be a minimum of consensus on certain social institutions and values. The difficult problem that social science has not even started to study empirically is how much consensus? How much in scope, intensity, spread across cleavage lines, on each of the aspects mentioned.

Once elected, a democratic government, to be legitimate and effective, should be able to rely on a basis of support fulfilling, to a greater or lesser extent, the following conditions:

1. It should not be limited to the supporters of the party, or coalition of parties, in power. A significant minority of the opposition approving of the government policies "in general"—while believing that their party could do it better or that their own particular interests would be better served by their party—will facilitate political compromise and make attacks on the legitimacy of the opponent a dangerous weapon.

2. No important basis of cleavage in the society—socioeconomic, religious, ethnic, regional, and others—can, without danger, be unanimous or nearly unanimous in its rejection of the government. The degree of "near unanimity" tolerable will depend on the nature of the cleavage, its numerical strength, degree of organization and activation, the intensity of its feelings, and the relations between the bases of cleavage and the party system. To give an ex-

ample, an intensely felt regional-ethnic opposition uniting people across class lines can be very disturbing even when it represents only a minority of the total electorate. Under certain circumstances the links between such social bases of alienation and key institutions like the army, the bureaucracy, and such, become almost decisive.

3. The leader of a coalition government should have a strong position in his own party and not be threatened by large-scale shifts to other parties if he follows certain policies, enters particular coalitions, and so forth. The leader of a dominant party in a multiparty coalition system needs perhaps more than a leader in a two-party system to have his party behind him to keep the coalition together and himself in a leadership position.

4. The consensus on the government across party and other lines of cleavage should not be so great as to lead to the absence of meaningful issues, to the oblivion of the distinction between "ins" and "outs," and with it, political stagnation and apathy. The dangers of coalitions based on parties representing almost the whole electorate—outside of crisis situations—would fall under this (the Austrian case would deserve research in this context).[46]

These propositions are formulated with considerable hesitation since they stand on very different levels of generality and have not been systematically put to any test. Only cross-national comparative research, covering different types of societies and political systems, in situations of normality and of crisis, could advance our knowledge in this area. Here we will attempt to show how a secondary analysis of survey data can touch on these problems. The meaning of the data on Germany would be considerably enhanced if we had comparable tabulations for other countries, and for Germany at different periods of time.

The Federal Republic was born as a truncated state with limited sovereignty, evoking little enthusiasm and interest. The low consensus on the new state was reflected in the low interest in the new constitution, and the creation of the state itself (40 percent indifferent about the fundamental law and only 51 percent in favor of the creation, with 23 percent against).[47] Even the symbolic issues like the national flag divided—perhaps not so intensely as in the past—the people, with a majority of those with an opinion not identifying with the state flag. Trend data of the Institut für Demoskopie show how the identification with the system has been growing. The present national colors in 1949 were preferred to the Prussian black-white-red by 20 versus 37 percent; by 1956 the proportions had changed to 34 versus 25 percent.[48] When asked: "Do you think it is better for a country to have one party, so that there exists the maximum of unity or several parties, so that different opinions can be freely expressed?" in 1951 and 1956 the responses were, respectively: several, 61 and 76 percent; one, 22 and 11 percent; no party at all, 5 and 2 percent; and no opinion 12 and 11 percent.[49] Another question touches the legitimacy of the leadership, as the previous one dealt with that of the system, by asking if "the deputies in Bonn represent in the first place the interests of the population, or do they have other interests that are more important to them?" The first alternative was chosen in 1951 by 30 percent and in 1956 by 51 percent and the second respectively by 39 and 26 percent. As part of the consensus on the rules of the game, we can consider not only the rejection at the polls of parties not abiding by them, but the agreement on the undesirability of extremist opposition: when asked simultaneously about outlawing the KPD (Communists) and SRP (neo-Nazis) the proportions were almost identical, even when on separate polls the tolerance for the neo-Nazis tended to be slightly higher.[50] It would have been interesting to present these trend data broken as to various groups in the population and to relate the figures with the groups' experiences in the last decade. Such an analysis could have tested the proposition that the *efficacy* of a political system—that is the ability to satisfy the needs and expectations of its citizens—contributes to its *legitimacy*—the belief in its desirability and right to make decisions and to demand loyalty. As a comparable analysis of French survey data for the Fourth Republic could show how ineffectiveness—particularly in the Algerian question—contributed to the crisis of legitimacy in 1958.

The data on a relatively simple question about the Adenauer government will allow us to explore somewhat the "sociology of political consensus." The question was "Do you in general agree or disagree with the government policy of Adenauer?" The trend data on this question from the Institut für Demoskopie show that at the time—the third quarter of 1953—the approval (40 percent of the population, 73 percent of those having an opinion either way) was close to an all-time high, and that level was maintained with some slumps until early in 1956. However, in the period from the second quarter of 1953 until 1961 the agreement only once went below 40 percent, and the disagreement generally stayed between 20 and 25 percent, reaching a maximum of 30 percent and a minimum of 15 percent. We give these data to put our analysis in proper perspective: it refers to a moment of rather high support, but one that was not unique nor too far from the average for the Adenauer era.[51]

Consensus Across Party Lines

In 1953 Adenauer's government found support not only among the sympathizers in his own party, or those of the coalition partners, but also among those of minor parties outside the government, and, what is most important for the problem of consensus, in the ranks of the major opposition party. Approximately one-fourth of the SPD supporters expressed agreement, and only 36 percent rejected his policies (*Table 15*).

We can look at the same data in the other direction; among those agreeing with Adenauer in general, only 55 percent supported the CDU and 67 percent the coalition parties, while the SPD received 13 percent of their preferences.

Adenauer could count on a strong support within his own party (70 percent of all those preferring the CDU) and few opponents in it, something that may seem obvious, but might not be so if we consider the heterogeneous base of the party. In the coalition partners—the FDP and DP—we find a certain ambivalence that manifests itself in a larger number of "undecided" and "no opinion" in the FDP (the more noteworthy given the higher educational level) and in disagreement or "no opinion" among DP supporters. Given the weight of the CDU among the coalition supporters, the approval among them was 64 percent versus minorities of 5 percent critical and 11 percent undecided. If we turn to the overall attitude of the SPD supporters, the overt disapproval was 36 percent—equal to 62 percent of those with a decided opinion either way—and 22 percent gave a general approval. Among the more opinionated men, only little more than one-half of the SPD supporters disagree, and fully 28 percent express approval.

Table 15—Consensus on the Policies of the Adenauer Government Among the Supporters of Different Parties: Men and Women. ("Are you in general in agreement with the government policy of Adenauer?")

	Agree	Disagree	Undecided	No opinion		
CDU	70%	2%	9%	20%	100%	(1096)
FDP	54	7	20	19		(239)
DP	39	15	14	32		(100)
Total coalition parties	64	4	11	21		(1435)
Z	51	11	15	23		(53)
BHE	38	13	15	34		(142)
BP	34	15	16	36		(95)
Other	25	45	12	18		(72)
SPD	22	36	18	24		(836)
KPD	—	63	—	37		(19)
No preference	19	10	20	51		(814)
Total	40%	15%	15%	30%		(3466)

In summary, the government had the support of the majority of the population with an opinion; its leader had his own party strongly behind him; the overt opponents in the parties forming part of the coalition were a minority; and in the major opposition party those irreconcilable with its policies were not in a majority. There was considerable consensus across party lines but not so total as to blur them.

How does this compare with other European democracies? If we look at Italy, where another Demo-Christian leader became the symbol of postwar reconstruction and the DC—like the CDU—the indispensable and dominant element in any government coalition, we find much less consensus. Taking a 1954 DOXA survey[52] after De Gasperi's death—obviously a point of maximum approval—we find that the approval on the part of the opposition was considerably lower. We could not expect more than 5 percent approval among the Communists, but that only 18 percent of the PSI should consider that in general he had acted fairly well, while 26 percent disapproved completely and another 26 percent considered that he had committed many errors that could have been avoided, shows the intensity of the Left opposition. In contrast the support among the smaller coalition parties—PSDI, PRI and PLI—contrary to what one would expect in view of the frequent crises, show more agreement than the minor partners in the Bonn government. The approval within the DC, if we consider only those with an opinion either way, was somewhat less unanimous than for Adenauer within his constituency. However, the data on both leaders suggest that one should not underestimate the consensus that the center leadership of Christian Democratic parties can achieve among their heterogeneous following.

It could be argued that the supportive consensus—to use V. O. Key's expression—for a head of government should be higher than the tolerance of those supporting the parties in power for the leadership of the opposition. The latter then would be a better measure of the degree of dissensus, and this should be particularly relevant for West Germany, where the main opposition party never has won control of the Federal government, and its legitimacy in the days of Weimar was questioned by important segments of the society. Taking the answers to a sentence-completion question about the opposition leader Ollenhauer, asked in 1957, we find 50 percent of the SPD supporters favorable, 15 percent negative, compared to 15 versus 41 percent and 35 percent without opinion among those of the CDU. Compared with a similar question about Adenauer the number of those without opinion is much higher, but also—surprisingly—SPD supporters were considerably more hostile to him (55 percent) than those of the CDU to Ollenhauer (35 percent). Among "other parties" the position of both leaders is quite similar, with a somewhat more positive response to the Chancellor.[53]

Table 16—Opinions About the Probability That the Party in Power or in Opposition Could Endanger the Country's Welfare Among Their Respective Supporters in Germany, the U.K., and Italy (June–July 1959)*

Country	Opinion	Probably Wouldn't Happen	Might Happen	Probably Would Happen	Don't Know	No.
Germany	among SPD supporters about CDU	40%	32%	12%	16%	(235)
	among CDU supporters about SPD	33	30	17	20	(334)
U.K.	among Labour supporters about Conserv.	54	28	10	8	(376)
	among Conserv. supporters about Labour	25	37	34	3	(358)
Italy	among PCI supporters about DC	4.5	20.5	43	32	(55)
	among PSI supporters about DC	22	16	27	35	(44)
	among DC supporters about PCI	3	10	57	30	(353)
	among DC supporters about PSI	8%	17%	39%	36%	(353)

* The questions were:
The . . . party now controls the national government. Do you think that its policies and activities would ever seriously endanger the country's welfare? Do you think that this probably would happen, that it might happen, or that it probably wouldn't happen?
Let me ask you about some of the parties that might some day take control of the government: if the————party were to take control of the government how likely is it to seriously endanger the country's welfare? (and the same list of alternatives).
I am indebted to S. Verba for calling these data to my attention.

How does Germany stand in comparative perspective on this consensus about a basic legitimacy of the main competitors for power? We noted already the wide support that Adenauer could find in the opposition, but there remains the question, often raised and left open by the CDU's dominance of the Federal government: Would this basic trust be extended by CDU supporters to an SPD government? Survey data cannot substitute the actual historical experience, but an hypothetical question, particularly when the responses can be compared with other countries, can be revealing. The data (*Table 16*) suggest that among CDU supporters there is a large number undecided on the question of whether or not an SPD government "could seriously endanger the country's welfare" than among British Conservatives;

but the number of those who say it "would probably happen" is twice as large—and here comes a surprise—among British Conservatives faced with the prospect of a Labour government. The contrast with the attitudes of DC supporters, not only about a PCI, but even a PSI, government, shows the range of responses in Europe to a question like this and also shows the very different relation of the two Demo-Christian parties to their opponents on the Left. It is noteworthy that, as in Germany but at a much lower level, the supporters of the Left are more willing to grant legitimacy to a DC than the latter's supporters to parties of the Left. Unfortunately, we don't have corresponding data for the past and we don't know how stable such opinions may prove under stress, but we feel the data we have form a good indicator of how the SPD—despite ugly words during the campaigns—gained legitimacy in Germany since World War II among its opponents.

Naturally, consensus across party lines is not characteristic of party members and the involved and active partisans, but of the less committed and interested followers. This is the case with the SPD attitude toward Adenauer, but even among the more partisan supporters, the rejection is not unanimous. Thus among male party members—a small minority in Germany—78 percent disagree and still 6 percent agree; among the supporters attending meetings frequently, the proportions are 71 and 12 percent; among those attending such rallies sometimes 51 and 30 percent; while among those almost never talking politics, the figures go down to 31 and 24 percent—the difference becoming very small compared to the politically interested. (In all this we have ignored those with no opinion or undecided).

Consensus Across Class Lines

Given the social bases of parties, we can also expect considerable consensus across class lines. Despite the natural occupational cleavages, in no group do those who explicitly disagree exceed 20 percent, but in some those undecided or with no opinion are sizable (*Table 17*). The approval ranges from 64 percent among free professionals to a low of 26 percent among farm laborers and 31 percent among workers. A majority of professionals, upper white-collar employees, and civil servants express approval. As we would expect in terms of their preference for the SPD, the most critical groups—combining those who disagree and those undecided—are manual workers (36 percent), farm laborers (31 percent), and lower white-collar workers. Taking only the men—obviously more opinionated—those disagreeing explicitly are fewer than 25 percent except among manual workers (31 percent), with the lower white collar exactly 25 percent. On the other side, the explicit agreement, among men, ranges from 68 percent among professionals to 32 percent among workers. These data suggest that the partisan cleavages are more marked than the "class cleavages." The crosscutting of both cleavages—as discussed previously—obviously contributes much to limit the political significance of differential positions in society.

A comparison with the De Gasperi question should be fruitful. It is not easy, however, since housewives are not included, though working women might be, and the proportions who "don't know" vary between the two countries. Taking only those who have a decided opinion either way—among the occupationally active in Italy and among men in Germany—the range is from 95 percent German professionals approving to 64 percent of the farm laborers, followed by 68 percent of lower white collar and 70 percent of manual workers; in Italy from 88 percent among employers to 49 percent among farm laborers and 54 percent among workers, 57 percent artisans, and 79 percent among employees. Clearly the polarization between workers and middle–upper-class occupations is more marked, and the hostility of the farm laborers—the *braccianti*—obviously due to their numerical importance has quite different political consequences from that of a few farmhands in Germany. But also in Italy the consensus across occupational lines is greater than across party lines.

Table 17—Consensus on the Policies of the Adenauer Government Among Different Social Strata (by Occupation of the Respondent or the Head of Household, Men and Women)

Occupation	Agree	Disagree	Undecided	No opinion		Agree Among Those with an Opinion Either Way
Free Professions	64%	5%	15%	16%	(61)	93%
Upper white collar	59	10	14	18	(153)	86
Farmers	42	8	14	36	(418)	85
Artisans	49	7	17	27	(235)	85
Civil servants	56	14	12	18	(281)	81
Businessmen	50	13	10	27	(239)	79
Lower white collar	42	15	15	28	(398)	74
Farm laborers	26	9	23	42	(65)	74
Urban workers	31%	20%	16%	33%	(1578)	61%

* The questions used were the same as in Table 16.

To summarize these comparisons, we may note that when we apply a similar method to the German and Italian data the range of approval goes:[54] Among parties—CDU 98 percent to a low of 38 percent among the SPD and 36 percent among minor opposition parties and nil among the KPD supporters; in Italy it goes from 84 percent among DC supporters to a low of 6 percent among Communists, 27 percent among the PSI, and 35 percent among the neo-Fascists. Among occupational strata the range in Germany— among men only—from 95 percent among professionals, to 64 percent among farm laborers, followed by lower white-collar workers 68 percent and manual workers 70 percent; in Italy from 88 percent among employers to 49 percent among farm laborers and 54 percent among workers. The extreme differences among occupational groups of some importance—that is, ignoring farm laborers—in Germany are 31 percentage points, in Italy 39, taking the *braccianti,* and 34 with the industrial workers.

The preceding discussion raises the issue of whether the consensus across class lines is only a reflection of partisan alignments within each group. Our data show that this is certainly not the case.

Two hypotheses can be suggested about the attitudes of supporters of a party from different strata on issues or the government's policies. One, that those deviating from the modal pattern of their group—the one most congruent with its interests or identifications—are still immersed in a *climate of opinion* favorable to the other party and, therefore, will be less decided in their identification with the positions of the party of their choice. The other, that since the deviation from the modal pattern of one's group carries with it social sanctions, those doing so can be expected to feel more strongly about issues and to be more critical of the party dominant in their group. We would expect those bringing themselves to the decision to break with their milieu to be more committed than those for whom their party choice is more a matter of tradition or habit than a conscious decision. We will call the second hypothesis the *"renegade"* hypothesis, using the term in the sense of Simmel, when he wrote:

> He exhibits a characteristic loyalty to his new political, religious, or other party. The awareness and firmness of this loyalty (other things being equal) surpass those of persons who have belonged to the party all along. . . . The special loyalty of the renegade seems to me to rest on the fact that the circumstances under which he enters the new relationship, have a longer and more enduring effect than if he had naively grown into it, so to speak, without breaking with a previous one.[55]

Let us look at some facts to see if they fit the *group climate of opinion* or the *renegade* hypothesis. How do workers supporting the CDU and salaried middle-class men supporting the same party stand toward Adenauer's government policies? And, inversely, salaried middle-class and working-class SPD supporters?

The less-decided approval of Adenauer by the working-class than salaried middle-class CDU supporters (77 versus 86 percent) would fit the *group climate* hypothesis. The same could be said about the CDU middle-class

Table 18—Consensus on the Policies of the Adenauer Government Among Men: by Occupation and Party

Workers:	Agree	Disagree	Undecided	No opinion	
SPD	22%	49 %	17 %	12%	(295)
CDU	77	2	10	11	(124)
Bourgeois parties	35	18.5	18.5	28	(43)
Salaried middle class					
SPD	22	55	15	8	(73)
CDU	86	2	5	7	(113)
Bourgeois parties	73%	12.5%	12.5%	2%	(48)

supporters who are more decided in their approval than CDU workers (*Table 18*). The greater hostility of the salaried middle-class followers of the SPD than among the workers in the same party (55 as against 49 percent disagreeing) would fit the *renegade* hypothesis. (Incidentally, the CDU workers are not more undecided or without opinion than their SPD fellow workers, something that goes against the traditional cross-pressure thesis;[56] true enough, the table shows a higher proportion of such responses among the CDU workers than among the salaried CDU supporters but this difference could be explained by the education and interest differences between workers and salaried employees. By contrast the attitude of workers favoring Bourgeois parties [FDP, DP, BP] fits better into the cross-pressure interpretation.)

Why should different hypotheses be applicable to apparently similar situations? A further task would be to specify the conditions in which one or the other would be valid. The type of specification we should look for is, like this one, suggested by the data: the higher the education and political interest of a group, the more likely it is that its deviants will act like renegades and that the group climate of opinion will be more important in the case of uneducated, uninformed, and apolitical groups. It is not by chance that the image of the renegade has been central in the history of thought and been applied not least by Michels, to members of the intelligentsia breaking away from their class or their faith. The often less politically interested Catholic worker supporting the CDU cannot but reflect the critical Socialist climate of opinion, without however being swayed away from a party supported by many of his environment and to which he has traditional loyalties bolstered by many formal and informal group pressures. The more educated civil servant or employee deviating from the dominant climate of opinion perhaps has to be more convinced of his decision.

Religion and Consensus

The Protestant-Catholic, Secularist-Clerical, cleavage contribute—as we tried to show—to the political fragmentation of Germany and toward making a two-party system along lines of class or socioeconomic cleavage unlikely. However, in European perspective those religious cleavages contributed only mildly to the cultural and political fragmentation—to use Almond's term.[57] Already then, we noted that they also act as a factor of integration, creating across class and party lines a climate of opinion that contributes to the consensus that has characterized postwar West Germany.

Overlapping group affiliations, in this case class position and religious affiliation, contribute to reduce the emotion and aggressiveness of political cleavages, without—against the cross-pressure hypothesis—leading to an escape into apathy. This "crossing of social circles" was described by Simmel when he wrote:

> The individual may add affiliations with new groups to the single affiliation which has hitherto influenced him in a pervasive and one-sided manner. The mere fact that he does so is sufficient, quite apart from the nature of the groups involved, to give him a stronger awareness of individuality in general, and at least to counteract the tendency of taking his initial affiliations for granted.[58]

The "web of group affiliations" weakens the commitment to positions of any single group, while cumulative cleavages make for rigid positions. Those whose family and friends support another party cannot be violently partisan about their divergent choice and see only evil in a party supported by those close to them.

In view of this, we would expect that Catholics in all parties will be more likely to favor the policies of a Catholic chancellor than Protestants (*Table 19*). This is actually the case except for the DP among men. Catholic men supporting the SPD and FDP—sometimes denounced as "secularist" parties in Catholic circles—do not behave as renegades but are subject to a Catholic climate of opinion. In the case of the SPD, this is true both for working-class and middle-class supporters. In the case of women—where the religious identification is much more important for the electoral decision—those who support one of the Bourgeois parties (FDP, DP) or the refugee party are less pro-Adenauer than Protestant women supporting the same parties. In their case we can say the renegade hypothesis describes the facts more adequately. It is significant that among SPD women the difference by religion is smaller than among men, but it is still there. In the case of the Bavarian Party—a party to which the Church cannot object—the same pattern persists.

Table 19—Support for Adenauer Among Various Groups by Class Religion and Political Party: Men Only

Percentage in each cell indicates proportions agreeing

		MANUAL WORKERS			
	Going to church		Not going to church		Total
CDU					
Catholics	81	(48)	73	(37)	79 (85)
Protestants	75	(16)	72	(21)	73 (37)
SPD					
Catholics	31	(32)	28	(87)	29 (119)
Protestants	32	(41)	13	(11)	18 (152)
		URBAN MIDDLE CLASS			
CDU					
Catholics	92	(77)	78	(31)	87 (108)
Protestants	83	(35)	76	(21)	80 (56)
SPD					
Catholics	50	(14)	25	(28)	33 (42)
Protestants	23	(22)	21	(33)	22 (55)

Our data allow us to go even farther, both among urban middle-class and working-class supporters of the SPD: the Catholics are more favorable to Adenauer than the Protestants, and this is true even when we compare groups of similar religious practice among workers and middle-class persons —except for regular church-going Catholic middle-class men (for them undoubtedly the SPD choice has to be a conscious one based on disagreement with the policies of the CDU government), who are slightly more hostile than the equally religious Protestant men of their class. Among the four groups compared, they are the only ones who act like renegades.

On the other side among CDU supporters of both classes, a Protestant identification, and consequently milieu, weakens the commitment to the policies of the party chairman, even when not much. Among both strata and religious groups, religious practice strengthens the CDU identification. Independently of religion and practice, middle-class CDU supporters are more favorable to the Center-Right party leader than those of the working class.

We can explore this hypothesis using a body of independent data collected in 1961 using a different indicator:[60] strength of party identification (see *Table 20*).

The Catholic supporters of the CDU—both among men and women—are more likely to answer "convinced adherent" than "prefer at present" when asked: "Would you say that you are a convinced adherent of ——— (party they intend to vote for) or that you are inclined in favor of that party because in the present situation it is most adequate?" On the contrary, among the supporters of the FDP, Catholic men are less committed to the party than Protestants, probably because their choice was more a temporary protest vote against Adenauer, without a break from the Catholic climate of opinion. On the other side, the Catholic women, when supporting the FDP, matched the renegade hypothesis more. We also found this attitude in 1953 in their position toward Adenauer: for them, given the greater significance of religion

Table 20—Party Preference in the 1961 Bundestag Election, Religion and Strength of Party Identification: percentage "convinced adherent"*

Party Preference	Religion	MEN Convinced Adherent	No.	WOMEN Convinced Adherent	No.
CDU	Catholic	34%	(172)	41%	(253)
	Protestant	26	(61)	25	(95)
FDP	Catholic	13	(9)	60	(5)
	Protestant	41	(29)	28	(32)
SPD	Catholic	40	(85)	24	(67)
	Protestant	32%	(68)	28%	(123)

* The remainder up to 100% are those who "prefer at present" or, in a few cases, who express no opinion. For the source of these data see footnote 59.

for women, their vote represents a more conscious break with the subculture. The SPD Catholic women were still influenced by that subculture, while the men—supporting probably the SPD earlier and more consciously—were somewhat more among the convinced adherents. There are indications that the strong adherence is found among workers, but not among white-collar employees. Furthermore, these Catholic men were almost all nonpracticing. It would be interesting to see if, despite this the attitude toward Adenauer among them—at a moment of popularity—would still have been affected by the climate of opinion, as our data seem to suggest.

The simultaneous effects of class, religious identification and practice, and party, can be summarized in two figures: 92 percent of the middle-class churchgoing Catholics supporting the CDU agreed with Adenauer, and only 13 percent of the working-class SPD Protestants not going to church did so. If the correlations between class, religion, religious practice, and party were much higher than they are in Germany, the dissensus could reach such a degree of polarization.

The web of group affiliations certainly contributes decisively to the integration of German society. The attitudes toward Christian Democratic governments in Italy suggests that there too, among all parties except the Monarchists, a religiously tolerant position—reflecting some religious identification

—correlates with a less unconditional disapproval, and this is true even for the Communists (*Table 21*).

Table 21—Approval of the Government—Dominated by the DC—in the Last Five Years Among Italian Men of Different Attitudes Toward the Role of the Church and Supporting Different Parties

ATTITUDE TOWARD THE GOVERNMENT

Party preference	Attitude toward Church (pos. + neg. —)	Unconditional approval	In general it acted well	Mediocre without many errors	Serious errors that could have been avoided	Disapprove completely	Don't know	
PCI	+	—	—	25%	75%	—	—	(4)
	—	—	—	5	25	58%	13%	(85)
PSI	+	5 %	20 %	35	10	5	25	(20)
	—	1	5	22	39	21	12	(128)
PSDI	+	2.5	37.5	45	15	—	—	(40)
	—	—	5	39	39	5	11	(56)
DC	+	8	56	21	2	1	13	(140)
	—	7	40	27	8	—	19	(118)
PLI	+	—	29	43	29	—	—	(14)
	—	—	4	52	28	12	4	(26)
PMP or PNM	+	—	27	18	27	18	9	(11)
	—	—	25	22	34	9	9	(32)
MSI	+	—	29	14	43	14	—	(7)
	—	—	15	8	61	15	—	(13)
Don't know, indifferent	+	2	24	34	8	4	29	(48)
	—	2	20	17	14	10	37	(104)
Total	+	5	41	29	10	2	13	(293)
	—	2 %	15 %	23%	27%	16%	18%	(654)

We have defined as positive to the role of the Church those who approve of its taking a position on at least four of seven issues ranging from civil marriage and morality of the movies and TV, school and trade union questions, to internal politics. The question on approval of the government is the same quoted in the text above.

These data are from a national survey made April 2–12, 1958, by DOXA. For a detailed report see *Bolletino della DOXA*, 12 (11–13), (May 24, 1958). I am grateful to Professor P. Luzzatto Fegiz for making these data available to me for secondary analysis.

A democratic society, therefore, should favor such crosscutting of group affiliations and avoid the existence of overly organized and closed subcultures, as tended to be the case in the interwar years, when "people played chess or football according to their political affiliations and seldom met on any common ground," to use an observation made by Mannheim comparing Continental and British parties, "parties do not represent totalitarian organizations of particular strata; party lines are not the only or the essential dividing lines through the entire life of the nation."[60]

NOTES

1. For a sociological analysis of German social structure and democracy, see T. Parsons, "Democracy and the Social Structure in Pre-Nazi Germany," *Journal of Legal and Political and Political Sociology*, 1, pp. 96–114, reprinted in *Essays in Sociological*

Theory, (2d ed.; New York: The Free Press, 1958), pp. 105 ff.; R. Dahrendorf, "Demokratie und Sozialstruktur in Deutschland," *European Journal of Sociology,* 1 (1) (1960), pp. 86–120; and Otto Kirchheimer, "German Democracy in the 1950's," *World Politics,* 13 (2) (Jan. 1961), pp. 254–66. The work by Ralf Dahrendorf, *Gesellschaft und Demokratie in Deutschland* (Munich: R. Piper, 1965) is the latest and most important contribution to the problem.

2. There is an extensive and important literature on German political parties. For a brief summary in English, see Sigmund Neumann, "Germany: Changing Patterns and Lasting Problems," in Sigmund Neumann (ed.), *Modern Political Parties,* (Chicago: Univ. Press of Chicago, 1956), pp. 354–92. For a "genealogical tree" of parties, see p. 392, and also in Erwin Faul (ed.), *Wahlen and Wähler in Westdeutschland,* (Villingen: Ring Verlag, 1960), p. 116.

The study by Neumann, *Die deutschen Parteien: Wesen und Wandel nach dem Kriege,* (Berlin: Junker & Dunnhaupt, 1932), a classic with detailed bibliography, is essential for understanding the party system of Weimar. For the postwar period, Max G. Lange *et al., Parteien in der Bundesrepublik. Studien zur Entwicklung der Parteien bis zur Bundestagswahl* (Stuttgart: Ring Verlag, 1955), is a basic source.

3. The political and ideological development of the German working class within that context is studied from a sociological perspective by Guenther Roth in *The Social Democrats in Imperial Germany: A Study in Working Class Isolation and National Integration* (Totowa: Bedminster Press, 1963).

4. For the idea of "institutionalized class conflict," see R. Dahrendorf, *Soziale Klassen und Klassenkonflikt in der industriellen Gesellschaft* (Stuttgart: F. Enke, 1957), pp. 234 ff. and *passim,* and the works of T. H. Marshall and H. Schelsky, with whom this conception originated.

5. For cross-national comparisons of the socio-political composition of the national electorates of the fifties, see the path-breaking article by Mattei Dogan, "Le vote ouvrier en Europe occidentale," *Revue française de sociologie,* 1 (1960), pp. 25–44. For a comparison between Germany and the United States, see Morris Janowitz, "Soziale Schichtung und Mobilität in West-Deutschland," *Kölner Zeitschrift für Soziologie und Sozialpsychologie,* 10 (1958), pp. 1–38, especially pp. 7, 28. The article also contains data on social structure and political behavior.

6. For such detailed comparisons, see M. Dogan, *op. cit.,* and Chap. 4 in Juan J. Linz, *op. cit.*

7. For the social bases of West German parties, see Erwin Faul and Wolfgang Hirsch-Weber, "Die Stimmabgabe einzelner Bevölkerungsgruppen," in W. Hirsch-Weber and K. Schütz (eds.), *Wähler und Gewählte* (Berlin: Verlag Franz Vahlen, 1957), pp. 190–293. Chapters 5 and 7 are particularly relevant to this paper.

8. For a detailed analysis of the social bases of Italian parties see Mattei Dogan, "La Stratificazione Sociale dei Suffragi in Italia," in Alberto Spreafico and Joseph La Palombara (eds.), *Elezioni e comportamento politico in Italia* (Milan: Edizioni di Comunitá, 1962).

For France see the estimate of working class MRP support in J. D. Reynaud and A. Touraine, "La représentation politique du monde ouvrier" in M. Duverger (ed.), *Partis Politiques et Classes Sociales en France* (Paris: A. Colin, 1955), p. 34, and Richard Hamilton, *The Social Bases of French Working Class Politics* (unpublished Ph.D. diss., Columbia Univ., 1963), based on data of the Institut Français d'Opinion Publique (IFOP), kindly made available for secondary analysis by Prof. Jean Stoetzel. For a systematic comparison of the French and Italian electorates see the chapter by Mattei Dogan in this volume.

9. See the chapter by Robert T. McKenzie and Allan Silver, in this volume, also some of the data in Mark Abrams, Richard Rose, and Rita Hinden, *Must Labour Lose?* (Baltimore: Penguin Books, 1960).

10. It is impossible to refer here to the extensive literature on the salaried middle class from the early writings of Lederer and Marschak; those of the depression period by Kracauer, Dreyfuss, Speier and Geiger; or to the recent works of Croner, Neundörfer, Girod, Crozier, and C. W. Mills *et al.* In this context the reference is to Theodor Geiger, *Die soziale Schichtung des Deutschen Volkes* (Stuttgart: F. Enke, 1932), and his articles in *Die Arbeit* "Die Mittelschicht und die Sozialdemokratie," 8(8) (Aug. 1931), pp. 619–35 and "Panik im Mittelstand," 7(10) (1930), pp. 637–54.

11. Institut für Demoskopie survey data, Elisabeth Noelle and Erich P. Neumann (eds.), *Jahrbuch der öffentlichen Meinung 1947–1955* (Allensbach am Bodensee: Verlag für Demoskopie, 1956), p. 176, and DIVO, *Der Wähler vor der Bundestagswahl* (Frankfurt-am-Main, 1957), p. 152.

12. The absence of such a *Volkspartei* parallel to the Catholic *Zentrum* among the Protestants was seen as the basis of the Nazi success by Geiger when he wrote: "It would seem as if National Socialism, similarly to the *Zentrum*—only with numerically greater success—would be able to penetrate all strata as a general popular movement (*Volksbewegung*). At the left, Social Democracy and Communism would be its limits of expansion. In the middle position, because of the similarity in social structure, the *Zentrum* is called to be the decisive antagonist of the NSDAP, something that the comparison of the election results in Catholic and Protestant districts always shows," *op. cit.,* p. 112.

13. John Bonham, *The Middle Class Vote* (London: Faber & Faber), 1954, pp. 170–73) gives 14 percent. M. Dogan, "Le vote ouvrier en Europe occidentale," *op. cit.,* 22 percent, and Robert R. Alford, *Party and Society* (Chicago: Rand McNally, 1963), Table B–1, p. 348, roughly 20 percent.

14. Data from IFOP and INED (Institut National d'Etudes Demographiques) surveys analyzed by Richard Hamilton, *op. cit.*

15. "The Labor Movement in Germany," in Hans J. Morgenthau (ed.), *Germany and the Future of Europe* (Chicago: Univ. of Chicago Press, 1951), p. 101.

16. We consider both the Catholics going to church regularly and the Protestants going regularly or at least irregularly as "church-going," since the obligation has a different meaning for the two.

17. Erwin Faul, "Soziologie der westdeutschen Wählerschaft," in Erwin Faul (ed), *Wahlen und Wähler in Westdeutschland, op. cit.;* pp. 135–315, pp. 272–73. See also the DIVO 1957 study and Wolfgang Hartenstein et al., "Die Septemberdemokratie," *Die neue Gesellschaft* 5 (1) (Jan.–Feb., 1958), pp. 15–16, Table 5.

18. All these aspects have been analyzed in detail in J. Linz, *The Social Bases of West German Politics," op. cit.,* Chap. 5 to 13, pp. 206–461.

19. Bonham, *op. cit.,* p. 52.

20. Data from national surveys not designed with such theoretical distinctions in mind do not allow such regrouping, nor the type of analysis of the social structure based on census and similar data carried out by Geiger in his *Soziale Schichtung des deutschen Volkes* (*op. cit.*); on the other hand, they permit political behavior to be linked directly with background characteristics. The studies of Renate Mayntz, "Gedanken und Ergebnisse zur empirischen Feststellung sozialer Schichten." *Kölner Zeitschrift für Soziologie und Sozialpsychologie,* VIII (1956), and Erwin K. Scheuch, "An Instrument to Measure Social Stratification in Western Germany," *Transactions of the Third World Congress of Sociology,* VIII, pp. 185–9, show how much more sophisticated analyses of the stratification system are possible—particularly for the middle strata—that could be very fruitful for political sociology.

21. *See* footnote 10, this chapter.

22. *Op. cit.,* particularly the differences in the appeal of the DDP (Deutsche Demokratische Partei), the DVP (Deutsche Volkspartei), and the DNVP (Deutschnationale Volkspartei), their splinters, the Wirtschaftspartei and the NSDAP.

23. "Die Mittelschichten und die Sozialdemokratie," *Die Arbeit,* 8 (8) (Aug. 1931), pp. 619–20.

24. K. Adenauer, "Leitsätze christlicher Sozialpolitik. Das Sozial- und Wirtschaftsprogram der CDU," *Wesfalenpost* (Soest) 1 (36) (Aug. 27, 1946), quoted by Gerhard Schulz in "Die CDU—Merkmale ihres Aufbaus," in Lange et al., *Parteien der Bundesrepublik* (*op. cit.*), p. 78.

25. Unfortunately it is difficult to get comparable data for the late Weimar Republic and the present to document changes in social position and mentality, and even more so to link them with political behavior and attitudes. Changes in the social origin of employees in similar position—perhaps more often downward mobile in the past, now more upward mobile or, what is sociologically particularly interesting, recruited from "white-collar-worker" families—would be very important for all those theses that explained the radicalization of that stratum in terms of "status politics" and in accounting for the moderate position today. Or one might consider the different impact

of generational experiences: war and its aftermath, interrupted studies, and the like on the middle class in the 1920's and early 1950's, not to mention the different interpretation given to historical events and their impact by people in similar position. Some of the data on politics and generations for workers and white-collar employees suggest a lessening of status consciousness and political cleavage between the "blue" and the "white" collar workers (see Chap. 27 of my study, *The Social Bases of West German Politics, op. cit.*).

26. For a discussion of the different position of men and women in the white-collar labor force, see Ludwig Neundörfer, *Die Angestellten, Neuer Versuch einer Standortbestimmung* (Stuttgart: Enke Verlag, 1961) pp. 43–8, 77–8, 110–13, 148–60.

27. For comparisons between the income of "white" and "blue" collar workers, see Neundörfer, *op. cit.,* pp. 148–60.

28. This index of "work satisfaction" is described in J. Linz, *The Social Bases of West German Politics, op. cit.,* Appendix V, pp. 941–45. The questions used were: if they would choose the same occupation again; find their work interesting or monotonous; would prefer their present enterprise rather than another or being indifferent where to work; and if the boss only gives orders or talks with the employee.

Surprisingly enough there has been almost no research linking work satisfaction—studied by industrial sociologists and psychologists—and studies of political behavior. A noteworthy exception is A. Kornhauser *et al., When Labor Votes: A Study of Auto Workers* (New York: University Book, 1956), pp. 183–200. Richard Hamilton, *op. cit.,* deals systematically with this problem.

29. Richard Centers, *The Psychology of Social Classes. A Study of Class Consciousness* (Princeton: Princeton Univ. Press, 1949), p. 170 and Table 71 on p. 172.

30. Edmund Dahlström, *Tjänstemännen, näringslivet och samhället. En attitydundersökening* (Stockholm: Studieförbundet Näringsliv och Samhälle, 1954), reviewed by S. Rokkan, in *Kölner Zeitschrift für Soziologie,* 7 (2) (1956), pp. 247–52.

31. This is a central theme in S. M. Lipset, M. Trow, and J. Coleman, *Union Democracy* (New York: The Free Press, 1956), Chap. 8, pp. 154–75. In an analysis of the politics of workers in plants of different size I have in part replicated some of the findings of Lipset *et al.,* see *The Social Bases of West German Politics, op. cit.,* pp. 400–407.

32. *White Collar* (New York: Oxford Univ. Press, 1956), p. 227.

33. M. Dogan, in the paper on French and Italian politics in this volume.

34. There have been a number of excellent ecological studies of rural politics for the prewar period, particularly Rudolf Heberle, *From Democracy to Nazism. A Regional Case Study on Political Parties in Germany* (Baton Rouge: Louisiana State Univ. Press, 1945). The persistence of a- if not anti-democratic attitudes among the peasantry could be documented with public opinion data. The limited successes of neo-Nazi groups have been largely rural. In view of this the continuous and increasing support for the CDU is specially significant: it ties to a democratic party a group whose democratic convictions are not too strong. In a sense the situation is similar to that of the workers with authoritarian attitudes that support democratic parties of the Left that Lipset has pointed out.

35. The comparison of religious cleavage between classes in different societies and their relation to politics deserves much more study. A secondary analysis of data of the Institut National d'Etudes Démographiques—INED—"Une enquête sur l'opinion publique à l'égard de la limitation des naissances," by Alain Girard and Raul Samuel, *Population,* 11 (3) (1956) suggests that the gap in practice between classes in France and Germany may well be almost the same, in which case many of the arguments based on the dechristianization of the working class in Latin Europe versus the ability of the more progressive Catholicism of central-western Europe to hold its loyalty would have to be restated. The difference would be more in the general level of secularization of *all classes.* It is impossible to present the data here in detail. I am very grateful to Alain Girard for having made these data available for secondary analysis.

36. To use the famous slogan of Julius Bachem in 1906. For the Protestant political tradition fusing with the old *Zentrum* in the CDU, see the works on German parties by Neumann and Bergsträsser and K. Buchheim, *Geschichte der Christlichen Parteien in Deutschland* (Munich: Kösel, 1953) and a Heidelberg doctoral dissertation by W.

Braun. *Evangelische Parteien in historischer Darstellung und sozialwissenschaftlicher Beleuchtung,* 1936. See also the study of Gerhard Schulz, in Lange, *op. cit.,* and the monographs by Wieck on the founding of the CDU. This should not obscure the role of nonreligiously motivated politicians in the founding and development of the party.

37. Max G. Lange, "Die FDP—Ein Versuch einer Erneuerung des Liberalismus," in M. G. Lange (ed.), *Parteien in der Bundesrepublik, op. cit.,* pp. 351–6.

38. UNESCO Institute data. Our own data show the FDP more than twice as strong among the university-educated Protestants as among the Catholics, while the difference is less marked in all other educational groups. The FDP shares this appeal to the secularized upper bourgeoisie with the Italian Liberals.

39. These estimates come respectively from W. Hartenstein and K. Liepelt, "Party Members and Party Voters in West Germany," in S. Rokkan (ed.), *Approaches to the Study of Political Participation* (Bergen: Christian Michelsen Institute, 1962) Table 4, p. 49, and A. J. Heidenheimer, "La structure confessionelle, sociale et régionale de la CDU," *Revue Française de Science Politique,* 7 (3) (1957), p. 365.

40. *Ibid.*

41. Another indication that the laicism-clericalism conflict in Germany is less marked than in France can be seen from the fact that when asked: "What do you consider better, that children should be educated without distinction of religion in the same school or that there should be two different types of schools, one for Catholics and another for Protestant children?" (E. Noelle, E. P. Neumann, *Jahrbuch der öffentlichen Meinung 1947–55,* Allensbach, Verlag für Demoskopie, 1956, p. 224) those favoring one school for everybody—and mind this means not a "laic" school—were 49% of the CDU supporters, 79% of those of the SPD and 81% of the FDP. In France the difference between parties on the question was greater with 84% MRP, 77% UNR, 73% Independents, 49% RGR, UDSR, 22% SFIO and 11% PCF for *freedom* of teaching; even if we compare only parties not on the extreme like the RGR and the Independents the difference is almost as great as between Socialists and Demo-Christians in Germany. Data from Alain Girard and H. Bastide, "Les problèmes démographiques devant l'opinion," *Population* (1960) pp. 245–288, p. 285. The question was: "In your opinion, is it better that there should be only state schools or both state and free schools (*écoles libres,* meaning religious schools)?"

42. Data from a report by the research center of the Dutch Labor party quoted by Michael P. Fogarty, *Christian Democracy in Western Europe 1820–1953* (Notre Dame: Notre Dame Univ. Press, 1957), p. 359. For more detailed data from a Netherlands Institute of Public Opinion survey—distinguishing religious practice—see S. M. Lipset, *Political Man* (Garden City: Doubleday, 1960), pp. 244–246. In some surveys the contribution of the nonbelievers to the support of the Socialist party (PvdA) is even higher.

43. The French data are from a 1952 survey by the Institut Francais d'Opinion Publique (IFOP), *Sondages* 14 (4) (1952), "La France est-celle encore Catholique?" and have been recalculated using IBM cards kindly made available by Prof. Stoetzel of the IFOP.

44. Georg Simmel, "The Web of Group Affiliations," trans. by R. Bendix in *Conflict —The Web of Group Affiliations* (New York: The Free Press, 1955), p. 151.

45. The importance of the dual problem of the cleavage and consensus was emphasized by S. M. Lipset in "Old and New Frontiers of Political Sociology," in R. K. Merton (ed.), *Sociology Today* (New York: Basic Books, 1959), pp. 81–114. B. B. Berelson, P. F. Lazarsfeld, and W. N. McPhee, *Voting* (Chicago: Univ. of Chicago Press, 1954), chapters 9 and 14 gave early attention to this problem in their research. V. O. Key, Jr., *Public Opinion and American Democracy* (New York: Knopf, 1961), presents in chapter 2, entitled "Consensus," useful theoretical distinctions and a discussion of methodological problems. Among contemporary political theorists, R. A. Dahl's *Preface to Democratic Theory* (Chicago, Univ. of Chicago Press, 1956) is particularly relevant (see mainly pp. 357–66). M. Janowitz and D. Marvick, *Competitive Pressure and Democratic Consent* (Ann Arbor: Bureau of Government, Institute of Public Administration, Univ. of Michigan, 1956) is a sociological contribution to the problem.

46. See R. A. Dahl (ed.), *Political Oppositions in Western Democracies* (New Haven, Yale Univ. Press, 1966), especially the chapter on Germany by the late Otto Kirchheimer.

47. Elisabeth Noelle and Erich P. Neumann, *Jahrbuch der öffentlichen Meinung 1947–1955* (Allensbach: Institut für Demoskopie, 1956), p. 157.

48. Elisabeth Noelle and Erich P. Neumann, *Jahrbuch der öffentlichen Meinung 1957* (Allensbach: Institut für Demoskopie, 1957), p. 173.

49. *Ibid.*, p. 258.

50. E. Noelle and E. P. Neumann, *Jahrbuch der öffentlichen Meinung 1947–1955, op. cit.*, pp. 272–75.

51. E. Noelle and E. P. Neumann, *ibid.*, pp. 172–3, and *Jahrbuch . . . 1957, op. cit.*, pp. 182–3. E. P. Neumann and E. Noelle, *Umfragen über Adenauer. Ein Porträt in Zahlen* (Allensbach: Verlag für Demoskopie, 1961), pp. 44–7.

52. Pierpaolo Luzatto Fegiz, *Il Volto Sconosciuto dell' Italia. Dieci Anni di Sondagi DOXA* (Milan: A. Giuffré, 1956). pp. 534–40.

53. E. P. Neumann and E. Noelle, *Umfragen über Adenauer, op. cit.*, p. 29.

54. The Italian data from the DOXA survey quoted above. We combined those "approving unconditionally" and those saying "on the whole he did well" vs. those saying "I disapprove completely" and "made mistakes that could have been avoided," leaving out the few with no opinion or ambivalent, to avoid the problem created by the larger number with no definite opinion in Germany and to simplify the comparisons.

55. Georg Simmel, "Faithfulness and Gratitude," in K. Wolff (trans. and ed.), *The Sociology of G. Simmel* (New York: The Free Press, 1950), pp. 379–95. See also Robert K. Merton, "Continuities in the Theory of Reference Groups and Social Structure," in *Social Theory and Social Structure* (2d ed.; New York: The Free Press, 1957), pp. 295–6.

56. P. F. Lazarsfeld, B. Berelson, H. Gaudet, *The People's Choice* (New York: Duell, Sloan & Pearce, 1944), p. 53, and B. Berelson, *et al.*, *Voting, op. cit.*, pp. 128 ff. See also S. M. Lipset, *Political Man* (Garden City: Doubleday, 1960), pp. 203–13.

57. Gabriel A. Almond, "Comparative Political Systems," *Journal of Politics*, 18, reprinted in Heinz Eulau, *Political Behavior* (New York: The Free Press, 1956), pp. 40–1. See also S. M. Lipset, "Party Systems and the Representation of Social Groups," *European Journal of Sociology*, 1 (1) (1960), pp. 3–38, for the multiple cleavages and the party systems of a number of countries—particularly the case of France, pp. 16–22.

58. G. Simmel, "The Web of Group Affiliations, *op. cit.*, p. 151.

59. Data from a study done in the summer of 1961 (before the Berlin wall) by DIVO for the Institute for Political Science and the Research Institute for Sociology at the University of Cologne in six selected constituencies, kindly made available to me for secondary analysis by Erwin Scheuch.

60. Karl Mannheim, *Freedom, Power and Democratic Planning* (London: Routledge, 1951), p. 32.

Three

Northern Europe

Seven

Cleavages in Finnish Politics

Erik Allardt and Pertti Pesonen[*]

An emphasis on social structure seems to suggest that political cleavages be classified as either structural or nonstructural. Maybe this distinction appears to neglect the fact that all cleavages presuppose some kinds of groupings. But some political cleavages correspond to ones differentiating social groups within which solidarity and cohesion already exist on other than purely political grounds, while certain other such cleavages lack any such correspondence. Because the latter cleavages can be perceived only in the sphere of politics, they are here referred to as nonstructural. Of course, they may reflect psychological differences, but they do not reflect any division of the body politic into social groups that are characterized by a personal feeling among their members of belonging together in most walks of life.

Finnish history points to one political cleavage which has been at least periodically of quite nonstructural nature. At certain times the differences of opinion on Finland's proper foreign policy have defied attempts to trace them back to differences between solidary social groups. Moreover, the attitudes on foreign policy have not always correlated with the dimension of nationalism. For instance, some strong nationalists have preferred compliance

---

[*] The first two sections are by Pertti Pesonen, the remainder by Erik Allardt. The analyses reported refer to elections *through 1962 only*.

with Russian demands, while some others have favored an uncompromising foreign policy. Likewise, both nationalist and internationalist arguments have been presented to support a friendly policy.

Among structural cleavages, the one based on social class has been of crucial importance. But it has been by no means the only one. The historical review given below notes how the differences of the Finnish-speaking majority and the Swedish-speaking minority have sometimes politically overshadowed matters concerning social class. Additional political cleavages, which have been structural without being based on social class, have also existed. For discussions of this type it is crucial to know precisely under what conditions the political cleavages of different kinds are likely to result in strongly disruptive conflicts. Some light might be thrown upon the problem by a discussion of the case of Finland, whose political scene has contained both nonstructural and various kinds of structural political cleavages.

PAST AND PRESENT CLEAVAGES

The Parliament of Finland proclaimed the country's independence December 6, 1917. Following this declaration, it was but a matter of weeks before the nation experienced the most extreme result of social and political cleavage: a civil war which lasted from January to May, 1918. The governmental army cleared Finland of the Russian military detachment which had remained in the country but also fought against the Red Guard, the armed force set into being by the revolutionary wing of the Finnish Social Democrats. This severe conflict quite obviously cast its shadow over Finnish society for two decades. For instance, the Social Democratic Party, which was consistently accorded the widest electoral support among the parties, remained in opposition until 1937, with only one exception, in 1926–27. Subsequently, partly by reason of the patriotism of Finnish labor in the wars of defense which began in 1939, the Socialists have been "not only tolerated, but even accepted," to quote the phrase of a veteran Social Democrat.

In a greatly simplified explanation of the causes of the civil war, at least some mention must be made of the bad social conditions which the economy and the legislation of the country had been unable to correct, and the rapid dissemination of a radical kind of Socialistic ideology among a wide sector of the population. But neither of these factors had occasioned an important political cleavage in the country's legislature at the turn of the century. The reason for this is self-evident: the traditional Diet of the four Estates had by then become outdated, and no longer corresponded to the current needs of the country.

However, Russia's momentary weakness and Finland's internal restlessness, instanced notably in the General Strike of 1905, led to a reform of the Diet in 1906. Had the reform been effected earlier, it might have been milder in nature. But by 1906 the principles of universal suffrage and an equal and secret ballot were no longer challenged either by the government commission that drafted the new bills or by the Diet. Instead, discussions centered around such questions as correct voting age, qualifications of women for political activity, and size of constituencies. When a new Parliament Act was passed in 1928, only minor amendments to that of 1906 were introduced. The unicameral legislature of two hundred members and the adopted principles of popular representation needed no change.

At the 1904 election, only 125,000 persons had been entitled to vote, but in the general election of 1907 the universally enfranchised adult population, women included, numbered 1,273,000. Thus, in the first years of the century the most important political dividing line was that which separated the politically privileged minority of the nation from its nonfranchised majority. This dividing line also bore some relationship to its social counterpart, that separating the upper strata of the society from the "common people."

There is no doubt that the peasantry belonged to the "common people" in 1617, when the new Diet Act authorized the already existing division of the people of the united countries of Sweden-Finland into the four Estates. Neither was Finland's Diet appreciably outmoded for its social background in 1809, when the Finnish people swore allegiance to the new Grand Duke of Finland, the Russian Tsar, who in return made Finland an autonomous state within the Russian Empire. But during the nineteenth century the social cleavage structure of the country soon underwent change. While the population increased rapidly, the peasant population rose in social status, and in many areas gradually became identified with the upper strata. In the meantime, an agrarian proletariat of tenant farmers, cotters, and farm laborers increased in numbers, and furthermore, a class of industrial workers was coming into being.[1]

The old Diet experienced two sharp political cleavages, both reminiscent of a typical two-party pattern. Neither one of these was directly based on social class. The native population spoke two different languages. A minority of about one-seventh spoke Swedish, which was, however, the official language of the country by reason of the former political union with Sweden; this tongue was also spoken by most of the country's educated inhabitants. After revival of the sessions of the Diet in 1863, the Finnish National Party soon became established. Its primary aim was that of attaining equality of the two language groups, and subsequently that of ensuring superiority of the language of the majority. The party's political opponent, the Swedish National Party, began its work in 1870, and has been in existence ever since. Both parties controlled two chambers in the Diet of four Estates.

The last two sessions of the Diet were overwhelmingly characterized by another political cleavage. The Russification policy of Tsar Nicholas II had assumed its full force in 1899. Disagreement on the correct policy of Finland toward Russia caused the new and serious political cleavage. The Constitutionalists adhered strictly to the law of Finland, whereas the Compliers were ready to yield on all counts which in their view did not affect Finland's vital interests. The majority of the Compliers were Fennomans, while the Constitutionalists included the Young Finnish Party, which had split from the former, and the Svecomans. Nevertheless, the strongest opposition to Tsarist Russia was afforded by the Labor Party, which had been founded in 1899.

The very beginnings of the Finnish workers' movement had been moderate both in purpose and in composition of participation. But the Labor Party differed from the other parties in many respects. First of all, it had the very rare opportunity of working within the old Diet. Second, it had by the end of 1906 about 100,000 enrolled members[2] and thus was the first mass party on the political scene, since the others had been only quite loose groupings of political leaders. Third, it accepted a definite political doctrine of international origin, Socialism. Moreover, it was the first party to declare that it represented one social class alone. This last principle was not of minor importance, if one remembers the theory implied in the Diet Act of 1869, according to which each chamber of the Diet was presumed to represent the people as a whole, and not only the interests of their respective Estates.[3] In 1903 the party assumed its present name, the Social Democratic Party.

The Social Democratic Party professed to monopolize representation of the lower strata of the population. In the campaign of 1907, this gave it an initial advantage in the fight to gain the support of the newly enfranchised. Furthermore, it was the first party with any experience in dealing with the masses. Among industrial workers, the backing given the party was so obvious that most of its efforts were concentrated among the lower strata of the rural electorate, a fact that would also exert a long-lasting effect on the social background of Finland's political parties.

In the first election of the unicameral Parliament, a total of five major parties appealed to the electorate. In addition to the above-mentioned Social Democrats and the two Finnish parties, they comprised the Swedish People's Party, which had assumed its present name in 1906, in an effort to emphasize the newly felt need to appeal to a wider range of the electorate, and the Agrarian Union, also founded in 1906 and having as sole aim the gaining of rural votes. The campaigning was effectively carried out, and the recorded turnout of 70.7 percent was unsurpassed in the sixteen elections that followed; only since 1945 has the Finnish electorate gone to the polls in greater proportions.

The results of the election caused a drastic political change in the Finnish legislature. The first distribution of seats in Parliament, and the percentage distributions of the popular vote in 1907 were as follows:[4]

| | | POPULAR VOTE (percent) | | |
Parties	Mandates	Total	Urban	Rural
Social Democrats	80	37.0	33.3	37.6
Finnish Party	59	27.3	20.2	28.5
Young Finnish Party	26	13.7	13.1	13.7
Swedish People's Party	24	12.6	26.3	10.5
Agrarian Union	9	5.8	0.3	6.7
Christian Labor, etc.	2	3.6	6.8	3.0
Total	200	100.0	100.0	100.0
		(899,347)	(120,765)	(770,050)

It was quite unexpected that Finland's Social Democrats, ten years younger than the Swedish Socialist Party and twenty years younger than the Danish, should prove to be the strongest Socialist party in Europe. Still one might also argue that its support might have been even more substantial. The "unprivileged" population, including industrial and farm laborers, the unemployed, and also the cotters and tenant farmers, was in 1905 calculated as embracing 62.4 percent of the population (56 of the urban, and 63 of the rural).[5] But current electoral studies have shown that among the lower classes there often exists a general tendency toward a low poll turnout. A recent analysis of the election of 1907 also provides a reminder of three other obstacles that the Social Democrats were not quite able to surmount: the unpopularity of their antireligious attitude, the radical social and even more radical language program of the comparatively successful Finnish Party, and also the appeal of the Agrarian Union to the lower rural classes.[6] On the other hand, Socialism's wide acceptance in the rural areas during and as a result of the General Strike of 1905, was basic to its success in predominantly rural Finland. In this connection, one also notes that the share taken by the Swedish Party in the votes was not far removed from the proportion of the Swedish minority in Finland, which points toward the Socialists' relative lack of success among the Swedish-speaking population.

The Finnish Parliament did not fulfill the expectations of the voters. Possibly the language question, which did not interest the Social Democrats, and the arguments concerned with the policy toward Russia, prevented the Parliament's concentration on attempts to solve urgent social problems. But it is more important that in fact only the form of a democratic Parliament existed, an absolute veto on legislation and the right to give executive orders being vested in the Russian Tsar. Moreover, the earlier "dispute between the Tsar and the Finnish people took on the character of a dispute between the two nations now that Russia had a Parliament of its own."[7]

When eight general elections had been held during the period 1907–17, the country's party pattern was confronted with reorientation. However, the changes were not many in number. Only the Finnish Party and the Young Finnish Party were by now obsolete, and in their place two new non-Socialist parties were founded in 1918, the National Coalition (Conservative) and the National Progressive (Center) Party. Since then, Finland's party pattern has generally included six parties. Of these, the four non-Socialist parties have already been mentioned. The only change was the replacement of the Progressive Party by the Finnish People's Party in 1951. For most of the time the Left has been divided between the Social Democrats and the Communists. The latter party was started in Moscow in 1918; played its part in Finnish politics from 1920 as the Socialist Labor Party and the Workers' and Small Farmers' Party; and was outlawed in 1930 but again legalized in 1944 by the terms of the armistice with the Allied Powers; since then it has also led a front organization known as the Democratic Union of the Finnish People (SKDL). In the 1930's the Finnish political scene included an extreme Right-wing, the Patriotic People's Movement (IKL), which twice gained fourteen seats. Recently, an opposition group has broken away from the Social Democratic Party, and since the 1958 election another one from the Agrarian Union.

Table 1 gives the results of four of the fourteen general elections in independent Finland; the first, those immediately preceding and following World War II, and the most recent one. Naturally such a "sample" of election results leaves many political fluctuations out of account. Nevertheless, the net changes in four decades have been sufficiently meager to justify the conclusion that in direct contrast to some other countries with a system of proportional representation, Finland's party situation has proved rather stable.

Table 1—Results of the Finnish General Elections of 1919, 1939, 1945, and 1962

| Parties | DISTRIBUTION OF MANDATES | | | | PERCENT DISTRIBUTION OF POPULAR VOTE | | | | | | | | | | | |
| | | | | | Total | | | | Urban | | | | Rural[a] | | | |
	1919	1939	1945	1962	1919	1939	1945	1962	1919	1939	1945	1962	1919	1939	1945	1962
Swedish People's Party	22	18	14	14	12.1	9.6	7.9	6.4	24.6	14.4	11.9	8.2	9.7	8.2	7.2	5.6
Swedish Leftist	—	—	1	—	—	0.5	0.5	—	—	1.1	1.0	—	—	0.3	0.3	—
National Coalition (Conservatives)	28	25	28	32	15.7	13.6	15.0	15.0	21.7	18.4	20.4	21.9	14.0	11.4	11.9	10.5
National Progressive/ Finnish People's Party (1962)	26	6	9	13	12.8	4.8	5.2	6.3	14.2	8.9	10.1	11.1	17.3	3.5	3.3	3.6
Agrarian Union	42	56	49	53	19.7	22.9	21.3	23.0	1.3	1.7	2.1	3.3	20.6	29.7	26.8	34.0
Small Holders/Small Peasants (1962)	—	2	—	—	—	2.1	1.2	2.2	—	0.2	0.1	0.4	—	2.8	1.7	3.1
Social Democratic Party	80	85	50	38	38.0	39.8	25.1	19.5	38.1	49.3	25.9	24.1	38.3	37.4	24.9	17.2
Christian Labor/ Social Democratic Opposition (1962)	2	—	—	2	1.5	—	—	4.4	0.0[b]	—	—	5.2	0.1[b]	—	—	4.0
Democratic Union of the Finnish People (Communist)	—	—	49	47	—	—	23.5	22.0	—	—	28.2	24.0	—	—	23.8	21.2
Others[c]	—	8	—	1	0.2	6.7	0.3	1.2	0.1	6.0	0.3	1.8	0.0	6.7	0.1	0.8
Total	200	200	200	200	100.0	100.0	100.0	100.0	100.0	100.0	100.0	100.0	100.0	100.0	100.0	100.0
(Millions of votes)					(1.0)	(1.3)	(1.7)	(2.3)	(0.2)	(0.3)	(0.6)	(0.8)	(0.8)	(1.0)	(1.1)	(1.4)

Source: Official election statistics.

a Rural municipalities and townships.

b These votes are mainly included in the above figures for Agrarian Union.

c In 1939, all these mandates and most of the votes were given to the "Patriotic People's Movement" (Extreme Right); in 1962 the seat was gained by the Liberal Union.

In the opinion of some scholars, this is an indication of the adjustment of political cleavages to the prevailing social ones.

The development that can be followed by means of *Table 1* might be summarized, party by party, in the following manner. In relation to the others, the Swedish People's Party has experienced a slow but consistent decrease in popular support. The Progressives soon lost their backing among the rural electorate, which inevitably weakened their total national standing. The Conservatives lost rural support between the two world wars, but these losses were not so severe as those suffered by the Progressives. For the Agrarians, the election of 1919 was quite successful, a reminder of the Act of 1918, which contained provisions enabling 46,470 tenant farmers and 45,250 cotters to become landowners.[8] Since then, the Agrarian Union has been, without exception, the major non-Socialist party. The Left has gained proportional strength in the cities; after World War II, the Socialist parties received a majority of the urban vote and well over 40 percent of the votes of the rural electorate. The election of 1945 signalized a definite swing to the Left; subsequently Social Democracy has made a slight gain in urban areas in comparison with Communism. In rural communes, one notes a minor relative loss as regards them both in contrast to the increase in the share of the Agrarians.

One might describe Finland's present multiparty system as being basically of the Scandinavian type. But in many respects it has its peculiarities. The system includes a politically organized language minority. The Agrarian party has been able to retain its strength, despite inception of the era of rapid industrialization and urbanization. In 1958, the proportion of Communist voters (23.2 percent) was even higher than that in Italy (where the Communists then received 22.7 percent of the votes cast in the election of the Chamber of Deputies). Nevertheless, the Finnish electorate has no greater inclination to vote Labor than those of the other Scandinavian countries; only twice, in 1916 and in 1958, has the Left acquired a majority in the Finnish Parliament. An additional flavor was given to the general election of 1962 by two of the three largest parties having acquired independent, newly separated opposition wings.

The fact that a multiparty system provides many possibilities for interparty conflicts does not of course abolish the need to reach majority decisions, which have, in turn, at least temporary integrating effects on some parties. A majority makes legislative decisions, and the principle of parliamentarism requires majority support for the State Council (Cabinet) as well. There have been periods of government by rather consistent coalitions and their oppositions. Thus, during the years 1950–57 it was mainly Agrarians and Social Democrats that cooperated in the State Council. But the Conservatives and the Communists were far from forming a unified opposition. Indeed, the Finnish Parliament is but seldom clearly divided into parties in power and opposition. Sometimes, as in 1959–62, the Parliament tolerates a minority Cabinet of one party. At a time when external danger threatened in 1939–44, the comprehensive cabinet coalitions were able to work almost without opposition at all. However, when Cabinets are formed, some conclusions may be drawn as to where the sharpest political cleavages exist. Conservative President Svinhufvud refused in 1931–37 to appoint Social Democratic ministers; since 1948, the Communists have been continuously in opposition because no other party is willing to cooperate with them.

Although Finnish society has its political conflicts, the underlying social structure is less heterogeneous than that of many other European countries. In this connection, two things may deserve emphasis. First of all, even half a century ago Finnish society was in many respects homogeneous. For example, in 1900 no less than 98 percent of the population adhered to the Lutheran Church, and the 1,336 persons, whose mother tongue was Lappish, constituted the nation's largest racial minority group.[9] Second, during the first six decades of the twentieth century the differences of many social characteristics within the population further weakened.

As can be seen from *Table 2,* the minority language has lost proportional importance. From 1900 to 1960, the Swedish-speaking population remained rather constant in number, while the Finnish-speaking population increased by 75 percent. The relative decline of the language of the minority also corresponds to the election results shown in *Table 1.* This tendency has no doubt lessened the importance of the language cleavage, which still was a major political issue in the 1930's. Legislation and the changing language composition of the civil service have worked to the same effect. The Constitution Act of 1919 states that both Finnish and Swedish are the national languages of the Republic, and the country's language legislation is based on the principle of equal treatment of the members of the two language groups. Accordingly, according to the 1960 census, the 548 locally self-governing communes were grouped by official language for the ten-year

Table 2—Absolute and Percentage Distributions of Finland's Population by Mother-Tongue, in 1880–1960

Year of Census	Finnish	Swedish	Other languages	Total
1880	1,756,000	295,000	8,000	2,061,000[a]
1900	2,353,000	350,000	10,000	2,713,000
1920	2,754,000	341,000	10,000	3,105,000
1940	3,328,000	354,000	14,000	3,696,000
1960	4,108,000	331,000	7,000	4,446,000
1880	85.2%	14.3%	0.4%	99.9%
1900	86.1	13.6	0.3	100.0
1920	88.7	11.0	0.3	100.0
1940	90.0	9.6	0.4	100.0
1960	92.4%	7.4%	0.2%	100.0%

Source: Statistical Yearbook of Finland (1962), Table 20.
[a] Includes persons whose language was unknown.

period 1963–72 as follows: 457 had Finnish and 44 Swedish as the only official language, while 47 were bilingual, of them 13 having a Finnish and 34 a Swedish majority.[10]

To find conditions which are likely to have led to social cleavages, one should now generally confine examination to various dissimilarities of an economic nature. Industrialization began in Finland later than in the major industrial nations, late also in comparison with the other northern countries of Europe. Nevertheless, rapid industrialization is now, and has for some tens of years been, the most prominent economic trend in Finnish society, accompanied especially between the two world wars by an increase in agricultural production. In 1920, 65 percent of the economically active population still made their living in agriculture, but the corresponding figure was only 35 percent in 1960. During the same 40-year period, industrial population rose from 15 to 31 percent, and the groups occupied in commerce, transport, and communications from 6 to 18 percent.[11]

This development has been a necessary prerequisite for the rising standard of living. The increased national income, in turn, has been followed by a trend toward more equalized distribution of wealth, because since World War II above-average increases have occurred in workers' real wages. The following index numbers show the rapidity of this recent development:[12]

	1926	1939	1962
National production per capita	100	137	239
Industrial workers	100	128	308
Male workers in agriculture	100	125	263

The constant of Pareto, which was 1.84 in 1938, rose to 2.57 in 1945. The latter measure may well have indicated the most equal distribution of income so far recorded anywhere.[13] Moreover, graduated income taxation has most heavily burdened those Finns with higher earned income, while the position of the least well-to-do citizens has been improved by an advanced social policy. Simultaneously, the ownership of real property and stocks has also become more common, and the Finnish colonization policy has for a long time favored the formation of small but numerous independent farms. In 1950, only 21 percent of Finnish farms comprised more than 10 hectares (ca. 25 acres) of arable land. Consequently, the considerable loss of population from agriculture has not decreased the number of landowners, but has merely freed labor power to engage in other occupations. It was calculated that in 1959 1,604,000 occupants, members of the family and relatives, lived on farms. This number amounted to 36 percent of the population, and averaged 4.13 persons per farm. But in addition only 46,000 persons, or 0.12 per farm, were permanently employed on the farms.[14] Mechanization has quite recently generally altered agricultural technique: there were fewer than 15,000 tractors in 1950, but about 90,000 in 1960.

Many further figures might be presented to support the general statement that Finnish society has become more and more homogeneous. A majority of the population still lives in what are administratively defined as rural communes, but the differences between "rural" and "urban" concepts are shrinking.[15] Mass communications cut down cultural differences: the number of licensed radio receivers is more than one to four persons and that of TV sets one to nine persons. Easy transportation diminishes geographical distances. Geographical mobility, especially to urban areas, is considerable: only one-fourth of the present inhabitants of Helsinki or Tampere were born in their city, the majority being born in rural communes. In the sphere of labor relations, established cooperation also suggests increased homogeneity. The principle of collective bargaining still looked remote in the 1930's, but was accepted by the employers during and after World War II.[16] State arbitration has lately become an essential part of the negotiating procedures of Finnish labor-market organizations.

But differentiating factors also remain and evolve in Finnish society. Economic development has not attained equal stages of progress in all parts of the country. The population is heavily concentrated in the south and also in the west; in the thinly populated northeastern areas only 18–22 percent are engaged in industry, while in the southwest the corresponding proportion is 32–39 percent. Industrial occupations now compete with agriculture for predominance. And in the treatment of social cleavages, shrinking differences may not always be interpreted as signs of shrinking conflicts. The diminished class differences may be accompanied by increased class consciousness. Modern mass communications and organizational and cultural centralization may be accompanied not only by a more homogeneous culture, but also by easier responses and deeper cleavages within the society, whenever conflicts arise at the national level of social and political leadership.

THE CURRENT PARTY SITUATION AT LEADERSHIP LEVEL

The old cleavages across the dimension of Radicalism-Conservatism has separated the Socialist and non-Socialist parties from each other, both in Parliament and in the municipal boards of trustees. In recent years, however, some non-Socialist parties have shown a tendency to resent the use of the traditional joint expression "bourgeois" parties. The Socialist parties, in turn, accuse each other of cooperating with the "bourgeois" or the "reactionaries." This theme marked for months the lengthy campaign preceding the presidential election of 1962. The candidate of the Social Democrats, Olavi Honka (who abandoned his candidacy in November 1961), had been nonpolitical, but was also known to have supported the Conservatives. He was also nominated by the Conservatives and three other non-Socialist parties as well: in other words, by the groups which in the Electoral College of 1956 largely voted in common for the Social Democratic candidate in opposition to the successful candidate, Urho Kekkonen. The election of the latter was then mainly due to the support provided by the non-Socialist Agrarians and the Communists. In 1962, however, his reelection was jointly voted by the "bourgeois" electors, while the opposing Left was divided into three separate groups.

The President of Finland exercises such vast political powers, that a contest for his office can result in significant political cleavages. Nevertheless, the most many-sided and focal political battle ground is the legislature, where fuller information on differences within and between the parties, and the cohesive forces at work, is obtainable through the behavior of the representatives of the various parties during the process of legislative decision-making. Such a study, utilizing parliamentary records, has been made of the Finnish Parliament of 1948–51.[17] This work shows four major groupings of parties, one of them running in parallel with the above-mentioned presidential cleavage of 1956. The three others were termed by the author the "Right-Left," the "Communist-non-Communist," and the "rural-urban" voting blocks. When only the four biggest parliamentary groups were taken into consideration in the study, the distribution of the 397 roll-call votes was the following:[18]

Agarian and Conservative vs.		
Social Democrat and Communist	194	(49%)
Communist vs. all others	83	(21%)
Agrarian and Communist vs.		
Social Democrat and Conservative	47	(12%)
Agrarian vs. all others	46	(12%)
The three other combinations	26	(6%)
Unanimous	1	(0%)
	397	(100%)

The traditional Socialist-non-Socialist cleavage was in fact the most apparent factor differentiating the votes given in Parliament. Most matters thus voted upon were concerned with social policy, the defense budget, and state-owned industry. All the proposals which induced three groups to vote against the Communists had originated from the Communist group. They dealt with the economic and social conditions of workers. In most decisions on agricultural and forestry matters or about urbanization, the Agrarians in turn stood alone against the majorities of other parliamentary groups, while some of the divisions in which the Agrarians and Communists cooperated may also be interpreted as signs of rivalry between these two parties in conferring benefits on the rural population.

The above distribution nevertheless contains no information on conformity within a party in Parliament. By utilization of the index presented by Stuart Rice, the following measurements of average party cohesion were obtained:[19]

	Index of Cohesion	(Number of Mandates)
Communists	95.1	(38)
Agrarian Union	87.3	(56)
Social Democrats	86.6	(54)
National Coalition	84.0	(33)
National Progressive	82.0	(5)
Swedish People's Party	74.5	(14)

It is not peculiar to the Finnish Parliament alone, that the Communists constitute the most cohesive group. The least cohesion existed among the Swedish members, which is also quite in accord with expectations, as long as the language question is not frequently made a voting issue. However, the general impression gained from the above index numbers is the relatively high degree of cohesion within all the parliamentary groups. The predominant Socialist-non-Socialist division generally created their highest relative unanimity. When the Communists or the Agrarians stood alone facing the opposition of other groups, they achieved a maximum of their cohesion. On the other hand, the greatest deviation from group opinion occurred among the Conservatives, Swedes, and Communists, when the interests of agriculture became a matter for voting.[20] The rural-urban or agricultural-industrial cleavage thus tends clearly to cross parliamentary party lines.

Because the Finnish system of proportional representation slightly favors large parties, some so-called electoral unions are formed for each election in those constituencies where the cooperating parties might otherwise lose representation. Deep political cleavages prevent such cooperation, and a review of the elections again proves that the Socialist-bourgeois and the Communist-anti-Communist cleavages have been the deepest ones. The Communists and the Social Democrats simply do not form electoral unions in general elections either with each other or with any non-Socialist parties.[21] On the other hand, the National Progressive, now the Finnish People's Party, has formed forty-two electoral unions with the Agrarians and twenty-eight with the Conservatives between 1919 and 1962. There have also been six electoral unions consisting of Agrarians, Conservatives, Progressives, and the Swedish People's Party.[22]

Long-range platforms are an obvious guide to the ideological cleavages of party systems. A detailed content analysis of the eight Finnish party programs has been completed recently.[23] Considering both the substantive and the structural aspects of the documents, and viewing the orientation, attitude, motivation, and argumentation of party ideologies, the analysis finds the two Communist programs consistently different from those of the Conservatives, Swedish People's Party, and the Finnish People's Party. But the party "spectrum" is far from being unidimensional. The Communist Party of Finland and the Democratic Union of the Finnish People differ from the six others as regards the desire to maintain Finland's constitution, parliamentary domocracy, and social order. Emotionally toned Marxist expressions are used by both the Social Democrats and the Communists. There are scale-like orders of the parties; there are also unique features of the Swedish People's Party. Occasionally the ideologies form a Right, a Center, and a Left, while the attitudes on economy are of four distinct types. The Conservatives and the Swedes defend the capitalistic system and oppose government control; the Finnish People's Party, Agrarians, and Small Peasants defend the system but favor control; the Social Democrats like the control but dislike the system; and the Communist platforms abandon state control as a useless means to their ends.

In order to analyze Finnish political culture—cleavages and integrating factors included—another line of approach has recently been adopted in a study of leading politicians. It was assumed by Karen Erickson that formal expression is given to the values and ideologies of a political system by its leaders, and that such concepts give order and direction to action and behavior within the system. Her analysis of the values and ideologies of Finnish political leadership, mainly the members of Parliament, is in progress.[24] The questions are concerned with state activities along with those of institutions, groups, and forces which influence the making of political decisions. Specifically, seven problem areas have emerged as a result of the answers obtained in interviews: extent of governmental activity, foreign policy, social welfare, employment, industrialization, political cooperation, and representation.

According to the preliminary findings of this study, Finnish party alignments are temporary and provisional. Although party groupings and the differences of opinion often coincide, there is sufficient crossing of party lines on the extent to which the government should participate in economic and social welfare, and the means of implementing a foreign policy of neutrality, to suggest a new alignment of fewer parties. Reliance on law appears to be the most important integrating factor in the Finnish political system. Moreover, group interests are perceived by the political leaders not as discrete entities whose sum comprises the national interest, but rather as being subordinated to an image of the national interest which cuts through established groups. However, it is undetermined how closely the leadership agrees on the nature of this image. The material also indicates that in Finland political leadership opinion is moderate rather than conservative or radical; interest-group leaders tend to hold less moderate opinions than do leaders in formal governmental organs or even in political parties.

Interest groups and political parties are, however, quite intertwined one with the other. According to interviews with the members of Parliament who were elected in 1951, most members thought of themselves as representing at least one economic interest. The two interests shared in common by the Social Democrats and Agrarians were the cooperative movement, with forty-five and forty-three adherents respectively, and the small farmers' organizations, represented by five members in each group. But even in these areas, the members of the two belonged to different organizations. The two large national organizations of consumers' cooperatives were so distinctly differentiated on political grounds that no overlapping existed across parliamentary group lines. No other common economic interests at all was shared by the Social Democrats and the non-Socialists. No non-Socialist member represented the trade unions, and no Social Democrat, the white-collar organizations and employers' interests. On the other hand, the four non-Socialist parties had more common ground. Apart from the small farmers' organizations, all the interests represented by Agrarians were also shared by some Conservative and Swedish members, whereas of the four groups only Agrarians contained no representation of industrial employers' organizations. The Finnish People's Party was peculiar in that it comprised the relatively heaviest representation of white-collar interests, but none of the agricultural producers and employers.[25]

In general, Finnish members of Parliament become affiliated with their interest groups and other organizations before their election. Of the members elected during the years 1919–39, 36 percent had held a position in governing bodies of cooperatives prior to their election, 30 percent had been active in organizations of producers and private entrepreneurs, 25 percent in farmers' organizations, 21 percent in various youth organizations, 19 percent in trade unions, 12 percent in defense organizations, 11 percent in temperance and social-improvement associations, and so forth. The Socialist-non-Socialist cleavage was again the main differentiator of interests. But there was also other correlations of party and interest-group affiliations.[26] Some economic interests could be identified with a certain party, but many more with some group of parties competing to advocate the interest concerned.

It is of major interest in any representative government to learn not only from which spheres of interests but also from which social strata in general the "representatives of the people" are recruited. A well-known tendency of electorates is to vote for candidates who are above their own social level, and the social background of the Finnish Parliament has proved to be no exception to this general rule. Successful candidates in parliamentary elections can be classified as follows:[27]

	1907–17	1919–39	1958	Population in 1950
Upper class	37%	43%	44%	3%
Middle class	30	25	26	21
Peasantry	20	24	24	19
Workers	13	8	7	52
	100%	100%	100%	95%

Accordingly, the working class has not only been quite underrepresented proportionally, but has also shown a slight tendency to decrease in membership in Parliament. The number of peasant members rose until the 1930's, and is nowadays exceptionally high in comparison with other legislatures. But if a similar comparison be made, the Finns have hardly been prone to consult lawyers on election days, since the number of members with legal training has in general amounted to only 10 percent of all members, and currently comprises twenty members (10 percent). Another group of advocates is more common: many representatives of Socialist parties are either officials of parties and interest groups or journalists employed by the labor press.[28]

Table 3—Social Class and Education of the Members of Parliament Elected in 1958, by Party

	Communists	Social Democrats	Agrarian	Center	Conservatives	Swedish	Total
Social Class							
Upper class	9	16	20	6	27	9	87
Middle class	17	29	2	2	—	2	52
Peasantry	12	4	26	—	2	3	47
Workers	12	2	—	—	—	—	14
	50	51	48	8	29	14	200
Education							
University level	3	8	16	6	26	8	67
Secondary school	6	5	—	—	—	2	13
Vocational school	12	18	20	2	3	3	58
Adult educational institution	8	12	5	—	—	—	25
Elementary school	19	8	7	—	—	—	35
No information	2	—	—	—	—	—	2
	50	51	48	8	29	14	200

Source: Martti Noponen, "Piirteitä kansanedustajien sosiaalisesta taustasta," Politiikka (1959), pp. 99, 102. Regular Social Democrats and members of Social Democratic opposition group are combined.

Information on the social background of the members of Parliament is given by party in *Table 3*. The parties are quite different in this respect. Only the Socialist parties, and of these mainly the Communists, have elected workers to Parliament. But the upper and middle classes are in a majority in every group except the Agrarians, where the farmers dominate slightly. In this connection, a reminder is necessary that some farmers are here classified as "upper class."[29] The Conservatives constitute the group with most upper-class representatives; the majority also have a university degree. In both respects their closest rival is the Finnish People's Party. But higher education is rare among the Communist members, a tendency also shown in the combined group of Social Democrats.

In a survey of the social background, external information sometimes gives only a vague idea of class and other group identifications. Probably some of the inhabitants of Helsinki still rather identify themselves with other communities, and a social rise does not necessarily cut a person's emotional and other ties with his previous class. If one eliminates the social rise experienced by members of Finnish Parliaments during the period 1919–39, by considering instead the social class of their parents, quite a new picture is provided of the members' social backgrounds. It is close to being a sample of the Finnish society one generation earlier; and social class also distinctly differentiates as to party. About 70 percent of the representatives of Socialist parties, but very few non-Socialists, were born to working-class parents, while most Agrarian representatives had farming fathers.[30]

Social class or occupational-group interests also seem to constitute the major differentiator of political parties in the perceptions of the Finnish electorate. Such a conclusion was reached in December 1955, when a sample of students was asked why they favored their particular party, and also in May 1958, when a cross-sectional sample of the inhabitants of Tampere answered an inquiry on the most agreeable feature of their chosen party.[31] Almost all the Communists of Tampere conceived of their party as a defender of the workers' interests. This was also a typical Social Democrat's answer, although some of them replied—as did many supporters of the Finnish People's Party —that their party "keeps in the middle of the road." The last-mentioned party was regarded by its supporters as a defender of white-collar interests, while Agrarians favored their party because of its furthering of rural and farming interests. Most student supporters of the Swedish People's Party mentioned the minority language group. However, in both samples the Conservative supporters were likely to emphasize their party's patriotism, general interests, and able leaders.

In the Tampere survey, another question was asked concerning the worst characteristic of the least agreeable party. The opponents of the Conservatives criticized that party as the representative of the upper classes, as discriminating against the workers and as being too militaristically minded, while Communists were thought of by their opponents as a "glaringly radical" party, lacking patriotism and furthering foreign interests. The Agrarian Union was disliked by its opponents because of the excessive favor accorded its own class interests. The Finnish People's Party, in turn, was accused of uselessness, and opponents disliked the Social Democratic opposition because it caused disruption.

In October 1958, the Finnish Gallup Poll asked a national sample for opinions on the good and bad aspects of all parties, irrespective of the interviewees' own party preferences. Nevertheless, it proved easiest to get a positive opinion about the interviewee's own party, which was also the most difficult one for him to criticize. The most unanimous criticism was that attached to the Agrarians—their advocacy of one-sided group interest. But that party was also praised by supporters, and some nonsupporters, for the very same reason. The criticism of the Communists had more ideological support. Their party was seen not only by others but even by some of its own supporters as traitorous to its own country, unreliable, and too violent. The Social Democrats were criticized by the electorate for their internal dissensions.[32]

Such surveys indicate that Finnish political parties are different not only at leadership level, or according to the stereotyped cartoons and slogans, but also in the minds of the electorate. To a large extent the differentiation is due to images of the class basis and class interests of the parties. But important ideological differences are also sensed which are not related to social cleavages.

In addition to differentiating party images, the perceived distance between different parties is of interest in a multiparty system because it would reveal to what extent the political cleavages at leadership level are paralleled among the electorate by similar cleavages of a political nature. Some information on this may be obtained from the material in the Tampere survey where, however, the Agrarians were few in number and no candidates of the Swedish People's Party have run for election. As an indirect measure of these distances, one might use the opinions on policy matters. The Communist and "bourgeois" supporters had opposing preferences, as did their parties, and there was relatively little deviating opinion. But the group of Social Democratic supporters was difficult to locate. For example, equally many Social Democrats favored socialization and desocialization. When a sample of voters was asked in Helsinki in 1962 to classify each party as Socialist, bourgeois, or neither, the Social Democrats were most obviously considered Socialist, while Communism was thought by many to be "neither." Yet another classification into Left wing, Center, and Right wing placed only the Communists and the Social Democratic opposition in the Left wing. In the popular image, the place of the Social Democrats was closer to the Center. Likewise, the Swedish People's Party, Agrarian Union, and Finnish People's Party were generally perceived as bourgeois but Center.[33]

The sample in the Tampere survey was also given a list of all the parties, and asked to arrange them in order of preference. In general, the favored and disliked parties were more differentiated than the middle ones, which appeared to be harder to place on the continuum of preference. *Table 4* gives data on the second and last choices of the interviewees by their party preference. The supporters of non-Socialist parties usually had no difficulty in naming the most disliked party, the Communists. The Communists, also named by the Social Democrats more often than any other party, had in their turn the most aversion to the Conservatives. But many supporters of all leftist parties also picked the Swedish People's Party as the least liked. The seemingly uncompromising attitude which distracted the leaders of the two Social Democratic camps did not at that time exist among the backers of Social Democrats. The Socialist–non-Socialist cleavage also seems to have greatly diminished in the minds of the non-Socialists, while the "class struggle" attitude was mainly concentrated among the Communist backers.

To some extent *Table 4* reflects all the major national political cleavages which were revealed by the roll-call behavior of the legislators. Of the leftist parties, the Communists were closer to the Agrarians, while strongly adhering to the Socialist–non-Socialist dichotomy. A dislike of the party of the minority language was common in this Finnish-speaking area. The most obvious political cleavage in Tampere was, however, the Communist–non-Communist conflict. Only 11 percent of the Social Democrats rated the Communists second, while 38 percent rated them last. Putting the two Social Democratic groups together, and discounting them as number two preferences, their second parties were distributed as follows: 21 percent Communist, 58 percent one of the non-Socialist parties, and 21 percent don't know. In the minds of the Social Democrats, the Communist–non-Communist cleavage was thus clearly more predominant than the division of the electorate into Socialists and non-Socialists.

Table 4—Party of Second and Last Choice, by Party Preference, Among Adult Population of Tampere in 1958 (in percentages)

	Communists	Social Democratic Opposition	Social Democrats	Agrarians	Finnish People's Party	Conservatives	Aggregate
	(108)	(25)	(164)	(10)	(30)	(93)	(433)
Second Choice							
Communists	•	8	11	—	3	—	5
Social Democratic Opposition	27	•	38	10	—	2	22
Social Democrats	30	56	•	60	43	26	20
Agrarians	14	4	10	•	3	4	9
Finnish People's Party	3	8	13	—	•	50	17
Conservatives	5	4	9	10	43	•	8
Swedish People's Party	1	—	—	10	—	5	2
Don't know	20	20	19	10	8	13	17
	100	100	100	100	100	100	100
Most Disliked							
Communists	•	16	38	60	87	79	40
Social Democratic Opposition	6	•	4	—	—	2	3
Social Democrats	8	—	•	10	—	—	2
Agrarians	3	20	13	•	7	3	8
Finnish People's Party	4	4	2	—	•	—	2
Conservatives	33	12	9	20	—	•	13
Swedish People's Party	19	32	16	10	3	5	15
One of the Social Democrats	4	—	—	—	—	1	1
Don't know	23	16	18	—	3	10	16
	100	100	100	100	100	100	100

Source: Pertti Pesonen, *Valtuutus kansalta.* (Helsinki: Söderström, 1965), English version *The Election in Finland* (New Haven, Yale Univ. Press, 1967).

SOCIAL CLASS, POLITICAL CLEAVAGES, AND SOCIAL CONFLICTS

It is an historical paradox that the modernization of European societies and the lessening of ascriptive values has occurred simultaneously with the growth of social class as an important source for political diversity. In the Scandinavian countries particularly, class conflicts have been considerably lessened, if not completely eliminated; at the same time, social class accounts for more of the variation in party preference than some decades ago.

However, it may appear much less paradoxical when comparing the effects of class-based cleavage and other cleavages. Such a comparison produces generalization in which the simultaneous appearance of the lessening of class conflicts and the growing importance of class as a source for variation in political opinions can be explained. As seen from *Table 5,* social class is an important source for variation in party preference. Another important dividing line exists between the urban and rural population, but this cleavage is built into the stratification system, because farmers conceive themselves as a separate group and are conceived as such by others. The importance of social class is also revealed by the fact that occupation and self-identification as criteria for class give almost identical results. Overlapping between the two criteria is negligible.

Table 5—Party Preference by Social Class Defined by Occupation and by Class Identification in a Finnish National Sample*

Party Preference	CLASS BY OCCUPATION			CLASS BY SELF-IDENTIFICATION		
	Farmer (308)	Worker (421)	White collar (133)	Farmer (323)	Worker (411)	White collar (116)
Social Democrats	3%	34%	14%	3%	36%	12%
Communists	9	34	5	9	35	2
Agrarians	54	5	5	53	4	6
Bourgeois (three parties)	17	11	61	17	10	65
No preference	17%	16%	15%	18%	15%	15%

Source: Gallup Poll, 1958.
* Party preference is here defined on the basis of a rather complicated battery of questions dealing with actual voting in the last elections and voting intentions at the time of the interview (October 1958). If the interviewee said that he did not vote in 1958 or declined to say whether he did, he was asked how he would vote at present. If he still did not reveal his preference, he was asked how he voted in 1954. This way of eliminating persons without a party preference is certainly problematic in more than one respect, but the most troublesome fact is that some of the Communist voters try to hide their party preference by not revealing it on any direct question or by saying that they voted for the Social Democrats. This has been clearly shown by Finnish Gallup in earlier polls. Therefore, control questions, which only Communists as a rule answer positively, have to be used in order to pick out Communists from the Social Democratic and the "no preference" groups.

When restricting the comparison to those who reveal party preference, it appears that 64 percent of the farmers prefer the Agrarian Party, 80 percent of the workers prefer one of the two Socialist parties, and 76 percent of the white-collar people prefer one of the three bourgeois parties. Looking at the data another way, it appears that 85 percent of those preferring the Agrarian Party are farmers, 82 percent of those supporting the Socialist parties are workers, whereas only 45 percent of those who prefer one of the bourgeois parties belong to the white-collar group. The supporters of the bourgeois parties include large numbers of farmers and workers. This is particularly the case in the Swedish People's Party, which also tries to represent the Swedish-speaking minority who live mainly in urban and rural areas of western and southern Finland. The Swedish-speaking population's rather heavy vote for the Swedish People's Party is one of the main exceptions to the class-based political division. A second exception is that of the farmers in one particular area who give heavy support to the conservative National Coalition Party instead of supporting the Agrarians. The third notable exception is most important for its effect on Finnish politics: the workers as a social class are politically divided into Communists and Social Democrats.

Large numbers of Swedish-speaking fishermen, small farmers, and workers vote for the Swedish People's Party and not for the Swedish candidates in the Socialist parties. This is particularly true for Swedish-speaking farmers. Generally, the higher the proportion of Swedish-speaking people in a commune, the more the Swedish farmers and workers vote for the Swedish People's party. The party has a bourgeois platform, but the members represent a wide scale of ideologies and interests ranging all the way from rather radical Liberalism to strong Conservatism. Although linguistic differences have not been important in postwar politics, Swedish-speaking voters have maintained their traditional party allegiance. The absence of strong conflict on matters concerning language and loyalty to the Swedish party has led to a certain lack of interest in social change by the Swedish-speaking population. Although the majority of the Swedish-speaking Finns are farmers or fishermen, they have a slightly higher proportion of upper and middle-class persons than the Finnish-speaking majority. The Swedish minority has become a conservative force in the postwar period, favoring the status quo in Finnish society.

The second notable exception to class-based cleavage is almost completely due to the political traditions of one region. As many as 21 percent of all farmers who reveal their party preference do not vote for the Agrarian Party. Among those farmers who vote for the Conservatives, 85 percent are from the southern parts of the Pohjanmaa region (the province of Vaasa) in western Finland. A distinguishing trait of much of this region is the almost complete absence of a stratification system. The region is mainly populated by independent farmers. No urban centers dominate life in this region. The farmers are small and, perhaps even more important, the variation in the size of farms is slight. They are mainly run by the farmer and his family without aid of farm workers. This has been the historical pattern for the region, whereas the greater part of the country had a crofter system from the nineteenth century until almost late 1920. Big farmers leased small areas to crofters, who were obliged to do a certain number of day's work per year. However, the crofters' tenure was uncertain, and they could be fired at the big farmer's discretion.[34]

A rather decisive factor underlying the conservatism of the farmers of South Pohjanmaa is their influence on the formation of the modern social and political order, and which has developed into pride and strong feeling for the legitimacy of that order. During the so-called Liberation War in 1918, which turned into a civil war between "Whites" and "Reds," the White forces started their operations in South Pohjanmaa, where in many places almost all of the male population joined the White army. The South Pohjanmaa farmers have been perceived as the real backbone of the existing social system by conservative urban people. South Pohjanmaa's religious development has also been important. During the nineteeth century the region was the center of a strong religious movement of a fundamentalist nature. Instead of producing sects, these religious movements have stayed within the

Lutheran Church (which attracts over 90 percent of the Finnish population) and have strongly influenced the church's religious patterns. South Pohjanmaa farmers not only vote for the conservative National Coalition Party to a much higher degree than other farmers, but the Agrarian representatives for South Pohjanmaa in the Parliament also have a more conservative record than their party colleagues from most of the country.[35] During the 1930's a strong anti-Communist movement with Fascist inclinations, the Lapua, started in a commune which is also the center of the strongest religious movement in the region.

It is worth noting that the above-mentioned exceptions to class-based voting means the existence of crisscrossing cleavage lines. However, it is hardly reasonable to say that these nonclass cleavages have led to an increase of more instrumental attitudes in politics or to greater willingness to compromise or negotiate. It seems more reasonable to state that instrumental adaptation presupposes institutionalized rules for the handling of conflicts. In modern Finnish society, social institutions concerned with instrumental adaptation are either based on social class, such as labor-market organizations, or they do not have any particular relations to cleavages in the social structure. The latter is true for many governmental or state-sponsored organs concerned with social and economic policy. Cleavages other than those based on social class or the related difference between rural producers, farmers, and consumers tend to lack institutional arrangements for the handling of conflicts when they occur. Accordingly, nonclass cleavages often lead to strongly emotional expressions and do not as a rule seem to increase consensus in the society. This seems to be particularly true for the most important exception to class-based cleavage, namely, the one between Social Democrats and the Communists.

During the twentieth century, until World War II, the dominating dividing line in Finnish politics was the class-based cleavage between the Socialists and others. At the time of the Civil War in 1918 there was only one Socialist Party, the Social Democrats. Likewise, in the 1930's, when the Communist Party was forbidden, the Social Democratic Party was the only existing Socialist Party. In many respects the classical dividing line between Socialists and others has ceased to be the big source of conflict. Most of the earlier Socialist objectives, such as social-welfare measures and the rights of the labor unions, have been incorporated into the social system and are accepted by most people. Today, Social Democrats are considered very respectable even in bourgeois circles, but in the 1930's the situation was different. Today the class-based cleavage line between Socialists and others has a rather different effect than it had in the past. The acceptance of the labor movement has led to an institutionalization of class cleavage, and thus, to a lessening of class conflicts.

Many sociologists have stressed that the existence of multiple crisscrossing cleavage lines prevents basic cleavages from becoming strong disruptive conflicts and crises of legitimacy. Coser assumes quite explicitly that multiple crisscrossing cleavage lines prevent the breakdown of consensus and basic cleavages along one axis.[36] In his theory of mass society Kornhauser has shown how the existence of intermediate bodies, such as voluntary associations and independent mass media between primary personal relations and the national social system is a condition for a pluralist society and a stable democracy. He refers, among other things, to the fact that strong intermediating voluntary associations produce crisscrossing cleavage lines which makes it impossible for a single group to dominate their member's lives.[37] However, the Weimar Republic was full of crisscrossing cleavage lines and still it led to crises of legitimacy and the overthrow of the democratic system. Kornhauser is certainly right when he argues that intermediating bodies were lacking in Germany at that time. Nevertheless, the assumption of the conflict-lessening effects of crisscrossing cleavage lines disregards the nature of social institutions. It can justifiably be stated that any cleavage which lacks institutional rules for handling conflicts can lead to crises of legitimacy. Cleavages which have resulted in institutions concerned with instrumental adaptation and the solving of conflicts according to rules, tend to diminish the chances for strong conflicts and a complete change of the system. In Finnish society this may at least be an explanation of the fact that class cleavage is legitimate and taken for granted. Instead of being an anachronism related to the old ascriptive society, this pattern has continued with the modernization of society. In the case of the cleavage between Social Democrats and Communists, however, the conflict is strong and there are no institutional arrangements to lessen it. The different branches of the labor movement, such as the trade union movement, the adult education association, and the worker's sport movement, which could act as mediating agencies, are split along ideological lines. The appearance of a third Socialist Party, the Social Democratic Opposition, has lately only widened the gap between Social Democrats and Communists.

THE SPLIT WITHIN THE WORKING CLASS

The split in the working class between Social Democrats and Communists is one of the dominating features of contemporary Finnish politics. It is also one of the features which makes political life in Finland so different from the situation in the other Scandinavian countries. In contrast to the fairly well integrated Social Democratic Parties of Denmark, Norway, and Sweden, the Finnish Social Democratic Party has to compete with the Communists for popular support and is also ridden with internal conflicts. Lately, the opposition within the party has emerged as a separate group in Parliament and it also ran separately in the municipal elections of 1960. The weakness of the Social Democratic Party comes out clearly in studies of voting participation. Generally, the greater the support for the biggest party in a commune, the higher the voting participation in the commune. This means that voting participation is usually very high in communes where just one political party dominates. This applies, however to all parties but the Social Democratic Party.[38] The same is also true for voting within the labor unions.[39] The best explanation is perhaps the cross-pressure hypothesis.

Cross-pressures are rare in areas where one political party is dominant, but the crisscrossing lines among the Social Democrats make the situation exceptional within that party.

The political situation for the Social Democratic Party is difficult. In order to compete with the Communists for working-class support, it has to display a certain radicalism. On the other hand, because they are the foremost competitors of the Communists, the Social Democrats are sometimes allied to the bourgeois parties. Further, the Agrarians, although a parliamentary minority, run the Finnish cabinet and are hostile to the Social Democrats. Whether the absence of Social Democrats from the cabinet is the result of Agrarian hostility or Russian pressure is a moot point. As a matter of fact, the Social Democrats cooperated with the Conservatives in the presidential campaign of 1962 in order to oust Agrarian President Kekkonen.

In view of the political situation of the Social Democratic Party, it is interesting to compare the social base of Communist and Social Democratic support. A crucial question is how the two have been able to compete with each other for the support of new voters. The term "new voters" as used here does not refer to those attaining voting age but particularly to the citizens of the relatively isolated areas of northern and eastern Finland, in which voting participation has increased considerably since World War II, According to the Gallup Poll of 1958, there are no differences in the age distribution among workers supporting the Communists and workers supporting the Social Democracts.

The well-known generalization that women tend to be more conservative than men is also supported by Finnish evidence.

Table 6—Working-Class Men and Women According to Party Preference in 1958 (in percentages)

Party Preference	Men (218)	Women (206)
Social Democrats	32%	36%
Communists	41	27
Agrarians	6	4
Bourgeois	6	16
No preference	15	17

Working-class women support Communism less than men, and give more support to the bourgeois parties; however, the differences are rather small. It is important to note that the question of women's rights is not a political issue. Finnish women have long had a comparatively favorable position judged both by law and custom. The most outstanding example of female emancipation is the fact that the country was the first in Europe to grant women political suffrage. Likewise, a comparatively high proportion of women are enrolled in the universities.

The picture, however, gets more complicated with the introduction of the urban-rural dichotomy as a new variable. Working-class women from urban areas are inclined to give comparatively little support to the Communists. In fact, support for the Communists and the bourgeois parties are virtually equal among urban working-class women. With men, the situation is different. Urban working-class men are divided evenly between the Social Democrats and Communists, but the Communists get strong support from the rural working class. One of the peculiarities of Finnish Communism is its rather strong rural character. Fifty percent of the working-class people living in rural areas outside villages prefer the Communists, whereas only 19 percent indicate preference for the Social Democrats. In the cities, however, the corresponding percentages are 33 and 46 respectively.

Table 7—Working-Class Men and Women from Rural and Urban Areas According to Party Preference in 1958 (in percentages)

| Party Preference | MEN | | WOMEN | |
	Urban (100)	Rural (116)	Urban (101)	Rural (104)
Social Democrats	39	26	39	33
Communists	38	43	19	34
Agrarians	—	12	1	8
Bourgeois	10	3	24	8
No preference	13	16	17	17

In a large country with a small population, such as Finland, the opportunities for social mobility, social participation, and educational training are rather limited for those who do not live close to urban areas. A great proportion of Finland's small farmers make their living not only from farming but also from lumberwork. These farmers are counted as workers here, as they are in Finnish labor statistics. In the North and the East particularly the farmers have to take nonfarm jobs in the winter. In these areas the Communists also have their heaviest support, as seen from *Table 8,* in which the country has been divided into the South and West and North and East.

Table 8—Working-Class Party Preference in 1958 by Urban and Rural Areas in the South and West and North and East of Finland (in percentages)

| Party Preference | URBAN | | RURAL | |
	South & West (167)	North & East (34)	South & West (122)	North & East (98)
Social Democrats	42	26	36	21
Communists	29	26	34	45
Agrarians	1	—	7	14
Bourgeois	15	24	8	2
No preference	13	24	15	18

The Communists have their strongest backing among rural working-class people in the North and East. However, the majority of the Finnish population lives in the South and West. This can be seen from the number of respondents in the different groups.

Social and economic conditions, as measured by indices of per-capita income, unemployment, social welfare, and so forth are also much better in the South and West than in the North and East.

Three conclusions are warranted by *Table 9*. First, workers who during the preceding year were unemployed tended to support the Communists more often than the Social Democrats. Second, particularly in the South and West, the gainfully employed tended to support the Social Democrats. Third, judging from the number of respondents, unemployment is comparatively much more common in the North and East than in the South and West.

The employment statistics give additional support to the third conclusion. Only a relatively small proportion of the unemployment in Finland can be ascribed to industrial labor. The unemployment problem is mainly a question of agrarian underemployment. Small farmers, unless they do not wish to remain at a standard of living considerably below that of industrial workers, must supplement their incomes by nonfarm labor. An estimated total of nearly 20 percent of the total labor force is comprised of farmers who are engaged in temporary nonfarm work, mainly lumbering.

Table 9—Party Preference by Employment Status Among Working-Class People from the South and West and the North and East in 1958 (in percentages)

Party Preference	SOUTH & WEST		NORTH & EAST	
	Self or somebody in the family unemployed during last winter (73)	Nobody in the family unemployed (216)	Self or somebody in the family unemployed during last winter (60)	Nobody in the family unemployed (72)
Social Democrats	25	45	20	24
Communists	44	27	53	29
Agrarians	3	3	7	14
Bourgeois	9	13	2	12
No preference	19	12	18	21

Judging from *Table 9* the number of people who had been unemployed during the winter of 1958 is rather great. It may be an overestimate. However, the unemployment figures for the postwar period do not primarily measure economic hardship but rather a state of alienation from the ordinarily accepted ways of earning a living. The policy of the Finnish government has been to arrange work for all the unemployed on public projects. In fact, almost all of the unemployed are so engaged, and according to a study by Jouko Siipi,[40] their salaries are sometimes comparable to those of normally employed workers. To be unemployed means merely that a person is registered as unemployed and has to resort to governmental unemployment work sites. Accordingly, unemployment means restrictions as to freedom of action and the possibilities of working where one chooses.

It can generally be stated that nationwide political-behavior studies which do not take the differences between the South and West and North and East into account are doomed to be failures. Party preferences according to income composition is rather different in the two halves of Finland, as seen in *Table 10*.

It appears that the better-paid workers in the South and West contribute to the heavy support for the Social Democrats, whereas the poorer workers in the North and East account for the heaviest support for the Communists.

As seen from the number of respondents in the different groups, the workers are, in general, better paid in the South and West.

Even if the Communists have heavier support in rural than in urban areas, as well as heavier support in the North and East than in the South and West, they have rather strong support in both areas. In Finnish political terminology this difference corresponds to the labels of industrial Communism and backwoods Communism. Finnish Communism is strongest in the woodlands, but since a smaller part of the population lives in the rural areas of the North and East, there are, in an absolute sense, more Communists in the South and West.

Table 10—Party Preferences According to Annual Income in the Working Class in the South and West and North and East (in percentages)

Party Preference	SOUTH AND WEST		NORTH AND EAST	
	Less than 400,000 Marks (150)	More than 400,000 Marks (122)	Less than 400,000 Marks (91)	More than 400,000 Marks (28)
Social Democrats	33	50	21	36
Communists	33	28	40	39
Agrarians	4	2	11	7
Bourgeois	14	11	7	7
No preference	16	9	21	11

In an earlier paper, one of the present authors[41] indicated that whereas Social Democracy in the whole country and Communism in the South and West can to some extent be explained by early Socialist traditions, Communism in the North and East does not go back to these traditions. The vote for Social Democrats in both areas, as well as the vote for Communists in the South and West in the general election of 1954, correlate positively with the Social Democratic vote in 1916 and with the percentage of Reds killed in the Civil War in 1918. However, in the North and East, the Communist vote in 1954 shows only zero correlations with these variables of common Socialist tradition. The strong support for the Communists in the northern and eastern areas is of a more recent origin. Whereas the northern and eastern areas before World War II had the lowest voting percentages, voting participation after the war has tended to be very high in the Communist strongholds in the North and East. The Social Democratic Party has not been able or even tried to conquer the votes of these groups of newcomers in politics. The Social Democrats' effective competition with the Communists has been mostly restricted to areas where the Social Democrats have traditionally had support. This may be seen as a weakness, but it is perhaps best interpreted in terms of the structural base of the two parties. By tradition, the Social Democrats strongly represent the interest of the urban wage earners and consumers. The new groups in politics, the rural poor people from the North and East, however, are in a sense both wage earners and producers. They may be subsistence farmers, but they profit from the subsidies the government provides for farmers.

REGIONAL DIFFERENCES IN THE
SOCIAL BASES OF THE
FINNISH POLITICAL PARTIES

The dividing line between the South and West and the North and East is also important in other aspects of the Finnish political and social structure. In historical studies it has been shown that political traditions seem to affect the political climates of the two halves of Finland.[42] The northern and eastern parts have always had more radicalism, even within the agrarian and bourgeois blocks. In the South and West the social system of earlier times was heavily village-centered, whereas in the North and East, with its extremely low density of population, it was very much based on the extended family.[43] There are some studies indicating that the village-centeredness in the South and West created extremely strong village cohesiveness as late as the latter part of the nineteenth century. This was particularly true in South Pohjanmaa where, as has been indicated, the political climate is very conservative. On theoretical grounds one can assume that strong village cohesiveness results in support for the status quo, but no studies of the impact of these differences in the social structure have been carried out.

In Finnish parliamentary elections, the principle of proportional representation is applied within sixteen different electoral districts among which the 200 mandates are distributed in proportion to the districts' respective population.

The dividing line (see *Figure 1*) between the South and West and North and East is drawn in such a way that about two-thirds of the total area of Finland belongs to the northern and eastern half of the country. Still the North and East has a much smaller part of the population than the South and West. In 1958 the electoral districts in the South and West elected 126 members while those in the North and East elected 74 members to the Parliament. Although the Communists, as the map indicates, are particularly strong in the North and East, more Communist representatives are still elected from the South and West (29 out of 50 in 1958).

The areal units on the map are neither electoral districts nor precincts, but the 550 communes of the country. The communes, both rural and urban, are the smallest administrative units in the country and have a certain amount of self-government. Because of the long historical tradition of dividing the country into communes, they are also natural social areas in the sense that people identify themselves and others by referring to the communes as their places of birth and residence.

The commune has been used as the analytic unit in an ecological correlation and factor analysis which will be presented shortly. It aims at describing the differentials in the social bases of the political parties in the South and West and the North and East. The Aaland Islands, which have a large amount of self-government and elect only one person to the Parliament, have been omitted from the analysis.

Factor analysis has been used because it provides a possibility of simultaneously handling the many variables which may affect political behavior. Because it is mainly a technique for reducing the variation in many observed variables to the variation in only a few basic ones (the factors), it can be used to pick out those key factors which can lend themselves to closer analysis. Here we are using the results only for a brief description of the social background of Finnish parties. This can be done by looking for the factors in which the variables indicating support for a particular political party have high factor loadings. The variables measuring party support (variables 1–7 in *Table 11*) have therefore not been used in the interpretation of the factors. These variables indicate the vote for each party in the 1950's, with one exception. Since the Swedish Party runs only in six electoral districts, the proportion of Swedish-speaking people in each commune has been used as a measure.

The rationale behind the decision to avoid the use of the variables measuring party support during the 1950's in the interpretation of the factors is, of course, the fact that these are the variables which we would like to explain. From the point of view of the methodology of factor analysis, this is a rather questionable procedure. However, in this particular case, the procedure seems to be acceptable. All factors in *Table 11* also have high loadings in variables other than those measuring party support in the 1950's. This enables one to make the interpretation on the basis of those other variables.

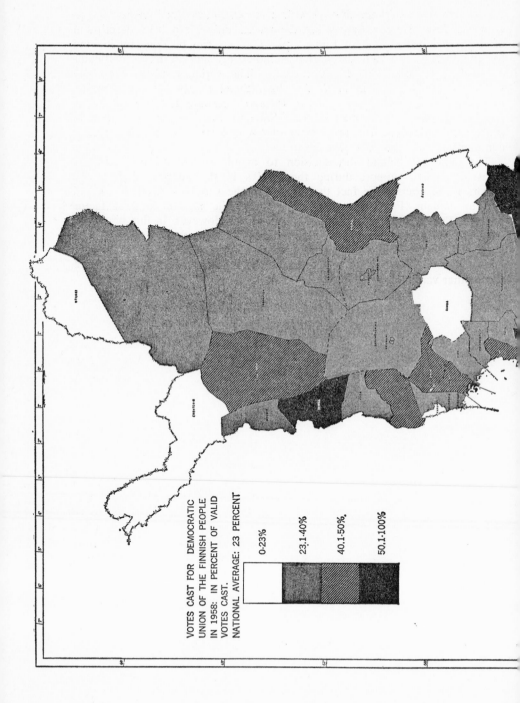

VOTES CAST FOR DEMOCRATIC
UNION OF THE FINNISH PEOPLE
IN 1958: IN PERCENT OF VALID
VOTES CAST.
NATIONAL AVERAGE: 23 PERCENT

0-23%

23.1-40%

40.1-50%.

50.1-100%

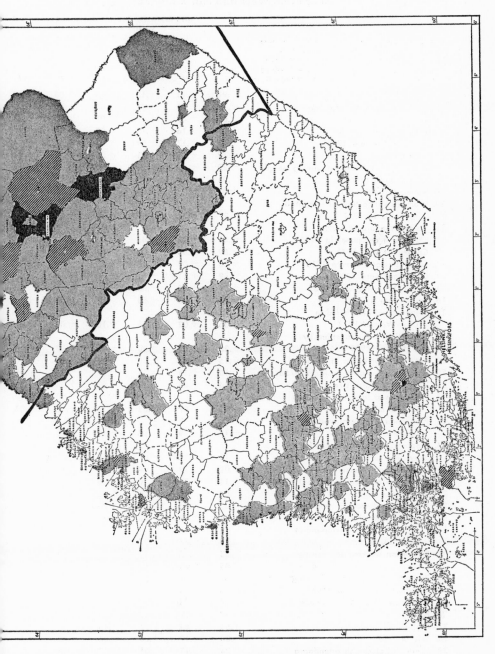

*Figure 1—The Electoral Support of the Communists in 1958,
by Commune, in Percent of Popular Vote.*

Table 11—The (Orthogonally) Rotated Factor Matrices for South and West and North and East

THE ROTATED FACTOR MATRICES
SOUTH & WEST

Variables[a] (unless year indicated the measures are from the 1950's). All variables reflect relative frequencies (for instance, the number of Reds killed in the war in 1918 per 1,000 of the total male population in each commune).	I	II	III	IV	V	VI
1. Communist vote in 1951	+.91	+.13	+.13	+.04	−.05	+.12
2. Social Democratic vote 1954	+.17	+.25	+.20	.00	−.23	+.52
3. Agrarian vote 1954	+.09	−.49	+.49	+.01	−.35	+.03
4. Communist vote 1954	+.89	+.16	+.13	.00	−.06	+.07
5. Conservative vote 1954	+.17	+.17	+.81	+.06	+.02	+.24
6. Liberal vote 1954	+.19	+.32	+.41	+.35	−.23	+.44
7. Proportion of Swedish-speaking people	−.20	+.40	−.58	−.06	+.32	−.12
8. Voting turnout 1954	+.01	+.10	−.08	−.78	−.10	−.02
9. Voting turnout 1958	+.07	−.02	+.01	−.85	−.06	−.04
10. Women's voting turnout compared to men's in 1951	+.27	−.17	+.37	+.14	+.04	+.10
11. Vote of the largest party (in each commune) in 1958	−.41	−.11	−.45	−.03	−.04	−.44
12. Communist vote 1945	+.89	+.08	+.05	+.01	−.04	+.16
13. Social Democratic vote 1916	+.63	−.09	+.16	−.26	−.09	+.44
14. Communist vote 1929	+.69	+.21	+.11	+.06	−.15	+.03
15. Social Democratic vote 1939	+.71	+.15	+.05	−.10	−.19	+.32
16. Fascist vote 1936	+.12	+.03	+.83	−.07	−.04	+.21
17. Frequency of Reds killed in Civil War in 1918	+.36	+.02	+.16	−.10	+.03	+.66
18. Proportion of farms settled by crofters in 1910	+.36	−.51	+.20	−.13	+.17	+.28
19. Vote for prohibition in 1931	+.15	−.04	+.39	−.49	−.28	−.20
20. Rise in Communist vote in 1948/58	−.18	+.15	+.21	−.11	−.31	+.08
21. Variance in farm size	+.24	+.05	+.11	+.09	+.03	+.22
22. Proportion of farms smaller than 50,000 m²	+.05	−.07	−.08	+.16	−.15	−.07
23. Proportion of persons working in agriculture	−.14	−.79	+.02	−.08	+.08	−.36
24. Proportion of people cared for by the commune	+.18	+.18	−.07	+.10	−.18	+.23
25. Proportion of unemployed in 1931–32	+.02	+.19	−.09	−.18	−.68	+.10
26. Proportion of unemployed in 1948–53	+.14	+.27	+.10	−.06	−.68	+.09
27. Income per capita	+.04	+.63	−.08	+.08	+.04	+.34
28. Proportion of manual workers	+.30	+.56	−.06	+.04	−.16	+.43
29. Population density	+.21	+.78	+.08	+.11	−.11	+.29
30. Proportion of people working in retail trade	+.19	+.77	+.27	+.05	−.11	+.15
31. Proportion working in industry	+.33	+.67	−.09	−.01	−.18	+.28
32. Proportion of electrified homes	−.05	+.78	−.10	−.24	+.05	−.17
33. Proportion of crowded dwellings	+.28	−.28	+.23	−.10	−.03	+.66
34. Migration into the commune	+.22	+.25	+.21	+.12	−.13	+.74
35. Migration out of the commune	+.17	+.02	+.28	+.15	−.05	+.72
36. Frequency of library loans	+.07	+.69	.00	−.06	+.03	−.04
37. High-school attendance	+.03	+.64	+.26	−.16	−.08	−.24
38. Suicide rate	+.08	+.19	+.28	−.06	−.12	−.03
39. Frequency of church attendance	−24	−.18	−.01	−.12	+.11	−.15
40. Frequency of people taking Holy Communion	−.12	−.10	+.10	−.09	+.06	−.09
41. Sunday-school attendance	−.21	−.19	+.07	−.01	−.22	−.36

* All variables were normalized before the correlation coefficients were computed. The normalization has been done separately for the South and West and the North and East. The method of factoring has been Thurstone's centroid factor method and the centroid structures have been rotated by the Quartimax orthogonal solution. The matrices have been run at the Illiac, the University of Illinois electronic digital computer, by the courtesy of Professor Charles E. Osgood.

THE ROTATED FACTOR MATRICES
NORTH & EAST

Variables (unless year indicated the measures are from the 1950's). All variables reflect relative frequencies (for instance, the number of Reds killed in the war in 1918 per 1,000 of the total male population in each commune).

	I	II	III	IV	V	VI
1. Communist vote in 1951	+.89	+.04	−.07	+.18	+.15	−.06
2. Social Democratic vote 1954	−.44	+.28	−.67	−.24	+.04	+.04
3. Agrarian vote 1954	−.08	−.49	+.67	+.21	−.28	−.04
4. Communist vote 1954	+.88	+.02	−.05	+.17	+.20	−.08
5. Conservative vote 1954	−.40	+.64	−.16	−.05	−.01	+.02
6. Liberal vote 1954	−.08	+.47	+.03	−.29	+.44	+.03
7. Proportion of Swedish-speaking people	.00	+.73	+.01	−.07	−.08	−.12
8. Voting turnout 1954	+.25	−.05	+.09	+.80	+.08	−.02
9. Voting turnout 1958	+.30	−.21	+.15	+.74	+.20	.00
10. Women's voting turnout compared to men's in 1951	−.12	−.27	−.27	−.56	−.07	+.05
11. Vote of the largest party (in each commune) 1958	−.01	−.41	+.58	+.32	.24	−.06
12. Communist vote 1945	+.80	+.07	−.20	+.07	−.03	−.13
13. Social Democratic vote 1916	+.09	+.02	−.81	+.02	−.22	+.03
14. Communist vote 1929	+.78	+.08	+.09	+.09	−.01	+.20
15. Social Democratic vote 1939	+.11	+.19	−.86	−.07	−.10	−.01
16. Fascist vote 1936	−.11	+.26	−.07	+.18	+.12	+.10
17. Frequency of Reds killed in Civil War 1918	−.06	+.35	−.49	+.04	−.22	+.28
18. Proportion of farms settled by crofters in 1910	+.06	−.44	−.28	−.08	−.13	−.17
19. Vote for prohibition in 1931	+.14	+.17	+.20	+.52	−.26	−.33
20. Rise in Communist vote in 1948/58	+.10	+.05	+.30	+.07	+.63	+.05
21. Variance in farm size	+.17	+.18	−.21	+.05	+.08	+.01
22. Proportion of farms smaller than 50,000 m²	+.12	−.01	−.05	−.17	+.25	−.07
23. Proportion of persons working in agriculture	+.04	−.84	+.20	+.03	+.04	−.01
24. Proportion of people cared for by the commune	+.20	−.09	−.51	−.27	−.20	+.11
25. Proportion of unemployed in 1931–32	+.27	+.08	+.10	+.21	+.63	+.09
26. Proportion of unemployed in 1948–53	+.34	+.02	+.47	+.25	+.38	−.07
27. Income per capita	+.18	+.61	−.09	+.01	+.06	+.13
28. Proportion of manual workers	+.20	+.64	−.37	−.08	+.17	+.12
29. Population density	−.06	+.54	−.26	+.09	−.07	+.28
30. Proportion of people working in retail trade	+.03	+.71	−.09	+.04	+.23	−.17
31. Proportion working in industry	+.16	+.82	−.20	+.03	−.02	+.08
32. Proportion of electrified homes	+.05	+.76	−.01	+.18	+.04	+.11
33. Proportion of crowded dwellings	+.20	−.55	−.08	+.01	+.40	+.06
34. Migration into the commune	+.11	+.55	−.20	−.21	+.11	+.42
35. Migration out of the commune	−.05	+.42	−.10	−.15	+.03	+.54
36. Frequency of library loans	+.13	+.39	+.01	+.04	.00	+.09
37. High-school attendance	+.03	+.51	+.07	+.20	+.25	−.44
38. Suicide rate	−.01	+.20	−.14	−.06	−.15	−.02
39. Frequency of church attendance	−.16	+.13	+.07	+.04	−.19	−.05
40. Frequency of people taking Holy Communion	−.14	+.03	−.13	−.15	+.03	−.03
41. Sunday-school attendance	−.30	−.18	−.23	+.03	−.09	+.28

The factors can be labeled as follows:

South and West

Factor I. *The factor of Socialist Traditions.* Highest loadings in the following variables: Communist vote in 1945 (+.89), Social Democratic vote in 1916 (+.63), Communist vote in 1929 (+.69), Social Democratic vote in 1939 (+.71).

Factor II. *The Modernization factor.* Highest loadings: proportion of people working in agriculture (−.79), income per capita (+.63), population density (+.78, proportion of people working in retail trade (+.77), proportion working in industry (+.67), proportion of electrified homes (+.78), frequency of library loans (+.69), high-school attendance (+.64).

Factor III. *The factor of Nationalist Conservatism.* Highest loadings: women's voting turnout (+.37), vote of the largest party (−.45), fascist vote in 1936 (+.83), vote for prohibition in 1931 (+.39).

Factor IV. *The factor of Political Passivity.* Highest loadings: voting turnout in 1954 (−.78), voting turnout in 1958 (−.85), vote for prohibition in 1931 (−.49).

Factor V. *The factor of Social Security.* Highest loadings: rise in Communist vote in 1948–58 (−.31), proportion of unemployed in 1931–32 (−.68), proportion of unemployed in 1948–53 (−.68).

Factor VI. *The Mobility factor.* Highest loadings: frequency of Reds killed in Civil War (+.66), proportion of crowded dwellings (+.66), migration into the commune (+.74), migration out of the commune (+.72).

North and East

Factor I. *The factor of Communist Traditions.* Highest loadings: Communist vote in 1945 (+.80), Communist vote in 1929 (+.78), proportion of unemployed in 1948–53 (+.34), Sunday-school attendance (−.30).

Factor II. *The Modernization factor.* Highest loadings: proportion of people working in agriculture (−.84), income per capita (+.61), proportion of manual workers (+.64), population density (+.54), proportion of people working in retail trade (+.71), proportion working in industry (+.82), proportion of electrified homes (+.76), proportion of crowded dwellings (−.55), migration into the commune (+.55), high-school attendance (+.51).

Factor III. *The factor of Rural Traditionalism.* Highest loadings: vote of the largest party (+.58), Social Democratic vote in 1916 (−.81), Social Democratic vote in 1939 (−.86), frequency of Reds killed in Civil War (−.49), proportion of people cared for by the commune (−.51), proportion of unemployed in 1948–53 (+.47), proportion of manual workers (−.37).

Factor IV. *The factor of Political Activity.* Highest loadings: voting turnout in 1954 (+.80), voting turnout in 1958 (+.74), women's voting turnout (−.56), vote for prohibition in 1931 (+.52).

Factor V. *The factor of Unsecurity.* Highest loadings: rise in Communist vote in 1948–58 (+.63), proportion of unemployed in 1931–32 (+.63), prohibition of unemployed in 1948–53 (+.38), proportion of crowded dwellings (+.40).

Factor VI. *The Mobility factor.* Highest loadings: vote for prohibition in 1931 (−.33), migration into the commune (+.42), migration out of the commune (+.54), high-school attendance (−.44).

No attempt to compare the factors of the South and West and the North and East systematically will be made here. Instead, we will focus on the description of the social base of the political parties by looking for the factor loadings of the variables measuring party support.

Table 12—Factor Loadings of Variables Measuring Party Support in the South and West and North and East

SOUTH & WEST

FACTORS

Variables Measuring Party Support:	Socialist Traditions	Moderni- zation	Nationalist Conservatism	Political Passivity	Social Security	Mobility
Social Democratic vote in 1954	+.17	+.25	+.20	.00	−.23	+.52
Agrarian vote in 1954	+.09	−.49	+.49	+.01	−.35	+.03
Communist vote in 1954	+.89	+.16	+.13	.00	−.07	+.07
Conservative vote in 1954	+.17	+.17	+.81	+.06	+.02	+.24
Liberal vote in 1954	+.19	+.32	+.41	+.35	−.23	+.44
Proportion of Swedish-speaking people in 1950	−.20	+.40	−.58	−.06	+.32	−.12

NORTH & EAST

	Communist Traditions	Moderni- zation	Rural Traditionalism	Political Activity	Insecurity	Mobility
Social Democratic vote in 1954	−.44	+.28	−.67	+.24	+.04	+.04
Agrarian vote in 1954	−.08	−.49	+.67	+.21	−.28	−.04
Communist vote in 1954	+.88	+.02	−.05	+.17	+.20	−.08
Conservative vote in 1954	−.40	+.64	−.16	−.05	−.01	−.01
Liberal vote in 1954	−.08	+.47	+.03	−.29	+.44	+.03
Proportion of Swedish-speaking people in 1950	.00	+.73	+.01	−.07	−.08	−.12

Several interesting, although tentative, conclusions can be drawn from *Table 12. First,* since many political parties have high loadings for several factors, the table indicates that their social base is often of a rather complicated nature. For instance, the Liberal Party in the South and West seems to have support in milieus characterized by Modernization as well as in those characterized by Nationalist Conservatism, by Political Passivity, and by Mobility. *Second,* some parties seem to have an entirely different background in the South and West and the North and East. In the South and West the support for the Conservative Party is clearly related to what has been labeled Nationalist Conservatism, whereas in the North and East it is most clearly related to Modernization. *Third,* at least one party seems to have a rather similar structural base in the two halves of Finland. The Agrarian Party's support has high negative loadings in the Modernization factor in both the South and West and the North and East. Similarly, it seems to be related in both areas to some kind of traditionalism, although this takes the form of Nationalist Conservatism in the South and West and

Rural Traditionalism in the North and East. *Fourth,* the Communist support seems to be more strongly related to traditions than the Social Democratic support. However, the traditions are of a very different nature in the South and West, where the Communist support is particularly related to common Socialist traditions, than in the North and East where the traditions are purely Communistic. As seen from *Table 11,* the Communist traditions in the North and East do not seem to have anything in common with Socialist traditions measured, for instance, by the votes for the Social Democratic Party in 1916 and 1939. According to *Table 12,* the support for the Social Democratic Party in 1954 has a rather strong negative loading ($-.44$) in the factor of Communist Traditions. *Fifth,* the support for the Social Democratic Party is either strongly related to Mobility as in the South and West or negatively related to Traditionalism as in the North and East.

The conclusions are quite tentative. The most reliable is the first. Most of the variables measuring party support are strongly loaded on several factors. This suggests that the social bases of the political parties are not very clear-cut and that their support comes from groups living under rather dissimilar conditions, It does not apply to Communism in the present factor analysis, but to some extent, this seems to be due to the inclusion of quite a few Communist variables in the factor analysis. Even in social class, as an important source for party alignment today, there are several types of criss-crossing lines within the parties.

FACTORS THAT REDUCE STRUCTURAL STRAINS IN FINNISH POLITICAL LIFE

Finnish political life cannot be described completely in terms of party system and support for different parties, albeit political parties act through the Parliament, and the Cabinet, of course, is composed of politicians. However, since the President of the Republic enjoys wide executive powers, political support for the President has to be taken into account.

The formers of the Finnish constitution had a "dualistic" conception of government. In a country with a parliamentary system and presumably a plurality of parties, the office of the President was planned to counter-balance certain shortcomings of parliamentarism. The political scientist Sven Lindman has summarized the constitutional rules as follows:

> Most of the administrative duties were imposed upon the Cabinet, which was responsible to Parliament, whilst certain important powers were reserved for and assigned to the President (who was described as the holder of the "Supreme Executive Power"). The President's prerogatives included the unlimited right of dissolution, the right to initiate legislation (i.e., the right to decide whether a bill projected by the Cabinet should be brought before Parliament or not), and the right to refuse sanction to a bill voted by Parliament (this veto may be broken by a simple majority after new elections). He also obtained the right to issue decrees regulating the execution of laws, and decrees on certain matters which are traditionally regulated in an administrative way in

Finland. Within certain limits, he was invested with the power to direct foreign policy. And he was to appoint a number of high civil servants as well as the Army officers. The members of the Cabinet were appointed by him, though he had to observe the provision made by the constitution for their enjoying the confidence of Parliament.

Lindman concludes that the investment of large powers in the office of the President has not counterbalanced the expected weaknesses of parliamentarism. Finland has had the characteristic features of many European political systems: a split-party system, unstable cabinets, and so forth. On the other hand, the President has not been unimportant, although he has often exercised his influence through informal channels.[44]

Table 13—Vote Intentions for the Presidential Candidates in the Election of 1956 According to Party Preference and Social Class (in percentages)

The Candidates	SOCIAL DEMOCRATS			COMMUNISTS			AGRARIANS			OTHER (Bourgeois)		
	Farmer (54)	Worker (348)	White collar (53)	Farmer (18)	Worker (112)	White collar (1)	Farmer (310)	Worker (82)	White collar (29)	Farmer (67)	Worker (113)	White collar (153)
Social Democratic candidate (Fagerholm)	22	49	53	11	4	—	1	4	—	9	5	4
Communist candidate (Kilpi)	—	1	—	22	40	100	1	—	—	—	—	—
Agrarian candidate (Kekkonen)	22	12	6	22	27	—	76	77	62	12	10	5
Bourgeois candidates (Tuomioja, Törngren, Rydman)	30	14	28	—	4	—	4	7	28	65	69	83
No preference	26	24	13	45	24	—	18	12	10	14	16	8

Source: Gallup Poll, December 1955.

The President is, as the saying goes, supposed to stand above the parties and the actual political cleavages. In practice, this seems to depend very much on the general political situation. Some of the presidential election campaigns have been hard and bitter. Twice, the final votes in the electoral college, which in the last instance elects the President, has been 151 to 149 (1931 and 1956). On the other hand, in times of external danger the President has been elected almost unanimously. The great powers of the President have not in any way tended to reduce the number of parties. However, it may be safely said that the support for and attitudes toward the President produce a cleavage that crisscrosses ordinary party lines. This can be seen in *Table 13,* which presents data from a national sample.

The number of Communist voters is all together too small, because the data have not been corrected as explained in the note to *Table 5.* However,

Table 13 certainly shows the existence of crisscrossing cleavage. The attitudes toward the candidates are, compared with party preference, less dependent on social class, although social class still explains part of the variation. This can be seen from *Table 14,* in which the party preferences in 1958 within the working class are compared with the presidential preferences of 1955.

Table 14—Working-Class Respondents According to Party Preference in 1958 and Preference for Presidential Candidate in 1955 (in percentages)

Party Preference 1958		Preference for Presidential Candidate 1955	
Socialist	80	Socialist candidates	45
Agrarian	7	Agrarian candidate	29
Bourgeois	13	Bourgeois candidates	25

It is apparent that the attitudes toward the presidential candidates are less tied to social class than to party preference. Due to the complicated international situation, there are no available survey data for the presidential campaign in 1961 and the presidential election in early 1962. However, during 1961, up to the month of November, Finland faced a two-party situation in the presidential campaign. President Kekkonen, who won the last election by support of the Agrarians, the Communists, and some dissenting electors from the Finnish People's Party and Swedish People's Party, was in 1961 particularly supported by the Agrarians, the Social Democratic opposition, the Communists, and by dissenters in all political parties. In November 1961 the grave international situation caused a drastic change in the preparations for the elections. The presidential candidate nominated by the Social Democrats resigned, and in most circles the reelection of Kekkonen was regarded as a necessity from the point of view of foreign policy. It is not easy to point out the differences between Kekkonen's adherents and opponents objectively. According to his adherents, the differences between the two blocs were based on different attitudes toward foreign policy. The opponents of Kekkonen, on the other hand, emphatically denied any differences in foreign policy attitudes. According to them, the real issue concerned the fact that Finnish politics during Kekkonen's reign was torn by strong interparty struggles and hostilities.

However, the question remains: Do the cross-pressures created by differences in support for the President and party make for depoliticization or calming down of political issues? It is not easy to give a straight answer. As has been said earlier, the solving of political problems presupposes institutional rules which can be applied in conflict situations. In case there are strong cleavages around the President, the conflicts may be much more difficult to handle than, say, conflicts in economic matters which can be solved through the political parties and the labor-market organizations. This seems to have been true for the presidential campaign in 1961. The debate concerning the President was very keen. It does not seem reasonable to say that the crisscrossing cleavage lines created by the difference between party preference and attitudes toward the President resulted in a greater willingness to negotiate.

The fact that there have been strongly partisan views concerning President Kekkonen does not provide a real answer to our question. In many sociological analyses in recent years, it has been repeatedly shown that not all conflicts can be regarded as dysfunctional from the point of view of the maintenance of the social system. It is reasonable to say that maintenance of Finland as an independent country rests mainly on two functional requirements: (1) adaptation of the foreign political situation and the handling of neighbor relations, particularly with Soviet Russia and (2) maintaining a certain degree of integration and internal cohesion. In terms of these two criteria for functionality, the conflicts around the presidential election reflect a kind of division of labor in Finnish politics of today. President Kekkonen's adherents have stressed the necessity of adaptation to the political situation that emerged after World War II, whereas his opponents have stressed the need for internal cohesion. Thus, the conflicts can be interpreted as a step in the country's adaptation to a new situation and as a move toward an equilibrium which was greatly disturbed by World War II.

It is not easy to discuss the consequences of a two-party system in Finnish politics. A two-party system would provide better possibilities for fulfilling the functional necessity of integration, whereas a multiparty system provides better possibilities for adaptation to new international situations. It seems possible that a two-party system would, in the long run, provide for a much more stable government than Finland has had in the past. On the other hand, in a country such as Finland, the need for adjusting to new international situations may require the emergence of new men and earlier noncommitted parties for handling the phases of adaptation. The need for new actors is perhaps harder to fulfill in a two-party system where the two involved parties, to some extent, display a rather similar policy with only minor nuances. In this fashion, stability itself can become a danger to the maintenance of the system.

In any case some degree of integration is needed for maintaining the system. What are the factors which maintain cohesion and integration in Finnish society? Considering that Finland has survived the war and the postwar period, such factors presumably exist.

It has been pointed out earlier that cleavages which have no particular institutions for the handling of conflicts can easily lead to bitter conflict. But rules, of course, are not enough. An additional requirement is a belief in the legitimacy of these rules. In other words, what is considered legitimate by almost all members of Finnish society?

As in most small borderlands with powerful neighbors, nationalism has been strong in Finland. During an earlier period, national independence, under any social system, was the value on which consensus rested. This has been particularly true during times of external threat. During the Winter War of 1939–40, the Finnish nation was, for all practical purposes, completely united.

However, nationalism has undergone great changes in the postwar period. Despite the debate around the role of foreign policy in the presidential campaign, explicit hostile attitudes and expressions toward Soviet Russia are regarded to an increasing degree as unsuitable and even condemnable. People may disagree on whether Finland should take initiatives in showing friendly gestures toward Russia or should adhere to a passive and very strict neutrality, but the crucial fact is the increasing rejection of hostile attitudes toward Russia. Combined with the positive evaluation of national independence, this gives Finnish society a certain internal cohesion.

However, there are other changes in what has been called Finnish nationalism. It should be mentioned first that there are differences in the evaluation of national independence among the supporters of different parties. Survey studies indicate that national independence as a social value, when compared to other values, is much less strongly stressed among the Communists than among the supporters of other parties. However, supporters of the Communist Party also seem to give importance to national independence. Political observers have often stressed that the Communism displayed by the masses is very insular and merely takes the form of protest against social conditions without being rooted in ideology.

Observations and analyses suggest also that national independence is changing from being an end in itself toward being a means for securing some other goals. In this sense Finnish nationalism is starting to resemble the type of national pride or patriotism which prevails in Scandinavia today. In a study of the attitudes toward national defense, Antti Eskola has shown that there is a positive correlation between the stress on national independence and satisfaction with the socioeconomic conditions in every political party. Likewise, there is a positive correlation between the stress on national independence and what Eskola labels "the aptitude to give specific criticism." Those who are able to criticize specific conditions in their commune of residence are apt to stress national independence. Specific criticism is a kind of behavior which is, apparently, a sign of integration.

The most interesting result, however, concerns age. There are certain patterns which are strikingly similar among young people within all political parties. First, what can be labeled "instrumental patriotism" (national independence as a means to other goals) is particularly characteristic of the young age groups. The percentage of those who think that social welfare is more important than national independence is virtually the same among supporters of all parties in the age group of seventeen to twenty-five. For older people, there are great differences between Socialists and others.[45]

There are also other studies showing the differences between the age groups. In a monograph on the Conservative Party, Onni Rantala has produced rather interesting data.[46, 47]

Although a similar study has not been done within the other bourgeois parties, it seems reasonable to assume that the same kind of differences would occur. The younger members of the bourgeois parties are more in favor of the kind of welfare state which the Socialists have pleaded for than are older members. One may call it "creeping Socialism" or not, but the fact remains that this results in a certain consensus in society. At the same time age is not an issue in the sense that age groups organize and put forward conflicting demands. People of the same age group are of course more likely to meet than people from different age groups. The younger age groups have, on such occasion, a common meeting ground in their rather similar political attitudes.

Another factor related to integration may be pointed out: regional, local, and almost tribal identity seems to be a rather important feature in the Finnish social structure. Relatively independent local government has a long tradition in Finland. Today the communes are the partially independent local units. As has been shown in an earlier paper by the present authors,[48] this gives the citizens many possibilities for participating in formal decision-making. In 1956 a count showed that the 417 Finnish-speaking rural communes (communes with a large majority of Swedish-speaking inhabitants were excluded) had

Table 15—Opinion and Attitudinal Differences According to Age Among the Members of the Conservative National Coalition Party (in percentages)

	AGE		
Issue or Attitude	16–29 (46)	30–49 (141)	50– (113)
Does not like to stress the importance of traditions	46	33	33
The nation's economy should be planned at least as much as it already is	21	11	12
The care of sick people should at least partly be paid for by the state	87	71	70
The state should initiate more social welfare measures	30	5	6
The expenses for national defense should not be increased	17	8	4
Social radicalism being above the average according to a Guttman scale	74	40	59

9,382 municipal councillors—who had elected 3,253 governing board members—and a total of 114,675 other trustees. When eliminating those who are counted twice, 5 percent of the Finnish-speaking rural electorate are involved in decision-making. A similar count shows that in the municipal elections of 1956 there were 33,000 members and vice-members on the electoral boards, and about 450,000 persons needed to sign the petitions required before candidates are permitted to run for election. Usually inhabitants take a rather strong pride in their communes. The communes constitute important reference groups and thus provide a common meeting ground irrespective of party alignment.

There is no higher level of formal self-government (except the Aaland Islands), but it is still true that some larger geographical areas are important bases for identity in the Finnish society. Earlier, the old tribal division of Karelians, Ostrobothnians, Tavastians, and so on played a significant role, but today regional identity is formed mainly on the basis of so called economic areas. Lately, regional societies have arisen which, albeit not yet formally introduced into the constitution as governing bodies, have sometimes had a rather decisive influence on the economic and social life in their regions. In a way, the rather informal nature of identities with the economic regions has prevented them from becoming strongly politically divided. On the other hand, the local governments are in most communes strongly influenced by party politics. This reflects a general tendency: local government in the *communes* was less influenced by party politics at an earlier time than now. Recent statistics show that the communal elections are more and more tied to national party politics. Thus, in the municipal elections of 1956 only 1.6 percent of the elected councillors were not formally tied to any political party.[49]

Lately there has been much discussion about the fate of communal self-government, since the state has encroached upon many local functions. According to the Swedish political scientist Gunnar Heckscher, citizen participation in decision-making in Sweden has been transferred more and more from the local societies to large-scale organizations and voluntary associations.[50] This is also true for Finland, although voluntary associations are often formed on a local base and local identity is the uniting factor. The number of voluntary associations has been rapidly growing. This is a very crucial point for the future of Finnish society. According to Kornhauser, a great number of nonpolitical associations forming intermediate bodies between the elite and the nonelite is a condition for a stable democracy.[51] In Finland the situation is not very clear-cut. There are associations which function as intermediating bodies. On the other hand, many of those associations which in the other Scandinavian countries are not tied to party politics are very heavily political in Finland. The sports movement has been divided into two blocs, a bourgeois and a Socialist one, the latter also being divided into two groups. The cooperative movement, which plays a rather important role in the Finnish economy, is likewise divided into a bourgeois and a Socialist camp. To this may be added the labor movement which, as earlier shown, has been split along ideological lines.

When looking for other conditions usually connected with a stable political system, it can be pointed out that the groups employed in nonmanual work are rapidly growing. Likewise, the standard of living has improved very rapidly. Between 1951 and 1959 the volume of industrial production in Finland increased proportionally more than it did in the other Scandinavian or Anglo-Saxon countries. The same was true for the total national product.[52] Of course, Finland's starting point was lower, but it seems safe to say that the social and economic conditions are rather rapidly approaching the general Scandinavian level.

Therefore, we may conclude that in spite of strong conflicts in Finnish politics today, there are many signs of a development similar to that which has already happened in the other Scandinavian countries. The changes both in the nature of patriotism and the rapid improvements in economic and social conditions at least point in this direction, provided Finland's international situation remains unaltered.

It may be noted that concern over Finland's political development still differs from that in Denmark, Norway, and Sweden. In the latter countries, many political scientists have displayed a concern for growing depoliticization. In Finland the contrary has been true. There is a common basis for concern. A democratic system is endangered both by a high degree of emotional or expressive behavior, as in Finland, and by political disinterestedness, which follows when the political debate focuses on minor technical matters.

NOTES

1. Eino Jutikkala, *Suomen talonpoika kautta aikojen* (*The Finnish Peasant Through the Ages*) (Helsinki, 1946), pp. 184–5; Jussi Teljo, *Suomen valtioelämän murros* (*The Breaking of Finland's Political Life*) (Porvoo-Helsinki, 1949), p. 11.

2. Hannu Soikkanen, *Sosialismin tulo Suomeen* (*The Coming of Socialism to Finland*) (Porvoo-Turku, 1961).

3. K. R. Brotherus, *Suomen valtiollisen järjestysmuodon kehitys* (*The Development of Finland's Constitution*) (Porvoo-Helsinki, 1963), p. 63.

4. *Elections pour la Diète en 1907 et en 1908*. The numbers of voters are given in brackets. Some rural and urban voters are excluded by reason of voting outside their own electoral area.

5. Edvard Gylling, "Katsaus viime eduskuntavaaleihin" (A Review of the Recent General Election), *Työväen kalenteri 1908* (Helsinki, 1907).

6. H. Soikkanen, *op. cit.*, pp. 364–5.

7. Eino Jutikkala, "The Road to Independence," in Urho Toivola (ed.), *Introduction to Finland 1960*, p. 34.

8. Jutikkala, *Suomen talonpoika . . . , op. cit.*, p. 193.

9. *Statistical Yearbook of Finland 1955* (Helsinki, 1955), Tables 19, 21.

10. Decision of the Council of State on the language classification of administrative and self-governing areas during 1963–72, *Suomen asetuskokoelma* No. 687 (Dec. 28, 1962).

11. *Statistical Yearbook of Finland 1962* (Helsinki, 1963), Table 24.

12. Olavi Riihinen, "Kuinka Suomen kansan elintaso on kohonnut" (How the Standard of Living of the Finnish People Has Risen), *Keskisuomalainen*, 1961:4, and consultation with Mr. Paavo Grönlund.

13. Gunnar Fougstedt, "Inkomstens fördelning i Finland" (The Distribution of Income in Finland), *Ekonomiska samfundets tidskrift*, 1948, pp. 251–6; Odal Stadius, "Inkomstnivelleringen och dess följder" (The Equalization of Incomes and Its Consequences), *Förhandlingar vid nordiskt nationalekonomiskt möte i Stockholm den 20–22 juni 1949* (Stockholm, 1949), pp. 56–8.

14. *Maataloustilastollinen kuukausikatsaus* (*Monthly Statistics of agriculture*), 1961:4, p. 16.

15. As regards living conditions, at the turn of the century rural communes averaged 2.40 persons per room, but Helsinki only 2.09 persons; in 1950, hardly any differences existed (1.53 and 1.47); O. Riihinen, *op. cit.*

16. Carl Erik Knoellinger, *Labor in Finland* (Cambridge: Harvard Univ. Press, 1960, pp. 95–105.

17. P. G. Nyholm, "Havaintoja eduskuntaryhmien koheesiosta vaalikaudella 1948–51" (Some Aspects on the Cohesion of the Finnish Parliament Groups in 1948–51), *Politiikka* (1959), p. 16; and *Suomen eduskuntaryhmien koheesio* (with summary: "The Cohesion of Party Groups in the Finnish Diet") (Helsinki, 1961), especially pp. 50–69.

18. P. G. Nyholm, "The Cohesion . . . ," *op. cit.*, p. 55.

19. Stuart Rice, *Quantitative Methods in Politics* (New York, 1928), pp. 208–9; P. G. Nyholm, "The Cohesion . . . ," *op. cit.*, p. 35.

20. P. G. Nyholm "The Cohesion . . . ," *op. cit.*, pp. 87–91.

21. The only exceptions have been the "United Labor" electoral union of Communists and Social Democrats in the northern Oulu electoral area in 1924, and the cooperation of the Communists in 1945 with a minor party of small landholders.

22. Onni Rantala, *Vaaliliittoyhteistyö Suomen eduskuntavaaleissa 1907–58* (*Multiparty Electoral Unions in 1907–58*) (Tampere, 1963); and *General Election of Finland in 1962*, p. 50.

23. Olavi Borg, *Suomen puolueideologiat* (*The Ideologies of the Finnish Parties*), (Helsinki: Söderström, 1964). Seven of the parties are mentioned in Table 1, for 1962. The Social Democratic Opposition has not adopted a party program while the Communist Party of Finland and the Democratic Union of the Finnish People have separate ones.

24. Karen Erickson, "Leadership Opinion In Finnish Politics." Diss., Harvard University, in preparation.

25. Lolo Krusius-Ahrenberg, *Kring intresserepresentationen i vår riksdag* (*The Representation of Interests in Our Parliament*), Report No. 4 of the Research Institute of the Swedish Business College in Helsingfors, (Helsinki, 1955).

26. Martti Noponen, "Kansanedustajien sosiaalinen tausta Suomessa vuosina 1907–1939" (The Social Background of the Members of Parliament in Finland in 1907–1939), unpublished Licenciate diss., Univ. of Helsinki, 1961, Table 37. For a summary see M. Noponen and P. Pesonen "The Legislative Career in Finland" in E. Allardt and Y. Littunen (eds.), *Cleavages, Ideologies and Party Systems* (Helsinki: Westermarck Soc., 1964), pp. 441–463.

27. M. Noponen, *op. cit.*, p. 305; Armas Nieminen, "Yhteiskuntaluokat" ("Social Classes"), *Oma maa IV* (Porvoo, 1958).

28. Martti Noponen and Pertti Pesonen, "The Legislative Career in Finland," UNESCO Conference on Comparative Political Sociology (Tampere, 1963), pp. 15, 18.

29. Geographical structure differentiates the Agrarians even more than other parliamentary groups. Only five of the forty-eight Agrarian representatives, but a majority of every other group, lived in urban municipalities in 1958.

30. M. Noponen, "The Social . . . ." *op. cit.*, p. 309.

31. Pertti Pesonen, *Valitsijamiesvaalien ylioppilasäänestäjät* (*Student Voters in the Election of the College of Presidential Electors*) (Vammala/Helsinki, 1958), and *Valtuutus kansalat* (*A Mandate from the People*) (Helsinki: Söderström, 1964).

32. Olavi Borg, "Monipuoluejärjestelmän ideologisten peruserojen kuvaamisesta" (On the Concepts Describing Basic Ideological Cleavages in a Multi-Party System), *Politiikka* (1963), pp. 6–11.

33. Preliminary material of the Finnish Gallup Institute.

34. S. M. Lipset, *Agrarian Socialism* (Berkeley: Univ. of California Press, 1950). The Region of South Pohjanmaa provides a very interesting case for comparison with the Canadian province of Saskatchewan. Social conditions in both regions have in some respects been similar, but whereas Saskatchewan is the only province in the whole of North America which has a Socialist majority, the region of South Pohjanmaa is strongly conservative. An important difference is that the Saskatchewan farmers have been strongly influenced by the world market situation.

35. L. Krusius-Ahrenberg, *op. cit.*

36. L. A. Coser, *The Functions of Social Conflict* (New York: The Free Press, 1956).

37. W. Kornhauser, *The Politics of Mass Society* (New York: The Free Press, 1960), pp. 74–101.

38. E. Allardt, *Social struktur och politisk aktivitet* (*Social Structure and Political Activity*) (Helsinki: Söderström, 1956), pp. 40–9.

39. A. Heikkilä, *Ammattiosasto ja jäsenten aktiivisuus* (*Activity within Labor Unions*), unpublished Master's thesis, Univ. of Helsinki, 1960.

40. J. Siipi, *Maaseutuväestö ja työttömyys* (with an English summary: *Rural Population and Unemployment*), Publication No. 13 of the Institute of Social Policy of the University of Helsinki.

41. E. Allardt, "Social Factors Affecting Left Voting in Developed and Backward Areas," Paper prepared for the Fifth World Congress of the International Political Science Association in Sept. 1961.

42. E. Jutikkala, *Suomen historian kartasto* (*Atlas of Finnish History*), with texts in Finnish and English (Porvoo: WSOY, 1949).

43. E. Haavio-Mannila, *Village Fights,* Publication No. 3 of the Institute of Sociology, Univ. of Helsinki, 1958.

44. S. Lindman, "The Dualistic Conception of Parliamentary Government in Finland," in *Democracy in Finland* (Helsinki, 1950).

45. A. Eskola, *Yhteiskunnan säilyttämistä ja puolustamista koskevat arvostukset* (*Attitudes Concerning the Maintenance of Society and National Defense*), (Helsinki, Suomen Sotatieteellinen Seura, 1962).

46. O. Rantala, *Konservatiivinen ja radikaalinen asennoituminen* (*Conservative and Radical Attitudes*) (Tampere, 1960).

47. O. Rantala, *Konservatismi ja sen kannattajat* (*Conservatism and Its Supporters*) (Helsinki: Tammi, 1960).

48. E. Allardt and P. Pesonen, "Citizen Participation in Political Life: Finland," *International Social Science Journal*, 12 (1) (1950): 27–39.

49. J. Nousiainen, *Suomen poliittinen järjestelmä* (*The Political System of Finland*) (Porvoo: WSOY, 1959), p. 233.

50. G. Heckscher, *Staten och organisationerna* (Stockholm, 1946).

51. W. Kornhauser, *op. cit.*, Chap. 3.

52. O. Niitamo, "Suomen teollisuus" (The Industry of Finland), *Tuotantouutiset,* No. 5, 1960.

Eight

Geography, Religion, and Social Class: Crosscutting Cleavages in Norwegian Politics

Stein Rokkan

This is an attempt to analyze the principal sources of cleavage in the Norwegian political system and to account for changes and persistencies in the alignments of the Norwegian electorate since the emergence of national parties in the 1880's. The quality of the data and the precision of the analyses will vary significantly from decade to decade, and much of what is said will remain conjectural until tested and reinterpreted through detailed inquiries. Most of the discussion of the early elections will have to be limited to crude collations of published statistics: there are a few scattered analyses of the politics of particular localities, but so far no attempts at systematic comparisons of data across the entire nation.[1] The more elaborate tabulations in this paper all bear on data for the elections since 1945; these have been subjected to detailed scrutiny within the program of political research at the Michelsen Institute and the Institute for Social Research[2] and have been studied both through ecological methods[3] and through the use of survey techniques.[4] Within the confines of a chapter in an international symposium, it will clearly not be possible to go into the technicalities of these various analyses and to discuss findings for the full range of variables in the study designs. Only a few of the more "telling" tables will be presented and all of them will bear in one way or another on the discussion of two cross-cutting dimensions of the Norwegian party system—the *territorial* and the *functional*.

A FUNDAMENTAL THEME IN
NORWEGIAN POLITICS:
OPPOSITION TO CENTRAL AUTHORITY

In a stimulating paper presented at the Fifth World Congress of Sociology, Seymour Martin Lipset analyzed the critical sequences in the building of the "first new nation," the United States of America,[5] and made a case for systematic comparisons of such processes of initial political growth. He highlighted the basic similarities in the ranges of problems faced by the leaders of nation-states upon the achievement of territorial independence: the issues and the dilemmas confronting the American elite after 1783 could fruitfully be analyzed and elucidated in the same conceptual framework as those confronting the statesmen and politicians of the new states now emerging from colonial dependence in Asia and Africa.

It is tempting to discuss developments in Norway in this comparative perspective. Norway was, it is true, an old nation and had already reached a high level of political unity and cultural cohesion in the thirteenth century. Later, however, it had fallen under foreign dominance and had, from 1536 onward, for most practical purposes been ruled as a colonial territory under the Danish crown.[6] The country was administered by a corps of officials educated in Copenhagen, and its trade was dominated by burghers of foreign descent operating under Royal protection. Danish rule was never despotic, however, and the authorities could generally count on loyal acquiescence to their rule, not least among the peasants who made up the vast majority of the population. There was little direct discrimination against Norwegians, and careers in the Royal administration, in the Church, and in the academies were open to bright and industrious sons of burghers and peasants. These educated Norwegians rarely felt fully at home in Danish society, however, and during the eighteenth century an increasing number of them voiced opposition to Danish rule. There were also many signs of unrest among the peasants,[7] and by the end of the century there was widespread talk about the reestablishment of an independent Norwegian nation. But no organized efforts got under way until Napoleon tried to blockade the Continent and thereby made communications between Denmark and Norway more and more hazardous.

The national rising in 1814 was largely a response to changes in external conditions. Shortly after the defeat of Napoleon in Germany, Bernadotte invaded Holstein and forced the Danish king to cede Norway to Sweden. The reaction in Norway was quick and remarkably effective. The Danish prince, Christian Frederick, became the rallying point for a strong movement of independence and defiance.[8] The leaders in this movement were all officials or members of the urban patriciate, and the great majority were of foreign descent and had few and often only impersonal ties with the native peasantry: in the terminology of the twentieth century they essentially made up a class of privileged settlers, of *colons.* Yet they were fully committed to the cause of Norwegian autonomy: Denmark was not a *metropolis,* a mother country they could withdraw to. Some of them considered it safer to work for a union with Sweden, but there was general agreement that a new Norwegian state must be established, with full sovereignty at least in its domestic affairs. What was even more important, this oligarchic elite had been increasingly swayed by the liberal ideas of the philosophers of the Enlightenment[9] and had come to accept the principle of popular sovereignty. They felt a heavy responsibility for the national community as a whole and were deeply concerned to ensure legitimacy for their actions through the explicit consent of a united people. The Constitution they agreed on in May 1814 is a remarkable document, remarkable for what it tells us about the ideals and the strategies of the elite at the time, but equally remarkable for the possibilities it opened up for future developments. It ensured the legitimacy of the central government and provided the basis for the continued rule of its officials, and yet at the same time set the stage for the mobilization of forces of protest and opposition within the still inarticulate strata of the subject population.

The new nation established through this instrument was at an early stage of economic development. Not even 10 percent of the population lived in incorporated cities, perhaps another 5 percent in agglomerations around coastal trading centers, sawmills, mines, and iron works. The remainder of the population was scattered through the countryside and lived as peasants and fishermen only marginally tied to the money economy of the cities and the centers of trade.

The Constitution of 1814 recognized the basic division between city and country but showed no concern for proportional representation. There was no question of numerical democracy: there was to be representation by *Estates* but within the framework of a unitary national assembly. The cities made up one set of constituencies and their representatives were to be elected in two steps by the qualified holders of burgher rights and by owners of real estate of a given minimum value. The rural districts of each province made up separate constituencies and their representatives were to be chosen by colleges elected by the peasants: the freeholders and those who had leased registered land for more than five years.

These two Estates, the *burghers* and the *peasants,* made up the bulk of the electorate; of the 59,000 registered on the rolls in 1814 they easily made up 98 percent. The remaining 1–2 percent made up the core of the new system, however: they were the official estate, *embedsstanden.* The King's officials were given full franchise, even after retirement, both in the cities and in the provinces, and they were in fact able to dominate the rural as well as the urban electoral colleges for several decades.

The contrast between city and country was accentuated through the provisions for electoral ratios. In the cities there was to be one elector for every fiftieth registered voter and one representative for every fourth elector—this gave a ratio of 1:200. In the country districts the ratio was set at 1:1000. This blatant overrepresentation of the cities was kept within bounds, however: if the voters in the cities, at that time well under 10 percent of the total electorate, were to send more than one-third of the representatives to the National Assembly, amendments were to be introduced to ensure a strict 1:2 ratio of urban to rural representatives in future elections. This provision, however, was not taken very seriously in the first decades after 1814. The gradual increase in the population of the cities produced a more and more marked overrepresentation of their electorates, but concerted action against this numerical injustice was not taken until the peasants had finally begun to mobilize their forces in opposition to the political and economic dominance of the cities.

Peasants and Officials

At first the enfranchized peasants tended to vote for their "betters." For close to two decades after 1814 the rural electoral colleges sent more officials than freeholders to Parliament. The first movement of rural protest came in 1832. There was a perceptible increase in participation in the countryside and a decisive change in the recruitment of representatives: the proportion of freeholders and other farmers rose and the proportion of officials declined. The movement slowed down later in the thirties and in the forties, but the direction of the change was unmistakable:[10]

Representatives from Rural Districts

PERCENT CLASSED AS

	Freeholders and other farmers, sheriffs, parish clerks	Governmental officials	Attorneys	Others
1815–27	45	47	2	6
1830–42	59	31	4	6
1845–57	63	29	2	6
1859–74	74	17	6	3

Representatives from the Cities

	Burghers	Officials	Attorneys	Others
1815–27	45	48	5	2
1830–42	34	60	5	1
1845–57	32	50	8	10
1859–74	35	50	8	7

This slow but steady process of rural mobilization went on at roughly the same pace throughout the national territory: only the three northern provinces, the least developed and the most markedly "colonial" in character, lagged conspicuously behind in the recruitment of representatives from the peasant Estate.

It has been conjectured that the peasants would have entered national politics in much greater force in the thirties, forties, and fifties if the officials had not opened up another and more immediate field for the exertion of these new energies—*local self-government*.[11] Under the Danish regime, most of the decisions on local affairs had been taken by the Royal officials, at best upon consultation with a *ting* of the peasants in the community. These autocratic practices continued for more than two decades after the new constitution had given the peasants their rights of representation: they were free to enter the National Assembly but they were given no possibilities of taking direct part in the running of their immediate local communities. It is again interesting to see that the initiatives required to bring about a change toward democratic practices were taken by groups of *officials* and not by representatives of the peasants themselves. The cabinet minister who introduced the bill proposing the introduction of local self-government through elected officeholders centered his argument on the need to give the peasants a greater share of responsibility in the administration of their communities and to provide a sound political education for those of them who were later to serve in the national legislature.[12] The peasant representatives in the *Storting* at first showed remarkably little interest in such reforms, but once they saw these possibilities for action they pressed hard for the fullest possible measure of self-government.

Their motives were simple and eminently practical: they had come to see the administrative apparatus of the new nation-state as a threat to the traditional ways of life of the rural communities; they wanted to keep this apparatus in check and they wanted to shift the burden of taxation from the subsistence economy of the countryside to the money economy of the cities and the trading centers. They came to realize that this cause could be advanced at two levels: in the *Storting*, through their efforts to keep central expenditure at a minimum and to curtail the rights and privileges of government officials; in each *local community*, through direct control of the field administrators. This determined opposition to central authority was the common denominator of the policies of the peasants on entering the political arena; beyond that they were frequently at loggerheads and unable to act in concert. The Norwegian peasantry was deeply divided by region and by locality; there were fundamental differences in economic conditions and rural traditions and the unity achieved in opposition to the common enemy proved difficult to maintain once the officials had been forced to give in and submit to parliamentary control. The peasants had united in the defense of the periphery against the center, but there was as yet no positive ideology underlying their policies. Their outlook was basically local and provincial: they showed no concern for the survival of the nation as an integrated unit of action and they cared even less for international affairs.

No attempt has as yet been made to document in detail the entry of the peasants into local politics after the introduction of elective councils in 1837, but there can be little doubt that these local institutions offered much more effective channels of mobilization and activation than the elections to the *Storting*. Whether in fact the opening up of these new channels reduced the pressure for representation in the electoral colleges and in the National Assembly is of course very difficult to say: the hypothesis has not been tested statistically and the difficulties of data-gathering are quite forbidding. Whatever the factors at work, it remains certain that it took several decades before the peasants pushed on to the next step: the organization of a disciplined party of opposition and the development of a broad basis of national electoral support.

Two developments set the stage for a decisive change in the balance of political forces in the Norwegian system:

> 1. The growth of a *nationalist-populist ideology* in defense of the traditional language and culture of the rural communities and in opposition to the powerful influences from the central cities and their educated elites.
> 2. The emergence of a *radical-democratic movement in the cities*, also defending traditional Norwegian values against what was taken

to be foreign influence, but primarily directed against the power of the central administrative elite and against the dominance of the Swedish government in the Union of the two nations.

The rural movement gave the opposition party a mass basis and a distinctive ideological justification, but the urban radicals gave it political direction and leadership and brought about the decisive change from a policy of mere resistance to a drive for power and supremacy in the system.

The peasants had at first confined their opposition to matters of economy and local administration and made few or no attempts to challenge the supremacy of the official Estate: they generally accepted the language and the cultural traditions of the King's officials as superior to their own and they conformed as far as they could to the standards of public conduct set them by this urban, and to them often foreign, elite. It is true that the puritan revivalism of the Hauge movement had mobilized many peasant families, particularly in the West, against one group of the King's officials, the clergymen of the established state church, but it took several decades before this opposition over religious practices and principles found direct political expression. The first significant signs of change came in the 1830's: the peasants began to assert themselves in the *Storting* and now found support in intellectual and literary circles.

The Romantic Movement had finally reached Norway and found a deep and lasting resonance in the literature and scholarship of the new nation. The emphasis on the continuity of history and the cult of the *Volk* prompted a series of thorough reassessments of the situation and the destiny of the Norwegian state and brought about a profound change in the dominant conceptions of the cultural prerequisites of nationhood. Just like so many intellectuals in the decolonized territories of the twentieth century, the poets, historians, and linguists of this new nineteenth century nation became passionately concerned to establish the historical necessity of independence and to substantiate the ties with a glorious past. Norway had been a strong and unified nation-state in the Middle Ages, but had suffered a "four hundred year eclipse" under Danish rule. How had it been able to retain its cultural identity, to survive as an entity during all these generations? Once the question was raised, the answer became obvious: the *peasantry* had ensured the identity of the nation, while the urban patriciate and the officials had brought in foreign manners and ideas and a foreign language and had threatened to undermine the cultural foundations of the nation.

This populist ideology found its most immediate expression in the movement to give Norway *a new language*. The history of the Norwegian language-forms tells us a great deal about the cultural conditions of nation-building. The official languages of the nation-states of the West were the products of five sets of developments: the growth of *stable networks of communication* across the aristocratic lineages and between them and the court of the realm, the development of distinct *clusters of trade relationships* among cities, the *centralization of the administrative apparatus,* the growth of a *national system of higher education,* and the emergence of the *printing trade* after Gutenberg.[13] None of these conditions was present in Norway in the century after Gutenberg, and the result was clear cut: the country did not develop an official language of its own during the centuries when the other nation-states of the West developed theirs. The Black Death had cut down the leading aristocratic lineages, the cities tended to be more active in foreign than in domestic trade, and the country as a whole came under Danish rule and administration during the century after Gutenberg. Copenhagen became the center of higher learning and acquired a monopoly of printing: Copenhagen controlled the process of linguistic standardization within the two-nation realm. The spoken dialects of the Norwegians were reduced to the level of provincial vernaculars, and the Copenhagen elite set the rules and the standards of orthography and grammar and, at least among the officials and the burghers of the cities, even influenced the pronunciation in day-to-day discourse. The Reformation was a major factor in this development: the translations of the Bible and the accelerated dissemination of tracts, catechisms, and educational texts gradually acquainted most of the peasant population with Danish in its written form and set it apart as a language of prestige and power. This did not change overnight with independence in 1814. The country continued to be ruled by the officials; they all had their training in Copenhagen and saw no possible alternative to written Danish as the official language of the new state. The Danish standards of spelling and grammar were simply taken for granted: it was a language for writing and printing and had its own separate functions, completely distinct from the functions of everyday speech. Danish was, after all, not a foreign language: Norwegians might not readily understand it when spoken by Danes, but the city people, at least in the East and in Bergen, had few difficulties with written Danish as an expression of the "high" language of Church and State. The discrepancies between the written language and the spoken dialects were much more marked in the countryside, particularly in the inner valleys and in the West, and these regional differences in the conditions of communication were gradually to produce important cleavages in the politics of the new nation.

The cultural ties with Denmark were bound to weaken after 1814. The development of an independent university in Christiania divorced the new elites from spoken Danish and made them more aware of the discrepancies between the written forms and what they considered to be standard educated Norwegian. By mid-century, a movement of gradual reform got under way. More and more of the literary and cultural leaders began to alter the spelling to conform more directly to the speech of the educated classes in the cities and an increasing number of distinctly Norwegian words and phrases found acceptance in the official language. The result was the development of an independent *riksmål*, a distinctly urban language which, during the first half of the twentieth century, found general acceptance in the commercial and industrial centers throughout the country and, at least numerically, became the dominant one.

Such a gradual process of accommodation between the written and the spoken language was hardly possible in the countryside, particularly not in the regions of the most isolated peasantry, in the inner valleys and in the West. In these regions the gradual mobilization of the peasants finally led to a *linguistic revolt*. More and more of them came into contact with the culture of the cities, and many a peasant's son tried to enter this new world by establishing himself in a trade or by acquiring an education. Some succeeded, but many felt awkward and inferior in communicating with officials and cityfolk and felt the need to establish their cultural identity through a language of their own. A young peasant's son, an autodidact of genius, Ivar Aasen, saw this need and saw what was to be done. He undertook a detailed study of Norwegian peasant dialects and constructed on this basis a *standard rural language,* the *landsmål.* This may have had its elements of arbitrariness, but it had one decisive advantage: it gave the majority of peasants a distinct cultural identity, a language they could recognize as the nation's own. Aasen took his point of departure in the Norse of the old sagas and simply asked himself: What would standard Norwegian have looked like in his day if it had been given a chance to develop independently, if in fact the Danes had not taken over the control of the administration and the church in 1536? Many romantics would have answered: the purest Norwegian had survived among the isolated peasantry of the valleys and across the fjords, and any standard language must build on the dialects of the communities that had upheld the cultural identity of the nation during the centuries of Danish rule. Ivar Aasen was not an antiquarian, however; he was clearly anxious to establish links to the past, but he was equally anxious to strengthen the basis for a movement of cultural integration across the valleys and across the fjords, to create an efficient common language for the nation. He was a romantic but he was also keenly aware of social and geographical realities: he wanted to create a new symbol of historical identity but also hoped to form an efficient instrument of practical communication.[14]

The emergence of this standard rural language gave further strength to the peasant opposition and prepared the ground for the final drive for power. But the peasants were also driven forward by important allies in the cities; by nationalist intellectuals and by radical dissidents within the broader middle class emerging in the process of further urbanization. As in so many other countries, the leadership in this urban movement was taken by independent *lawyers,* university-trained professionals who had not entered the administration and who made much of their living from defending the rights of burghers and peasants against the officials. This "lawyer's party" in the *Storting* became a force in politics in the years after 1848.

A coalition with the peasant opposition was essential, and attempts were made in 1851 and again in 1859 to organize a distinctive party in Parliament and to ensure disciplined action against the Cabinet. The "Reform Club" set up in 1859 met with violent opposition, however: the dominant political culture emphasized territorial representation and individual judgment and went counter to any attempt to establish collective agreements among representatives of different districts. But this was only a temporary setback; the fight for united action continued outside Parliament. The first mass movement in Norwegian politics had already emerged in the aftermath of the continental upheavals of 1848—a network of "Workers' Associations" grouping at its peak in 1851 close to 30,000 members, mainly among journeymen, cotters, and smallholders of the East.[15] This movement proved a failure, however; at its peak it threatened mass demonstrations in the capital and its leaders were arrested and imprisoned in the end. The peasants moved much more cautiously and did not develop a nationwide network of political associations until 1865. These "Friends of the Peasant" reached a membership of some 21,000 and spread to the South and West as well as the East. The primary aim of the association was to influence the voters and the electors in the rural constituencies and to ensure the election of trusted opponents of the officials and the King's government. The leader of the urban opposition, Johan Sverdrup, soon saw the importance of this movement and established an alliance in 1869. This was the first step toward the formation of a united opposition party, the *Left,* as it soon came to be called, and it also marked the beginning of the great struggle for power in the Norwegian system.

The Left Defeats the Officials

The struggle took fifteen years. It got under way in earnest in 1869 and it ended with the impeachment of the King's Cabinet in 1883 and the formation of the first parliamentary government in Scandinavia on June 26, 1884: the King gave in and asked the leader of the opposition to form a Cabinet responsible to the dominant party in the *Storting,* the Left.

The struggle ranged over a number of issues, but the core question of the conflict concerned the relationship between the Legislative Assembly and the Executive.

The struggle proceeded at two levels: first, it focused on a proposal to *break down the barriers of communication* between legislators and Cabinet ministers; second, and decisively, it centered on the *King's right to veto decisions taken by the Storting.*

The Constitution of 1814 had instituted a clear-cut division of powers and established the prerogatives of the King and his council. The *Storting* was to pass laws, impose taxes, authorize expenditures, and control the administration, but was barred from any influence on the King and his Council of State. The King appointed his ministers just as he appointed other officials of the state, and the ministers were to retain complete independence from the legislators: they were not even allowed to take part in legislative deliberations. The King could refuse to sanction decisions of the *Storting,* but at least as far as ordinary laws were concerned, this veto was explicitly stated to have "suspensive" force only: if three successively elected assemblies had adopted the same decision it would become valid law even without the King's consent.

The opposition chose its point of attack with great skill: they proposed to give Cabinet members the right to take part in the deliberations of the *Storting* and rallied a large majority for such an amendment to the constitution. Amendments to this effect had been proposed again and again since 1821, but had been rejected by one Assembly after another out of fear of the persuasive powers of the articulate and knowledgeable officials in the King's Council. In 1872 the tables were finally turned: the new allies in the *Storting* had gained in self-confidence and were convinced that they would hold their own against any member of the Cabinet.

The Executive was forced into a corner and was deeply divided over its strategy of defense.[16] After a protracted struggle in the Cabinet, a majority of the Norwegian Ministers advised the Swedish King to veto the amendment. A bitter fight ensued between Parliament and government. The Left opposition grew in strength and determination year by year, but stuck strictly to the rules of the game laid down in the Constitution: they brought up the amendment after each successive election, passed it with overwhelming majorities and then waited for the veto from the King. The possibility of direct promulgation was raised in 1877, but caution prevailed: the opposition wanted a verdict by the people and made the election of 1879 a virtual referendum on the veto powers of the King. The response was overwhelming and, in June 1880, the *Storting* declared the amendment to be valid law without the King's consent.

The tension between representatives and officials now reached its climax, and the country was on one or two occasions on the verge of civil war: there were ugly rumors of a *coup d'état* aided by the Swedes,[17] and the Left on its side encouraged the organization of a network of riflemen's associations to serve as a popular militia against the armed forces of the officials.[18] Both sides appealed to the Constitution, however, and were concerned to establish their rights through due process of law. The defenders of the Cabinet, the *Right* as they were by now generally called, were the first to call for impeachment proceedings under the Constitution. They wanted to put the decisions of the *Storting* and the Cabinet to a judicial test, and they hoped that the Court would uphold their claim that the King had an absolute veto against amendments in the Constitution. The Left at first did not want to bring the matter to a head through impeachment proceedings; instead they carried out a systematic campaign of legislative harassment and hoped to force the Conservative government to resign over budgetary difficulties. This did not work out, however, and the leaders of the Left finally came around to the idea of impeachment proceedings. Again, they did not want to act without the verdict of the people at the polls: the election of 1882 became the first expressly partisan contest in Norwegian history and mobilized practically twice as many voters as in the "prepolitical" elections before 1879.

The verdict was again clear-cut: the Left controlled more than two-thirds of the *Storting* and was free to set the terms of the impeachment proceedings as they wanted. The Constitution provided that such proceedings be conducted before a "Court of the Realm," composed of one political section and one juridical: on the one side the elected representatives in the "upper division" of Parliament, the *Lagting,* and on the other the appointed judges of the Supreme Court. To ensure their supremacy in this mixed court the leaders of the Left packed the *Lagting* with staunch opponents of the government and then proceeded to impeach eleven members of the Cabinet. The deliberations lasted for a year and were followed with intense interest throughout the country. The verdicts were in themselves never in much doubt: the members of the Cabinet would be judged to have acted contrary to the Constitution and would be divested of their offices. The real issue centered on the King's reaction to such verdicts—would he ignore them, appoint another Conservative government from among his officials, or would he introduce parliamentary rule? The King and his advisers were long uncertain and worked with several alternative plans. In the end they decided, after a series of complex maneuvers, to entrust the government of the country to the Left. The Right was paralyzed through divisions among several leaders and factions and an overture to the Left seemed at the time to be the only way of saving the Union from serious disruption.

The victory of the Left, however, could not save the Union. On the contrary, it heralded a swelling tide of opposition to the Swedish King and to the dominance of Swedish officials in the conduct of foreign affairs of the two countries.

The Act of Union signed in 1815 had left the two countries fully independent of each other in their domestic affairs; they each had their own, and very different, constitutions, their separate administration, finance, and defense, and their own judiciary, Cabinet, and Parliament. The two countries were only joined to each other in a personal union under one king, and the real problem in the maintenance of such a union lay in the organization of common consular and diplomatic services. On this point the act gave the Swedes a distinctly dominant position: the King and his Minister in Stockholm were given full powers over the conduct of foreign affairs. There were few disagreements on overall policy toward the Great Powers in the nineteenth century and therefore little danger of a disruption of the Union on that count. The critical issues did not concern basic policy, but the outward signs of representation and the problems of external communication—the flag of navigation and the consular services in foreign ports. Incipient conflict over these eminently practical but still highly emotional issues occurred in the thirties, but there was no evidence of serious movements of secession before the eighties. Tension began to mount in the sixties over Swedish pressures for revisions in the Act of Union and for an integration of defense forces. These efforts of amalgamation came too late, however. The accelerating mobilization of the peasantry of both countries into national and domestic politics made any attempts to establish new links across these cultural entities hopeless.[19]

The Left government formed in 1884 had taken a conciliatory line and its leader, Johan Sverdrup, in fact proved a loyal supporter of the King. This attitude, however, spelled his ruin. He proved a great deception to the radical democrats and nationalists in his party, and he was not able to keep the victorious alliance together for more than a few years. By early 1888 the Left was split in two warring factions: the "Pures" and the "Moderates." The Union was only one of a series of issues in this split, but it proved the most important one in the struggles of the nineties. The Pures took an uncompromising stand for greater independence, while the Moderates sided with the Right in advocating caution in dealings with the Swedes. The Pures won a clear victory in 1891 and voted to set up a separate consular service for Norway. The King vetoed this law in 1892 and the decisive fight over the Union was on.

The two countries were on the verge of war in 1895 but happily decided to pursue the negotiations. The delay helped to dampen the bitterness of the opposition between Pures, Moderates, and the Right; there was a distinct movement toward the "Center"[20] and the Right finally accepted the need for a separate consular service. This basic change in the structure of Norwegian politics at the turn of the century prepared the ground for the final denouement in 1905. It was a broad coalition of the Center which achieved the independence which the Left had advocated and the Right had feared. The Union was no longer an issue; new cleavages had emerged in Norwegian

Table 1—Cities vs. Rural Districts in Norwegian Politics 1815–1882: Population, Electorate, Registration, Votes, and Seats

Year	Estimated Population (thousands)		Total Qualified for Franchise (thousands)		Registered (thousands)		in per cent of Qualified		Votes Cast in per cent of Registered		Seats		Ratio Votes: Seats	
	Cities	Rural	Cities	Rural	Cities	Rural	Cities	Rural	Cities	Rural	Cities	Rural	Cities	Rural
1815	78	807	No data	No data	6	54	No data	No data	No data	No data	26	57	No data	No data
....														
1829	99	1009	″ ″	″ ″	6	55	″ ″	″ ″	64.8	43.0	30	51	139.8	464.4
1832	102	1050	″ ″	″ ″	7	59	″ ″	″ ″	59.3	46.8	31	64	126.1	427.9
1835	105	1090	″ ″	″ ″	7	60	″ ″	″ ″	63.6	51.0	31	65	135.4	470.7
1838	111	1124	″ ″	″ ″	7	63	″ ″	″ ″	64.8	48.6	31	67	144.8	455.2
....														
1859	200	1373	17	103	11	67	40.2	29.5	60.2	45.6	50	67	135.6	454.1
1862	220	1419	17	105	11	68	33.7	28.1	52.0	43.4	37	74	155.4	397.2
1865	236	1466	18	109	11	70	29.1	26.4	46.2	41.1	37	74	140.9	386.7
1868	259	1477	18	109	11	70	29.9	30.5	47.8	47.6	37	74	148.3	449.4
1870	272	1486	19	109	11	70	23.8	29.5	40.3	45.8	37	74	122.7	433.9
1873	289	1502	21	110	12	70	31.8	28.0	53.9	44.2	37	74	176.4	417.2
1876	308	1521	23	114	13	71	31.1	25.7	54.5	41.1	37	74	189.1	396.6
1879	365	1516	24	115	15	72	40.0	28.4	65.5	45.2	38	76	254.6	431.0
1882	382	1539	26	120	19	80	61.5	46.9	82.6	70.1	38	76	417.1	740.5

Note: "Cities" is used here as a translation for kjøpsteder, incorporated urban districts under royal charter. "Rural districts" (landdistrikter) include ladesteder (market towns) as well as herreder (rural communes). This distinction applies to all the tables in this chapter.

politics and were soon to overshadow the old ones between the Left and the Right.

The Emergence of National Parties and the Mobilization of the People

The critical contest for power between the Left opposition and the Conservative defenders of the old regime triggered off a process of mass mobilization into politics and this process soon acquired its own dynamics: the process changed the conditions of political activity and set the stage for the emergence of new alignments, new cleavage lines in the system. Any attempt at an interpretation of the Norwegian party system must start out from this basic fact: the system had lost its equilibrium, and new elements were continuously brought in on either side to achieve some balance, however precarious and however questionable in the long run.

These changes in the character of the political system can be documented statistically.

Let us first consider the long period of equilibrium from 1814 to 1872. *Table 1* gives the basic data from the official statistics of elections.[21]

By the standards of 1815 Norway was a remarkably democratic country. There are no official estimates of the total number of enfranchised for the first regular election to the *Storting,* but if we go by the ratios of enfranchised to registered established for later elections, we would estimate the total number of residents qualifying for suffrage at some 8,500 for the chartered cities (*kjøpsteder*) and some 82,000 for the rural districts (market towns, *ladesteder,* and rural communes, *herreder*). In percentage of the total population this would mean roughly 11 percent in the cities and 10 percent in the rural districts. No other western European country seems to have reached this level so early and been able to stay there. France, of course, had its brief exposure to universal manhood suffrage in 1792[22] but the *régime censitaire* introduced with the Restoration limited the suffrage to some 72,000 out of a population of close to 30 million.[23] In Great Britain the total electorate went up to 500,000 before the First Reform Act of 1832, and this came to between 2 and 3 percent of the population.[24] Among the northern countries Norway was the first to institute a wide suffrage. Denmark followed in 1849 and enfranchised most of the men over thirty: only servants, paupers, vagrants, and bankrupt citizens were excluded. Sweden maintained its four-estate regime up to 1866, but the great reform of that year did not go very far in the direction of equalitarian democracy; not quite 6 percent of the population was given the right to take part in the direct elections for the Lower Chamber and some 11 percent in the municipal elections for the Upper Chamber. The wider municipal franchise was markedly unequal, allowing as it did for a multiplication of votes as a function of income.[25]

Comparisons of levels of "democratization" should preferably be based on some standard definition of a "maximal" electorate in the given nation: calculations from the total population may be misleading, particularly in analyses of time series, since the percentages may be affected by changes in demographic structure. For the nineteenth century the best measure of "maximal" electorate would seem to be the number of resident *men* over the standard age of voting, in Norway then twenty-five. Unfortunately, the census breakdowns do not always give precise figures for this "maximal" electorate, but estimates based on interpolations between censuses suggest the following changes in levels of "democratizations" in Norway:[26]

| | Men 25 and over (thousands) | | | | Qualified: (percent) | | | Registered: (percent) | | |
Year	Total	Cities	Rural	Election	Total	Cities	Rural	Total	Cities	Rural
1815	201	18	183	1815	(45)	(47)	(45)	29	31	29
1825	245	24	222	1826	(39)	(39)	(39)	26	25	26
1845	302	33	268	1844	(35)	(32)	(36)	23	23	23
1865	388	51	337	1865	33	35	32	21	22	21
1875	396	61	335	1876	34	37	34	21	21	21
1891	431	87	343	1891	46	47	46	32	35	32
1900	474	119	355	1900	—	—	—	93	88	95

With all their uncertainties these figures tell us something important about the process of democratization in Norway: the Constitution of 1814 gave political citizenship rights to more than two-fifths of all men aged twenty-five and over but, as the population grew and as more and more moved out of the primary sectors of the economy, there was a distinct decline in the levels of enfranchisement, both in the rural districts and in the cities. It took some seventy-five years and a process of intensive political mobilization before the system again reached the original level.

The system was at its nadir of participation in the 1860's: only one man in three qualified for the franchise, only one man in five had actually been entered on the electoral rolls, and only one man in ten went so far as to vote. The magistrates controlling the electoral rolls clearly felt no need to encourage citizens to take the required oath to the Constitution and to get themselves registered; the defenders of the official estate saw no advantage in massive participation and were concerned to keep such struggles as might occur over representation within the narrow bounds of the established local elites. By 1870 the turnout among the registered was at its lowest ever: 40 percent in the cities; 46 percent in the rural districts. But by 1873 the first signs of the coming wave of mobilization could already be detected: the vote rose to 54 percent in the cities but stayed as low as ever in the countryside. The next thrust came at the election of 1879: the turnout rose to 65.5 percent in the cities but still stayed very low in the rural districts. There the decisive breakthrough did not come until the fiercely partisan election of 1882; then the turnout level suddenly rose from 45 percent to 70 percent.

Even more important than this rise in participation among those already admitted was the increasing pressure to *bring more adults into the system:* first, by getting more of those already meeting the franchise criteria registered, second, by advancing new claims of qualification within the old rules, and third, by pressing for changes in the very rules of admission.

With the intensification of the electoral struggle in 1879 came a variety of pressures to get more of the eligibles on the registers. There is evidence of widespread passive, if not active, resistance to such pressures among the officials in charge. A standard complaint among the organizers in the opposition was that the magistrates kept such short and erratic office hours that it was impossible to get through the formalities.[27] Even in the cities, where access to officials should be a simple matter, there was very little change in the registration figures in 1879. By 1882, however, the officials had clearly lost out: not only had the Left intensified its pressures but even the Right now recognized the need to mobilize its potential to the hilt. The result was that the proportion of registered rose from 61 to 74 percent in the cities and from 63 to 67 percent in the rural areas.

This pressure to increase registration was accompanied by a variety of attempts to establish new claims to political citizenship within the rules of the Constitution. The old franchise criteria left one major opening: all owners of registered rural land qualified whatever the size of value of the property, and it was therefore possible to establish one's rights as a citizen by acquiring some worthless strip of land and getting it registered as a holding. There are no detailed estimates available of the extent of this practice during the crucial years of initial mobilization; however, there is a good reason to believe that a sizable share of the increase in the rural electorate from 1879 to 1882 (115,410 to 119,911) was due to such purchases of land for political purposes, and there is some evidence that the practice continued up to 1885.[28]

By that time, however, the first step toward mass suffrage had already been taken: the *Storting* had decided to add to the old franchise criteria of status and property a new criterion of *minimum income*. This new criterion did not exactly open the gates to the masses, but it did allow a steady increase in the electorate over the next fifteen years. The decision was based on detailed studies of the consequences of a variety of alternative arrangements and was not a rash step taken under the pressure of the heated political controversies of the day: in fact, a number of proposals for extensions of the franchise had been considered in the 1870's, and the Central Bureau of Statistics had been asked to undertake a special census of all taxpayers in the country to determine for each proposal the likely composition of the new electorate.[29] *Table 2* gives a simplified summary of the conclusions of this study; it first sets out the composition of the urban and the rural electorate as it was by the old criteria in 1876 and then presents an estimate of what the composition would be under a set of new criteria equivalent to those actually adopted from 1885 onward. These data tell us a great deal about the conditions for political conflict in Norway and deserve some comment.

To simplify the analysis I have grouped the occupations distinguished in the statistical report into four groups:

"Governmental Establishment"
"Burgher" Estate
"Peasant" Estate
"Underprivileged"

These four groups correspond roughly to the original franchise criteria of 1814—the basic categories of politically privileged citizens were officials, burghers, and peasants. But the system was not a rigid one; it left several openings for active outsiders. In the cities it was possible to acquire suffrage

Table 2—Changes in the Occupational Composition of the Electorate and the Storting: Estimates for 1876, 1885, 1900

| | 1876 | | | | | | 1885 | | | | 1900 Manhood suffrage | | | |
| | All male taxpayers | | Franchise of 1814 Qualifying for franchise | | Elected to Storting | | First extension Qualifying for franchise | | Elected to Storting | | Electorate: men 25 and over | | Elected to Storting | |
	Cities	Rural	Cities	Rural	Cities	Rural	Cities	Rural	Cities	Rural	Cities	Rural	Cities	Rural
Totals = 100%	(49,386)	(205,112)	(23,581)	(112,117)	(37)	(74)	(35,411)	(138,047)	(38)	(76)	(103,319)	(336,319)	(38)	(76)
Governmental establishment:														
—King's officials	2.8	0.4	5.8	0.8	56.8	8.1	4.0	0.6	44.7	13.2	1.5	0.3	26.3	10.5
—lower officials and local govt. employees	6.9	2.2	4.3	1.7	8.1	28.4	7.9	2.4	10.5	26.3	7.7	2.4	15.8	23.7
"Burgher" Estate:														
—merchants and others in business	15.6	2.0	26.7	1.7	24.3	10.8	22.4	2.2	15.8	2.6	13.6	3.9	21.1	5.3
—lawyers	0.3	—	0.7	0.1	8.1	4.1	0.7	0.1	18.4	7.9 }	1.5	0.2 }	7.9 }	2.6
—other free profess.	0.5	—	0.4	—	—	—	0.5	0.1	5.3				5.3	1.3
"Peasant" Estate														
—freeholders	0.4	47.7	0.7	85.0 }	—	45.9 }	0.5	69.7 }	—	44.7 }	1.0	32.1	—	47.4
—leaseholders	0.1	4.7	—	5.9	—		0.1	5.5	—		—	3.0	—	—
—adult family memb.	—	1.4	—	0.8	—	—	—	0.2	—	—	—	—	—	—
—fishermen	1.6	3.9	1.0	0.8	—	—	1.0	1.8	—	—	1.9	8.9	—	—
"Underprivileged"														
—cotters	—	14.0	—	0.2	—	—	—	2.4	—	—	—	7.1	—	—
—workers	42.0	13.6	22.5	1.3	—	—	27.6	8.6	—	—	50.3	25.6	—	2.6
No occupation, pensioners (føderåd)	0.5	5.1	0.5	0.4	—	—	0.8	1.3	—	—	—	7.4	—	7.4

Note: The estimates for 1876 and 1885 are based on a special tax census carried out by the Central Bureau of Statistics to determine the effects of each of the alternative proposals for extension of the suffrage, see Statistiske Oplysninger om de fremsatte Stemmeretsforslags Virkning (Christiania, Det statistiske Centralbureau, C. No. 14, Parts I–II, 1877). The estimates for 1885 are based on the assumption that franchise would be given to all men twenty-five and over who either satisfied the old franchise criteria or had a minimum income of 800 kroner in the cities or 480 kroner in the rural areas (the actual limit set in 1884 was 500 kroner for the rural areas but no calculation for this level was made in 1876). The totals given refer to the actual tax-paying population in 1876 and do not take into account later increases in population and income. This explains the differences between these totals and the figures for those actually enfranchised in 1885 (Table 3). The estimates for 1900 are based on the census of that year (Norges Off Stat., IV, 124). The census gives higher figures for men twenty-five and over (127,000 in the cities and 349,000 in the rural areas) than the electoral statistics give for the totals enfranchised (see Table 4): this may be assumed to be largely due to slow registration, labor mobility and a slight difference in the age limits applied. The distributions for the occupations of the representatives are based on the official classifications but these are sometimes problematic because of multiple positions.

through ownership of real estate, and the minimum value was set so low that this was not a privilege of wealth, at least not in the smaller cities. As a result a substantial number of salaried employees and manual workers were actually enfranchised under the old criteria. The basic principle of the constitutional provisions had been to reserve the franchise to economically independent heads of households and to exclude residents who depended on others for their livelihood. The ownership clause, however, cut across this principle and in fact allowed more than 40 percent of the salaried and more than 25 percent of the wage earners in the cities to qualify for the vote. The "underprivileged" were not let into the system all of a sudden: there was a gradual process of civic incorporation and this clearly affected the later history of mobilization and polarization.

The process was not a uniform one throughout the country, however: the criteria of political citizenship were set in economic terms and differences in the rates of economic growth and urbanization had distinct consequences for the process of civic incorporation.

Under the original rules of 1814 the economically expanding cities were bound to keep the inflowing wage earners out of their political systems: it was difficult for such newcomers to acquire housing of their own and there was in practice no other way for them to gain suffrage. In the smaller cities the workers were more likely to have built their own little dwellings and consequently to qualify for the vote. With the introduction of an income criterion in 1884 all this changed: there was a sudden influx of working-class voters in the large cities, a much slower movement in the other cities.

The wage earners fared much worse in the countryside and there even the reform of 1884 did not go very far toward full suffrage:

	Six largest cities	Other cities	Rural districts
Workers on tax rolls	9,878	10,855	56,667
—enfranchised under 1814 criteria	21%	30%	2%
—enfranchised under 1884 criteria	53%	46%	27%

The landless rural proletariat was far worse off economically than the urban working class and did not enter the electorate in force until 1900. The households of the cotters and the farm laborers were the last to be represented in the political system and they also, as we shall see from later tables, lagged far behind in the process of mobilization.

The income criterion introduced in 1884 almost doubled the electorates of the largest cities but increased the electorates in the smaller ones and in the rural districts by less than a quarter. The reform essentially served to incorporate into the political system the potentially most influential of the still disfranchised strata, the better-off employees and workers economically mobilized through urbanization and initial industrialization, but politically alienated under the old franchise rules. The reform of 1884 still kept tens of thousands of workers outside the system, but the majority of these were spread through the countryside and could not so easily be mobilized for concerted action:

	Six largest cities	Other cities	Rural districts
Male taxpayers in 1876	24,765	24,621	205,112
Of these:			
—enfranchised by 1814 criteria	44%	52%	55%
—enfranchised by 1884 criteria	77%	67%	67%
Taxpayers still disfranchised	5,766	8,209	67,065
Of these:			
—salaried employees	9%	9%	2%
—manual workers	80	77	36
—cotters (husmenn)	—	—	27
—fishermen	—	6%	10
—retired peasants (føderåd)	—	—	13%

These, of course, are estimates based on the tax census of 1876: they do not take into account the continuing economic mobilization of the population through the expansion of trade, the revolution in transportation, the burgeoning industries. It is easy to see from *Table 3* that the criteria introduced in 1884 made for a continuous expansion of the electorate in a period of economic growth. Without any formal change in the franchise rules, the electorate rose from 182,400 in 1885 to 238,000 in 1897. The process of economic mobilization went on *pari passu* with the process of political mobilization and, so to speak, built up toward the climax in 1898—the introduction of general suffrage for all men over twenty-five.

Table 3—The Process of Mobilization 1876–1897: Increases in the Total Qualified, in Registrations, and in Votes, in the Initial Period of Party Growth

	CITIES				RURAL DISTRICTS			
Election	Electorate (qualified for franchise)	Registered in p.c. of electorate	Votes cast in p.c. of electorate	in p.c. of registered	Electorate (qualified for franchise)	Registered in p.c. of electorate	Votes cast in p.c. of electorate	in p.c. of registered
1876	22,529	57.0	31.1	54.5	114,001	62.6	25.7	41.1
1879	24,191	61.0	40.0	65.5	115,410	62.7	28.4	45.2
1882	25,789	74.4	61.5	82.6	119,911	67.0	46.9	70.1
1885	35,806	71.5	59.8	83.7	146,602	66.4	48.4	72.8
1888	37,285	71.7	56.2	78.4	150,712	67.4	46.1	68.3
1891	40,888	74.2	63.4	85.5	156,977	69.7	49.0	70.4
1894	54,528	86.1	80.7	93.8	179,891	80.3	71.4	88.9
1897	58,523	85.5	77.7	90.9	179,592	81.3	67.8	83.4

The figures in *Table 3* indicate that the new entrants of 1885 did not register at the same rate as the citizens already enfranchised: there were slight drops in the overall registration levels in the cities in 1885 and 1888. The system had reached a plateau and a new thrust of mobilization did not get under way until 1891 in the cities and not until 1894 in the rural districts. The system reached its peak of mobilization in the election of 1894. This was not only an occasion for the expression of partisan loyalties but also, under the threat of an imminent struggle with Sweden, a major demonstration of national identity.

This crescendo of mobilization made it impossible to resist the further extension of the franchise: the *Storting* reached its decision in 1898, and the first election under manhood suffrage was held in the year 1900.

Table 2 gives the composition of the urban and the rural electorates in 1900 and tells us a great deal about the changes in the conditions of electoral competition. In the cities more than half of the eligible voters were now manual workers, about 20 percent were lower middle-class private or public employees, about 10 percent were artisans of various kinds, and only some 15 percent belonged to a bourgeoisie of businessmen, professionals, and officials. In the rural districts the freehold peasants no longer made up the majority of the electorate; they now had to face the potential threat of an equal number of cotters and workers.

The lower classes had entered the political arena, but their impact was not immediate. There still remained, it is true, two provisions reminiscent of the earlier *régime censitaire:* all accountable men aged twenty-five and over were entered on the electoral rolls, but their rights might be *temporarily suspended* if they had received public assistance or were in bankruptcy proceedings. These provisions affected only a small percentage of the electorate, but they had a deep symbolic meaning for the militants of the working-class movement: the stigma of poverty might still debar a man from his national citizenship rights.

It took some time, however, before the latest entrants actually made use of their new rights and had a direct impact on the balance of power in the system. The new electoral arrangements had opened up the gates to the masses. They no longer needed to register through an oath to the Constitution: all they had to do was to get themselves to their polling station and cast their ballot. But vast numbers of the enfranchised working class clearly did not make use of these opportunities at the first elections after the introduction of manhood suffrage. The Norwegian statistics do not allow breakdowns for turnout by class and occupation of the kind available for Sweden,[30] but it is not difficult to calculate from the overall figures in *Table 4* that the turnout must have been very low among the new entrants in the elections of 1900 and 1903:

| | 1900 | | 1903 | |
	Cities	Rural	Cities	Rural
Total votes cast	65,000	173,000	72,000	168,000
Estimated distribution between				
—established electorate	45,000	122,000	45,000	122,000
—new entrants	20,000	51,000	27,000	46,000
Estimated turnout				
—established electorate				
(1897 figure)	78%	68%	78%	68%
—new entrants	44%	33%	52%	28%

The drop in total turnout after the introduction of manhood suffrage was more marked in the rural districts than in the cities. There was a distinct lag in the rate of political mobilization in the countryside and this lag became even more pronounced with the extension of the suffrage to the *women,* first on an income basis for the elections of 1909 and 1912, later on the same conditions as the men. *Table 4* shows how much easier it proved to mobilize the urban women than the rural. The discrepancies in turnout levels stayed at 19–20 percent for fully two decades, and the decisive breakthrough in rural mobilization did not come until the election of 1930, a contest largely fought over issues of fundamentalism and secularism between the old parties and the new giant of Norwegian politics, the Labor party.[31]

Table 4—The Lag in Rural Mobilization after the Introduction of Manhood Suffrage: Differences in Turnout Levels Between Rural Districts and Cities, 1900–1961

| | Total Electorate (thousands) | | | | Overall Turnout | | Differences Cities—Rural Districts | | |
| | Cities | | Rural | | | | | | |
	M	W	M	W	Cities	Rural	Total	Men	Women from 1909
1900	104	—	336	—	62.8	51.6	11.2	11.2	
1903	111	—	346	—	64.7	48.7	16.0	16.0	
1906	116	—	354	—	70.7	58.7	12.0	12.0	
1909	122	96	363	199	72.9	59.0	13.9	7.0	26.5
1912	130	106	372	219	72.8	61.1	11.7	4.3	24.0
1915	142	190	390	412	69.4	54.9	14.5	7.8	21.9
1918	152	202	411	437	71.3	54.9	16.4	8.8	24.6
1921	175	229	462	487	76.9	64.0	12.9	6.7	19.6
1924	181	240	483	510	80.1	65.4	14.7	8.5	21.0
1927	190	251	508	537	76.9	64.3	12.6	6.4	19.3
1930	198	263	532	558	81.6	75.7	5.9	2.0	9.8
1933	213	278	568	586	81.8	73.9	7.9	3.8	12.3
1936	229	294	605	616	87.5	82.4	5.1	2.3	8.3
1945	258	320	715	708	80.6	72.6	8.0	4.8	11.5
1949	320	395	733	724	86.4	79.2	7.2	4.3	10.4
1953	336	408	767	748	84.0	76.9	7.1	4.2	10.2
1957	340	411	786	762	82.5	76.3	6.2	3.9	8.7
1961	347	417	799	777	82.8	77.3	5.5	3.4	7.7

Electoral Equality and the Defense of the Periphery

The Norwegian Constitution of 1814 had enfranchised the peasantry but kept it within bounds: one vote in the cities weighed as much as five votes in the countryside. *Within* the constituency the principle was one man, one vote, one value, but *across* constituencies there were gross inequalities.

In the first phase, these inequalities helped to keep the system in balance: the officials and the burghers were overwhelmingly outnumbered by the peasants but were able to maintain full control of the system as long as the electoral ratios ensured urban overrepresentation and as long as a majority of the peasants still voted for their "betters."

In the next phase the system began to get out of balance: the leading cities grew rapidly but their claims on representation were countered by strong opposition from the leaders of the mobilizing peasantry.

The electoral mechanics of this change were simple enough. Under the original provisions of 1814, an increase in the number of registered citizens in a constituency would result in a proportional increase in its number of electors and therefore of representatives. An upper limit was set, however, to such increases in city representation. The Constitution stated that the ratios were to be changed if the total number of city representatives were to exceed one-half of the number of rural representatives. This was safe enough in 1814; there was then barely one citizen registered in the cities to ten in the country constituencies. But as the cities grew they sent more and more representatives to the *Storting* and went far beyond the original 1:2 ratio. By 1859 the cities had acquired fifty seats and the rural districts sixty-seven, and the peasants finally took action to defend their rights. The 1:2 urban-rural ratio was strictly enforced, and each constituency was to send a fixed number of representatives to the *Storting,* unaffected by changes in the number of registered. The tables had been turned: the 1:2 ratio had originally served to ensure urban overrepresentation but now this "peasant clause," as it came to be called, became a bulwark in the defense of the rural interests in an increasingly urban society.

Table 5 tells us something about the consequences of this decision. This gives the ratios of enfranchised to representatives and of voters to representatives for the two leading cities, for the other cities, and for the rural constituencies.

In 1885, the cities were still markedly overrepresented. The only exception was the capital; there the continuing inflow of population had steadily increased the numbers of citizens behind each representative. The other cities had not yet been affected to this extent. Even in the second city, Bergen, it still took only half as many citizens to elect a representative as it did in the surrounding country districts. This did not change fundamentally with the introduction of manhood suffrage in 1900. The capital became even more underrepresented, but Bergen and the other provincial cities were still distinctly better off than the rural districts. Bergen eventually grew faster than the smaller cities and by the 1920's was slightly underrepresented by comparison with the average country constituency. But the 1:2 rule essentially hurt the metropolitan center of the nation and served to protect the smaller provincial cities: a vote in the capital weighed about one-third of a vote in these provincial places in 1885, and with the increasing concentration of the population at the center this numerical injustice became increasingly pronounced.

Voices for a reform were heard again and again in the *Storting* but the provincial interests invariably won out against the center. The basic argument for continued overrepresentation of the provinces was very simple[32]— the capital was the seat not only of the government and central administration, but also of the most important organs of opinion and the largest interest organizations. A citizen at the center consequently had far easier access to the channels of decisive influence than a citizen in the distant periphery of the nation. Representation was not only of population, but of territory; the law of elections should reflect a concern for balance among the regions as fully as a concern for justice by numbers. Contrary to what later occurred in Denmark,[33] there were no attempts in Norway to develop any exact formula for the weight of the territory versus the weight of the citizens in deciding on the distribution of seats, but the compromises reached in the *Storting* clearly resulted from vague notions of the need to balance the one criterion against the other. Thus, as will be seen from *Table 5,* the northernmost of the

Table 5—Inequalities of Representation 1885–1961: Ratios of Electorate: Representatives (E:R) and Voters: Representatives (V:R), in the Cities and the Rural Provinces

Election	Christiania[a]/Oslo		Bergen		Other Cities		All Rural Provinces		Finnmark	
	E:R	V:R	E:R	V:R	E:R	V:R	E:R	V:R	E:R	V:R
1885	2,643	1,563	941	458	1,049	445	1,929	933	1,590	340
1900	10,200	6,395	3,208	1,961	1,788	1,060	4,425	2,282	2,580	1,807
1912	17,816	11,852	7,239	5,369	3,689	2,846	7,202	4,400	5,017	2,825
1924	21,659	18,378	10,737	8,658	5,682	4,362	9,927	6,496	5,969	3,356
1936	27,527	24,203	13,593	11,554	6,893	6,017	12,216	10,038	8,094	6,392
1949	45,195	39,389	15,707	13,358	8,428	7,192	14,457	11,489	10,284	6,957
1961	26,639	22,241	15,880	12,657	E:R 14,582		V:R 11,350		10,408	7,301

[a] Christiania formed a constituency with two minor cities through 1903.

provinces, Finnmark, was consistently favored in the apportioning of seats, not only because of its large territory and its low density, but also because of its position at the farthest periphery of the nation.

The 1:2 "peasant clause" survived a number of onslaughts and was not given up until 1952. The process of urbanization had continued throughout the near-century since the 1859 reform, and the administrative divisions between urban and rural communes had lost some of their sociological and political significance. The urban and rural sections of each province were merged into one multimember constituency and the seats reapportioned to these new units. Again, however, the *Storting* acted to defend the periphery against the center: Oslo was given almost double the number of seats it had held before, but it still took two votes in the capital to balance one vote in the provinces.

SEVEN PHASES IN THE DEVELOPMENT OF THE ELECTORAL CLEAVAGE SYSTEM

We have described the initial process of political mobilization in Norway and analyzed the developments which led up to the introduction of universal manhood suffrage in 1900. We have tried to show how the process of urbanization and economic mobilization affected the basic conditions of the political struggle and how the expansion of the electorate from 1879 to 1900 set the stage for new alignments within the system. We shall now proceed to describe the system of party division and electoral cleavages which emerged after 1900.

The history of electoral politics in Norway may schematically be set out as a sequence of successive changes in the structure of cleavages and alignments within the national polity.[34]

We may conveniently distinguish five dimensions of conflict in the system:

(1) the *territorial* opposition (*T*) between capital and provinces, between center and periphery;

(2) the *sociocultural* (*SC*) conflict between the academically educated, "Europeanized" officials and patricians in the cities and the increasingly status-conscious, articulate, and nation-oriented peasants in the rural districts and their descendants in the expanding cities;

(3) a *religious* opposition (*R*) between the secularism and tolerant liberalism of the established urban population and the orthodox and fundamentalist Lutheranism of large sections of the rural and recently urbanized population;

(4) an economic conflict in the *commodity market* (*CM*) between the buyers and sellers of agricultural and other primary economy products, again essentially a conflict between the urbanized and the persistently rural interest sectors;

(5) finally, an economic conflict in the *labor market* (*LM*), first between employers and wage earners and, later primarily in the larger units of the economy and in the public sector, between employers and salaried employees.[35]

Table 6—Sequences and Phases in the Development of Electoral Alignments 1882–1961

Phase	Conditioning Events	Elections	Major Party Alternatives								Cleavage Lines					
											T	SC	R	CM	LM	Other
I	Struggle for parliamentary supremacy	1882–85			Left				Right		X	X				
II	Victory of Left, extension of suffrage	1888–97			Left	Mod.			Right		X	X	X			foreign policy
III	Manhood suffrage, struggle over Union	1900–18	Lab.	Wk.dem.	Left			Nat. Lib.	Right		X	(X X)			X	
IV	Industrialization, Proportional Representation	1918–30 CP ('23–)	Lab.	Soc.dem. ('19–'27)	Left		Agr.	Nat. Lib.	Right		X	(X X)	X	X		
V	Economic crisis	1933–36 (CP)	Lab.		Left	Chr.	Agr.	Common-wealth	Right	Nat. Soc.	X	X	X	X	X	
VI	World War	1945–57 CP	Lab.		Left	Chr.	Agr.		Right		X	X	X	X	X	foreign policy
VII	Cold War	1961–	Soc. P. Lab.		Left	Chr.	Agr.		Right		X	X	X	X	X	EEC

The sequences of phases in the development of electoral alignments can be schematically set out as in *Table 6*.

Tables 7–10 set out the aggregate election results for each of these phases and show the contrasts in alignments between cities and rural areas and between the center and the provinces.

In the first phase, 1882–85, the salient cleavages were territorial and sociocultural: the Left was strongest in the rural areas of the provinces and the Right was strongest in the capital, in the cities in the East and in the Trøndelag, and in the surrounding countryside (*Tables 8 and 10*). The striking difference between Bergen and Christiania reflects a persistent territorial opposition and to some extent also a difference in the character of the alliances within the local elite. Ulf Torgersen's analysis of the recruitment of electors suggests a markedly lower level of status polarization in Bergen than in the capital.[36]

The Left acceded to power in 1884 but did not survive as a united party for more than four years; it split up into a "Pure" wing of radical nationalists and a "Moderate" wing of spokesmen for traditional religious and moral values. This split cut across the earlier territorial cleavage and produced a temporary alliance between conservatives at the center and fundamentalists in the periphery. The Moderates were concentrated in the Southwest: they had their only urban strongholds in the cities of Stavanger and Haugesund and they derived most of their support from the coastal communities in that region. The contrasts between these outer districts and the agricultural communities in the inner fjords and valleys were indeed striking, and there is much evidence to suggest that the differences between Moderates and Pures in fact reflected contrasts in community norms and traditional ethical attitudes. It is difficult to assemble reliable data for detailed statistical tests of these differences for this early phase, but Øidne's analyses[37] and our work on the geography of the Christian vote (see *Table 18*) at least provide prima facie evidence of such a relationship between community culture and political alignment.

This three-party system was not destined to last. The struggle over the Union with Sweden and the introduction of manhood suffrage set the stage for a series of changes in political alignments. The threat of a war with Sweden dampened the opposition between Left and Right, and the entry of the workers into national politics changed the character of the cleavage system. Concerted efforts were made to establish a broad "Unionist" front against the emerging working-class movement,[38] but the earlier conflicts between the center and the provinces, the urban culture and the rural, were far from resolved and in fact proved markedly more divisive than straight class issues throughout the period up to 1918. The continuing mobilization of the peasantry generated a series of new claims on the central decision-makers and the initial mobilization of the lower classes in the cities and in the countryside often cut across the old cleavage lines and created a complex system of party divisions. The old Left was torn over such issues of class politics as workers' rights and social security, but the earlier division between Pures and Moderates subsided and the core of the party united in defense of the rural "counter-culture": it fought for the full recognition of the *landsmål* as a national standard language, for the strengthening of lay control over the

Table 7—Election Results 1882–1965: Votes Cast for Each Major Party Grouping in Percent of All Registered in the Cities and the Rural Districts*

	Labor[a]		Left[b]		Moderates[c]		Right[e]		Agrarians	
	Cities	Rural	Cities	Rural	Cities	Rural	Cities	Rural	Cities	Rural
Indirect Elections:										
1882			36.0	47.2			45.9	22.0		
1885			37.8	49.3			45.1	22.3		
1888			28.0	29.4			46.0	21.9		
1891			37.9	36.9			47.1	32.7		
1894	1.1	—	46.0	44.9			46.3	43.5		
1897	2.0	—	45.7	44.3			42.9	38.5		
1900	7.2	1.6	30.5	30.5			29.0	21.3		
1903	13.7	4.4	22.3	23.7	3.9	16.1	32.6	21.9		
Direct Elections										
1906	20.9	6.1	20.9	33.0			31.2	16.1		
1909	22.7	7.9	15.3	20.3			31.4	19.9		
1912	27.4	11.3	16.5	27.2			26.7	17.4		
1915	27.9	14.3	16.6	23.0			26.1	12.6		
1918	24.0	15.0	9.6	21.0			33.5	10.1	—	3.7
1921	29.7	16.5	8.9	17.8			37.4	15.9	—	12.5

Direct Elections	C.P. Cities	C.P. Rural	Labor[a] Cities	Labor[a] Rural	Left[b] Cities	Left[b] Rural	Soc. People's Cities	Soc. People's Rural	Christians Cities	Christians Rural	Agrarians Cities	Agrarians Rural	Right[c] Cities	Right[c] Rural	Nat. Soc. Cities	Nat. Soc. Rural
1924	6.3	3.3	27.8	14.9	8.3	16.4					—	13.3	36.7	16.4		
1927	4.0	2.1	32.4	21.6	8.6	14.2					—	14.3	30.8	11.4		
1930	2.2	0.9	29.0	22.1	10.8	18.4					0.3	17.4	38.8	16.5		
1933[d]	2.2	1.0	35.8	28.2	10.5	14.6			—	0.9	0.2	15.0	27.6	11.9	2.6	1.3
1936[d]	0.8	—	40.0	33.6	10.6	15.1			0.8	1.3	—	13.8	29.1	14.6	2.4	1.2
1945[d]	13.8	7.1	32.9	30.3	9.4	10.9			4.9	6.5	—	8.5	20.5	9.8	—	—
1949[d]	6.4	4.0	39.9	35.9	11.0	10.9			3.3	8.6	—	9.9	24.8	9.3	—	—
1953	5.0	3.5	38.9	35.7	8.2	7.7			6.1	9.4	0.3	10.5	25.2	9.7	—	—
1957	3.2	2.3	40.3	36.4	7.6	7.5			5.8	9.0	0.3	10.6	25.0	9.7	—	—
1961	2.6	2.1	38.4	36.0	6.8	7.1	2.8	1.4	5.6	8.5	0.3	10.8	25.7	10.9	—	—
1965	1.2	1.1	37.7	36.0	9.2	8.6	6.0	4.4	5.5	7.8	2.5	12.8	24.7	13.1	—	—

* The strength of each party or party group has been expressed as percentages of all registered voters at the given election. Registration was voluntary through 1897; from 1900 onward it was automatic on the basis of population records.

a Includes various "workers' lists" 1894–1903 and the Social Democratic party (Labor's Right wing) in 1921 and 1924.

b Includes the "Worker Democrats," later the "Radical People's Party."

c All the official statistics for party distributions for this period add the Moderates to the Right; only in one document prepared for the Storting (Indstilling S. XX, 1890) is there an attempt to estimate distributions for the three parties and this is for 1888. With the "Right" are also counted the "Unionist" party of 1903 and 1906 and the Frisinnede (National Liberals) from 1909 to 1936.

d A minor party, the "Commonwealth Party," in some ways similar to the Social Credit party in Canada, was nationally active in 1933, 1936 and 1949 and appeared under a different name (in Bergen only) in 1945. It gained these percentages of votes from the electorate:

	1933	1936	1945	1949
Cities	2.4	3.6	0.4	0.8
Rural Districts	0.6	2.9	—	0.7

Table 8—The Election Results in the Country Districts: Regional Contrasts During the Early Phase 1882–1897

	(total votes and percentages)					
	1882	1885	1888	1891	1894	1897
Oslofjord area						
Total vote[a] = 100%	(10,905)	(14,184)	(13,258)	(16,100)	(23,630)	(22,419)
Left	56.6	54.8	36.0	49.4	43.4	46.4
Moderates[b]	—	—	9.2	—	—	—
Right (and Mod.)	43.4	45.2	54.8	50.6	56.6	53.6
East Inland						
Total vote = 100%	(14,302)	(17,127)	(16,654)	(19,700)	(31,930)	(32,360)
Left	70.5	67.5	49.4	56.1	54.6	55.5
Moderates	—	—	16.6	—	—	—
Right (and Mod.)	29.5	32.5	34.0	43.9	45.4	44.5
South and West						
Total vote = 100%	(20,589)	(25,641)	(25,540)	(25,750)	(44,940)	(43,847)
Left	69.1	76.2	35.6	45.2	47.0	50.8
Moderates	—	—	43.1	—	—	—
Right (and Mod.)	30.9	23.8	21.3	54.8	53.0	49.2
Trøndelag						
Total vote = 100%	(5,685)	(7,884)	(8,166)	(8,900)	(11,320)	(11,651)
Left	76.8	66.9	57.5	65.7	61.5	64.1
Moderates	—	—	7.8	—	—	—
Right (and Mod.)	23.2	33.1	34.7	34.3	38.5	35.9
North Norway						
Total vote = 100%	(4,080)	(4,910)	(4,995)	(5,600)	(9,500)	(10,680)
Left	75.0	78.5	62.2	67.0	61.6	62.0
Moderates	—	—	15.7	—	—	—
Right (and Mod.)	25.0	21.5	22.1	33.0	38.4	38.0

[a] Minor parties excluded.
[b] Separate data for Moderates are available for 1888 only.

church, and for legislation against the sale of alcohol. The concentration on issues of cultural defense gave the party a dominant position in the South and the West but made it increasingly difficult for it to keep its earlier clientele in the other regions, particularly in the cities.

In the East, the Trøndelag, and the North, the entry of the lower classes had had a much more direct effect on the alignments of leaders and followers. The Labor Party, originally the political wing of the burgeoning trade union movement, gradually moved into the heart of the political struggle and in 1903, at the second election after the introduction of manhood suffrage, sent its first representatives to the *Storting*. It is deeply significant that these first representatives all came from the far North, from the economically most backward areas of the country. In these provinces the smallholders, the cotters and the fishermen, had for centuries depended for their living on privileged owners of port facilities who bought their produce and controlled their credit. The introduction of manhood suffrage coincided with a number of changes in the coastal economy—the installation of the first industrial plants, the motorization of the fishing fleet—and the result was an explosive mobilization of protest against the controlling class and the established system. The Labor Party had built up its initial organizational strength in the capital and in the central areas of the East but its political breakthrough came in the extreme periphery. This alliance between the rural proletariat and the urban working class proved a great force in Norwegian politics and was soon to bring about a series of changes in the entire system of party alignments.

For the old Left the entry of the lower classes and the Labor Party into the political arena posed a number of difficult problems of ideology and of strategy. The party leaders found it impossible to agree on the same lines of action in the cities and the countryside, in the East and the West, and the result was a series of splits. In the East, particularly in the inland provinces, a working-class movement of the old Left[39] had some success in the years before and during World War I, but the business followers of the party feared the consequences of a move toward Socialism and again and again sided with the Right on issues of economic policy: this splinter group, the *Frisinnede,* eventually merged with the Right yet tended to represent a more conciliatory ideology emphasizing the need for basic consensus across party lines.[40]

During the same period, 1906–20, the old Right gradually changed from a party of the official "establishment" toward a party defending the emerging community of business and industrial leaders and advocating the freedom of economic enterprise from interference by the state.[41] The party never made a complete break with its past, however; it retained important elements of the ideology of the strong and neutral state defended by the King's officials against the Left, but at the same time took over elements of the laissez-faire liberalism of the business community. The struggles between the "Burkean" and the "Liberalist" wings of the party in the 1950's reflect this early realignment within the party.

Whatever the ideological direction it took, the party was never able to establish lasting strongholds outside the cities and the surrounding areas. In contrast to the British Conservative Party, the Right in Norway, as in the other Scandinavian countries, was never able to bring about an alliance of urban and rural elites and to create the basis for a broad national movement. The efforts to build up a "Unionist" party against the Socialists in the years immediately after 1905 came to nothing: the century-old conflict between urban power and rural aspirations could not be solved within one party, and the division between the Right and the Left remained roughly what it had been in 1884, a split along the territorial-cultural axis.[42]

These realignments took place over a period of some fifteen years, from 1906 to the beginning of the economic crisis after World War I. This was a period of rapid economic growth. A number of new industries were built up, not only in the cities and their suburbs but also, largely as a result of developments in hydroelectric and electrochemical technology, in isolated places in the rural periphery. Increasing numbers of smallholders and fishermen moved out of their traditional environment and took jobs on construction sites, in transportation and in manufacturing. This rapidly recruited labor force found it difficult to adapt to the rigors of industrial life and developed strong resentments against the management and owners of industries. A syndicalist movement, to some extent influenced by the American IWW, established itself rapidly after 1912 and gained control over many of the local branches of the Labor party. Class antagonisms became increasingly acute, not least under the impact of the experiences of inflation and a get-rich-quick mentality during World War I. The result was a thoroughgoing radicalization of the Labor party: it was the only one of the Scandinavian Socialist parties

Table 9—Regional Contrasts in Party Polarization 1900–1961: Data for the Rural Districts

	1900	1903	1918	1921	1927	1930	1936	1945	1957	1961
Oslofjord area										
Valid votes = 100%	(31,895)	(34,259)	(88,054)	(118,598)	(156,101)	(187,534)	(238,352)	(260,412)	(253,503)	(272,022)
Soc. (CP + Lab. + Soc.dem.)	—	6.8	34.2	32.3	43.3	35.9	46.5	51.8	53.0	53.5
Left (and Christians)	49.5	37.3	16.3	9.8	6.3	8.9	7.1	17.3	14.8	13.5
Agrarians	—	—	4.4	16.4	17.7	18.7	12.6	8.2	10.2	10.4
Conservatives	50.5	55.9	44.7	41.5	32.6	36.6	30.8+2.2[b]	22.7	21.1	22.6
Polarization score[a]	—	.63	.83	.88	.92	.89	.92	.81	.83	.85
East Inland and Trøndelag										
Valid votes = 100%	(59,357)	(58,984)	(170,186)	(218,849)	(239,945)	(284,370)	(337,604)	(354,282)	(411,241)	(419,717)
Soc. (CP + Lab. + Soc.dem.)	8.4	11.8	34.3	30.9	42.9	38.6	49.3	60.1	58.9	59.2
Left (and Christians)	58.7	48.6	39.1	25.6	19.9	19.8	14.9	16.6	14.1	13.0
Agrarians	—	—	9.2	21.4	26.2	26.2	20.8	14.8	17.1	17.3
Conservatives	32.9	39.6	15.1	21.4	10.9	15.3	11.4+1.9	8.6	9.7	10.5
Polarization score	.41	.51	.56	.67	.73	.73	.81	.81	.83	.84
South and West										
Valid votes = 100%	(63,031)	(57,166)	(111,587)	(184,802)	(189,865)	(244,890)	(289,944)	(297,594)	(355,722)	(361,604)
Soc. (CP + Lab. + Soc.dem.)	0.4	1.3	14.8	14.0	21.9	16.7	24.1	33.9	36.5	36.9
Left (and Christians)	55.1	51.4	59.0	44.1	38.2	41.1	37.8	41.3	37.3	36.1
Agrarians	—	—	9.3	22.7	26.7	27.2	19.5	13.9	15.6	15.1
Conservatives	44.5	47.3	16.2	18.5	13.2	15.0	13.9+0.6	9.9	10.6	11.9
Polarization score	.45	.49	.34	.42	.48	.44	.51	.52	.56	.58
North										
Valid votes = 100%	(16,658)	(15,096)	(51,217)	(75,582)	(104,174)	(78,604)	(134,972)	(111,441)	(154,448)	(158,005)
Soc. (CP + Lab. + Soc.dem.)	—	28.9	40.4	32.5	45.5	32.1	46.3	66.5	60.3	60.6
Left (and Christians)	73.5	47.9	54.8	26.1	22.9	26.3	16.6	13.8	16.8	15.8
Agrarians	—	—	1.8	13.8	10.0	11.9	8.2	3.7	8.5	9.0
Conservatives	26.5	17.7	2.3	26.9	21.6	29.7	18.7+0.6	16.1	13.9	14.6
Polarization score	—	.47	.44	.70	.75	.70	.80	.86	.82	.83

[a] This gives the Socialist + Conservative (inclusive of the National Liberal and, in 1936, the National Socialist) vote as a ratio of the total vote cast for all major party groups except the Agrarians (disregarded in this context since they express another dimension of representation.)
[b] National Socialist vote.

Table 10—Election Results in Cities: Regional Contrasts 1882–1961

	THREE PRINCIPAL CITIES[a]			OTHER CITIES		
	Christiania/ Oslo	Bergen	Trond- heim	Oslo- fjord	East Inl. and Trøndelag	South, North and West
1882						
Tot. vote	(3,124)	(1,838)	(1,896)	(2,191)	(2,930)	(3,989)	(775)
Left	23.8	68.6	42.0	37.7	38.8	56.9	56.8
Right	76.2	31.4	58.0	62.3	61.2	43.1	43.2
1888						
Tot. vote	(5,935)	(2,077)	(1,856)	(2,670)	(3,282)	(4,157)	(829)
Left	25.0	53.3	44.3	34.9	38.9	35.0	48.4
Moderates	0	13.2	0	0	0	18.4	0
Right	75.0	33.5	55.7	65.1	61.1	46.6	51.6
1897						
Tot. vote	(16,844)	(4,851)	(3,200)	(5,045)	(5,995)	(7,583)	(1,620)
Soc.	3.9	4.3	—	—	—	—	—
Left	48.7	58.8	52.0	43.2	50.5	52.6	57.3
Mod. + Right	47.4	36.9	48.0	56.8	49.5	47.4	42.7
1903						
Tot. vote	(24,841)	(9,244)	(5,249)	(7,603)	(8,622)	(12,694)	(2,883)
Socialist	27.0	22.2	27.7	5.8	16.4	10.6	27.9
Left	21.8	36.8	21.1	37.3	33.0	48.0	47.2
Right and Mod.	51.2	41.0	51.2	56.9	50.6	41.4	24.9
Polarization[b]	0.78	0.63	0.79	0.63	0.67	0.54	0.53
1927						
Tot. vote	(128,693)	(40,958)	(22,874)	(37,935)	(40,325)	(52,513)	(11,470)
Socialist (CP + Lab.)	49.4	47.8	50.8	48.7	51.0	39.3	51.5
Left	29.1	21.3	7.9	8.6	9.0	27.8	22.3
Right[c]	46.8	31.0	41.3	42.7	40.1	32.9	26.2
Polarization	0.97	0.79	0.92	0.91	0.91	0.72	0.78
1930						
Tot. vote	(140,735)	(45,866)	(26,011)	(41,195)	(43,309)	(60,988)	(13,780)
Socialist (CP + Lab.)	42.2	38.3	36.4	36.9	32.2	28.9	45.5
Left + Agr.	3.4	24.0	4.0	11.8	19.2	34.7	22.4
Right[c]	54.3	37.7	59.6	51.3	48.6[d]	36.4[d]	32.1
Polarization	0.97	0.76	0.96	0.88	0.81	0.65	0.78
1936						
Tot. vote	(168,426)	(57,451)	(30,324)	(49,507)	(54,193)	(76,771)	(17,694)
Soc. (CP incl.)	51.3	39.2	49.2	50.9	49.7	37.3	49.6
Lib. + Chr.	2.7	26.9	4.5	12.1	9.7	28.7	16.6
Right[c] (incl. NS)	44.8	22.0	41.2	36.4	39.6	28.7	24.8
Polarization	0.97	0.69	0.95	0.88	0.90	0.70	0.82
1945						
Tot. vote	(170,900)	(57,954)	(29,713)	(54,969)	(55,879)	(77,847)	(14,234)
Soc. (CP incl.)	56.7	53.1	63.9	58.7	62.1	52.3	63.6
Lib. + Chr. + Agr.	13.4	26.2	11.6	15.8	11.5	27.4	17.8
Right	29.9	17.8	24.4	25.5	26.4	20.3	18.6
Polarization	0.87	0.73	0.88	0.84	0.89	0.73	0.82
1957						
Tot. vote	(278,590)	(62,512)	(32,745)	(63,772)	(72,491)	(99,634)	(32,997)
Soc. (CP incl.)	50.6	51.1	61.0	56.8	59.5	47.2	61.3
Lib. + Chr. + Agr.	11.2	24.7	12.6	13.1	16.5	32.0	16.3
Right	38.2	24.2	26.3	27.7	22.8	20.8	22.0
Polarization	0.89	0.75	0.87	0.87	0.83	0.68	0.84

Table 10 (continued)

	THREE PRINCIPAL CITIES[a]				OTHER CITIES		
					East Inl. and Trøndelag	South, North and West	
	Christiania/ Oslo	Bergen	Trond-heim	Oslo-fjord			
1961							
Tot. vote	(287,665)	(62,962)	(31,756)	(62,845)	(65,375)	(93,717)	(24,497)
Soc. (CP + SP + Lab.)	51.7	53.0	61.1	57.1	59.6	46.8	60.9
Lib. + Chr. + Agr.	9.8	24.8	11.6	12.0	14.9	30.3	16.1
Right	38.5	22.2	27.3	30.9	25.5	22.9	23.0
Polarization	0.90	0.75	0.89	0.89	0.86	0.70	0.85

[a] Christiania and Trondheim made up constituencies with minor neighboring towns through 1903. The only figures available are for these slightly larger units.
[b] Soc. + Cons./Soc. + Left (incl. Chr.) + Cons.
[c] This includes votes for the *National Liberals* through 1936.
[d] Includes joint "burgher" lists.

to muster a majority for joining the Communist International when the showdown came in 1919.[43] By contrast to the developments in the other countries, the split-off in Norway came on the Right wing and not on the Left: a Social Democrat party was formed of the dissidents who voted against the Third International in 1919, and gained about one-quarter of the total working-class vote at the elections of 1921 and 1924. The majority Labor Party proved a highly insubordinate ally of the Communists in Moscow, and by 1923 it had had enough: the result was another split, this time to the Left.[44] The election of 1924 saw three working-class parties competing for votes: the Communists, the central Labor Party, and the Social Democrats. At the next general election, in 1927, the Right-wing splinter returned to the fold and Labor polled 36 percent of the votes—it was now the largest party in Parliament and constituted a serious threat to the established powers in the nation.[45] The Communist Party remained in opposition on the Left but soon dwindled to insignificance: it had a renaissance in 1945, but again failed to develop a broad organizational basis for its activities and petered out in the 1950's.

The victory of the revitalized Labor Party in 1927 shook the system to the core and triggered off extensive countermovements, both in the cities and in the countryside. The election of 1930 was a distinct setback to the Labor Party; as will be seen from *Table 9* it did not lose much of its established support (the strength of the parties is given as a percentage of all eligible voters in that table, not of votes cast) but was unable to compete with its opponents for new votes. As will be seen from *Table 4* the turnout rose to its highest point since the introduction of universal suffrage, 81.6 percent in the cities and 75.7 percent in the countryside. This was essentially the result of widespread efforts to mobilize the *women* voters to the defense of the traditional moral and religious values against the threats of secularism and Socialism.

The economic crisis of 1930–31 changed the mood of the country, however, and Labor soon recovered from the setback. The party launched a determined drive for power and reached its first goal in 1935: it took over the government and introduced a number of measures to relieve the economic situation and to improve the conditions of the workers and the peasants. It still did not command a majority in the *Storting,* but its reservoirs of support were not exhausted: the turnout was still low in many working-class neighborhoods in the cities and among smallholders and fishermen and their families in the countryside, and there was much to be achieved through systematic organization, both through the unions and through the local party branches. The election of 1936 was without comparison the hardest-fought contest in Norwegian history: the turnout rose as high as to 87.5 percent in the cities and 82.6 percent in the countryside. The Labor Party came very close to a majority in the East, the Trøndelag, and the North, but was still weak in the South and West. The class antagonisms and the resultant polarization between Socialists and Conservatives had not manifested themselves with equal force in all regions of the country. As can be seen from *Tables 9 and 10* the process reached its maximum as early as 1921 in the central region around the capital, took considerably longer in the eastern valley regions, in the Trøndelag and the North, but never got very far in the South and the West. This is a fact of crucial importance in the Norwegian political system: a number of the tables in the analytical sections of this study will focus on this crosscutting of geographical and cultural cleavage lines with the socioeconomic.

The steady growth of the Labor Party had important repercussions for the alignments of the opposition parties. The old Left was divided over conflicts of interest and ideology along several axes, not only along the territorial-cultural-religious as in the 1880's, but along an economic-functional axis as well.

The Left had been able to stave off a split of the 1888 type through a series of compromises: it had allowed the orthodox Lutherans to establish a divinity school of their own in 1906 and had opened the state church to its graduates in 1913; it had favored strict legislation on the production and sale of alcohol and had organized the referendum that brought in total prohibition in 1919. But the fundamentalists of the West found it increasingly difficult to stay within the old party: the abolition of prohibition after the referendum in 1926 and the rapid rise of the Labor Party after 1930 increased their opposition to all signs of secularization and set the stage for the formation of a distinctly religious party. A Christian People's party first appeared in 1933 and continued the traditions of the Moderates of the nineties: this can be seen both from the two maps in *Fig. 1* and from the series of parallel figures for voting strength in *Table 18*.

By that time the old Left had also been split along an economic cleavage dimension: the conflict between rural and urban interests in the community market (*CM in Table 6*) had triggered the formation of a distinct economic interest party, the Agrarians, first in a few isolated constituencies in 1915, later as a regular nationwide organization. This party sapped much of the strength of the old Left in the richer rural areas of the East Inland and in the Trøndelag and also made considerable inroads in the agricultural areas of the South, the West, and the North.

This development added a further dimension to the Norwegian cleavage system: two economic-functional cleavages (*CM* and *LM* in the table) cut across each other and across two (or three) territorial cultural ones (*T-SC* and *R*).

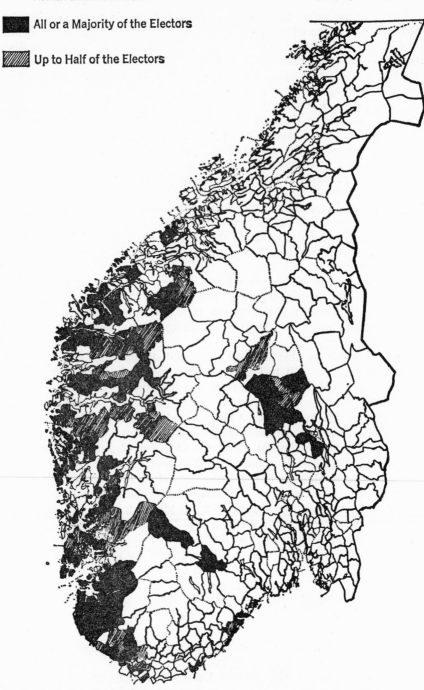

The Moderates in 1891

■ All or a Majority of the Electors

▨ Up to Half of the Electors

*Figure 1—Maps for the Strength of the Moderates in 1891
and the Christians in 1953: Southern Norway Only.*

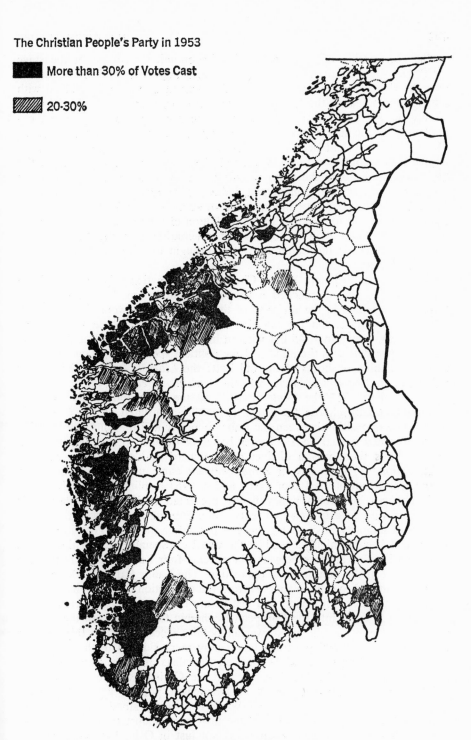

The Christian People's Party in 1953

■ More than 30% of Votes Cast

▨ 20-30%

Figure 1 (continued)
Source: G. Øidne, Syn og Segn, *63(3) 1957, pp. 107–08.*

The crosscutting of the two functional-economic cleavages set the stage for a triangular conflict: Labor opposed both Agrarians and Conservatives over the rights of wage earners, but Labor was at the same time allied with the Agrarians against the Conservatives on the need for controls in the commodity market and for the protection of the primary economy against exploitation by the urban bourgeoisie and against competition from abroad.[46] The Labor Party had been able to bridge the urban-rural cleavage in Norwegian society but as a result was caught between conflicting pressures: the Oslo-based radicals in the party wanted to challenge the right of all owners and employers, whether commercial, industrial, or rural, while the victorious moderates in the party saw the need for an alliance of workers, smallholders, and fishermen and for a policy of reconciliation of urban and rural interests.[47] The natural result of this conciliatory orientation was the "Red-Green" agreement of 1935: the Labor Party was brought to power with the support of the Agrarians.

With the establishment of the Christians as a nationwide party in 1945 the Norwegian system reached a temporary equilibrium. For sixteen years to come the voters in the majority of the constituencies were faced with six distinct alternatives. On the Socialist Left they could choose between the *Communists,* strong in 1945 but without importance after 1948, and the governing *Labor* Party. In the middle of the political spectrum they could choose among the three offshoots of the old Left: the *Liberals* (still retaining their old name in Norwegian, *Venstre*), the *Christian People's* Party, and the *Agrarians* since 1958 the *Center* Party). At the other end of the spectrum they could finally choose the *Right* (generally translated as the *Conservatives*). The opposition between the Labor majority and the four non-Socialist parties reached a peak in 1949 over issues of detailed price regulation but in the 1950s there was a distinct trend toward de-ideologization and de-politicization.[48] This policy of *rapprochement* came under heavy fire from the neutralist Left of the Labor Party, and in 1961 a splinter party advocating basic changes in foreign policy finally presented itself to the voters: this *Socialist People's* Party won two seats in the *Storting* and reduced the Labor Party to a minority position for the first time after the war. The situation in Parliament became highly unstable; the two Left Socialists found themselves in the position of arbiters between the seventy-four Labor members and the seventy-four in the non-Socialist opposition. The Labor Party decided to stay in power but had to rely on support from the opposition on the right in carrying out its policies. This happened just before the storm broke over the issue of Norwegian entry into the European Economic Community. In this fight—the bitterest experienced in Norwegian politics since the early thirties—the Labor government and the trade union movement sided with the Conservatives in advocating entry, while the Left Socialists and the Agrarians came out strongly against it. The Liberals and the Christians were split and the old-established regional contrasts in Norwegian politics again manifested themselves.[49] The Southerners and Westerners again stood out as the defenders of the cultural autonomy of the provinces against the encroachments of the center. This time the enemy was not just in Oslo, but, what made it much worse, in the distant bureaucratic centers on the European continent.

But there was more to come: President De Gaulle's "No" to the entry of the British, and therefore also the Norwegians, into the EEC, set the stage for a "repolarization" of Norwegian politics and by the summer of 1963 had brought the country to the brink of a serious political crisis. The Labor Party could no longer count on the support of any of the four opposition parties; it was thrown to the mercy of the two Left Socialists. An administrative scandal in the wake of a mining disaster broke the back of the Labor government; it was voted out of power for the first time in twenty-eight years.[50] For four hectic weeks the country was governed by a coalition of the four non-Socialist parties. The wounds of the bitter fight over the European issue healed quickly and the four were able to agree on a progressive program of continued reform, not very different in its basic orientation from the policies already pursued by the Labor Party. The old governing party met the crisis with admirable courage and launched a program further toward the Socialist left than at any time since the twenties. The result was a temporary victory: the two Left-wing dissidents came to heel and voted the Labor Party back into power, but the old leadership had clearly begun to lose control over developments within the movement. There were many signs of disaffection among the young,[51] and the polls began to suggest a gradual decline in the strength of the party. The election of September 12–13, 1965, confirmed this trend. The Labor Party was set back from 46.8 to 43.2 percent of the valid votes and the Left Socialists moved up from 2.4 to 6.0 percent. This was no landslide but in a multiparty PR system even small changes in voting strength may radically change the situation in Parliament. Labor lost six of the seventy-four seats, while the Left Socialists stayed at the two-member level despite its gains at the polling booths. The result was a clear-cut majority for the four non-Socialist parties—80 over 70.[52] It took some time before they could reach agreement on a coalition government but prudence and patience prevailed and the four gradually found it possible to work together in harness despite the many sources of friction and *malaise*. They continuously avoided decisive action on any of the thorny issues of cultural and religious policy and departed only imperceptibly from established Labor policy on such issues as taxation, credit control, and the maintenance of state industries. This was a distinct innovation in Scandinavian politics: the experiment was eagerly watched both in Denmark and in Sweden, and there was much speculation about the chances for similar developments in those countries.

THE TWO PERIPHERIES: THE SOUTH/WEST AND THE NORTH

Our sketchy review of the electoral alternatives and the distributions of votes since 1882 has underscored the persistence of regional differences in political alignments in Norway.

The South and, even more markedly, the West, have stood out again and again as the regions of the strongest cultural resistance to centralizing and urbanizing forces and have offered the most effective barriers against the spread of polarized class politics. The map in *Fig. 2* for the strength of the Labor Party in the fifties brings this out with great clarity.

Lower Quartile: The 170 Communes Polling Less Than 22.6% Labor
The Two Middle Quartiles: 22.7 — 41.6%
Upper Quartile: The 170 Communes Polling More Than 41.6% Labor

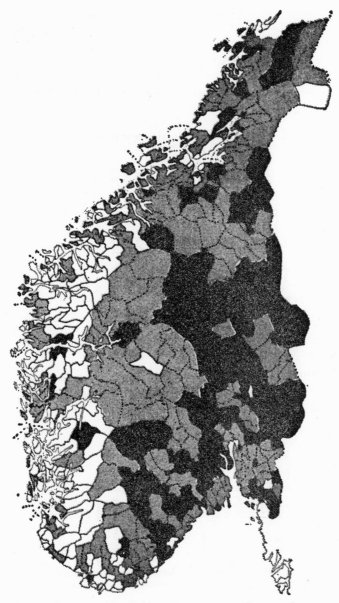

*Figure 2—The Strength of the Labor Party in the Rural Communes:
Votes in Percent of Total Registered in 1957.*

Table 11—Socialist-Conservative Polarization in 1957: Contrasts Between Communes at Different Levels of Urbanization and Industrialization

Communes in	Density	Industrialization: 1950 census	No. of comm.	Total electorate = 100%	CP + Lab.	Left	Chr.	Agr.	Cons.	Polarization score[a]
						Votes cast for: (percent)				
East and Trøndelag	Low	Low: under 23.1%	129	211,262	40.0	4.9	7.6	17.9	6.5	.79
		Medium: 23.2–35.7%	90	250,642	43.9	4.7	6.4	14.9	9.3	.83
		High: 35.8%+	36	131,933	50.6	3.6	6.1	9.4	10.6	.86
	High	High	34	232,312	47.7	5.3	6.3	3.6	17.6	.85
	Cities	Low: under 37.1%	7	52,635	46.3	5.1	5.7	1.1	22.6	.86
	+ towns	High: over 37.1%	26	485,575	44.6	5.0	5.0	0.2	28.3	.88
South and West	Low	Low	131	138,199	20.6	12.7	16.4	17.1	6.0	.48
		Medium	85	119,657	23.6	14.0	15.4	14.4	6.2	.50
		High	35	84,524	31.9	11.3	15.5	9.6	6.2	.59
	High	Low	4	7,083	15.9	14.7	16.1	5.7	10.1	.46
		Medium + High	24	120,674	36.3	13.7	10.6	5.0	11.4	.66
	Cities	Low	9	40,513	33.9	17.9	9.6	0.2	17.8	.65
	+ towns	High	11	161,596	40.4	14.2	7.8	0.4	17.8	.73
North	Low	Low	71	108,631	36.5	4.7	7.4	6.6	8.3	.79
		Medium	25	55,665	38.8	5.4	6.4	7.3	8.3	.80
		High	7	22,422	49.4	3.6	6.4	6.2	6.2	.85
	High	Low + Medium	10	20,071	43.8	4.3	5.0	2.1	12.7	.86
		High	3	9,914	57.2	4.3	3.6	0.3	11.8	.90
	Cities	Low	10	38,263	45.9	8.2	4.5	0.3	17.6	.83
	+ towns	High	1	4,805	54.9	4.7	3.4	0.2	10.7	.89

[a] Polarization score calculated as in Tables 9 and 10.

By contrast, the North has stood out as the polarized periphery. Economically the most backward of all the regions, it has a persistent record of radicalism and was the first to send Labor representatives to the *Storting* after the introduction of manhood suffrage in 1900.

But these are impressions from comparisons of aggregate figures. How far do these contrasts stand up to detailed scrutiny community by community? How far do the differences in politics between different communities reflect differences in social structure and in the level of economic growth, and how far do they reflect differences in local cultural traditions?

We are not in a position to give precise answers to such questions for the early elections; yet we have assembled a considerable body of information on variations between communities since World War II, and we shall use the data from this "ecological archive" to throw light on the character of regional differences in Norwegian politics.[53]

Our punched-card archive currently consists of commune-by-commune data for all local and national elections from 1945 to 1965; census data for 1950 and 1960; educational, agricultural, industrial, and fiscal statistics; data from a church-attendance count; data on local party organizations and party memberships; and data on nominees to lists for the *Storting* elections. So far we have used the data in this archive for descriptive rather than analytical purposes. The bulk of the tables presented in this chapter present similarities and differences in distributions on political variables between communal units classified in terms of one, two, or three geographical, socioeconomic, or cultural variables. In the cruder descriptive presentations (e.g., *Table 11*) we have simply aggregated electorates and votes within each group of communes and given percentage distributions for these aggregates. These then express averages weighted for commune size but give no indication of ranges of within-group variation. In some of the tables (e.g., *Table 12*) each commune

Table 12—Regional Differences in Socialist Support Outside Industry: by the Proportion of Large Forestry Units in each Commune

Region	P.c. of Actives in Forestry 1950	P.c. of units over 1,000 da.	N= 100%	Index CP + Lab. — Ind.[a]		
				Q₁	Md	Q₃
East and	Under 2.1	Under 2.5	53	8.5	14.–	20.1
Trøndelag		Over 2.5	44	9.9	19.2	27.1
		Under 2.5	22	9.5	15.6	24.9
	Over	2.5–11.8	94	15.4	24.7	32.5
		Over 11.9	76	25.5	33.4	48.2
South and	Under 2.1	Under 2.5	187	−9.3	1.–	10.–
West		Over 2.5	53	−4.6	2.2	15.4
	Over	Under 2.5	2		12.5	
		Over 2.5	33	5.7	14.3	27.1
North	Under 2.1	Under 2.5	73	35.3	43.5	57.1
		Over 2.5	31	23.2	31.2	40.8
	Over	Under 2.5	4		36.1	
		Over 2.5	8		41.4	

[a] The difference for each commune between the percent of the economically active in mining, manufacturing and construction by the 1950 census and the percent of the *electorate* voting CP or Labor in 1949.

counts as one unit irrespective of the size of its electorate: this allows statements about the range of variation for given political attributes within each group of communes.

In the bulk of the analyses the dependent variables are straightforward political variables such as turnout or strength of a given party expressed as a percentage. Only in one case so far have we tried out an index based on an assumption about some constant source of support for a given party: this is our "*CP + Lab. − Ind.*" score which simply gives the difference, negative or positive, between the Socialist strength in the electorate and the proportion of the labor force in manufacturing, mining, or construction. This score is based on the crude assumption that 100 percent of the votes from "industrial" households go to the CP or to Labor. This assumption, of course, is unrealistic: this can easily be seen from the distributions found for each occupational group in a nationwide survey (*Tables 17 and 18*). Nevertheless, the score gives a very clear picture of differences between regions and types of communes and has proved of distinct heuristic value in our research. We hope in our future work to develop a scheme of *alternative assumptions about the political preferences of each socioeconomic stratum* and to test these assumptions through analyses of commune-by-commune discrepancies between calculated and observed distributions of the vote. Calculations of this type have recently been tried out with some success in France,[54] and the potentialities of the technique have been ingeniously demonstrated on Swedish data in a recent article by Gösta Carlsson.[55]

Our first set of ecological tables focus on the *territorial and the socioeconomic structure* of the communes within each of the basic divisions of the country.

A comparison between *Tables 9 and 10* will show that the political differences between the South/West and the other regions are less pronounced in the *cities* than in the rural districts. Our crude score for Socialist-Conservative polarization gives these differences between the South/West and the other regions for 1957:

	Oslofjord	East Inland, Trøndelag	North	South/West
(1) Principal cities	.89	.87	—	.75
(2) Other cities	.87	.83	.84	.68
(3) Rural districts	.83	.83	.82	.56
Diff. (1) − (3)	.06	.04	.02	.19

The differences between the regions are clearly most marked in the countryside. *Table 13* goes into further detail and shows that the contrasts are most pronounced in the sparsely populated, preindustrial communes, but tend to disappear in the urbanized and industrialized areas. It is in the low-density, low-industry communes, the typical primary-economy communes, that we find the most distinctive patterns of regional politics. The crucial difference lies in the balance of strength between the offshoots of the old Left and the working-class parties. In the South and the West the three Middle parties are still dominant, in the East and the Trøndelag and even more markedly in the North they have been overshadowed by the Socialists:

Least industrialized communes in	Socialists	Strength in 1957 Middle parties	Conservatives
South and West	20.6	46.2	6.0
East and Trøndelag	40.0	29.4	6.5
North	36.5	18.7	8.3

Clearly the Socialists have been able to mobilize very important electoral resources in the rural areas of the East and the North but have found it much more difficult in the South and West. Where did they find these resources in the East and the North and why did they fail in the South/West? Our further tables seek to throw light on these questions.

We shall consider in turn three sources of primary-economy strength: the households of actives in *forestry,* the households of *smallholders and farmers,* and the households of *fishermen. Table 12* gives rough estimates of the likely contributions of Socialist votes from the forestry sector of the primary economy. In the East and the Trøndelag the Socialist parties clearly derive the bulk of their rural strength from the forestry labor force: the greater the number of actives in forestry in a rural commune, the greater the number of Socialist votes from nonindustrial households. In the South and the West there is a similar trend, but there are only a few typical forestry communes and these add very little to the total electoral resources of the Socialist parties in this region. In the North there is no consistent trend in the data: the very few forestry workers in that region clearly do not make a difference for the Socialist parties.

The table also tells us of differences in residual sources of electoral support for the Socialist parties. In the South and the West the communes with the lowest proportions of actives in forestry will generally only return Socialist votes from industrial households; indeed, in close to half of them the Socialists do not appear to have exhausted their industrial potential.[56] In the East and the Trøndelag, Socialists can count on sizable support from households in other sectors than industry and forestry, and in the North this is in fact the normal situation. We shall explore these further sources of support in later tables.

Why such differences between regions? One line of explanation focuses on *status inequalities* and *class hatred* as crucial variables: the rural communities of the East, the Trøndelag, and the North have tended to be much more hierarchical and have offered much stronger incentives to class politics than the equalitarian communities so frequently found in the South and the West.

This hypothesis could be tested in a variety of ways. In our first attempts at analysis we have used *the sizes of holdings* in forestry and agriculture as indicators of socioeconomic differentiation within communities.

The South and the West stand out as regions of small holdings and of minimal variations in the size of units. As seen from *Table 12* there are very few forestry communes in these regions. The thirty-five communes with more than 2.5 percent of their active population in forestry are practically all in the South; in the West the forestry sector is minimal and the small variations in the numbers of forestry workers appear to be of no political significance. Variations in *agriculture* count much more, and the statistics of agricultural censuses offer striking evidence of regional differences in community structure. The agricultural census of 1959[57] gives these regional variations in the size of farm units:

	Total rural holdings over 5 decares	Mean size in decares	Proportion of units over 100 decares
East and Trøndelag	108,981	61.01	18.4%
South and West	74,757	35.99	3.4%
North	42,237	30.11	1.7%
The Nation	225,975	46.95	8.9%

How would we expect such differences in the structure of the primary economy to be reflected in political behavior? Here it is essential to distinguish between absolute and relative size. In absolute terms we might expect the holders of small units to suffer economic hardship and to be easily swayed by class ideologies. In relative terms, the political weight of the size of the holding will vary with the community context: holders of small units will react one way in situations of direct dependence on large farms and forest estates in their own community, quite another way in communities where their

Table 13—Regional Differences in Socialist Support Outside Industry: by the Proportion of Large Farms in Each Commune

Region	P.c. of farms over 100 da.	N= 100%	Index CP + Lab. — Ind.[a]		
			Q₁	Md	Q₃
East and Trøndelag	Under 1.5%	23	14.1	26.7	39.1
	1.6–10.8%	88	19.4	29.7	40.-
	10.9–28.3%	104	14.6	23.9	33.7
	28.4 +	74	9.6	15.-	22.8
South and West	Under 1.5%	141	− 3.4	5.-	14.1
	1.6–10.8%	112	−12.-	0.5	10.3
	10.9 +	21	−10.2	2.4	13.7
North	Under 1.5%	70	34.5	43.7	57.9
	1.6–10.8%	42	25.6	34.8	45.3
	10.9 +	4		29.-	

[a] For explanation see Table 12.

neighbors are all roughly equals. In the South and the West the holdings tend to be very small by the standards of the East, but in the majority of communities they are *all* small by such standards and there is therefore very little basis for class resentment and class cleavage in local politics. In the East and the Trøndelag, holdings vary much more in size, both within and across localities, and there will be much more pronounced tendencies toward a class polarization of the votes in the primary economy. In the East and the Trøndelag the result is quite clear cut: the Socialist "surplus" is much larger in communes with a number of large forestry units. The explanation seems relatively simple: large forestry units require wage labor and most of the workers will tend to be seasonally employed and eke out their living through small agricultural holdings of their own. *Table 13* appears to confirm this interpretation for the East: the Socialists are strongest in communes with a majority of small farm holdings and much weaker in communes with a large number of fair-sized farms. Clearly the rural structures most likely to prove polarizing are those made up of marked majorities of smallholders, forestry workers, and other seasonal laborers dependent on a few dominant forest owners and large-scale farmers. In such communities age-old antagonisms between the "populace" and the "lords" will almost invariably find political expression in heavy Socialist surpluses.

Class antagonisms also explain the high level of polarization in the North. In these provinces the smallholders and the fishermen had for centuries depended for their living on owners of port facilities who bought their produce and controlled their credit. With the extension of the suffrage in 1900 resentments against this system of economic dependence soon found political expression, and the Labor Party very quickly established itself as a serious contender for power in the far North. The first five Socialists to be elected to the Storting all came from the North, four of them from the fisheries districts of Tromsø and Finnmark, one from the new industrial center at Narvik. In the elections which followed, the Socialists spread throughout the Northern provinces and increased their votes almost continuously. By 1927 the two Socialist parties had reached a clear majority position in the region and after the setback in 1930 continued toward a position of absolute dominance. The split between Communists and Labor was of little importance in the thirties, but in the election just after World War II the CP established itself as a major wing of the working-class movement of the North. Its votes fell markedly after the events of 1948, but the party lost much less in the farthest North near the Soviet Union than in the rest of the country:

	CP/Labor ratios		
	1945 CP/ Lab.	1949 CP/ Lab.	1961 (CP + Left Soc.)/ Lab.
All rural districts	.23	.11	.10 (Left Soc. in 5 of 18 provinces)
Nordland	.23	.10	.19 (Left Soc. list)
Tromsø	.23	.09	.05 (no Left Soc.)
Finnmark	.38	.28	.20 (no Left Soc.)

We hope to go into details of an analysis of the Communist-Labor ratios in another context.[58] In this chapter we shall in most cases concentrate on the total Socialist strength and seek to identify major sources of variation in this total.

In *Table 14* we have classified all the rural communes by one of our criteria of peripheral status; this is a score which we first developed in an analysis of turnout variations[59] but which has also proved useful in explorations of regional differences in party support. The political distinctiveness of the North stands out very clearly in this table: the peripheral communes in the East, South, and West are all markedly less polarized than the central ones, but in the North the periphery differs very little from the other rural communes in the region.

Table 15 classifies the communes by the proportion of those economically active in fisheries and shipping; this is essentially a measure of the coastal versus inland character of the geography. Again the North stands out as the most polarized region. Even in the typical fisheries districts polarization is as

Table 14—Differences in Party Strength Between Central and Peripheral Areas Within Each Region:
Data for 1957

Region	Accessibility^a	No. of communes	Electorate 1957 N = 100%	CP	Lab.	Left (percent)	Chr.	Agr.	Cons.	Polarization^b
East and	High	97	464,014	2.9	43.4	4.4	6.3	9.0	14.1	0.85
Trøndelag	Medium	163	335,707	3.2	41.0	4.9	6.7	14.9	7.6	0.82
	Low	29	26,428	0.8	32.7	7.2	10.8	14.7	5.1	0.68
South and	High	48	173,204	1.2	30.6	13.8	13.0	7.4	9.7	0.61
West	Medium	193	261,199	0.6	24.2	12.7	15.1	13.7	6.3	0.53
	Low	34	35,734	0.02	17.8	12.7	17.0	18.6	6.1	0.45
North	High	11	19,753	3.1	37.7	4.6	5.0	4.6	11.9	0.85
	Medium	49	122,613	3.9	37.6	4.9	6.6	5.9	8.6	0.81
	Low	56	74,337	2.3	35.3	4.5	7.2	6.6	7.9	0.80

Votes Cast For (percent) spans columns CP, Lab., Left, Chr., Agr., Cons.

^a A score for average accessibility originally developed for analyses of electoral turnout and based on (1) the percentage of the 1950 population in "house clusters" (2) the percentage of children of school age taught in central boarding schools within the commune because of distances from their homes, (3) the percentage of school children taught in one-class or two-class schools (because of low density of population).
^b CP+Lab.+Cons./CP+Lab.+Left+Chr.+Cons.

high as .79 as against .75 for the East and the Trøndelag and as little as .43 for the South/West. The contrast between the two coastal areas is indeed highly revealing: in the North the Socialists mobilize close to 60 percent of the votes cast and the Conservatives are strongest among the opposition

Table 15—Differences in Party Strength Between Inland and Coastal Communes (Measured by the Percent of Actives In Fisheries and Shipping—Low-Density Communes Only)

Region	P.c. in Fisheries, Shipping, 1950	No. of Comm.	Electorate =100%	CP+Lab.	Middle (percent)	Cons.	Polarization^a	Chr. in p.c. of Middle Parties	All Non-Soc.
East	Under 2.5	182	451,432	46.4	25.5	7.1	0.85	23.5	18.4
and	2.5–15.9	43	82,230	38.2	28.8	11.8	0.77	31.0	21.9
Trøndelag	Over 16.0	30	60,175	34.1	25.2	15.7	0.75	36.9	22.7
South	Under 2.5	63	74,260	27.1	43.9	5.0	0.60	26.0	23.3
and	2.5–15.9	107	156,977	24.8	42.7	6.4	0.53	36.3	31.6
West	Over 16.0	77	111,143	19.8	42.6	6.5	0.43	45.3	39.3
North	Under 2.5	11	6,384	44.6	17.5	6.9	0.85	26.3	18.9
	2.5–15.9	16	15,764	42.3	19.2	6.2	0.82	24.5	18.5
	Over 16.0	76	45,553	36.9	18.4	8.3	0.79	43.5	29.4

Votes for (percent) spans CP+Lab., Middle, Cons.; Election of 1957 spans Chr. in p.c. of Middle Parties, All Non-Soc.

^a (CP+Lab.+Cons.)/(CP+Lab.+Left+Chr.+Cons.)

parties; in the South/West the offshoots of the old Left mobilize close to two-thirds of the valid votes and the Conservatives are the weakest of the non-Socialist parties. In both regions the Christian People's Party finds its surest sources of strength in the coastal communes; these are, as we shall see in later tables, areas of intensive religious activity and as a result more likely to add to the electoral potential of the Christians.

Throughout our work with the ecological data we have been concerned to cross-check our interpretations through parallel analyses of data from cross-sectional sample surveys. The design and size of the samples will not allow as detailed regional breakdowns as an analysis of official statistics, but even the crude classifications possible within a normal-sized nationwide sample will provide useful guidance in interpreting the ecological findings.

In *Table 16* we have grouped the respondents in our nationwide survey of 1957[60] into ten occupational categories and for each of these given the distri-

Table 16—Regional Contrasts in Party Preferences Within Major Occupational Groups (Survey Data for 1957)

Total Cross-Section	N	CP	Intended Vote 1957 Lab.	Left	Chr.	Agr.	Cons.	Unclear	Non-voter
Sample	1546	1%	40	6	7	7	14	12	13
East, Middle North	1125	2%	45	3	6	5	15	12	12
South, West	421	x	27%	12	9	12	12	11	17
Primary: all	407	1%	31	6	9	22	7	9	16
EMN	283	1%	41	4	7	17	7	8	15
SW	124	—	9%	13	13	33	6	9	18
Farmers	171	1%	14	10	9	38	9	9	11
EMN	98	1%	19	6	7	37	8	17	20
SW	73	—	7%	15	11	40	10	8	10
Smallholders, fishermen	138	1%	34	4	11	12	7	9	22
EMN	100	2%	42	2	8	8	10	8	20
SW	38	—	13%	8	18	24	0	10	26
Workers	98	1%	56	4	5	6	3	8	17
EMN	85	1%	64	2	5	3	3	8	13
SW	13								
Nonprim. manual: all	644	2%	58	3	4	1	7	10	13
EMN	479	3%	61	3	4	1	7	11	11
SW	165	1%	50	5	7	4	7	7	20
Manufacturing	285	1%	64	3	4	1	4	12	11
EMN	214	2%	65	2	3	1	5	13	9
SW	71	—	58%	7	8	3	0	7	17
Crafts	106	3%	55	2	6	1	8	7	19
EMN	77	3%	60	1	5	0	8	9	14
SW	29	3%	41	3	7	3	10	0	31
Other	253	2%	54	4	4	2	10	11	13
EMN	188	3%	57	4	4	1	9	11	11
SW	65	—	45%	5	5	5	12	11	18
Nonmanual: all	464	x	23%	8	9	1	32	16	11
EMN	336	1%	26	4	9	1	34	15	10
SW	128	—	14%	19	9	3	25	18	12
Self-employed	53	—	21%	2	11	2	24	21	19
EMN	38	—	18%	—	8	3	26	24	21
SW	15								
Salaried, public	130	—	30%	15	12	2	22	14	5
EMN	93	—	40%	10	12	0	20	14	4
SW	37	—	5%	30	14	5	27	14	5
Salaried, private	189	1%	25	5	8	2	33	15	11
EMN	139	1%	27	1	9	1	38	15	7
SW	50	—	20%	14	6	4	20	16	20
Employer	92	—	10%	9	3	0	46	17	15
EMN	66	—	11%	5	5	0	50	12	18
SW	26	—	8%	19	0	0	35	31	8
No occup. (present or past) given	31	—	32%	6	10	0	10	16	26

Note: Respondents have been classified by the *occupation of the head* of the household. If the head was no longer economically active, he was classified by his past occupation.

butions of intended votes in the two principal divisions of the country: the East, the Middle, and the North versus the South and West. As suggested by our ecological analyses the differences between the two divisions proved most pronounced for smallholders and fishermen (44 versus 13 percent Socialist), and for workers outside manufacturing industries and construction (61 versus 45 percent). Interestingly enough the regional contrasts also proved marked for public employees (40 versus 5 percent). This clearly reflects long-term differences in the channels of recruitment of local leadership. The old Left recruited much of its leadership among lower public officials, sheriffs, teachers, newspapermen, and once in power placed increasing numbers of supporters in public employment. The continued dominance of the Middle parties has kept these channels open in the South and the West, while the dominance of the Labor Party in the other regions has made for substantial changes in the politics of public employees.[61]

Table 17 offers further confirmation of our interpretation of the ecological

Table 17—Differences in Class Voting Between Communes of Different Economic Structure Within Two Contrasting Regions (Survey Data for 1957)

Occupation of Head	Residence	Region	N =100%	Soc.	Intended Vote 1957 Middle party	Cons.	Unclear, non-voter
Worker	City or	SW	77	61 %	8	9	22
	town	ETN	230	63	7	9	21
	Industrialized	SW	31	45	30	3	22
	rural comm.	ETN	161	65	6	5	24
	(30% or more in ind.)						
	Other rural	SW	70	33	24	4	39
		ETN	173	64	10	4	22
Independents in primary economy	Industrialized rural comm.	SW	25	4	68	8	20
	(25% or more in ind.)	ETN	40	32.5	30	2.5	35
	Other rural	SW	86	10	58	6	26
		ETN	158	32	35	11	22
Middle class (salaried, indep. outside primary econ.)	Cities, towns, heavily industrialized rural comm. (40% +)	SW	84	13	25	29	33
		ETN	228	26	11	39	24
	Other rural	SW	44	16	42	18	25
		ETN	108	29	18	25	28

findings: the differences between the South/West and the other regions tend to disappear in the cities and the most urbanized communes but are particularly marked for workers in the least industrialized areas (33 versus 64 percent Socialist) and for farmers and fishermen (9 versus 32 percent). The rural communes are much less class-polarized in the South/West than elsewhere: the offshoots of the old Left recruit their support from cross-sections of the local citizenry and tend to express territorial and cultural opposition rather than class interests.

THE CULTURAL DISTINCTIVENESS OF THE SOUTH/WEST

So far we have focused our analysis on structural variables. In simple summary, we have tried to identify the structural conditions for the maintenance of territorial politics in peripheral localities and we have focused our explorations on two sets of community characteristics: the type of primary economy predominant in the community and the size distribution of the local holdings. Schematically, the findings of our analysis can be set out in this fourfold table for the sources of party strength in the primary-economy communities:

		COMMUNITY STRUCTURE	
		More hierarchical	More equalitarian
TYPE OF	*Inland:* *agriculture/* *forestry*	East/Trøndelag: Socialist and Agrarians the strongest	South and West: Liberals and Agrarians the strongest
PRIMARY *ECONOMY*	*Coast:* *fisheries*	North: Socialists and Conservatives the strongest	South/West: Christians the strongest

The entries in each of the cells represent statistical tendencies, but these are not very marked and there is a great deal of variance still to be accounted for. The socioeconomic distinctiveness of the South and the West may explain some of the deviations from the average national alignments, but the bulk of the variance can only be explained in cultural terms. To determine the weight of such cultural variables is not a simple matter, however. We have been able to assemble a variety of information on the overall contrasts between the regions and among the provinces within the regions, but to determine the importance of these differences in cultural conditions locality by a locality has proved highly problematic. Our findings, therefore, can hardly be more than suggestive of promising lines of further inquiry.

Ever since the emergence of mass politics, the South and the West have given greater support than any other regions to three sets of policies:

(1) They have constituted a bulwark for defense of Lutheran orthodoxy and pietistic fundamentalism against the radicalizing and secularizing influences of the cities.

(2) They have offered a fertile soil for temperance and prohibition movements.

(3) They have been the strongholds of the rural language movement against the standard *riksmål* identified with the capital and the urban bourgeoisie.

In *Table 18* we have assembled some evidence from official statistics of the persistence of such differences over time. In their language policies, in their stand on temperance and prohibition, and in their support of distinctly

Table 18—Persistent Differences in Cultural Orientations
(Selected Statistics 1888–1961 for Each of the Six Regions and for the Provinces of the South and West)

| Region Province | "CHRISTIAN" SHARE OF THE OLD LEFT[a] | | | | Teetotalists[b] per 1,000 adults 1923 | Votes for Prohibition[c] 1926 | Language[d]: p.c. of school districts using | |
| | 1888 | | 1961 | | | | | |
	Left + Mod.	Mod. in p.c. of L. + Mod.	Middle parties	Chr. in p.c. of Middle			landsmål 1910	nynorsk 1956/57
Oslofjord	45.2	20.3	24.0	34.2	18.4	26.2	0	0
East inl.	66.0	25.1	21.5	24.2	25.9	35.4	13.5	35.7
South Tot.	68.7	53.0	48.7	34.8	79.4	74.8	28.8	48.5
Aust-Agder	63.0	45.1	41.4	41.8	41.5	71.0	42.8	49.7
Vest-Agder	73.4	58.7	54.9	30.4	112.8	79.2	18.5	47.5
West Tot.	82.2	55.3	51.8	38.1	93.7	76.3	47.4	94.0
Rogaland	84.8	75.4	54.2	36.7	71.6	81.3	23.7	85.8
Hordaland	77.7	61.1	46.0	40.3	72.4	70.9	57.7	95.1
Sogn og Fj.	77.0	55.6	51.5	29.2	104.4	71.4	57.8	99.8
Møre og Romsd.	90.0	33.4	57.4	41.9	129.9	82.9	42.0	93.1
Trøndelag	65.3	11.9	36.3	27.7	82.8	60.8	14.2	42.9
North	77.9	20.2	25.5	36.3	33.9	53.2	4.4	13.1

[a] The percentages for the Left, the Moderates/Christians, and the Agrarians (the three Middle parties) are calculated on the basis of the total valid votes cast, not on the basis of the total electorate.

[b] NOS VII, 129, Tab. 29. These statistics were unfortunately discontinued after 1923; see NOS VII, 196, p. 51x.

[c] NOS VIII, 14, p. 3. The distributions for the first referendum in 1919 are of less interest in this context since the votes in the rural districts were so overwhelmingly for prohibition at that time:

| | CITIES AND TOWNS | | RURAL COMMUNES | |
	For	Against	For	Against
1919	44.5	55.5	70.1	29.9
1926	30.3	69.7	51.7	48.3

[d] For 1910: NOS V, 218, Tab. 1, p. 3. For 1956-57: NOS XI, 344, Tab. 14, p. 19. The 1910 table gives figures by district only while later statistics also indicate the number of children in nynorsk schools. The national figures for 1956-57 were 49.0 percent of the districts, but only 33.5 percent of the children: the nynorsk districts are clearly less densely populated than the others.

Christian parties, the South and the West have continuously tended to differ from the rest of the country ever since the beginning of competitive national politics.

This does not mean that the two regions have always pulled together on all such questions nor that the localities within each region have all pulled in the same direction. Our crude differentiations by province within each region tell a story of complex variations both over time and across localities. The two provinces of the South have differed considerably: Aust-Agder has been closer to the East in the level of class polarization, but has at the same time been a stronghold of revival movements and dissident free churches and has, since 1949, returned disproportionately high numbers of votes for the Christian People's Party; Vest-Agder, by contrast, went heavily Moderate in 1888, but has not proved very fertile soil for the Christians in the elections since 1945. The outer coastal areas of the West were stronger in their fundamentalism than in their rejection of the urban language: the stronghold of the Moderates in 1888, the province of Rogaland, was very slow in introducing *landsmål* in its schools (see the figures for 1910). The *nynorsk* movement is strongest in the least urbanized of the provinces, Sogn og Fjordane, but this is the least fundamentalist of the provinces: it still has the lowest percentage of Christian votes of its Middle party total. The northernmost of the Western provinces, Møre og Romsdal, was early a stronghold of the teetotalist movement, but gave very few of its votes to the Moderates in 1888; today, however, it has the highest share of Christian votes in the region, though marked divisions have persisted between the fundamentalist south and the more secular north of the province. There is no one-to-one fit between the levels of support for the three sets of policies at any given time: what makes the South/West such a characteristic division of the country is the parallel development of three distinct cultural movements, all directed against standards and practices seen to be spreading from the central areas and the cities. These movements did not always pull together, but their net impact on national politics was unmistakable: they all stood for the defense of rural values against the centralizing forces triggered off through economic development and the strengthening of governmental agencies.

Gabriel Øidne has drawn up maps for the strength of the Moderates in 1891 and the strength of the Christians in 1953 and found a close correspondence area by area (*Fig. 1*). Our own statistical tests indicate very little influence of the early political traditions in the fisheries communes, but a definite impact in the agricultural ones. The Christians get a high share of the votes in the coastal districts whatever the strength of the Moderates, while in the agricultural communes they tend to be stronger where the Moderates were strong and weaker where they were weak. The differences are particularly striking in the provinces of Rogaland and Hordaland and are only slight in the provinces to the north. In these the Moderates were much weaker and, given the electoral system then in force, it makes it much more difficult to measure their exact local strength. It is possible that our results are artifacts of the method used in comparing party strengths over such long periods, but the crude statistics available for the early period make further checks very difficult. Clearly in order to pursue these detailed ecological studies of continuities in religious and political traditions it will be essential to assemble commune by commune and period by period information on memberships in religious associations and temperance movements, and this will, if at all possible, require a major effort of data collection. So far we have only been able to work with data from a church-attendance count carried out in 1956[62] and with the official statistics for the language form used in local primary schools. Highly suggestive data have recently been made available on memberships in temperance organizations,[63] but these unfortunately are only available for units made up of several contiguous communes.

Table 19—Frequencies of Attendance at Church Services and Religious Meetings: Differences Among Six Regions of Norway Found in the 1957 Survey*

			REPORTED ATTENDANCE 1957 (PERCENT)					
			(1) attends church, attends meetings	(2) attends church, never meetings	(3) never church, attends meetings	Total (1)+(2)+(3) attends one or the other	(4) never church, never meetings	NA
Region	Sex of respondent	N =100%						
Oslofjord	Tot.	478	6	8	9	24	67	9
	M	220	4	8	8	20	71	9
	W	258	8	9	10	27	64	9
East inland	Tot.	298	6	12	7	26	69	5
	M	145	2	10	2	14	79	6
	W	153	11	14	12	37	59	4
South	Tot.	97	16	8	13	38	47	14
	M	46	17	7	9	33	52	15
	W	51	16	10	18	43	43	14
West	Tot.	324	10	12	10	32	61	7
	M	172	10	14	8	32	61	7
	W	152	10	10	12	32	61	7
Middle	Tot.	221	6	8	8	22	74	5
	M	112	7	7	3	17	79	5
	W	109	5	9	14	27	69	4
North	Tot.	128	7	9	11	27	72	1
	M	67	9	6	9	24	76	—
	W	61	5	13	13	31	67	2

* The question was "How many times during the last month have you (a) been to church service? (b) been to religious meetings? (c) listened to a service on the radio? The marginal response distributions were:

	Never	Occasionally, varies	1–3 times last month	Every Sunday	More frequently	NA, other
Church	76%	2	16	1.5	0.5	4
Meetings	77%	2	13.5	1.5	1	5
Radio	17%	14	20	30	12	8

But even our cross-sectional sample surveys from the 1950's tell us about persistent differences in cultural orientations among the regions.

Table 19 summarizes information from our nation-wide survey of 1957 on regional variations in church attendance and in participation in religious meetings. Religious participation is clearly most widespread in the South and in West. In these regions, some 22–25 percent of the adults interviewed re- reported that they would go to church at least once a month: this compares with 14 percent for the East and the Trøndelag, 16–18 percent for the Inland and North. The contrasts are much less for attendance at religious *meetings* outside the Church: the South and West still score highest but the differences are barely significant.

Attendance figures tell only part of the story: politically, the crucial variable is the *direction* of the religious commitment. The Lutheran State Church can claim the formal allegiance of some 95 percent of all Norwegians, but about three-quarters of these members are completely passive. They do not oppose the teaching of religion in the state schools, and they do not challenge the traditional privileges of the Church; yet they generally do not attend services except at such high points of the life cycle as christenings, confirmations, marriages, and burials. Only about a quarter of the adult population takes an active part in religious life and most of their energy is channeled not through the immediate bodies of the Church but through a variety of lay organizations: women's club, charitable organizations, societies for the support of missions. Religious life in Norway has ever since 1814 been marked by a polarization between the government-appointed clergymen and the activists in revival movements, mission organizations, and "Free Churches." The conflict between the established Church and the fundamentalist organizations paralleled very closely the conflict between the King's officials and the old Left: there was the same rejection of central authority and the same assertion of the values and traditions of rural life against the corruption of the cities. Much has changed since the early conflicts over the control of the Church, but membership in mission societies is still a telling indicator of religious orientation and as such also politically significant.

Table 20 gives a breakdown of a nationwide sample by type of religious membership and again underscores the regional contrasts in religious life. In

Table 20—Membership in Religious Association: Survey Data for Differences Between Occupational Groups in the Two Contrasting Divisions of the Country.

Region	Occupation of head	Type of locality	Sex	N= 100%	Member of State Church, no assoc.	Mission societies	Other in State Church	Dissenter	NA
East, Trønde- lag, North	Worker	Total	M	281	90%	4	3	2	1
			W	283	82	7	6	5	1
		Urban	M	111	91	1	3	3	2
			W	119	83	4	7	6	–
		Rural	M	170	88	6	3	2	1
			W	164	81	10	5	4	–
	Smallholder, farmer		M	87	92	5	–	2	–
			W	111	60	31	3	5	–
	Middle class		M	169	88	5	4	4	–
			W	167	81%	7	5	5	1
South, West	Worker	Total	M	92	91%	3	4	1	–
			W	86	74	13	8	5	–
		Urban	M	34	94	–	6	–	–
			W	43	88	2	9	–	–
		Rural	M	58	90	5	3	2	–
			W	43	60	23	7	9	–
	Smallholder, farmer		M	56	82	13	–	5	–
			W	55	45	45	3	5	2
	Middle class		M	69	84	9	1	4	1
			W	59	76%	15	4	5	–

its cities, the South/West differs very little from the rest of the country, but very striking differences are found for women in the rural communes. In the South/West 30 percent of the women in rural working-class households are found to belong to some religious association within the Church. The figure for the other regions is 15 percent. The difference is also marked for women in smallholders' and farmers' households—48 versus 34 percent. Perhaps more significant are the differences in the support of the orthodox and fundamentalist "mission societies": 23 versus 10 percent and 45 versus 31 percent. These societies tend to be stronger in all strata of the South and the West and, as we shall see, make up the core of the Christian People's Party.

We have not yet been able to include in our ecological archive commune-by-commune information on the membership strength of the temperance organizations and our nationwide survey of the fifties did not cover the variables in this area as thoroughly as required for the present purposes.[64] Fortunately a membership count undertaken for 1960 by Arne Dolven gives us a clear picture of these regional variations and also allows some further differentiations by clusters of communes. The basic findings of this count can be set out as follows:[65]

TOTAL MEMBERSHIP FOR ALL TEMPERANCE ORGANIZATIONS COVERED

	Mean for region	Range of means for areas (handelsområder) within each region	Range of means for handelsdistrikter (smallest data units)
East	2.03	1.15–3.99	0.25– 6.16
South	7.98	6.79–8.85	2.84–17.75
West	6.00	2.68–8.59	1.85–17.34
		(N. Møre) (S. Møre)	
Trøndelag	3.43	3.23–3.95	0.95– 6.81
North	1.86	1.54–2.35	0.44– 4.57

We have so far been able to document the cultural distinctiveness of the South and West on three scores: frequencies of religious attendance, number of memberships in religious associations, and number of memberships in temperance organizations. The contrast in local language options is equally marked and can be readily documented: *Table 18* gives a straightforward account of variations among regions and among provinces and could without any difficulty be followed up by detailed tables for ranges of variation at the level of the commune. There are problems about the interpretation of such official figures, however. The decisions on the language to be used in the local primary school need not always reflect the wishes and the usages of the majority: such decisions tend to be in the hands of a few articulate community leaders and quite particularly the local teachers. A check against data from sample surveys of the adult electorate is therefore of great interest. In the nationwide sample survey carried out in 1957, we asked each of our sampled citizens which language form he or she used "when writing." The intention was to elicit open answers to a question about actual linguistic usage. *Table 21* gives a classification of the responses and a breakdown by region, by type of community, and by occupation of the head of the household. The survey suggests that the *nynorsk* counter-language is much weaker in actual usage than in the schools; the official statistics for 1957 indicated that about one-

Table 21—Differences in Language Preference Between the Regions (Survey Data for 1957)*

			N= 100%	Riksmål	Bokmål[a]	Landsmål, Nynorsk	Other Answers[b]
Total Nationwide Sample			1546	65%	19	12	4
East	Urban	Total	359	81	14	1	4
		Workers	190	83	11	1	6
		Middle class	169	79	17	1	3
	Rural	Total	394	71	15	7	7
		Workers	170	76	13	2	9
		Middle class	142	76	17	2	7
		Farmers, etc.	82	63%	15	14	5
South, West	Urban	Total	199	63%	24	12	2
		Workers	101	66	20	13	1
		Middle class	98	59	29	11	1
	Rural	Total	218	33	11	50	5
		Workers	69	35	18	45	1
		Middle class	42	29	17	50	5
		Farmers, etc.	107	34%	7	53	7
Trøndelag, North	Urban	Total	84	85%	14	1	0
		Workers	41	93	7	–	0
		Middle class	43	77	21	2	0
	Rural	Total	261	54	39	5	2
		Workers	88	59	35	3	2
		Middle class	49	53	37	8	2
		Farmers, etc.	124	52%	42	6	2

* Question: "Which language form do you prefer to use when you write?"
[a] Includes four respondents stating they preferred "samnorsk."
[b] These were: five respondents, "a mixture," six, "both forms," three, "what I was taught at school," thirteen, "ordinary language," thirty-six, NA and Refuse.

third of all children in rural schools were taught in *nynorsk*, whereas the survey suggests that only one-sixth of the adults living in rural community actually use the language. Similar differences have been found in responses to questionnaires administered to recruits to the armed forces. The *nynorsk* movement can no longer stem the flow of communications and conformity pressures from the urban centers, but it can still count on strong and articulate minorities in each community to control local decisions on the choice of language. This appears to be the most plausible interpretation of the discrepancies found in the data.[66]

The breakdown of survey responses give us a clear picture of the sources of *nynorsk* strength:

	Oslofjord	East Inland/ Trøndelag	North	South/West
Urbanized, industrialized areas	Negligible	Negligible	Negligible	One of every six
Primary-economy areas —farm households	One of every twenty	One of every six	Negligible	Half of the households
—other households	Negligible	Negligible	Negligible	Half of the households

It is in fact almost exclusively in the South and the West that we find homogeneous *nynorsk* communities: communities where the entire local culture is marked by the ideology of rural defense and where all adults except a few "strangers" speak and write *nynorsk*. Outside the South and West the primary-economy communities are more likely to be linguistically divided: the farmers and the teachers brought up in the ideology of rural opposition will stick to *nynorsk,* while employees, businessmen, and members of the professions may speak a local dialect, but are more likely to be swayed by the pressures of the urban language norms, at least when writing.

How do these differences among the regions affect the strength of the political parties? We are currently carrying out detailed regression analyses of the available ecological data[67] but unfortunately cannot report on the findings here. We have to confine ourselves to a few suggestive tables from sample surveys carried out in 1957.

Table 22 suggests that active participation in religious services and meet-

Table 22—Differences in Party Preference Between High-Frequent and Low-Frequent Participants in Religious Activities
(by Region, Type of Locality, and Sex)

Region	Locality	Frequency of Attendance at Services/ Meetings[a]	Sex	N =100%	Intended vote 1957 Socialist CP+Lab.	Middle Lib.+Chr.+Agr.	Cons.	Chr. in p.c. of Middle	All Non-Soc.
ETN	Cities	Higher	M	21	29	20	24	50	29
			W	40	30	20	15	100	57
		Lower	M	170	57	5	20	38	7
			W	178	44	8	26	40	10
	Rural	Higher	M	40	35	38	10	66	52
			W	61	33	34	7	68	56
		Lower	M	280	54	14	12	29	18
			W	261	46	15	10	20	12
SW	Cities	Higher	M	21	0	77	10	56	49
			W	21	33	24	19	79	44
		Lower	M	75	42	18	20	22	11
			W	64	34	17	16	12	6
	Rural	Higher	M	25	36	32	8	63	50
			W	25	16	36	8	67	55
		Lower	M	78	27	39	12	8	6
			W	71	17	44	0	14	14

[a] The "higher" attenders are those who stated they went to a church service or a religious meeting at least *twice* a month. For questions and marginal response distribution, see Table 19.

ings is a fair predictor of political position. In all the urban areas we find markedly heavier support for the three Middle parties among the religiously active than among the passive; commitment to the Church and the mission societies helps to lower the polarization between Socialists and Conservatives and also adds significantly to the strength of the Christian People's Party within this intermediary sector of the political spectrum. In the rural communes the regional contrast again comes out quite clearly. In the East, Trøndelag, and North the three offshoots of the old territorial-cultural Left prove much stronger among the religiously active than among the passive. In the South/West there is no such difference; in these regions the Middle parties have achieved a dominant position and do not depend as much on the religiously most active groups in each community. The Christian share of the Middle party total, however, does depend on the level of religious participation, in fact even more markedly in the South/West than in the other rural areas. To put the finding in general terms: in the East, Trøndelag, and North, the basic cleavage line cutting across the tendency toward class polarization is religious, while in the South and West there is a general pattern of cultural rejection of class politics.

Table 23 adds further information on the political consequences of memberships in religious associations. The members of the orthodox "Inner Mission" and related associations give the strongest support to the Christian People's Party, and on this score there is very little difference between regions; the greater strength of the Christian in the South/West simply reflects the higher level of membership in such fundamentalist movements. Controls for occupation suggest that the effects of religious membership on Middle-party support are particularly marked among the smallholders and fishermen of the East, Middle, and North; in these regions the religiously active are the least extreme in their politics and tend to shun both the Socialists and the Conservatives. In the South/West the overall level of polarization is lower and the effect of religious membership is less pronounced in the countryside. Other factors, such as language preference and membership in teetotalist organizations, are equally likely to increase the votes for the Middle parties. It is interesting to note, however, that in the middle-class strata membership in religious associations proves a very good predictor of political allegiance in all regions of the country: this goes for the East, Middle, North division (where 31 percent of the middle-class members vote Christian as against 5 percent of the nonmembers) as well as for the South/West (where the discrepancy is 33 versus 3 percent).

The nationwide cross-section interviewed in 1957 is too small to allow detailed breakdowns for more than one cultural indicator at a time: this is why *Tables 22* and *23* concentrate on religious variables only. Fortunately we have at hand local data for the South/West which allow cross-classifications by all the three cultural indicators discussed in this section. In the local sample surveys carried out in the Stavanger area in 1957[68] we asked questions not only about language choice and religious activity, but also about stand on the temperance issue. The question asked was very straightforward: "Do you consider yourself a temperance man?"[69] In *Table 24* we have cross-classified the three indicators and controlled for the occupation of the head of the household. The results are indeed striking: within the working-class sample we find the Socialists (CP grouped with Labor) weakest among the religiously active temperance people opting for *nynorsk* (33 percent) and strongest among the religiously passive *bokmål* people, whether with the temperance movement or not (83 and 72 percent). These three indicators account for the bulk of the deviations from straight class voting in the Stavanger area. The only party to gain from these deviations are the Christians; at least in the working class their strength appears to be almost exclusively a function of such cultural and moral commitments. The strength of the Liberals is much more difficult to explain: the party has its followers not only in all strata, but also in all the distinct cultural and religious groupings.

Table 23—Party Preference and Religious Membership
(Overall Differences Between Occupational Groups in the Two Divisions of the Country)

Region	Occupation	Religious Affiliation	N=100%	Socialist	Middle	(Of Which Chr.)	Cons.	Unclear, Uncertain, Nonvoter
East, Trøndelag, North	Worker	Member	74	43%	19	(15)	8	30
		Not member	486	67	6	(2)	6	21
	Primary independent (farmer, fisherman)	Member	51	22	55	(22)	8	16
		Not member	147	36	27	(3)	10	28
	Middle class	Member	49	16	33	(31)	20	30
		Not member	285	29	11	(5)	37	24
South, West	Worker	Member	30	33	27	(17)	7	33
		Not member	148	50	17	(5)	6	28
	Primary independent	Member	39	5	67	(21)	5	23
		Not member	71	11	56	(8)	7	25
	Middle class	Member	24	8	45	(33)	21	26
		Not member	103	16%	27	(3)	25	32

This comes out even clearer in the figures for the sample of farmer and middle-class households. The Liberals find sizable support in all the groups distinguished through the cross-classification of the three indicators; the Christians derive most of their support from the religiously active; and the Conservatives hardly gain a single vote in the *nynorsk* circles, and only a few among the temperance people. The parties at the two poles of the political spectrum, the Socialists and the Conservatives, are both weak among the religiously active and among *nynorsk* speakers; they both uphold urban secular values in politics and attempt to keep questions of private morals out of public debate. But the two parties differ very much on the temperance question. The Labor Party has always had a strong temperance wing,[70] while the Conservatives have upheld the urban traditions of convivial drinking and fought bitter fights with the Middle parties over restrictive alcohol policies.

The data we have at hand do not tell us whether the patterns of variations found in the samples interviewed in the Stavanger area would hold for the other regions of the country.[71] The marginal frequencies for each of the three indicators as well as for the principal parties would be very different in a nationwide sample and the findings for the Liberals and the Christians are likely to prove very different in the East, possibly also in the Trøndelag and the North, from what we find for the South/West; this, at least, is what our ecological analyses suggest. The urbanized wing of the old Left, the present Liberal Party (it is still, of course, called the "Left," but we translate it by the term "Liberal" in discussing developments since the thirties) stands for different value and policy positions in the two divisions of the country; we shall discuss some evidence for this in the concluding section below. The contrast between the radical "Oslo" Liberals of the East and the more moderate Liberals of the South and West clearly reflect their very different position in community politics. In the South and West the old Left and its various offshoots have been in power since the 1880's, and the more urbanized of the followers of this movement no longer distrust central authority to the extent the party did at the beginning. At the center, by contrast, the old Left lost out to the power-holders in the labor movement, in farming, and in business and, in addition, shed some of its religiously active clientele to the Christians. The result was a fundamental radicalization and an increasing openness to the ideological claims of alienated opponents of all established power.

ECONOMIC DEVELOPMENT, OCCUPATIONAL MOBILITY, AND ELECTORAL CHANGE

Our analysis has concentrated on the spread of polarized politics from the centers to the peripheries of each region of the country. We have studied a process of change, and we have tried to pinpoint some of the factors making for differences in the rates of such change.

In our discussion so far we have used *polarization* as a shorthand term for any change toward an accentuation of distinctions of class and status in the alignments of the mobilized citizenry. In one set of analyses we have simply

Table 24—The Three Cultural Indicators and the Vote (Data for the Stavanger Area on the Impact of Language Commitment, Religious Activity, and Stand on the Temperance Issue on the Vote: by Occupation)

Language	Religious Activity[a]	Temperance Stand[b]	WORKING CLASS							FARMERS AND MIDDLE CLASS						
			N=100%	Soc.	Lib.	Chr.	Agr.	Cons.	Other	N=100%	Soc.	Lib.	Chr.	Agr.	Cons.	Other
Bokmål	High	Yes	175	47%	11	13	1	4	24	106	9%	31	21	9	16	14
		No	76	63%	11	1	0	11	14	77	10%	32	3	12	30	13
	Low	Yes	52	83%	2	0	0	4	11	39	20%	18	10	8	18	26
		No	123	72%	10	1	0	4	13	103	29%	21	1	4	33	11
Nynorsk	High	Yes	46	33%	13	30	11	0	13	63	3%	21	25	38	0	13
		No	12	5	(2)	(1)	(1)	(1)	(2)	19	11%	10	5	53	16	5
	Low	Yes	8	(2)	(1)	0	(4)	5	(1)	18	0%	28	6	55	0	11
		No	20	50%	10	0	15	5	20	15	20%	13	0	47	7	13

a Index based on church attendance, attendance at religious meetings, listening to religious services on the radio, membership in religious associations. The maximum score was 8. In the table, the "low" category scored 0 or 1.
b Respondents classified on the basis of responses to the question "Regner De Dem som avholdsmann?" ("Do you consider yourself a temperance man?").

traced a series of changes over time in the total strength of the most distinctly class-based parties, the Socialists and the Conservatives. These tabulations tell us a great deal about differences among regions and among localities in the *net outcome* of the process of change, but do not get us very far toward an understanding of the *realignments within each stratum of the enfranchized citizenry*. When we have assembled ecological data for all communes for a longer span of time, say from 1900 to 1960, we may be in a position to specify in greater detail the conditions for an acceleration of realignments by class and status,[72] but even then it is bound to prove difficult to pinpoint the exact locus of change within each community. We hope, however, to be able shortly to apply to Norwegian data the very promising procedure worked out for Swedish provincial statistics by the sociologist Gösta Carlsson.[73] Instead of correlating aggregated attributes for each of the units, he proceeds by testing out a series of alternative models of voter alignments: so many percent of stratum A voting for party P, Q, R . . ., so many percent of stratum B, and so on. He then calculates for each province and for a long series of elections since the first one under manhood suffrage in 1910 the expected results for each party and compares them with the actually *observed* results. This gives him a basis not only for a choice among his models but also for estimates of probable changes in the alignments of the voters over time. His primary finding is that the remarkable gains of the Social Democrats since 1910 can only in part be explained through the changes brought about in the composition of the electorate through industrialization and urbanization; roughly two-thirds of the gain must be attributed to increasing mobilization *within* each stratum, not only in the industrial working class, but also in the rural proletariat and in the urban middle classes. Such long-term analyses are much easier in Sweden than in other countries: the official electoral statistics have for decades given details of the class composition of the electorate at each election. Parallel analyses for Norway will be much more costly and less precise because of the intervals between elections and censuses, but will nevertheless repay the effort.

While we wait for the results of such detailed diachronic analyses, we shall have to make do with such shortcuts to information as we find at hand. Data from *sample surveys* can give us tolerably precise estimates of the political alignments of the principal strata of the electorate but unfortunately cover much too short periods of time. In Norway there are no extant tabulations from surveys of individual political behavior before 1949.[74] We may, however, stretch our time series through the use of *recall data;* this is what we have done in *Tables 25–28.*

Using data for two generations we have been able to estimate the extent of class voting for four successive periods since the beginnings of partisan conflict in Norwegian politics:

(1) the period of early mobilization before and after the introduction of universal suffrage;

(2) the period of rapid industrialization and consequent Socialist growth;

(3) the period of the depression and Labor's rise to power;

(4) the period of stabilization and deideologization under the rule of the Labor Party.

The groups distinguished in *Tables 25 and 26* clearly overlap to some extent, but the trends from one group to the next are remarkably consistent. Obviously we cannot be sure that the samples we have constructed of fathers of children born before and after 1907 are without bias; differential fertility

Table 25—Changes in Class Polarization: Estimates for Four Periods Based on Survey Data for Father's and Own Occupation and Preferred Party

	N = 100%	Socialist	Middle Parties	Cons.	Unclear, Uncertain, Non-voter
1890s–1920s Respondent born before 1907 Father's occupation and vote:					
Manual worker	242	38%	24	9	29
Smallholder, fisherman	60	10	43	17	30
Farmer	171	5	59	17	18
Salaried	58	5	29	50	16
Independent, self-empld.	54	19	26	37	19
1910s–1930s Respondent born 1907–1927 Father's occupation and vote:					
Manual worker	332	59	14	8	18
Smallholder, fisherman	60	45	25	10	20
Farmer	145	8	66	8	18
Salaried	70	21	20	33	26
Independent, self-empld.	60	20	35	27	18
1930s–1940s Respondent born 1907–1927 Own (spouse's) occupation and first vote:					
Manual worker	334	73	13	5	9
Smallholder, fisherman	64	53	30	6	11
Farmer	68	24	60	7	9
Salaried	140	41	31	20	9
Independent, self-empld.	67	28	33	24	15
1950s Respondent born after 1927 Own (spouse's) occupation and first vote:					
Manual worker	154	60	11	5	25
Smallholder, farmer	31	23	29	6	42
Salaried	76	33	20	24	24
Independent, self-empld.	11	(4)%	(1)	(2)	(4)

among the fathers and differential mortality among the children will clearly have affected the chances of inclusion through such recall procedures. We have tried in various ways to check the amount of bias introduced through this procedure, but since we did not have any information about the father's year of birth, any estimates of sampling bias will of necessity be very crude. Both the occupational and the political breakdowns do move in the right directions from period to period, however, and this gives us some confidence in the results.

**Table 26—Changes in the Occupational Composition
of the Socialist Vote 1890s to 1950s
(Estimates from Survey Data in 1957)**

	N = 100%	Farmers, Smallholders	Workers	Salaried Employees	Independent, Self-employed
1890s–1920s Resp. born before 1907: father's party Socialist	119	13	76	3	8
1910s–1930s Resp. born 1907–1927: father's party Socialist	267	15	74	6	5
1930s–1940s Resp. born 1907–1927: own first vote Socialist	372	13	65	15	5
1950s Resp. born after 1927: (a) voted before 1957: first vote Socialist	99	5	72	20	3
(b) first voters 1957: intended to vote Socialist	29	7	72	17	3

The changes in occupational structure from period to period tell us a story of rapid economic growth:

Stratum	I		II		III		IV	
Primary sector								
—independents	39%		30%		19%		11%	
—workers		11%		12%		8%		5%
Manual workers: total	41		49		49		56	
—secondary and tertiary		30%		37%		41%		51%
Salaried employees	10		10		21		28	
Independents: secondary and tertiary	9		9		10		4	
Total: actives with reported occupations	99%		98%		99%		99%	
N = 100%	594		678		678		274	

This simple summary reflects two distinct movements of change;

(1) from the primary economy into the secondary and the tertiary;
(2) from manual wage work into salaried clerical, technical and professional work.[75]

The political effects of these changes can be read out of *Table 25.*
The findings can be simply summarized as follows:

(1) in the primary economy at first very little difference between the political distribution for the lower stratum of smallholders and fishermen and the higher stratum of farmers, but from around 1910 onward a rapid process of radicalization in the lower stratum and consequently a high level of rural polarization;

(2) among manual workers at first a fair spread of political preferences between Labor and the old Left but then from around 1910 onward a marked change toward greater and greater Socialist predominance;

(3) among the salaried employees at first a distinct distrust of the Socialists, but with the growth of Labor to a position of dominance in the system a definite change toward an even spread of political preferences between the major party groupings (the decline in the percentage for Labor in the youngest generation after World War II appears to be largely due to the lower turnout and the higher percentage of nonresponse among the young, primarily women employees);

(4) among the self-employed and the employers a remarkably high percentage of Socialist sympathizers (19–28 percent) throughout the four periods: a number of independent artisans and builders clearly have felt closer to ordinary workingmen than to the bourgeois middle class.

These findings force us to give further consideration to our statements about the process of polarization in Norway. Clearly the Norwegian system was gradually polarized in the sense that an increasing proportion of the voters in the lower manual strata united behind Labor. *But there was no corresponding polarization of the upper strata.* This distinguishes the Norwegian case from the British. To illustrate this difference we shall adopt the simplifying 2 x 2 procedure developed by Alford in his comparisons of Great Britain, the United States, Canada, and Australia.[76]

If we dichotomize both by class (manual or lower rural versus nonmanual and higher rural) and by party (Socialist versus non-Socialist), we get these series of 2 x 2 tables for the four periods of Norwegian politics:

		TOTAL SAMPLE				SECONDARY AND TERTIARY SECTORS ONLY		
		Soc.	Non-s.	N = 100%		Soc.	Non-s.	N = 100%
Period I	Manual/ lower	45%	55	214	Manual	55%	45	132
	Nonmanual/ higher	9%	81	233	Nonmanual	14%	86	93
	Index:	36				41		
Period II	Manual/ lower	70%	30	319	Manual	75%	25	202
	Nonmanual/ higher	18%	82	220	Nonmanual	27%	73	101
	Index:	52				48		
Period III	Manual/ lower	77%	23	361	Manual	73%	27	280
	Nonmanual/ higher	37%	63	247	Nonmanual	41%	59	185
	Index:	40				32		
Period IV	Manual/ lower	77%	23	123	Manual	78%		
	Nonmanual/ higher	43%	57	76	Nonmanual	45%	55	65
	Index:	34						

Alford's calculations from British survey data gave results such as these for the total samples:

	1945		1951		1957 (I)	
	Lab.	Cons.	Lab.	Cons.	Lab.	Cons.
Manual	68%	40	65%	35	67%	33
Nonmanual	31%	69	23%	77	24%	76
Index	37		42		43	

By Alford's index of class voting[77] the Norwegian pattern has not differed very much from the British, but this is only because the index is indifferent to the *direction* of the deviance from straight class voting: the index simply indicates how close the political alignment is to the class alignment. If we look closer at the tables we will find a *radical reversal of the sizes of the deviant cells:*

(1) in the earlier periods (I and to some extent also in II) the Norwegian alignment resembled the British in that the political distinctiveness of the working class was low and the class distinctiveness of the Labor Party high;

(2) in the later periods, however, the size of the "rightward" manual cells was reduced (from 55 percent for the total sample in the first period to 23 percent in the later ones), and the size of the "leftward" nonmanual cell increased (9 to 43 percent) producing a pattern very different from the British.

The British Labour Party was never able to gain more than about two-thirds of the votes cast by members of working-class households and only rarely enlisted support from more than one-quarter of the middle class. A direct comparison with Norway is difficult because of the greater importance of the primary sector: in Britain under 5 percent of the active population, in Norway some 25 percent in the 1950's. If for purposes of comparison we exclude the primary sector completely we find that the Norwegian Labor Party is stronger than its British counterpart both in the working class (overall figures for 1957 sample: 79 percent of votes cast) and in the middle class (32 percent). In Britain the Conservatives were able to keep in power so long because of their hold on the working class. In Norway, a much less industrialized and much less urbanized country, the Labor Party could not hope to reach the majority point solely on the basis of its appeal to the working class: it had to rally support not only among the smallholders and fishermen in the primary sector but, what proved even more decisive, within the new and continuously expanding middle class of salaried employees. It is easy to document the success of these efforts: it can be calculated from *Table 16* that the party can count on some 40 percent of the votes from the households of *public* employees (about half of the vote in the East, Middle, and North, but less than 10 percent in the South and West) and some 30 percent from the households of *private* employees. *Table 25* tells us how this came about: the decisive increase in Labor strength in the new middle class came in the thirties, the decade during which the party rose to power. *Table 26* shows the consequences for the composition of the Labor Party electorate: in the early phase of growth only 3 percent of the party's supporters belonged to the new middle class, but by the 1950's one-fifth of the new voters rallying behind the party came from this class.

Tables 27 and 28 give us some clues to an understanding of this process of change. The new middle class could not be recruited exclusively from the old; sons and daughters moved in both from the primary economy and the

Table 27—Occupational Mobility and Political Change
(Data from the Nationwide Survey in 1957)

Father's Occupation	Own or Head's Occupation	Father's Vote	N = 100%	Own Vote in 1957			
				Soc.	Middle	Cons.	Unclear Uncertain Nonvoter
Worker	Worker:	Soc.	269	80%	2	3	14
		Non-s.	81	52	11	13	24
Worker	Primary Independent:	Soc.	22	59	23	0	17
		Non-s.	32	25	31	6	37
Worker	Nonmanual:	Soc.	74	49	16	12	23
		Non-s.	52	21	21	37	21
Primary independent	Worker: independent:	Soc.	42	88	5	0	7
		Non-s.	115	30	29	13	28
Primary independent	Primary independent	Soc.	19	68	10	0	21
		Non-s.	142	12	58	11	18
Primary independent	Nonmanual:	Soc.	14	57	28	7	7
		Non-s.	81	10	31	28	30
	Worker:	Soc.	30	73	3	0	23
	Nonmanual	Non-s.	45	24	22	22	32
Nonmanual	Primary independent:	Soc.	5				
		Non-s.	18	17	56	17	—
Nonmanual	Nonmanual:	Soc.	28	46	0	21	32
		Non-s.	123	9%	22	54	15

working class. *Table 27* classifies the respondents in the 1957 survey by their fathers' and by their own occupation and shows the effects of such socioeconomic mobility or stability on political alignments. What we find is that family

Table 28—Party Preferences of Salaried Employees by
Father's Occupation and Union Membership
(Nationwide Survey of 1957)

Father Worker		N = 100%	Consistent Socialist	Uncertain, Wavering Not voting	Consistent Non-Soc.
LO member		43	51%	30	19
	M	22	58	19	23
	W	21	43	43	14
Non-LO union		33	33	24	42
	M	18	34	23	44
	W	15	33	27	40
Not organized		53	28	40	32
	M	23	30	26	44
	W	30	27	50	23
Father Middle Class					
LO		28	50	29	21
	M	12	67	16	16
	W	16	38	38	25
Non-LO		42	10	19	71
	M	23	17	17	65
	W	19	0	22	78
Not org.		86	9	28	64
	M	38	5	31	63
	W	48	12%	24	64

loyalties in politics have weighed very heavily even for the upward mobile.

Let us look at the two sets of movements in the system and estimate the amount of political change brought about in each case:

	PERCENT DEVIATING FROM FATHER'S VOTE (voting for opposite party grouping)	
Movements into working class	*Father Socialist*	*Father Non-Socialist*
—peasant origins	5	30
—working class origins	5	52
—middle class origins	3	24
Movements into middle class		
—peasant origins	35	10
—working class origins	28	21
—middle class origins	21	9

Movement into the working class appears to have brought about the largest number of generational shifts in political allegiance. This is just another reflection of the basic change toward increasing uniformity of party support in this stratum. Movement into the middle class has produced much more mixed results: surprisingly few shifts *away from* Socialism and curiously many shifts *to* Socialism, at least among those of working class origins. *Table 28* provides an important clue to the strength of the Labor Party in the new middle class. Whatever the origins of the salaried employee, he or she is most likely to vote Socialist if a member of a regular labor union, and least likely to vote Socialist if a member of a dissident middle-class union or not organized at all. The salaried employees in Norway have never been able to unite behind one central union in the way their Swedish counterparts have done.[78] The new middle class has always been split between Labor-oriented unions within the LO (the *Landsorganisasjon*), and a variety of minor bargaining organizations set up independently of this dominant federation,[79] and a heavy proportion of them, particularly in commerce and small business, have never been unionized. It is among these members of dissident middle-class unions and among the unorganized that family background proves politically decisive. While there is hardly any difference by social origins among the LO members, the working class–middle class differential is very marked indeed in the two other groups:

	DIFFERENCES BETWEEN SALARIED EMPLOYEES OF WORKING CLASS VERSUS MIDDLE CLASS ORIGIN		
	In percent consistently Socialist	*In percent wavering, uncertain*	*In percent consistently non-Socialist*
Self or spouse member of dissident union	+23	+5	−29
Neither self nor spouse in any union	+19	+12	−32

These data point to two crucial conditions for the development of a distinctive middle-class wing of the Labor Party: more and more sons and daughters of working-class families have moved upward, and many of them have been able to stay in the same organizational environment as their fathers because the LO unions cut across the class lines. To some extent this movement is also a direct consequence of Labor's rise to power; not only has the party placed an increasing number of workers' sons and daughters in municipal and central government employment at the salaried and profes-

sional levels, but the very growth of the public sector since the 1930's has
created an increasing number of openings for such upward mobility. The
movement has not been restricted to the public sector, however. Our data
suggest that a similar process has taken place in the private sector, although
with less distinctive electoral results. Many working-class women who have
moved into private salaried positions have tended to be uncertain about their
politics and to waver between opposite positions.

It is tempting to interpret the softening of ideological oppositions in the
fifties in these terms:[80] the battle for the "middle ground" in the social structure exerted restraints on all parties, not only Labor but also on the Conservatives.

To put Labor's situation in a nutshell, it has been able to count with great
confidence on core support from the households of unionized workers, but
to gain a parliamentary majority it has had to keep up strong appeals on two
fronts: on the one hand the poorer smallholders and fishermen in the peripheries of the nation, on the other the rising new middle class in the urban
centers. The vote potential in the peripheries has been declining, but it would
still be highly hazardous for the party to alienate this group of supporters.
The result has been a series of complex compromises over policies in the
primary sector of the economy. The urban and industrial interests within the
party have been pushing very hard for efforts to increase the efficiency of
farming and fishing and to cut out marginal units, but party leadership has
been very much restrained in their policies in this sector, not just because it
depends on smallholders and fishermen for about 12 percent of its votes, but
even more because these groups can appeal to the far-larger group, about
30 percent, who grew up in these environments and still feel some loyalty
to these interests even after moving into other walks of life. This source of
influence on party strategy is bound to decline, however, with continuing
economic growth. The crucial battles are currently fought over the votes of
the rising middle class. In the fifties there were distinct tendencies toward a
softening of class appeals and greater recognition of the need for differentiated scales of rewards. Svennik Høyer[81] has recently completed a content
analysis of the editorials of nine major newspapers during four campaigns
before *Storting* elections. He finds an overall reduction in the intensity of the
political appeals, a decrease in the use of blanket ideological terms such as
"socialism," "liberalism," and "capitalism," and, perhaps most significantly,
a decrease in the number of distinct policy issues dealt with within the same
editorial. This he takes to indicate a general reduction in the concern about
ideological oppositions across the entire field of politics and a corresponding
increase in the tendency to deal with political issues through piecemeal discussion. The interesting thing about this analysis is that he has been able to
show that this process of *"Entideologisierung,"* to use the standard German
phrase, has proceeded furthest in the newspapers with the broadest and socio-
economically most diverse readership. The closer a newspaper gets to dominating its community through its household coverage, the more sensitive it
will be to the divisions of political allegiance and the less explicit will it tend
to be in its political preferences.

Such a softening of ideological appeals may have had its short-run advantages but it is a strategy fraught with grave risks; there can be little doubt
that the downward trend in Labor memberships in the fifties[82] and the rise

of such splinter groups as the Socialist People's Party reflected disenchantment in the core groups of supporters. The Swedish Social Democrats recognized the risks of the "soft" strategy early in the fifties and soon found a
powerful alternative: break down the old status divisions between manual
workers and salaried employees and establish a *joint platform* for the defense
of their interests against their employers.[83] The party decided to focus its
action on issues which united the workers and the new middle class and found
the perfect answer in the proposal for retirement pensions based on earnings
during the best years of employment. This plan met a widely felt need for
improvements in old age benefits and at the same time recognized the justification of differential pension rights reflecting the established wage and salary
hierarchies. The issue was fought out in a national referendum in 1957 and
later in the *Riksdag,* and there is definite evidence of the success of this
strategy, not only in strengthening the Social Democrats, but also in broadening their middle-class appeal.[84]

The Norwegian Labor Party was for a long time reluctant to adopt this
strategy. Until 1961 the Labor Party had felt no urgent need for such a
change in strategy, and the Common Market issue delayed the effect of the
defeat that year. The decisive change did not come until the summer of 1963;
the Labor government was defeated after twenty-eight years in power and,
in order to take over the government again, was forced to present a much
more radically Socialist program than at any time during its rule as the
majority party. One major plank in this new program was a new pensions
scheme on the lines of the Swedish plan. This helped the party over the
immediate difficulties and brought it back into power, but it did not prove
such a boost to the organization and the membership as it had for the Swedish
Party. The Norwegian Liberals were not split over the pensions issue in the
way their Swedish friends had been, and the Norwegian Conservatives did
not offer any resistance to the scheme in the way their Swedish allies had.
Quite to the contrary, the Norwegian Liberals had for years advocated a
scheme along these lines and the Norwegian Conservatives had shown a great
deal of concern for the plight of the aged. In fact, when the Labor Party lost
out in 1965 and the four non-Socialist parties took over the government of the
country, there were only insignificant signs of disagreement over the scheme;
the new Government pushed on with the details of the pensions legislation
and the scheme was unanimously adopted by the *Storting* in 1966. The hopes
of the Labor Party had been dashed; the pensions plan may have helped to
keep the two Left-wingers under control but it did not gain the party even
an inch of ground in the battle for the political center. In fact the results of
the 1965 election showed that the party had chosen the wrong strategy in a
"low-threshold PR democracy": overconcentration on the battle for the
middle ground generates movements of disaffection and opposition on the
extremes of the political spectrum. The Downs model may have its validity
for plurality systems;[85] it breaks down in a low-threshold multiparty system.

Our analysis of the data for the crucial election of 1965 is still under way
and we can only report a few initial findings.[86] Looking first at the aggregate
figures for the country as a whole, we find that the total Socialist share of
the vote fell back by only 1.2 percentage points from 1957 to 1965: from
51.7 to 50.5 percent of the valid votes cast. But this total was without
political significance. The decisive change in the majority-minority balance

resulted from the spread of these Socialist votes on more and more competing lists. The total "Left splinter" votes (CP in 1957, CP plus SP in 1961 and 1965) increased from 6.5 percent of the Socialist total in 1952 to 12.7 percent in 1965, and the great majority of these votes were wasted below the threshold of representation.[87] The Socialist People's Party presented lists in six constituencies in 1961 and gained two seats: in 1965 it presented lists in all the twenty constituencies and nearly tripled its vote, but still stayed at the two-member level. Some of these added votes no doubt came from defectors from the CP, now down to a miserable 1.4 percent, but the bulk of the increase seems to have come from younger men and women from Labor Party environments who no longer felt committed to the cause of their fathers. Our cross-tabulations by type of commune suggest that the Labor Party lost fewer votes in the fisheries districts and the least urbanized countryside than in the industrial areas and the cities. The Left Socialists made more headway in the urbanized communes, but the net losses for the three-party bloc were nevertheless heaviest in the cities. Further analysis suggests that the Socialist bloc held its own in the still mobilizing periphery, the communes with the most marked increases in turnout, but lost out in the already highly politicized and polarized areas. The hypothesis we hope to explore in some detail in our analysis of the survey data collected before and after the election is that most of the changers in the economically advanced communities were younger, geographically and socially mobile voters. In these groups the rates of defection from traditional Labor loyalties seem to have been quite marked—mostly, it is true, toward the radical Socialist People's Party, but often also to the Liberals. Perhaps the single most important development in 1965 was the shift in the balance of electoral strengths on the non-Socialist side. The Liberals had been losing ground in the Oslofjord region for several decades but now suddenly came back in great force. The result was three new mandates for a "middle" party in the most polarized of the regions. By contrast the Conservatives made heavy inroads in the typical "middle party" districts of the South and West; there was a marked tendency toward continued polarization in the periphery but a reversal toward differentiated politics at the center. This double movement helped the non-Socialist bloc toward a clear victory in the battle for seats; they made their most significant gains in the constituencies where the payoff was highest. There has been much speculation about the extent to which this was the result of "strategic voting": how many non-Socialists defected from their traditional party to vote for a coalition list just below the threshold point? This raises tricky issues in analysis; we hope to be able to explore this in detail in our work with the survey data for this important "realigning" election.

SUMMARY: THE TWO BASIC
DIMENSIONS OF NORWEGIAN POLITICS

Our analysis of Norwegian developments has centered on two themes:

1. We have tried to pinpoint sequences in a process of *nation-building,* of increasing integration and standardization across localities differing in their social structure and in their cultural orientations.

2. We brought together data for an understanding of the *political repercussions of economic growth,* of urbanization, industrialization, and "bureaucratization."

The original lines of cleavage in the Norwegian system were *territorial* and *cultural:* the provinces opposed the capital, the peasantry fought the officials of the King's administration, the defenders of the rural cultural traditions spoke against the steady spread of urban secularism and nationalism.

Three developments brought about a decision change in the cleavage system during the first two decades after the establishment of universal suffrage:

(1) the entry of the bulk of the peasantry into the national money and credit economy and the concomitant shift from an attitude of negative resistance against the tax-collecting state toward a positive emphasis on the role of the national government in meeting the claims of the rural population;

(2) the emergence of a nation-wide movement of working class protest, not only in the cities and the industrializing countryside, but also in the forestry and fisheries communities of the Eastern and Northern provinces;

(3) the transformation of the original Right from an organization for the defense of the established administration of the state to a party essentially defending the claims of the urban middle class and the emerging business community against the encroaching apparatus of the national government.

These functional-economic lines of conflict cut across the earlier territorial-cultural ones and produced a complex system of alliances and oppositions:

(1) in the cities and the industrializing communities in the countryside the electorates were increasingly polarized between a Socialist Left and a Conservative Right;

(2) in the highly stratified forestry and fisheries communities of the East, Trøndelag, and North, there was a similar, although slower, process of polarization, even in the extreme peripheries of the outlying provinces;

(3) but in the more equalitarian primary economy communities of the South and West, the forces of territorial defense remained strong and vigorous and resisted effectively the pressures toward a polarization of local political life.

The striking difference between the South/Western and the Northern peripheries essentially reflects a difference in the timing of the crucial waves of mobilization: in the South and West the breakthrough came during the second half of the nineteenth century and found expression in a number of religious and cultural movements of resistance against the centralizing urban forces; in the North the breakthrough came with the introduction of manhood suffrage and took the form of a movement of violent social and economic protest, not primarily against the center of the nation but against the local property owners and employers.

In the South and the West the struggle centered on the symbols of community identification—the religious creed and the language. The mobilized peasantry fought all signs of liberalism within the state church and rejected the standard urban language brought into their communities by the clergymen, officials, teachers, and traders. The rural counter-language, the *landsmål,* became the rallying symbol for a broad movement of cultural defense, not only in the South and West but also in the old peasant communities of the eastern valleys. In the other regions of the country, the movement never rallied such decisive community support: in these regions the functional cleavage lines soon emerged as the dominant ones, and the earlier territorial contrasts lost in importance.

But the territorial strains were still present, and the Common Market issue brought them out in full daylight; the "functional" antagonists, the LO and the Conservatives, were united in their advocacy of entry, while the offshoots of the old territorial Left were either deeply split or entirely against any application for full membership. Our reanalysis of Gallup data collected at different points during the campaign for and against entry[88] suggests an intriguing system of alliances:

(1) on the pro-EEC side, the Labor voters, primarily in the cities and outside agriculture and fisheries, the Liberals in southern and western cities and the Conservatives everywhere;

(2) on the anti-EEC side, the Left Socialists and the smallholders and fishermen of the Labor Party, the Liberals of the eastern cities and to some extent in the western countryside, the Christians of the South and West, and Agrarians practically everywhere.

In one way this was a revival of the alliance of the seventies and eighties: alienated urban radicals joined with the peasantry of the provinces in an attack on the "establishment." But the central authorities had changed in character: the radical-peripheral alliance was no longer directed against the King's administration and its ties with the Swedish government but against a complex pluralistic network of trade unions, business organizations, and governmental authorities and their ties with the organs of European integration. The stakes were different, but the game had retained something of its old structure.

The opposition against entry proved stronger at the mass level than among party leaders, but the mobilization of opinion had at least been strong enough to bring about a compromise: a *Storting* decided by a three-fourths majority to apply for membership, but stipulated that the people were to be consulted in a referendum before any terms of affiliation were accepted.[89] But history decided otherwise: General de Gaulle called off the campaign on January 14, 1963, and the issue disappeared from Norwegian politics, at least for a few years. Functional-economic cleavages came to the fore again and the old divisions within the bourgeois opposition lost some of their importance: the result was the first serious Cabinet crisis for twenty-eight years.

NOTES

1. For a listing of early electoral studies, see S. Rokkan, "Norway," a chapter in S. Rokkan and J. Meyriat (eds.), *International Guide to Electoral Statistics, I, National Elections in W. Europe* (Paris: Mouton, 1967).

2. Accounts of this program will be found in S. Rokkan and H. Valen, "Parties, Elections and Political Behaviour in the Northern Countries," in O. Stammer (ed.), *Politische Forschung* (Cologne: Westdeutscher Verlag, 1960), pp. 103–36; S. Rokkan. "Political Research in Scandinavia 1960–65: Norway," *Scandinavian Political Studies,* 1 (1966), pp. 266–80, and S. Rokkan and H. Valen, "The Norwegian Program of Electoral Research," forthcoming in *Scandinavian Political Studies,* 2 (1967).

3. See especially S. Rokkan and H. Valen, "The Mobilization of the Periphery," in S. Rokkan (ed.), *Approaches to the Study of Political Participation* (Bergen: Michelsen Inst., 1962), pp. 111–58; S. Rokkan and H. Valen, "Regional Contrasts in Norwegian Politics," in E. Allardt and Y. Littunen (eds.), *Cleavages, Ideologies and Party Systems* (Helsinki: Westermarck Society, 1964), pp. 162–238.

4. The most complete analysis so far undertaken of Norwegian survey findings is presented in H. Valen and D. Katz, *Political Parties in Norway* (Oslo: Universitetsforlaget, 1964); this focuses on a local survey in the southwest of Norway. Among analyses based on the nationwide survey carried out in 1957 these deserve particular attention: S. Rokkan and A. Campbell, "Citizen Participation in Political Life: Norway and the United States of America," *Int. Soc. Sci. J.*, 12 (1) (1960), pp. 69–99, reprinted in J. Meynaud (ed.), *Decisions and Decision-Makers in the Modern State* (Paris: UNESCO, 1957); S. Rokkan and P. Torsvik, "Der Wähler, der Leser und die Parteipresse," *Kölner Zschr. Soziol*, 12 (2) (1960), pp. 278–301. A detailed panel survey of a nationwide cross-section was carried out in 1965 and is currently under analysis.

5. Subsequently printed in S. M. Lipset, *The First New Nation* (New York: Basic Books, 1963).

6. The official historical version is that Norway was a territory within the integral Danish-Norwegian state; see such standard constitutional texts as F. Castberg, *Norges Statsforfatning* (3d ed.; Oslo: Aschehoug, 1966), I, pp. 78–90. Whatever the juridical niceties, the fact remains that policy for this territorial entity was determined in the Danish chancelleries and that control of the education and graduation of future officials of the realm was centralized at the University of Copenhagen. In these terms the situation in Norway was not essentially different from the nineteenth-century colonies defined as "departments" or "provinces" of the mother country. What distinguished Norway from, say, Algeria, was the independence of the patriciate from the trading networks of the dominant metropolitan center: the openness toward other centers of commerce and industry in Europe made Norway much less of a "colony" in any economic sense.

7. For details see Bryn J. Hovde, *The Scandinavian Countries 1720–1865* (Ithaca: Cornell Univ. Press, 1948), I, pp. 195–205.

8. The events in 1814 have been described in great detail in numerous historical treatises. A standard Norwegian source is Sverre Steen, "1814," *Det frie Norge*, I (Oslo: Cappelen, 1951).

9. For illuminating discussions of the background see Hovde, *op. cit.*, and J. A. Seip, *Det opinionsstyrte enevelde,* (Oslo: Universitetsforlaget, 1958).

10. These figures are taken from the first statistics of recruitment ever published in Norway: J. N. Mohn, "Storthingerne 1815–1874 belyste ved Statistik," *Norsk Retstid*, 1874 (48) pp. 761–776. Further details on recruitment are given in the monumental history of the Norwegian Parliament, Alf Kaartvedt, Rolf Danielsen, *et al.*, *Det Norske Storting gjennom 150 år* (Oslo: Gyldendal, 1964), especially I, pp. 146–9 and II, pp. 80–93. A punched-card archive for biographical information on all members of the Storting has recently been established at the University of Bergen and will allow much more detailed analyses of changes in recruitment channels.

11. For details see *Minneskrift til formannskapslovenes 100-års jubileum: 1837–14, January, 1937* (Oslo: Gyldendal, 1937); T. Hjellum, *Partiene i norsk lokalpolitikk* (Oslo: Gyldendal, 1967).

12. See Steen, "Konge og Storting" *Det frie Norge*, V (Oslo: Cappelen, 1962), pp. 300–30.

13. For discussions of the importance of the printing trade in the development of national consciousness, see H. A. Innis, *The Bias of Communication* (Toronto: Univ. of Toronto Press, 1951), pp. 28 ff., and, in a highly speculative vein, Marshall McLuhan, *The Gutenberg Galaxy* (London: Routledge, 1962), pp. 218–39. For a general account of the role of linguistic standardization in processes of nation-building, see E. Haugen, *Language Conflict and Language Planning. The Case of Modern Norwegian* (Cambridge: Harvard Univ. Press, 1966), Chap. I.

14. For further details see A. Burgun, *Le développement linguistique en Norvège depuis 1814* (Christiania: Videnskapsselskapet, 1919–21); E. Haugen, *op. cit.*, "Con-

struction and Reconstruction in Language Planning: Ivar Aasen's Grammar," *Word* 21 (2) (Aug. 1965), pp. 188–202.

15. On this early movement of working class protest, see J. Friis, *Marcus Thrane* (Christiania: Steen, 1917), and E. Bull, *Arbeiderklassen i norsk historie* (Oslo, Tiden, 1947).

16. This conflict has been analyzed with consummate skill in Jens Arup Seip, *Et regime foran undergangen* (Oslo: Tanum, 1945).

17. For details on the preparatory steps taken by the army, see A. Kaartvedt, *Kampen mot parlamentarisme 1880–1884* (Oslo: Universitetsforlaget, 1956), pp. 307–12.

18. See Kaartvedt, *op. cit.*, pp. 131–7.

19. For an attempt to interpret the deepening schisma between Norway and Sweden in the light of Karl Deutsch's model of the processes of communication underlying the consolidation of territorial nation-states, see R. Lindgren, *Norway-Sweden: Union, Disunion and Scandinavian Integration* (Princeton: Princeton Univ. Press, 1959).

20. See R. Danielsen, "Samlingspartiet og unionen," *Historisk tidsskr.*, 41 (4) (1962), pp. 303–20.

21. For details of the sources of data for the early elections see S. Rokkan, "Norway," in S. Rokkan and J. Meyriat (eds.), *op. cit.*

22. For information on the electoral arrangements during the Revolution, see G. D. Weil, *Les élections législatives depuis 1789* (Paris: Alcan, 1895); G. Lachapelle, *Les régimes électoraux* (Paris: Colin, 1934); and P. Campbell, *French Electoral Systems and Elections 1789–1957* (London: Faber, 1958). For details on franchise statistics, see R. R. Palmer, *The Age of Democratic Revolution: The Challenge* (Princeton: Princeton Univ. Press, 1957), Appendix V, pp. 522–8.

23. See P. Campbell, *op. cit.* For further details on the period 1831–48, see S. Kent, *Electoral Practices under Louis Philippe* (New Haven: Yale Univ. Press, 1937).

24. See Charles Seymour, *Electoral Reform in England and Wales* (New Haven: Yale Univ. Press, 1916. For further literature, see D. Butler and J. Cornford, "Britain," in S. Rokkan and J. Meyriat (eds.), *op. cit.*

25. For detailed estimates of the size and composition of the Swedish electorate after 1866 see G. Wallin, *Valrörelser och valresultat. Andrakammarvalen i Sverige 1866–1884* (Stockholm: Ronzo, 1961), Chap. I.

26. The figures in parentheses are estimates: they assume that the ratios of the registered to the qualified were the same for the early elections as for 1859. This, of course, cannot be taken for granted without further checking of the accessible sources of information. We are currently exploring various possibilities of analysis in the extant census materials from 1801, 1825, and 1845 and hope to be able to add further precision to our estimates in a later report. The data at hand suggest that our estimates tend to be too high for the cities (probably because of the gradual increase in the numbers of lower-class citizens qualifying as owners of real estate) and more accurate for the rural districts (where the franchise criteria were not given in monetary terms and where the "thresholds of incorporation" accordingly did not vary with changes in the value of the currency).

27. Detailed examples of such practices were given by H. E. Berner in 1880 (see H. Meyer, *Den politiske arbeiderbevegelse i Norge* [Oslo, DNA, 2nd ed., 1935], p. 88) and by N. Mejdell, *Nyt tidsskrift*, 1 (1882), pp. 596–607. For a broader treatment see Danielsen, *Det norske Storting gjennom 150 år*, II, pp. 26–47.

28. A first detailed account of *myrmandsvaesenet* (the peat bog buying) was given by the pioneering compiler of electoral statistics, John Utheim, in *Valgmandsvalgene og Storthingsvalgene 1882* (Kristiania: Cammermeyer, 1883), pp. 62–64. The estimate of the size and composition of the 1885 electorate in Table 4 is based on a special tax census of 1876 (see below): at that time there were in the rural areas 112,000 who qualified under the old rules and an additional 26,000 who would qualify if an income minimum of Kr 480 were introduced as a further criterion of franchise. In fact, when this criterion (to be exact, the minimum was set at Kr 500, not Kr 480 as assumed in 1876) was introduced in 1885, the rural electorate rose to 146,600, roughly 8,600 more than estimated; even allowing for the continued rise in monetized income in the countryside, it seems clear that a sizable percent of this increase in enfranchisement must have come about through politically motivated purchases of land.

29. *Statistiske Oplysninger om de fremsatte Stemmeretsforslags Virkning* (Christiania: Statistisk Centralbureau, C. No. 14, 1877).

30. For details on Swedish electorate statistics, see E. Janson, "Sweden," in S. Rokkan and J. Meyriat (eds.), *op. cit.*

31. For further details on the participation of women in Norwegian politics, see S. Rokkan and H. Valen, "The Mobilization of the Periphery," *op. cit.*

32. For a review of arguments for the overrepresentation of the periphery, see S. Rokkan and S. Høyer, *Samfunnsvitenskapelige undersøkelser omkring den kommende folkeavstemning* (Bergen: Chr. Michelsens Inst., 1962); this deals specifically with arguments against "one man-one vote" nationwide referendums.

33. For comment on the Danish constitutional provision, see Alf Ross, *Dansk Statsforfatningsret* (Copenhagen: Nyt Nordisk Forlag, 1960), pp. 249–275.

34. This account of the development of the Norwegian party system represents an extension of the corresponding section of S. Rokkan and H. Valen, "Regional Contrasts in Norwegian Politics," *op. cit.*

35. In terms of the model presented in the Introduction to this volume, the *T, SC,* and *R* cleavages are varieties of type 1 and reflect strains generated through the *National* Revolution, while the *CM* (type 3) and *LM* (type 4) cleavages reflect strains produced through the *Industrial* Revolution.

36. See Ulf Torgersen, "Sosiale klasser, politiske partier og politisk representasjon i norske bysamfunn," *Tss. samfunnsforskning,* 2 (3) (Sept. 1961), pp. 162–81, and *The Formation of Parties in Norway: The Problem of Left-Right Differences* (Oslo: Institute for Social Research, 1966), mimeo.

37. The first attempt at electoral geography in Norway was due to the geologist Andreas M. Hansen. In his *Norsk folkepsykologi* (Christiania: Dybwad, 1899), he tried to link up the strength of the fundamentalist Moderates with the anthropological characteristics (skull shape, hair and eye color) of the local population. See further S. Rokkan and H. Valen, "Regional Contrasts," *op. cit.* Some sixty years later the geographer Gabriel Øidne set out to produce another set of social, cultural, and political maps to trace continuities in local political tendencies, but unfortunately never published more than the one article, "Litt om motsetninga mellom Austlandet og Vestlandet," *Syn og segn,* 63 (3) (1957), pp. 97–114.

38. See Rolf Danielsen "Samlingspartiet og unionen," *op. cit.,* also his useful review of early party developments in "Framveksten av de politske partier i de nordiske land på 1800-tallet," *Problemer i nordisk historieforskning* (Oslo-Bergen: Universitetsforlaget. 1964), pp. 131–40.

39. See T. Aasland, *Fra arbeiderorganisasjon til mellomparti* (Oslo: Universitetsforlaget, 1962).

40. See Ulf Torgersen, *The Anti-Party Ideology: Elitist Liberalism in Norwegian Social and Political Structure* (Oslo: Institute for Social Research, 1966), mimeo; also his contribution "Våre helter og høvdinger," to the special issue, "Fascismen i Norge," *Kontrast,* 2 (3) (1966), 29–36.

41. For illuminating accounts of the processes through which the old Right changed its character from 1903 to the 1930's, see Kaare D. Tønnesson, "Et departement 'med det rette sinnelag for naeringslivets vel'," *Hist. tss.,* 44 (1) (1965), pp. 1–16, and Ulf Torgersen, *Landsmøtet i norsk partistruktur 1884–1940* (Oslo: Institute for Social Research, 1966), mimeo, especially pp. 47–57.

42. This contrast has been discussed in further detail by S. Rokkan in "Electoral Mobilization, Party Competition and National Integration," in J. Palombara and M. Weiner (eds.) *Political Parties and Political Development* (Princeton: Princeton Univ. Press, 1966), pp. 241–65.

43. The classic analysis of these contrasts is still E. Bull "Die Entwicklung der Arbeiterbewegung in den drei skandinavischen Ländern," *Arch. f. Geschichte des Sozialismus* 10 (1922), pp. 329–61.

44. See especially K. Langfeldt, *Moskvatesene i norsk politikk* (Oslo: Universitetsforlaget, 1962).

45. For an account of these developments, see T. Roset, *Det norske Arbeiderparti og Hornsruds regjeringsdannelse i 1928* (Oslo: Universitetsforlaget, 1928).

46. S. S. Nilson, in a paper at the First Nordic Conference on Political Science (Voksenåsen, Oslo, June 1966) has objected to our "polarization score" as underesti-

mating the extent of class dominance in politics because it leaves out the votes for the Agrarians. Our rationale for the score is very simple: the Agrarian vote was in *all* regions an expression of conflict in the *commodity* market and was only in *some* regions (mainly in the richer farming areas of the East) at the same time a reflection of conflict in the *labor* market. Since we wanted a measure that could be used in all regions, we chose to disregard the Agrarians. In our future analyses we hope to establish a better indicator of class polarization by first estimating the proportion of Agrarian votes likely to have come from the households of farmers regularly dependent on hired labor.

47. This conflict gave rise to a fascinating debate between advocates of a *class* party of ideologically committed members and a *national* (*folk*) party aggregating the votes of a wide variety of dissatisfied citizens, whether workers, employees, artisans, shopkeepers, peasants, or fishermen. The best contemporary analysis of these conflicting strategies was due to Dag Bryn and Hallvard Lange, "Klasse eller folk," *Det 20 de århundrede*, 31 (3) (March 1930), pp. 67–75. Their analysis stresses the extraordinary contrast between the *organizational* and the *electoral* strength of the party: as a membership body the party was predominantly urban and concentrated in Oslo; as a body of voters, it was predominantly rural and provincial. This theme has recently been developed in further depth by Ulf Torgersen, *Landsmøtet, op. cit.*, pp. 85–98.

48. For general discussions of trends in these directions, see the articles by Ulf Himmelstrand and Ulf Torgersen in S. Rokkan (ed.), *Approaches to the Study of Political Participation* (Bergen: Michelsen Institute, 1962).

49. See the concluding section of Rokkan-Valen, "Regional Contrasts," *op. cit.*

50. For further details see S. Rokkan, "Norway: Numerical Democracy and Corporate Pluralism," in R. A. Dahl (ed.), *Political Oppositions in Western Democracies* (New Haven: Yale Univ. Press, 1966), pp. 70–116.

51. See particularly the concluding chapter of A. Zachariassen, *Fra Marcus Thrane til Martin Tranmael* (Oslo: Arbeiderpartiets Forlag, 1962).

52. For an initial analysis of the 1965 election, see S. Rokkan and T. Hjellum, "Norway: The Storting Election of September 1965," *Scandinavian Political Studies* 1 (1966), pp. 237–46.

53. On the development of this facility, see S. Rokkan and H. Valen, "Archives for Statistical Studies of Within-Nation Differences," in R. L. Merritt and S. Rokkan (eds.), *Comparing Nations* (New Haven: Yale Univ. Press, 1966), pp. 411–18.

54. For details of recent developments in electoral ecology see S. Rokkan, "The Comparative Study of Electoral Statistics," introduction to S. Rokkan and J. Meyriat (eds.), *op. cit.*

55. G. Carlsson, "Partiförskjutningar som tillväkstprocesser," *Statsvet. ts.* 66 (1963), pp. 172–213.

56. In an unpublished monograph written within our program, Erling Saeter has shown for the southern and western regions that the Socialists have had least success in mobilizing their industrial potential in areas with high proportions of *small industrial units* and with high proportions of *women* in the industrial labor force.

57. N.O.S. XII. 79, *Jordbruksteljinga i Norge, 20. juni 1959*, I (1961), Table 1. Our calculations refer to holdings of 5 da. or more.

58. For a cursory review of information on the politics of the far north see Nils Ørvik, *Europe's Northern Cape and the Soviet Union* (Cambridge: Harvard Univ., Center for International Affairs, 1963).

59. See S. Rokkan and H. Valen, "The Mobilization of the Periphery," *op. cit.*, p. 116.

60. For details of the design of the study see S. Rokkan, *The Nation-wide Election Survey 1957: Basic Tables* (Bergen: Michelsen Institute, 1960).

61. The most extensive study so far undertaken of the politics of the "new middle class" in Norway is due to Egil Fivelsdal, *Funksjonaerenes syn på faglige og politiske spørsmål* (Oslo: Universitetsforlaget, 1964).

62. For a first report on the results see G. Spilling, "Resultater av kirketelling og opinionsundersøkelse," *Kirke og kultur* 62 (1957), pp. 385–99. A first summary table by region and type of locality is presented in Rokkan-Valen, "Regional Contrasts," *op. cit.*, pp. 187 and 222–3.

63. A. Dolven, "Norsk avholdsrørsle," *No. tss. alkoholspørsmål*, 15 (4) (1963), pp. 185–228.

64. All these three cultural variables were explored in greater detail in the nation-wide panel survey conducted in 1965. H. Valen will report on the findings in a forthcoming article.

65. Recalculated from A. Dolven, *op. cit.* The delimitation of the five regions in this analysis does not tally completely with the usage in the other tables of this chapter, but this does not affect the direction and significance of the differences.

66. For further statistics on the strength of the *nynorsk* movement, see Haugen, *op. cit.*, Appendix 1, pp. 309–15.

67. See the examples of multiple regression analysis in Rokkan-Valen, "Regional Contrasts," *op. cit.*, pp. 179–83. Reports on further analyses covering a broader range of ecological data are in preparation.

68. For detailed reports on these surveys see Valen-Katz, *op. cit.*, Chap. 6 and Appendix A.

69. The responses to this question have been analyzed in further detail in S. Brun-Gulbrandsen and J. Wallace, "Regner De Dem som avholdsmann?" *No. tidsskr. alkoholspørsmål* 15 (3) (1963), pp. 129–55.

70. The temperance issue in fact counted heavily in the struggle for power in the Labor Party from 1912 to 1927; this has been brilliantly analyzed at the leadership level by U. Torgersen in *Landsmøtet, op. cit.*, pp. 73–85. This interpretation of the temperance movement as an expression of "peripheral protest" against the spread of the "money and credit" culture from the urban centers opens up an important perspective for comparative research. For a parallel study of development in the United States, see Joseph Gusfield, *Symbolic Crusade: Status Politics and the American Temperance Movement* (Urbana: Univ. of Illinois Press, 1963).

71. The nationwide panel survey carried out in 1965 will allow much more detailed analysis of the cultural dimensions of the vote in Norway and pinpoint the most significant differences among the regions.

72. For a programmatic statement of the need for such longitudinal studies, see S. Rokkan, "Electoral Mobilization, Party Competition and National Integration," *op. cit.*

73. G. Carlsson, "Partiforskjutningar som tilllväkstprocesser," *op. cit.*

74. The first academic survey was carried out in 1949 and was reported by Allen H. Barton in *Sociological and Psychological Problems of Economic Planning in Norway*, Ph.D. diss., Columbia Univ. 1954.

75. The survey data tally fairly well with the aggregate census figures for the principal occupational categories:

Distribution of Active Population by Major Categories

	Total = 100% (thousands)	Independent		Salaried	Workers		No Info.
		Primary	Other		Primary	Other	
1875	736	28	10	5	24	28	5
1900	887	23.5	10	8	28.5	37	3
1950	1388	15.5	9.5	19.5	10.5	44	1
1960	1409	19.4		24.9	55.7		—

Source: Population censuses and, for 1960, E. Fivelsdal, *op. cit.*, Table 1.1.

76. See R. Alford, *Party and Society* (Chicago: Rand McNally, 1963), and his chapter in the present volume.

77. For a discussion of the Index of Class Voting see Alford's presentation of his Table 2 in his chapter above. The corresponding table in *Party and Society* (p. 85) is unfortunately marred by misleading misprints (Types II and III).

78. For accounts of differences in union structure, see Walter Galenson, *Labor in Norway* (Cambridge: Harvard Univ. Press, 1949), and "Scandinavia," in *Comparative Labor Movements* (Englewood Cliffs: Prentice-Hall, 1952). For details on divisions within the new middle class in Norway, see E. Fivelsdal, *Funksjonaerenes syn, op. cit.*

79. Precise estimates of the extent of this split are fraught with difficulties because of

differences in the classification of occupations; see the discussion in S. Rokkan, "Norway: Numerical Democracy and Corporate Pluralism," *op. cit.*, pp. 98–9.

80. For further elaboration, see S. Rokkan, "Norway: Numerical Democracy," *op. cit.*, pp. 89–105.

81. S. Høyer, "Pressens økonomiske og politiske struktur," *Tss. samfunnsforskning* 1965 (4), pp. 221–42, and his forthcoming report in *Scandinavian Political Studies* III (1968).

82. On the decline in membership figures, see Ulf Torgersen, "The Trend Towards Political Consensus," in S. Rokkan, *Approaches to the Study of Political Participation, op. cit.*, and A. Zachariassen *Fra Marcus Thrane til Martin Tranmael, op. cit.*, concluding chapter.

83. See especially B. Molin, *Tjänstepensionsfrågan. En studie i svensk partipolitik* (Gothenburg: Akademiförlaget, 1965), and his article, "Swedish Party Politics: A Case Study," *Scandinavian Political Studies* I (1966), pp. 45–58.

84. See B. Särlvik, "The Role of Party Identification in Voters' Perception of Political Issues: A Study of Opinion Formation in Swedish Politics 1956–1960," paper, Fifth World Congress of Political Science, Paris, 1961; see also his "Political Stability and Change in the Swedish Electorate," *Scandinavian Political Studies*, I (1966), pp. 188–222.

85. See Anthony Downs, *An Economic Theory of Democracy* (New York: Harper & Row, 1957), and the discussion of "thresholds" in PR systems in S. Rokkan, "Electoral Systems," *International Encyclopedia of the Social Sciences,* forthcoming.

86. For early reports see S. Rokkan, H. Valen, and A. Amundsen, "Stortingsvalget 1965," *Samtiden* 74 (8) (1965), pp. 463–80, and S. Rokkan and T. Hjellum, "Norway: The Storting Election of September 1965," *op. cit.*

87. For details of the workings of the electoral system see Rokkan-Hjellum, *op. cit.*

88. See Rokkan-Valen, "Regional Contrasts," *op. cit.* pp. 199–201.

89. A plan for a detailed study of this referendum was prepared by S. Rokkan and S. Høyer (*Samfunnvitenskapelige undersøkelser omkring den kommende folkeavstemning,* Bergen, Michelsen Institute, Nov. 1962, 29 pp.) but had of course to be shelved after January 14, 1963.

Four

The Emerging Nations

Nine

Patterns of Politics
in Present-Day Japan

Joji Watanuki

This chapter will attempt to interpret the pattern of politics in present-day Japan, paying special attention to the political allegiance of the white-collar group. Political characteristics for this group show certain tendencies peculiar to modern Japan, and which might aid in the understanding of the more general pattern of politics. In the interpretation, I have tried to introduce multi-contextual considerations as much as possible. Although this chapter is essentially a mono-contextual study, by introducing such multi-contextual considerations,[1] we can expect a more sophisticated interpretation concerning the pattern of politics in this particular case, and we can contribute to knowledge of other societies which are relatively highly industrialized but still moving and changing under the impact of the industrialization process.

What is the meaning of "multi-contextual" considerations? In terms of stages of industrialization, Japan passed the initial stages long ago; now she may be compared in many ways with present-day Italy or France. But she is an industrialized society in what is called the non-Western world, and this uniqueness has meaning beyond her geographical location. Lucian Pye has tried to present an analytical scheme for understanding non-Western political process; he presents seventeen characteristics of such a process.[2] Although Japan is not non-Western in the sense of passing from traditional society to industrialization, we find that eight characteristics out of the seventeen which Pye enumerated still persist in present-day Japan to a considerable degree but for different reasons than Pye suggested. Although this article will not deal historically with problems of initial industrialization and its political consequence in Japan, we will pay attention to certain limiting factors still working in current Japanese politics which arose from her position as a late-comer in the world race to industrialize and as a member of the non-Western world.

VOTING BEHAVIOR:
THE PATTERNS[3]

The pattern of voting behavior in modern Japan points up four characteristics[4] different from the general tendencies usually found in western European societies.

First, if we classify political parties on a continuum of Left-Right,[5] usually there is demonstrated a tendency for low-income groups to vote for leftist parties.[6] In the case of Japan, however, on the basis of nationwide poll data, it is difficult to recognize clearly any relationship between income group and party choice.[7] If there is any, the relationship seems to be very weak.

Second, with regard to party choice of certain occupational groups, the high rate of support for leftist parties (predominantly for the Japan Socialist Party) among the white-collar group is striking. As shown in *Table 1* in the white-collar group, support for the Socialists exceeds that for the Liberal

Table 1—Party Choice Among Occupational Groups (November 1960) (in percentages)

	Liberal Democrats	Socialists	Democratic Socialists	Miscellaneous	Nonpartisan Candidates	"Don't Know"	Nonvoter
Farmers and fishermen	70.1	17.5	3.6	0.3	0.3	1.4	6.8
Merchants and small manufacturers	64.8	19.6	4.0	0.6	1.2	—	9.7
White-collar	31.8	44.0	4.9	1.5	0.4	0.4	17.0
Manual workers	31.0	43.2	1.1	2.7	2.1	5.2	14.7
Housewives	51.2	25.2	5.4	0.3	0.6	3.2	14.0

Source: Answers to the question, "For which party did you vote in the election of the Members of House of Representatives in 1960?" gathered by a nationwide sample survey conducted by *Shinbun Yoronchosa Renmei* (Public Opinion Survey League for the Presses) just after the election.

Remarks: In this sort of public opinion survey, the ratio of people who answer that they voted for the Communist Party is usually 1 percent or less (the actual vote for the Communist Party is usually three percent of the total votes). Perhaps this research agency included the answers for the Communist Party into the category of "Miscellaneous" because of the small number of such answers.

Democratic Party. The Japan Socialist Party, in terms of its ideology and rhetoric at least, can be regarded as a left-wing Socialist Party, the counterpart of which we cannot find in western European societies (except perhaps Nenni's Socialist Party in Italy). Although it is not statistically significant in the table, if we add the support for the Democratic Socialists to that for the Socialists, support for these two parties among the white-collar group is greater than support by manual workers. Although the intellectuals' inclination to be more radical, to support more the (relative) Left than the other strata, is a rather universal phenomenon in Western societies, it should be noted that the white-collar group in Western societies support the Right-wing Socialists to a considerable degree, along with some support for the Conservatives or the Liberals. The high rate of support for the Socialists, especially for the Left Socialists among the Japanese white-collar group as a whole, is not paralleled in any western European society.

A third correlation in the analysis of voting behavior is made in terms of educational level. In most industrialized societies, the higher the level of education, the higher the voting rate. But correlation between educational levels and party choice remains vague in the case of Japan. In most Western societies, there is a fairly clear correlation between educational level and party choices—the more educated tend to support the Left (*Table 2*).[8]

Table 2—Party Choice and Educational Level (November 1960)
(in percentages)

	Liberal Democrats	Socialists	Democratic Socialists	Miscellaneous	Nonpartisan Candidates	"Don't Know"	Nonvoter
Low educational level[a]	57.0	22.2	4.0	0.6	0.4	1.9	13.9
Medium educational level[b]	46.2	34.8	5.0	0.7	0.9	0.7	11.6
High educational level[c]	39.2	35.0	7.7	—	2.1	—	16.1

Source: Same as Table I.
[a] Low educational level: those who finished sixth or eighth grade elementary-school work (before World War II) and those who finished ninth grade junior-high-school work (after World War II).
[b] Medium educational level: those who were graduated from eleventh grade middle school (before World War II) or twelfth grade senior high school (after World War II).
[c] High educational level: those who graduated from various forms of higher educational institutions (before World War II) or universities and colleges (after World War II).

Fourth, the universal tendency for younger groups to support the Left and older groups to show a more conservative inclination[9] is clearly illustrated in Japan's case. As shown in *Table 3*, there are three political generations in Japan.

Table 3—Party Choice and Age Groups (November 1960) (in percentages)

Age	Liberal Democrats	Socialists	Democratic Socialists	Miscellaneous	Nonpartisan Candidates	"Don't Know"	Nonvoter
20–29	37.6	37.1	5.1	1.2	0.3	0.5	18.1
30–39	50.1	32.2	4.9	0.4	0.3	0.3	11.3
40–49	59.4	23.0	5.1	0.2	1.0	2.0	9.4
50 +	62.8	15.0	3.7	0.5	0.9	2.6	14.5

Source: Same as Tables 1 and 2.

Those in their twenties (born between 1930 and 1940) and educated after World War II show a high rate of support for the Socialists.[10] Those in their thirties and forties tend to vote for middle-of-the-road parties. Those in their fifties and older are distinctly conservative. Incidentally the size of the 20–29 group is roughly equal to the group 50 +. Thus the radical 20–29 group and the conservative 50 + group balance out around the middle-of-the-road 30–49 group.

VOTING BEHAVIOR:
SOME EXPLANATIONS

How can we properly explain these four characteristics of voting behavior by various groups in present-day Japanese society?

The lack of clear correlation between income groups and party choice can be explained in terms of two factors. The first factor is technical: It is difficult to evaluate the income of Japanese farmers accurately by usual questionnaire-type survey techniques, because a considerable part of what otherwise would be their household expenses is covered by the crops they raise. Therefore, because opinion polls cannot allocate much time or space to subtle distinctions, many farmers are included in the low-income group even though their actual income might be quite high. As stated before, farmers predominantly are supporters of the Liberal Democratic Party. This naturally makes the correlation between income level and party choice ambiguous.

However, apart from such a technical problem, it is still true that the Liberal Democrats command the majority of support among lower strata in rural villages and also substantial support among urban lower strata. In rural villages, the reasons for this support are partly due to the economic structure of agriculture and partly due to the social structure of the village in Japan. Japanese agriculture is predominantly based on small-owner cultivators. Even the poor Japanese farmers are small farmers cultivating their own land with family labor. In this respect, the political situation in the rural sector of Japan is quite different from that of Italy, where vast numbers of tenant farmers and agricultural workers are organized by leftists, mainly Communists. Even in France and Sweden, where small farming is the dominant form, considerable numbers of agricultural workers are employed, and many of them are supporters of the Socialists.[11] The conservativeness of this kind of small peasantry has been repeatedly pointed out by various writers. In addition, the social structure of the Japanese rural village offers the opportunity for the dominance of conservative values. Need for cooperation in the control of water for irrigation, common worship of village Shinto gods, common ties to the same Buddhist temple, concentrated physical location of houses in a narrow area, networks of extended family ties and other conjugal ties, and the administrative practice of utilizing the village as an administrative unit (a practice long established and maintained from the feudal past through the process of modernization in the Meiji period, 1868–1911)—these conditions had created a high degree of village solidarity and (especially before land reform after World War II) hierarchical interpersonal relationships.[12] The Conservatives have taken advantage of this solidarity and pattern of hierarchy which, although shaken by land reform, still remains, especially in mountainous villages where landlords who own and run the forests still dominate the village. In such areas, support for the Conservatives has solidified, and infiltration by the leftists has been thwarted. The poorer the farmer, the more he is vulnerable to the political values in the village[13] and to pressure from powerful people who have good reasons for being conservative.[14]

In cities, we see a fairly clear correlation between income level and party choice, i.e., the lower the income level, the more support for the Socialists. But as *Table 4* shows, the Conservatives are getting fairly strong support among people in the lowest income bracket.[15] This phenomenon is neither strange nor peculiar to present-day Japan. A similar tendency is reported in Sweden;[16] and in Japan's case, those in the lowest income group live in an environment where traditional values are prevalent, so that it is no wonder that they show an inclination to suport the Conservatives.

Recently a Buddhist faction called *Sōka Gakkai* (Value Creation Society) gathered its followers and, in local elections and the election for the House of Councilors, ran its own candidates. These received four million votes. According to available survey data, this group is recruiting its followers mainly

Table 4—Party Choice and Income

PARTY CHOICE (PERCENT)

Monthly Income	Liberal Democrats	Socialists	Democratic Socialists	Other Answers (including "Don't know")
0	37	38	6	19
0–10	33	33	6	28
10–15	26	43	3	28
15–20	25	50	4	21
20–30	32	48	4	16
30–40	39	47	4	10
40–50	37	43	7	13
50–60	52	33	6	9
60–80	49	29	6	16
80–100	69	12	9	10
100 & over	79	8	5	8

Source: A survey conducted by Minshushugi Kenkyukai among samples of males over twenty years living in Tokyo Ward Districts in February 1961.
Remarks: The unit of monthly income is 1,000 yen (about $3.00 U.S.).

(but not exclusively—we can find intellectuals and high income people such as an actress, a professional baseball pitcher, the wife and daughter of a *Todai* professor among its followers, but these are small in number) from the uneducated, lower-income group and among unskilled manual workers. The age composition of its followers is interesting: the *Sōka Gakkai* boasts the strength of youth organizations. Actually, according to survey data in a lower-class residential section of Tokyo,[17] about half of this group's followers are youths in their twenties. Two comments may be ventured: politically, half of these youths, who compose the followers of the *Sōka Gakkai,* are recruited from potential supporters for the leftists. The other half are drawn from potential supporters for the Conservatives. Hence, the effects of political activities of the *Sōka Gakkai* can work equally unfavorably to the leftists and the Conservatives. Second, the growth of *Sōka Gakkai* can be regarded as a sign of the partial collapse of traditional values. The *Sōka Gakkai* attacks, although vaguely, the corruption of the establishment, emphasizes the immediate benefits which can be gained by believing in its values, and, within its hierarchy of positions, emphasizes the principle of achievement, which attracts especially those youths who have low educational achievement levels and cannot expect much promotion in their jobs. As S. M. Lipset put it, it is universal that

> Once the lowest strata are broken from their allegiance to traditional values and come to believe that a change for the better is possible, they tend to back a political tendency which offers an immediate and relatively uncomplex solution to their problem.[18]

Let us now try to explain the comparatively high ratio of support for the leftists among white-collar workers in Japan. Why do the Japanese manual workers support leftist parties only to the same extent as (or even to a lesser extent than) do the white-collar workers? The manual worker group in Japan, although statistically regarded as a homogeneous group, is really highly heterogeneous. If we look at the manual worker group in terms of the size of enterprises where they work, and the locality where they live, we are struck by the correlations with their party choice (see *Table 5*). Those who are employed in medium-size enterprises and especially in small family enterprises show a tendency similar to their employers—a tendency toward the old middle class

Table 5—Party Choice Among Various Strata of Manual Workers (in percentages)

I. In Tokyo Wards Districts

	Liberal Democrats	Socialists	Democratic Socialists	Others ("Don't Know," No Response)
Workers in large enterprises[a]	9	76	5	10
Workers in medium and small enterprises	20	57	4	19
Artisans	39	30	6	24
Workers without stable job	33	40	2	25

II. In a local city near Kobe (Miki City, population 38,000)

	Liberal Democrats	Socialists	Democratic Socialists	Communists	Others ("Don't Know," No Response)
Workers in large enterprises[b]	21	46	19	—	14
Workers in medium enterprises[c]	47	35	11	—	6
Workers in small enterprises[d]	46	37	7	—	10

III. In an industrial city in Northern Kyushu where the biggest steel mill in Japan is located (Yawata City, population 330,000).

	Liberal Democrats	Socialists	Democratic Socialists	Communists	No Votes	Others ("Don't Know," No Response)
Workers in large enterprises[e]	8	78	5	1	7	1
Workers in medium and small enterprises	22	57	2	4	14	1

Source: (1) A survey conducted by Minshushugi Kenkyukai among samples of males over twenty years in Tokyo Wards Districts in February, 1961. (II) A survey conducted by the author in February, 1962. (III) A survey conducted by the author in December, 1960.
  [a] Those which employ over 500 employees.
  [b] Those which have over 500 employees.
  [c] Those which have 50–499 employees.
  [d] Those which have 1–49 employees.
  [e] Those which have over 500 employees.

in their party choice and also in their social attitudes. The majority of those workers are not organized in labor unions, and they are living in an environment where traditional values are prevalent. Although this sort of tendency in terms of party choice and social attitudes is rather universal,[19] what is characteristic of Japan's case is the vast number of such "Tory" workers. According to the author's estimate, the Liberal Democrats are getting roughly five million votes from this group of manual workers and their families (see *Chart 1*).[20] The voting behavior of "Tory" workers lowers the average ratio of workers' support for the leftist parties in the nationwide survey data. If we

Chart I
The Japanese Voters, 1960

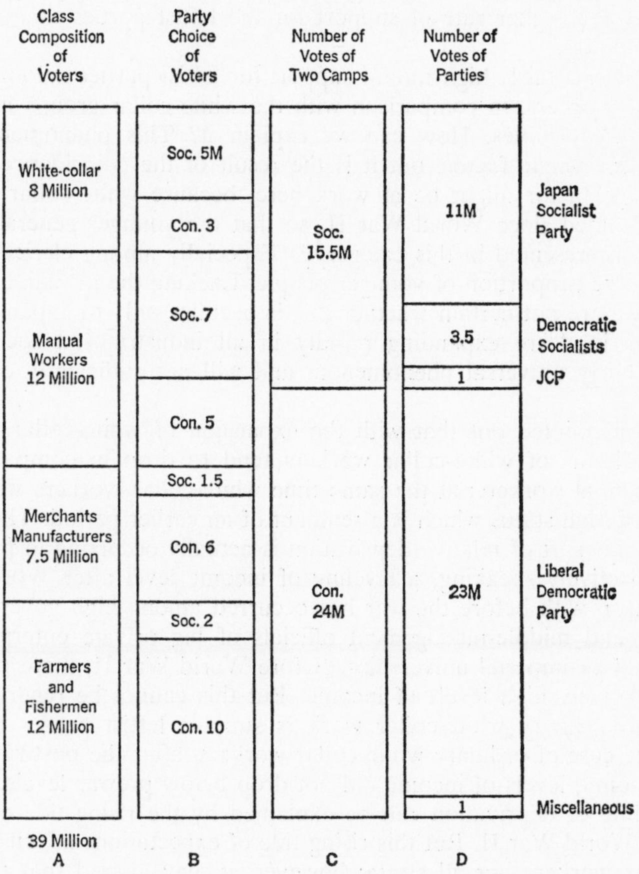

Class Composition of Voters	Party Choice of Voters	Number of Votes of Two Camps	Number of Votes of Parties	
White-collar 8 Million	Soc. 5M		11M	Japan Socialist Party
	Con. 3	Soc. 15.5M		
Manual Workers 12 Million	Soc. 7		3.5	Democratic Socialists
			1	JCP
	Con. 5			
Merchants Manufacturers 7.5 Million	Soc. 1.5			
	Con. 6	Con. 24M	23M	Liberal Democratic Party
	Soc. 2			
Farmers and Fishermen 12 Million	Con. 10			
			1	Miscellaneous
39 Million				
A	B	C	D	

Note: This chart is made on the basis of the following assumptions and procedures:

1. Total number of electorate is about 54 million, 73% of whom voted in 1960; thus 39 million votes were cast.

2. To make the chart simple, we assume that female voters voted in the same way as their husband or father. In Japan's case, this has been substantiated by opinion polls. This is different from the Italian case, where women strongly favor the Christian Democrats, regardless of male preference.

3. The voting rate of farmers, small merchants, and manufacturers is higher than that of white-collar and manual workers. The sizes of the classes of voters in column A are estimated by taking into consideration this different rate of voting and using the Census statistics on the occupational composition of male population gainfully engaged in economic activities.

4. In columns B and C, Communist and Democratic Socialist votes are combined with those of Socialists. Also, miscellaneous minor parties and independent candidates votes are included in Conservative (cf. D).

compare the party choice of workers who are working in big enterprises or plants with that of the white-collar group as a whole, or with that of the white-collar contingent in the same enterprise or plant, then clearly those manual workers show a higher rate of support for the leftist parties than the white-collar workers do.

Still we have a fairly high rate of support for leftist parties among Japanese white-collar workers, in comparison with the white-collar groups in all western European societies. How can we explain it? This phenomenon is not caused by any single factor, but it is the result of the coincidence of many. First, the age factor might be at work here, because white-collar jobs have rapidly expanded since World War II, so that the younger generation might be strongly represented in this category.[21] Especially among clerical workers, we find a large proportion of younger people. Lacking the available comparative data, we are not certain whether this is peculiar only to Japan, but since white-collar jobs are expanding rapidly in all industrialized societies, this may be a fairly universal phenomenon, and will not sufficiently explain the tendency.

It is often pointed out that with the expansion of white-collar jobs, economic conditions of white-collar workers tend to drop in comparison with those of manual workers; at the same time white-collar workers will cling to the image of high status which is a remnant of an earlier period. The question is whether this sort of relative deprivation is actually occurring in present-day Japan. Objectively speaking, a leveling of income level after World War II in comparison with before the war has occurred among high government officials, top and middle-management officials of big private enterprises, and professors of ex-imperial universities. Before World War II, these people had enjoyed relatively high levels of income. But this cannot be regarded as the reason that ordinary white-collar workers support leftist parties today, because in the case of ordinary white-collar workers, after the postwar recovery of the economy, levels of income did not drop below prewar levels. The subjective feeling of deprivation can be explained by the rising tide of expectations after World War II. But this rising tide of expectations affected not only white-collar workers but all strata; however, it may argued that the impact of the rising tide of expectations would be strongest among white-collar workers because they are more exposed to mass media and to urban living. Housing shortages, congestion in public transportation, high prices of land for housing—these conditions undoubtedly contribute to the discontent and the demand for more planning and intervention by the government. But again these conditions affect all strata of society.

Another factor influencing the voting behavior of white-collar workers is the rapid and widespread unionization and subsequent spread of egalitarian values among the white-collar group after World War II. It is hard to tell what percentage of white-collar workers are now organized, because in Japan, labor unions were organized on the basis of plant or enterprise and include both manual and white-collar workers within one organization, except in the case of metal and coal mines. White-collar workers (because of the union shop concept) automatically become members of the labor union of each plant or enterprise if one exists. Even in an enterprise where the majority of the employees are white-collar (e.g., in banks, schools, and public offices), unions were organized rapidly after World War II and maintained to the present. As a matter of fact, public servants are one of the most highly unionized groups (67.2 percent). Because of their mixed membership, because of their emergence just after World War II, when destruction and poverty made everyone equal, and because of their nature as unions, labor unions have emphasized egalitarian values and solidarity (although often in practice this means solidarity due to being employees of the same enterprise). It has been pointed out that in the British and Swedish cases, white-collar unions tend to emphasize and try to maintain the difference between their interests and those of manual workers, in terms of interests such as wages, working hours, vacations, promotions, and so forth. Politically they are often led by "liberal" rather than Socialist leaders. However, in terms of their instrumental interests —legal recognition of labor unions, the right to strike, and so on—they show solidarity with manual workers' unions.[22] What is different in Japan is that, although white-collar workers feel a difference in status and certainly want to maintain and enlarge it whenever possible, this sort of demand has no legitimacy in Japanese labor unions, with their mixed membership and their ideology which emphasizes solidarity. This is not to say that Japanese white-collar workers conform completely to this egalitarian value and ideology. As a matter of fact, they do feel that they should be treated differently from manual workers and often are discontented because their mixed-membership union is dominated by such workers and does not represent their interests well; often the white-collar workers split the union in the case of prolonged and intensified strikes. What we wish to suggest is that, where labor unions emphasize egalitarian values, chances are greater that the white-collar group will behave solidly with manual workers, at least officially, and in doing so, internalize the norm of solidarity to some degree. We also do not wish to suggest that membership in labor unions among white-collar employees guarantees their active participation to union activity. On the contrary, generally speaking, they are inactive members. There are, however, several militant unions which are composed mainly of white-collar members; also one can find active union members and leaders from the white-collar group in unions with mixed membership. In this context, we will introduce a fourth factor: resentment toward the status hierarchy among lower white-collar workers, especially those working in government bureaucracies.

In spite of post–World War II reforms, the promotion to higher positions in government bureaucracies is open only to those who graduated from particular universities (mainly ex-imperial universities). Those graduates can expect rapid promotion and various fringe benefits attached to higher positions. Those who are excluded from this privileged route of promotion naturally feel discontentment toward such a system, and the younger they are, the more they feel discontented. Moreover, before World War II, until 1918, only the imperial universities had been legally *the* universities, and even after that, there had existed two kinds of institutions of higher learning. One was the university, and another was the "higher institution for professional training," which required shorter years of study, and therefore was more accessible to those from poorer families. These two had resulted in a legitimate hierarchy of schools and their graduates. After World War II, the educational reform standardized all institutions of higher learning, giving them the same legal status as the universities. However, in practice now, differential treatment according to the particular universities concerned still strongly exists.[23] This fosters more discontent and resentment among those alienated from the privileged route than in pre–World War II days. In the Union for Taxation Stations' Personnel, the Union of Clerks in Judicial Administration, the Union of Employees of Agricultural Ministry, and among clerks in postal service and in railways within the Postal Workers' Union and National Railway Union, this sort of resentment is the basis for members' support for militant union activities and ideologies. To some extent, this resentment and discontent can be suppressed and transformed into conformity with the status hierarchy: Those who are alienated from the privileged route of promotion can expect some kind of lesser promotion by age seniority. To become active in militant union activity naturally jeopardizes one's position with respect to promotion, and many refrain from being marked as militant.

Those who are privileged (i.e., those who are graduated from first-class universities), on the other hand, are not necessarily supporters of the Liberal Democrats. Often they become politically apathetic and do not vote. But when they vote, there are more who vote for the Socialists than for the Liberal Democrats (at least in the 30–39 group). Thus we find that a fifth factor at least hinders the white-collar workers from becoming ardent supporters of the Liberal Democrats: that is the attitudes and values unfavorable to the traditionalism and anti-intellectualism of the Liberal Democrats. All opinion polls show positive correlation between occupational group and attitude toward traditionalism. The white-collar group as a whole most strongly exhibits attitudes favorable to traditional values.[24] Education has much to do with these attitudes. The more they are educated, the more these members are unfavorable to traditionalism. But this again is not peculiar to Japan. Generally speaking, higher education fosters rational and liberal thinking; Samuel Stouffer reported about United States society that, the higher the educational level of a group, the more tolerant and liberal to political deviation it would be.[25] We have seen that age can be correlated with attitudes to traditionalism. The younger generation has an attitude unfavorable to traditional values in comparison with the older generation. In Japan this tendency is stronger than in other societies. And peculiarly, in Japan these rational and liberal attitudes, which are unfavorable to traditionalism and to anti-intellectualism, are expressed as support for the leftist parties—mainly for the Socialists.[26] To express this another way: it is an expression of distrust toward the Conservatives, i.e., the Liberal Democrats. At the core of this problem is the nature of political alternatives in present-day Japan, a problem we will touch upon in the following section.

JAPAN'S "CULTURAL" POLITICS

If we dare to characterize the basis of political alternatives in present-day Japan with a single concept, we might suggest "cultural politics" or "value politics."[27] By "cultural politics" I mean politics in which the cleavages caused by differences in value systems have more effect on the nature of political conflict than the cleavages caused by economic, or status, differences.

This is not to deny the working of economic or status interests in Japanese politics, but rather to emphasize the relative dominance of cultural or value factors and the superimposition and effects of these factors on others.

As shown above, the governing conservative party—the Liberal Democratic Party—is recruiting its support mainly from older members of the middle class and younger workers influenced by this class in terms of traditional values. In addition, there are people—entrepreneurs, executives, and higher civil servants—whose vested economic or personal interests in the status quo lead them to support the Liberal Democratic Party. Economic motivations among farmers, merchants, and small manufacturers, or even among manual workers, will also result in support for the Liberal Democratic Party. Such support is understandable, for, as the governing party, the Liberal Democrats can distribute various concrete rewards such as subsidies, construction of roads and bridges, tax cuts, and other legislative measures and executive actions. The attraction of these kinds of rewards seems to be increasing.[28] Yet there also exist vast psychological resources of traditional values which the Liberal Democrats can use, especially on occasions when such issues as education, labor, and police come to the forefront as political issues.

The Socialists surely depend on organized labor as the basis for organization and financing. Ideologically the Socialist Party claims that it is a class party representative of all laboring people. It is commonly regarded as the guardian of the interests of organized labor. Certainly it supports various welfare measures in order to establish itself as the guardian of all laboring and underprivileged people. However, its cause is weakened by the Liberal Democratic Party, which admits the necessity for such welfare measures, and whose welfare policies as the governing party are incorporated into legislative statutes; thus the Liberal Democrats can boast of their achievements in this respect too. Even among organized laborers (or employees of big enterprises who are relatively favorably treated in comparison with those manual workers who are employed in medium- and small-size enterprises), support for the Socialists is not given because of intense economic discontent or belief in the expected economic effects of a Socialist regime.[29] Among the issues on which the Socialists and the Liberal Democrats have bitterly disagreed, noneconomic considerations have played an important role—e.g., the problem of revision of the 1947 Constitution, revision of various reform measures introduced after World War II, especially in the fields of education, police, and labor legislation. The Liberal Democrats have wanted to revise these in a direction more compatible with traditional values and, at the same time, in the direction of stronger, more centralized state power (particularly in the field of education). Some ultraconservative elements among the Liberal Democrats have been voicing openly more drastic revision of these measures than the leaders of the Liberal Democrats want to accept; this element among the Liberal Democrats has caused some support for the Socialists. The Socialist Party has vigorously opposed attempts to revise these reform measures, and many intellectuals have expressed strong opposition to such revision; we can say that the considerable support by white-collar workers for the Socialists is based on distrust of the Liberal Democrats concerning these matters.

Possible reasons for the importance of "cultural politics" or "value politics" are the following: (1) the existence of sharp cultural cleavages due to ethnic or religious heterogeneity in the society; (2) the rapid changes in society resulting in massive changes in values; (3) the relative economic prosperity (whereas economic discontent might motivate people to political participation); (4) the relative absence of status discontent due to rigid status demarcations.

Japan lacks the first condition, while in France and Italy, for example, the cleavage between clericalism and anticlericalism has plagued politics for a long time and to the present. The second condition is found in societies which are undergoing the rapid process of modernization and industrialization, and in such cases, poverty, misery, and resentment toward rigid status demarcations inherited from previous periods usually play their roles in politics. However, in Japan, a broad basis for rational, antitraditional values and ideologies already developed long before World War II. For instance, the development of institutions for higher education was amazing long before World War II,[30] and the labor movements have a long history going back to the early twentieth century. Yet, officially, traditional or even mystical ancient values and ideologies had dominated (combined with ultranationalism and militarism) especially after 1930. After World War II, when restrictions on antitraditionalism were removed, antitraditional values, ideas, and ideologies gained momentum, and the spokesmen for such ideas took advantage of reform measures introduced by the occupation authorities as the bulwark against the resistance and counterattack by the traditionalists. On the other hand, the traditionalists had reasons for wanting to revise post–World War II reform measures; they contended that most of these measures were imposed from outside, and did not fit the "actual situation in Japan"; traditional values still strongly remained in rural sectors and among older middle-class people in cities. Surely, they argue, it is a condition of stability to make legal institutions congruent with value patterns. Such strongly held views, based on a degree of support, contribute to the intensification of cultural politics in present-day Japan.

The status factor, as S. M. Lipset points out, has a bearing on the intensity of political conflict in society (i.e., the more rigid the status demarcation line is, the more class-conscious people become). Japan is an interesting case to study in this regard.

In all interpersonal ties, hierarchical relationship and values have been emphasized (e.g., rigorous and meticulous use of honorific words and sentences, subordination to superiors even in one's private life, and so on).

After the Meiji Restoration (1868), which abolished the feudal status, the new government created the legal status of nobility. It gave this status of nobility to ex-feudal lords, relatives and higher servants of the imperial family, and, later, to those military men, industrialists, and higher bureaucrats who had contributed to the regime, glorifying this status as the guardian group of the imperial family.

Before World War II, in formal organizations, especially in government bureaucracy, a rigid distinction between higher and lower positions was established. The basic idea was that the higher the position, the closer it was to the Emperor, and therefore the more it shared the glory of the Emperor. In private enterprises, although such a mystique was lacking, the status demarcation between administrative personnel and workers was quite rigid, and hierarchical patterns defined every relationship within the formal organization.

In the face of these strong and widespread status demarcations, nevertheless, the status system in prewar Japan had been fairly open. Whoever graduated from the imperial universities and passed the examination for higher governmental positions could expect to be promoted to high government office, almost regardless of birth status. Both in government bureaucracies and private enterprises, lower white-collar and manual workers could expect their sons to climb to higher status by giving them higher education.[31] As for the nobility, it was a newly created status without tradition and reputation comparable to European nobilities; since this status was conferred on many generals, industrialists, and politicians, it was rather an achieved-honor system than an ascribed status system.

After World War II, the nobility was legally abolished and economically badly stricken. Also, in formal organizations, strict demarcation of status considerably lessened. Although, some privileged status and promotion routes still remain, the weakening of status lines is causing resentment among white-collar workers with lower "educational careers" and impelling them toward vigorous union activity. In coal mines and other industries, authoritarian labor management remains and stimulates militant union activity such as the "work-shop struggle." However, in general, we do not attach much importance to status demarcations as stimuli to militant class politics. Certainly such hierarchical interpersonal relationships remain strong everywhere, and we can see the pattern even within universities, labor unions, and the like although weakened already and weakening more and more. The political consequences of hierarchical interpersonal relationships, which are part of traditional values, are the solidification of conservative support in the society. Thus in Japan's case, status relationships do not greatly stimulate militant class-conscious action; on the contrary, they contribute to support of the conservatives by large segments of the population.

As for the results of the emphasis on "cultural politics," the following should be mentioned: generalization of issues and intensification of conflict. Clearly, in present-day Japanese politics, the issues are connected, interpreted, and perceived as part of a wider context of values, principles, and emotions. This occurs particularly concerning issues of education, police and other internal security, and labor legislation.[32] Because of the generalized effect of cultural politics, conflicts are more intensified than they would be if factors of economic discontent and status were the only influences. On the other hand, when cultural cleavage is superimposed on intense economic discontent or status resentment, extreme political conflict, emotional and generalized, can result, and changes in total social structure can occur. At the present moment, it appears that the first case applies to present-day Japan. Many observers talk of the polarization of Japanese politics; an equal number speak of the stability of Japanese politics. One can talk about the stability of Japanese politics in several ways: for instance, the Liberal Democrats hold the majority of votes and seats, so coalition formation is not necessary; regardless of intensified conflict around various issues, there is little prospect that election results would change drastically in the short run. In these terms, we can talk about the stability of Japanese politics, and this stability may be said to coincide with cultural factors which change slowly.

PROSPECTS FOR THE FUTURE

The source of support for traditional values and also for the Liberal Democratic Party is the group of older citizens in the middle classes—small farmers and self-employed merchants and manufacturers—and also those who have low educational achievement levels. With the rapid growth of the economy, the predominance of older members in the middle classes will decrease. This trend will certainly determine traditional values and the Liberal Democratic Party. However, how rapidly will it occur? According to the estimate made in the "Income Doubling Plan" of the government, by 1970 the number of those engaged in agriculture will decrease by 30 percent, and the number of self-employed merchants and manufacturers will decrease by 10 percent, in comparison with figures for 1956–8. On the other hand, the number of employees in secondary and tertiary industries (including both manual and white-collar workers) is estimated to increase by 80 percent. When we apply this estimate to the figures shown in *Fig. 1,* assuming that all other factors remain equal, then we can estimate that the Conservatives (predominantly the Liberal Democrats) will command 26 million votes and the Leftists (the Socialists, the Democratic Socialists, and the Communists) 24 million votes. Thus, the number of votes for the opposing "camps" will become fairly equal by 1970, but the Conservatives can expect to remain in the majority.[33] Moreover, among the Leftists, it is uncertain how big a share of the 24 million votes the Socialists would get, although at present there is little sign that the Democratic Socialists would expand at the expense of the Socialists.

With changes in occupational structure, would the pattern of politics change? Again assuming all other things equal, two comments might be made: First, since the size of manual and white-collar groups will grow, and the size of the older middle class will decrease, the influence of white-collar and manual workers in the support of the Liberal Democrats would rise. This could bring about some change in a more "liberal" direction among the Liberal Democrats, because manual and white-collar workers, however traditional or conservative in comparison with those who support the Socialists, are different from the old middle classes. They have interests in common with those manual and white-collar workers who support the Socialists. Second, it is probable that the Liberal Democrats, acknowledging this change in occupational structure, would have to begin to "modernize" party structure and activity. Already the necessity for such modernization has begun to be recognized by some leaders of the Liberal Democratic Party. However, there are factors which hinder the realization of such attempts. The basis for the Liberal Democratic Party in the local communities consists predominantly of old middle-class people; as changes threaten their position, they will become more conservative, even reactionary, being hostile to the organized workers (including the white-collar group). In view of the changing occupational structure, at least some of the leaders of the Liberal Democrats would become more "liberal," but the grass-roots activist subleader has little stimulus to become "liberal"; on the contrary, he has reason to be more conservative. Thus it is doubtful that the Liberal Democrats could extensively modernize their party structure and activity.[34] The Socialists seem contented with the "natural" growth of support for their party, for the traditional and anti-intellectual aspect of the Liberal Democrats alienates white-collar workers, organized laborers, and more educated and young people. However, to increase its support beyond that "natural" tendency is particularly difficult for the Socialists, especially if the present economic prosperity continues. Since the psychological basis of support for the Socialists is largely inspired by distrust of the traditional and anti-intellectual position of the Liberal Democrats, the Socialists can gain more attention by radical rhetoric than by moderate views. Although the influence of orthodox Marxism on the ideology of the Socialists shows signs of weakening, the radical character of the ideology of the Socialists will not vanish in the near future.

Another important consideration affecting the pattern of future Japanese politics would be the possibility of change in the political allegiance of the older members of the middle classes, especially the farmers. However far the process of industrialization in Japan proceeds, it is inconceivable that the size of the portion of the middle class would drop to the percentage demonstrated in Britain or the United States. The cases of Sweden and Norway provide a pattern in which conservative and traditional forces from the old middle class formed a particular interest group which exerts influence in government. Can we expect such a pattern in Japan's case? Can we expect farmers to become concerned about their particular economic interest because of the precarious position of agricultural in an industrial society, to establish a special interest group, apart from the traditional and conservative political camp, and form some "neutral" camp? The pattern of politics would change totally and approach that of Scandinavia. Although there are some slight signs that Japanese farmers are becoming more benefit-conscious instead of tradition-bound, the probability of radical change in this direction is slight.

Needless to say, many factors are involved in any prediction of future change in the pattern of politics in Japan.[35] We have attempted only to understand more fully some of these factors.

NOTES

1. That is, this chapter is intended to be a mono-contextual study which contains some elements of multi-contextual study. I intend also to go beyond mere description of patterns and to inquire into causal factors. In this sense, this chapter is meant to be comparative.

2. Lucian W. Pye, "The Non-Western Political Process," *Journal of Politics,* 20 (August 1958), pp. 468–86. But later in his book, *Politics, Personality and Nation Building* (New Haven: Yale Univ. Press), in which that article was included as a chapter, he chose the word *transitional* instead of "non-Western." The characteristics among the seventeen which Pye enumerated which might be found in present-day Japan are "1. The political sphere is not sharply differentiated from the sphere of social and personal relations," "2. Political parties tend to take on a world view and represent a way of life," "4. The character of political loyalty gives political leaders a high degree of freedom in determining politics." "8. There are sharp differences in the political orientation of the generations." "9. Little consensus exists as to the legitimate ends and means of political action," "11. Roles are highly interchangeable," "15. The affective

or expressive aspect of politics tends to override the problem-solving or public-policy aspect."

3. In Japan, official election statistics do not give us information about the various sociological characteristics of the voters. The data used in the following analysis are mainly those of various public opinion polls.

4. We can add one more characteristic which concerns the voting rate. Usually in western European societies, the voting rate in cities is higher than in rural districts. In Japan, the voting rate is higher in rural districts than in cities. The reason for this is that in rural districts the pressure to vote is high because of the strong village solidarity and the idea that voting is regarded as an obligation to the community.

5. In Japan, this continuum would include: on the extreme Left the Japan Communist Party, then the Japan Socialist Party as Left-wing Socialists, then the Democratic Socialist Party as Right-wing Socialists; on the right, the Liberal Democratic Party appears as a coalition of various conservative factions. The extreme rightist parties are split, and their votes are negligible.

6. S. M. Lipset, *Political Man* (New York: Doubleday, 1960; Doubleday Anchor, 1963), Chap. 7.

7. Data concerning correlation between income level and party choice is usually omitted from the publications of the opinion survey data. For available published data, see Nihon Shakaigakkai Chosa-iinkai (ed.), *Nihon Shakai no Kaisoteki Kozo* (Tokyo: Yuhikaku, 1958), p. 308.

8. In this connection, it may be argued that, since the chances for higher education have expanded after World War II owing to education-reform programs, those who are in the bracket of "higher educational level" will be largely members of the younger generation; their party choice might be more influenced by the age factor than by the educational factor. However, contrary to the belief that post-World War II Japan established a tremendous member of universities and colleges at a single stroke, the fact is that higher educational institutions in Japan had developed already before and during World War II. Therefore, the age distribution of those with "higher educational level" is not necessarily so skewed to the direction of the younger generation. What expanded amazingly after World War II was middle-level education (senior-high-school system). Consequently, the age distribution of those in the bracket of medium educational level is heavily in the twenties, and we certainly can see the influence of the age factor in the party choice of this group. Age distribution and educational levels are summarized below:

	20–29	30–39	40–49	50–59	60 +
High educational level	31%	28%	22%	15%	4%
Medium educational level	44	27	17	7	5
Average	29%	24%	19%	14%	14%

Source: A nationwide sampling survey conducted by *Tokeisuri Kenkyujo* (Institute of Statistical Mathematics, Ministry of Education) (Tokyo: Shiseido, 1961), p. 471, Table 13.

9. S. M. Lipset, *op. cit.*, Chap. 8.

10. Whether this generation would retain their inclination to support the Left in their old age remains to be seen. There would be a number of "defections" as they climb the social ladder and take on more mature roles. But also it is probable that the life style of this generation would remain radically different from that of other generations. Whether the Conservatives can absorb large numbers from this generation depends on various factors, such as whether the Conservatives can "modernize" their party.

11. According to the labor statistics, in Japan the number of males employed in agriculture and forestry in 1962 was 370,000; a considerable part of this figure represents forest workers. In contrast to this, in Italy, the number of male agricultural workers in 1962 was 1,200,000 (Istituto Centrale di Statistica. *Bollettino Mensile di Statistica*, Aug. 1963). Most of these are organized under CGIL. See Joseph La Palombara, *The Italian Labor Movement: Problems and Prospects* (Ithaca: Cornell Univ. Press, 1957), p. 108. For France, see J. A. Laponce, *Government of the Fifth Republic* (Berkeley & Los Angeles: Univ. of California Press, 1961), pp. 66, 328. With regard to Sweden, see Dankwart A. Rustow, "Scandinavia: Working Multiparty Systems," in Sigmund Neu-

mann (ed.), *Modern Political Parties* (Chicago: Univ. of Chicago Press, 1956), p. 181.

12. See Tadashi Fukutake, "Social Character of the Village Community," in *Man and Society in Japan* (Tokyo: Univ. of Tokyo Press, 1962), pp. 78–101.

13. To keep peace within itself and to act as a unit are some of the important political norms of the village community. This is what Lucian Pye called the "communal basis of politics." After World War II, just before land reform, farmers' unions or farmers' leagues were rapidly organized in Japan. In order to keep peace in the villages, often all farmers in the village—including landlords and part-time farmers who engage in farming only on Sundays and holidays—preferred to join that farmers' union or farmers' league. These farmers' unions or leagues lost their strength rapidly after land reform. In local elections, the village community usually recommends the candidate for what all the villagers are expected to vote. In extreme cases where the campaign is intensified, in order to block infiltration from the candidate of other villages, watchers are posted on the roads at the entrances to the village.

14. We should not overlook the role of traditional values in this point. The lower the stratum is, the less educated and the more its members hold traditional values—subservience to the superiors, conformity to village norms, and so on. These values internally motivate people to vote for the Conservatives, even when pressures from outside are weak or nonexistent.

15. Again, a technical problem should be noted. Especially in Japan where age is one of the main factors in determining the wage, younger people are disproportionally included in the lower-income bracket. Considering this age factor, which reinforces the tendency for support of the leftists, we can assume that poor older people are strongly inclined to the Conservative view.

16. See Dankwart Rustow, *The Politics of Compromise—A Study of Parties and Cabinet Government in Sweden* (Princeton: Princeton Univ. Press, 1955), p. 141.

17. A survey conducted by sociology students of the University of Tokyo. *Sōka Gakkai-Gendai Nihon ni okeru Taishu Soshiki to Taishuundo,* (1963) mimeo.

18. S. M. Lipset, "Socialism—Left and Right—East and West," *Confluence,* 7 (2) (Summer 1958), p. 187.

19. S. M. Lipset, *Political Man, op. cit.,* Anchor ed., pp. 252–4.

20. According to the statistics, in 1960, 54.8 per cent of employees in all industries (excluding agriculture and fishing, domestic service, public service, and other service industries) are working in enterprises with less than thirty employees. Roughly speaking, over half the workers are under the strong influence of traditional values which stem from the influence of their employers and from their living environment. Therefore, the Political Organization for Medium and Small Size Enterprises (*Chushokigyo Seijirenmei*) boasts that it can represent over twelve million votes, including the votes of families of employers, those of employees and their families. But actually this organization succeeded in organizing only a fraction of this stratum.

21. See the following breakdown of occupational groups according to age (in percentages):

	20–29	30–39	40–49	50–59	60 +	
Professional and administrative	26	27	25	17	5	100 (N = 144)
Clerks	53	26	14	6	1	100 (N = 271)
Laborers	47	26	16	8	3	100 (N = 173)
Lower laborers	22	24	30	17	7	100 (N = 96)
Average	29	24	19	14	14	100 (N = 2,369)

Source: Tokeishuri Kenkyujo, *op. cit.,* p. 472.

22. David Lockwood, *The Blackcoated Worker* (London: Allen & Unwin, 1958), pp. 195–6. Walter Galenson, *Trade Union Democracy in Western Europe* (Berkeley & Los Angeles: Univ. of California Press, 1961), p. 84.

23. Individuals who graduated from evening colleges, working in some government organization or private business during the day, have quite precarious status. In most cases, they are officially not treated as graduates from the colleges. This causes discontentment among those graduates who, in general, have ability to learn and desire to climb the social ladder more than many usual university students. In 1961, nearly 90,000

students enrolled in evening colleges, about 12 percent of the total number of university students.

24. For more detailed data and discussion on this matter, see Yoshiharu Scott Matsumoto, "Contemporary Japan—The Individual and the Group," *Transactions of the American Philosophical Society*, New Series, 50, Part I, 1960.

25. Samuel A. Stouffer, *Communism, Conformity and Civil Liberties* (New York: Doubleday, 1955).

26. In this connection, we should question the prospects for the Democratic Socialist Party which is a moderate Right-wing Socialist party. Isn't it probable that this party could get the political allegiance of the white-collar workers because it is the party opposed to the Liberal Democrats, and its moderate Socialistic idea might be more congruent with the political and social attitudes of the white-collar group? As far as survey data show, there is no sign that the Democratic Socialists are succeeding in getting the political allegiance of the white-collar workers. The support for the Democratic Socialists is scattered almost evenly among various occupational, educational, and age strata. In the recent election for the House of Representatives in November 1963, the Democratic Socialists increased their seats from 17 to 23, although their share of the total votes decreased from 8.8 percent to 7.4 percent. Considering the fact that at this election, the Democratic Socialists didn't run candidates in about half of the constituencies, and at the previous election of 1960 it ran candidates in almost all constituencies, the result of the recent election can be interpreted as a victory for the Democratic Socialists, however small it was. Because no survey data on the recent election is available at the present time, I am not certain that support for the Democratic Socialists among the white-collars increased or not. In the recent election, the Socialists increased their share in the total votes from 27.6 to 29.0 percent. It would be reasonable to assume that the tendency of political allegiance among various strata did not change during 1960–63. The obstacle for the Democratic Socialists in getting strong support from the white-collar, from the educated, and from the younger generation has been the image that it is the party led by the old, both in age and behavior, an image symbolized by Mr. Nishio, the founder and the chairman of the party. This image cannot be easily changed.

27. I have borrowed this concept from Richard Hofstadter's article, "Pseudo-Conservatism Revisited: A Post-script—1962," in Daniel Bell (ed.), *Radical Right* (New York: Doubleday, 1963), p. 82. He introduces the concept as a supplement to his previous one of "status politics," in explaining the phenomenon of the rise of radical right in present-day United States society. His intention in introducing the new concept seems to be to correct the overemphasis on psychological factors due to status anxiety in the concept of "status politics."

28. Traditionally it has been said that the three essential characteristics for successful candidates were the three *ban*, i.e., *Jiban, Kaban*, and *Kanban*. *Jiban* meant solid territory, from which the candidate could expect firm support without much campaigning because of his status as a traditional notable there. *Kaban* meant a briefcase full of money for buying votes. *Kanban* was a signboard, or the ability to impress his name on the electorate. Today, instead of these three *ban*, people talk about three *ki*, i.e., *Rieki, Soshiki*, and *Ninki*. *Rieki* is benefit, *Soshiki* is organization, and *Ninki* is popularity. *Rieki* is definitely different from *Kaban*, that is different from buying the votes directly. It consists of distributing such rewards as government subsidies, construction of roads and bridges by government and local funds, and favorable legislation. These symbols are related to forms of support based on traditional ties and represent what Riesman referred to as "traditional types of apathy."

29. According to an opinion survey of organized workers under *Sōhyō* (General Council of Labor Unions, which is a leftist national federation of labor unions) and *Chūritsu-rōren* (Federation of Independent Unions, which closely cooperates with *Sōhyō*), those who believe in the possibility of improvement in their living standard under the Socialist regime number only 40 percent, while over 60 percent vote for the Socialists. On the other hand, with regard to the problem of the revision of the 1947 Constitution, 90 percent are against the revision, i.e., against the stand of the Liberal Democratic Party. This survey was quoted in an article by Hajime Shinohara and Keiichi Matsushita, "Nihon Shakaito no Shisojokyo," *Chuokoron*, December 1962.

30. It has been said often that both the number of universities and the number of

students enrolled in universities increased ten times as a result of post–World War II educational reforms. At present there are 500 universities and colleges (including junior colleges) and 760,000 students. As far as this statement concerns institutions legally recognized and formally designated as "university" or "college," it is correct. However, if we take into account various forms of higher-learning institutions which had existed before World War II and were reorganized as "universities" or departments of a "university" after World War II, the statement is misleading. For instance, in 1930, we had 230,000 students enrolled in 413 higher-learning institutions, as shown below.

	Number of institutions	*Number of students*
Universities	46	69,605
High schools*a*	32	20,551
Higher specialized training schools*b*	162	90,043
Various teachers' schools*c*	173	49,119
Total	413	229,318

Source: Gakusei Hachiju Nenshi (Tokyo: Ministry of Education, 1954), pp. 1058–74, Tables 9–15.

a These were higher preparatory schools for later specialized studies in universities. Their character had much in common with liberal arts colleges in the United States.

b These were four-year schools, for which eleven years of previous education was required for entrance.

c During World War II the status of these teachers' schools was raised to the same status with that of higher specialized training schools, and after World War II, these were reorganized as teachers' colleges.

31. The Japanese word used in such a context is *gakureki*, which means one's "educational career." It means not merely the level of education, but the particular school from which one graduated. It includes not only the quality of education at that school, but also the personal relationships among graduates from the same school.

32. Some would prefer to explain this generalization of issues in terms of the prevalence of ideologies. For instance, in an article on present-day Japanese politics, Herbert Passin has put it as follows: "As in any country where politics is so ideological, compromise is difficult, and all issues tend to take on a total character. . . . No issue stands alone, to be dealt with piecemeal and *ad hoc,* but as part of a matrix of issues, inter-dependent and naturally reinforcing. . . . This quality of all-out, uncompromising struggle is the most disturbing feature of the political climate of Japan today." (Herbert Passin, "The Sources of Protest in Japan," *American Political Science Review,* Vol. LVI, No. 2, June 1962, p. 393.) I prefer the concept of "cultural politics" to "ideological politics." Certainly cultural cleavage and ideological conflict reinforce each other, but it seems to me that cultural cleavage is the cause and ideological conflict is the effect. Moreover, although the leftists have a superabundance of ideologies strongly influenced by Marxist ideas, the Liberal Democrats seem to be plagued by a lack of coherent ideology. Especially in the lower levels of the party, local subleaders and activists lack ideology, yet they "feel" deep distrust and even hatred toward what seems to be a destroyer of traditional values. They interpret Socialist opposition in terms of their traditional value frame, and they generalize the issues.

33. In the recent election of November 1963, little changes has occurred in seats and share of votes among political parties. The Liberal Democrats gained 283 seats and 22.5 million votes (54.7 percent of the total votes), compared with 296 seats and 23 million votes at the previous election in 1960. On the other hand, the Socialists gained 144 seats and 12 million votes (29.0 percent of the total votes), compared with 145 seats and 11 million votes in 1960. Although the vote for the Socialists increased by 1 million, considering the increase of votes for Conservative independent candidates (2 million in comparison with 1 millon in 1960 election), the total share of votes— Conservatives versus Leftists—showed amazingly little change, in spite of the continuous change in occupational structure. Under the multiple-member-constituency system, election results depend on various factors—the quality of candidates, techniques of campaigning, and so on. A few factors relevant in the context of this paper may be men-

tioned: First, the voting rate at this election was barely 70 percent compared with 73.5 percent in the previous election. This 3.5 percent drop in voting rate means an approximate increase of 2 million nonvoters, and according to survey data on the voting rate, these 2 million votes include younger, educated, urban voters who might have been inclined to vote for the Socialists. Second, the issues at this election were mainly economic —the opposition parties saw the rising prices of everyday commodities as a sign of failure of the governing party's economic policy. In comparison with the previous election, which was held after the turmoil over the Japan and United States Security Treaty, and the assassination of the Secretary-General of the Socialist Party by an ultra-Rightist youth. The climate of politics at this election of 1963 was less tense. The so-called "low posture" of the governing Ikeda Cabinet of the Liberal Democrats during the two-and-a-half years certainly contributed to the decrease in political stimuli which otherwise might have incited a feeling of distrust of the Liberal Democrats and mobilized support for the Socialists.

34. I have omitted discussion of structures of political parties in Japan, since they have been discussed in detail by Robert A. Scalapino and Junnosuke Masumi, *Parties and Politics in Contemporary Japan* (Berkeley & Los Angeles: Univ. of California Press, 1962).

35. For instance, one major factor that I have not discussed is the population structure. The drop in birth rate and the extension of life expectancy will cause the ratio of older people to rise amazingly, especially after 1970. How will the political allegiance of older people change? Will they cling to traditional values; become discontented because of alienation or poverty; or be contented with social welfare measures? Such changes will affect the relative strength of the Conservatives and the Socialists, and also patterns of politics as a whole. The most influential and unpredictable factor is an external one—the nature of the international situation. Generally speaking, a tense international situation can result in consensus formation or a lessening of internal conflict, or it can intensify existing internal political conflict. In Japan's case at present, the problems of foreign policy contribute to the intensification of political conflict (or, I should say, they are utilized as a tool and expression of cultural politics).

Ten

The Politics of Uneven Development:
The Case of Brazil*

Glaucio Ary Dillon Soares

INTRODUCTION

The empirically oriented sociologist writing a paper on any aspect of Brazilian society is faced with two difficult problems: the lack of reliable survey data and the deficiencies of census materials. Empirical social science in Brazil is very recent and scarcely institutionalized, and adequate field political surveys using modern techniques probably do not total more than a dozen. On the other hand, census-type data have severe limitations, for the censuses before 1940 are not to be relied upon; the same is true for electoral statistics before 1945. Therefore, quantitative historical analysis is severely hampered, and this chapter will necessarily be limited to the postwar period.

The central aim of this chapter is to relate regional differences in Brazilian politics with underlying socioeconomic differences. It is hoped that the conceptual development of this basic hypothesis, plus the accumulation of both unsystematic descriptive data and organized statistical data will indicate the usefulness of the model. It is further hoped that this internally differentiated political model, based on varying socioeconomic structures, is applicable to other Latin American countries undergoing rapid and uneven socioeconomic change.

The Brazilian Party System

Some basic information on present Brazilian political parties and electoral laws may be useful at this point. In 1945, after the fall of the Vargas regime, political parties were allowed to compete freely for the first time in many

* The author would like to acknowledge the secretarial assistance received from the Department of Sociology and Anthropology, Washington University at St. Louis and from the Institute of International Studies, University of California at Berkeley.

years. Several parties presented candidates in the 1945 elections, and since then few basic changes have been introduced. The Brazilian Communist Party (*Partido Comunista Brasileiro,* PCB) was outlawed in 1947, other parties disappeared, some combined to form a new party, and entirely new ones were created. Recent news indicates that in the 1962 elections there were thirteen parties competing for power.

Brazil has adopted proportional representation for the Congress and for State and Municipal legislatures. The first is called the *Congresso* or *Câmara Federal;* the second are the *Assembléias Legislativas Estaduais,* one for each state; and the last are called *Câmaras Municipais,* one for each *município*—the political-administrative subdivisions of every state—except Guanabara.

The number of representatives elected in each state for the federal Congress is determined by its population, but the larger the population, the smaller the ratio of representatives to population. Thus, the most populated states are underrepresented and the least populated ones, overrepresented.

The Brazilian electoral system departs from the American single-member-district system due to the fact that each *município* does not have "its" representative. Congressmen are elected by the state as a whole. Each state has an electoral quotient (*quociente electoral*—number of registered voters in the state divided by the number of state representatives). For instance, Sergipe in 1958 had 123,737 voters and seven representatives—therefore an electoral quotient of 17,364 (123,737/7). The Brazilian Labor Party (*Partido Trabalhista Brasileiro,* PTB) received only 13,203 votes, and thus did not elect a single representative. However, the National Democratic Union (*União Democrática Nacional,* UDN) and the Social Labor Party (*Partido Social Trabalhista,* PST) formed an electoral alliance and received 58,434 votes. The alliance was then granted three representatives. But the votes of the parties that elected no representatives and the other parties' remainders accumulated to form a larger, overall state remainder. This is usually equivalent to the electoral quotient for one or two, or even more, representatives. The procedure is to assign the first one to the party with the largest remainder, considering *only* those parties that elected at least one representative.

On the other hand, each state has three representatives in the Senate and the president is elected by direct popular vote. However, the most important feature of the system is that illiterates cannot legally vote in Brazil.

The Model

Since the mode of analysis employed here will be to correlate socioeconomic variables with political ones, one approach would be to develop censal measures of socioeconomic variables, on the one hand, and political ones, on the other, and correlate these, using the states or even the *municípios* as units. It would be then implicitly assumed that these variables are continuous by nature, for at least theoretically there could be a state (or a *município*) at any point between the two extreme values of the above continuous variables. For the sake of precision the *município* should be taken as the unit of analysis, due to the fact that there is a great deal of internal differentiation *within* each state.

However, instead of employing that approach, geographically contiguous, underdeveloped states will be considered as a group and contrasted to another group of more developed states. Obviously a great deal of information will be lost. Not only the interstate variance within each of these groupings, but also the intermunicipal variance within each state will not be considered. The basic reasons for this approach are the following:

1. The central purpose of this paper is to present a *comprehensive* description of the impact of uneven development upon Brazilian politics, *not* to give a precise evaluation of the extent of this impact. It is believed that this can best be done by comparing political data in two areas highly differentiated in socioeconomic terms.

2. Moreover, geographical continuity is necessary for developing the idea of political culture and for stressing its dependence on socioeconomic factors.

3. The electoral data which seem most relevant to the hypothesis are given by state. This eliminates the possibility of using the *município* as a unit.

Although acknowledging the limitations inherent in this model and the value of the information lost, this model is deemed more appropriate to the purpose at hand. Therefore, it will suffice to present data in such a way as to emphasize the great distance between the two areas, in terms of both economic and social development. The reader will immediately become aware of the immense unevenness of Brazilian economic development, the extent of which is probably unparalleled in already industrialized countries. After this introductory presentation, attention will be shifted to political differences and, in succeeding sections, it will be suggested that these socioeconomic variations not only engendered differences in specific political variables but have really produced two entirely different political cultures. A brief description of these two political cultures will then be given.

As stated above, the extent of these differences is seldom, if ever, found within stable, industrialized nations. Furthermore, even *among* industrialized nations such differences are of a smaller magnitude. Nominal income per capita has a tremendous range among Brazilian states. 1955 estimates give Piauí 2,319.00 cruzeiros and Guanabara (then Distrito Federal) 28,995.00 cruzeiros per capita, more than twelve times higher than Piauí's. Among industrialized nations there is less than half as much variation. These variations are worth taking into consideration as a warning to those who treat Latin American countries as if they were homogeneous units.

The two areas to be considered are distinct geoeconomic regions and will be labeled *Northeast* and *Southeast*. They include 75 percent of the Brazilian population. The former will include the following states: Maranhão, Piauí, Ceará, Rio Grande do Norte, Paraíba, Pernambuco, Alagôas, Sergipe, and Bahia; whereas the latter compromises Rio de Janeiro, Guanabara, São Paulo, Paraná, Santa Catarina, and Rio Grande do Sul. Other states, representing only 25 percent of the population, will be left out due to intervening variables that would create serious problems of classification.

SOCIOECONOMIC DIFFERENTIALS

As indicated above, the socioeconomic differences between the two areas are impressive. Furthermore, with respect to most standard measures of social and economic development, the states composing the two areas do not overlap.[1] On the other hand, differences between regional *averages* do not tell the full extent of inequality and unevenness, for even *within* regions there is considerable variation. Therefore, considering the two areas together, socioeconomic differences between more advanced and lesser states can outrun differences between regional averages by many times. In 1955, the then Distrito Federal (presently State of Guanabara), with less than 3 million inhabitants, had about the same gross product as the entire Northeast, but only about one-sixth of its population. But differences are not only economic in character: in 1950, 84 percent of the population ten years and older was literate in the Distrito Federal; in Alagôas this figure was less than 24 percent; urbanization rates range from 97 percent in the Distrito Federal to 5 percent in Maranhão, in accordance with the census criterion; differences in average length of life exceeded ten years between the top and bottom states. Therefore, as specified before, any description of socioeconomic differences based on regional averages is necessarily inaccurate and loses a great deal of significance.

Another point to be made here is that many of these differences, being large enough as they are, have not decreased substantially since 1947.[2] Recently a strong effort has been made to cope with these problems by creating an institution with adequate financial support whose main function is to accelerate economic development in the Northeast, the SUDENE. Nevertheless, it is unlikely that actual differences in the *level* of development will be eliminated, or even very substantially reduced, within the next one or two decades.[3]

Urbanization and Industrialization

The first set of differences refers to what has been called the urban-industrial syndrome. However, the unqualified use of the word *syndrome* may be misleading in the sense that it overemphasizes the consistency among the several dimensions involved. The author has suggested in another article that the very incongruency between urbanization and industrialization is extremely helpful in explaining *both* radical leftism and extreme conservatism. When industrialization does not keep pace with urbanization, there is a mass of unemployed and underemployed with aspirations heightened by urban living and with no possibility of satisfying these aspirations even to a minimal degree, then leftist radicalism finds fertile soil.[4] In spite of the chronic shortage of urban industrial labor openings in the large Northeastern cities, miserable rural living conditions and periodic intense droughts force these men to migrate.

In accord with the census criterion, about 3,720,000 of the 17,970,000 Northeastern inhabitants were urban dwellers in 1950. On the other hand not fewer than approximately 9,680,000 of the 21,670,000 Southeasterners lived in urban areas. In terms of percentages, this indicates an urban population of 20.7 percent in the Northeast and of 44.7 percent in the Southeast —more than twice the Northeastern figure. Data for industrialization indicate similar patterns: *Table 1* shows that the percentage of the labor force in the primary sector (agriculture, and so forth) is 77 percent for the Northeast and only 48 percent for the Southeast, thus showing the dependency of the

Northeastern population on agriculture. On the other hand, those employed in manufacturing represent only 6.9 percent of the Northeastern labor force, but no less than 19.7 percent of the Southeastern labor force.

Table 1—Regional Differences in Urbanization and Industrialization, 1950 (in thousands)

	(a)	(b)	(b/a)	(c)	(d)	(d/c)	(e)	(e/c)
Northeast	17,973	3,719	20.7%	4,843	3,730	77.0%	332	6.9%
Southeast	21,671	9,679	44.7%	6,319	3,031	48.0%	1,245	19.7%

Source: *Anuário Estatístico do Brasil* (Rio de Janeiro: IGBE, 1956)
a, total population; b, urban population; c, labor force, 10 years and over (not included: unclassified, housewives, and students); d, labor force in forestry, agriculture, and farming; and e, labor force in manufacturing.

Following Marxian lines of thought, this reveals that relatively *more* of those leaving agricultural activities in the Southeast go into secondary activities and that this should be taken as an effective indicator of a meaningful difference in the degree of industrialization. In this sense, the Southeast is *becoming* an industrial society, whereas the Northeast remains pretty much a rural, agricultural, nonindustrial society. Nevertheless, it is necessary to keep in mind that these indicators are not fully consistent, allowing for a certain incongruency. Most data for economic development, mainly income per capita (which, incidentally, was Cr$4,511.00 in the Northeast and Cr$18,382.00 in the Southeast, for 1955), tend to ignore the incongruency, thereby artificially emphasizing the degree of consistency. Given this picture, the Northeast is behind in all aspects of the development syndrome. The next task is to see if there are concomitant variations in other, less economic aspects of development.

Education and Land Distribution

One variable of great importance for political analysis is education, for it has been found to correlate (negatively) with authoritarian traits,[5] with political preferences,[6] and the like. In other articles the author has attempted to demonstrate the usefulness of education as an indicator of social development.[7] However, what is important here is that education is related to ideology, interest, and participation.[8]

On the other hand, it has been found in *industrialized* societies that the less educated tend to adopt radical ideologies more often than the more educated. However, when one jumps from the personal level to larger units of analysis, seemingly contradictory facts may appear, such as the lack of leftist radicalism in the less educated areas. Two explanations may be anticipated here: on the one hand, it is clear that *both* education and political radicalism correlate with other variables such as industrialization and urbanization and, when the latter are held constant, the relationship between the two former may weaken, disappear, or even reverse. On the other hand, extremely low education—widespread illiteracy—may favor the permanence of a traditional culture, inhibit the development of an effective system of mass communication, and contribute to maintain a low degree of social change. Ideological leftist radicalization is therefore inhibited. Leftist ideologies not only face the obstacle of an aggressive traditional culture but are also further inhibited by inefficient communication and very low participation. The educational differences should thus prove to be significantly different between the two areas.

Table 2—Regional Differences in Education, 1950

	(a)	(b)	(b/a)	(c)	(c/a)	Literacy Range
Northeast	12,393	3,721	30.0%	18,585	0.15%	23.65%–33.63%
Southeast	15,669	10,269	65.5%	116,439	0.74%	52.47%–84.48%

Source: As above.
a, total population, 10 years and over (in thousands); b, literates, 10 years and over (in thousands); c, college graduates.

Table 2 clearly shows the educational gap between the Northeast and the Southeast. Whereas only 30 percent of the Northeastern population ten years and older are literate, those who can read and write account for 65.5 percent of the equivalent Southeastern population. The low range of variation in the Northeast shows that this is a widespread and quite uniform phenomenon. When considering college graduates, differences are also impressive: less than two out of a thousand have a college degree in the Northeast, a very low rate as compared with the Southeast, where more than seven do so. When it is considered that the urban areas are included in the overall Northeastern figures and that there is a tremendous urban-rural educational differential, then it immediately follows that the Northeastern rural population is almost entirely illiterate.

Low educational rates have always been incongruent with Brazil's stand on other development-associated indicators, and to a certain extent they constitute an obstacle to other aspects of economic development.[9]

Table 3—Regional Differences in Land Distribution, 1950
(areas in 1,000 ha.)

	(a)	(b)	(b/a)	(c)	(c/a)	(d)	(d/a)
Northeast	58,341	11,675	20.0%	23,019	39.5%	6,123	10.5%
Southeast	57,647	16,525	28.7%	20,311	35.2%	3,199	5.5%

Source: Mayer et al., Reforma Agrária, Questão de Consciência (3rd ed.; São Paulo: Editôra Vera Cruz, 1961), Anex II.
a, total area privately owned; b, area of holdings with less than 100 ha.; c, area of holdings with more than 1,000 ha.; d, area of holdings with more than 10,000 ha.

Another aspect of relevance for analysis of political behavior is the pattern of land ownership. It is hypothesized here that the latifundia are both cause and consequence of traditionalism, both general and political. Nevertheless, if traditionalism declines before the land ownership system is changed, then the heightening of the level of aspirations, in sharp contrast to the low standards of living, will probably result in the emergence of violence, for the soporific effects of traditionalism will no longer be present. Looking at *Table 3*, it is evident that the two areas are approximately equal in size of privately owned properties. But there are meaningful differences in the proportion occupied by small and large properties: whereas the smaller properties (less than 100 ha.) represents 20 percent of the total in the Northeast, they account for 28.7 percent of the total in the Southeast. On the other hand, the latifundia are more meaningful in the Northeast than in the Southeast, particularly the very large ones, with 10,000 ha. or more. This is even more important when one takes into consideration that the fertile land is much more scarce in the Northeast and that the latifundia usually hold the best land. It is interesting to note that the proportion of medium large properties (1,000 to 10,000 ha.) is slightly *higher* in the Southeast. This is probably due to production of coffee, but, whereas coffee farm workers are well paid, the peasants working in the Northeastern latifundia have one of the lowest standards of living on earth.

Even though it is fairly obvious that both areas are characterized by extreme inequality in ownership of land, differences between them are meaningful. Furthermore, these differences acquire new meaning when it is known that in the Northeast there are approximately 14 million persons living in rural areas, 2 million more than in the Southeast. Furthermore, there are 3,700,000 members of the labor force engaged in agriculture and related affairs in the Northeast, against 3 million in the Southeast. Therefore, not only is land inequality more accentuated in the Northeast, but this also acquires further significance when one considers that the region is heavily dependent on agriculture and farming, and when one considers that, compared to the Southeast, the rural population of the Northeast is larger and that there are more members engaged in agriculture and related activities.

However, this is even more impressive when it is known that the *percentage* of land in use is considerably lower in the Northeast. Not including Bahai and Sergipe, the Northeast has only 38 percent of the total privately owned land in agriculture or pasturage, whereas in the Southeast (excluding Rio de Janeiro and Guanabara) this percentage is 66 percent. No less than 52 percent of the land in the former group of states is either unused (28 percent) or covered with forests (24 percent), whereas in the Southeastern region this percentage is only 29 percent (13 percent unused and 16 percent dedicated to forests).[10] For the purposes of this chapter, however, the most important finding is that the latifundia present a much higher percentage of unused land than the smaller properties.[11] Correlational analysis of ecological data shows that inequality in land distribution correlates *negatively* with indicators of *both* social and economic development and *positively* with illiteracy.[12] Factor analysis of the same data suggests that there is a general factor of economic development that is clearly bipolar. The various indicators of inequality in land distribution, *together with illiteracy,* have a heavy *negative* loading on this factor.

Following the foregoing line of thought, it is legitimate to hypothesize that inequality in land distribution is detrimental to economic development. However, it may be counter-argued that differences in industrial development are perhaps more important and that rural-agricultural poverty is only a specific aspect of general underdevelopment, which is to be explained in terms of lack of industrialization. *Table 4* shows that differences in agricultural income are *greater* than differences in industrial income, both on a per-capita and per-hectare basis. Furthermore, although the agricultural product is an important source of gross income *both* in the Northeast and in the Southeast, it obviously is much more important in the former.[13] In other words, agriculture is more important for the Northeastern economy than industry, as compared with the Southeast. Differences in per-capita income are also more pronounced in agriculture than in industry between the two regions. Simply stated, the Northeast is the least productive as compared with the

Table 4—Regional Differences in Income, 1955
(in cruzeiros)

	General[a]	Per Capita Industrial[b]	Per Capita Agricultural[c]	Per Hectare Agricultural[d]
Northeast	4,511.00	30,111.00	8,989.00	575.00
Southeast	18,382.00	67,261.00	40,004.00	2,103.00

Source: as above, pp. 45, 291.

a, gross product/total population; b, industrial product/labor force in manufacturing; c, agricultural product/labor force in agriculture and related activities (primary sector); d, agricultural product/total area of privately owned properties. Population data for 1950.

Southeast, exactly in the sector that is most important to its economy. Given these data, what can be hypothesized in terms of economic sociology about their impact upon social organization?

Backwardness and Social Organization

It has been hypothesized that one feature of extreme backwardness is its impact on social organization, including organization of an adequate system of communication.[14] This probably reveals itself not only in the lack of formal organization, but of informal organization as well. It is clear that in a predominantly agricultural society, with lack of capital and other severe problems that characterize the Northeast, cooperation would be the most elementary step to cope with these problems. Voluntary agricultural cooperative are entitled to many legal privileges in Brazil and are the logical solution for many poor farmers in facing their common problems. It would be legitimate to expect farmers and landowners to join in business-type organizations and peasants to associate with agricultural trade unions that would protect their interests. However, this does not occur.

Apparently, family rivalries, an elitist conception of life, and high ethnocentrism have prevented landowners from organizing themselves to cope with common problems. In 1955 there were 1,170 registered cooperatives in the Northeast and 1,949 in the Southeast. This gives a ratio of 35 cooperatives per 100,000 members of the agricultural labor force in the Northeast, as against 64 in the Southeast. But the above data do not reveal the full extent of the real differences, for Southeastern cooperatives are oftentimes very large and the Northeastern ones more often than not are small ones. Thus differences in membership/population ratios are likely to be even more significant. On the other hand, it is clear that if the tremendous problems referred to are not enough to stimulate cooperation, factors in addition to those mentioned are probably involved. The two most important appear to be:

1. The *latifundista* is oftentimes an absentee and his lands, being extensive, allow for a comfortable urban living for him and his family, in spite of low productivity per hectare.
2. The *latifundista* is not an entrepreneur. Property is taken for granted; land is a source of prestige and a comfortable income. Expanding business, for purposes other than prestige and ownership satisfaction, and improving productivity are *not* his concern.

On the other hand, extreme backwardness, extreme poverty caused at least partially by inequality in land distribution, and widespread illiteracy, which is associated with the previous factors, have inhibited the peasants from organizing around their own interests. And, as it will be pointed out later on, the *latifundistas'* paternalistic attitudes toward the peasant have contributed to create a sentimental bond of loyalty of peasant to landholder. In these conditions, the peasant cannot visualize his interests as different from the landowner's, and even less can be perceive his interests as *opposed* to those of the landowner.

Widespread illiteracy is probably a very important variable in explaining the lack of class organization. Several studies show that both formal and informal participation is strongly associated with status—educational, occupational or other. However, Northeastern illiteracy rates cannot be properly understood outside the context in which they occur. Land inequality implies income inequality, which in turn suggests the existence of a large population with very low incomes. When this is at the subsistence level, children's work is needed and education becomes an unaffordable luxury. This helps to establish a vicious circle: the prevailing structures maintain widespread illiteracy; conservative politics help to preserve these structures; illiteracy favors apathy, religion, and traditional values, which in turn immunize and sterilize the peasants against class organization and the germ of ideological rebellion.

Lack of cooperation and of class organization are taken here only as illustrations of a general lack of social organization. For purposes of political analysis, the important point is that the factors mentioned inhibit class organization—to be further discussed later on.

Socioeconomic Differentials: Conclusion

In this section a picture of the tremendous unevenness between two large Brazilian regions was presented. These areas represent more than 75 percent of the Brazilian population. The remaining states have not been included due to classificatory problems and for the sake of comprehensiveness and geographical continuity.

Differences in the degree of urbanization and industrialization, using population statistics, have been shown. In addition, it has been suggested that these differences are linked to differences in educational level and in inequality of land distribution, which in turn add to existing differences in overall economic development. The significance of education for the analysis of political behavior has been touched on and the meaning of land inequality in a predominantly rural society has been emphasized.

In all respects, the Northeast appears as an extremely backward region. Little urbanized and even less industrialized, the Northeast is still predominantly rural and land production represents a sizable proportion of the total regional income. In a brief analysis, it was suggested that the land is unevenly distributed and that this relates to the proportion of unused or poorly used land.

The pattern of land distribution implies a sharp stratification, resembling a Marxian two-class system. Current sociological theory has suggested that this pattern provides fertile ground for class conflict in the absence of intervening, inhibiting variables. It is postulated that tradition is one such variable preventing the emergence of class conflict in an otherwise conducive situation. Traditional values, widespread illiteracy, and low communication facilities prevent the peasants from contacting ideologies of conflict. In a general sense, extreme backwardness, illiteracy, land inequality, religious dogma, traditionalism and political conservatism interact to inhibit social organization in general and class organization in particular. This is reflected in the political system, as will be emphasized in the further sections of this article.

POLITICAL DIFFERENTIALS

In this section there will be an attempt to demonstrate how socioeconomic differentials have contributed to differentiate the two areas politically. The measurable differences refer to party strength, alliances, electoral participation and, to a lesser degree, electoral dispersion.

Again, it will be seen that it is not by chance that these differences occur together, but are rather closely linked to other aspects of social structure and cannot be understood separately. The analysis will begin with differential party strength.

Party Strength

On the basis of previous suggestions with regard to socioeconomic differentials and their links to the political system, it would be expected that Northeastern politics are dominated by conservative parties. Qualitative inspection suggests that two of the four main parties, the Social Democratic Party (*Partido Social Democrático,* PSD) and the National Democratic Union (*União Democrática Nacional,* UDN) are conservative and rural-based, although the UDN has been trying to attract the urban middle classes with some degree of success. The Brazilian Labor Party (*Partido Trabalhista Brasileiro,* PTB) is essentially labor-oriented and the Social Progressist Party (*Partido Social Progressista,* PSP) in many areas is also working-class oriented, although ideologically less well-defined than the PTB. It is contended here that these parties do not have equal acceptance in developed and underdeveloped regions and, furthermore, that they do not perform the same function in each region.

Another notable feature of the Brazilian party system is lack of party loyalty and of adherence to party programs. Indeed party programs are generally thought of as being of little relevance and no special attention will be paid to them. Outstanding exceptions may be the Brazilian Communist Party (*Partido Communista Brasileiro,* PCB, outlawed in 1947), the far-Right Popular Representation Party (*Partido de Representacão Popular,* PRP), the Brazilian Socialist Party (*Partido Socialista Brasileiro,* PSB), and the PTB, but again this varies regionally. It is postulated that in the backward areas there exists widespread nonideological, instrumental use of political parties. The politics of these areas may be characterized by traditionalism, with the prolonged rule of dominant families, usually of landlords and small-town economic elites. Although highly symptomatic changes have recently been observed, during the period analyzed the models seems to apply. On the other hand, the politics of the developing areas may be characterized by class cleavage and the increasing role of ideology in determining political behavior. To a certain extent this model approaches the one commonly used to describe politics in industrialized areas.[15] Data will be presented in support of these hypotheses.

On the basis of previous suggestions regarding socioeconomic differentials and their linkage with the political system, it is to be expected that Northeastern politics are dominated by conservative parties. This is clearly the case, but with two qualifications:

1. The pattern is not completely static, i.e., it allows a certain amount of change and evidence of this change will be presented.

2. The pattern does not apply to the larger cities. These, living under chronic unemployment and underemployment are indeed the most radical spots in the country. The last qualification will be dealt with more extensively later on.

Looking at *Table 5* it becomes clear that the conservative parties have a

Table 5—Regional Differences in Congressional Seats Distribution, 1954 (in percentages)

	PSD	UDN	PTB	PSP	Small Parties	Total
Northeast	39.8	28.8	9.3	9.3	12.7	99.9 (118)
Southeast	26.2	19.0	26.2	11.1	17.5	100.0 (126)

Source: Tribunal Superior Eleitoral *Dados Estatísticos*, 3° vol., la parte (Rio de Janeiro, no date), p. 99. In this and other tables percentages do not total 100% due to rounding.

much stronger position in the Northeast, where they account for almost 70 percent of all representatives elected for the Congress, whereas in the southeast they account for only 45 percent.

There was a change between the 1945–7 and the 1950 elections, when the conservative parties lost many seats throughout the country, mainly in the Southeast. However, changes have been moderate since then.

The preferential appeal of the PTB for the Southeastern voter is perfectly clear and supports the previous discussion, fitting the stated hypothesis: while retaining 26.2 percent of all seats in the Southwest, it received only 9.3 percent in the Northeast. The PSP, which was said to be also labor-oriented, but less defined ideologically, seems to appeal slightly more to the developed areas. This last difference is not statistically significant, but it has been confirmed repeatedly in other elections.

Another difference of the same kind is found when data are analyzed for the state legislatures in 1950:

Table 6—Regional Differences in the Distribution of Seats in State Legislature, 1950

	PSD	UDN	PTB	PSP	Small Parties	Total
Northeast	32.7	30.9	6.3	7.4	22.7	100.1 (379)
Southeast	26.7	18.6	25.2	10.4	19.2	100.1 (318)

Source: As above, 2° vol., p. 46.

The two conservative parties, PSD and UDN, held more than 63 percent of all seats in the Northeast and a little over 45 percent in the Southeast. Thus the pattern seems clear: a respectable majority given to these parties taken together in the Northeast and a little less than a majority in the Southeast. This is not a phenomenon peculiar to any specific electoral level (federal, state, and so on), nor was it a peculiarity of a given electoral year. It repeats itself every electoral year at all levels.

The PTB, on the other hand, had relatively four times as many seats, in the Southeast as in the Northeast, a striking difference. The PSP confirmed the finding presented above: a milder tendency toward larger representation in the Southeast. The only important modifications refer to small parties, now with a slightly larger representation in the Northeast. This will be discussed later.

Thus by and large, the picture remains the same: a large concentration of seats in the hands of the two largest conservative parties, this concentration being more pronounced in the Northeast; a labor preference for the Southeast, this preference being more pronounced for the main labor party, the PTB.

Table 7—Regional Differences in the Distribution of Congressional Seats, 1962 (in percentages)

	PSD	UDN	PTB	PSP	Small Parties	Total
Northeast	32.4	29.4	25.7	2.9	9.6	100.0 (136)
Southeast	20.7	16.6	30.2	7.1	25.4	100.0 (169)

Source: Anuário Estatístico do Brasil, 1963 (Rio de Janeiro: IBGE, 1963).

Data for the 1962 congressional elections reveal pretty much the same picture: the PSD and the UDN drew a much larger support in the Northeast than in the Southeast. The PTB, PSP, and the small parties, on the contrary, received larger support in the Southeast. However, the 1954–62 period did witness some changes. First of all, the PSD lost considerable support in both areas, whereas the PTB made significant advances. These advances were most impressive in the Northeast, where the PTB jumped from 9.3 percent in 1954 to 25.7 percent in 1962. These gains seem to have been obtained mainly at the expense of the PSD and the PSP. The UDN kept its position in the Northeast, but lost considerable strength in the Southeast. This loss may have favored the Christian Democrats, who jumped from two to seventeen congressmen in the Southeast—a nine percentage point increase, from 1.6 to 10.6 percent.

The 1962 data confirms the previous findings: the Northeast is still dominated by the traditional conservative parties, by comparison with the Southeast. The PSD and the UDN alone account for no less than 61.8 percent of the Northeastern congressional seats, as opposed to only 37.3 percent in the Southeast. The PTB continued to draw more support in the Southeast but did make substantial gains in the Northeast. Part of this gain probably stems from the deterioration of the PSP in the Northeast: although the PSP disintegrated in both regions, the process was stronger in the latter. If the disintegration continues, the PTB is expected to make further gains at the expense of the PSP, specially in the Southeast, for the Northeastern PSP has little more to lose.

In spite of the confirmation of the previous *structural* differences between the Northeast and the Southeast, the winds of change seem to have touched the Northeast. However, this process of change seems to be concentrated in two of the most developed Northeastern states: Pernambuco and Bahia. The PTB increased its representation in these two states from seven to twenty-one congressmen, a 24-percentage-point jump, from 14.3 to 38.2 percent. Thus, structural differences in the degree of economic development seem to provide a partial explanation for the modernization of the political process whose beginnings were observed in 1962.

Any interpretation of these findings has to take into consideration the class structure in the two areas. The Southeast has a sizable industrial working class which gives a sure support to labor-oriented parties, mainly the PTB. In the Northeast, the working class is much smaller and concentrated in the state capitals and a few other large cities. Therefore, in terms of the total vote, the conservative parties dominate, for they receive urban support from the middle and upper classes and complete support in the upper-class-dominated rural areas, even though they often lose in municipal elections in large cities.

Regional Differences in Party Alliances and Coalitions

Party alliances and coalitions are another aspect of differential politics in the two analytical areas under consideration. Indeed they have an important meaning for developing the concept of differential political cultures. In a previous paper, the author tried to develop two theories to cope with the problem of explaining why parties engage in electoral coalitions. For the sake of identification, these theories will be called (1) economic and (2) cultural-ideological.[16] They aim to present a comprehensive view of some factors which increase the likelihood that party alliances and coalitions will occur. What is important to notice is that a set of testable hypotheses was derived therefrom and tested with the available data; the results gave strong support to the theories—theories which, incidentally, are not mutually exclusive.

The first theory was conceived after a hint given by a careful reading of Duverger's classical *Political Parties* and MacRae's article on the differential behavior of representatives elected in "close" and "safe" elections.[17] The general principle may be simply stated as follows:

> It is always preferable to be elected without coalitions (subsidiary goal), but when being elected (primary goal) itself is endangered then it is advisable to enter into an alliance with another party, for this will increase the likelihood of being elected.

A few testable hypotheses may be derived from the theory:

1. Smaller parties should elect relatively more representatives than should larger, via alliances and coalitions.

2. In majority elections (where, other things being equal, the probability of being elected is smaller than in proportional elections), there should be a higher percentage elected by alliances and coalitions than in proportional ones.

3. In federal elections, there should be a higher percentage elected by alliances and coalitions, as compared with state elections, for there are almost three times more seats in any state legislature than there are representatives of that state in the Congress.

These hypotheses were tested with relative facility and the data strongly suggested their acceptance. But there is a second theory, more relevant for the purposes of this paper. This theory was first elaborated as a result of integrating several readings dealing with the uncompromising attitudes of both political and religious radicals,[18] combined with the observation of homogeneous block voting of radical political parties in roll-call votes, and the simple observation of the uncompromising attitude of persons committed to an ideology. Ideology is conceived here as a belief system with two components—one with an explanatory view of reality and another with an evaluation of reality, and sometimes, an ideal state of affairs. An ideology is a cohesive and internally logical set of beliefs explaining reality and guiding action. Examples of ideologues are orthodox Marxists, orthodox Freudians, and extremely rigorous Catholics. This led to thinking of an ideological, black-or-white, uncompromising orientation in life, as differentiated from the nonideological, open, lack-of-unitary orientation which would be characterized by a less integrated belief system, or by a set of parallel, loosely related, belief systems. The last case hypothesizes a person with various belief systems that would *not* be dependent upon some common central authority.

Impressionistic descriptions of rural-traditional politics pictured very clearly that the prevailing ideology, a religious one, pervaded *all* classes and was not characterized by ties to any specific political parties. Actually, party ties would be unnecessary, for Catholic ideology has the strong support of the ruling elite, which in turn dominates *all* parties, with the exception of the Communist Party. Due to various reasons to be discussed later, the more "political" ideologies did not pervade politics in these areas, being successfully prevented from reaching them and being unknown by their inhabitants. Thus, no class-based ideology ever developed in these areas and political parties were ideologically empty, sheer *instruments* of the elites. Therefore, a nominal political party affiliation did not represent or indicate a strong identification or ideological commitment, being indicative only of an accepted institutional coverage for electoral purposes. Thus, uncompromising attitudes raised by class-based political ideologies could not grow in these areas.

If these assumptions are true, then the politics of traditional areas as defined herein should be more likely to accept electoral alliances than the politics of developing areas. Alliances and coalitions *are* compromises with one's own ideological orientations and, other things being equal, the stronger one's commitment to a given ideology, the stronger the resistance to this kind of electoral and ideological co-optation, to use Selznick's term.[19] *Table 8* shows the striking differences between the two regions with regard to the proportion of congressmen elected by party alliances and coalitions in the 1954 elections; whereas in the Northeast no less than 61.9 percent of all Northeastern congressmen were elected by party alliances and coalitions, only 8.7 percent of the Southeastern congressmen were so elected. It should be pointed out that the data refer to *elected* candidates, not to *all* candidates, but this is of relatively small significance in a proportional system. Looking at *Table 8* it is possible to see that the same pattern existed in the 1958 elections for the State Legislatures: 17.1 percent of those elected to State Legislatures in the Northeast did so via party alliances, whereas in the Southeast only 2.4 percent did so. Incidentally it is also apparent that both in the

Northeast and in the Southeast the proportion of men elected via alliances was smaller at the state level and higher at the federal level, as hypothesized above.

Table 8—Regional Differences in Party Alliances and Coalitions, Federal Congress 1954, and State Legislatures, 1958 and 1962

	CONGRESS		STATE LEGISLATURES, '58		STATE LEGISLATURES, '63	
	Seats	Alliances[a]	Seats	Alliances	Seats	Alliances
Northeast	118	73 (61.9%)	392	67 (17.1%)	419	130 (31.0%)
Southeast	126	11 (8.7%)	336	8 (2.4%)	377	49 (13.0%)

Source: Citations and 4° vol., p. 57.
[a] Alliances in this table also include coalitions.

Although this does not mean that the assumptions were correct (the same events could be explained by alternative theories), the fact that they were predicted from the theory and that they *could* have falsified it surely enhances reliance on the theory. It is therefore worth proceeding with these theoretical assumptions.

It should first be pointed out that it has *not* been suggested that Southeasterners are authoritarian and dogmatic while Northeasterners are not. On the contrary, due to lack of education and severe punitive upbringing it is likely that on the average the Northeastern population is far more authoritarian than the Southeastern. Does this affect politics and in particular party alliances and coalitions? The answer is no, for various reasons. In the first place, it is possible that Northeasterners satiate their need for "authority and structure" and for a dogmatic belief system by means of intense religious activity. On the other hand, the vast majority of the population—the uneducated majority—does not participate in politics anyway, and when it does, it does so submissively, oriented from the outside. It does not influence political decision-making processes. In brief, Northeastern politics are entirely dominated by the ruling elites and, when the large rural population participates in politics, it does so under the guidance and orientation of the rulers. Parties have no meaning for the rulers except as family property and electoral instruments providing institutional control at election times. Outstanding exceptions to this are the PCB and to a smaller extent, the PTB. Nevertheless, it is necessary to reemphasize that large cities are clearly an exception to this pattern.

It has been suggested that Southeastern politics are much more ideological than Northeastern politics, and as such they display two factors opposed to any kind of compromise in general and political compromise in particular:

1. They are class-based and it is more often than not hard to compromise when class interests are at stake.

2. They reveal a dogmatic *political* belief structure as a result of strong ideological commitment which is also opposed to compromise.

No direct evidence can be presented to demonstrate that these are the reasons why Southeastern political life is less characterized by coalitions and alliances. However, the above postulates are part of the theory which helped to predict the observed differentials.

Current theories would predict that the Southeast has a more complex occupational structure and that this would, in accordance with interest group theory in a proportional system,[20] lead toward a certain amount of electoral dispersion. Electoral dispersion is to be understood in terms of its two components: the number of parties competing and/or electing candidates and the evenness of the vote distribution among the various competing parties. A study using a precise measure of this concept has shown that urbanization is related to electoral dispersion.[21] Here, very brief indications in terms of the components will be given.

Stratification complexity is related to interest complexity. New interests require political representation and, oftentimes, this means a new party. On the other hand, given the increased role of ideology, small ideological parties representing dissenting minorities should appear more consistently in "ideological" areas than in "nonideological" ones. Current theories state that these small ideological parties are seldom electorally backed by the less educated, for they represent only a long-term investment, without any possibility of immediate reward through gaining power. Although in a proportional system this is less marked—it is easier for smaller parties to be represented—the fundamental fact that voting for small parties is a hopeless vote, in terms of higher ambitions, persists. Therefore, these parties are dependent upon a small, ideologically sophisticated minority. These minorities are likely to be found in the educated middle classes, which are much larger in the Southeast, as compared with the Northeast. If the assumptions are correct, other things being equal, small parties are more likely to be supported in the Southeast. One way of checking the correctness of the foregoing is by simply investigating how many parties elected at least one representative. Data suggests that in the Northeast there is a smaller number of states where five or six parties elected at least one candidate, both for the Congress and state legislatures. In 1954, 1958, and 1962, five out of the nine Northeastern states had less than five parties represented in the Congress, whereas in 1954 and

Table 9—Regional Differences in Electoral Dispersion, State Legislatures, 1950, Federal Congress, 1954 and 1958
(percent of the total number of seats obtained by the two largest parties in each state)

	State Legislature, 1950	Congress, 1954	Congress, 1958
Northeast	72.6 (379)	67.8 (118)[a]	70.3 (118)
Southeast	58.5 (318)	62.7 (126)	58.7 (126)

Source: As above.
* Totals over which the percentages were extracted.

1958 only two out of six Southeastern states did so. In 1962, Santa Catarina was the only Southeastern state with less than five parties represented in the Congress. In 1954, five of the nine Northeastern states had less than six parties represented in the state legislatures, whereas all Southeastern states had at least six parties represented.

It is fairly clear that more parties elect at least one representative in Southeastern elections as compared to Northeastern ones. Another way of assessing dispersion is simply to examine the proportion of the total vote obtained by the two major parties. Looking at *Table 9* it is seen that consistently the two largest parties (which, needless to say, could be entirely different in one state and another) had a larger percentage, over the total number of seats, in the Northeast. Therefore, however inconclusive the data may be as an indicator of dispersions, it seems that the available indications are in the predicted direction. However, more important is the problem of participation, so far as the purposes of this chapter are concerned.

Regional Differences in Political Participation

It is believed that widespread illiteracy affects participation in all senses, not only electorally (recall that illiterates cannot vote in Brazil), but in other spheres as well. Nevertheless, available data refer mainly to electoral participation, and they reveal that not only does the Southeast have a higher voting proportion of the total population, but that the relative difference is widening.

Table 10—Regional Differences in Electoral Participation 1950, 1954, 1958, and 1962 (in thousands)

	1950 (a)	1950 (b)	(b/a)	1954 (a)	1954 (b)	(b/a)	1958 (a)	1958 (b)	(b/a)
Northeast	17,973	2,458	13.7%	19,655	2,774	14.1%	21,498	3,096	14.4%
							1962 (a) 22,429	1962 (b) 3,526	(b/a) 15.7%
Southeast	21,671	3,834	17.7%	24,248	4,773	19.7%	1958 (a) 21,171	1958 (b) 6,694	(b/a) 24.6%
							1962 32,747	7,353	24.3%

Source: As above.
Remarks: 1950 from census data; 1954, 1958 from Population estimates.
a, total population; b, voters.

Thus the proportion of voters to population in the Northeast was 13.7 in 1950, 14.1 in 1954, 14.4 in 1958, and 15.7 percents in 1962—a very slow increase as compared with the Southeast, where the corresponding percentages would be 17.7, 19.7, 24.6, and 24.3 percents in 1962. The 1954, and specially the 1958 Southeastern percentages should be somewhat lower, because the 1960 census showed that previous figures underestimated the total Southeastern population. Furthermore, one should take into consideration that the Southeastern *population* is growing faster than the Northeastern due to internal migration and much lower morbidity rates, even though fertility rates are usually higher in the Northeast. Therefore increasing percentage differences gain significance: in 1950 the ratio of Southeastern/Northeastern voters was 156; in 1954, it increased to 172; in 1958 it reached 216; and it increased even further in 1962 to 226. These drastic changes occurred in a twelve-year period only.

Other data could be added to demonstrate how much lower is the degree of social mobilization in general and political mobilization in particular.[22] In all aspects the Southeast appears as a more activated society, with a higher degree of participation. Thus it is possible to construct two ideal models, one of an apathetic, nonparticipant society, where basic needs are continuously at stake and little or no time is left for "dilettante" activities, such as politics. This, of course, is linked with illiteracy and extreme poverty, which are in turn partially dependent on inequality, herein expressed in terms of land distribution. The Northeast approaches this model.

Nevertheless, the Southeast is far from approaching the "positive pole" model. It has appeared as an active, participant society, only *by contrast* with the Northeast, and it would be naive to believe that it approaches the model of a participant society.

One very important point has to be made here: it may be the case that social mobilization in general, including political participation and economic development, are *not* linearly related. The existing body of evidence does relate economic development with social mobilization in a seemingly linear way. But it may also be suggested that extreme *political* participation is symptomatic of class conflict and political restlessness, which are likely to occur in rapidly *industrializing* societies and not in stable, industrialized ones.[23] In this sense, it seems that the Brazilian Southeast should present higher rates of electoral participation than it actually does. But there are reasons to explain why it does not. In the first place, Brazil in general has a high rate of population growth, and that means a high proportion of the population under voting age. These have not been taken into consideration in the previous table, in the sense that they were not subtracted from the total. A second reason is given by the incongruent position of illiteracy with respect to other socioeconomic indicators. Judging by the latter, Brazil should have much lower rates of illiteracy, and this applies both to the Northeast and to the Southeast. In a recent study by the United Nations, Brazil is systematically placed fifth on a six-point scale in all but one indicator of socioeconomic development—education—where Brazil is classified in the last category.[24] The same would apply to the Southeast, for its literacy rate is below what would normally be expected judging by other socioeconomic indicators. That plus the age composition of the population explains why electoral participation rates are so low.

The Politics of Backwardness: Tradition

As stated before, one of the main contentions of this chapter is that politics in Brazilian underdeveloped areas is characterized by traditionalism. Traditionalism is here conceptualized as a broad value orientation, with heavy emphasis on its particularistic,[25] ascribed,[26] and sacred[27] dimensions, as opposed to universalistic, achieved, and secular. This value orientation is protected by the prevailing socioeconomic conditions and in turn helps to maintain them. As such, they fit a specific pattern of social organization and cannot be understood without reference to it. For centuries this social organization pattern has remained the same in Brazilian rural areas. Practically absolute illiteracy, lack of social and political participation, and almost complete submission on the part of the slaves and peripheral peasants, has contrasted with a small, sophisticated ruling aristocracy. Political power was clearly a consequence of status and land ownership. It was, and to a certain extent still is, regarded as a "natural" inherited role of the ruling family members. Because the landowners never regarded the slaves as a political force, and oftentimes did not regard the peasants as such, local politics was essentially a family business. The *município* more often than not included more than one leading family and, when it did not, it frequently exhibited an internal dissension within the leading family into two groups. Oftentimes one of these families affiliates with the UDN and the other with the PSD, but they sometimes are distressed by the party's state or national decisions and simply choose from among the other parties a convenient label for continuing with the same traditional family politics.

The political orientation is particularistic in character. In this sense, it is deeply influenced by interpersonal relations as opposed to universalistic, ideological orientations. The peasant votes for the landowner's candidate *qua* his candidate (when the candidate is not the landowner himself or a close member of the family). The ruling elite, on the other hand, takes political leadership for granted. It is a role ascribed to the well-born male, not something to be achieved. This *élitiste* conception of politics is also accepted by the peasants, to say nothing of the ruling elite itself. This conception, coupled with a particularistic value orientation, helps to explain the nonideological, *instrumental* use of political parties and public property as well.

The Sacred Dimension

Weber has defined traditional authority as follows:

> Traditional authority rests on the belief in the sacredness of the social order and its prerogatives as existing of yore. Patriarchal authority represents its pure type. The body politic is based on communal relationships, the man in command is the "lord" ruling over obedient "subjects." People obey the lord personally since his dignity is hallowed by tradition; obedience rests on piety. Commands are substantively bound by tradition.[28]

The politics of backwardness resembles this ideal-type. *Both* the social order and the landlords' undisputed right to authority and power testify to this. The church, obviously, does not endorse the existing order *per se,* but it contributes to its maintenance by strongly opposing those ideologies that might bring about revolutionary changes or any kind of radical change. Therefore, it *implicitly* contributes to preserving the existing order. On the other hand, the landlord often has paternalistic functions. He baptizes the peasant's sons, being a godfather; he gives "extra" rewards to the peasant, who has such a low level of aspiration that he is deeply gratified and feels indebted if his little daughter is given a doll. He takes poverty for granted and has no long-term plans or aims. F.P.R., a peasant working on a farm in Minas Gerais (a state not included in any of the two groups) said:

> Well, us has to work, because us will never be rich. All that is left for us is to get old, if God helps. Don't you think so? Sometimes some folks make it in the lottery and then lose everything again.[29]

And then, referring to the possibility of fooling the boss, when asked about his conception of a good worker, he stated:

> To fool the boss is to fool God. I live here 14 years and I never pulled a trick on nobody. The poor has to help the boss, because he is the one who is going to lose if he doesn't. My job is to grow the crop and I know when one should do certain things using the time that God give.

It is apparent that the Weberian definition of traditional authority to a large extent is applicable here. Hard life is taken for granted and inequality is uncontested. A certain fatalism is detectable.[30] Change and continuation are explicitly attributed to God's will; by implication so is the present state of affairs. Obviously, this outlook is hardly compatible with ideological rebellion.

In such a stagnant system, change has to come from the outside. And, in fact, a growing number of monographs is concerned with these early changing patterns in Brazilian municipal politics.[31] However, this represents a long-term investment for a political party and only recently the first returns of these investments began to be collected. In most of these instances, however, parallel changes in the municipal socioeconomic structure facilitated the political returns. One study showed very clearly the stagnant situation of a *município*, Barroso, Minas Gerais, where for almost 250 years local politics were dominated by two opposed leading families, who joined forces for the first time two years after a factory had been installed in the *município* and were defeated for the first time in history four years later.[32] The parties' history in this *município* is linked with the political wanderings of the families' leaders and all seven parties functioning in 1958 had been created by members of one of the two families.[33] The *instrumental* use of political parties by these leading families is exceedingly clear. Parties are created to mobilize support for a family member, being sheer electoral instruments devoid of ideological content. Many exist only during the campaign. There is intense interparty mobility and persons are often candidates for one party in one election, shift to another party in the following elections, to a third party in the elections after that, sometimes returning to the original party.[34]

However, some indications of change can be observed: in Barroso, even though other labor parties were used as electoral instruments by Geraldo Napoleão, one of the local family leaders, and the PTB proper came very close to this, the PTB is now a working-class party. It is class-based, it has a selective recruitment, it has an ideology. Phenomena like the ones observed in Barroso are not exceptions: they are happening in hundreds of Brazilian *municípios*. In the more deprived Northeastern areas, the peasants have been organized from the outside in the Communist-oriented *Ligas Camponesas*. However, traditionalism is still the main deterrent to this ideological rebellion. And yet, unless socioeconomic conditions change drastically before traditionalism does, this seems to be a battle against time. Barroso is a mild example. Perhaps a better one would be to say that that poor peasant's daughter, when referring to the landlord—the same one that her father respected as he would respect God—stated:

> I want to leave the country because in the country the farm worker and his family are slaves of the landowner; the time for slavery has already gone, but he who stays here stays as a slave.

The Politics of Development: Class and Ideology

If tradition and other nonideological orientations characterize the politics of backwardness, the politics of development are characterized by the increased role played by class and ideology. This section will attempt to show that if, as stated before, socioeconomic status and other class-associated variables are poor predictors of political behavior in rural, backward areas, the opposite is true for developing areas. *Both* socioeconomic status and social-class identification—herein interpreted as a broad, general ideological orientation towards society—are useful predictors of party affiliations and other types of political behavior as well.

A considerable number of studies have shown that status is associated with party preferences in several countries.[35] In a previous paper[36] it was shown that socioeconomic status, as measured by education and occupation —both separately and additively—was strongly correlated with preference for the presidential candidates in the Brazilian 1960 elections. The present data pertain to the same survey, and *Table 11* shows that the previous results are confirmed at the party level:

Table 11—Socioeconomic Strata and Party Preferences

Party Preference	I	II	III	IV	V	VI	VII
UDN (conservative)	56.3	54.5	51.2	38.2	32.5	20.2	18.4
PTB (labor)	11.1	10.9	17.2	28.8	28.5	39.9	42.3
Other Parties	9.6	13.9	13.5	11.8	17.1	14.2	14.8
None	9.6	8.9	9.0	10.6	13.8	12.0	12.2
DK's, no answer	13.4	11.8	9.1	10.6	8.1	13.7	12.3
TOTAL	100.0%	100.0%	100.0%	100.0%	100.0%	100.0%	100.0%
NUMBER	(135)	(101)	(244)	(510)	(123)	(401)	(196)

I—Professionals and High Administrative (10 or more persons under supervision); II—Middle Administrative (between 5 and 10 persons); III—Lower Administrative and Supervisory (less than 5 persons); IV—Routine Non-manual; V—Manual Supervisory; VI—Skilled Manual; VII—Unskilled Manual.

Table 11 clearly shows a monotonic increase in the percentage of the total vote given to the conservative UDN as socioeconomic status increases. Two breaks may be observed: one between categories III and IV and the other between categories V and VI. This can be interpreted as an indicator of a relatively small internal differentiation in the top three categories, relative proximity of white-collar workers and foremen and a relatively small differentiation of workers' political attitudes following skill lines.

Contrary to the UDN, the PTB decreases with increasing status, but strata I and II, and strata IV and V, show no differences. Again the two breaks can be perceived: the percentage given to the PTB jumps eleven percentage points from categories III to IV and from V to VI.

Both preferences given to other parties and lack of party preference show no definite pattern, but a manual-nonmanual dichotomy shows that manuals tend comparatively more towards other parties and also to have no party preference.

Social class identification,[37] on the other hand, shows a similar pattern. Qualitative interviews suggested that the categories used by the population at large to describe one's own class varied. The main alternatives were used to build a pre-coded question which included six classes: high or wealthy; upper-middle, lower-middle, working, poor, and operative (*alta ou rica, alta classe média, baixa classe média, classe trabalhadora, classe pobre, e classe operária*). Whereas identification with the poor class seems to be empty of ideological connotations, identification with the working class and the operative class are symptomatic of ideological *cadres*. The PTB usually campaigns in terms of *both* classes, but Communist propaganda is directed mainly towards "operários," which stand for industrial workers. For the time being, these classes will be lumped together and called "working," as opposed to the merging of the upper or wealthy (which had only a few cases) and the two middle classes (upper and lower), which will be called "middle." At each occupational level, class identification helps to predict party preference:

Table 12—Socioeconomic Status and Class Identification Influence Party Preferences Cumulatively

Socioeconomic Strata

Class	I–II		III		IV		V		VI		VII	
	M	W	M	W	M	W	M	W	M	W	M	W
UDN	58.4	47.8	54.3	28.6	46.1	28.2	37.9	24.5	26.1	18.3	31.1	14.0
PTB	10.4	17.4	14.4	31.4	24.7	34.2	18.2	39.6	29.3	42.9	26.7	45.3
Other	11.9	4.4	11.5	25.7	10.5	12.9	21.2	13.2	17.4	16.3	24.4	12.0
None	7.9	17.4	9.6	5.7	9.5	13.4	9.1	15.1	9.8	12.6	6.6	16.0
DK's	11.4	13.0	10.1	8.6	9.2	11.4	13.6	7.5	17.4	10.0	11.1	12.7
Total	100.0	100.0	99.9	100.0	100.0	100.0	100.0	99.9	100.0	100.0	99.9	100.0
Number	(202)	(23)	(208)	(35)	(295)	(202)	(66)	(53)	(92)	(301)	(45)	(150)

M: Middle; W: Working

Table 12 indicates that for all occupational strata, it holds that those identifying with the middle class give higher percentages of the total preferences to the UDN, and lower to the PTB, than those identifying with the working class. On the other hand, within each class occupational status is still related to party preferences, although not in a strict linear way. Incidentally, lack of party preference seems to be positively associated with working class identification, but no clear relationship with socioeconomic status can be observed.

However, *Table 12* uses crude class identification categories and one wonders whether the more refined categories mentioned above would make any additional difference. The answer is yes: among skilled workers, for instance, the PTB receives 24.4 percent, in the upper middle class (including a few cases of upper class identification), 33 percent in both the lower middle class and the working class, 38 percent in the poor class and 56 percent in the operative class. Thus, class identification with its more refined categories is a powerful instrument in the prediction of political behavior and attitudes.[38]

Perhaps this instrument can be used to understand the process of ideologization of the rural population migrating to the cities. Previous studies have suggested that the rural migrant in Brazil changes some of his political views after urbanization.[39] Simão suggests that he first turns PTB and then goes Communist.[40] The present study does not have data bearing directly upon this hypothesis, for by the time the survey was carried out the Communist Party had been outlawed for thirteen years. But looking at reference group theory[41] and applying it at the class level,[42] it is possible to hypothesize that due to the tremendous urban-rural inequality in wealth and general progress, the rural migrant thinks of himself as upwardly mobile, for the comparison of his present economic status with the past one gives him a feeling of relative reward. This may happen even though he is at the bottom of the urban-stratification ladder.[43]

However, the urban middle and upper strata offer a different frame for comparison. Soon enough the migrant perceives that he is underprivileged, but he still retains some satisfaction derived from the comparison with his past life. The realization that he is underprivileged and the contact with the surrounding environment leads many of them to lean towards the PTB. However, the higher standards of living observed probably raises the aspiration level of many. To the extent that these aspirations are not satisfied, the migrant is open for extreme leftist ideologization. Many never undergo such a process due to other factors, such as strong religious feelings. But others do, and these probably would vote and express preference for the Communist Party if the party were allowed to compete. The present data possibly would express this tendency with an increase in PTB preferences with length of urbanization among unskilled workers, but not necessarily among skilled ones, for the probability that their aspirations are fulfilled is higher. On the other hand, it should also be noted that there is an increase in operative class identification, which should be stronger among unskilled than among skilled workers. *Table 13* presents the data bearing upon these hypotheses.

Table 13—The Effect of Urbanization Upon Class Identification and Party Preferences

| | Number of Years Lived in Rio | | | |
| | UNSKILLED | | SKILLED | |
	Less than 20	20 or more	Less than 20	20 or more
Identification				
Operative Class	21%	31%	21%	27%
Working Class	37%	40%	29%	31%
Poor Class	21%	10%	23%	17%
% PTB	32%	50%	38%	37%
Number	(62)*	(42)	(92)	(72)

* Totals over which the percentages were extracted.
This table includes persons born outside of Rio only.

Analyzing the data in *Table 13,* the hypotheses formulated above seem to survive. Identification with the operative class goes up with increase in years of residence in both cases, but more among unskilled workers, even though the differential increase is statistically not significant. On the other hand, identification with the poor class goes down and identification with the working class goes up in both cases. Finally, the percentage of the PTB preferences goes significantly up with length of urban living among unskilled workers, but not among skilled workers.

Therefore, it seems that feelings of relative reward are replaced by feelings of relative deprivation as urban living makes socioeconomic inequality more visible. The rewarding comparison with a rural life which fades more and more into the past gives place to a damaging comparison with other persons' standards of living higher than one's own. The level of aspirations is reactivated by these comparisons and is heightened. Upward mobility to the more skilled levels with their financial and prestige rewards tends to restore a balance between relative rewards and deprivations. When upward mobility does not occur, there is an unbalance in favor of the negative, deprived feelings. However, religion and other variables may inhibit leftist radicalization even when strong feelings of relative deprivation are present.

The urban workers, however involuntarily, engage in strike practices and collective bargaining.[44] Many of them follow national and international news. The ideological jargon is ever present in the daily talk of many. These aspects are entirely absent from the peasants' lives.

On the other hand, the urban middle class is a sure consumer of political news—national or otherwise. Education and urban living brought heavy emphasis on universalistic and achievement values. Patronage is strongly fought. The national alliance between the PTB and the PSD has won several elections and these governments have been criticized by the middle class, above all on the grounds of corruption and patronage. *Moralismo* is the urban middle-class ideological issue and the *urban* UDN made it its flag. Economic liberalism and anti-Communism are other ideological orientations of the urban middle class in Brazil.

The politics of development therefore is ideological politics. A party cannot enter into electoral practices aimed at gaining a given class's support without losing part of its original followers. Class polarization in certain cities like Rio de Janeiro and Recife is apparent. Political parties attract given classes through their ideological program and after that are bound to those classes' interests; otherwise they will lose their support. As other parties compete for this support, the parties try to strengthen even further the existing links. However, the politics of developing areas are not identical to the politics of developed areas. In the latter, interest politics prevail with groups and classes competing for and aiming at larger shares of the national cake. In the politics of development present interests are oftentimes sacrificed in favor of ideological objectives of ideal states of affairs, ideologically recommended and in whose favor sacrifice of present interests are made. As the ideal state of affairs is ideologically defined, and as these ideologies have a strong differential class appeal, it seems legitimate to state that the politics of development is the politics of class and ideology.

Political Differentials: Conclusion

This section aimed at showing that the Brazilian Northeast and the Brazilian Southeast present various political differences and that these differences can be understood in terms of a systematic theory.

Politics in the Northeast is the politics of backwardness—the politics of tradition. It was shown that meaningful differences in terms of participation, alliances, electoral dispersion and party strength contribute to picturing two entirely different political *cultures*. The politics of backwardness was then described in terms of its overall value orientation, herein labeled traditionalism, with heavy emphasis on its particularistic, ascriptive and sacred dimensions. The linkage between this kind of politics with the socioeconomic structure in general, and the class structure in particular, was emphasized.

Survey data were used to illustrate the politics of development, which is characterized by the increased role of class and ideology as predictors of political attitudes and behavior.

THE POLITICS OF UNEVEN
DEVELOPMENT: CONCLUSIONS

The present chapter hypothesizes that within any given country huge internal unevenness in economic development may be sufficient to provoke political differences to a similar extent. Furthermore, it has been suggested that these *quantitative* economic differences lead to *qualitative* political differences, in the sense that they lay the grounds for two entirely different political *cultures*.[45]

Each of these cultures ideally should be described by inclusion of the whole array of relevant variables that stand at specifiable relationships to each other.

Rural economy obviously is predominantly agrarian and the class structure of rural areas is based on land ownership, tending towards a two-class system. The tremendous inequality which characterizes these areas provides for a close similarity to the Marxian model. Furthermore, a very low educational level and punitive upbringing probably contribute to the creation of a peasant modal personality which is pretty much authoritarian and dogmatic. Why, then, are these areas politically conservative? A few suggestions that are not mutually exclusive can be made:

a) High traditionalism inhibits ideological rebellion against the *status quo* by
   1) preventing a perception of the class interests as different, to say nothing of opposition;
   2) providing strong legitimacy both for the class structure and elite politics;[46]
   3) discouraging the organization of radical leftist parties, which receive faster and higher returns for the same investment by concentrating in the urban areas;[47]
   4) preventing widespread political participation and creating an overall atmosphere of complete apathy.
b) Intense religious activity inhibits ideological rebellion against the *status quo,* by
   1) providing a dogmatic global ideology, which satisfies the hypothesized "need for dogma, authority and structure";
   2) building a negative predisposition against radical leftist ideologies.

The politics of inequality and backwardness may be viewed as a highly explosive situation where revolutionary outbursts are inhibited by the above mentioned factors. If these break before the prevailing situation does, the explosion is likely to occur.

In urban areas, on the other hand, another race seems to take place and their political future seems pretty much dependent on the result of this race. As aspirations are much higher, and traditionalism much lower than in rural areas, the race is between the growth and aspirations of the working class and their satisfaction. "Lefticization" seems inevitable, for class organization is not inhibited and mass communications are available for the transmission of new ideologies. Furthermore, after the process of industrialization has been going on for a while, an existing working class acts as a transmitter of these values to the incoming migrants. The latter, of course, bring built-in values which sometimes inhibit *extreme* lefticization and the acquiring of an ideological, class-conflict perspective. Probably the fact that the Church does not oppose the PTB, but does oppose Communism and Socialism, helps to explain why most newcomers are readily indoctrinated by the Labor parties —whereas those who become Communist or Socialist take much longer to do so.[48]

However, Labor parties may not provide a strong enough outlet for aggression when there are intense frustrations like the ones provoked by the gap between high aspirations and lack of advancement and unemployment. Therefore, the process of radicalization seems to be dependent upon the race between urbanization, which heightens the level of aspirations for more and more people, and industrialization, which satisfies them. Brazil's extreme cases of urbanization higher than industrialization, Recife and Rio de Janeiro (presently capitals of the states of Pernambuco and Guanabara) provide the illustration: in 1945 and 1947 the Communist Party had its top successes in these two cities.

The final national politics is largely a by-product of the interaction between these two political cultures. The interests of such cultures often collide, and one would expect that the politics of development, based upon a larger and more active population, should systematically prevail. However, the Brazilian electoral system does not provide representation in the Congress and the Senate proportional to the number of voters, nor to the population, of each state. There is a diminishing number of congressmen per thousand population. Thus the least populated states are overrepresented and the most populated states are underrepresented. As the most populated states tend also to be the most developed ones, due to heavy immigration from other states and lower mortality and in spite of a lower birth rate, one can easily see that the politics of backwardness is overrepresented in the legislative powers.

Thus, taking the 1960 census and the 1962 election results, we see that there were approximately 160,000 persons per elected congressman in the Northeast, as opposed to over 190,000 in the Southeast. If one takes the voting population, differences are even more striking. Whereas the Northeast needed only about 25,000 voters to elect a congressman, the Southeast needed approximately 47,000, almost twice the Northeastern figure.

The disparity in the Senate is even stronger: there were 830,000 Northeasterners per senator, as opposed to 1,820,000 Southeasterners. Taking the voting population, figures are still more impressive: only 130,000 votes are needed to elect a senator in the Northeast, as opposed to no less than 440,000 in the Southeast.

Thus, the Brazilian electoral system overweights the political power of the politics of backwardness. Given the fact that fewer persons are able to vote in the Northeast, we see that relatively few landlords and rural political chieftains have an amazing influence in national decisions. No wonder that the Brazilian Congress and Senate have been unable to approve reform bills of any consequence, specially those dealing with agrarian and agricultural issues.[51]

However, the president is elected by a majority vote. This shifts the relative balance of power toward the Southeast. Thus, whereas Brazil has consistently had an ultraconservative Congress, presidents and vice-presidents have been systematically to the Left of the Congress. Thus it is doubtless that Getúlio Vargas, Jânio Quadros, and João Goulart were substantially more reform-minded than the Congress.

A further consequence of this nonproportional representation is the extreme flexibility of the Congress due to its lack of ideological orientation. The instrumental aspect of congressional pragmatic politics has enabled it to survive every major crisis in Brazilian politics. Getúlio Vargas was ousted by the military, Café Filho and Carlos Luz were equally ousted, Jânio Quadros resigned, or was forced to do so, and Goulart was prevented from taking effective presidential powers—until a plebiscite based on a *majority* vote reinstated him—and was finally ousted by the military in April 1964. Yet the Congress has systematically compromised, shifted positions, and accommodated to the new situations, being allowed to continue its existence. This ability to give without dignity, to compromise for the sole sake of political power, which characterize nonideological politics, is the ultimate reason why the Congress as an institution has survived every major crisis during the last eighteen years.

The regional differences underlined in this paper may help to explain certain contradictions in Brazilian politics (and, perhaps, Latin American politics) where intellectuals, students, and the urban lower classes promote considerable political agitation, whereas the most deprived areas remain strongly conservative. Parties, on the other hand, are cut across by these regional differences, taking completely different roles in different areas. The explanation lies perhaps in the fact that the country's politics cannot be analyzed in terms of one homogeneous unit. Socioeconomic differentiation engenders two distinctive political *cultures,* herein labeled the politics of backwardness and the politics of development. When these are taken as separate, their comparative analysis may contribute to an understanding of the politics of uneven development.

NOTES

1. The only exception would be urbanization, where Pernambuco stands higher than Paraná, S. Catarina, and R. G. Sul, in accord with the census criterion.

2. One study suggests that between 1947 and 1960 real income per capita increased by 56.2 percent in Brazil as a whole and by 64 percent in the Northeast. The same study suggests that this trend toward diminishing inequality started only after 1952. See H. Rattner, "Contrastes Regionais no Desenvolvimento Economico Brasileiro," in *Revista de Administracão de Empresas,* 11 (June 1964), pp. 133–66. However, the same study shows that real income grew slower in the Northeast, and that the per-capita figures reflect the differential population growth. In spite of a higher birth rate, the Northeast has managed to keep a lower rate of population growth by means of mass migration toward the other regions of the country.

3. Robock also points out that since 1955 the Northeastern percapita income has tended to grow somewhat faster, relative to other Brazilian regions. Nevertheless, 1960 estimates of per capita income show the Northeastern figures to be US $140.00, as compared with US $410.00 in the south and a US $240.00 average for Brazil (See S. H. Robock, *Brazil's Developing Northeast.* Washington: Brookings Institution, 1963).

4. For an attempt to formulate a theory linking the *incongruency* of socioeconomic indicators with political radicalism, see G. A. D. Soares, "Desenvolvimento Econômico e Radicalismo Político: Notas para uma Teoria," in *Boletim de Centro Latino Americano de Pesquisas em Ciências Sociais* (May 1961), pp. 117–57. See also "Congruency

and Incongruency among Indicators of Economic Development: an Exploratory Study," paper presented to the International Conference on Comparative Social Research on Developing Countries: Intracountry Discontinuities in the Process of Economic and Social Development in Latin America (Buenos Aires: Sept. 1964).

5. See S. M. Lipset, *Political Man* (New York: Doubleday, 1961), Chap. IV; M. Janowitz and D. Marvick, "Authoritarianism and Political Behavior," *Public Opinion Quarterly,* 17 (1953). Janowitz and Marvick suggest that education and authoritarianism are negatively correlated only in the middle class.

6. See M. Lipset, *ibid.,* Berelson, *et al., Voting* (Chicago: Univ. of Chicago Press, 1954); G. A. D. Soares, "Classes Sociais, Strata Sociais e as Eleicões Presidenciais de 1960," *Sociologia* (Sept. 1961), pp. 217–38.

7. See Soares, "Desenvolvimento . . . *op. cit.,* and "Desenvolvimento Econômico e Radicalismo Político: o Teste de uma Hipótese," *América Latina,* 5 (July–Sept., 1962), pp. 65–83.

8. See Berelson, *op. cit.*; S. M. Lipset, *op. cit.,* Part II; Paul F. Lazarsfeld *et al., The People's Choice* (New York: Duell, Sloan & Pearce, 1944), and G. A. D. Soares, "Interesse Político, Conflito de Pressões e Indecisão Eleitoral," in *Síntese Política, Econômica e Social* (Jan. 1960), pp. 5–34.

9. For an analysis showing how a low educational level has inhibited further economic development in Brazil, see R. Moreira, *Educação e Desenvolvimento no Brasil* (Rio de Janeiro: CLAPECSO, 1960).

10. Data from Mayer, *et al., op. cit.,* p. 267.

11. See, for suggestions in this direction, S. Schattan, "Estrutura Econômica da Lavoura Paulista," in *Revista Brasiliense* (Nov. 1959), and "Nota Sôbre a Estrutura Econômica da Lavoura Paulista" in *Revista de Ciencias Econômicas* (June, 1960).

12. These correlations can reach .70, as between the proportion of the privately owned land occupied by properties with 1,000 ha. and over, and the industrial income per capita.

13. The Northeastern gross national product in 1955 was Cr$ 80,915 million, of which Cr$ 33,530 million (41.4 percent) came from the primary and Cr$ 9,997 million (12.4 percent) came from the secondary sector. Southeastern data show that gross income ran about Cr$ 398,361 million, with the primary contributing 30.4 percent (Cr$ 121,253 million) and the secondary contributing 21 percent (Cr$ 83,740 million). Therefore, the Northeast is much more dependent on agriculture and less on industry, as compared with the Southeast.

14. E. Banfield, *The Moral Basis of a Backward Society* (New York: The Free Press, 1958), gives a description of how extreme backwardness limited social organization in southern Italian communities. Needless to say, southern Italian communities would look relatively well off by comparison with Brazilian northeastern ones.

15. See S. M. Lipset, *op. cit.,* Chap. 13. An important difference, however, is the assumed increase in the importance of ideology. If anything, the role of ideology seems to be declining in fully developed industrial societies. D. Bell, *The End of Ideology* (New York: The Free Press, 1960).

16. See G. A. D. Soares, "Alianças e Coligações Eleitorais: Notas para uma Teoria," in *Revista Brasileira de Estudos Politicos,* 17 (July 1964), pp. 95–124.

17. See M. Duverger, *Los Partidos Políticos* (Mexico City: FCE, 1957) and D. MacRae, "The Relation Between Roll Call Votes and Constituencies," in Eulau, *et al.* (eds.), *Legislative Behavior* (New York: The Free Press, 1959).

18. T. W. Adorno, *et al., The Authoritarian Personality* (New York: Harper & Row, 1950); H. J. Eysenck, *The Psychology of Politics* (London: Routledge, 1954); M. Rokeach, *The Open and Closed Mind* (New York: Basic Books, 1960); and S. Rydenfelt, *Kommunismen i Sverige* (Lund: Universitetsbokhandeln, 1954).

19. See P. Selznick, *TVA and The Grass Roots* (Berkeley: Univ. of California Press, 1949).

20. For a comprehensive exposition of interest group theory, see D. Truman, *The Governmental Process* (New York: Knopf, 1951).

21. See G. A. D. Soares, and A. M. Noronha, "Urbanização e Dispersão Eleitoral," in *Revista de Direito Público e Ciência Política* (July–Dec. 1960), pp. 258–70.

22. For a development of the social mobilization concept, see K. Deutsch "Social

Mobilization and Political Development," *American Political Science Review,* 55 (Sept. 1961), pp. 493–514.

23. This point has been made before by S. M. Lipset, *op. cit.;* H. Tingsten, *Political Behavior: Studies in Election Statistics* (London: P. S. King 1937); W. H. M. Jones, "In Defense of Political Apathy," *Political Studies* (Feb. 1954), pp. 25–37; and G. A. D. Soares, "Participação Eleitoral e Separação de Poderes," *Revista de Direito Público e Ciência Política* (Jan. 1960), pp. 36–66. Another study shows that political participation and ideological radicalism are positively correlated; see G. A. D. Soares, *The Active Few* (Berkeley: Institute of International Studies, 1964), mimeo.

24. See United Nations, *Informe Sobre la Situación Social en el Mundo,* 1961, pp. 52–3..

25. The definition of particularism adopted here was given by Parsons: "The standards and criteria which are independent of the particular social relationship to a particular person may be called universalistic, those which apply by virtue of such a relationship on the other hand are particularistic," in "The Professions and Social Structure," *Essays in Sociological Theory* (New York: The Free Press, 1954), pp. 41–2.

26. The adopted definition of ascription is also Parsonian: "The valued results of the actions of individuals," in "An Analytical Approach to the Theory of Social Stratification," *op. cit.,* p. 75.

27. For a conceptual development of this idea, see H. Becker, "Sacred and Secular Societies Considered with Reference to Folk-State and Similar Classifications," in *Social Forces,* 28 (May 1950), pp. 361–76.

28. Weber, M., "The Three Types of Legitimate Rule" (trans. by Hans Gerth) in Etzioni, A. (ed.), *Complex Organizations* (New York: Holt, Rinehart and Winston, 1961), p. 7.

29. These interviews were collected in relatively developed rural areas, by comparison with the Northeastern ones. The author is indebted to Professor Joseph Kahl for the use of this and subsequent quotations.

30. Kahl, J., in "Urbanização e Mudanças Ocupacionais no Brasil," in *América Latina,* V (Oct.–Dec. 1962), pp. 21–30 produced a traditional syndrome of which fatalism is the dominant trait. Rural villagers usually had a much higher score in the various component scales than urban ones of similar education. *Both* status and place of residence were good predictors. And again, Kahl's study was in a relatively well-developed rural area.

31. See, for instance, Carvalho, O., *Ensaios de Sociologia Eleitoral* (Belo Horizonte: Estudos Sociais e Políticos, 1958), "Os Partidos Políticos de Minas Gerais e as Eleições de 1958"; Sampaio, N. S. "Eleiçoes Bahianas"; and Castro, F. F., "A Campanha Eleitoral de 1958 no Piauí," all three published in *Revista Brasileira de Estudos Políticos,* 8 (Apr. 1960). Cf. also Sampaio, N. S., *O Diálogo Democrático no Bahia* (Belo Horizonte: Estudos Sociais e Políticos, 1960); and Diniz, S. G., "Quatorze Anos de Eleições na Vila do Pará, M.G. (1861–1875)," *Revista Brasileira de Estudos Políticos,* 17 (June 1964), pp. 139–191.

32. Cf. Silva, L., "Implicações Políticas do Desenvolvimento Industrial em Barroso-M.G.," *Revista Brasileira de Estudos Políticos,* 9 (July 1960).

33. *Idem,* pp. 244–245.

34. For an interesting description of Brazilian municipal politics, see Leal, V. N., *Coronelismo, Enxada e Voto—o Município e o Regime Representativo no Brasil* (Rio de Janeiro, 1948).

35. Lipset, *Political Man,* analyses in detail of most of these studies.

36. Cf. Soares, G. A. D., "Classes Sociais, etc.," *op. cit.*

37. For an early work which developed the idea of class identification, see Centers, R., *The Psychology of Social Classes* (Princeton: Princeton University Press, 1949).

38. Data from the same survey have been utilized by the present author to show that social class identification influences party preferences even when *both* respondent's and father's occupation are held constant. Cf. Soares, G. A. D., "Mobilidade Ocupacional e Comportamento Político" (Instituto de Ciências Sociais da Universidade de Brasil: mimeographed, 1961).

39. Cf. Simão, A., "O Voto Operário em São Paulo," *Revista Brasileira de Estudos Políticos,* 1 (1956), pp. 130–141.

40. In accordance with Simão, *op. cit.*

41. For a theoretical development of this theory, cf. Merton, R. and A. Kitt, "Contributions to the Theory of Reference Group Behavior," in Merton, R. K., *Social Theory and Social Structure* (New York: The Free Press, 1957, rev. ed.).

42. For an application of reference group theory at the class level, cf. Bott, E., "The concept of class as a reference group," *Human Relations,* VII (1954), pp. 259–286.

43. Rural migrants seem to be at a disadvantage in the urban stratification pyramid. Cf. Lipset, S. M. and R. Bendix, *Social Mobility in Industrial Society* (Berkeley: The University of California Press, 1959), and Soares, G. A. D., "Desenvolvimento, etc.," pp. 128–132.

44. Cf. Lopes, J. R. B., "O Ajustamento Do Trabalhador À Indústria: Mobilidade Social Motivação," in Hutchinson, *op. cit.*

45. An approach similar to the present one, where the author tries to explain a wide variety of dependent behavior, was undertaken by Lambert, L., *Os Dois Brasis* (Rio de Janeiro: CBPE, 1959).

46. For a development of the concept of political legitimacy, cf. Lipset, S. M., "Some Social Requisites of Democracy, Economic Development and Political Legitimacy," *American Science Review,* 53 (1959), pp. 69–105.

47. The Communist Party never developed a strong organizational network in the rural areas. During the past five years, however, intense activity aiming at the political mobilization and radicalization of the peasant has been developed, culminating with Julião's famous *Ligas Camponesas.*

48. This process is probably faster in countries like France and Italy, where there is a large, institutionalized, radical leftist party. Small leftist parties are uncertain, *long-term* investments for the voter, a condition which only the intellectual's ideological commitment is able to accept.

49. For a development of this argument, see G. A. D. Soares, "El Sistema Electoral y la Reforma Agraria En El Brasil," *Ciências Políticas y Sociales,* 29 (July–Sept. 1962), pp. 431–44.

Eleven

Class, Tribe, and Party
in West African Politics

Immanuel Wallerstein

In a colonial situation, political parties are born to protest and to seek change. For this reason, they were not encouraged in West Africa by the colonial authorities. Indeed, at first, they were not permitted. Before World War II, proto-parties existed in some of the few municipal centers where elections of a nontraditional variety were held: places such as Dakar (Senegal), Freetown (Sierra Leone), Accra (Gold Coast), and Lagos (Nigeria).

In all of these centers the suffrage was limited: in the British territories, by a property franchise; in French areas to those who were "citizens." The status of citizen was conferred in Senegal to those who were *originaires* of the four communes, a categorization not too different in its consequences from one chosen on the basis of property. Thus, the voters were a handful of urbanites, the most educated and Westernized in West Africa.[1] They were involved in the modern money economy, largely as civil servants, merchants, and professional men, and represented a small minority of the total African population. The governmental posts they filled by their votes were scarcely a determining element in the political structure of the colony. Hence, a handful of men voted occasionally for posts of little power.

This handful was a middle-class group, situated in prestige, power, style of life, and often income between a small ruling caste of European officials and the vast majority of the African population.[2] Their politics consisted largely of attempts to secure, reinforce, and extend their privileges within the colonial system. Such political cleavages as existed were largely grouped around personality differences, although occasionally an undertone of different economic interests was present. Sklar notes, for example, of wartime Lagos politics:

> The Yoruba population was politically divided on class or quasi-class lines. By and large, traditionalistic, predominantly Muslim, indigenous masses followed Macauley and the Nigerian National Democratic Party, while the Westernized, predominantly Christian, cosmopolitan (i.e., drawn from several provinces—Ijebu, Abeokuta, Oyo and Ondo— in addition to the Colony [of Lagos]) rising class followed the N.Y.M. [Nigerian Youth Movement]. Indeed the N.Y.M. in Lagos relied upon the "detribalized" working class, many of whom were Ibos, for its mass support.[3]

The situation Sklar is describing is, however, rather late, at the point of transition to the period of mass anticolonial politics. In the early days West African political associations were in the hands of a small elite, mostly lawyers and tended, in Hodgkin's words, to be "exclusive clubs for the professional and prosperous business classes which were now emerging."[4]

The grievances of these political associations were directed against the colonial authorities, whose system created both political and economic limits to the aspirations of this middle class, and against the traditional chiefs whose ways seemed onerous and irrelevant to this urbanized group. In the organs of limited deliberation that were established, such as the *Conseil Colonial* in Senegal or the Gold Coast Legislative Council, the major division was between the nominated traditional members and the elected representatives of the urban middle class.[5] The colonial government often gave tacit support to the former for fear of the ultimate consequences of the demands of the latter. The middle-class elements were more interested in extending the powers of the legislators than extending the suffrage. Indeed, in some cases, they were explicitly opposed to the latter. The most striking example is Sierra Leone, where the middle-class element formed a distinct caste, the Creoles, who were descended from returned slaves. Their organization, the National Council of Sierra Leone, declared as late as 1951 in an electoral manifesto: "We object to foreigners (i.e., non-Creoles, the Protectorate Africans) preponderating in our Legislative Council."[6]

Most observers agree that West African nationalism, then, was at least initially, a "middle-class phenomenon,"[7] and that

> Nationalism, in one of its aspects, clearly expresses the dissatisfaction of an emerging African middle class with a situation in which many of the recognized functions, and rewards, of a middle class—in the commercial, professional, administrative and ecclesiastical fields (were) in the hands of 'strangers' . . . The demand for African control of the State power (was) in part a demand for unrestricted access to these functions.[8]

The defining feature for inclusion in the middle class is uncertain, the new elites having a dual origin—the development of the economy and of the educational system. These two groups—the moneyed and the educated—are closely linked, but the overlap is not perfect. Mercier insists, in fact, that "the use of the term 'social class' risks in the majority of cases giving a completely false perspective." At most one can talk of "social classes in germination."[9] He notes, further, that many studies distinguish between classes along a continuum that is in fact only the "level of schooling."[10] Seurin suggests distinguishing between three kinds of bourgeoisie: administrative, commercial, and rural.[11] Using such categories, the administrative bourgeoisie, or civil servants, would most clearly coincide with the educated group. In French West Africa, they remained "the most important (political) group."[12] In British West Africa, the professional and business groups, however, played the larger role, partly because there they were a much larger group than in the French territories (with the exception of Senegal), partly because the British tradition of administration forbade political activity to civil servants.

The exact contours of the "middle class" may have varied from territory to territory. Yet, it was an identifiable group who indeed developed a reasonably marked class consciousness, in the sense that they realized they had a set of economic interests, separate from that of the European ruling elite and separate from that of the African peasant masses. They acted on this realization and created political associations to pursue these class interests. There are, however, two qualifications to be made to this statement. First of all, traditional systems of stratification still existed and still had an effect, albeit a declining one, upon men's social action, even those of the educated urbanite. Here we may note, however, a trend over time to translate traditional social status into modern social status.[13] The second qualification is that class and ethnic group were not necessarily distinct categories. We have already mentioned the case of the Creoles. Mercier notes the correlation between ethnic affiliation and profession, style of life and degree of Westernization.[14] Zolberg argues of the Ivory Coast that "economic differences coincide with traditional cleavages; there are now rich and poor tribes. . . ."[15]

World War II, by altering both the political and economic contexts, created a new situation in which political action would take new forms. The proto-nationalist, exclusive groupings of the "middle class" were to be superseded by or transformed into mass nationalist movements. The social composition of the leadership was to get more complex, the lines of class and tribe submerged somewhat in a revolutionary situation, and an ideology of national unity would be propagated by the new parties.

World War II was critical to West African political development in two ways. The economic expansion caused by wartime activity, and which continued after the war, led to the multiplication of junior cadres—junior clerks, mechanics, skilled artisans, health personnel, primary-school teachers—who began to form in the various territories a sizable "lower middle class." For the first time, enough leadership, with some training in modern ways, was available to man a mass nationalist movement. Furthermore, this group of men found not merely the colonial administration a barrier to their personal development, in terms of career and income, but were frustrated also by the older, more educated middle-class of higher civil servants, professionals, and wealthier merchants.

Second, these new cadres emerged at a time when the world political scene was changing radically. The bipolarization of the world and the success of nationalist movements in Asia created a favorable climate for anticolonial activity. Both the British and French governments were aware that methods of colonial administration could no longer continue as before. This led first of all to the expansion of both economic investment and educational activity, which led in turn to the creation of still more cadres at every level of education. In the case of French West Africa this included university graduates for the first time. Before World War II, they had been practically nonexistent, except in Senegal. This led also, albeit somewhat more reluctantly, to constitutional reform, which resulted, under the pressure of the nationalist movements that would be created, in the eventual decolonization of the area.

The various constitutional reforms of the early postwar years meant that West African politics had now become a serious matter. Everywhere parties were formed to contest the new elections. Rather, one should say electoral committees were formed; these were often grouped around a personality or an ethnic group. This kind of committee, with no real organizational structure, membership, or continuing activity, has been called a "patron party" or "elite party."[16]

Within a few years, however, various mass movements had emerged quite different from these electoral committees: the interterritorial *Rassemblement Démocratique Africain* (RDA) in much of French West Africa; the *Convention People's Party* (CPP) in the Gold Coast; the *National Council of Nigeria and the Cameroons* (NCNC) and the *Action Group* (AG) in Nigeria; the *Bloc Démocratique Sénégalais* (BDS); the *Comté de l'Unité Togolaise* (CUT); and the *Sierra Leone People's Party* (SLPP). There were many differences in structure, contours of membership, and political effectiveness of these parties. Their common denominator was that they all eventually came to power as incarnations of the spirit of nationalism and that they all sought to recruit support from all sectors of the community. Furthermore, they all, to a greater or less degree, sought to represent a "modernizing" point of view, but they also represented in many cases a reaction against the prewar educated elite, who now seemed too moderate in their nationalism, and too rooted in the privileges of the colonial system.

The new electoral systems brought into the political arena not only urban-ites but the rural masses, and the attempts by the mass parties to organize the peasantry were increasingly successful and either diminished the political role of traditional chiefs sharply or forced them to devise formulas of com-promise with the parties.[17] The mass parties ranged widely in attitudes toward the chiefs from the extreme hostility of the *Parti Démocratique de Guinée* (PDG-RDA) to the high degree of collaboration represented by the SLPP. Nevertheless, all the mass parties had an anti-chieftain element in their ideology, however muted, by virtue of their basic democratic and egalitarian option. The stronger the structure of the party, the more evident this anti-chieftain bias became. For this reason, in most areas the prewar split between the educated elite and the chiefs tended to be submerged in their common opposition as privileged groups to the new mass parties, the basic class split of postwar West African politics. As Schachter notes:

> In some areas, in spite of their many differences, a prewar town elite holding the highest positions permitted to Africans in the colonial system, and the official "chiefs" already conscious that the presence of Europeans stabilized their position, made common cause in patron parties against mass party leaders. The line-up of "haves" against their "have-not" challengers was evident in the epithets exchanged at election time. Urban patron party leaders called mass party leaders "vagrants" (Guinea) and "veranda boys" (Ghana); in the countryside patrons underlined that their rivals were "slaves" or "strangers."[18]

Mass nationalist movements were not, however, class parties. They could not be in a population most of which consisted mostly of peasants still living partially in a subsistence economy. Rather, these parties were national move-ments with populist undertones, led by emerging middle-class, largely urban, elements with strong grievances against the colonial administration[19] The degree to which these populist grievances were also directed against an indigenous urban elite varied with the strength of this elite, but the complaint of the nationalists that there was a group of men (senior civil servants and professionals) who were insufficiently militant was standard.

This populist cause included in large measure the African commercial classes, who saw their economic interests hindered by the colonial system. As Kilson observes:

> The nationalists arrived at the conclusion that to remove colonial rule is to open the way for the economic development of their countries in general, and for the growth of African industries in particular. . . . By emphasizing a functional relationship between economic development and state power, West African nationalists were able to attract the support of many African businessmen who expected the future independent West African states substantially to assist their growth.[20]

It included as well the new rural bourgeoisie, the African cash-crop planters. Their participation in the nationalist movement was most striking in the Ivory Coast, where there was a class of European planters who had received favored treatment by the colonial regime before and during World War II. The new mass parties also included the urban salaried workers in both the governmental and private sectors, many of whom were to be organized in trade unions, more or less linked to these parties. The parties thus collected all those with grievances and organized them into a revolutionary movement.[21]

West African colonial society in the postwar years can be looked at as a complex fabric of economic-interest groups, many of whom were coming into existence and expanding in size as a result of economic development. The fact that the political structure prevented these emergent "middle classes" from attaining personal goals which seemed to them technically realizable led to a bipolarization of the society. On the one side were the European ruling elite, allied in some cases with a small urban educated group, and those traditional rulers who had become virtual clients of the colonial administration. On the other side were the bulk of the middle-class elements, supported by the peasantry and an urban quasi-proletariat—quasi in the sense that they were often rural migrants retaining their links to the land to which they would eventually return. The anticolonial nationalist revolution presents thus an almost classic revolutionary pattern, where "the emergent or new and rising class refers to an actual social aggregate, engaged in class action and characterized by a growing sense of class consciousness."[22] The ultimate outcome was the attainment of a new political structure, an independent state. The precise patterns of this new structure, however, were determined in part by the particular class and ethnic distributions of each state and in part by the policies of the colonial power.

The basic reaction of the colonial ruling elite to the emergence of a mass nationalist movement was to encourage and promote divisions within it, partly on class grounds but largely on ethnic and regional bases. Parties based on these latter, more traditional, criteria risked having a widespread appeal to the peasantry, who, being largely outside the money economy, felt no necessary national or class consciousness. The period from 1945 to 1960 was characterized by a struggle between the colonial ruling elite and the emergent middle-class elite for the loyalty of the peasant masses. The essential doctrine of the colonial ruling elite was that the meaningful social entity remained the tribe (and, by extension, the region). By upholding this traditional definition of the situation, they hoped to maintain their power by control via their clients, the chiefs. The nationalist movement defined the situation as a "class struggle" in which the only "objective" members of the ruling class were Europeans and a handful of African client professionals and chiefs. Thus, African society was "classless," which was another way of calling for the revolutionary unity of the oppressed majority. The middle-class definition of the situation was to prevail, thus enabling the nationalist movement, given the favorable world context, to achieve a relatively rapid and nonviolent change in the basic political structure.

If virtually all West African countries arrived at independence with a single, dominant nationalist party, they reached this point by many different paths. In the Gold Coast (Ghana) the old established urban elite of lawyers, doctors, and businessmen, who had been the spokesmen of Gold Coast nationalism since 1897, founded the *United Gold Coast Convention* (UGCC). They sought to turn the organization into a mass movement and found that the leadership therefore escaped them. Under the leadership of the Secretary-General, Kwame Nkrumah, the younger and more radical elements broke away from the UGCC in 1949 to form the *Convention People's Party* (CPP), which made its prime demand "self-government now." In Apter's words, the "membership of the CPP was primarily the partially educated, the Standard VII boys, those whose roots with rural areas were not dissolved but whose urban affiliations made possible quick and effective organization."[23] In many of the villages these same partially educated young men assembled in the CPP to oppose the local chiefs. The split between the old urban elite, the intellectuals, and many of the chiefs on the one hand and the emerging town and village elites, of medium education, would remain the central focus of Gold Coast politics through independence, and even after.

A similar split developed in Senegal. There the old elite of the four communes developed a special juridical status. They were French "citizens" (as opposed to "subjects") long before 1946, when all French Africans acquired this attribute. They had long participated in the election of a deputy to the French Parliament. The most radical of their groups was the Senegalese section of the SFIO founded in 1936 during the Popular Front by Lamine Guèye. After the war, the SFIO sought, as did the UGCC, to claim the new political power. They were undone by the extension of the suffrage to the former "subjects," living in the rural areas and as laborers in the cities. Robinson explains thus the dissensions within the SFIO:

> Their causes were complex. In part, they represented the jealousy of the newly-enfranchised citizens of the bush (the former subjects) at the continued domination in the party councils and in the distribution of the spoils, of the old citizens' cliques; in part the natural hostility of the countryside to the towns; in part the rivalry of different ethnic groups and local associations, most of which were against the old citizens who had so long enjoyed a privileged position; in part dissatisfaction with the preoccupation with questions of political and juridical status which characterized socialist policy as represented by Lamine Guèye and his friends, and a demand, however vaguely felt,

for more emphasis on the immediate social and economic problems of the hitherto less favored subjects.[24]

These dissensions led to the formation in 1948 of the *Bloc Démocratique Sénégalais* (BDS) by Léopold Senghor and Mamadou Dia. Unlike the CPP however, the BDS was based essentially in rural areas, because the French traditional system of administration had consolidated the urban middle cadres, and especially the civil servants,[25] behind the old urban elite. Ancient privileges had become transformed into value patterns.[26] The consolidation of urban areas led to the consolidation of rural areas.[27] The BDS organized its strength in collaboration with the traditional rulers[28] who, in Senegal, are principally Moslem religious leaders. Senghor is reported to have said: "It was the Imams in the mosques who made our triumph."[29] Thus, the BDS was less urban-oriented and less antitraditional authority than the CPP, and therefore less radical in terms of its anticolonial militance.

Sierra Leone was in many ways quite similar to Senegal. Here too, there had existed for over a century, an urban group with special privileges, less judicially ensconced, but taking the even more solidifying form of an ethnic group, the Creoles. Postwar constitutional change took the form of extending the suffrage to the rural areas (known as the Protectorate, as opposed to the Colony which was Freetown and its environs).[30] In 1950, the Creoles formed an exclusive party, the *National Council of Sierra Leone*. In 1951, several Protectorate groups along with some Colony elements merged to form the Sierra Leone People's Party (SLPP) which quickly proved itself the majority party. Here the radicalism and the drive to modernization was even more muted by its close alliance with the chiefs, brought about the formal Colony-Protectorate (or urban-rural) split. Kilson explains the relative conservatism of the SLPP as follows:

> The long period of conflict between the Creole and Protectorate Africans had made the latter fully predisposed to any political organization which might emerge among themselves as against the former. All that was required of such an organization was that it oppose the long-standing supremacy of Creoles in Sierra Leone society. It was not necessary to develop a body of political principles or a nationalist ideology which would appeal to the masses and secure their support. So-called Creole supremacy, in short, became the main if not the sole political issue posed by S.L.P.P. leaders, and in posing this issue, they gained nearly complete support of the Protectorate masses.[31]

The politics in Gambia followed a similar pattern of division between Colony and Protectorate, the *People's Progressive Party* playing a role similar to that of the SLPP. In Gambia, however, the conflict was less acute. There was no ethnic group in the Colony similar to the Creoles, and the strong Islamization of the country helped bridge the rural-urban gap.

In the Ivory Coast, the prewar urban elite was tiny indeed and concentrated in an ethnic group, the Agni, not located in the capital. This elite formed a party, the *Parti Progressiste,* but they were overwhelmed right from the beginning by the mass party, the *Parti Démocratique de la Côte d'Ivoire* (PDCI-RDA). The basic split was not rural-urban as in Senegal, Sierra Leone, and Gambia. It was rather a coalition, like the CPP, of urban and rural emerging elements against the colonial administration, and their allies among the educated elite and the chiefs (both much weaker, however, in Ivory Coast). Politics did not start with an urban privileged group, overwhelmed by the hinterland by an extension of the suffrage. Political parties, from the beginning, had to "coordinate a widely scattered electorate."[32] There was, however, one crucial difference with the Gold Coast situation. The existence of a privileged European planter group led to the organization in 1944 of the *Syndicat Agricole Africain,* led by Félix Houphouet-Boigny, and representing the demands of the African cash-crop farmers for equal treatment. It was this group which formed the basis for the creation of the PDCI, thus giving middle-class farmers rather than middle-class urbanites the leadership of the nationalist movement,[33] explaining the later relative conservatism of the PDCI and why no split between the nationalist movement and the rural bourgeoisie occurred, as it did in the Gold Coast in 1954.

In Guinea, there was virtually no prewar urban elite. Nor was there a significant class of cash-crop farmers. Politics had to start from zero. The very few educated persons entered the civil service. The emerging urban elements found themselves organized in the trade union federation, the CGT, which from the beginning formed the backbone of the PDG. The nationalist leader, Sékou Touré, was originally the Secretary-General of the CGT. The later anticolonial radicalism of the PDG, which contrasted with that of its sister party (co-member of the RDA), the Ivory Coast PDCI, is explained by these structural factors. The party coalitions in Guinea, the Ivory Coast, and the Gold Coast were substantially the same, but the leadership in Guinea and the Gold Coast was urban, and the split between the mass party leadership and the intellectuals and professionals remained acute, unlike the Ivory Coast, as Schachter explains:

> In postwar Guinea most of those who had been prewar students in the dominant French West Africa secondary school, the École Normale William-Ponty, wanted to keep the only paying jobs open to them. These were invariably in the civil service and so they had little alternative, prior to 1956, but to go into "administrative" parties. . . . the mass party in Guinea, the *Parti Démocratique de Guinée,* was led by the products of the lower state schools, who accused Ponty graduates of "betraying the masses," and called them "valets of the administration." . . . In the Ivory Coast, by contrast, Ponty graduates took the lead both in regional "patron" parties and in the mass party, the *Parti Démocratique de la Côte d'Ivoire.* There Ponty graduates found alternatives to administrative employment in cocoa and coffee farming. Consequently, in Ivory Coast political cleavages did not relate closely to differences in the diplomas achieved by members of the elite.[34]

Togo developments might have resembled those of the Gold Coast, had it not been for the special situation of being a trust territory, coupled with a tribal irredentism. In 1946, the *Comité de l'Unité Togolaise* (CUT) was constituted as a political party. The social origins of its leadership were similar to that of the UGCC in the Gold Coast: the old elite of civil servants, professionals, and businessmen. This leadership had, however, been active in the *All-Ewe Conference,* a group that was organized in the Gold Coast and in both

British and French Togoland. The links of the CUT with the Gold Coast opened these men to the nationalist currents operating there. Combined with the fact that Togo as a trust territory was destined to become self-governing, this meant that the CUT outspokenly avowed independence (and reunification, first of Eweland, later of the two Togolands) as its objective. This demand for independence was unique at that time among the parties in the French areas of West Africa. Despite this advanced position, the younger elements of the CUT split off in 1951 to form *Juvento,* ostensibly a youth movement. This was a split reminiscent of that of the CPP with the UGCC, and over the same issue: nationalist militance.[35] Before *Juvento* could develop into a full-fledged mass nationalist party, French fears of CUT demands, however moderate they seemed to *Juvento,* led to the ouster of CUT from the local legislative bodies and elective posts, thus throwing *Juvento* back into an alliance with the CUT. When later the administration parties were swept away in the tide of Togolese nationalism, the nationalist movement was firmly in the hands of the CUT, that is, of the old urban elite. This urban elite, however, was not indebted to traditional rulers because the Ewe in the south who were the backbone of the CUT never had important chiefs and the northern chiefs had been induced by the French to create an administrative party in opposition to the CUT.[36] Dahomey has a social structure similar to that of Togo. The old elite founded the *Union Progressiste Dahoméenne* (UPD) in 1946. The party, however, split, largely on ethnic lines. The younger, more radical, new elites tried in 1955 to start a new party built around the remains of the UPD called the *Union Démocratique Dahoméenne* (UDD), which attempted to assert its militance by affiliating to the RDA, from which the UPD had split in 1948. The UDD was, however, not able to bridge the ethnic divisions which had split the parties rather evenly in a tripartite fashion. A unified national party was only achieved after independence, and it only lasted until the overthrow of the government in 1962.

The inland, savannah countries under French administration (Niger, Upper Volta, Sudan—now Mali, and Mauritania) did not have an urban educated elite like Senegal or the Gold Coast, or even like Dahomey and the Ivory Coast. In all these territories, the traditional chiefs wielded considerable authority, more than in the coastal territories under French rule. Such elites as existed were mostly civil servants. In the Sudan, the new urban elements allied themselves with a traditional commercial class in opposition to feudal chiefs, a small bourgeoisie of higher civil servants and merchants very Westernized in style of life but with strong links to traditionalist elements.[37] This was to be the basis of the ultimate success of the *Union Soudanaise* (US-RDA). In both Niger and Upper Volta, the new urban groups and anti-traditional elements were also to be found in the RDA. However, in both countries, splits in the local RDA, reflecting differences on major policy questions in the interterritorial RDA and linked to the question of militance, led a relatively more conservative wing to purge a trade union oriented, relatively more radical wing. In Mauritania, the new elites were simply too weak and the traditional rulers too strong to enable the former to come to power.

Nigeria presents the strangest picture of all, because the federal structure of the country led to an anomalous party development, unlike the "normal" West African pattern. The *National Council of Nigeria and the Cameroons*

(NCNC) was rounded in 1944. It represented a middle-class attempt to create a mass structure, which paralleled, indeed preceded, such attempts in other West African territories. It became strong in the southern half of Nigeria. In 1945, the Richards Constitution definitively created three regions in Nigeria, the North, West, and East (the latter two being in the south). This meant that the meaningful political structures were regional as well as federal.[38] In 1951, a new group was formed in opposition to the NCNC based on the leadership of the Nigerian Youth Movement. It was the Action Group (AG), a party that grew out of a Yoruba cultural society, the Egbe Omo Oduduwa, the Yorubas being the principal ethnic group in the Western Region. The AG was created in part because the Egbe was too conservative. Its effect on Nigerian politics as a whole, however, was that it represented a regional-ethnic opposition to an NCNC accused of being Eastern-based and Ibo-dominated, rather than a breakaway of radical elements.[39] The Ibos were the principal ethnic group in the Eastern Region and Nnamdi Azikiwe, the leader of the NCNC, was an Ibo. Tribal rivalries, as we shall see, are not unusual in West African politics. This one was, however, constitutionally reinforced by a regional structure. Thus, in terms of social composition and even ideology, the NCNC and the AG presented somewhat similar images, both dominated by the new urban middle class, but retaining reasonably good relations with (albeit control over) traditional elements.

The bastion of strength of traditional rule in Nigeria was to be found in the Emirates of the Northern Region. Indeed, these were the most powerful traditional rulers to be found anywhere in West Africa. They did not need to seek an alliance with urban professionals, as in the Gold Coast, to safeguard their power. They relied on the regional structure and gave their blessing to a moderate popular party, the *Northern People's Congress* (NPC), founded in 1949, which made its appeal on the basis of northern particularism. The Emirates, however, had a traditional feudal structure in which the Hausa majority were ruled by Fulani overlords. The NPC, which in the context of the North represented an attempt by certain educated elements to encourage a quite moderate degree of modernization, saw its radical elements break away in 1950 to form the *Northern Elements Progressive Union* (NEPU). NEPU is allied on the federal level with the NCNC. In the North, its action is based on a traditional class conflict, as Sklar notes:

> Among the underprivileged masses of Hausaland, radicalism has been persistent among certain occupational groups, notably, petty traders and urban dwellers of comparable status who constitute the rank and file of the populist Northern Elements Progressive Union, e.g., craftsmen, shopkeepers, tailors, butchers, etc.[40]

Yet, even with universal manhood suffrage, the NPC has been able to repel decisively the onslaught of NEPU. They have done this by welcoming into high posts in the party structure non-Fulani businessmen who are *talakawa* (traditional commoners) despite their new economic wealth:

> Generally the merchants are populist in their social attitudes and sympathetic to the feelings of the people among whom they live. Their influence in behalf of the NPC countervails NEPU appeal to *talakawa*

values. . . . It is a paradox of Northern social development that traditional class consciousness dulls the political edge of modern class
struggle.[41]

Thus we have seen that, in almost every instance, the political struggle in
postwar West Africa reflects some clear divisions over economic interests, although the details have varied widely according to the strength and structure
of the middle class, the juridical framework, and the strength of traditional
rulers. In fact, however, only the emergent middle classes of the towns can be
said to think in class terms to any substantial degree. The peasants, who are
the majority of the population, act everywhere primarily in terms of tribal
loyalties. The activation of such tribal loyalties in the modern political arena
has been a commonplace of West African politics. Colonial regimes have often
encouraged it; traditional rulers have often employed it. Sometimes the
emergent middle class elements of "backward tribes" have seen it as a path
to power. In any case, all the nationalist movements have had to contend with
it and surmount ethnic divisions insofar as they hoped to be successful in
their objectives.

The nationalist movements collected grievances and sought to place emphasis on those which united them against the main enemy, the colonial power.
Ethnic regional parties divided the nationalist movement and thus served to
vitiate its effects. In the early period of active struggle with the nationalist
movements in West Africa, the colonial authorities gave active support to
such ethnic "administrative" parties. This was particularly true of the French
administration. A classic instance was the Ivory Coast where, in the 1951
elections, there were at least five ethnic-regional parties enjoying administrative
support against the RDA, each appealing to its own sector.[42] Similarly, in
Togo, the French encouraged against the CUT not only the *Parti Togolais du
Progrès* but also a special group for the northern areas (of different ethnic
background than the Ewe who dominated the CUT), the *Union des Chefs et
des Populations du Nord.*[43] In Dahomey, the split in the UPD led to the
creation of the *Groupement Ethnique du Nord-Dahomey,* as well as the *Parti
Républicain du Dahomey* which appealed primarily to the Fon in the southeast. By 1957, the CPP in Ghana faced six regional-ethnic opposition parties.
The PDG in Guinea faced four main regional parties in the early postwar
years. In Nigeria, the ethnic parties usually allied themselves with one of the
two southern nationalist parties. The ethnic minorities in the East would
usually ally themselves with the AG and those in the West with the NCNC.

The phenomenon of regional-ethnic parties occurred throughout West
Africa. One can distinguish, however, two varieties which have opposite economic bases: the assertion of separate identity of the poorer region (or backward group), and that of the richer region. The poorer region usually is the
home of a group considered culturally backward, although of course there are
situations in which both sides have opposite evaluations of cultural prestige
levels. The antagonisms that manifest themselves here may predate the colonial
era. Instances of such an attitude can be found in the northern savannah regions of those coastal states which are economically and educationally dominated by the southern forest regions: the Ivory Coast, Ghana, Togo, Dahomey,
and Nigeria. In all these cases, the northern areas are Islamized, as opposed to

a Christianized and more Westernized south. Each of these countries has seen a northern regional party emerge.[44] In Senegal, such a movement flourished in the Casamance,[45] and in Mauritania in the Vallée du Fleuve.[46]. In 1947, such a movement among the Mossis in the Ivory Coast led to the reconstitution of Upper Volta as a separate territory.[47]

In Christian-pagan countries, Moslems, who occupy lower-status positions, felt threatened and organized political associations.[48] Christian-pagan minorities have reacted in the same way in Moslem areas.[49] In some cases, ethnic political reactions can be traced in part to the economic expansion of a politically dominant group.[50] In all these cases, the objective of political organization by the weaker group was to ensure a maximum of local autonomy, thus servicing the local emergent middle-class elements as well as the traditional rulers, both of whom are threatened by advance of the educated members of the dominant group. It also was a method of obtaining political leverage so as to increase their share of the distribution of national income and social expenditures.

The case of separatism of the richer region is more acute, more spectacular, and often more successful. If the relatively rich region coincides with the region relatively high in modern education and the region supplying a large proportion of the political personnel of the nationalist party, no problem is posed. Often, however, for reasons of geographic or historic accident, this was not the case. The three clearest examples in West Africa are the separatist movements of the Ivory Coast, the Western Region of Nigeria, and Ashanti in Ghana. The Ivory Coast as a territory within the Federation of French West Africa, and the Ivory Coast PDCI as a party within the French African RDA, led the fight, successfully, for the breakup of the federation. The main arguments were economic. The grievance was that the Ivory Coast subsidized other territories in the federation only to find that the benefits went disproportionately to Senegalese who had a larger educated elite and in whose territory resided most federal agencies.[51] The Western Region offered somewhat similar arguments concerning tax redistribution within the Federation of Nigeria. This was reflected in the breakaway of the AG from the NCNC. Western separatism (of the rich region) combined with Northern separatism (of the poor and educationally backward region) were largely responsible for the tripartite federal structure of Nigeria as it came to independence. The NCNC had stood for a strong central government with a minimum of seven constituent units.

Ashanti in Ghana was the richest region because of cocoa production. It also was the area of a people with a highly complex culture who were in the process of conquering the coastal Fanti and Ga at the same time the British established their rule. A feeling that they were unduly subsidizing the rest of Ghana, combined with the educational and political dominance of the coastal tribes, led to the breakaway in 1954 of the National Liberation Movement (NLM) from the CPP, a movement that ultimately was unsuccessful. Both the AG in Nigeria and the NLM in Ghana had strong roots in the cultural reassertion of a traditionally complex society. Relative economic deprivation combined with the threat of cultural de-classment led to ethnic-regional separatism. A comic-opera replica of Ashanti separatism in Ghana was the attempt by the Agni of Sanwi in the Ivory Coast to secede in 1959. The Agni had feelings toward the politically dominant Baoulé similar to those of the Ashanti toward the Fanti. The Agni were too a relatively rich area and originally more advanced in terms of Western education, an advantage they feared they were losing.

The position of the Agni approaches that of the Creoles in Sierra Leone or the residents of Bathhurst in Gambia—the defense of the interests of an old elite. Here we see clearly how ethnic regionalism of the rich region and class parties of the old bourgeoisie are in fact two variants of the defense of privileged groups.

The nationalist parties, faced with ethnic-regional claims, which often were masked economic claims, tended to treat these claims at their face value and sought to make the emotional appeal of cultural reassertion an ally rather than an enemy. They looked for ways of giving representation and recognition to these claims. They tried in fact to make these forces a channel for their own objectives. Such groups as the NCNC in Nigeria and the BDS in Senegal were in fact, at the beginning, primarily a federation of organizations including various ethnic-regional associations.[52] The NCNC and the BDS, however, in time shifted to a structure of regularly constituted party sections. Even more extreme was the example of the PDCI in the Ivory Coast which was constructed, in the words of one of its leaders, as a "federation of tribes."[53] In Sierra Leone, the SLPP used the chiefs and native authorities in the protectorate as its main mode of intraparty communication. Even where ethnic-regional groups were not formally recognized in the party structure, party leaders took care to include in proper dosage persons representing all the major ethnic groups.[54] Conversely, dissidents from the party tended to assert themselves in ethnic terms. As Zolberg remarks of the Ivory Coast:

> With an eye on future elections, leaders who left the party sought to create new political organizations. They had no choice but to voice their appeal in ethnic terms.[55]

Of course, the assiduous attention and even deference to ethnic claims ran counter to the ideological position of most nationalist movements. Open recognition of these claims could only weaken the hands of modernizing elements, as well as risk the disaffection of rival ethnic groups. Thus, the Senegalese nationalist leader, Mamadou Dia, claimed that the associations linked to the BDS in Senegal were "more regional than ethnic in character."[56] Sklar observes of the NCNC in Nigeria:

> NCNC leaders cannot afford to acknowledge publicly that the Ibo State Union may perform an occasionally useful role of intra-party conciliation. Historically, the NCNC is as much Yoruba as it is Ibo . . . Yet the Ibo constituencies of the East form a solid block of electoral support and the NCNC is acutely sensitive to charges of "Ibo domination."[57]

Still, the nationalist party, if it wanted to be a national party, had no choice but to collect ethnic support. A resolutely antitraditionalist party such as the PDG of Guinea found it very difficult to make headway in the Fouta-Djalon, where chieftaincy was still strong. At first, the PDG could only recruit the "captives" (*roundé*) and recent immigrants.[58] Ethnic-administrative parties, the SFIO and later the *Bloc Africain de Guinée,* had their strongholds here.

The PDG succeeded in obtaining support in this area only after the son of an important chief, Diallo Saifoulaye, "like Lafayette . . . left his privileges to join the democratic cause."[59]

The realities of political organization often forced more concessions on the nationalist party leaders than they desired to make. A PDCI leader, described the reasoning behind the party structure in the Ivory Coast:

> During the elections of 1945 and 1946 we have found that the ethnic associations that existed in the city of Abidjan functioned efficiently for electoral purposes as well. In preparation for the battle that we would be waging, we thought that it would be necessary to create highly solidary units, equivalent to Communist cells in France. Ethnic organization was the most natural and the most practical for this purpose. Regardless of where they lived and worked in the city, people of the same tribe came together for social purposes. So we transformed the ethnic associations into party subcommittees. Where they did not exist, we helped the tribes to organize original ones. Only in this way could we communicate with the members, collect dues, and pass down party directives in the various local languages.[60]

The consequence of this strategy was a more rapid initial success for the party but a long-range weak party structure.

The attempts of nationalist parties to overcome ethnic rivalries by judicious dosage often merely transferred the scene of these rivalries from interparty battles to intraparty battles. In the Ivory Coast PDCI, for example, Zolberg cites one explanation of the 1959 battle in the party congress over the election of the Secretary-General in these terms:

> Others refer to a showdown between the alliance of Baoulé and Western groups, who considered themselves "true" Ivory Coasters, and the alliance of border groups from the East near Ghana, the North-West near Guinea and Soudan, and foreign Africans living in the country.[61]

Differences within the NCNC often reflected the particularisms of both the Aro and the Onitsha and the tensions that have existed historically between them and the Ibo.[62] This was, however, infinitely preferred by nationalist movements to the situation in the Western Region of Nigeria where the AG and the NCNC built on and fed traditional rivalries.[63] Interparty ethnic rivalry both weakened the drive for de-colonization and took more violent forms.

Urban modernizers, then, in order to make the mass party into an effective anticolonial weapon tried to create intertribal coalitions. To do this, they could not always impose the terms they would have preferred. Often instead of building party cells, they made alliances with traditional chiefs or did a bit of both. Obviously, this would affect the nature of the mass parties. In northern Nigeria, the NPC was greatly indebted to the emirs and the Sufi brotherhoods[64] and could for this reason scarcely qualify as a mass party, although it received the majority of the votes and party activity was reasonably extensive. In Sierra Leone, the SLPP felt compelled to work through the chiefs in the rural areas and to share power with them. In fact, the result was a sort of division of domain, national affairs being left in the hands of an urban, educated group and rural local affairs in the hands of the chiefs.[65]

Kilson calls this "the strategy of integrating traditional rulers into the [party's] leadership structure."[66] In the Western Region of Nigeria, the relative strength of the modern Yoruba elites meant that though they were allied in the party with the traditional chiefs, they dominated the policy councils of the party.[67] The relationship of the BDS and the Islamic religious leaders in Senegal was similar. In many of the French areas, however, the French administration had installed nontraditional authorities as *chefs de canton*. These chiefs were more easily ignored or swept aside by the nationalist parties, especially after they compromised themselves in the postwar period by support of "administrative" parties. This was the case particularly of parts of Guinea, the Ivory Coast, the Sudan (Mali), and Togo.

The basic aim of the nationalist movements was to overcome *tribal* differences within the African community. Their attitude to *class* differences was more ambivalent. They utilized antagonisms against a small upper elite, but this had many dangers. For one thing, the middle-class status of the nationalist leadership was ultimately not too different from that of the small upper elite. For another, the small upper elite had needed skills. Thus, as time went on, the class-struggle ideological overtones of nationalism came to be blunted by a new unifying doctrine of anticolonialism. As long as two parties existed, however, the class lines were never entirely effaced. As Hodgkin argues:

> Where two or more parties co-exist within a single State, the divisions between them have to be explained in relation to a variety of factors— including ethnic, religious and cultural differences and oppositions, conflicts of economic interests, the play of external influences, personal antagonisms, and so forth. But conflicts of an ideological kind are seldom entirely absent, and may be a factor of the first importance. . . .
> Mass parties tend, on the whole, to be exponents of radical ideologies, and elite parties of conservative or traditionalist ideologies.[68]

If, at the moment of independence, nationalist parties were tending to efface class as well as tribal differences, the problems of the postindependence period strongly accentuated this trend. The party, came to power in an independent, sovereign state, had many weapons at its command to consolidate its power. The various elements of the bourgeoisie—administrative, commercial, and rural—were all highly dependent on the state. A new subcategory of professional politicians, a sort of political bourgeoisie, was even more obviously at the mercy of the party. The traditional chiefs no longer could count on any protection from the colonial authorities. The governments could use the power of political appointment or golden ambassadorial exile to bring leaders of former ethnic-administrative opposition parties into line. They could also manipulate the electoral systems to assure the elimination of opposition representation in the legislatures.

The reasons why the new West African nations felt such a need to create one-party states derived from the structural problems of national integration in new polities.[69] The drive for a one-party state has been accompanied by a theory to justify it, particularly explicit in the various parties that once were linked in the RDA (of former French Africa). The original claim that the class war was irrelevant to the African political situation was made by the

RDA in 1951.[70] Or, as Assane Seck has put it, "the class struggle manifests itself, not between this (middle) class and the African masses, but between all the Africans and the Europeans."[71] The theory was much elaborated by Sékou Touré in Guinea between 1958 and 1960.[72]

The arguments of a classless society as the basis of a one-party state has coincided with a reinforced nationalism that has involved antagonisms not only to Europeans but to "stranger" Africans as well. The question of who in fact controls power and the allocation of privilege in a one-party state has thus far been lightly passed over in ideological formulations. Frantz Fanon has recently argued that in fact in West Africa "the single party is the modern form of the dictatorship of the bourgeoisie without a mask, without pretence, without scruples, cynical."[73] His argument is based on the following analysis:

> The colonized bourgeoisie which comes to power uses its class aggressiveness to take over the positions previously held by strangers. . . . It brandishes energetically the notion of the nationalization of cadres, of the Africanization of cadres. . . . On their side, the town proletariat, the mass of unemployed, the small artisans . . . side with this nationalist attitude. . . . If the national bourgeoisie is in competition with Europeans, the artisans and the small trades launch battle against nonnational Africans. In the Ivory Coast, this takes the form of riots which are in fact racist against Dahomeans and Voltaics. . . . If the Europeans represent a limitation on the voracity of the intellectuals and the businessmen of the young nation, for the mass of the urban population competition is represented principally by Africans coming from a different nation. In the Ivory Coast, it is Dahomeans; in Ghana, Nigerians; in Senegal, Soudanese.[74]

There is almost no data available yet with which to analyze the relationship of position in traditional class structure and the modern class structure, although there seems to be a correlation.[75] Even "proletarian" organizations like trade unions are dominated by persons of traditionally high status. For, disproportionately, traditionally high status has been translated into modern education and, as Little argues, "the (social class) system, as a whole, has its main genesis in literacy and in the opportunities afforded by literacy."[76] If the upper castes, as a group, where they existed, have tended to furnish much of the new emerging classes, this has not prevented conflict between those whose immediate interests lie more with one system than another— thus, the politics of chiefs versus emerging middle classes. The emerging middle classes are, nevertheless, relatively open to talent, and access via education or politics is possible to others. The immediate economic struggles in the post-independence period remain as struggles within this middle class —for example, the administrative bourgeoisie (organized in trade unions) versus the political bourgeoisie (the government and party functionaries) allied sometimes with a rural planter class (Ivory Coast) or with urban businessmen (Nigeria).

The single political party has become an instrument of these emergent groups collectively to organize the nation for greater production and to mediate the claims of redistribution of income *among* the emergent classes. A true party system must await the large-scale entry of the population into the money economy (peasants becoming cash-crop farmers or urban laborers) in sufficient numbers, and having sufficient income level, to support combative instruments for their economic interests. The social structure of West African countries has not yet evolved quite to this point.

NOTES

1. For example, Garigue observes that in Dahomey in the five *communes mixtes* between the two world wars, "the elected members were practically always drawn from among the 'Creole' population." (P. Garigue, "Changing Political Leadership in West Africa," *Africa*, 24 (3) (July 1954), p. 228.) Creoles were Europeanized Dahomeans of partial Portuguese and Brazilian descent.

2. "The term 'middle' introduces an idea of moderation between extremes. The middle class would therefore be that class which has characteristics in common with the popular masses on the one hand and a so-called privileged group on the other, but these characteristics are less marked. Understood in this fashion, the notion of middle class does not seem to me altogether alien to ancient African societies, at least in the savannah regions of West Africa where the social structures were strongly hierarchical. . . . Today . . . this social structure has been swept away. . . . Nevertheless, since before the second World War, a new middle class has been emerging in French West Africa, quite different from the traditional middle class and formed primarily of civil servants. . . . Intermediate between the African masses and the Europeans, this group . . . had a certain social prestige. . . . In addition, alongside these civil servants, some new elements began to be seen: free professionals (lawyers, doctors, etc.), merchants and planters who tend to constitute an economic force proud of owing nothing directly to the Administration. . . . Thus fortified, the middle class in formation has acquired self-assurance and, by obtaining partial satisfaction for its demands, has improved the material conditions of civil servants and white-collar workers in the private sector." Assane Seck, "La formation d'une classe moyenne en Afrique Occidentale Française," INCIDI, *Développement d'une classe moyenne dans les pays tropicaux et subtropicaux*, XXIXe Session, Sept. 13–16, 1955. (Brussels, 1956), 159–62.

3. Richard L. Sklar, *Nigerian Political Parties* (Princeton: Princeton Univ. Press, 1963), p. 55.

4. Thomas Hodgkin, *Nationalism in Colonial Africa* (London: Muller, 1955), p. 141.

5. See R. Schachter, "Single-Party Systems in West Africa," *American Political Science Review*, 55 (2) (June 1961), p. 241, and M. Wight, *The Gold Coast Legislative Council* (London: Faber & Faber, 1946), *passim*.

6. See M. Kilson, "Sierra Leone," in J. S. Coleman and C. Rosberg (eds.), *Political Parties and National Integration in Tropical Africa* (Berkeley & Los Angeles: Univ. of California Press, 1964), p. 96.

7. M. Kilson, Jr., "Nationalism and Social Class in British West Africa," *Journal of Politics*, 20 (2) (May 1958), p. 376.

8. T. Hodgkin, "The African Middle Class," *Corona*, 8 (2) (Feb. 1956), p. 88. See also G. Balandier: "The growing awareness which comes about as a result of the new economic and cultural relations leads to reactions which have a directly political meaning. The latter are the doing of social categories who feel the colonial situation as a *limit* to their development or of those who find themselves both 'uprooted' and deprived as a result of the transformations they have undergone." The social categories cited are the indigenous bourgeoisie, indigenous planters, educated elites and African proletariats." ("Contribution à l'étude des nationalismes en Afrique noire." *Zaire*, 8 (4), April 1954, p. 384.) See also J. L. Seurin: "In the least favored territories the "political class' was recruited primarily from among 'intellectuals,' this group being almost identical with the 'civil servants' (for example, in Mauritania). . . . In the more favored territories (although the proportion of civil servants is larger) other socioprofessional groups (liberal professions, commerce, planters) furnished the political personnel." ("Elites sociales et partis politiques d'A.O.F.," *Annales africaines*, 1958, p. 151.)

9. P. Mercier, "Aspects des problèmes de stratification sociale dans l'Ouest Africain," *Cahiers internationaux de sociologie*, New Series, 17 (1954), p. 50.

10. *Ibid.*, p. 48.

11. J. L. Seurin, *op. cit.*, p. 144

12 *Ibid.*, p. 151.

13. G. Jahoda found that the fathers of nearly one-quarter of the students at the University College of the Gold Coast held some traditional positions. He also gives the following table of father's occupations, which demonstrates how sharp class patterns were already by 1954.

Occupation	All adult G.C. males	Fathers of students
Agriculture and fishing	70%	26%
Manual work (independent artisans, skilled workers and laborers)	23	8
All other	7	66

"The Social Background of a West African Student Population, I," *British Journal of Sociology*, 4 (4) (Dec. 1954), pp. 361–62.

14. *Op. cit.*, pp. 62–3.

15. A. R. Zolberg, *One-Party Government in the Ivory Coast*, (Princeton Univ. Press, 1964), p. 29.

16. For a development of the distinction between patron parties and mass parties, see R. Schachter, *op. cit.*, pp. 295–6. *See* also T. Hodgkin, *Nationalism . . . , op. cit.*, pp. 139–68. Hodgkin makes a distinction between congresses and parties which is based primarily on Nigerian politics and which holds up less well as a generalization. In his later book, *African Political Parties* (London: Penguin African Series, 1961), Hodgkin distinguishes between elite and mass parties (pp. 68–75), which resembles the categories of Schachter.

17. Seurin notes: "When beginning in 1946 the system of African political parties develops, the very principle of elections, seen with favor by the new political forces, would seriously undermine chieftaincy. . . . The traditional relationship of 'clientele' in African villages tended increasingly to favor the new elected politicians and as a result acted to the detriment of customary chiefs. Thus, the ancient political structures have been profoundly upset." (*Op. cit.*, p. 139.)

18. R. Schachter, *op. cit.*, p. 300.

19. Kilson notes three reasons why the middle class monopolized the leadership: "Firstly, the middle class, and especially its professional component, have had a monopoly over the intellectual tools necessary for comprehending the complex forces that make for change in a society that is advancing towards modernity. . . . Secondly, members of the middle class have had the wealth and influence necessary, and sufficient leisure, to pursue a part-time political career. . . . Thirdly, the professional and intellectual elements among the middle class were quick in developing an awareness of their interests in the new social system that emerged out of the Western impact, and of the relationship of these interests to the colonial system." ("Nationalism . . . ," *op. cit.*, p. 377.)

20. *Ibid.*, 386.

21. Schachter observes: "Mass party organizers sought out grievances, expressed them in the market place, coordinated them. Then blamed European rule for forced labor, taxes, abuses of official 'chiefs,' racial discrimination, poverty. Out of these grievances they welded their massive demonstrations against colonial rule. Most patron party leaders were too linked with the established authorities to play this muckraking role." (*Op. cit.*, p. 304.)

22. R. Sklar, *op. cit.*, p. 480. Sklar cites four objective criteria to identify members of the new and rising (emergent) class: "high-status occupation (notably professionals, educators, substantial businessmen, and senior functionaries in the civil service and in public or private enterprise), high income, superior education (especially in the cases of professionals, civil servants, and teachers), and the ownership or control of business enterprise." (pp. 480–1).

23. D. Apter, *The Gold Coast in Transition* (Princeton: Princeton Univ. Press, 1955), p. 167. Standard VII is the tenth year of schooling, the last year of primary

school in the system prevailing at the time. For a discussion of the split between the UGCC and the CPP, see I. Wallerstein, "Ghana face au présent," *Présence africaine,* New Series 18–19 (Feb.–May 1958), pp. 184–94.

24. K. E. Robinson, "Senegal: The Elections to the Territorial Assembly, 1957," in W. J. M. Mackenzie and K. E. Robinson (eds.), *Five Elections in Africa* (Oxford: Clarendon, 1960), p. 313.

25. "The larger number of 'civil servants' among PSAS [by 1957, this was the new name of the SFIO] candidates also exemplifies the extent to which it had derived its support from those who had 'arrived' and perhaps also the extent to which it was once, in Senegal, the *parti de l'administration," Ibid.,* p. 361.

26. "Socialists, even those in small trading posts, were contemptuous of the rural masses; 'they don't know why they are voting,' as one of them remarked." *Ibid.,* p. 342.

27. "While Lamine Guèye campaigned with difficulty, dressed formally in well-pressed suit and tie, Senghor wore khaki shorts and sunglasses, sat on the floor of the huts, and ate what he was served: 'the deputy in khaki,' he was affectionately called by Senegalese war veterans." T. Hodgkin and R. Schachter, "French-Speaking West Africa in Transition," *International Conciliation,* No. 528 (May 1960), p. 408.

28. It did largely because in the rural areas of Senegal "what has elsewhere been termed a 'rural bourgeoisie' has not emerged and the most favored economic categories coincide, by and large, with the upper strata of the traditional or semi-traditional type (heads of sects), or with those artificially created on the same model by the colonial administration." P. Mercier, "Evolution of Senegalese Elites," *International Social Science Journal,* 8 (3) (1956), p. 443.

29. Cited in W. J. Foltz, "Senegal," in J. S. Coleman and C. Rosberg (eds.), *op. cit.,* p. 22.

30 The extension was not accomplished in entirety immediately, D. J. R. Scott observes: "The exclusion of Protectorate women was also necessary as a support for the principle of two stages in the advance to universal suffrage. . . . The roots of this concept lay in the Colony, where it was necessary to reassure conservative opinion that the existing electorate would not be swamped at once. . . ." ("The Sierra Leone Election, May, 1957," in W. J. M. Mackenzie and K. E. Robinson (eds.), *op. cit.,* p. 182.)

31. M. Kilson, "Sierra Leone Politics, I: The Approach to Independence," *West Africa,* No 2246, June, 18, 1960, p. 688. For an account of how the recent changes have affected the makeup of the Sierra Leone legislature, see A. T. Porter, "The Social Background of Political Decision-Makers in Sierra Leone," *Sierra Leone Studies,* New Series, No. 13 (June 1960), pp. 2–13.

32. A. R. Zolberg, *op. cit.,* p. 84.

33. "The effect of these measures of economic discrimination was to throw the African planters into determined opposition to the French administration, an attitude distinguishing them from their counterparts in Ghana, for example. The Ivory Coast planters took the initiative in the anti-colonial struggle after the war. It is doubtful whether they would have done so if the administration had followed a policy of neutrality towards them, or favored them." (R. Schachter, *op. cit.,* p. 310.)

34. R. Schachter, *op. cit.,* p. 298.

35. As Pauvert notes, the *Juvento*-CUT split represented "differences between generations and between socio-economic strata," these two categories overlapping. (J. C. Pauvert, "L'évolution politique des Ewe," *Cahiers détudes africaines,* 2 (1960), p. 187.)

36. For a good account of Togo politics until 1956, see J. S. Coleman, "Togoland," *International Conciliation,* No. 509, (Sept. 1956).

37. See J. Delval, "Le R.D.A. au Soudan Français," *L'Afrique et l'Asie,* 16 (4) (1951), 54–67.

38. For an account of the Richards Constitution and its consequences, see J. S. Coleman, *Nigeria: Background to Nationalism* (Berkeley: Univ. of California Press, 1958). Chap. 12.

39. On the contrary, the NCNC relationship to the AG tended to become that of the radical group against the old elite in the Western Region: "The Action Group has attracted to their party not only the new political elite in the Yoruba towns . . . but also the Obas [chiefs] . . . The local politicians and the Obas have the support too of many of the local businessmen. Thus the Action Group is supported by a greater part of those whose prestige ranks highest in the town. The NCNC, on the other hand,

since becoming the opposition party, has endeavored to foster the discontented elements in each town and often contains an ill-mixed assortment of educated doctrinaire
left-wing nationalists, letter-writers and title-claimants." (P. Lloyd, "The Development of
Political Parties in Western Nigeria," *American Political Science Review,* 49 (3)
(Sept. 1955), p. 703.

40. R. Sklar, *op. cit.,* p. 335.

41. *Ibid.,* p. 329.

42. They were the *Bloc Démocratique Eburnéen* (southern Lagoon tribes), *Parti
Progressiste* (Agni and Abron), SFIO (Bété), *Union des Indépendants de la Côte
d'Ivoire* (Baoulé hostile to Houphouet-Boigny), *Entente des Indépendants de la Côte
d'Ivoire* (Moslems of the savannah). Later a number of these groups merged into a
party called the *Parti de l'Union Française.* See R. Schachter, *op. cit.,* p. 342.

43. See J. S. Coleman, "Togoland," *op. cit.,* p. 38.

44. *Northern People's Congress* (Nigeria); *Groupement Ethnique du Nord-Dahomey*
(later *Mouvement Démocratique du Dahomey,* and *Rassemblement Démocratique
Dahoméen*); *Union des Chefs et des Populations du Nord-Togo; Northern People's
Party* (Ghana); *Entente des Indépendants de la Côte d'Ivoire.*

45. The *Mouvement Autonome Casamançais* which later reemerged as the only
significant regional base of the nonethnic, radical nationalist *PRA Sénégal.*

46. The *Union Nationale Mauritanienne,* which was affiliated with the *Parti de la
Fédération Africaine* and called for the adherence of Mauritania in 1959 to the Federation of Mali, then composed of Senegal and the Sudan (now the Republic of Mali).
The Vallée du Fleuve is the southern area of Mauritania where live the Negro
minority, many of whose ancestors had been slaves to the majority of Moors. Adherence to the Federation of Mali would have meant for these people being part of a
political structure dominated by Negro peoples.

47. The Mossi came, and still come, to the southern Ivory Coast as migrant
laborers. They have, however, a strong traditional structure. In the reconstructed
Upper Volta, they represent about one-half the population and thus effectively have
self-control. Upper Volta, when reconstituted, included portions of Niger and the Sudan,
but the bulk of the territory had been part of the Ivory Coast since 1932, when Upper
Volta was dismembered.

48. "Such support as the Ghana Muslim Association Party was able to attract lay
primarily among the *lumpenproletariat* inhabiting the zongos of Accra and Kumasi. . . ."
(T. Hodgkin, *African Political Parties, op. cit.,* p. 67).

49. "In the lower Northern Region of Nigeria the separatist United Middle Belt
Congress is based mainly on Christian congregations" R. Sklar, *op. cit.,* p. 466. In
Guinea, the *Union Forestière* represented in part a reaction of Christianized (pagan)
évolués in Kisai country against the PDG which was identified with the Malinke
Islamized "superior" group, see Y. Person, "Soixante ans d'évolution en pays Kissi,"
Cahiers d'études africaines l, (1960), especially pp. 106–110.

50. This was the case of the Bété who reacted against Dioula and Baoulé acquisition
of land rights in their territory and joined the SFIO to indicate their dissatisfaction
with the RDA led by Baoulé and Dioula. H. Raulin notes of Daloa, a Bété center,
that opposition lists "succeed in regrouping behind a program of support for local
interests a certain number of malcontents essentially characterized by their autochtho-
nous origin and economic weakness" *Mission d'études des groupements immigrés à la
Côte d'Ivoire,* fasc. III. "Problèmes fonciers dans les regions de Gagnoa et Daloa" (Paris,
ORSTOM, 1957), p. 127. This was also the case in the Southern Cameroons where the
separatist parties grew up originally in protest against Ibo economic expansion and the
NCNC, which was identified with the Ibos.

51. "The sense of economic grievance runs deep in the Ivory Coast and it exists on
all levels of society. There are few sections of articulate Ivory Coast opinion who do
not feel that their territory has been exploited by its ex-partners in the federation.
Africans in other parts of French-speaking Africa tend to regard this as simply another manifestation of the "bourgeois" mentality dominant in the Ivory Coast. So it
may be. But whatever it is called, it has long roots. . . ." E. Berg, "The Economic
Basis of Political Choice in French West Africa," *American Political Science Review,*
54 (2) (June 1960), p. 405.

52. "The BDS had as affiliates, in addition to individuals, the Mouvement des

Forces Démocratiques Casamançais, the Union Générale des Originaires de la Vallée du Fleuve, La Collectivité Lébou, l'Union Générale des Peulhs" (K. E. Robinson, *op. cit.,* p. 336). In Nigeria, the NCNC included at its inaugural meetings 101 tribal unions as well as a host of other voluntary associations. See J. S. Coleman, *Nigeria, op. cit.,* pp. 264–265.

53. Cited in A. R. Zolberg, *op. cit.,* p. 116. See also pp. 277–8. The PDG in Guinea almost found itself in the same predicament. From 1947–49, ethnic associations were directly represented in the executive. In 1951, after the reconstitution of the PDG along nonethnic lines, Secretary-General Madeira Keita termed the previous policy "a grave political error." (B. Charles, "Un parti politique Africain: le Parti Démocratique de Guinée, *Revue française de science politique,* 12 (2) (June 1962), p. 313.

54. In Guinea, for example, four of the principal leaders at the moment of independence came from the four major ethnic groups which correspond to the four major regions: Sékou Touré, Malinké; Diallo Saifoulaye, Fulani, of Fouta-Djalon; Béovagui Lansana, forest peoples; Bengaly Camara, coastal Soussou.

55. *Op. cit.,* p. 129.

56. K. E. Robinson, *op. cit.,* p. 337.

57. *Op. cit.,* pp. 461–2. The Action Group, of course, is more openly attached to its ethnic origins, being itself an ethnic-regional split off from the NCNC "In theory, the Egbe [Egbe Omo Oduduwa, a Yoruba cultural organization] is nonpartisan and its relationship to Action Group is wholly unofficial; in practice its service to the Action Group is beyond compare. The two associations are virtually inseparable in rural areas of Yorubaland." (*Ibid.,* p. 465.)

58. R. Schachter, *op. cit.,* p. 301.

59. *La Liberté,* (PDG journal, Conakry), December 27, 1955, cited in *ibid.,* p. 302.

60. Quoted in A. R. Zolberg, *op. cit.,* p. 116.

61. A. R. Zolberg, "Politics in the Ivory Coast, 3: The Machine at Work," *West Africa,* No. 2255 (August 20, 1960), p. 939.

62. See R. Sklar, *op. cit.,* pp. 151–7, 190–230.

63. See P. Lloyd, "The Yoruba Town Today," *Sociological Review,* 7 (1) (July 1959), pp. 56–7.

64. "Among the Muslims of the upper North, a majority of the adherents of the leading *Sufi* brotherhoods, namely the *Qadriyya* and the *Tijaniyya* support the NPC. But a militant 'left-wing' of *Tijaniyya,* known as the *Yan Wazifa,* 'is a radical influence in both religion and politics'; many of its adherents support the opposition NEPU" (R. Sklar, *op. cit.,* pp. 466–7.)

65. "What this amounts to, in fact, is a division of governmental offices between the SLPP leaders and the Paramount Chiefs, with the SLPP being assured of the Chief's support in maintaining office at the central level . . . while the Chiefs are assured of the SLPP's support in preventing encroachments upon their traditional status, the contemporary significance of which is seen in the Paramount Chief's success at converting traditional status into modern pecuniary gains." (M. Kilson, "Sierra Leone Politics, II: The Approach to Independence," *West Africa,* No. 2247 [June 25, 1960], p. 703).

66. "Sierra Leone" in J. S. Coleman and C. Rosberg (eds.), *op. cit.,* p. 124. Kilson further comments on the degree to which SLPP parliamentary candidates have kinship links with chiefly families.

67. "In the Western Region, traditional authorities bow to the political leadership of the rising class of businessmen, professionals, civil servants, educators, and so on. In the North, businessmen generally define their interests in terms of collaboration with the politically dominant chiefs and administrative elite." (R. Sklar, *op. cit.,* p. 353.)

68. *African Political Parties, op. cit.,* 167–8.

69. This question is treated in I. Wallerstein, *Africa: The Politics of Independence* (New York: Vintage Books, 1961), Chap. V.

70. See "Manifeste du R.D.A.," *Afrique noire,* December 6, 1951.

71. *Op. cit.,* p. 163. Seck, while not technically in an RDA party, has been active in Senegalese nationalism, being currently a leader of the radical nationalist *PRA—Sénégal.*

72. See I. Wallerstein, "The Political Ideology of the PDG," *Présence africaine,*

12 (40; Engl. ed.: 1st trimester; 1962), pp. 30–41; also M. Keita, "Le Parti unique en Afrique," *Présence africaine,* 20 (Feb.–March 1960), pp. 3–24.

73. *Les damnés de la terre* (Paris: Maspéro, Cahiers Libres, No. 27–28, 1961), p. 124.

74. *Ibid.,* pp. 118–19.

75. Foltz finds, for example, in Senegal that only three of the seventy-nine deputies of the governing *Union Progressiste Sénégalais* (successor of the BDS) are of lower traditional caste status, and only one member of the political bureau of the radical nationalist opposition party, *PRA—Sénégal.* (Unpublished manuscript)

76. K. Little, "Social Change and Social Class in the Sierra Leone Protectorate," *American Journal of Sociology,* 54 (1) (July 1948), p. 21.

Selected Literature on Parties and Elections

Robert Alford, *Party and Society. The Anglo-American Democracies* (Chicago: Rand McNally, 1963)

Erik Allardt, *Social struktur och politisk aktivitet* (Helsingfors: Söderström, 1956)

Erik Allardt and Y. Littunen, (eds.), *Cleavages, Ideologies and Party Systems* Helsinki: Westermarck Society, 1964)

A. J. Allen, *The English Voter* (London: English Universities Press, 1964)

Gabriel Almond and James Coleman (eds.), *The Politics of the Developing Areas* (Princeton: Princeton University Press, 1960)

Gabriel Almond and Sidney Verba, *The Civic Culture: Political Attitudes and Democracy in Five Nations* (Princeton: Princeton University Press, 1963)

Daniel Bell, (ed.), *The Radical Right* (Garden City, New York: Doubleday and Co., 1963)

Mark Benney, A. P. Gray, and R. H. Pear, *How People Vote* (London: Routledge and Kegan Paul, 1956)

Lee Benson, *The Concept of Jacksonian Democracy: New York as a Test Case* (Princeton: Princeton University Press, 1961)

Bernard Berelson, Paul Lazarsfeld, and William McPhee, *Voting* (Chicago: University of Chicago Press, 1954)

Wolfgang Birke, *European Elections by Direct Suffrage* (Leiden: A. W. Sythoff, 1961)

John Bonham, *The Middle Class Vote* (London: Faber and Faber, 1954)

Karl D. Bracher, *Die Auflösung der Weimarer Republik* (Stuttgart and Dusseldorf: Ring Verlag, 1954)

Eugene Burdick and Arthur Brodbeck (eds.), *American Voting Behavior* (Glencoe: The Free Press, 1959)

Creighton Burns, *Parties and People* (Melbourne: Melbourne University Press, 1961)

D. E. Butler, (ed.), *Elections Abroad* (London: Macmillan, 1959)

D. E. Butler, *The Electoral System in Britain* (Oxford: Clarendon Press, 1963)

D. E. Butler and Anthony King, *The British General Election of 1966* (London: Macmillan, 1966)

Angus Campbell, Philip Converse, Warren Miller, and Donald Stokes, *The American Voter* (New York: John Wiley, 1960)

Angus Campbell, Philip Converse, Warren Miller, and Donald Stokes, *Elections and the Political Order* (New York: John Wiley, 1966)

R. M. Chapman, W. K. Jackson, and A. V. Mitchell, *New Zealand Politics in Action* (London: Oxford University Press, 1962)

Ricardo Cruz Coke, *Geografía electoral de Chile* (Santiago de Chile: Editorial del Pacífico, S. A., 1952)

Allan Cole and Naomichi Nakanishi, *Japanese Opinion Polls with Sociopolitical Significance, 1947–1957,* I (Medford: Fletcher School of Law and Diplomacy, Tufts University, 1960)

James S. Coleman and Carl G. Rosberg (eds.), *Political Parties and National Integration in Africa* (Berkeley and Los Angeles, University of California Press, 1964)

John C. Courtney (ed.), *Voting in Canada* (Toronto: Prentice-Hall of Canada, 1967)

Robert Dahl, (ed.), *Political Oppositions in Western Democracies* (New Haven: Yale University Press, 1966)

H. Daudt, *Floating Voters and the Floating Vote* (Leiden: Stenfert Kroese, 1961)

Torcuato Di Tella, *El sistema político argentino y la clase obrera* (Buenos Aires: Eudeba, 1964)

W. Dittman, *Das politische Deutschland vor Hitler* (Zurich: Europa Verlag, 1945)

M. Dogan, *La stratificazione sociale dei suffragi in Italia* (Milan: Edizioni di Comunità, 1962)

Georges Dupeux, *Le Front populaire et les élections de 1936* (Paris: Armand Colin, 1959)

Maurice Duverger (ed.), *L'influence des systèmes electoraux sur la vie politique* (Paris: Armand Colin, 1950)

Maurice Duverger, *Political Parties* (New York: Wiley, 1954)

Maurice Duverger, *Sociologie politique* (Paris: Armand Colin, 1966)

Heinz Eulau, *Class and Party in the Eisenhower Years* (New York: The Free Press, 1962)

E. Faul (ed.), *Wahlen und Wähler in West-deutschland* (Villingen: Ring Verlag, 1960)

P. L. Fegiz, *Il Volto Sconosciuto dell'Italia* (Milano: Dott. A. Giuffré, 1956)

Michael P. Fogarty, *Christian Democracy in Western Europe* (London: Routledge and Kegan Paul, 1957)

Lawrence H. Fuchs, *The Political Behavior of American Jews* (Glencoe: The Free Press, 1956)

Gino Germani, *Política y sociedad en una época de transición* (Buenos Aires: Paidos, 1962)

François Goguel, *Géographie des élections françaises de 1870 à 1951* (Paris: Armand Colin, 1951)

François Goguel (ed.), *Nouvelles études de sociologie électorale* (Paris, Armand Colin, 1960)

François Goguel and Georges Dupeux, *Sociologie électorale* (Paris: Armand Colin, 1951)

Léo Hamon (ed.), *Les nouveaux comportements politiques de la classe ouvrière: entretiens de Dijon* (Paris: Presses Universitaires de France, 1962)

Rudolf Heberle, *From Democracy to Nazism* (Baton Rouge, La.: Louisiana St. Press, 1945)

F. A. Hermens, *Democracy or Anarchy?* (Notre Dame: University of Notre Dame Press, 1938)

Wolfgang Hirsch-Weber and Klaus Schutz, *Wähler und Gewählte* (Berlin: Verlag Franz Vahlen, 1957)

S. Hoffman, *Le mouvement Poujade* (Paris: Armand Colin, 1956)

José Luis Imaz, *Motivación electoral* (Buenos Aires: Instituto del Desarrollo Económico y Social, 1962)

V. O. Key, Jr., *The Responsible Electorate* (Cambridge: Harvard University Press, 1966)

Uwe Kitzinger, *German Electoral Politics* (Oxford: The Clarendon Press, 1960)

Enid Lakeman and J. D. Lambert, *Voting in Democracies: A Study of Majority and Proportional Election Systems* (London: Faber, 1955)

Robert Lane, *Political Life. Why People Get Involved in Politics* (Glencoe: The Free Press, 1959)

J. La Palombara and Myron Weiner (eds.), *Political Parties and Political Development* (Princeton: Princeton University Press, 1966)

G. E. Lavau, *Parties politiques et réalités sociales* (Paris: Armand Colin, 1953)

Paul Lazarsfeld, Bernard Berelson, and Hazel Gaudet, *The People's Choice* (New York: Columbia University Press, 1948)

S. M. Lipset, *Agrarian Socialism* (revised edition, Garden City: Doubleday Anchor Books, 1968)

S. M. Lipset, *Political Man. The Social Bases of Politics* (Garden City: Doubleday, 1960)

S. M. Lipset (ed.), *Students and Politics* (New York: Basic Books, 1967)

W. J. M. Mackenzie and Kenneth Robinson (eds.), *Five Elections in Africa* (London: Oxford University Press, 1960)

J. Maquet and M. d'Hertefelt, *Elections en société féodale* (Brussels: Academie Royale des Sciences Coloniales, 1959)

William N. McPhee and William A. Glaser (eds.), *Public Opinion and Congressional Elections* (New York: The Free Press, 1962)

John Meisel, *The Canadian General Election of 1957* (Toronto: University of Toronto Press, 1962)

John Meisel (ed.), *Papers on the 1962 Election* (Toronto: University of Toronto Press, 1964)

Robert Michels, *Sozialismus und Fascismus in Italien* (München: Meyer & Jessen, 1925)

Lester Milbrath, *Political Participation* (Chicago: Rand McNally, 1965)

R. S. Milne and H. C. MacKenzie, *Marginal Seat 1955* (London: Hansard Society, 1958)

K. W. J. Post, *The Nigerian Federal Election of 1959: Politics and Administration in a Developing Political System* (London: Oxford University Press, 1963)

Lucian W. Pye, (ed.), *Communication and Political Development* (Princeton: Princeton University Press, 1963)

D. W. Rawson, *Australia Votes* (Melbourne: Melbourne University Press, 1961)

Peter Regenstreif, *The Diefenbaker Interlude. Parties and Voting in Canada* (Toronto: Longmans, 1965)

S. Rokkan, (ed.), *Approaches to the Study of Political Participation* (Bergen: Chr. Michelsen Institute, 1962)

Richard Rose, *Politics in England* (Boston: Little Brown, 1964)

Sven Rydenfelt, *Kommunismen i Sverige. Ett samhällsvetenskapligt studie* (Lund: Gleerup, 1954)

Robert A. Scalapino and Junnosuke Masumi, *Parties and Politics in Contemporary Japan* (Berkeley: University of California Press, 1962)

E. E. Schattschneider, *The Semi-Sovereign People* (New York: Holt, 1960)

Erwin Scheuch and Rudolf Wildenmann, *Zur Soziologie der Wahl* (Cologne: Westdeutscher Verlag, 1966)

Andre Siegfried, *Tableau politique de la France de l'Ouest* (Paris: Armand Colin, 1913)

T. E. Smith, *Elections in Developing Countries: A Study of Electoral Procedures Used in Tropical Africa, Southeast Asia, and in the British Caribbean* (London: Macmillan, 1960)

Ithiel de Sola Pool, Robert Abelson, and Samuel Popkin, *Candidates, Issues, and Strategies. A Computor Simulation of the 1960 Presidential Election* (Cambridge: The MIT Press, 1964)

A. Spreafico and J. La Palombara (eds.), *Elezioni e comportament politico in Italia* (Milan: Comunità, 1963)

Otto Stammer (ed.), *Politische Forschung* (Cologne: Westdeutscher Verlag, 1960)

Hugh Thorburn (ed.), *Party Politics in Canada* (Toronto: Prentice-Hall of Canada, 1963)

Herbert Tingsten, *Political Behaviour: Studies in Election Statistics* (London: P. S. King, 1937; Totowa: Bedminster, 1966)

Joseph Trenaman and Denis McQuail, *Television and the Political Image* (London: Methuen, 1961)

H. Unkelbach, *Grundlagen der Wahlsystematik* (Göttingen: Vandenhoeck und Ruprecht, 1956)

H. Valen and D. Katz, *Political Parties in Norway* (Oslo: Universities Press, 1964)

G. Vedel, *La dépolitisation: Mythe ou réalité* (Paris: Armand Colin, 1962)

B. Vogel and P. Haungs, *Wahlkampf und Wählertradition* (Köln und Opladen: Westdeutscher Verlag, 1961)

Systematic Index

This index is organized in rough conformity with the analytical distinctions developed in the Introduction: it essentially serves to link up the general analysis attempted by the Editors with the concrete descriptions in the country-specific chapters.

I. Types of Parties

The references in parentheses are to the types of party-forming cleavages distinguished on pp. 14–25 of the Introduction.

II. Institutional Frameworks

III. Major Parties: Country by Country

IV. *Dimensions of Voter Alignment*

Alphabetic Index